HANDBOOK OF PEDIATRIC PSYCHOLOGY AND PSYCHIATRY

Volume II

HANDBOOK OF PEDIATRIC PSYCHOLOGY AND PSYCHIATRY

Volume II

Disease, Injury, and Illness

Edited by

Robert T. Ammerman

Allegheny University of the Health Sciences
Pittsburgh, Pennsylvania

John V. Campo

University of Pittsburgh School of Medicine

Allyn and Bacon

Boston   London   Toronto   Sydney   Tokyo   Singapore

Series editor: Carla F. Daves
Series editorial assistant: Susan Hutchinson
Manufacturing buyer: Suzanne Lareau

Copyright © 1998 by Allyn & Bacon
A Viacom Company
Needham Heights, MA 02194

Internet: www.abacon.com
America Online: keyword: College Online

Library of Congress Cataloging-in-Publication Data

Handbook of pediatric psychology and psychiatry / edited by Robert T.
  Ammerman and John V. Campo.
  p. cm.
  Includes bibliographical references and indexes.
  Contents: v. 1: Psychological and psychiatric issues in the
pediatric setting — v. 2: Disease, injury, and illness.
  ISBN 0–205–16560–5 (v. 1). — ISBN 0–205–27601–6 (v. 2).
  1. Child psychiatry—Handbooks, manuals, etc. 2. Child
psychology—Handbooks, manuals, etc. I. Ammerman, Robert T.
II. Campo, John V.
  [DNLM: 1. Child Psychiatry. 2. Mental Disorders—in infancy &
childhood. 3. Child Development Disorders, Pervasive. WS 350
H23595 1998]
RJ499.3.H364 1998
618.92′89—dc21
DNLM/DLC
for Library of Congress   97–42736
               CIP

The editors and contributing authors have endeavored to present drug selection, doses of drugs, and schedules of treatment in accordance with the standards generally accepted at the time of the writing of this volume. Nevertheless, as new information becomes available, changes in treatment and in the use of drugs may become necessary. The reader is advised to carefully consult the instruction and information material included in the package insert of each drug or therapeutic agent before administration for, among other things, any change in indications and dosage, and all warnings and precautions. It is the reader's responsibility to determine the FDA status, to check the package insert, and to evaluate the acceptability regarding current standards for practice for each drug or treatment contemplated for clinical use. This advice is especially important when using, administering, or recommending new or infrequently used drugs and drugs lacking FDA approval for pediatric use. The editors, contributing authors and publisher disclaim all responsibility for any liability, loss, injury, or damage incurred as a consequence, directly or indirectly, of the use and application of any of the contents of this volume.

Printed in the United States of America

10 9 8 7 6 5 4 3 2 1 02 01 00 99 98

To Caroline, Patrick, and Evan

—RTA

To my parents, my wife, and my children

—JVC

CONTENTS

FOREWORD

The reader may wonder, and rightfully so, why the editors would request a pediatrician to write the foreword to these excellent volumes dealing with pediatric psychology and psychiatry. A colleague of similar discipline or specialty is usually honored in this way. I, therefore, feel both honored and privileged to do so.

Although not usual, it is certainly most fitting that a pediatrician be given the opportunity to comment upon a book addressing the broad range of developmental, psychiatric, behavioral, and medical conditions in which pediatricians are, or should be, involved.

The relationship between pediatrics and the behavioral sciences, psychology, and psychiatry continues to be a special one. Consider that child growth and psychological development is the basic science of pediatrics, and recall that child psychiatry developed independently, not as an offspring of adult psychiatry, but more as a cousin of pediatrics. Almost 70 years ago, the first child psychiatry clinic was established in an academic pediatric department (Leo Kanner; Johns Hopkins University, 1930). Recently, the relationship between pediatrics and child psychology and psychiatry have become strengthened, as evidenced by increased collaboration in practice and educational settings, and among our professional organizations.

Primary care physicians, especially pediatricians, play a major role in the provision of mental health services. A high percentage of problems encountered in pediatric practice are psychosocial in nature. Pediatricians have known that 85 percent or more of their time practicing pediatrics is spent giving advice, guidance, and counseling for psychological or development problems. Such activities constitute the art of pediatrics based on science. The early diagnosis of psychiatric illness with appropriate and timely referral is also the art and science of psychiatry and clinical psychology.

The title, *Handbook of Pediatric Psychology and Psychiatry*, may erroneously imply that the work is relatively superficial and entirely clinically oriented. Not so! Each chapter is a complete review of a subject or condition, providing current research findings and references. A case illustration is included in each chapter; a very helpful feature bridging current knowledge and understanding of diagnosis and treatment with a clinical example.

Current knowledge and understanding of the psychopathology of mental illness is certainly a prerequisite for good diagnosis and management; without clinical application the patient and family are unlikely to be helped. The late Dr. Dennis Cantwell (1990) expressed this so well:

> The scientifically minded artist (thinks) scientifically and empirically but will acquire and use clinical skills effectively. The scientifically minded artist accepts the fact that the same time one is searching for ultimate truth, one must frequently take therapeutic action based on data that are known to be inadequate. (pp. xv–xvi).

There is also a place for pediatricians working together with mental health professionals. I have had the great privilege and opportunity to work in a psychiatric setting shoulder to shoulder with a wide variety of mental health professionals. Such ideal arrangements are currently being threatened by the economic environment of medicine. It is an ideal that we should continue to strive to achieve.

I am pleased to have been given the opportunity to introduce these outstanding books edited by two outstanding teachers and practitioners. This comprehensive and in-depth, yet practical, treatise should be in the libraries of pediatric generalists, and all behavioral pediatricians and child mental health providers.

The conditions presented and explored in these texts affect the most vulnerable of the vulnerable, those children and adolescents who suffer from psychological conditions and serious mental illness. The care and nurturing of such children is among our most important human activities. The editors and contributors are dedicated to this activity, and the questions they raise that are still unanswered will be left to our younger colleagues. They, students, residents, fellows, and faculty, will be helped by these books in their pursuit of answers.

I take this opportunity to thank my many colleagues in child and adolescent psychology and psychiatry who have made invaluable contributions to the education of pediatricians in training and in practice, and to my own career development—and for their patience.

REFERENCE

Cantwell, D. P. (1990). Foreword. In B. D. Garfinkel, G. A. Carlson, & E. B. Weller (Eds.), *Psychiatric disorders in children and adolescents*. Philadelphia: W.B. Saunders.

GEORGE D. COMERCI, M.D., F.A.A.P.
Former President of the American Academy
    of Pediatrics
Clinical Professor of Pediatrics and
Past Professor of Pediatrics and of
    Family and Community Medicine
University of Arizona College of Medicine

PREFACE

The idea for this book grew out of our sometimes heated, but always collegial, discussions about various issues in psychology and psychiatry, which began during our years in training, and continued as our careers developed. Several observations emerged from our discussions, which eventually became the focal point for a book.

First, both psychology and psychiatry have become partners of primary care physicians in pediatrics and family medicine, as well as a variety of sub-specialists. The pediatric primary care provider has been increasingly recognized as the "gatekeeper" for behavioral health services for children and adolescents, and the primary care setting appears to be the place where such intervention is most likely to take place. Most children are seen by their primary care medical provider within a given year, and there appears to be considerable overlap between so-called mental health problems and physical problems, with relevant examples including accidents and injury prevention, maltreatment, chronic physical illness, somatization, and psychophysiologically reactive disorders such as migraine.

A variety of psychiatric disorders occur concurrently with health problems. Emotional and behavioral disorders quite commonly first present in pediatric medical settings, often with medically unexplained somatic symptoms, and children and adolescents with psychiatric disorders may be higher utilizers of medical services. It is also relevant that psychiatric symptoms may be closely associated with or caused by physical disease. Psychiatric symptoms or disorders can negatively impact the course of physical disease as a result of influences on the behavior of children and families, and sometimes a direct physiologic effect on the disease process itself. The ex-citing developments of the past several years in behavioral medicine, psychopharmacology, and the psychobiology of illness have stimulated research and highlighted the richness and complexity of conceptualizations of mind and body.

The biomedical model of illness and disease has been responsible for many of the major achievements of modern Western medicine, though it soon became clear that many individuals experience subjective distress or illness in the absence of the clear-cut physical pathology or physical signs generally associated with disease. This resulted in a psychological model of illness developing alongside the biomedical model and the development of parallel systems of care delivery, one based on the biomedical model and focused on "legitimate" illness and its treatment, and another based on a presumed psychological model and focused on "mental illness," which has been considered somehow "illegitimate," a result of some sort of sociomoral failure on the part of the patient and family, and a source of great stigma and potential embarrassment. While it is true that much has changed in our views of psychiatric illness, much has stayed the same, and stigma remains with us. The practical and theoretical problems and inconsistencies of modern practices such as mental health "carve-outs" regarding health care insurance appear to be derivative of the false dichotomy that has been perpetuated in the traditional health care delivery system. It is clear that we are living in exciting times, which have presented both challenges and opportunities for psychology and psychiatry, and it appears to be somewhat ironic that the economics of modern health care may actually provide the impetus for successfully addressing the issue of stigma and integrating the various disciplines that function in medical settings, regardless of their supposed orientation regarding the mind-body split that has been pervasive in Western medicine.

Another consequence of our discussions over the years has been the shared conviction that the traditional distinctions between pediatric psychology and psychiatry are unrealistic and largely in error. Pediatric psychology and psychiatry appear to be complementary disciplines, each with its own unique strengths and areas of emphasis, but disciplines with extensive areas of overlap and much in common. We share much of the same literature, have a commitment to the comprehensive care of children and adolescents, and utilize an ecological perspective in which it is recognized that biological, psychological, and social variables interact in complex ways to bring about the clinical presentation of children in both medical and mental health settings. Dramatic shifts in the way health care is provided, driven primarily by financial imperatives, require partnerships between pediatric psychology and psychiatry and call for new models of pediatric health care, such as truly integrated medical and mental health services. The future demands a new collegiality and sense of collaboration across the disciplines engaged in the care of children and adolescents, as well as flexibility and a shared sense of purpose.

The two volumes of *Handbook of Pediatric Psychology and Psychiatry* reflect the interdigitation of pediatrics, psychiatry, and psychology. Unlike most volumes on this topic, in which each discipline has its own reference books written by similarly trained professionals primarily using their own literatures, this book established bridges connecting psychology, psychiatry, and pediatrics. This is evident in the chapter topics, which are comprehensive and broad in scope. Separate chapters are included on psychiatric disorders (Volume I) which frequently present in pediatric settings, in addition to chapters on pediatric illnesses and conditions (Volume II) which have psychological and psychiatric components. Sections on general issues (e.g., consultation and liaison, cultural issues) and special topics (e.g., child maltreatment, pain) are also included. Most of the chapters are coauthored by both psychologists and psychiatrists, and many also include pediatricians. Lastly, most of the chapters follow a standardized format within each section, which ensures that pediatric medical, psychological, and psychiatric issues and perspectives are addressed. Case illustrations are included to highlight multidisciplinary assessment and treatment. In sum, we have striven

to compile a handbook that is state of the art clinically, has a strong empirical foundation, and is relevant and useful to pediatricians, psychologists, psychiatrists, and other professionals who care for children and adolescents.

We are especially saddened by the untimely death of Dr. Marla Hooks, the coauthor with Dr. Elizabeth McCauley of the chapter, "Affective Disorders." It is clear that she was an extraordinary person. She was trained in both pediatrics and psychiatry, and had been the recipient of many honors, including a fellowship with the Health Services Research Institute for Minority Faculty through the Association of American Medical Colleges. In addition to her many strengths as a wife and mother, she showed great promise professionally, both clinically and academically. We extend our condolences and deepest sympathy to her husband, her children, and other family members, as well as to her many friends and colleagues. Dr. Hooks will be greatly missed, and we are proud that her contribution is appearing in this book.

We would like to acknowledge the help, assistance, and encouragement that we have received from numerous individuals in putting together this book. First and foremost, we thank the contributors for sharing with us their experience and expertise. Their enthusiasm for assembling writing teams across disciplines was both gratifying and inspiring. We extend our appreciation to Mylan Jaixen and Carla Daves, our editors at Allyn and Bacon, who from the beginning have understood and supported our efforts to create a multidisciplinary text for pediatric psychology and psychiatry. Their unswerving patience and understanding in the face of inevitable delays are especially noteworthy. We gratefully acknowledge the administrative support provided by Nancy Simpson, Cindy DeLuca, Roberta Farren, Patricia O'Donnell, Maryann Ruffing, Ann Huber, Stuart McKenna, and Sue Hutchinson (at Allyn and Bacon). Our appreciation also goes to the following reviewers for their comments on the manuscript: Karla Doepke, Auburn University; Kevin J. Armstrong, Western Michigan University; and Jennifer Johnson, University of California, Irvine. Finally, we are thankful for our friendship, and especially grateful for the love, support, and patience of our respective wives and families, the figurative glue which has served to hold this project together.

Robert T. Ammerman
John V. Campo

Pittsburgh, Pennsylvania

ABOUT THE EDITORS
AND CONTRIBUTORS

Robert T. Ammerman (Ph.D., University of Pittsburgh, 1986) is Associate Professor of Psychiatry, Allegheny University of the Health Sciences, Allegheny Campus, and Director, Mental Health Services in Childhood Disabilities, Department of Psychiatry and Allegheny Neuropsychiatric Institute, Allegheny General Hospital (Pittsburgh, PA). He is a Diplomate in Behavioral Psychology from the American Board of Professional Psychology. He is the recipient of grants from the National Institute on Disabilities and Rehabilitation Research, Vira I. Heinz Foundation, Children's Trust Fund of Pennsylvania, National Institute on Drug Abuse, National Institute on Alcoholism and Alcohol Abuse, and the Staunton Farm Foundation. His research interests are child abuse and neglect, psychopathology in children and youth with disabilities, psychosocial impact of congenital neurological syndromes, and adolescent substance abuse.

John V. Campo (M.D., University of Pennsylvania, 1982) is Assistant Professor of Psychiatry and Pediatrics at the University of Pittsburgh School of Medicine. He is Director of the Center for Pediatric Psychiatry and Medicine Module at the Western Psychiatric Institute and Clinic, and Director of the Behavioral Science Division at the Children's Hospital of Pittsburgh. He is board certified in pediatrics, psychiatry, and child and adolescent psychiatry. His interests include medically unexplained physical symptoms in children and adolescents, the association between psychopathology and physical disease, and models of delivering pediatric behavioral health care within medical settings.

Alia Antoon (M.D., D.C.H., University of Baghdad Medical School, Baghdad, Iraq, 1963, Diploma of Child Health from the Royal College of Surgeons, London, England, 1968) is Assistant Clinical Professor in Pediatrics at Harvard Medical School, Boston, Chief of Pediatrics and Ambulatory Services, Shriners Burns Institute, Boston, and Assistant in Pediatrics, Massachusetts General Hospital, Boston. She is a Diplomate of the American Board of Pediatrics and the American Board of Pediatric Endocrinology and Metabolism. Major research interests are metabolic studies in post-burns, and effects of growth hormone on healing in children with burns and oxygen consumption in the brain.

Ronald L. Blount (Ph.D., West Virginia University, 1985) is Associate Professor of Psychology at the University of Georgia. The primary focus of his research is on the assessment and treatment of children's distress during acute painful medical procedures. He is also interested in coping styles, children's adaptation to chronic illness, and other aspects of pediatric psychology.

Ronald T. Brown (Ph.D., Georgia State University, 1978) holds faculty appointments in the Department of Pediatrics, Psychiatry and Behavioral Sciences, and Rollins School of Public Health at Emory University. Dr. Brown has been the recipient of several National Institutes of Health, Office of Education, and other foundation grant awards related to pediatric psychology and psychopharmacology. Dr. Brown's research interests include childhood cancer, sickle cell disease, and attention deficit hyperactivity disorders. He is a fellow of the

American Psychological Association and is the author of over 116 empirical articles and book chapters.

Robert D. Canning (Ph.D., Pacific Graduate School of Psychology, 1993) is Staff Psychologist for the VA Sacramento PTSD Clinical Team and Clinical Instructor of Psychiatry at the University of California, Davis Medical Center. Following receipt of his doctorate, he completed an NIMH post-doctoral fellowship in Psychiatric Epidemiology at the University of Pittsburgh School of Medicine. During his fellowship, Dr. Canning investigated the psychosocial well-being and psychiatric morbidity of caregivers to adult heart transplant patients. His current interests center on psychiatric comorbidity and treatment of combat veterans suffering from chronic PTSD.

Michael P. Carey (Ph.D., Louisiana State University, 1988) is Associate Professor of Psychiatry at the Medical College of Ohio, where he also serves as Co-Director of the Northwest Ohio Consortium Internship Training Program for Professional Psychology and Director of The Child Psychology Service at Kobacker Center. Dr. Carey also serves as the Associate Director on the adolescent inpatient unit at MCO. His research interests include developmental psychopathology, especially as it relates to anxiety, depression, disruptive behavior disorders, and child abuse, with a particular interest in the treatment of obsessive-compulsive disorder.

David S. Chedekel (Ed.D., Boston University, 1971) is Chief Psychologist at the Shriners Burns Institute (Boston) and a member of the staff of the Department of Psychiatry at Massachusetts General Hospital. He is also an Instructor in Psychology at Harvard Medical School. He has co-authored several articles and two book chapters in the area of emotional factors associated with burn injuries. His current research interests include psychological adaptation of adolescent burn victims, post-traumatic stress disorder and body image issues in burned children, and behavioral factors related to burn injuries.

Alan M. Delamater (Ph.D., University of Georgia, 1981) is Associate Professor of Pediatrics and Psychology and Director of Clinical Psychology in the Department of Pediatrics at the University of Miami School of Medicine. His research focuses on the behavioral and psychological aspects of chronic illness in children and adolescents, including the role of stress and coping processes and family functioning.

Arden D. Dingle (M.D., University of Medicine and Dentistry of New Jersey, New Jersey Medical School, 1986) is Assistant Professor of Psychiatry and Behavioral Sciences and Pediatrics at the Emory University School of Medicine. She is Director of the Child and Adolescent Consultation-Liaison Service at Grady Health Systems and is the Associate Director of Training in Child and Adolescent Psychiatry. Dr. Dingle's research interests include chronic physical illness and adolescent suicide.

Jacques Donders (Ph.D., University of Windsor, 1988) is Chief Psychologist in Mary Free Bed Hospital in Grand Rapids, Michigan. He received Diplomate status in Clinical Neuropsychology from the American Board of Professional Psychology in 1994. His research has focused on psychometric issues and prediction of outcome in children with acquired and congenital neurological conditions.

Elizabeth Dreelin (Ph.D., Fuller Theological Seminary, 1994) is a Clinical Psychologist and nurse. Currently, Dr. Dreelin is a post-doctoral fellow in pediatric psychology and Instructor in the Department of Psychiatry and Behavioral Sciences at Emory University School of Medicine.

Margaret S. Eidson (M.D., University of Miami, 1976) is Associate Professor of Clinical Medicine, Division of Pediatric Endocrinology/Diabetes at the University of Miami School of Medicine. She is board certified in Pediatrics and in Pediatric Endocrinology. Dr. Eidson received a Master of Nursing degree from Emory University in 1969 and taught Nursing at Georgia State University and at the University of Miami before entering medical school. She is now also Regional Director of the Diabetes/Endocrine Program for Children's Medical Services of Florida. She is particularly interested in problems of growth, disorders of sexual differentiation and development, congenital thyroid disorders, and Type I diabetes mellitus.

Ingemar Engström (M.D., Ph.D., University of Uppsala, Sweden, 1991) is Director of the Psychiatric Research and Development Unit in Örebro, Sweden. He is also a consultant in psychosomatic medicine, Department of Pediatrics, Örebro Medical Center Hospital. Dr. Engström's research interests include mental health in chronically ill children, especially children with inflammatory bowel disorders and other gastrointestinal diseases. He is also engaged in research on eating disorders and depressive disorders in children and adolescents.

Matthew R. Galvin (M.D., Indiana University, 1979) is Clinical Associate Professor of Psychiatry at Indiana University School of Medicine, where he also serves as Assistant Director of Psychiatric Services for Children and Adolescents and is active in outpatient and inpatient child and adolescent psychiatry. He has authored and co-authored psychoeducational books for children and their families, as well as research articles on moral development and the psychobiological sequelae of child maltreatment.

Leslie A. Gavin (Ph.D., University of Denver, 1990) is Assistant Faculty Member at National Jewish Center of Immunology and Respiratory Medicine, and an Assistant Professor in the Department of Psychiatry, University of Colorado Health Sciences Center. Her research focuses on family factors affecting childhood chronic illness, including family process, family illness management, and parental illness exaggeration and fabrication.

John P. Glazer (M.D., University of California, San Diego School of Medicine, 1972) is Head, Section of Child and Adolescent Psychiatry, and Director of the Pediatric Consult-Liaison Service at the Cleveland Clinic Foundation in Cleveland, Ohio. His special interests include pediatric oncology, organ transplantation, bioethics, and childhood bereavement.

Johanna Goldfarb (M.D., Johns Hopkins University, 1974) is Section Head in Pediatric Infectious Diseases at the Cleveland Clinic Children's Hospital. Her training in pediatrics includes residencies at the Cornell Medical Center, New York Hospital and at the Hershey Medical Center, Pennsylvania State University. Her training in infectious diseases was at Montefiore-Yeshiva Medical School, the Bronx, New York (1981–83). Her clinical practice includes the care of children with AIDS and other immune deficiencies. Her research is in clinical pediatric infectious disease.

Kathryn E. Gustafson (Ph.D., Ohio University, 1988) is Assistant Professor of Medical Psychology in the Department of Psychiatry and Behavioral Sciences, Assistant Professor of Psychology in the Department of Psychology: Social and Health Sciences at Duke University, and Clinical Associate in the Department of Pediatrics at Duke University. She has been a co-investigator and coordinator on a number of federally funded research grants with infants of very low birth weight and with children with cystic fibrosis and sickle cell disease. Her research and clinical interests are in the areas of child and family adaptation to chronic childhood illness, and ethical issues in clinical psychology.

Regina Smith James (M.D., University of California, Los Angeles, 1993) is a resident in the Child & Adolescent Psychiatry Program at the Cleveland Clinic Foundation. Dr. James's clinical and research interests are in the area of post-traumatic stress disorder and psychological adjustment to medical illness in the pediatric population.

Wun Jung Kim (M.D., Seoul National University, 1975; M.P.H., University of Michigan, 1985) is Associate Professor, Director of Training in the child and adolescent psychiatric residency, and Director of the Adolescent Inpatient Unit at the Medical College of Ohio. His research interests include epilepsy, adoption, and cross-cultural psychiatry.

Andrea Kuldanek (M.D., Wayne State University, 1977) is Medical Director of the Pediatric Brain Injury Program at Mary Free Bed Hospital and Rehabilitation Center in Grand Rapids, Michigan. Dr. Kuldanek has an extensive clinical practice providing care to children with neuromuscular disorders with emphasis on children and adolescents recovering from traumatic brain injury. She has also provided leadership in developing rehabilitation programs to address the needs of children and adolescents recovering from traumatic brain injury.

Bo L. Lindquist (M.D., Ph.D., University of Lund, Sweden, 1980) is Associate Professor of pediatrics at the University of Uppsala, Sweden. Dr. Lindquist's research areas include pediatric gastroenterology, especially inflammatory bowel diseases, coeliac disease, and interactive mechanisms between gut epithelium and intestinal bacteria. He is author and/or co-author of 50 original papers and 7 books.

Sharon L. Manne (Ph.D., Arizona State University, 1987) is Assistant Attending Psychologist at Memorial Sloan-Kettering Cancer Center and Assistant Professor of Psychology in Psychiatry at Cornell University Medical School. She is the author of over 25 empirical articles and book chapters, many dealing with childhood cancer, and is currently the recipient of a Research Career Development Award and a FIRST Award from the National Cancer Institute. Her research interests include children's acute pain and distress during invasive medical procedures, parent and child coping with childhood cancer, and parent-child cooperation with home care tasks performed during cancer treatment.

Barbara G. Melamed (Ph.D., University of Wisconsin, 1969) is Professor and Director of Behavioral Medicine and the Anxiety Disorders Clinic at Albert Einstein College of Medicine-Ferkauf Health Psychology Program, Yeshiva University, the Bronx, New York. She has authored *Behavioral Medicine: Practical Applications in Health Care* and *Child Health Psychology*. She is past president of the American Psychological Association Division of Health Psychology. Dr. Melamed is a former Associate Editor of *Health Psychology* and is on the board of many other journals. She is a Diplomate in Health Psychology from the American Board of Professional Psychology.

Daniel J. L. Quiggins (Ph.D., San Diego State University and University of California, San Diego, 1996) is a postdoctoral fellow at Children's Hospital of Michigan in Detroit. He is currently interested in investigating the risk and protective factors of adjustment in pediatric populations.

Alexandra L. Quittner (Ph.D., University of Western Ontario, 1987) is Associate Professor of Psychology at Indiana University, with adjunct appointments at the Indiana University School of Medicine. She currently holds a Research Career Development Award from NIH and is the principal or co-investigator on several research grants examining the effects of chronic illness on child and family adaptation. She has been engaged in the development of situation-specific measures of coping and a daily phone diary procedure, and is developing and evaluating the effects of family interventions for children and adolescents who have a chronic illness.

Lisa P. Rizzone (M.A., Tufts University, 1989) is a clinical and research fellow at Shriners Burns Institute, Boston Unit, and Massachusetts General Hospital. Through her clinical internship and work experience, Ms. Rizzone has developed an interest in children's and families' adaptation to burn injuries. She has published an abridged version of her thesis on PTSD in parents of burned children, as well as co-authored articles relating to emotional disorders, anxiety, issues of death, and PTSD in burned children.

Margaret L. Stuber (M.D., University of Michigan, 1979) is Associate Professor in the Department of Psychiatry and Biobehavioral Sciences at UCLA Neuropsychiatric Institute. She is the Director of the Pediatric Consultation Services, and the Associate Chair for Medical Student Education for the Department. Her primary research interest is the psychological sequelae of highly technical pediatric treatments, such as organ transplantation, in survivors and their families. Recently her work has focused on the use of a post-traumatic stress model in understanding the long-term emotional impact of life-threatening childhood illness on families.

Sally E. Tarbell (Ph.D., York University, 1984) is Assistant Professor of Psychiatry at the University of Pittsburgh Cancer Institute. She has developed pediatric psychology services in general and pediatric hospital settings. Her research focuses on the assessment and management of pediatric pain and on the impact of parental illness on young children.

Kenneth J. Tarnowski (Ph.D., University of South Carolina, 1984) is Professor of Psychology at the University of South Florida, Ft. Myers. He has published more than 100 articles in the areas of behavioral pediatrics, developmental psychopathology, and child and family behavior therapy. He currently serves as co-editor for *Children's Health Care* and serves on the editorial board of several other peer reviewed journals in clinical psychology, pediatrics, and psychiatry.

Robert J. Thompson, Jr. (Ph.D., University of North Dakota, 1971) is Professor and Head of the Division of Medical Psychology in the Department of Psychiatry and Behavioral Sciences and Professor of Psychology in the Department of Psychology: Social and Health Sciences at Duke University. He is a Fellow of the Division of Clinical Psychology of the American Psychological Association and is a Diplomate in Clinical Psychology of the American Board of Professional Psychology. He received the Distinguished Researchers Award of the Association of Medical School Professors of Psychology in 1993. His clinical and research interests focus on how biological and psychosocial processes act together in the development and adjustment of children with developmental and medical problems.

James Walter Varni (Ph.D., University of California, Los Angeles, 1976) is Professor of Psychiatry at the University of California, San Diego, School of Medicine, and Director of the Psychosocial and Behavioral

Sciences Program, Division of Hematology-Oncology, Children's Hospital and Health Center, San Diego. Dr. Varni is a Fellow of the American Psychological Association and the Society of Behavioral Medicine. Dr. Varni has published over 120 professional articles and book chapters on children and families, and two professional books on behavioral pediatrics. Dr. Varni is the recipient of the American Psychological Association Distinguished Research Contribution Award. His research focuses on the utilization of conceptual models in empirically identifying individual differences in adjustment to pediatric cancer and pediatric chronic pain, and cognitive-behavior therapy interventions in pediatric chronic physical disorders.

Marianne Z. Wamboldt, (M.D., University of Wisconsin, 1981) is currently the Director of Pediatric at Behavioral Health the National Jewish Center for Immunology and Respiratory Medicine, as well as Associate Professor of Psychiatry and Associate Director of Child Psychiatry at the University of Colorado Health Sciences Center. She has authored over 25 empirical articles and book chapters on the interaction of medical illness and psychological factors. Her current research is focusing on the genetic and environmental family risk factors for poor asthma outcome in children and adolescents.

Russell E. Ware (M.D., Duke University, 1983; Ph.D., Duke University, 1991) is Associate Professor at Duke University Medical Center. He is the Director of the Pediatric Hematology Research Laboratory Center. His research interests include basic and clinical investigations of hematologic disorders in children.

Frances J. Wren (M.B., B. Ch., B.A.O., University College, Dublin, Ireland, 1979; MRCPsych, 1988) is Assistant Professor of Psychiatry and Pediatrics at the University of Pittsburgh School of Medicine. She also serves as Medical Director of the out-patient program, Center for Pediatric Psychiatry and Medicine, University of Pittsburgh Medical Center, and as Staff Psychiatrist in the Behavioral Science Division of Children's Hospital of Pittsburgh. Dr. Wren's interests include the delivery of mental health care in pediatric medical settings and the interdisciplinary assessment and treatment of disorders of growth and weight gain, including pediatric obesity.

CHAPTER 1

PAIN MANAGEMENT

Kenneth J. Tarnowski
Ronald T. Brown
Arden D. Dingle
Elizabeth Dreelin

DESCRIPTION OF THE PROBLEM

Pain is a ubiquitous experience. Despite the fact that individuals, including children, can describe their pain experiences in detail, it has been difficult to arrive at an acceptable definition of the term. Historically, pain was conceptualized in terms of an emotion. With the advent of sensory physiology, pain was redefined in terms of sensory input. Although there have been considerable advances in pain theory, assessment, and treatment over the past two decades, controversy remains concerning how to best conceptualize emotional, cognitive, and sensory components.

There is consensus that a unidimensional focus (e.g., sensory) is of limited usefulness in defining pain. Such models have given way to complex multidimensional conceptualizations. Variants of these latter models emphasize the synergistic interplay among sensory, affective, neurochemical, and motivational factors (Melzack, 1973; Varni, 1981). Psychological factors that have been found to be of particular importance include suggestion, attention, anxiety, learning history, culture, attributed meaning of pain, and developmental status, including the ability to understand causes and consequences.

In 1959, Beecher described the sensory and reactive components of pain. Sternbach (1968) later described pain as a private and personal sense of hurt, signal of danger, and pattern of interacting sensory, affective, and motivational pain factors. Merskey (1980) described pain as an experience of hurt associated with tissue damage. Fordyce (1976) offered a behavioral conceptualization that described pain in terms of a pattern of responses to both nociceptive stimuli and contingencies operating in the environment. Jay (1985) recently conceptualized pain as the interaction of overt, covert, and physiological responses that can be stimulated by tissue compromise as well as other antecedent and consequent conditions. Because pain in young children appears to be inextricably intertwined with other types of negative affect, coupled with the language limitations evidenced by this age group, some investigators have proposed that the terms behavioral distress and pain be used interchangeably (Katz, Kellerman, & Siegel, 1980).

Types of Pediatric Pain

Based on duration, pain is typically differentiated into two basic types: acute and chronic. For some pediatric conditions, efforts to distinguish the two types of pain may have limited applied significance (Varni,

Katz, & Dash, 1982). There are, however, several relevant distinctions between acute and chronic pain in terms of etiology, neurophysiology, function, assessment, and response to treatment (Bonica, 1979).

Acute pain is an adaptive function signaling the presence of a noxious stimulus and prompts immediate response (e.g., limb withdrawal) and enhanced attention to potential sources of continued experienced distress. Most often such distress is self-limiting and the individual is able to localize the distress and respond in a way so as to mitigate further distress (e.g., rest, seek medical assistance). It is well known that the intensity of acute pain may not be closely related to the extent of tissue damage (e.g., severe pain with minor tissue damage). Varni (1981) has proposed that the severe intensity and anxiety associated with acute pain may be the variables that best distinguish it from chronic distress.

Chronic pain refers to pain of long duration, typically on the order of six months or more, that is more often caused by serious injury or progressive disease. Chronic pain may begin with an episode of acute distress or it may be of insidious onset. Importantly, in the case of chronic pain, there may be a lack or minimal degree of fear (Varni et al., 1982). Pain may be continuous or intermittent, continue after healing has occurred, involve adjacent body areas that were not original targets of disease or injury, and is characterized by a set of pain behaviors (e.g., facial grimacing, posturing) that are subject to social reinforcement and can become independent of organic etiology (Fordyce, 1976).

In addition to the acute-chronic distinction, Varni (1983) has proposed four categories of pediatric pain: disease-related pain (e.g., sickle cell anemia), trauma-related pain (e.g., burn injuries), procedure-related pain (e.g., bone marrow aspiration, burn debridement), and pain not related to an identifiable injury or disease state.

Cognitive-Developmental Considerations

A preliminary question that needs to be addressed concerns the issue of whether very young children experience pain. Conventional wisdom since the 1930s has essentially posited that infants did not experience pain, or perhaps only experienced a muted version which was attributed to immature cortical functions. Early child development investigators, including Peiper (1936) and McGraw (1941), employed a variety of measures including motor reaction time and onset of vocalization following exposure to noxious stimulation, as well as filmed recording to assess infant pain responses. Results

of these investigations suggested that infant pain responding was decorticate in nature. Although neuronal myelinization is incomplete at birth, it is well known that there is considerable individual variability in the rate of myelinization as well as cortical functional integrity (Swafford & Allen, 1968). Recent evidence (see review by Craig & Grunau, 1991) invalidates earlier proposals concerning the apparent lack of infant pain responsivity. Indeed, the available evidence on the issue does not support a view of child pain as a muted version of what older children or adults experience. Although children and adults may evidence qualitative and/or quantitative differences in response to specific noxious stimuli, this does not imply that children experience less subjective distress (Abu-Saad, 1981).

No doubt there are factors that complicate pain assessment and intervention with pediatric populations. Physical, emotional, and cognitive developmental variables influence what will be assessed and how such evaluations will be conducted. Although a detailed consideration of developmental factors is beyond the scope of the present chapter, it is imperative that clinicians be well acquainted with the literature on the developmental aspects of pediatric pain assessment and intervention (Bush & Harkins, 1991). In general, there is a need to be familiar with the range of reactions and response competencies that children exhibit with respect to pain expression and control at varying developmental levels. For example, specific infant expressions of pain include parameters related to crying, gaze patterns, postural changes, autonomic responding, and facial expression, in addition to specific neurological and endocrinological events. During the first two years, early developmental changes reflect evolution of nonverbal pain responding. Toddlers exposed to noxious stimuli often react with limb withdrawal in addition to a more diffuse behavioral response pattern typical of infants. Physical aggression, body rocking, clenched fists, and teeth-clenching are commonly observed responses. Preschoolers often display similar patterns of motor reactions but also begin to attach special meaning to pain experiences. In particular, preschool children begin developing causal and self-implicating hypotheses concerning the origins of pain. Older children evidence increased behavioral variability in response to noxious stimuli. This increased response variability is likely due, in part, to family and cultural variables which, for the most part, are learned phenomena. Factors such as anxiety, expectation, cognitive preparation, pain history, family and peer models become important variables that influence the behavioral expression of distress in older children and adolescents.

Of particular importance is a child's cognitive-developmental level. Thompson and Varni (1986) propose that children's cognitive-developmental status will have a marked influence on the perception and report of distress. An obvious difficulty in conducting assessments with young children concerns the limited communication skills of toddlers and prelingual children. Words to describe pain and hurt may be entirely lacking from the child's vocabulary. Knowledge of children's developmental status is critical to the use of appropriate language and explanations as well in the design of developmentally-sensitive intervention strategies.

Other investigators (Bibace & Walsh, 1980) offer health and illness conceptualizations that are based on the cognitive-developmental stages described by Piaget. Specifically, Bibace and Walsh classify children's conceptualizations of health and illness into six categories. Categories progress from notions of phenomonism and contagion at ages 2–6, to contamination and internalization at ages 7–10, to complex physiological and psychophysiological conceptualizations at age 11 and beyond. According to Thompson and Varni (1986), there is an absence of empirical data concerning the effects of cognitive-developmental level on pediatric pain assessment. However, there is consensus that cognitive factors must be acknowledged explicitly and incorporated into any assessment strategy that is considered to be developmentally valid.

INCIDENCE AND PREVALENCE

In general, data are available concerning the epidemiological characteristics associated with specific psychiatric disorders (e.g., attention-deficit/hyperactivity disorder) as well as common medical conditions (e.g., various forms of cancer). However, accrual of data concerning the epidemiology of pediatric pain presents obvious problems. Foremost is the fact that we are not really focusing on a fairly homogeneous and well-defined disorder per se. Rather, we are considering heterogeneous response patterns that are virtually ubiquitous and associated with a staggering array of conditions (e.g., sickle cell anemia), injuries (e.g., burns), and procedures (e.g., acupuncture). Indeed, pain symptomatology may be evidenced in conditions that range from the common cold (e.g., sinus pain) to chronic pain disorder (e.g., chronic back pain). Although a comprehensive review of the epidemiology of pain associated with even major disorders is beyond the scope of a chapter, a brief overview of some of the most common pediatric

conditions and procedures will serve to provide a general sense of the magnitude of the problem.

Procedure-related pain is encountered by all children. Immunizations and venipuncture are mandated procedures to which all infants and children will be subjected. A subset of children (most typically infants) are also circumcised. The majority of children have transient negative behavioral and emotional responses to such procedures. Healthy preschool and school-aged children continue to be subjected to the occasional injection or venipuncture and begin dental treatments, including amalgam restorations. Other forms of procedure-related pain are largely confined to suspected or documented cases of serious medical conditions (e.g., cancer). Specifically, leukemia is the primary cancer of childhood. Children suspected of such forms of illness will be required to have bone marrow aspirations (BMAs). Although a variety of forms of pharmacological and psychological preparation are typically used with BMAs, data suggest that more than 70 percent of children experience considerable pain (Zeltzer & LeBaron, 1982). In most instances, children with cancer may experience more difficulty with the acute pain associated with medical interventions and procedures than disease-associated pain (Jay, Ozolins, Elliott, & Caldwell, 1983). Other types of procedural pain are less well managed, and the percentage of children who experience severe distress for specific procedures is estimated to be greater than 90 percent (e.g., burn related debridement) (Tarnowski, 1994).

Data on recurrent pain in children and adolescents suggest that such problems are relatively common. For example, Oster and Nielsen (1972) and Apley and Naish (1958) reported prevalence rates of pediatric recurrent abdominal pain to be approximately 10 to 15 percent. Headaches are another common source of recurrent pain. The majority of children (75 percent) have experienced headaches by 15 years of age (Bille, 1962). Chest and limb pain are also frequent pediatric complaints that are most often evaluated in the context of pediatric primary care clinic visits. However, consistent data concerning the prevalence of such problems are lacking. Most of these concerns tend not to be related to an identifiable condition but rather are considered to be idiopathic.

In general, it has been estimated that approximately 30 percent of children suffer from recurrent pain syndromes including headaches, abdominal pain, and limb pain (McGrath & Hillier, 1989). Children affected by such problems typically present with a history of painful episodes that are without well-defined organic etiology, periods of good health, and an absence of pain in between episodes.

Chronic pain is relatively uncommon in children. However, children with specific diseases (including arthritis, hemophilia, and sickle cell anemia) can present with severe pain that may be recalcitrant to common forms of intervention. Most children with these conditions will experience protracted periods of distress over the course of their lives. As with other disorders, precise prevalence rates of pain are difficult to specify as different centers may serve different subpopulations (e.g., older children, patients with severe symptomatology). In addition, there may be differences in the overall approach to such cases such that children treated in different centers receive interventions that vary along important parameters (e.g., availability of multidisciplinary pain staff in regional medical centers). McGrath and Hillier (1989) note that other sources of chronic pain include (a) that associated with nerve damage in which pain persists beyond the time needed for healing; (b) injury-related chronic pain (e.g., orthopedic); and (c) pain as a consequence of psychological factors.

ASSESSMENT APPROACHES

A multidimensional assessment of pain is necessary across informants, settings, and time. Numerous strategies are available for evaluating pain in children that focus on cognitive-verbal, physiological, and behavioral-motoric responses (Tarnowski & Brown, 1995a). Such assessments should always be conducted within the context of a diagnostic interview. The patient's history and experience with pain should be obtained from multiple sources and, for this reason, multidisciplinary staffings are an integral component of any pain management program. Interviews, rating scales, questionnaires, and self-monitoring techniques comprise common methodologies used to evaluate cognitive-verbal responses to pain.

Rating Scales

Rating scales may be divided into three categories: (a) simple descriptive scales (SDS), (b) visual analogue scales (VAS), and (c) graphic rating scales (GRS). Employing scales is a basic strategy for assigning differential values to various pain experiences. The SDS is a scale that incorporates adjective anchors for the severity of pain, while the only VAS scale available includes adjective descriptors at the end points of the continuum. The GRS lists additional adjectives on a continuum without making specific reference to their exact point on the line. These methods have been employed frequently to evaluate pain in children and adolescents. Although

their ease of administration is clearly an advantage, some limitations include their capacity to assess only one dimension of pain and their failure to account for subjective aspects of pain. These measures have been utilized in the assessment of procedural pain (Hester, 1979; Hilgard & LeBaron, 1982), chronic pain associated with arthritis secondary to hemophilia (Varni, 1981), and acute pain related to burn injuries (Tarnowski, McGrath, Calhoun, & Drabman, 1987).

Graphic Assessment Approaches

Because cognitive level and language can be a limitation, particularly in younger children, graphic representations of pain (which include pain mannequins, drawings, and color models) also are employed in evaluating pain in children. One simple method of assessing pain is the use of a pain mannequin whereby the child is asked to designate a specific pain location by drawing an "X" on the outline of a human figure (Tarnowski & Brown, 1995a). In addition, children can be asked to draw a picture of their pain and of themselves while they are experiencing pain. Unruh and associates (Unruh, McGrath, Cunningham, & Humphrey, 1983) found that these types of pictures could be reliably and meaningfully categorized by content.

Color selection methods also have been used to assess pain intensity. Interestingly, children have been found to designate the color red to describe pain (Savedra, Tesler, Ward, Wegner, & Gibbons, 1981; Varni, Thompson, & Hanson, 1987).

Descriptive Approaches

As an integral aspect of the assessment of pain in children, it is important to conduct a careful and extensive interview regarding the child's experience of pain (Tarnowski & Brown, 1995a). Information should be obtained from multiple sources across settings. Important data for the consultant to acquire include information about the pain (e.g., severity, quality, location, duration, precipitants), how the child and the family cope with the pain, the child and family's previous experience with pain and its management, and the child's attributions about the pain and the related illness. Ross and Ross (1984) have indicated that the majority of children can provide excellent one-word pain descriptors, and their definitions of pain are usually unidimensional. Karoly (1991) observed that children can effectively use a combination of verbal and pictorial rating scales to monitor and describe their pain.

Diaries, questionnaires, and ratings by adults have been used to provide verbal descriptors of pain. Diaries are most appropriate for children at the concrete operational stage of development (children aged 8 to 12). Advantages of this technique include sensitivity to fluctuating patterns of pain, inclusion of affective and cognitive reactions, and the ability and ease of monitoring treatment effects. Several pain questionnaires have been developed for use with children as a comprehensive multidimensional assessment instrument for use in the study of acute and chronic pain (Thompson & Varni, 1986). Both the child and parent are requested to complete measures of intensity, location, and affective components of pain. The parent form also includes a comprehensive family history (Thompson & Varni, 1986). These measures have included the Pediatric Pain Questionnaire (Tesler, Ward, Savedra, Wegner, & Gibbons, 1983) and the Children's Comprehensive Pain Questionnaire (McGrath, 1987). Finally, parent, staff, and teacher ratings are frequently used to assess the symptoms of pain-related behavioral distress in the child. Such ratings have been found to correlate well with distress (Jay & Elliott, 1984) and cooperation during medical procedures.

Physiological Measures

Due to problems with methodology and validity, the use of physiological measures of pediatric pain has been infrequent. However, some physiologic measures may be useful clinically in the assessment of pain in children. These include measures of respiration, muscular tension, blood pressure, pulse rate, and skin resistance (Tarnowski & Brown, 1995a). A promising technique in the physiological assessment of pain is the measurement of beta-endorphins, which have been identified as being related to self-reports of pain in pediatric burn patients (Szyfrelbein, Osgood, & Carr, 1985). Finally, the availability of telemetric monitoring has increased the access of ongoing physiological assessment for children in pain.

Observational Techniques

The evaluation of behavioral-motoric responding usually consists of the use of raters who observe and record responses according to operational definitions. Operational definitions recast general descriptions of behavior (e.g., pain) into clearly observable aspects of behavior (e.g., crying). Primarily the following dimensions are quantified: frequency, time, duration, distance, occurrence per opportunity, or percentage of response components completed. An essential feature of this technique is the establishment of inter-observer reliability where the extent of agreement is documented (Tarnowski & Brown, 1995a). The prototypic observational scale is the Procedure Behavioral Rating Scale (Katz et al., 1980), which is a frequency recording system. This schema appears to be sensitive to both quantitative (frequency) and qualitative (response type) changes in children's responding. Several coding schemes are available and modifications have been employed depending upon the population being studied. Attempts also have been made to modify the original code (e.g., number of categories, weighted intensity ratings) in the interest of preserving its reliability and validity. The results of these changes have been mixed in terms of psychometric properties (Tarnowski & Brown, 1995a).

Clinical Assessment of Pain

Unfortunately, optimal assessment of pain as described above is rarely realized in clinical practice. There are a variety of reasons for this discrepancy between ideal and actual practice. Assessment of pain is a complex problem that occurs within a complicated and diverse environment. Often, the consultant contacted for the assessment and management of a child's pain usually is not the primary health care provider for that child and has been asked to participate in the child's care only after multiple other strategies have failed (Tarnowski & Brown, 1995a). The system and other health care professionals commonly cannot accommodate labor-intensive assessment techniques due to problems with understaffing, poor morale, and lack of sophistication about psychological techniques. In addition, patients and primary health care providers wish that complex issues would change immediately, which is not always possible. Very frequently, when patients do not feel satisfied with their treatment, they will express their frustration through resistance, non-compliance, and "doctor shopping." Finally, while the multidisciplinary approach to health care is considered the ideal, it can be difficult to implement, particularly if the pain consultant is not directly involved in the service activities (Tarnowski & Brown, 1995a).

Typically, assessment information is obtained by clinical interview (child, parent, and staff) as well as some form of self-report and informal behavioral observations. Data on specific physiological assessments for pain in children are sparse and are currently not clinically useful. In practice, the physiological data obtained during routine medical procedures (i.e., blood pressure and heart rate) can be usefully integrated with behavioral assessments of pain. While observational assessments appear to be the most sophisticated methodological approaches for assessing pain in children, they are not practical due to time, financial, and personnel constraints. However, other behavioral indices of the child's functioning are readily available, such as amount of ambulation time, frequency of medication requests, amount of time out of bed, repetitions of physical therapy, days of hospitalization, type and dosage of medication, and school days attended.

To be effective in the assessment of pediatric pain, the consultant should be an integral part of the multidisciplinary team caring for the patient (Brown, Dingle, & Koon-Scott, 1994). Pain evaluations should occur early in the general evaluation of the patient. A systematic approach needs to be established for the collection of data that is appropriate for the population and setting. This should include clinical interviews, self-report measures, observational information, and physiological data. Once data have been collected and synthesized, the consultant should review the information with the team. At this point, a consensus can be reached and an appropriate treatment plan developed, which also should be discussed with the child and family, while obtaining additional input from the family.

INTERVENTION STRATEGIES

Numerous approaches are available for managing pain in children. These modalities, which are reviewed below, range from pharmacotherapies, the most widely used, to behavioral and cognitive techniques.

Pharmacological Treatment

Antipyretics. Antipyretic agents are analgesics that are effective for relief of mild or moderate pain and exert their influence peripherally, rather than in the central nervous system (Pfefferbaum & Hagberg, 1993). Aspirin compounds and acetaminophen are commonly used for pain relief. They are the drugs of choice in controlling low-intensity pain and inflammation. Aspirin is administered orally, absorbed rapidly, and peak blood levels typically occur two hours after ingestion. The most common side effects are gastrointestinal upset and bleeding, although when administered with milk or food, the gastrointestinal effects are minimized. Because

aspirin inhibits the production of prostaglandin (Roth & Majerus, 1975), it is contraindicated for children with liver disease, hemophilia, and vitamin K deficiency. Aspirin also has been implicated in Reye syndrome and should be avoided in children with viral illnesses. Acetaminophen is frequently administered to children for symptoms associated with colds and influenza. It is not associated with gastrointestinal or hematologic side effects nor with Reye syndrome (Pfefferbaum & Hagberg, 1993). It does not have anti-inflammatory properties and is administered for moderate pain in children. Other peripheral agents being increasingly used for chronic pain include non-steroidal anti-inflammatory agents, which act similarly to aspirin (Pfefferbaum & Hagberg, 1993).

Opioid analgesics. Opioid analgesics, which include morphine and related compounds, constitute a class of drugs that are the primary pharmacological treatments for severe pain that is both acute and chronic (Pfefferbaum & Hagberg, 1993). Narcotics generally should be used when peripheral agents are ineffective or not tolerated. Despite their efficacy, these compounds have several adverse effects, such as respiratory depression, light headedness, dizziness, sedation, nausea, vomiting, constipation, sweating, tolerance, and dependence. Opioids can produce mental and physical dependency and have a high potential for abuse. Codeine is a weaker opioid analgesic. Synthetic derivatives of morphine and codeine are classified according to their structural similarity, their relative analgesic potency, their agonist (facilitating) or antagonist (blocking) relationship, their potential for abuse, and their adverse side effects. Commonly used synthetic agents include meperidine (Demerol), hydromorphone (Dilaudid), fentanyl citrate (Sublimaze), oxycodone (Percocet, Percodan), and -pentazocine (Talwin). These agents generally differ in their strength and their duration of action (Tarnowski & Brown, 1995a).

Adjunctive and combination drugs. To potentiate analgesic effects, opioids are sometimes combined with other medications (e.g., aspirin and related compounds, antidepressants, phenothiazines). Combinations of drugs are also useful for invasive medical procedures (McGrath, 1991). Psychotropic drugs alone (neuroleptics, anxiolytics) have frequently been administered to diminish anxiety that frequently accompanies pain in children, particularly during invasive medical procedures. McGrath (1990) noted that tricyclic antidepressants, when used as an adjunct to a cognitive behavioral program for depressed adolescents with headaches, are effective in decreasing the frequency and intensity of headaches.

Factors impeding pain management with pharmacotherapy. Over the years, there has been considerable concern about the possibility of addiction resulting from narcotic analgesia (McGrath, 1990, 1991; Pfefferbaum & Hagberg, 1993; Walco, Cassidy, & Schechter, 1994). In fact, survey data indicate that nearly 40 percent of physicians are alarmed about the risk of addiction with the use of narcotics in pediatric populations (Schechter & Allen, 1986). Walco et al. (1994) have maintained that it is important to differentiate between physical dependence (a physiologically determined state in which symptoms of withdrawal would occur if the medication was not administered) and addiction (a psychological obsession with the drug). Studies of pain management in children with sickle cell syndrome, who typically receive analgesia on a chronic intermittent basis, have found essentially no risk of addiction with the administration of narcotics (Morrison, 1991; Pegelow, 1992). To date, there is no empirical evidence to suggest that children are more susceptible to addiction than are adults (Walco et al., 1994).

Another issue of concern regarding management of pain with analgesics is the potential for deleterious side effects, especially respiratory depression or arrest associated with opioids (Walco et al., 1994). As Walco and associates have pointed out, the risk of respiratory problems is no more likely in pediatric populations than in adults when appropriate dosing and adequate monitoring are practiced.

Route of analgesia administration also can be a significant dilemma for children and may result in their not requesting pain analgesia for fear of receiving intramuscular injections (Pfefferbaum & Hagberg, 1993; Tarnowski & Brown, 1995a; Walco et al., 1994). In fact, fear of injections may cause children to minimize or even deny pain (Tarnowski & Brown, 1995a). Thus, pain medication should be administered in less aversive ways (i.e., either orally or intravenously) (Tarnowski & Brown, 1995a). Regardless of the route of administration, pain is often managed most effectively when medication is given on a regularly scheduled basis, especially for children with chronic pain.

When considering pharmacotherapy for pain management, the practitioner must carefully assess the etiology and severity of the child's pain in conjunction with the characteristics of the analgesic agent. For example, antipyretics are often used successfully for managing mild pain, while narcotics are frequently required to alleviate severe pain (Tarnowski & Brown, 1995a). In short, it is important to have ongoing management with frequent re-assessments to ensure that the pain is adequately controlled. Persistent pain can intensify behavioral problems and exacerbate emotional reactions such as anxiety and depression, thereby complicating treatment of pain.

Other Somatic Strategies

Surgical techniques. Because chronic, intractable pain is less common in children than in adults, surgery has been an infrequent method of treatment for pain relief. However, with increased life expectancy for many children with chronic diseases, surgical approaches may increasingly become a more accepted modality for managing pain. The primary surgical technique is the ablation of the involved nerve. However, as some experts have pointed out (Melzack & Wall, 1982; Tarnowski & Brown, 1995a) identifying and selectively destroying the affected nerve is frequently difficult. Moreover, neurosurgical techniques often only temporarily relieved pain.

Anesthetic blocks. When the ultimate goal is the numbing of a specific area, anesthetic blocks have been effectively utilized. Local anesthetics commonly are employed to manage pain during invasive medical procedures and minor surgery, including circumcisions, hypospadia repair, and hernia repair (Brown, 1985; Mather & Cousins, 1986; Schulte-Steinberg, 1980). Spinal analgesia has been recommended for children undergoing corrections for congenital anomalies, problems associated with prematurity, and neonatal respiratory disease, when general anesthesia is contraindicated. Nerve blocks, a form of regional anesthesia, provide localized anesthesia without the risk of general anesthesia or the side effects of narcotics. These approaches have been effectively employed to reduce pain during and after surgery (McGrath, 1990).

Electrical nerve stimulation. To treat pain in adults, electrical stimulation can be applied to the skin surface or by surgically implanted electrodes. The most common type of cutaneous nerve stimulation is transcutaneous electrical nerve stimulation (TENS). This technique may be useful for children with chronic pain where opioid analgesia cannot be administered (McGrath, 1990). Epstein and Harris (1978) employed TENS therapy to successfully reduce children's post-operative pain. Although this approach appears promising for pediatric populations, additional research efforts are needed to assess its efficacy and safety.

Pressure and massage. Children suffering from pain often appear to be consoled by massage, strokes, or other types of touch such as hugs. Moreover, such techniques usually offer children reassurance when they are experiencing pain. Although pressure applied to specific regions of the body may induce analgesia (McGrath, 1990), there have been no empirical studies that have examined the efficacy of therapeutic touch in pediatric pain populations.

Acupuncture involves the insertion of thin needles into designated pressure points. Gunsburger (1973) investigated the effectiveness of acupuncture therapy in children; these results were encouraging, yet further research is necessary to assess its efficacy and safety.

Behavioral and Cognitive Therapies

Contingency management. The premise underlying contingency management of children's pain is based upon the theory that children are reinforced by significant others for behaviors associated with pain (Masek, Russo, & Varni, 1984). Reinforcement for such behaviors is hypothesized to occur when children receive increased attention that is contingent upon their need for comfort and pain relief (McGrath, 1991). Thus, because these behaviors assume reinforcing properties, they continue despite the fact that the child assumes a dependent relationship with caretakers and becomes reliant upon procedures to alleviate pain.

When beginning a contingency management program, a careful assessment is conducted regarding factors that are believed to be reinforcing pain behaviors. These reinforcers may include diminished responsibility at home and at school for pain behaviors and greater emotional nurturance from family members and hospital staff. Thus, primary and secondary pain reinforcing behaviors are identified and targeted for intervention. Typically, a contingency management system is developed that rewards behaviors that are incompatible with pain, such as activity on the hospital ward, compliance with medical procedures to reduce pain, and resuming responsibility at home and at school. A heavy schedule of reinforcement is important, which is contingent on the child carrying out the desired targeted behaviors. Most important, the hospital staff and family members must be intimately and consistently involved in the program, as frequently, albeit inadvertently, they may be the reinforcers of the pain behavior (Tarnowski & Brown, 1995a).

Desensitization. Densensitization is most frequently employed in procedural related pain such as lumbar punc-

tures or bone marrow aspirations that may result in conditioned fears or anxiety (McGrath, 1991; Tarnowski & Brown, 1995a). Desensitization includes the identification of specific anxiety-producing events of a medical procedure. The anxiety elicited by the child is paired with a response such as relaxation that is incompatible to the anxiety. Eventually, a program is established that gradually exposes children to less anxiety-inducing aspects, while simultaneously teaching coping strategies designed to help the children relax and master control of the anxiety-producing situation (Wolpe, 1982).

Distraction. One commonly employed procedure for reducing pain, particularly for younger children, which may be easily implemented by parents and hospital staff, is the use of distraction. The theoretical tenet underlying distraction is inattention. Specifically, children's attention to another stimulus may directly diminish a neuronal impulse evoked by pain (McGrath, 1991). This has been supported in laboratory studies of animals in which neuronal activity evoked by continued noxious activity has been found to be directly associated with the animal's level of attention (Dubner, Hoffman, & Hayes, 1981; Price, 1988). Procedures of distraction may include playing video games, deep breathing, describing a unique object, singing, or talking about a favorite story (McGrath, 1990).

Imagery. Imagery, the process by which a child focuses intensely on the mental image of an experience or situation, has been demonstrated to be an effective means for children at all age levels to manage pain (Hilgard & LeBaron, 1984; McGrath, 1990). This procedure utilizes auditory, visual, and kinesthetic senses for generating physiological changes that produce relaxation (Tarnowski & Brown, 1995a). It has been suggested that imagery is most successful in the management of pain when children are allowed to create their own images. For example, McGrath (1991) presented a case study of a young girl with cancer who imagined magic sparkles, an invisible air to breathe in, who was better able to handle invasive medical procedures (McGrath, 1991).

Modeling. One frequently employed procedure involves the use of modeling, whereby a child learns vicariously by observing another child's behavior (Bandura, 1976). After many observations of this behavior, the child eventually acquires this desired behavior. This procedure has been especially efficacious in reducing fear and avoidant behaviors or pain when undergoing invasive medical procedures (Melamed & Siegel, 1980). Modeling has been demonstrated to be especially useful for reducing pain associated with injections, dressing changes, bone marrow aspirations, and lumbar punctures (McGrath, 1991). An important consideration in the use of modeling is the appropriate match between the model and the patient, where chronological age, previous history with medical procedures, and type of pain are similar (Tarnowski & Brown, 1995a).

Relaxation. Relaxation techniques have been used successfully in managing children's pain related to invasive treatments for cancer (Jay, Elliott, Ozolins, Olson, & Pruitt, 1985), burn injuries (Brown et al., 1994), sickle cell disease (Zeltzer, Dash, & Holland, 1979), and headaches (McGrath, 1983). The tenets underlying relaxation involve diminished sympathetic nervous system activity that results in decreased oxygen consumption and respiratory rate, increased skin resistance, and production of alpha waves (Benson, Pomeranz, & Kutz, 1984). During progressive muscle relaxation, children learn to tense and relax various muscle groups (i.e., legs or arms) to more specific areas. The effectiveness of relaxation techniques depends upon a child cognitive level, with younger children typically requiring more concrete examples. For example, McGrath (1990, 1991) described relaxation with young children who were asked to pretend that they were floppy relaxed dolls. Interventions employing relaxation include progressive muscle relaxation, yoga, meditation, and biofeedback (Tarnowski & Brown, 1995a).

Biofeedback. Biofeedback has often been employed successfully in the management of pain in children (Attanasio et al., 1985; Jessup, 1984; Turk, Meichenbaum, & Berman, 1979). It is a procedure whereby unobserved activity in the body is amplified and translated into either auditory or visual signals. The procedure allows children to receive immediate feedback pertaining to physiological parameters and thus teaches children to differentiate between relaxed and tense body states; these body states frequently have been found to be related to the presence or absence of pain. The clinical use of biofeedback has been most utilized for headaches, in which electromyogram activity in the frontalis muscle is monitored (McGrath, 1991). Although biofeedback is of potential clinical utility, several possible disadvantages include children's short attention span, cognitive limitations pertaining to the task, and young children's fear of the electrical equipment (Attanasio et al., 1985).

Stress inoculation. The stress inoculation model, which includes a package of cognitive-behavioral therapies in-cluding relaxation, imagery, and contingency management, was developed by Turk (1978). The goal of stress inoculation is to decrease observed and self-reported distress (Dahlquist, Gil, Armstrong, Ginsberg, & Jones, 1985). Stress inoculation has been employed successfully with children undergoing lumbar punctures, in whom decreases in anxiety and pain and concomitant reductions in pharmacotherapy have been observed at three- and six-month follow-ups (McGrath & deVeber, 1986). Similarly, in an investigation of pediatric patients receiving dental procedures, Nocella and Kaplan (1982) reported that children receiving stress inoculation exhibited fewer body movements in comparison to controls.

Ecologically Based Interventions

Family-focused interventions. Over the past decade, there has been a burgeoning interest in the family's adjustment and adaptation in pediatric chronic illness groups (Kazak & Nachman, 1991). More importantly, there has been an increased recognition regarding the role of the family in assisting the chronically ill child with coping and managing pain. One program involving the family in the management of pain has been developed by Kazak (1993), who employed a multimodal treatment package combining pharmacologic, cognitive, and behavioral therapies such as relaxation, distraction, and hypnosis. In this program, family members are increasingly involved in carrying out the individualized therapies; eventually they assume responsibility for the entire intervention program. Data from this program have been encouraging in supporting the integration of a systemic family approach in assisting the child with managing pain.

The importance of a systemic familial approach in managing pain is illustrated in a recent investigation. Sharpe, Brown, Thompson, and Eckman (1994) examined predictors of children's and mothers' coping strategies in managing chronic pain associated with sickle cell disease. Disease severity, socioeconomic status, child adjustment and adaptive behavior, maternal psychopathology, and family functioning were examined in mother-child dyads to assess the predictive potential of these factors on coping behavior. Less adaptive strategies of coping, including disengagement (employing less active and more passive strategies for managing pain such as wishful thinking, problem avoidance, and social withdrawal), were predicted primarily by internalizing symptoms (i.e., anxiety and depression) and a negative and pessimistic attributional style. More important, mothers who reported more active engagement strategies for coping (i.e., problem solving, cognitive restructuring, and social support) with their children's pain were more likely to endorse greater use of techniques to both prevent and effectively manage pain. Of particular importance in this investigation is that disease severity was not found to be predictive of coping strategies. Rather, familial factors, including maternal coping and psychopathology, were most predictive of children's ability to cope. This study is clinically relevant, as it underscores the importance of a family model for managing pain for children with chronic illnesses.

In a clinical application of the findings presented by Sharpe and colleagues (Sharpe et al., 1994), Tarnowski and Brown (1995b) present a case study of an adolescent with sickle cell syndrome where chronic pain had been a pervasive problem in the child's medical history. A systems approach was employed, with family members serving as coaches, which included basic education about the disease, pain management strategies (i.e., deep breathing, relaxation, and imagery) and delineation of both short- and long-term goals. Significant improvement in coping and less reliance on medical management (i.e., emergency room visits, pharmacotherapy) resulted.

School-based interventions. Consistent with the general literature in pediatric psychology, few studies have examined the efficacy of school-based interventions for children during chronic pain. Ross and Ross (1988) have described a psychoeducational program designed to facilitate the coping and behavioral management of chronic pain. A unique aspect of this program is that it addressed secondary prevention efforts to circumvent the development of chronic pain behaviors. Children were provided with information pertaining to the etiology and management of pain and strategies for coping with pain. That the data were encouraging in teaching the children to manage pain and prevent additional pain-related behaviors suggests the value of school-based interventions in this population (Ross & Ross, 1988).

Case Illustration

Clinical Presentation

T. H. is a 14-year-old African-American male with sickle cell syndrome. This disease, characterized by intermittent pain episodes, frequent infections, and poor blood cell production is a genetic recessive disorder involving abnormal red blood cells. These abnormal cells can cluster together and block normal blood flow. Individuals with sickle cell syndrome require chronic pain analgesia and have periodic exacerbations of their illness. The severity of this disease ranges from minimal to incapacitation problems that can lead to early death. Children with sickle cell syndrome can develop difficulties in adjustment due to the stressful demands of coping with recurrent medical problems and lifestyle restrictions.

Until age six, T. H. managed with only two hospitalizations, both of which were for pain crises. Although he had some difficulties with pain, T. H. and his family usually managed without seeking medical attention. However, when T. H. was approximately eight years old, he frequently began presenting in the emergency room with complaints of pain. Initially, T. H.'s pain crises could be managed in the emergency room. Soon, however, this intervention became inadequate and he required increasingly lengthy hospitalizations. Eventually, T. H. was hospitalized every month for about one week. Pain management became a major concern for T. H., his family, and the staff, who felt frustrated and disappointed regarding his numerous hospitalizations. Regardless of the treatment, T. H. continued to have frequent, severe episodes of refractory pain. After a hospitalization that lasted several weeks due to the fact that T. H. could not be weaned off opiates, the medical team consulted the pain consultation center.

Assessment Findings

At this time, T. H. was 11 years old. T. H. and his family were interviewed, and they completed several self-report measures. The consultant and the staff carefully observed T. H.'s behavior on the ward during times of different pain intensity. Evaluation results revealed a young-appearing, overweight child who gradually warmed up and became vocal and interactive. T. H. demonstrated a limited understanding of sickle cell syndrome. His pain was either nonexistent or severe, impairing, and unmanageable. T. H. could not quantify his pain, identify its location, progression or precipitants, or relate any management techniques that alleviated his pain with the exception of medication. T. H. had attended school only four days out of the previous six weeks; he primarily was spending his time at home watching television and eating snacks. T. H. had one friend, age seven, with whom he occasionally played video games. On examination, T. H. appeared anxious and depressed. T. H. had been raised by his maternal grandparents since the age of two when his mother was imprisoned. His grandmother died when he was eight years old. T. H. had no contact with his mother until her release from prison one month ago, at which time she informed him that she was going to resume taking care of him.

According to T. H.'s grandfather, his wife had been T. H.'s primary caretaker and the one responsible for managing his medical care. The grandfather had a limited understanding of sickle cell syndrome, and believed that it was a "bad disease that killed people." He did not believe that T. H.'s symptoms could be managed at home because any sign of pain indicated that T. H. might be dying. T. H.'s grandfather thought that T. H. was safest in the hospital and that only physicians could alleviate the pain that T. H. was experiencing.

T. H.'s mother missed multiple appointments without explanations, but eventually came to the clinic to meet with the consultant. She lacked any knowledge of her son's past medical history, stating repeatedly that sickle cell syndrome was not a major disease and only weak individuals needed medical assistance. She thought that T. H. should just start "acting like a man and be responsible for himself." She could not describe any circumstances in which hospitalizations would be appropriate.

Additionally, T. H. and his family described a situation of intense, prolonged conflict between his mother and grandfather. Both clearly disapproved of the other, would not disclose the reasons for their dislike, and blamed the other for T. H.'s medical problems. T. H. felt torn and often expressed his affection for his grandfather as well as his wish to get to know his mother better. On self-report measures, T. H. indicated attitudes and perceptions about his pain similar to those he expressed verbally. When charting the occurrence of his pain, T. H. recounted severe, unremitting pain that was not responsive to analgesics, and that suddenly remitted without any apparent connection to medical treatment. His grandfather's responses were consistent with the information from his interview. T. H.'s mother refused to complete the forms.

Behavioral observations were conducted by the pain consultant, the primary nurse, and the recreational therapist. T. H.'s behavior was noted to differ over the course of his hospitalization. Initially, he remained in bed with frequent complaints of pain and requests for analgesia. With time, T. H. became more mobile and began interacting with other children and staff on the hospital ward. However, when asked about his pain, T. H. continued to complain of severe, incapacitating pain and to demand medication. When engaged in activities or interacting with peers, T. H. appeared to function quite well. His pain appeared to be most problematic when demands were made upon T. H. T. H. demonstrated knowledge of few pain management strategies except for requesting analgesia and being distracted by ward activities.

Treatment Selection and Course

Following the pain assessment, the team met and agreed upon a comprehensive treatment plan that was discussed with T. H. and his family. It was decided that major areas of difficulty were (1) family conflict over T. H.'s care, which resulted in inconsistent management; (2) inability of T. H. and his family to quantify and qualify his pain and any changes or identify and employ active coping strategies other than a medical means of coping (i.e., use of the hospital and pain analgesia); and (3) the medical staff's frustration and anger with T. H. and his family.

The family agreed that T. H. would continue to reside with his grandfather. The family participated in a series of psychoeduational sessions about sickle cell syndrome, learning about effective strategies for pain management and appropriate uses of the hospital and analgesia. With the assistance of the consultant and the participation of T. H., a contract was developed describing how to manage T. H.'s symptoms at home. T. H. began working with the consultant on developing a vocabulary to describe his pain and behavioral techniques to manage it. T. H. also began individual psychotherapy to deal with his feelings and issues regarding his chronic illness and his family.

Several changes were implemented in T. H.'s medical management. For example, regular and frequent staff meetings were held to discuss his progress. A medication regimen was agreed upon; T. H. would receive analgesia on a regular schedule with a gradual tapering, based upon his response to the medication. The type of medication and dose were determined by T. H.'s level of symptomatology and his previous history of drug effectiveness. Criteria were established to evaluate T. H.'s degree of pain and the efficacy of his treatments. This was accomplished by means of staff observations and T. H.'s self-reports. A daily behavioral schedule was designed to provide structure and minimize secondary gain during the course of hospitalization. It was emphasized to the staff, T. H., and his family that the difficulties were chronic and that improvements would take considerable time.

T. H. responded to this plan; he was able to learn and begin utilizing various techniques to describe and manage his pain. His complaints of pain and demands for medication decreased. T. H. adhered closely to his hospital schedule. He was subsequently discharged with out-patient treatment that consisted of frequent medical visits, individual psychotherapy with associated family work, a detailed plan of pain management for use at home, and criteria for medication use and hospitalization.

Treatment and Follow-Up

T. H. was hospitalized over the next year, but the frequency and duration of hospitalizations declined significantly. Increasingly, T. H. developed the capacity to deal with his pain in multidimensional ways. He consistently began attending school and participating in extracurricular activities with peers. His family also complied with the treatment plan. T. H. continued in psychotherapy, discussing issues of independence and managing a chronic illness. T. H. was last hospitalized eight months ago; since that time, he occasionally has had episodes of pain, but the pain has been managed on an out-patient basis.

SUMMARY

There are numerous approaches available to physicians and psychologists for ameliorating pain in children and adolescents. Pharmacological agent(s) of choice should be selected following careful assessment and consideration of the properties of specific drugs, including dosing intervals, administrative route, side effects, and emanative effects. Although addiction potential requires consideration, clinical experience and research evidence suggest that this factor is often given too much weight in clinical decision making. Indeed, what is required is an increased educational emphasis to decrease the all-too-common undermedication problem and to dispel some of the common myths concerning the actual risks associated with pharmacological intervention with children. In general, nonsomatic intervention strategies have received considerable empirical support for use with adults. Unfortunately, additional outcome data are needed concerning pediatric populations. To date, a variety of behavioral and cognitive treatment strategies have been used to decrease distress and include those efforts aimed at increasing physical activity, reducing postural restrictions, decreasing muscular tensions, and enhancing control over noxious stimuli. In particular, multicomponent treatment packages modeled after stress-inoculation treatments (Turk, 1978) have demonstrated considerable potential. Other strategies, including family- and school-based interventions hold promise but await more formal clinical evaluation. Data suggest that broad-spectrum treatment approaches that combine drugs

with cognitive and behavioral methods are associated with the greatest probability of success.

Unfortunately, there is often considerable disparity between ideal and actual approaches to the assessment and treatment of pain in children and adolescents (Tarnowski & Brown, 1995a). The availability and effectiveness of multidisciplinary teams can make a critical difference in patient outcome. Such formal teams may not be established, readily accessible, or may be dysfunctional. Optimal evaluation and management methods hinge on experienced staff who are patient, empathic, diplomatic, and aware of the sociopolitical realities and constraints of the systems they are working in. No doubt, well-functioning multidisciplinary teams are better equipped to successfully negotiate the considerable personal and interpersonal stress and the ethical dilemmas that characterize work in this area. Empirical efforts are needed to guide the development, maintenance, and evaluation of such efforts.

REFERENCES

Abu-Saad, H. (1981). The assessment of pain in children. *Issues in Comprehensive Nursing, 5,* 327–335.

Apley, J., & Naish, L. (1958). Recurrent abdominal pains: A field survey of 1,000 school children. *Archives of Diseases in Children, 33,* 165–170.

Attanasio, V., Andrasik, F., Burke, E. J., Blake, D. D., Kabela, E., & McCarran, M. S. (1985). Clinical issues in utilizing biofeedback with children. *Clinical Biofeedback and Health, 8,* 134–141.

Bandura, A. (1976). Effecting change through participant modeling. In K. D. Krumboltz & C. E. Thoresen (Eds.). *Counseling methods* (pp. 248–265). New York: Holt, Rinehart, & Winston, Inc.

Beecher, H. K. (1959). *Measurement of subjective responses: Qualitative effects of drugs.* New York: Oxford University Press, Inc.

Benson, H., Pomeranz, B., & Kutz., I. (1984). The relaxation response and pain. In P. D. Wall & R. Melzack (Eds.), *Textbook of pain* (1st ed., pp. 817–822). Edinburgh, Scotland: Churchill Livingstone, Inc.

Bibace, R., & Walsh, M. E. (1980). Development of children's concepts of their illness. *Pediatrics, 66,* 912–917.

Bille, B. (1962). Migraine in school children. *Acta Paediatrica Scandinavia, 136* (suppl) 1.

Bonica, J. J. (1979). The need of a taxonomy. *Pain, 6,* 247–252.

Brown, R. T., Dingle, A. D., & Koon-Scott, K. (1994). Consultation. In K. J. Tarnowski (Ed.). *Behavioral as-*

pects of pediatric burn injuries (pp. 119–146). New York: Plenum Press.

Brown, T. C. K. (1985). Local and regional anesthesia in children. *Anesthesia, 407–409.*

Bush, J. P., & Harkins, S. W. (1991). *Children in pain: Clinical and research issues from a developmental perspective.* New York: Springer-Verlag.

Craig, K. D., & Grunau, R. V. E. (1991). Developmental issues: Preschool and school-age children. In J. P. Bush & S. W. (Eds.), *Children in pain: Clinical and research issues from a developmental perspective* (pp. 171–193). New York: Springer-Verlag.

Dahlquist, L. M., Gil, K. M., Armstrong, F. D., Ginsberg, A., & Jones, B. (1985). Behavior management of children's distress during chemotherapy. *Journal of Behavior Therapy and Experimental Psychiatry, 16,* 325–329.

Dubner, R., Hoffman, D. S., & Hayes, R. L. (1981). Neuronal activity in medullary dorsal horn of awake monkeys trained in a thermal discrimination task: III. Task-related responses and their functional role. *Journal of Neurophysiology, 46,* 444–464.

Epstein, M. H., & Harris, J., Jr. (1978). Children with chronic pain: Can they be helped? *Pediatric Nursing, 4,* 42–44.

Fordyce, W. E. (1976). *Behavioral methods for chronic pain and illness.* St. Louis, MO: C.V. Mosby.

Gunsburger, M. (1973). Acupuncture in the treatment of sore throat symptomatology. *American Journal of Chinese Medicine, 1,* 337–340.

Hester, N. (1979). The preoperational child's reaction to immunization. *Nursing Research, 20,* 250–255.

Hilgard, J. R., & LeBaron, S. (1982). Relief of anxiety and pain in children and adolescents with cancer: Qualitative measures and clinical observations. *International Journal of Clinical and Experimental Hypnosis, 30,* 417–442.

Hilgard, J. R., & LeBaron, S. (1984). *Hypnotherapy of pain in children with cancer.* Los Altos, CA: William Kaufmann.

Jay, S. M. (1985). Pain in children: An overview of psychological assessment and intervention. In A. R. Zeiner, D. Bendell, & C. E. Walker (Eds.). *Health psychology: Treatment and research issues* (pp. 167–196). New York: Plenum Press.

Jay, S. M., & Elliott, C. H. (1984). Behavioral observation scales for measuring children's distress: Effects of increased methodological rigor. *Journal of Consulting and Clinical Psychology, 52,* 1106–1107.

Jay, S. M., Elliott, C. H., Ozolins, M., Olson, R. A., & Pruitt, S. D. (1985). Behavioural management of children's distress during painful medical procedures. *Behaviour Research and Therapy, 23,* 513–552.

Jay, S. M., Ozolins, M., Elliott, C. H., & Caldwell, S. (1983). Assessment of children's distress during painful procedures. *Health Psychology, 2,* 133–147.

Jessup, B. A. (1984). Biofeedback. In P. D. Wall & R. Melzack (Eds.). *Textbook of pain* (pp. 776–786). Edinburgh, Scotland: Churchill Livingstone, Inc.

Karoly, P. (1991). Assessment of pediatric pain. In J. P. Bush & S. W. Harkins (Eds.), *Children in pain: Clinical and research issues form a developmental perspective* (pp. 59–82). New York: Springer-Verlag.

Katz, E. R., Kellerman, J., & Siegel, S. E. (1980). Distress behavior in children with cancer undergoing medical procedures: Developmental considerations. *Journal of Consulting and Clinical Psychology, 48,* 356–365.

Kazak, A. (1993, August). *Family adaptation related to procedural distress in childhood leukemia.* Paper presented at the annual meeting of the American Psychological Association, Toronto.

Kazak, A. E., & Nachman, G. S. (1991). Family research on childhood chronic illness: Pediatric oncology as an example. *Journal of Family Psychology, 4,* 462–483.

Masek, B. J., Russo, D. C., & Varni, J. W. (1984). Behavioral approaches to the management of chronic pain in children. *Pediatric Clinics of North America, 31,* 1113–1131.

Mather, L. E., & Cousins, M. J. (1986). Local anesthetics: Principles of use. In M. J. Cousins & G. D. Phillips (Eds.), *Acute pain management* (pp. 105–131). New York: Churchill Livingstone, Inc.

McGrath, P. A. (1990). *Pain in children: Nature, assessment and treatment.* New York: Guilford Press.

McGrath, P. A. (1991). Intervention and management. In J. P. Bush & S. W. Harkins (Eds.), *Children in pain: Clinical and research issues form a developmental perspective* (pp. 83–115). New York: Springer-Verlag.

McGrath, P. A., & deVeber, L. L. (1986). The management of acute pain evoked by medical procedures in children with cancer. *Journal of Pain and Symptom Management, 1,* 145–150.

McGrath, P. A., & Hillier, L. M. (1989). The enigma of pain in children: An overview. *Pediatrician, 16,* 6–15.

McGrath, P. J. (1987). The multidimensional assessment and management of recurrent pain syndromes in children. *Behaviour Research and Therapy, 25,* 251–262.

McGrath, P. J. (1983). Migraine headaches in children and adolescents. In P. Firestone, P. J. McGrath, & W. Feldman (Eds.), *Advances in behavioral medicine for children and adolescents* (pp. 39–57). Hillsdale, NJ: Lawrence Erlbaum Associates, Inc.

McGraw, M. B. (1941). Neural maturations exemplified in the changing reactions of the infant to the pin prick. *Child Development, 12,* 31–41.

Melamed, B. G., & Siegel, L. J. (Eds.). (1980). *Behavioral medicine: Practical applications in health care.* New York: Springer Publishing Company, Inc.

Melzack, R. (1973). *The puzzle of pain.* Harmondsworth, England: Penguin.

Melzack, R., & Wall, P. D. (1982). *The challenge of pain.* New York: Penguin.

Merskey, H. (1980). *Some features of the history of pain.* New York: Penguin.

Morrison, R. A. (1991). Update on sickle cell disease: Incidence of addiction and choice of opioid in pain management. *Pediatric Nursing, 17,* 503.

Nocella, J., & Kaplan, R. M. (1982). Training children to cope with dental treatment. *Journal of Pediatric Psychology, 7,* 175–178.

Oster, J., & Nielsen, A. (1972). Growing pains: A clinical investigation of a school population. *Acta Paediatrica Scandinavia, 61,* 329–334.

Pegelow, C. H. (1992). Survey of pain management therapy provided for children with sickle cell disease. *Clinical Pediatrics, 31,* 211–214.

Peiper, A. (1936). Hautschutzereflexe. *Jarlbuch Kinderheilkundle, 146,* 233.

Pfefferbaum, B., & Hagberg, C. A. (1993). Pharmacological management of pain in children. *Journal of the American Academy of Child and Adolescent Psychiatry, 32,* 235–242.

Price, D. D. (1988). *Psychological and neural mechanisms of pain.* New York: Raven Press.

Ross, D., & Ross, S. (1984). Childhood pain: The school-aged child's viewpoint. *Pain, 20,* 179–191.

Ross, D. M., & Ross, S. A. (1988). *Childhood pain: Current issues, research, and management.* Baltimore: Urban & Schwarzenberg.

Roth, G. J., & Majerus, P. W. (1975). The mechanism of the effect of aspirin on human platelets: I. Acetylation of a particulate fraction protein. *Journal of Clinical Investigation, 56,* 624–632.

Savedra, M., Tesler, M., Ward, J., Wegner, C., & Gibbons, P. (1981). Description of the pain experience: A study of school-age children. *Issues in Comprehensive Pediatric Nursing, 5,* 373–380.

Schechter, N. L., & Allen, D. (1986). Physicians' attitudes toward pain in children. *Journal of Developmental and Behavioral Pediatrics, 7,* 350–354.

Schulte-Steinberg, O. (1980). Neural blockade of pediatric surgery. In M. J. Cousins & P. O. Bridenbaugh (Eds.), *Neural blockade in clinical anesthesia and management of pain* (pp. 503–523). Philadelphia: J. B. Lippincott Company.

Sharpe, J., Brown, R. T., Thompson, N., & Eckman, J. (1994). Predictors of coping with pain in children with sickle cell disease and their mothers. *Journal of the American Academy of Child and Adolescent Psychiatry, 33,* 100–107.

Sternbach, R. (1968). *Pain patients: Traits and treatments.* New York: Academic Press.

Swafford, L. E. & Allen, D. (1968). Pain relief in the pediatric patient. *Medical Clinics of North America, 52,* 131–136.

Szyfrelbein, S., Osgood, P., & Carr, D. (1985). The assessment of pain and plasma B-endorphin immunoactivity in burned children. *Pain, 22,* 173–182.

Tarnowski, K. J. (1994). *Behavioral aspects of pediatric burns.* New York: Plenum Press.

Tarnowski, K. J., & Brown, R. T. (1995a). Pediatric pain. In R. T. Ammerman & M. Hersen (Eds.), *Handbook of child behavior therapy in the psychiatric setting* (pp. 453–476). New York: John Wiley & Sons.

Tarnowski, K. J., & Brown, R. T. (1995b). Psychological aspects of pediatric disorders. In M. Hersen & R. T. Ammerman (Eds.), *Advanced abnormal child psychology.* Hillsdale, NJ: Lawrence Erlbaum Associates, Inc.

Tarnowski, K. J., McGrath, M., Calhoun, B., & Drabman, R. S. 1987). Self-versus therapist-mediated debridement in pediatric burn injury. *Journal of Pediatric Psychology, 12,* 567–579.

Tesler, M., Ward, J., Savedra, M., Wegner, C., & Gibbons, P. (1983). Developing an instrument for eliciting children's descriptions of pain. *Perceptual and Motor Skills, 56,* 315–321.

Thompson, K. L., & Varni, J. W. (1986). A developmental cognitive-behavioral approach to pediatric pain management. *Pain, 25,* 283–296.

Turk, D. C. (1978). Cognitive behavioral techniques in the management of pain. In J. P. Foreyt & D. P. Rathjen (Eds.), *Cognitive behavior therapy* (pp. 199–232). New York: Plenum Press.

Turk, D. C., Meichenbaum, D., & Berman, W. H. (1979). Application of biofeedback for the regulation of pain: A critical review. *Psychological Bulletin, 86,* 1322–1338.

Unruh, A., McGrath, P., Cunningham, S., & Humphrey, P. (1983). Children's drawings of their pain. *Pain, 17,* 385–392.

Varni, J. W. (1981). Behavioral medicine in hemophilia arthritic pain management: Two case studies. *Archives of Physical Medicine and Rehabilitation, 62,* 183–187.

Varni, J. W. (1983). *Clinical behavior pediatrics: An interdisciplinary biobehavioral approach.* New York: Pergamon Press.

Varni, J. W., Katz, E. R., & Dash, J. (1982). Behavioral and neurochemical aspects of pediatric pain. In D. C. Russo & J. W. Varni (Eds.), *Behavioral pediatrics: Re-*

search and practice (pp. 177–224). New York: Plenum Press.

Varni, J. W., Thompson, K. L., & Hanson, V. (1987). The Varni-Thompson Pediatric Pain Questionnaire: I. Chronic-musculo-skeletal pain in juvenile rheumatoid arthritis. *Pain, 28,* 27–38.

Walco, G. A., Cassidy, R. C., & Schechter, N. L. (1994). Pain, hurt, and harm: The ethics of pain control in infants and children. *New England Journal of Medicine, 331,* 541–544.

Wolpe, J. (1982). *The practice of behavior therapy.* Elmsford, NY: Pergamon Press.

Zeltzer, L., Dash, J., & Holland, J. P. (1979). Hypnotically induced pain in sickle cell anemia. *Pediatrics, 64,* 533–536.

Zeltzer, L., & LeBaron, S. (1982). Hypnotic and non-hypnotic techniques for reduction of pain and anxiety during painful procedures in children and adolescents with cancer. *Journal of Pediatrics, 101,* 1032–1035.

CHAPTER 2

PREPARATION FOR MEDICAL PROCEDURES

Barbara G. Melamed

DESCRIPTION OF THE PROBLEM

Psychological and psychiatric studies indicate that illness and/or hospitalization can lead to or precipitate neurotic reactions (Freud, 1952). The experience of having invasive medical procedures by themselves does not determine the amount of distress. It may depend upon the age of the child, the anxiety of the parent, the pre-procedural coping skills, and the controllability and intensity of the medical event. It is also necessary to consider whether procedures are delivered in the hospital, requiring separation from family and friends, and eliciting fear of unfamiliar surroundings, in addition to anxiety about painful procedures. Another important consideration is the seriousness of the problem. Is the procedure likely to influence health and relieve pain and discomfort in a short-term acute procedure, or is this merely an ongoing diagnostic and treatment process for a long-standing chronic illness with strong debilitating effects? The physical burdens of an illness, such as special diets or regimens, may influence family functioning, including siblings' distress and financial strain.

Haggerty (1986) has shown that pediatrics, over the past four decades, has changed, with marked decreases in the numbers and percentages of children suffering from such common infectious diseases as polio, measles, rubella, and mumps. The bulk of hospital pediatric care has shifted during the past decade to emergency treatment of accident/injury/abuse, and to episodic readmissions of children with chronic, life-threatening diseases such as asthma, congenital heart disease, diabetes, and sickle cell anemia. The frequency of surgery to remove the tonsils and adenoids has decreased markedly. There is a transition to out-patient or one-day surgery (Starfield, 1991). This chapter considers the factors that predict which children become susceptible to problems associated with medical procedures, and provides examples of psychological treatment strategies that effectively improve adjustment.

In attempting to provide structure for the clinician, it is useful to conceptualize a coping process that takes into account the nature of the medical event, the coping resources within the family, the context within which medical care is delivered, and the stages through which the system must pass in coming to terms with and dealing with the illness or medical procedure.

McCubbin and Patterson's (1983) Double ABCX model, which was developed to represent the stages of coping in families with chronically ill children, is useful for conceptualizing responses to medical procedures. The stressor may be the need for a medical procedure that is possibly aversive, not only because of its invasive properties, but because the findings of the diagnosis may change the way the family system functions. Therefore, the stressor (A factor) must be viewed within the resources (B factor) that the family has available for meeting the demands of the stressor, and the definition (C factor) the family makes of the seriousness of the stressor. The family's subjective evaluation of the stressor is derived from previous experience in meeting such crises. A family's outlook can vary from seeing the medical procedure as a challenge or as an uncontrollable event that may strain the family's functioning. The X factor is the crisis, or the amount of disruptiveness, disorganization, or incapacitation in the family social system. It is rare that a medical procedure occurs as an acute, nonrepetitive aversive event. Most medical events occur in a context that incorporates previously experienced sounds, smells, and situations. Dental injections, which are highly feared by children especially when they are five to twelve years of age, have become associated over time with long treatment procedures, often restricting freedom of physical movement and verbal communication. Diagnostic tests, such as bone marrow aspirations, usually involve dealing with a course of events. Yet, children do not become adapted because of mere repeated exposure. The reactions of family and child are a result of long-time experience with the health care system. Visits to doctors and dentists are a necessary part of growing up. Pediatricians also find that 20 percent of all the visits for consultation about somatic conditions actually involve emotional and behavioral symptoms (Garralda & Bailey, 1990). Many of these children with psychological and psychiatric problems have high rates of referral to other medical specialists. Thus, pediatric-psychiatric liaison becomes a much needed collaboration. In addition, there are iatrogenic aspects of the medical setting that also arouse fears, among them fear of injections, of human blood, and of being touched by strangers. The medical setting can be seen as an arena in which children can develop the coping skills needed for dealing with uncomfortable or painful events. Children who have developed these skills in less serious situations may be better equipped to cope if they should be faced with hospitalization for a chronic illness that requires repeated uncomfortable or painful procedures.

Defining the Medical Procedure

Whether healthy or ill, a child's encounter with a medical procedure presents a complex set of stimuli that may compel a child's attention, elicit strong emotions, and evoke a broad range of coping strategies. These are likely to result in affective memories that may influence future encounters with the medical context (Steward, 1993). Thus, it is important to investigate how the children's memory of medical procedures can inform the medical staff to do a better job of preparation and follow up.

Medical procedures must be defined in the broadest context. They include any procedure conducted or supervised by medical personnel for the purpose of evaluating or modifying health status. Thus, standing in stocking feet on a scale, feeling the cold stethoscope pressing on one's chest or back as the doctor listens to the heart and lungs, experiencing the prick of a needle, being physically restrained by an X-ray machine or being placed in a CAT Scan or MRI with unusual, sights and sounds, are all part of the memory vividly coded as part of the kinesthetic, proprioceptive, and nociceptive experience. Thus, even though some medical procedures may not be strictly painful, the associated confusion, parent anxiety, and possible further treatment are part of the scenario. In addition, these procedures vary on the dimensions of relative painfulness, proximity of equipment and invasiveness and the ability of the child to cognitively understand the need for the procedure.

Identifying Stressors

Medical concerns include: (a) obtaining competent care; (b) understanding, clarifying, and verifying medical information; (c) the family's ability to follow through with prescribed home treatment; (d) the child's willingness to comply; (e) how to help the child endure or minimize pain; and (f) worry about results of the test and uncertainty of the prognosis. Anna Freud (1952) asserted that it is not the severity of the injury or illness that determines the relative stressfulness of an experience, but rather the meaning of it for the child. Although parent agreement on the relative stressfulness of specific medical procedures is high, children do not consistently rank order them. In addition, whereas pediatricians and children agree on the amount of pain experienced, parents tend to overestimate the amount of pain their children feel. Therefore, it is important to assess the judgments and distress of the child and understand their role in medical procedures. With experience, a child's judgment of the relative dangerousness of a particular medical procedure may diminish and future encounters may become less memorable. As children's maturity develops, they may play a larger role in the administration of a procedure, such as self-injections of insulin for diabetic children.

Identifying Resources and Coping

Resources are the psychological, social, interpersonal, and material characteristics of individual family members and the medical care system that are used by the child to meet the demands of the situation. In addition to the preexisting resources, new resources are those that must be learned or created to deal with the specifics of unique situations, such as lying still and breathing out during a bone marrow aspiration.

Coping reflects attempts by the child and family to adapt. Coping abilities vary as a function of the age of the child, previous experiences with similar situations, parental cohesiveness, and severity of the medical crises. Coping is an active process that changes with the demands of the situation within an intrapersonal (strengths and capacities of the person) and interpersonal environment.

INCIDENCE AND PREVALENCE

Each year more than 5 million children in the United States are hospitalized for diagnostic procedures. Over 45 percent of all children under the age of 7 have already been to the hospital at least once. About 15 percent of all children deal with a prolonged chronic illness (Drotar, 1981).

Children with illnesses once considered terminal, such as leukemia and cystic fibrosis, are now living longer and requiring more medical treatment. Those children who require repeated medical procedures, such as bone-marrow aspirations, may develop more anxiety and behavioral disturbances over time if they fail to cope initially.

Over one third of hospitalized children suffer transient or long-term psychological reactions including regressive behavior, increased dependency, excessive fears, anger, bedwetting, or social withdrawal. On the other hand, at least 24 percent of the children receiving medical invasive procedures reported improved self-esteem and coping behaviors after they had been hospitalized.

Often, parents attribute the onset of an emotional disturbance such as tics, enuresis, phobias, and behavior problems to an illness or to hospitalization. Such experiences in childhood may have effects that last into adulthood, in the form of attitudes toward physicians, illness, and body function (Blom, 1957). Experiences with invasive medical procedures that the parents had during their own childhood may influence their children's reactions to hospitalization. It has been shown repeatedly that anxious parents communicate their agitation to children who are anticipating medical procedures (Melamed & Ridley-Johnson, 1988). A recent study found that the interaction of mother and child traits, attitudes, and behaviors was the best predictor of how that child would respond in the waiting room before the doctor's examination and to such procedures as receiving an injection and undergoing anesthesia (Lumley, Abeles, Melamed, Johnson, & Pistone, 1990).

ASSESSMENT APPROACHES

The primary focus of this section is to identify how a functional analysis of the specific task demands and coping behaviors in sick or injured children and their families can lead to appropriate treatment. The experience of an acute medical procedure for emergency treatment, diagnosis, or ongoing care of chronic illness must be evaluated on the dimensions of predictability, controllability, and potential illness-alleviating properties. The context within which these procedures are experienced are another environmental factor to be considered. Treatments that takes place in the hospital, in an out-patient setting, or in the home provide different opportunities for reducing aversive qualities and maximizing comfort and cooperating. The provider-patient relationship is a critical determinant of whether or not the appropriate information is imparted at the right time by the appropriate caregiver to allow the patient to anticipate and adjust to potentially aversive procedures.

The quality of the mother-child interaction must be considered in the decision as to whether or not to include the parent in assisting in the procedure. Anxious mothers, especially those who judge their child as "difficult," are likely to induce agitation and anxiety by their presence (Greenbaum, Cook, Melamed, Abeles, & Bush, 1988; Lumley, Melamed, & Abeles, 1993). As more fathers accompany their children for medical appointments, their role must also be given consideration. In addition, many of today's working mothers cannot take the time off to meet the preventive health care needs of young children, let alone stay full-time with their hospitalized children. A babysitter or teacher may accompany a child to an out-patient emergency room. A child may interact with a variety of strangers (e.g., medical and graduate students, interns, residents, and faculty) in receiving services. In a teaching hospital, a child who has an in-patient elective surgery may meet on average 15 strangers who come in and out of their room in a 24-hour period. In addition, visitors of other patients, maintenance people, and others may come and go. Children must be evaluated in terms of their developmental skills, including ability to comprehend medical procedure, illness beliefs, and age-appropriate skills that may be interfered with by ongoing medical intervention. Previous personality disposition and current coping strategies may influence their ability to learn new methods for facing acute procedures. In addition, the physical condition itself must be explored for influences of disease progression, side effects of treatments, age of onset, duration of illness, and course of stressors in the care of chronic diseases.

Medical Issues

Length of Illness

Children with chronic illnesses and their families are exposed to highly stressful aversive events at different times during their development. Fifteen percent of all children will experience one or more chronic illnesses by age 15, and as many as 30 percent of these children may be handicapped by secondary social and psychological problems. Many children who previously would have died of cancer, cystic fibrosis, diabetes, and renal failure are reaching adolescence and adulthood due to advances in medical care. However, their quality of life involves adapting to an often complex treatment regimen, which causes them to feel alienated from their age group. Studies have supported the conclusion that although chronic illness can be seen as a life stressor for children, the disease process itself does not appear to be the primary cause of behavioral adjustment problems (Drotar, 1981). Most children show surprising resilience and regain a level of adaptive coping with minimal psychological intervention. However, the child who shows a protracted retreat from age-appropriate developmental tasks may be at risk for more serious psychological problems.

The impact of the illness depends on a number of factors including (1) features unique to the illness, its course, severity, visibility, and the degree of handicap it imposes; (2) specific attributes of the child, such as age of onset of the illness, intellectual and cognitive abilities, and social and emotional adjustment; (3) family resources, such as problem-solving skills, level of cohesion, adaptability to change, and openness of communication; and (4) support systems that are available to the child and his or her family, comprising extended family, friends, and community resources (Drotar, 1981; Sperling, 1978; Willis, Elliot, & Jay, 1982).

Controllability/Predictability

The degree of which medical experiences are perceived as controllable to children depends upon many factors. The child's previous experience in the situation can provide information about the control or lack of control and may affect the child's expectations regarding his or her ability to cope. For children who have repeated exposure to bone marrow and lumbar punctures, Katz and colleagues (Katz, Kellerman, & Siegel, 1980) have found that there are developmental differences in pain expression and tolerance. In addition, information provided in advance about the upcoming event may reinvoke an anxiety response that had previously been conditioned. Children also differ in terms of information and coping styles. Burstein and Meichenbaum (1979) found that children who tended to avoid playing with hospital-related toys one week before surgery were more anxious about hospitalization than those who chose to play with such toys.

Psychological and Psychiatric Issues

Effects of medical experiences are not uniform and depend on children's temperament and age, as well as their cognitive and behavioral styles. The degree to which the child and family perceive that they can control illness-related stressors may influence how they cope. The perception of the ability to cope depends on previous experience as well as current perception of controllability. The following areas must be assessed in order to determine whether a given child or family may need help coping with medical procedures: temperament, age, timing of preparation, previous experience, coping tasks, and parenting variables.

Temperament

Individual temperamental traits or behavioral styles that place a child at risk for poor coping consist of "difficult temperament" or tendency to "withdrawal" during stress. Lumley and associates (1993) demonstrated that children who have these temperament characteristics and whose mothers try to give them information do poorer during anesthesia for surgery than those who have the opposite characteristics. Difficult children cooperated more with separation and anesthesia induction if mothers had used distraction to help the children prepare for surgery.

Age and Sex

Younger children, particularly those less than five years old may be more vulnerable to separation from familiar adults than their older counterparts. Their knowledge of health, illness, and hospitalization is likely to be at a primitive level. Thus, they may fear more immediate physical events such as shots and restraints, whereas older children may have more abstract reasoning and fear more of the long-term consequences of illness, such as contagion or disfigurement. Younger children may have distorted ideas about pain and illness that heighten their apprehensions. Some children seem to believe that painful medical procedures, illness, and hospitalization are punishments for wrongdoing or the result of a deliberate desire of the practitioner to hurt them. Older children who are faced with severe pain may regress to a more primitive level of reasoning. While preschool children may be most threatened by medical or dental instruments, school-age children are likely to be more upset by their dealing with health practitioners themselves. In preschool children, fears about separation from their parents and anxiety about strangers may be more significant than physical fears. Adolescents, on the other hand, have fears about health and bodily integrity. Older children's fears are more likely to be the result of unpleasant memories of previous visits to the doctor or dentist. Thus, the information that is provided to help a child deal with an invasive medical procedure must be geared toward his or her level of thinking. Brown and colleagues (Brown, O'Keeffe, Sanders, & Baker, 1986) found that children use different coping styles depending upon age. Older children reported increased coping cognitions and used a greater number of different types of strategies. Positive self-talk was the most common coping strategy across all ages. Attention diversion was frequently the most widely used with injection situations. Catastrophizing strategies occurred most often with injections, during which children focused on negative affect, anxious anticipation, or rumination about the situation. Girls and boys tended to use similar coping strategies, but girls reported greater use of positive self-statements and tended to focus on negative aspects of the stressor.

Timing of Preparation

Older children, usually seven years of age or older, can benefit from advanced preparation about what to expect and instruction on how to handle the upcoming events. They have the abstract cognitive capacity to re-hearse events before they occur, and to try out coping strategies using imagery. Younger children, however, should not be prepared too far in advance of the upcoming preparation. Very young children may benefit from preparation that takes place in their homes and that involves mothers as preparatory agents. For example, it has been demonstrated that film modeling in advance of surgery reduced anxiety more in children aged seven and older a week in advance of their own hospitalization, whereas children under 7 years of age become more anxious, sweating more profusely during the admissions process (Melamed, Meyer, Gee, & Soule, 1976). In children having out-patient (ambulatory) surgery, distraction was more effective than giving them information about procedures in the absence of having time to learn how to cope with them (Faust & Melamed, 1984).

Previous Experience

Self-efficacy, or children's belief that they will cope successfully, may be influenced by how well they coped with similar experiences in the past. If the upcoming event is familiar and has been effectively handled in the past, then additional information may be unnecessary. However, this is not always the case. Children faced with repeated lumbar punctures and bone marrow aspirations, for example, in the treatment of a variety of cancers, may become more anxious and show less appropriate behavior in the face of the impending event. Even with elective surgery, it was found that hospital preparation by slide-audiotape did not improve adjustment and could even sensitize children who were too young or who had previous negative experiences (Melamed, Dearborn, & Hermecz, 1983).

Coping Tasks

Moos (1982) defined a useful framework for conceptualizing tasks typically required by children undergoing invasive medical procedures. The first group of tasks is primarily illness-related, and includes management of pain and other symptoms, coping with hospital and treatment procedures, and developing and maintaining satisfactory relationships with the medical personnel. The second group involves maintaining emotional balance (such as moderating anxiety), maintaining a sense of self-worth and competence, sustaining satisfactory relationships with significant others, and preparing for possible loss of functioning that may result from the illness.

Moderating Parenting Variables

The emotional contagion by which the parental anxiety is communicated to the child, both nonverbally and verbally, requires evaluation. If a parent is so distressed that they cannot help the child cope with the ongoing course of events, it may be better to restrict their role in the medical procedure. Many studies have demonstrated that the more fearful the parent, the more likely they will negatively affect the child's adjustment to the procedure (Greenbaum et al., 1988). However, if parents bring their own anxiety under control they may be valuable in helping the child modulate and cope effectively with the procedure.

Young children frequently demand the presence of their parent for routine medical procedures, such as inoculations and blood tests (Gonzalez et al., 1989). Although there may be an increase in distress and protest in young children during intravenous and inoculation procedures when the parent is present, this behavior is interpreted as a signal for seeking help (Gross, Stern, Levin, Dale, & Wojnilower, 1983; Shaw & Routh, 1982). Separation of young children from their mothers may lead to greater disruptiveness. Once maternal and child characteristics that put a child at risk are identified, it is possible to do brief relaxation training with mothers and train them to become more effective coaches for their children. Even in situations of intense and repeated pain, such as venipunctures or bone marrow and lumbar punctures, distraction can be a useful technique (Blount et al., 1992; Manne, Bakeman, Jacobsen, Gorfinkle, & Redd, 1994).

The immediate goals of psychological preparation are to prevent children's excessive anxiety, improve their cooperation with procedures, and hasten physical recovery. The long-term goal is to teach children coping skills for self-control, maintaining respect for health care providers, and having them become advocates of preventive health for their own children. Often, health care professionals can recognize cues of parental discomfort and offset possible negative influences by helping these parents acquire the information that they need to help children cope with medical experiences.

Medical Management Issues

The medical setting is a context that is useful both for the prevention of maladaptive anxiety disorders and for providing an opportunity to advance the integration of theories of stressful experience within a developmental perspective. In fact, children with early traumatic dental or medical experiences have been found to show a greater incidence of somatic disturbances and neurotic tendencies (Sermet, 1974; Shaw & Thoreson, 1974). Evidence based on retrospective report in the adult dental literature indicates that dental fears may be learned in childhood (Kleinknecht, Klepac, & Alexander, 1973). Fears of injections, choking, and medical sounds and smells are well represented in children 4 to 14 years of age. Several studies indicate that children who have early negative experiences with physicians or surgery have increased dental and medical anxiety later in development (Cuthbert & Melamed, 1982).

The management of a child's illness involves reports of the mother regarding symptom history, and clinical observation of the child with signs being measured through instrumentation, blood tests, and behavior. The proper management of the child depends upon appropriate diagnosis by the physician, correct choice of medical regimen, and the maintenance of compliance with medical and physical rehabilitation. If any of these steps are not fulfilled, then intervention and recovery will be impeded. If parents bring their child to medical professionals only when they are feeling bad or when infection occurs, then going to the doctor inevitably becomes linked with pain, interfering with the physician's being able to establish a trusting relationship. Thus, medical management must be considered within a complex model of information provision, feedback, reintegration of necessary changes in the patient's ongoing life activities, and feedback to the physician regarding changing physical status. It is only when open communication exists that the optimal trajectory is functioning. Assistance in information gathering, prescribing and obtaining relief from the distressing symptoms must be considered simultaneously with the promotion of healthy behavior and symptom monitoring. In the course of chronic illnesses, such as asthma, childhood diabetes, cystic fibrosis, or juvenile rheumatoid arthritis, good monitoring and regimen adherence reduce the exacerbation of controllable symptoms. Even minor elective surgery has associated uncertainty, potential risks of anesthesia problems, and should never be considered as "not serious" by the physician in communicating with the parent. In addition, age of the child and developmental cognitive maturity should determine to a large extent what role the child should play in assuring their own optimal care.

Psychological and Behavioral Treatments

The first step in determining whether psychological treatments are necessary is to define what the medical procedures involve. It is important to understand whether or not they are time limited, constitute discrete painful stimuli, and give the child control over their onset or offset. Next, in order to optimize the child's ability to withstand pain and prevent anxiety, the child's emotional and behavioral resources need to be ascertained. Has the child coped with this type of experience in the past? If so, what was done in order to maintain cooperation? The child's ability to tolerate drugs and the potential advantage of self-control procedures should be evaluated. If there is a sibling with whom the child has a good relationship, it is important to explore whether or not the other child can assist. Parental anxiety and concerns must also be considered. Parents' abilities to coach their child through a stressful procedure are very important, and may alleviate some of their own sense of helplessness that they could not prevent the occurrence of the illness.

Not every child needs preparation for routine medical procedures. Sometimes, if the child is too young, or not able to profit from information, guided rehearsal and assistance through the actual procedure is better than advanced preparation. There is a risk of sensitizing children who are not cognitively mature or who have already had a negative experience with the procedure.

There are at least three primary goals for psychological treatment: (1) encouraging trusting relationships, (2) providing emotional support, and (3) giving age-appropriate information that will be useful for developing coping strategies at the proper time prior to or during an invasive medical event. Each of these will be discussed below with illustrative examples provided from the literature.

Encouraging Trusting Relationships

Practitioners can put potentially frightening procedures in perspective by demonstrating the sights and sounds of the instruments on themselves or parents. The child can be encouraged to participate by holding instruments, or choosing which arm to use for the intravenous. Children given control over rest periods were found to be more cooperative during dental procedures (Corah, 1973). Routinely, the hospital staff should make an effort to know a patient's likes and dislikes at the time of admission. When staff use the child's name and talk about the child's hobbies and school interests, they personalize the visits and communicate interest and concern.

Parents should be allowed to stay for as much of the process as possible. Particularly, children who are afraid of strangers and unfamiliar surroundings and who are younger than eight should have the option of having a parent sleep in the room overnight. Children can be encouraged to bring a favorite toy or blanket to make the transition from home less traumatic. If the child will only be staying at the hospital for a short time, items that will provide immediate distraction (e.g., videogames) should be packed. Children in hospital settings should be encouraged to draw or talk freely about their fears and anxieties, so that the staff can normalize unusual hospital regimens. The child who comes prepared to establish friendly relationships with strangers who will provide medical care is more likely to be trusting. The child should not be lied to about the nature of the stressor. They should be encouraged to participate in the procedure, understand the positive benefits of treatment, and to use coping methods that they have learned to use successfully in other situations. Children should not be made to feel that they can embarrass their parents or fail to meet their parents' expectations. Such sayings as "Be brave . . . don't cry" should be discouraged.

Providing Emotional Support

Emotional support helps the patient reduce anxiety and builds confidence in the patient's ability to cope with pain. Research demonstrates that children need to be rewarded for specific cooperative behaviors as well as be corrected when they fail to give a required response. Reassuring physical touches, rather than words such as "It won't hurt too much," may help relax the child (Greenbaum, Lumley, Turner, & Melamed, 1993). The child and health care provider should agree on specific words, numbers, or hand signals that indicate a need for a rest period.

Providing Information

Knowing what to expect helps the child to anticipate how the procedure will feel and may provide ways that the patient can control the discomfort. In many cases, medical procedures are painful and children have little control over the length of time they must tolerate the procedure. In those cases, information should not be provided too far in advance of the actual situation. Specific information about how to behave is often better than detailed explanations about why certain things are done.

Some procedures, such as removal of a cast, are threatening but not painful. The child may be frightened by seeing the injured limb, by the noise and vibrations from the saw, the fear of being cut, or the burnt smell of the cast. In such cases, sensory information has been shown to be more effective than general information in preparing the child. For example, children from 6 to 11 years of age who received information concerning how the saw might sound and how the limb under the cast would look and feel exhibited less observable distress during removal of the cast than other children receiving no message or just general information (Johnson, Kirchoff, & Endress, 1975). A child's ability to benefit from information depends in part on previous experience in the situation and prior attempts at coping. Some children benefit from having a chance to play with hospital-related toys that allow them to depict a child undergoing the procedure. Film or peer modeling, in which the child observes other children successfully coping with the same procedures has also been found to be helpful. For children who are very frightened or too young to understand, distraction is often a better strategy for allaying fear, especially in the anticipation of the procedure. Thus, watching a pleasant television show, or telling jokes might be part of the treatment.

Imagery Procedures

The use of imagination can be helpful in creating an attitude of mastery. If children are encouraged to emulate favorite figures, or imagine themselves helping their hero by tolerating short-term procedures, pain and anxiety can be reduced. Illustrative of this approach would be to tell a child to imagine that they are on their favorite ride at Disney World, or opening birthday presents.

Modeling

This procedure provides the observer with exposure to aspects of the aversive situation through the eyes of another child. In addition to preparing children for restorative dental procedures, bone marrow aspirations, and lumbar punctures, this medium can be used to teach specific self-care skills, such as injection skills to diabetic youngsters. With modeling, the child has an opportunity to acquire behaviors in the absence of first-hand experience. By observing a live or filmed peer successfully undergo a medical procedure, the young patient learns appropriate and cooperative strategies to use during the medical situation. Participant modeling gives the child practice in the coping response and improves performance in the actual situation (Klingman, Melamed, Cuthbert, & Hermecz, 1984).

Modeling is recommended to prepare children who are inexperienced with routine medical procedures,

because both procedural information and cooperative behavior are portrayed. Learning about coping skills can also occur. Children report less anxiety and experience reduced physiological arousal if they view a hospital videotape prior to the experience (Melamed & Siegel, 1975). However, if the child has had a previous unpleasant experience, or is too young, this type of preparation may be contraindicated, as it may lead to sensitization. Particular attention must be paid to the timing of preparation media. Younger children should not be prepared too far in advance of the event. Children over seven years of age appear to benefit from advanced preparation (Melamed, Meyer, Gee, & Soule, 1976). In some cases, parents also receive preparation and can help their child get ready for the experience. Behavioral rehearsal can allow the child to have a cathartic experience prior to the actual situation. Studies have shown that mothers trained to be coaching assistants have children who adjust better during procedures and leave the hospital sooner (Peterson & Shigetomi, 1981; Zastowny, Kirschenbaum, & Meng, 1986).

Systematic Desensitization

If the child is very frightened, a more gradual approach is indicated. Particularly for an avoidant child when the other approaches have failed to work, systematic desensitization (SD) may be the treatment of choice. Children and adults have been treated successfully by exposing them either in imagination or real life to medical events. Fear of injections (Taylor, Ferguson, & Wermuth, 1977), dental treatment (Ayer, 1973), and intravenous procedures and hemodialysis phobias (Katz, 1974; Nimmer & Kapp, 1974) have been treated by desensitization. SD involves the construction of a graded hierarchy of anxiety-evoking situations that approximate the feared situation, such as receiving injections. At each step a competing response, such as muscle relaxation or emotive imagery, is paired with the feared scene. Although SD is usually effective with adults, it is less well-evaluated in children and it may be more practical to introduce them slowly to the real situation. For children with limited imagery ability or difficulty in relaxing, in-vivo desensitization is often better. This involves guiding the child through real life steps. For instance, it may be beneficial to gradually and systematically introduce the child to the dental chair, dental assistant, and sounds and smells of the operatory when there is no actual treatment undertaken. Sawtell, Simon, and Simeonsson (1974) demonstrated that the dental - assistant's friendly chat with the child outside of the dental operatory also reduced fear behavior. Again, the elements of building a trusting, emotionally supportive relationship should not be underestimated.

Hypnosis

Hypnosis has been used with some success in helping children adjust to bone marrow aspiration, and chemotherapy procedures (Kellerman, Zeltzer, Ellenberg, & Dash, 1983). Children can be more easily hypnotized by allowing them to create their own imagery (Gardner, 1974).

Distraction

Helping the patient think about something other than the procedure at hand has been highly effective (Manne et al., 1994). Illustrative examples include teaching the child to count the number of ceiling tiles, watch TV cartoons, or play videogames. Having mothers coach their children to use partyblowers to offset distress has assisted children to get through procedures associated with chemotherapy. It is also important to understand under what circumstances distraction works best. In one study comparing distraction and film modeling (Faust & Melamed, 1984), it was found that same-day surgery children were less anxious when shown a distracting film prior to surgery rather than a videotape modeling a child's experience. The need for immediate information in the absence of time to practice coping may make information more threatening. Again, it is essential to obtain the child's previous history of coping strategies that can be used effectively with minimal prompting.

Operant Reinforcement Procedures

Children should be reinforced by praise or by tangible reinforcers for appropriate behavior. This can be most helpful in teaching the child to discriminate the desirable behavior. Although this has been widely applied to increase compliant behaviors in medically related situations (i.e., drug-taking and oral hygiene), few efforts have been directed at reducing children's medical fears by various reinforcements.

Pharmacological Treatments

Adjunctive drugs. Dentists routinely use local anesthetics to reduce the pain involved in injection and drilling for routine restorative treatment. Ridley-Johnson and

Melamed (1986), in a review of the literature on this subject, argue against the continued use of the anesthetic once the child is able to tolerate the procedure. Obviously, the need for conscious sedation in the case of extractions is entirely different. Often suppositories are used to induce relaxation in toddlers and other youngsters prior to separation from the parent. Jay, Elliot, Katz, and Siegel (1987) demonstrated the effectiveness of combined cognitive therapy and diazepam in improving cooperation of children experiencing repeated bone marrow aspirations. In many settings where brief but painful procedures are indicated, conscious sedation is employed. The use of Patient Controlled Analgesia in the recovery phase of operations needs to be further explored. Often children are undermedicated for surgical procedures because of the mistaken belief that they do not experience the same pain as adults. There is evidence that the reporting of pain behavior may differ as a function of age of the child (Bush & Harkins, 1991). It is necessary to explore both verbal and nonverbal cues (grimacing, white knuckles) to determine the need for pharmacological treatments that may alleviate pain and distress. There are many methods of assessing pain in children, ranging from self-report to physiological measures (Karoly, 1991). In general, there is very little danger of children becoming addicted to pain medication.

CASE ILLUSTRATION

Injection Phobias

Fear of injections occurs in 10/100,000 individuals (Agras, Sylvester, & Oliveau, 1969). Injections remain the most common painful medical procedure experienced by children. It is a serious problem if left untreated in that it may lead to delay of preventive intervention in both pediatric and dental settings. Most children develop this fear in regard to receiving dental treatment where a topical is used to prevent discomfort. The three most frequent fears reported by children include injections, choking, and drilling (Cuthbert & Melamed, 1982). When children are rated as highly anxious prior to their immunizations, they are also most likely to be distressed during the procedure. Adult patients with injection phobias may avoid necessary diagnostic and medical treatment (catheters, hemodialysis) due to their anxiety about the invasive procedures. If left untreated, dental injection fears may generalize to other medical situations, including avoidance of hospital settings completely. In cases of children who require intravenous injections because of dialysis or cancer treatments, the fear may become injurious to their health. Children with acute lymphoblastic leukemia (ALL) are treated by frequent invasive medical procedures including intramuscular and intravenous injections, lumbar punctures and bone marrow aspirations. Children must learn to inhibit screaming and flailing or restraint may be required, further generating painful memories of the experience. Children who need to self-inject insulin in the care of their illness must learn how to prepare and safely administer their own medication. If they are anxious about finger pricks and fail to comply with blood glucose monitoring, they may develop complications in their metabolic stability by injecting incorrect doses at inappropriate times. Anticipatory fear can sometimes cause more physical and emotional discomfort than the stressor itself.

Clinical Presentation

The following case of an adolescent girl's difficulty with medical procedures was selected given that it was necessary to consider her previous medical experience and family factors in the treatment of her phobia of injections. The Casey family had just returned from a two year living experience in India, where the father was a career diplomat. In order to reenter the public school the children had to receive inoculations to satisfy board of health requirements. The 16-year-old daughter Cindy was terrified of needles and began having trouble concentrating and sleeping, and related these problems to her anticipation of receiving the inoculations.

Assessment Findings

Initial Interview

The 16-year-old youngster came with her mother for the intake interview. Cindy described her problem as a specific fear of injections, both when she is receiving them and when she observes others being injected. She said that she has always been afraid and faints at the onset of injection procedures. The only exception is when she has no time to anticipate the shot. Her attempts at overcoming this problem by talking logically to herself or by blocking the thoughts of the shot have been unsuccessful. She feels very limited by the problem since she wanted to consider a medical career. Even thinking about marriage and the required blood tests makes her become anxious. The history of the problem was not associated

with any specific traumatic event. Cindy's father also reported syncope and fear of fainting before shots.

Evaluation

The assessment evaluation consisted of administration of several questionnaires, in vivo testing of the fear in the dental operatory, and physiological reactivity to watching a videotape of intravenous and dental injections. In addition, Cindy's mother completed the Child Diagnostic Screening scale. A consultation with the neurologist was initiated to rule out an episode of epilepsy when the patient experienced a fainting response while observing children with diabetes self-inject.

Results from the questionnaires indicated a well-circumscribed fear of injections, needles, and related areas which had become generalized. For instance, she was afraid of dogs because if they had rabies and bit her she would need shots. In addition, the fear was elicited not only by the actual event of getting a shot, but also viewing of this and other medical procedures in movies or on television. Her reaction began with nausea, which then made her feel dizzy and faint. A fear of enclosed places, thought to be related to a sense of nausea, similar to that elicited by the threat of an injection threat led to her avoidance of tunnels, small rooms, and elevators. Her scores on the Fenz-Epstein questionnaire (Fenz & Epstein, 1965) indicated feelings of insecurity in addition to elevation on autonomic and muscular arousal dimensions. Although her total score on the total Fear Survey Schedule (Wolpe & Lang, 1964) was within normal limits, elevations were found on prospects of a surgical operation, medical odors, premature heart beats, witnessing surgical operations, doctors, and fainting and becoming nauseous. She completely skipped over items of human blood and animal blood. She reported that after seeing the beginning of a film in the eighth grade about giving blood, she fainted.

On the positive side, Cindy had many friends and hobbies, including horses, reading, swimming, and dramatics. Her profile score on the Mark-Matthews Phobia questionnaire (Marks & Matthews, 1979) indicated a specific blood-injury phobia. Her imagery ability was measured to be of average ability (Sheehan, 1967).

The mother's report of her problems as seen in the Child Diagnostic Screening Scale also revealed minimum problems. When questioning the parent about how this interfered with their functioning, it was reported that her concerns led to the careful planning of trips requiring immunizations. History of the family's illnesses was positive for heart disease. Cindy also had scoliosis and wore a Milwaukee brace from 12 to 14 years of age. At this time, she was occasionally teased by school mates, which made her feel socially isolated.

At the time of evaluation, the need for treatment was high, in that the youngster required immunization to be readmitted to high school after living abroad. Other factors that may have been adding to stress at the time were also evident. Her mother had recently had a hysterectomy with a negative biopsy. In addition, Cindy's 23-year-old sister had recently married and moved from the home.

Treatment Selection and Course

The first step of the procedure, given her refusal to go to the clinical laboratory for the immunization, involved imaginal flooding to scenes she associated with past fearful experiences in which she fainted during injections. To illustrate the personalization and concreteness of this process of reinstigating the memory prototype, a specific scene is described:

> You are 9 years old and you are in the doctor's office to get your gamma globulin shot. Everyone is in a large white room. Your heart beats faster as one by one your mom, sister, and brother go first and you are next. Your palms are sweaty and you feel nauseous. Your dad and the doctor and you enter a small dim room with a black flat table in the center. When your turn comes you are forced bodily on the table and you need to have the shot in your rear end. You feel tense all over. You are screaming and your fists are clenched so tight that you break a Barbie doll you are holding. You feel the air conditioning even though you are feeling hot all over, and you can smell the alcohol.

For this youngster, her role in the family has revolved around her injection phobia. They travel frequently because of the father's occupation and they often visit countries requiring immunizations. She apparently has become a focus of family attention as indicated by the second scene she created regarding immunization:

> Your family is sitting around the dinner table discussing a trip overseas to either Korea or India. If you go to Korea you do not need a shot, but if you want to go to India you must get immunized. As you start thinking about getting that shot for India you tense up all over. You feel hot and your stomach

feels sick and nervous. Even though you know it won't hurt much, you still feel trapped and depressed. You really prefer going to India, but having to get that shot makes you uncomfortable. You feel out of control.

Flooding consisted of creating three levels for each of these two high anxiety-provoking situations so that they could be presented within a graded exposure (in imagery), assuring success at the lowest level. So, for instance, in the first scene described above, having the choice of immunization in her arm rather than in her rear end reduced its impact. The patient is given five minutes of relaxation before each trial. This is to help her get into a state that would enhance vividness of imagery to the flooding scripts. Then sixty minutes is spent in presenting each step of the scene from the least to the most frightening until each can be imagined twice in succession. Each trial lasts approximately six minutes, with the therapist prompting her once per minute by giving her segments from her own words regarding the physiological reactions or cognitions associated with her fear. The patient gives fear ratings on a scale of 1 to 10, with 1 = "completely relaxed" and 10 = "as afraid as I've ever been." She also rates vividness on a 10 point scale from 1 = "no image at all," to 10 = "as vivid as though I were actually there." The patient is encouraged to try to experience all the fear that would actually be felt in the real experience.

The patient began to fall asleep during the third session. This may have been an avoidance response or habituation to the scene content. Physiological recordings taken during the imagery periods did reveal that her heart rate dropped over the three sessions. Her self-report ratings generally revealed only a moderate degree of vividness and her ratings did not correspond well with the hierarchy of fears. She said that she had some difficulty in taking the "imagery" seriously and this reportedly interfered with her feeling fearful. She also could not imagine the "smell" of the alcohol or "feel" the air conditioning.

Behavioral Test

Given the difficulty of having her reduce her fear by the flooding procedures, a decision was made to evaluate a hierarchical arrangement of low to highly fearful items including having her imagine that she was receiving the two injections she needed to re-enter school. Some of these scenes involved viewing two videotapes of injections being received by children. The second demonstrated self-injection procedures administered by young girls and boys who were dealing with juvenile diabetes. During this behavioral test, Cindy was cooperative in attempting to view needles and videotapes of injections. However she refused to watch blood being drawn from another patient and would not "stick" her own finger for blood (See Table 1.1). Her heart rate was variable. Table 1.1 presents the in vivo situations in the actual hierarchical order which was constructed.

Given her previous report of fainting, her blood pressure was monitored during all of these procedures. Her baseline blood pressure prior to the videotape of a child receiving a blood test was 120/80 mmHg. During the viewing the tape segment, it dropped to 90/69 mmHg. During the viewing of the diabetes videotape, the same precipitous drop in blood pressure was observed.

The patient was also seen by the dentist in a pediatric dental clinic. As she was being prepared to receive a novocaine injection, she began to faint, at which point her blood pressure dropped significantly. The dentist pushed her reclining chair back to elevate the client's feet and the fainting episode was terminated. She actually refused to receive the injection and tolerated the cavity restoration without the anesthetic.

As a continuing part of in vivo desensitization, she agreed to observe self-injection procedures. To assure medical supervision, we conducted this therapy on the juvenile diabetes in-patient unit under the supervision of a nurse. Cindy was able to watch one injection that took 10 minutes of preparation. As soon as another child was preparing, Cindy said that she felt faint and nauseous. She put her head down but looked as though she was going to fall out of her chair. The patient actually appeared to be having a seizure. She became rigid, her eyes rolled back in her head, and she became incontinent. With the help of the nursing staff, she was laid down on a couch and she awoke startled. She said she felt very tired and slept until her parents arrived to pick her up. We initiated a consultation with Neurology to evaluate her condition for possible seizure disorder versus vagal-syncope.

The neurologist evaluated Cindy's reported history of tonic-type convulsions that had been reported during infancy, and did an EEG. He felt that, with an unremarkable EEG and the fact that the patient did not hyperventilate, these episodes are likely to be signs of vaso-vagal syncope. The family history revealed that the grandfather had Parkinson's disease and may have had seizures. The father has syncope when he sees needles, and the mother also reported some episodes with syncope and rigidity. The neurological examination of the patient revealed no major cognitive, memory, or affective disturbances. Cranial nerves II–XII were entirely normal. Motor examination revealed good strength throughout. There was no weakness, fasciculation, or atrophy. The cerebellar testing was normal. Sensory examination including position sense testing was normal. Deep tendon reflexes were symmetrical and Cindy had a normal flexor plantor response.

The conclusion of the neurologist was as follows: "I certainly agree with you that with a history of vaso-vagal episodes one can see seizures if there is a rapid decrease of brain perfusion. It is interesting to note, however, that the father also has similar vaso-vagal problems when he sees needles. He does not seize however. One wonders therefore whether she could have a propensity for epilepsy which is associated with seizures in infancy and now a lower threshold with vaso-vagal syncope."

In order to rule out clear epileptic disorder, another EEG and a CT scan were conducted. These results were perfectly normal. He indicated that if behavior therapy was unsuccessful, some type of medication prior to the time she must undergo a procedure that has needles

Table 1.1. Patient's Injection Hierarchy

Least Anxiety Provoking

1. Doctor's examination table visible.
2. Observe injections in oranges.
3. Sit in dental chair.
4. View table of syringes and alcohol.
5. Touch instruments on dental tray.
6. View test tubes of blood.
7. Hold syringe.
8. In car on way to get shots.
9. Watching another patient waiting for a blood test.
10. Leave Fear Clinic to drive to clinic for shot.
11. Enter doctor's office at clinic.
12. Watch finger prick and blood drawn on another patient.
13. Wipe your own finger with alcohol for shot.
14. Watch dental injection on video.
15. Nurse swabs arm with alcohol for shot.
16. Your own finger prick is taken.
17. Watch syringe drawn up with immunizing fluid.
18. Videotape of child receiving shot before surgery.
19. Watch a laboratory test in blood laboratory.
20. Receive injection.
21. Receive second shot.
22. Immediately after shot.
23. Five minutes after shot.
24. Fifteen minutes after shot.
25. Told that she may need more shots.

Most Anxiety provoking

associated with it should be considered. Once the therapist felt satisfied that there was no seizure disorder, plans were made to generalize the successes she had had to the actual situation that brought her into treatment. Therefore, a trip was planned to accompany her to the health department clinic for the needed immunizations. This clinic visit was treated as part of the therapy. Components of her fear involved the waiting, the sights and smells of the clinic, and the presence of her brother. She was congratulated for her success. Therapy continued since there were possibly more immunizations required and the patient still feared medical procedures. She completed the therapy in 12 sessions.

Termination and Follow-Up

The patient felt proud of her ability to receive the required inoculations for immunization with the therapist. She chose to continue so that she could have dental treatment and future immunizations without being fearful.

The therapy demonstrated the need to consider the physiological as well as the verbal report of fear of injections. While systematic desensitization with in vivo exposure was the treatment that led to success, without monitoring blood pressure and merely proceeding in the typical manner the patient could have fainted or had a seizure in an unprotected situation. In addition, although the histrionic behavior and family modeling components could have led to the choice of a more psychodynamic approach, the importance of her receiving the immunizations before the start of the school semester prompted the behavioral approach. Treatment success, the awareness of her vaso-vagal syncope and the ability to use distracting imagery and relaxation training to get through the inoculations, left her feeling more competent and in self-control for future medical encounters.

SUMMARY

This chapter attempted to define what aspects of hospitalization or medical procedures tend to evoke the greatest anxiety in children. Medical procedures take place in a social context, and it is important to examine the effects of this. In addition to the uncertainty of events, most procedures involving injections or venipunctures provoke concern about pain. If children are separated from parents, this may heighten their sense of insecurity. Even though children may show more distress in the presence of their mother, children (particularly those between 5 and 8 years of age) express a preference for having the parent with

them during injections (Gonzalez et al., 1989). Thus, by a thorough functional analysis examining the anticipatory fears and coping abilities of both the children and their parents, a therapist can help select an appropriate intervention. The reduction of pain is clearly related to being able to form accurate cognitive expectations about procedures and increase the child's sense of control. Factors that also need to be considered in the selection of appropriate intervention strategies include the child's temperament and previous experiences in similar situations, the actual coping tasks required by the procedure, the timing of preparation, and the ability of the parents to assist in obtaining the child's cooperation.

Several interventions were described to promote trust of the practitioners and cooperation with the procedures. Giving information about what will occur, and how long the procedure will last, can help children anticipate their ability to cooperate and get through the situation successfully. Choosing an effective intervention requires knowledge about the child's coping repertoires and cognitive abilities, which enable the understanding and learning of new techniques. Distraction may be very effective for short, nonthreatening procedures such as cast removal or exploratory examination. However, the normal child who will possibly be experiencing some pain can benefit from film modeling, which portrays another child coping with the procedure. Behavioral rehearsal provides an opportunity to practice the method they may use to handle stress. Younger children benefit from more concrete opportunities to handle the instruments or play with hospital-related toys. Providing them with a way to signal when they need a break may enhance their sense of control. Parents of younger children may be taught how to help them use distraction and breathing techniques and serve as their coaches during the procedures. In children who have extreme apprehension and cry or scream in order to disrupt the procedure, another approach may be considered. With avoidant children, systematic desensitization and guided imagery have been quite useful. The therapist helps the children construct a hierarchy of the feared events. The children then practice remaining calm and relaxed as they imagine how they will behave during the various procedures. When the children are successful in imagery, then in vivo procedures allow them to experience this success in situations similar to those they must experience. Hypnosis may be used to help the child focus on the sense of relaxation or control achievable. For painful procedures, children can learn to shift the pain to a different location so that they can keep their limb still. It is important to remember that procedural pain does often occur and that it is important to consider analgesic medication so that the experience of pain does not become conditioned to the sights, personnel, or instruments used by physicians during medical procedures. In addition, there are times where anxiolytic drugs or sedation prior to or during a procedure are better than behavioral approaches. The importance of prevention of acute fears of medical procedures is stressed. In children who must face repeated injections during the course of a chronic illness, the need to reinforce their self-confidence by allowing them to participate in their own regimen with some assistance from their caretaker is essential.

REFERENCES

Agras, W. S. Sylvester, D., & Oliveau, D. (1969). The epidemiology of common fears and phobias. *Comprehensive Psychiatry, 10,* 151–156.

Ayer, W. (1973). Use of visual imagery in needle phobic children. *Journal of Dentistry for Children,* April, 1–3.

Blom, G. E. (1957). The reactions of hospitalized children to illness. *Pediatrics,* Sept., 590–600.

Blount, R. L., Bachanas, P. J., Powers, S. W., Cotter, M. C., Franklin, A., Chaplin, W., Mayfield, J., Henderson, M., & Blount, S. D. (1992). Training children to cope and parents to coach the during routine immunizations: Effects on child, parent, and staff behaviors. *Behavior Therapy, 23,* 689–705.

Brown, J. D., O'Keeffe, T., Sanders, S., & Baker, B. (1986). Developmental changes in children's cognition to stressful and painful situations. *Journal of Pediatric Psychology, 11,* 343–357.

Burstein, S., & Meichenbaum, D. (1979). The work of worrying in children undergoing surgery. *Journal of Abnormal Child Psychology, 7,* 121–132.

Bush, J. P. & Harkins, S. W. (1991). Conceptual foundations: Pain and child development. In J. P. Bush & S. W. Harkins (Eds.), *Children in pain: Clinical and research issues from a developmental perspective* (pp. 1–30). New York: Springer-Verlag.

Corah, N. (1973). Effects of perceived control on stress reduction in pedodontic patients. *Journal of Dental Research, 52,* 1261–1264.

Cuthbert, M. I., & Melamed, B. G. (1982). A screening device: Children at risk for dental fears and management problems. *Journal of Dentistry for Children, 49,* 432–436.

Drotar, D. (1981). Psychological perspectives in chronic childhood illness. *Journal of Pediatric Psychology, 6,* 211–228.

Faust, J., & Melamed, B. G. (1984). The influence of arousal, previous experience, and age on surgery preparation of ambulatory and inhospital patients. *Journal of Consulting and Clinical Psychology, 52,* 359–365.

Fenz, W. D., & Epstein S. (1965). Manifest anxiety: Unifactorial or multifactorial composition? *Perceptual and Motor Skills, 20,* 773–780.

Freud, A. (1952). The role of bodily illness in the mental life of children. *Psychoanalytic Study of the Child, 7,* 69.

Gardner, G. (1974). Hypnosis in children. *International Journal of Clinical and Experimental Hypnosis, 22,* 20–38.

Garralda, M. E., & Bailey, D. (1990). Paediatrician identification of psychological factors associated with paediatric consultations. *Journal of Psychosomatic Research, 54,* 303–312.

Gonzalez, J. D., Routh, D. K., Saab, P. G., Armstrong, F. D., Shifman, L., Guerra, E., & Fawcett, N. (1989). Effects of parent presence on children's reactions to injections: Behavioral, physiological and subjective aspects. *Journal of Pediatric Psychology, 14,* 449–462.

Greenbaum, P. E., Cook, E. W., Melamed, B. G., Abeles, L. A., & Bush, J. P. (1988). Sequential patterns of medical stress: Maternal agitation and child distress. *Child and Family Behavior Therapy, 10,* 9–18.

Greenbaum, P. E., Lumley, M. A., Turner, C. T., & Melamed, B. G. (1993). Dentist's reassuring touch: Effects on children's behavior. *Pediatric Dentistry, 15*(1), 20–24.

Gross, A. M., Stern, R. M., Levin, R. B., Dale, J., & Wojnilower, D. A. (1983). The effect of mother-child separation on the behavior of children experiencing a diagnostic medical procedure. *Journal of Consulting and Clinical Psychology, 51,* 783–785.

Haggerty, R. (1986). The changing nature of pediatrics. In N. A. Krasnegor, J. D. Arateh, & M. F. Cataldo (Eds.), *Child health behavior: A behavioral pediatrics perspective* (pp. 9–16). New York: John Wiley & Sons.

Jay, S., Elliott, C. H., Katz, E., & Siegel, S. E. (1987). Cognitive behavioral and pharmacologic interventions for children's distress during painful medical procedures: A treatment outcome study. *Journal of Consulting and Clinical Psychology, 55,* 860–865.

Johnson, J. E., Kirchoff, K. T., & Endress, M. D. (1975). Altering children's distress behavior during orthopedic cast removal. *Nursing Research, 24,* 404–410.

Karoly, P. (1991). Assessment of pediatric pain. In J. P. Bush and S. W. Harkins (Eds.), *Children in pain: Clinical and research issues from a developmental perspective.* (pp. 59–82). New York: Springer-Verlag.

Katz, E., Kellerman, J., & Siegel, S. E. (1980). Psychological distress in children with cancer undergoing medical procedures: Developmental considerations. *Journal of Consulting and Clinical Psychology, 48,* 356–365.

Katz, R. C. (1974). Single session recovery from a hemo-dialysis phobia: A case study. *Journal of Behavior Therapy and Experimental Psychiatry, 5,* 205–206.

Kellerman, J., Zeltzer, L., Ellenberg, L., & Dash, J. (1983). Adolescents with cancer: Hypnosis for the reduction of the acute pain and anxiety associated with medical procedures. *Journal of Adolescent Health Care, 4,* 85–90.

Kleinknecht, R., Klepac, R., & Alexander, L. (1973). Origins and characteristics of fear of dentistry. *Journal of the American Dental Association, 86,* 842–848.

Klingman, A., Melamed, B. G., Cuthbert, M. I., & Hermecz, D. A. (1984). Effects of participant modeling on information acquisition and skill utilization. *Journal of Consulting and Clinical Psychology, 52,* 414–422.

Lumley, M. A., Melamed, B. G., & Abeles, L. A. (1993). Predicting children's presurgical anxiety and subsequent behavior changes. *Journal of Pediatric Psychology, 18,* 481–497.

Lumley, M. A., Abeles, L. A., Melamed, B. G., Johnson, J. H., & Pistone, L. M. (1990). Coping outcomes in children undergoing stressful medical procedures: The role of child-environment variables. *Behavioral Assessment, 12,* 223–238.

Manne, S., Bakeman, R., Jacobsen, P., Gorfinkle, K., & Redd, W. (1994. An analysis of a behavioral intervention for children undergoing venipuncture. *Health Psychology, 13,* 556–566.

Marks, I. M., & Matthews, A. M. (1979). Brief standard self-rating for phobic patients. *Behaviour Research and Therapy, 17,* 263–267.

McCubbin, H. J., & Patterson, J. M. (1983). Family transitions: Adaptation to stress. In H. I. McCubbin and C. R. Figley (Eds.), *Stress and the family. Volume 1: Coping with normative transitions* (pp. 5–25). New York: Brunner/Mazel, Inc.

Melamed, B. G., Dearborn, M., & Hermecz, D. A. (1983). Necessary considerations for surgery preparation: Age and previous experience with the stressor. *Psychosomatic Medicine, 45,* 517–525.

Melamed, B. G., Meyer, R., Gee, C., & Soule, L. (1976). The influence of time and type of preparation of children's adjustment to hospitalization. *Journal of Pediatric Psychology, 1*(4), 31–37.

Melamed, B. G., & Ridley-Johnson, R. (1988). Psychological preparation of families for hospital treatment. *Developmental and Behavioral Pediatrics, 9,* 96–102.

Melamed, B. G., & Siegel, L. (1975). Reduction of anxiety in children facing surgery by use of filmed modeling. *Journal of Consulting and Clinical Psychology, 43,* 511–521.

Moos, R. H. (1982). Coping with acute health crises. In

T. C. Green and R. Meagher (Eds.), *Handbook of clinical health psychology.* New York: Plenum Press.

Nimmer, W. H., & Kapp, R. A. (1974). A multiple impact program for the treatment of an injection phobia. *Journal of Behavior Therapy and Experimental Psychology, 5,* 257–258.

Peterson, L., & Shigetomi, C. (1981). The use of self-control techniques to minimize anxiety in hospitalized children. *Behavior Therapy, 12,* 1–14.

Ridley-Johnson, R., & Melamed, B. G. (1986). Behavioral methods and research issues in management of child patients. *Anesthesia Progress, 33,* 17–23.

Sawtell, R., Simon, J., & Simeonsson, R. (1974). The effects of five preparatory methods upon child behavior during the first dental session. *Journal of Dentistry for Children, 41,* 37–45.

Sermet, O. (1974). Emotional and medical factors in child dental anxiety. *Journal of Child Psychology and Psychiatry, 15,* 33–321.

Shaw, D., & Thoreson, C. (1974). Effects of modeling and desensitization in reducing dental phobia. *Journal of Consulting and Clinical Psychology, 21,* 415–420.

Shaw, E. G., & Routh, K. (1982). Effects of mother's presence on children's reaction to aversive procedures. *Journal of Pediatric Psychology, 7,* 33–42.

Sheehan, P. W. (1967). A shortened form of Bett's questionnaire upon mental imagery. *Journal of Clinical, 223,* 380–389.

Sperling, E. (1978). Psychological issues in physical illness and handicap. In E. Geller (Ed.), *Psychological aspects of pediatric care.* New York: Grune and Stratton.

Starfield, B. (1991). Childhood morbidity: Comparisons, clusters, and trends. *Pediatrics, 88,* 519–526.

Steward, M. S. (1993). Understanding children's memories of medical procedures: "He didn't touch me and it didn't hurt." In *The Minnesota Symposia on Child Psychology,* Vol. 26 (pp. 171–225).

Taylor, C. B., Ferguson, J. M., & Wermuth, B. M. (1977). Simple techniques to treat medical phobias. *Postgraduate Medical Journal, 53,* 28–32.

Willis, D. J. Elliot, C. H., & Jay, S. M. (1982). Psychological effects of physical illness and its concommitants. In J. Tuma (Ed.), *Handbook for the practice of pediatric psychology.* New York: Plenum Press.

Wolpe, J., & Lang, P. J. (1964). A fear survey schedule for use in behavior therapy. *Behavior Research and Therapy, 2,* 27–30.

Zastowny, T., Kirschenbaum, D., & Meng, A. (1986). Effects on stress before, during and after hospitalization for surgery. Coping skills training for children. *Health Psychology, 5,* 231–248.

CHAPTER 3

CHILD MALTREATMENT

Robert T. Ammerman
Matthew R. Galvin

DESCRIPTION OF THE PROBLEM

Definitions

Few constructs have been as elusive and controversial in arriving at a clear definition as child maltreatment. A professional and societal consensus about what constitutes maltreatment simply does not exist, thus complicating the development of policy, allocation of limited intervention resources, and conducting of systematic research. Indeed, the National Research Council (1993) laments "that the absence of consistent research definitions seriously impedes the development of an integrated research base in child abuse and neglect" (p. 70). The same impediments interfere with the emergence of a coordinated clinical approach to identification, assessment, and treatment of child victims and their families. The authors go on to list the primary reasons for the failure to delineate clear definitions of maltreatment: (1) lack of societal consensus about what constitutes adequate or inadequate parenting practices; (2) unclear reference points regarding how maltreatment should be defined; (3) disagreement about standards of endangerment or harm that should be used in defining maltreatment; (4) different intended uses of definitions (e.g., formation of policy, criteria for inclusion in a research study); (5) the meaning of an act of maltreatment varies as a function of child's age, developmental level, and

culture; and (6) variations in social, emotional, and cognitive functioning between subgroups of children (e.g., toddlers vs. adolescents). Further complicating the picture is the differential criteria employed by various professional groups that work with children. For example, several studies (see Giovannoni, 1989) have shown that lawyers and physicians typically rely heavily on physical evidence in making a determination of maltreatment, whereas psychologists and social workers attend more to the child's emotional and behavioral presentation. Finally, because maltreatment is almost always perpetrated in private, professionals must rely on indirect indicators and symptoms in order to identify abuse and neglect. Varied methods and different sources of information can lead to strikingly divergent conclusions about the occurrence and topography of maltreatment (McGee, Wolfe, Yuen, Wilson, & Carnochan, 1995). As a result, arriving at a clear, concise, and universally accepted definition of maltreatment is an ideal that will probably never be obtained.

Despite the above limitations, progress has been made in broadly defining maltreatment. In general, maltreatment refers to acts of commission or omission that result or have a substantial risk in causing physical or emotional harm to the child. Four types of maltreatment are recognized: physical abuse, neglect, sexual abuse, and emotional abuse. Physical abuse includes hitting, punching, pushing and pulling, striking with an object, scalding or burning, or other acts that can physically harm the child. Neglect involves failure to provide adequate care to the child, such as poor hygiene, nutrition, education, supervision, and nurturance. Sexual abuse consists of incest, sexual assault, fondling, exposure to inappropriate sexual material, or other forms of sexual exploitation. Finally, emotional abuse pertains to verbalizations that belittle, terrorize, humiliate, or demean the child, thereby undermining the child's emotional development. Of course, numerous variations on the above definitions abound depending on the professional discipline or setting, and the uses to which the categories are put (e.g., legal vs. research).

Etiology and Theoretical Formulations of Maltreatment

Ecological Model

As the expansion of empirical research consistently revealed the multidimensional nature of child maltreatment, a variety of models were proposed in the 1970s and 1980s that attempted to integrate the causative variables implicated in physical abuse and neglect (see Ammerman, 1990), one of the most comprehensive being the ecological model (Belsky, 1993). This formulation, emerging from Bronfenbrenner's (1979) conceptualization of child development, identifies four levels of influence that combine and interact to bring about maltreatment. Moreover, a distinction is made between *potentiating* factors, which predispose the family to physical abuse or neglect, and *compensatory* factors, which protect the family from deterioration and eventual engagement in maltreatment. The first level, ontogenetic, comprises characteristics of the individual that contribute to or prevent maltreatment. Included here are such variables as high parental IQ (compensatory factor) and poor parenting skills (potentiating factor). The microsystem (second level) reflects those aspects of the family which increase (marital distress, children with behavior problems) or decrease (supportive relatives) the probability of maltreatment. Level three, the ecosystem, involves community and social forces, such as unemployment or the presence of service providers in the community. Finally, the macrosystem (level four) reflects cultural and societal influences, including acceptance of corporal punishment and economic prosperity.

The ecological model provides an important clinical backdrop in that it acknowledges the multiple pathways whereby child maltreatment is manifested, and it identifies variables that interact and differentially affect the probability of abuse or neglect. It is out of such an understanding that effective assessment strategies and interventions should emerge.

Social and Community Risk Factors

A number of authors have posited that stress stemming from socioeconomic disadvantage and paucity of community supports is a significant contributor to maltreatment (Garbarino, 1976; Trickett, Aber, Carlson, & Cicchetti, 1991). Specifically, the frustration engendered by the daily occurrence of stresses secondary to poverty, unemployment, and financial hardship adds to the likelihood of abuse and neglect. Several studies have demonstrated a link between maltreatment and low socioeconomic status (SES). For example, there is a disproportionate representation of low SES families in maltreated samples. Half of those reported for abuse and neglect receive public assistance (American Humane Association, 1985). Likewise, unemployment, educational underachievement, and low family income are related to intra familial violence in general (Straus et al., 1980).

Garbarino and colleagues (Garbarino, 1976; Garbarino & Crouter, 1978) have further elucidated the contribution of socioeconomic stress to child abuse and neglect. In an analysis of 58 counties in New York State, it was revealed that socioeconomic stress in combination with limited community resources accounted for 36 percent of the variance in predicting reports of maltreatment (Garbarino, 1976). In another study, Gaines, Sandgrund, Green, and Power (1978) found that increased life stress (resulting primarily from socioeconomic hardships) best discriminated between abusive, neglectful, and nonmaltreating mothers. Browne (1986) reported that stressful life events (e.g., unemployment) explained 13 percent of the variance in a regression equation predicting recidivism in maltreating parents. Additional lines of evidence supporting the role of stress in maltreatment come from the high incidence of abusive punishment in single-parent families (Sack, Mason, & Higgins, 1985), and the preponderance of maltreatment in families with more than two children (Russel & Trainot, 1984).

Despite the above-mentioned finds, the causative connection between stress and maltreatment is limited. Low socioeconomic status is neither a sensitive nor specific marker for child abuse and neglect. That is, most underprivileged families do not engage in maltreatment, and low SES is not a necessary condition for abuse and neglect. Therefore, stress stemming from social and community factors is but one pathway to the development of child maltreatment. While such variables are rarely the direct target of clinical intervention, it is critical that assessment and treatment be conducted with an understanding of factors that may interfere with successful response to individual and family interventions.

Parental Factors

During the 1960s, parental psychopathology was implicated as the primary cause of child abuse and neglect. The "psychopathology model" posited that maltreating parents were mentally ill, psychotic, sadistic, and had personality disorders (Spinetta & Rigler, 1972). This unidimensional formulation, however, has since been rejected (Wolfe, 1987). Only 10 to 15 percent of abusive parents are diagnosed with a specific psychiatric condition. Furthermore, no "abusive" personality type has emerged from comparisons between abusive and nonabusive parents. Yet, abuse and neglect constitute acts of physical violence and omission of care, respectively, on the part of parents. Thus, it is not surprising that attention continues to focus on the role of the parent in the etiology of child maltreatment.

Wolfe (1985, 1987) has extensively reviewed the literature on characteristics of abusive parents. Although no specific constellation of psychopathologies has been identified, several broad features have consistently been reported. In particular, abusive parents (relative to their nonabusive counterparts) appear to be socially isolated (Corse, Schmid, & Trickett, 1990), exhibit low self-esteem (Lahey, Conger, Atkeson, & Treiber, 1984), and have a low frustration tolerance (Wolfe, Fairbank, Kelly, & Bradlyn, 1983). In addition, they often display poor parenting skills (Trickett & Kuczynski, 1986), unrealistic expectations regarding their child's behavior (Azar & Rohrbeck, 1986), and greater perceived life stress (Mash, Johnston, & Kovitz, 1983). Abusive parents also have a greater proportion of negative to positive interactions with their children and other family members (Reid, Taplin, & Loeber, 1981).

Unfortunately, few studies have examined parents who engage solely in neglect. Those investigations that have been carried out, however, report that neglectful parents are lonely, isolated, immature, and have experienced deprived childhoods themselves (Polansky, Ammons, & Gaudin, 1985; Polansky, Gaudin, Ammons, & Davis, 1985). Gaudin (1993), in summarizing the work in this area, notes that research has generally supported the findings of Polansky and colleagues in grouping

neglectful mothers into five categories: impulse-ridden, apathetic-futile, mothers suffering from reactive depression, mothers with mental retardation, and psychotic mothers. Finally, drug and alcohol abuse is associated with child maltreatment in general, and neglect in particular (Famularo, Stone, Barnum, & Wharton, 1986).

As with social factors in the etiology of maltreatment, parental characteristics are limited markers for abuse and neglect in isolation. The above descriptions are not unique to maltreatment, and are found in many distressed but nonmaltreating families. Yet, parent variables are highly predictive of inadequate caretaking in high-risk families (Egeland & Brunnquell, 1979). Oliver (1993) argues convincingly that intrafamilial factors are overwhelmingly the most important contributors to physical abuse and neglect. Furthermore, parental deficits are typically the primary focus of interventions, although numerous authors strongly emphasize the need to consider the family and social context when treating maltreating parents (Wahler, 1980; Wolfe, 1987). Parental characteristics, therefore, must be viewed as an important (but not the only) influence in the development of maltreatment.

Child Factors as Contributors to Physical Abuse

Significant attention also has focused on the role of the child in the etiology of physical abuse (see Ammerman, 1991). It has been proposed that certain child features lead to parental frustration and add to the overall level of family stress, thus resulting in physical mistreatment. These "abuse-provoking" characteristics include prolonged and irritating crying (Frodi, 1981), oppositional and defiant behavior, and conduct problems (deLissovoy, 1979). Additionally, certain child populations are believed to be at increased risk for abuse because they exhibit many of these provocative behavior problems that exacerbate stress (Ammerman & Patz, 1996). Illustrative are premature or low birth weight infants, and children with physical disabilities, mental retardation, or poor health (Ammerman, Van Hasselt, & Hersen, 1988).

Deviant child behavior is a frequent precipitant of abuse (Kolko, Kazdin, Thomas, & Day, 1993). Prolonged crying in infants is often cited by abusive parents as a triggering antecedent of physical violence. Reporting on a series of investigations, Frodi (1981) determined that the especially irritating cry of premature newborns elicits negative emotional and physiological reaction in both abusive and nonabusive parents. Parent-child conflict, particularly involving child non-compliance and conduct disturbance, is another frequent precursor of physical abuse (Kadushin & Martin, 1981). However, prospective studies of abusive families have failed to demonstrate a significant causative role for child behavior problems in abuse. For example, Egeland and Brunnquell (1979) found that aspects of infant temperament (infant orientation, irritability and consolability), in contrast with parental characteristics, added little to a discriminant function differentiating adequate from inadequate care groups. Unfortunately, controlled prospective studies that examine the contribution of behavior problems to abuse in middle childhood and adolescence are unavailable. Given the unique developmental issues in toddlerhood through adolescence, it is too early to reject the importance of behavioral disturbances in the etiology of abuse in older children.

Ammerman (1991) argues that child factors contribute to physical abuse only in combination with other social or intra familial risk factors. He states that "under certain conditions, child factors may add to the overall likelihood of abuse" (p. 97). He goes on to urge that future investigations should not ask "do child characteristics play a role in the etiology of abuse," but rather "in which circumstances do child factors contribute to the overall likelihood of abuse?" (p. 97). In other words, the child does not cause his/her own abuse. Instead, it is argued that certain characteristics of children (e.g., behavior problems) interact with pre-existing risk variables to bring about physical abuse.

Sexual Abuse and Incest

In sharp contrast to the literature on physical abuse and neglect, the empirical data base on child sexual abuse is quite limited (see Tzeng et al., 1991). Clinical anecdotes and untested theoretical speculations abound, therefore providing few guideposts for understanding the etiology of sexual abuse. Exceptions do exist, as exemplified by the emergent literatures on characteristics of sexual molesters, impact of sexual abuse on children, and adult survivors of incest (see Ammerman & Hersen, 1992). However, a clear causal framework of sexual abuse does not exist.

In the past decade, theoretical formulations on sexual abuse have changed drastically. In the 1970s, family system models predominated (e.g., Justice & Justice, 1979), in which incest was viewed as symptomatic of general family dysfunction. All members of the family were allocated a role in bringing about sexual abuse: the father was characterized as patriarchal and domineering, the child victim was seductive, and the mother was enabling and denied the abuse. Since then, it has become evident the perpetrator is the primary instigator of sexual abuse. For example, the well-known Tufts study on sexual abuse (Gomes-Schwartz, Horowitz, & Cardarelli, 1990) revealed that 52 percent of sexual abuse involves aggression, thus dispelling the myth that child victims are universally "seduced" into participation. Moreover, this study also found that the majority of mothers, upon discovery of the abuse, were supportive of the child and antagonistic to the perpetrator.

Current theories of sexual abuse, which await empirical validation, emphasize the following factors that increase likelihood of sexual abuse. First, fathers are patriarchal, domineering, and likely to view their children as "property." They are emotionally and socially compromised, and may exhibit psychopathology and deficits in social skills. In extrafamilial sexual abuse, pedophilic tendencies (Kolko & Stauffer, 1991) on the part of perpetrators predominate. Second, factors that undermine family functioning facilitate sexual abuse. Included are social isolation, poor communication, and poverty. And third, vulnerable children are most likely to be victims of abuse. Children who are unable to resist, are easily threatened or intimidated, or are incapable of readily telling others of abuse, are potential victims. Faller (1993) offers an integrated model of sexual abuse in which perpetrators exhibit the prerequisite characteristics of being sexually aroused by children and having a propensity to act on these urges. Presence of additional risk factors from cultural (e.g., male dominance), familial (e.g., marital discord), environmental (e.g., unemployment), personality (e.g., low self-esteem), and past history (e.g., have been sexually abused as a child) domains contribute to the overall probability of sexual abuse occurring.

Relevance to the Pediatric Setting

Child abuse was first identified and empirically studied in the pediatric setting, so its relevance and importance to clinicians working in these environments cannot be overstated. The most severe forms of maltreatment typically present first to pediatricians and hospital-based clinicians and require acute medical treatment. Such locations are ideal for arranging longer-term psychiatric and psychological interventions, however, and many hospitals and emergency rooms now have procedures that facilitate identification and follow-up care.

The pediatric setting is also where some forms of maltreatment are first identified and treated. Illustrative are failure to thrive, in which infants fail to grow and develop as a result of neglect, and Munchausen's Syndrome by Proxy, in which children are intentionally injured or made ill by caregivers. A physical exam may also be crucial in the recognition of physical or sexual abuse, and in amassing evidence if criminal prosecution of perpetrators is warranted. Finally, because somatization and increased illness are potential sequelae of maltreatment, abused and neglected children may require increased medical attention and appear more often in pediatric clinics.

The pediatric setting is increasingly a multidisciplinary environment in which psychologists and psychiatrists interact with pediatricians and other child specialties in a consulting or more directly involved capacity. By its very nature, child maltreatment requires intervention from a variety of sources and individuals, necessitating a collaborative and integrated approach to care providing. Such professional relationships have been at the heart of the child abuse and neglect treatment community since its widespread recognition as a major societal problem, and provide a model for other medical conditions that are at the cusp of pediatrics, psychology, and psychiatry.

EPIDEMIOLOGY

Documenting the epidemiology of child abuse and neglect has been elusive. Because it is a private act, child maltreatment is rarely observed directly. Reports of perpetrators are often biased or suspect, and retrospective recollections by victims can be incomplete or distorted. Epidemiological studies have been extremely sensitive to methodological differences, resulting in a variety of findings reflecting such diverse approaches to data collection. Indeed, there is greater confidence in monitoring changes in rates of maltreatment over time using repeated applications of identical or similar methodologies. It is generally acknowledged that available statistics reflect the proverbial "tip of the iceberg," in that many cases of abuse and neglect go undetected. Broader definitions of maltreatment render identification that much more difficult. Finally, sound methodologies are expensive and labor-intensive to implement, resulting in only intermittent data collection (see National Research Council, 1993).

The most recent statistics available at time of publication are drawn from official reports of child abuse and neglect to state agencies in 1993 (National Center on Child Abuse and Neglect, 1995). According to this report, 1,018,692 children were substantiated or indicated victims of maltreatment, yielding an incidence of 15 children per 1,000. Neglect was the most common form

of maltreatment (49 percent), followed by physical abuse (24 percent), emotional or other forms of maltreatment (23 percent), and sexual abuse (14 percent). Over 2.3 million children were referred for investigation of possible maltreatment, demonstrating that child maltreatment is both over-reported (as suggested by the number of unsubstantiated reports) and under-reported (as suggested by the generally accepted view that most cases go undetected). The rate of reporting has increased 331 percent since 1976, documenting the increased awareness of child maltreatment in society in general, and among care providers to children in particular. Professionals (including health care personnel) accounted for 53 percent of reports. In terms of substantiated reports, the proportion of reports is negatively correlated with age. Victims were divided more or less equally between males and females. Fifty-four percent of victims were White, 25 percent were African-American, and 9 percent were Hispanic. The reader is referred to Knutson (1995) and the National Research Council (1993) for reviews of other epidemiological studies and their diverse results.

ASSESSMENT APPROACHES

Medical Issues

Child maltreatment often comes first to the attention of medical personnel, and it is in the pediatric setting that identification is most critical. As previously mentioned, the pediatric setting is the place where the most serious physical consequences of maltreatment will be observed and treated. Although most physical abuse does not result in permanent injury or require acute medical attention (see Wolfe, 1987), more serious forms of maltreatment in which fatality is possible or long-term health and development are threatened are often found in physicians' offices and emergency rooms. In the case of very young children, the medical setting may be the only place where community involvement occurs. Recent reviews (Johnson, 1996; Wissow, 1995) underscore the importance of identification in these settings, and provide guidelines for screening.

Table 3.1 presents potential signs of child abuse and neglect that should arouse suspicion in health care providers. Important sources of information include the physical examination and explanations (which, in the case of maltreatment, are typically inconsistent and implausible) for the injuries provided by caregivers. A comprehensive and careful history must be obtained,

Table 3.1. Signs and Symptoms That Should Arouse Concern about Child Abuse or Neglect

Subnormal growth

   Weight, height, or both less than the 5th percentile for age
   Weight less than the 5th percentile for height
   Decreased velocity of growth

Head injuries

   Torn frenulum of upper or lower lip
   Unexplained dental injury
   Bilateral black eye with history of single blow or fall
   Traumatic hair loss
   Retinal hemorrhage
   Diffuse or severe central nervous system injury with history of
      minor-to-moderate fall (<3m)

Skin injuries

   Bruise or burn in shape of an object
   Bite marks
   Burn resembling a glove or stocking or with some other
      distribution suggestive of an immersion injury
   Bruises of various colors (in various stages of healing)
   Injury to soft-tissue areas that are normally protected
      (thighs, stomach, or upper arms)

Injuries of the gastrointestinal or genitourinary tract

   Bilious vomiting
   Recurrent vomiting or diarrhea witnessed only by parent
   Chronic abdominal or perineal pain with no identifiable
      cause
   History of genital or rectal pain
   Injury to genitals or rectum
   Sexually transmitted disease

Bone injuries

   Rib fracture in the absence of major trauma such as a motor
      vehicle accident
   Complex skull fracture after a short fall (<1.2m)
   Metaphyseal long-bone fracture in an infant
   Femur fracture (any configuration) in a child <1 yr old
   Multiple fractures in various stages of healing

Laboratory studies

   Implausible or physiologically inconsistent laboratory results
      (polymicrobial contamination of body fluids, sepsis with
      unusual organisms, electrolyte disturbances inconsistent
      with the child's clinical state or underlying illness, wide
      and erratic variations in test results)
   Positive toxicologic tests in the absence of a known ingestion
      or medication
   Bloody cerebrospinal fluid (with xanthochromic supernatant)
      in an infant with altered mental status and no history of
      trauma

Reprinted by permission of *The New England Journal of Medicine,* L. S. Wissow, "Child Abuse and Neglect," Vol. 332, pp. 1425–1431, copyright 1995, Massachusetts Medical Society.

given that identification of maltreatment is often based on a pattern of symptoms (e.g., multiple bone fractures in various stages of healing) rather than a single, acute incident. Moreover, some of the physical signs of maltreatment may also be found in other conditions (illustrative is a pattern of old and new fractures in Wilson disease). Extensive documentation is necessary to facilitate the processes involved in reporting and obtaining services for the child and family.

In the case of physical abuse, bruises are the most common sequelae. Of particular import are bruises on parts of the body that are not usually injured accidentally, such as the back, buttocks, and back of the hands (Johnson, 1996). In contrast, bruises on the shins, forearms, hips, and brows are most often attributed to accidental injuries. Bruises caused by objects typically leave a distinctive mark, such as the outline of a belt buckle or the imprint of a hanger. Bruises can be dated by observing color; multiple bruises in various stages of healing are suggestive of physical abuse. Fractures may occur from wrenching or pulling, although blunt force can also lead to this type of injury. These injuries, too, can be dated, and a pattern of variously healing fractures is indicative of physical mistreatment. Finally, burns occur in about 10 percent of physical abuse (Johnson, 1996). Shape and pattern of burns provide clues as to their origin. For example, cigarette burns leave distinctive "punched-out" marks, while burns caused by immersion (most common in infants) in scalding water exhibit distinctive cut-off lines.

Head trauma and abdominal injuries are likely to result in serious injury, or death. Indeed, more that 95 percent of serious intracranial injuries in infancy are caused by physical abuse. In addition to blunt trauma, CNS injury may result from "shaken-baby syndrome," in which violent shaking leads to intracranial hemorrhage and cerebral contusions. Intra-abdominal injuries result from blunt force blows, resulting in ruptured spleen, liver, or other injuries to internal organs.

Neglect is identified by observation of the child's general health and hygiene. Developmental delays and failure to grow or gain weight at minimally accepted levels and rates are suggestive of neglect. Poor dentition and nutrition should arouse suspicion. In infants, an area of missing hair on the back of the head is consistent with infants having been left to lay on their backs most of the time. Finally, failure to obtain needed medical attention, administer necessary medications or other treatments, and frequent canceling of necessary medical appointments may indicate more pervasive neglect. Full assessment of neglect requires extensive social service involvement, typically involving a home visit and observation.

Sexual abuse can result in physical indicators identifiable by physical examination or laboratory tests. Trauma may cause overt physical injuries, and the presence of sexually transmitted diseases are suggestive of sexual abuse. However, the role of the physical examination in the identification of less traumatic forms of sexual abuse is unclear and a matter of considerable debate (Wissow, 1995).

Psychological and Behavioral Assessment

Assessment Strategies

The assessment of abuse and neglect, consistent with the ecological model, should consider several areas of individual and family functioning. Moreover, within each level of measurement (i.e., individual, family), numerous domains (e.g., psychopathology, social resources, parental attributions) are of interest to the clinician. Behavioral, cognitive, and affective elements need to be evaluated. All of these may contribute to and/or reflect family dysfunction in general, and child abuse and neglect in particular.

Optimally, assessment includes observation of family members in the natural home environment. Logistical limitations, however, often impede such an arrangement. For example, in some cases, child protective service agencies will have removed the perpetrator or the child from the home before their referral for treatment. Also, perpetrators may be especially guarded and unwilling to allow more intrusive assessment procedures.

In the absence of (or in addition to) a thorough home assessment, the clinician should utilize a combination of evaluative approaches. Self-report instruments, clinical observations, diagnostic interviews, and psychometric measures completed by others (e.g., teachers) are essential features of a multimodal assessment. No single type of assessment approach is adequate by itself and each has limitations. For example, self-report indices are prone to negative biases in abusive mothers (Reid, Kavanagh, & Baldwin, 1987). Interviews can be distorted by confabulation. Simulated observations can be so removed from the natural environment that they do not elicit the parent-child interactional patterns that are of most interest. Taken together, these shortcomings in specific assessment techniques highlight the need for multiple measures and approaches in abuse and neglect.

The perpetrator, the child victim, and the family are the primary foci of assessment. Of these, assessment of the perpetrator is most critical in eliminating maltreatment and reducing the likelihood of recidivism. Interactions between family members are also important in identifying coercive patterns that may contribute to the escalation of conflict and eventual violence. Family functioning must also be considered within the social and cultural contexts that may facilitate the emergence of maltreatment (e.g., poverty, acceptance of punitive disciplinary methods). Finally, the child requires careful evaluation. Because the effects of maltreatment vary considerably in terms of type, extent, and severity (see Knutson, 1995), the child will typically require support and extensive psychiatric and psychological intervention.

The psychological and psychiatric assessment of the parent, child, and family is discussed in the following sections. The measures described are drawn from both the clinical and research literature. This is *not* an exhaustive list of the possible measures for maltreatment. On the contrary, the varied clinical presentations resulting from abuse and neglect necessitate a broad, flexible, and creative approach to assessment. The approaches described are meant to be illustrative of the numerous strategies available to the clinician.

Psychiatric Diagnosis

The various forms of maltreatment (physical abuse, sexual abuse, and neglect), are often associated with different psychopathologies categorically diagnosed on Axis I and Axis II in the Diagnostic and Statistical Manual of Mental Disorders (DSM) multiaxial system. In DSM-III-R (American Psychiatric Association, 1987), Axis IV was used to encode psychosocial stressors including maltreatment as acute or enduring circumstances. In DSM-IV (American Psychiatric Association, 1994), Problems Related to Abuse or Neglect are actually encoded on Axis I as V-codes, whereas Axis IV is reserved for psychosocial and environmental problems, no longer separated into acute and enduring circumstances and no longer rated for severity. For our purposes, DSM-IV will be utilized to conceptualize consequences of maltreatment. However, research studies cited are based on DSM-III-R or DSM-III. Although potential sequelae of maltreatment involve all aspects of cognitive, social, emotional, and behavioral development, psychiatric diagnosis permits the isolation of psychopathological syndromes which, in turn, may have a known course and suggest various treatment alternatives. It is readily acknowledged that there is no single set of psychiatric symptoms that is unique to maltreatment; several patterns have emerged, and they are reviewed below.

The developmental implications of maltreatment are better appreciated if the clinician has also included in the history of present illness, the personal or family history, or the developmental history, an account of the experience in terms of pertinent variables: age at onset, duration, frequency, character, sense of violation, relationship to perpetrator, as well as protective and aggravating factors. In DSM-IV, examples of maltreatment are still given on Axis IV as problems with the primary support group, in effect permitting redundancy in characterizing maltreatment experiences. However, Axis IV is probably more useful to note stressors associated with "the continuum of caretaker casualty" (Sameroff & Chandler, 1975) such as rejection, harsh and inconsistent parenting or "witness abuse." Reportable maltreatment episodes lie at the extreme of this continuum which, in relatively subacute forms, may dominate the child's day-to-day reality, producing effects at least as pernicious as the reportable episodes themselves. More enduring circumstances associated with maltreatment include fears of retaliation from the alleged perpetrator or rejection from disbelieving family members for having reported, as well as the cascade of stressors associated with familial disruption once protective services are activated on behalf of the victim. In fact, potentiators and/or consequences of maltreatment may be identified in any of the problem areas encoded on Axis IV: primary support group, social environment, educational, occupational, housing, access to health care services and interaction with the legal system. Frequent exposure to urban violence and trauma constitutes another related enduring circumstance perhaps with similar sequelae.

Apart from its use for V-codes, Axis I in DSM-IV retains the distinction of being the axis for major psychiatric disorders. On Axis I, one discerns the emotional, cognitive and behavioral sequelae of maltreatment—provided the symptomatology is sufficiently extensive and severe as to warrant a categorical psychiatric diagnosis. Posttraumatic stress disorder (PTSD) is an obvious differential diagnostic consideration, particularly if the maltreatment experience is recent and relatively circumscribed. However, in more enduring adverse circumstances, as is the case for emotional unavailability, neglect, rejection, hostility and intermittent violence fostering hyper vigilance, stress responses may be transduced into chronic mood and, perhaps, anxiety disorders without associated PTSD symptoms. Conduct disorder is an important diagnostic consideration in boys who have been maltreated (Rogeness, Macedo, Harris, &

Fisher, 1986a). Dissociative disorder, psychosexual disorders, and, in cases of physical abuse, multiple personality disorder (Beitchman, Zucker, Hood, DaCosta, Akman, & Cassavia, 1992), are potential psychiatric sequelae of sexual abuse. Dissociative phenomena are probably more common among maltreated children than is clinically recognized.

A recent review of psychiatric diagnoses in maltreated children (Famularo, Kinscherff, & Fenton, 1992) summarized (1) maltreated children were more likely to present Affective Disorders or depressive symptoms, and PTSD; (2) dissociation in adolescence was significantly correlated with degree of stress or abuse experienced in childhood (multiple personality disorder at the extreme); (3) physical abuse was more associated with aggressiveness, whereas sexual abuse was more associated with runaway behavior, disturbed thinking, negative descriptions of human relationships, and greater preoccupation with sexuality. Famularo and associates (1992) compared 96 subjects ages 5 to 10, 61 of whom had been maltreated. Maltreatment was ascertained on the basis of removal from the home in the case of in-patients and 2 substantiated reports in the case of out-patients. The Diagnostic Interview for Children and Adolescents (DICA) was administered to children and their parents. A clinical diagnosis was also made. Compared to controls, maltreated children had increased incidence of attention-deficit/hyperactivity disorder (ADHD), oppositional defiant disorder, and posttraumatic stress disorder (PTSD). Thirty-nine percent of maltreated children had PTSD by the DICA-child's version, versus 21 percent by the parent's version. Conduct disorder and mood disorder were apparent on the parent's version but not the child's. Interestingly, while sexual maltreatment appears to be more often associated with PTSD than is physical abuse, both maltreatment conditions are associated commonly with diagnoses of ADHD (McCleer, Callagan, Henry, & Wallen, 1994). There is a frequent finding of learning disorders (now encoded on Axis I in DSM-IV) in maltreated children that may constitute an intrinsic vulnerability to maltreatment or may be a sequelae in some cases (Lewis, Lovely, Yeager, & Femina, 1988).

Axis II sequelae include adverse effects on intellectual functioning. Maltreatment is also implicated in the pathogenesis of borderline personality disorder (Famularo et al., 1992). An expansion of the scope of Axis II for heuristic purposes permits an appreciation of other sequelae identified in research in developmental psychopathology. Cicchetti and Toth (1995) have reviewed the literature on sequelae of maltreatment in the developmental domains of language (particularly inner state language), cognition, emotion, and self-other differentiation. The impression one has from available research is that maltreatment at an early age has the potential for altering the child's developmental trajectory both immediately and in ways that do not become apparent until stage-salient developmental milestones are neared.

Social-cognitive, social-emotional, and social-valuational development depend upon the interplay of security and autonomy. Maltreated children have problems in peer relations, especially regarding simple and complex equalities (Mueller & Silverman, 1989). In a study of 10 abused and 10 neglected and 20 nonmaltreated preschool children, it was found that the abused group was less likely than the comparison group to judge hypothetical behaviors with consequential hypothetical harm as not permissible (Smetana & Kelly, 1989).

The domains of moral development include conceptualization, moral emotional responsiveness, moral attachment, valuation and moral volition (Stilwell & Galvin, 1985; Stilwell, Galvin, & Kopta, 1991; Stilwell, Galvin, Kopta, & Norton, 1994). The domains of moral development affected by maltreatment have been the subject of preliminary investigations in psychiatrically hospitalized youth. Nineteen psychiatrically hospitalized boys with serious and persistent illness were grouped according to whether or not they experienced maltreatment before 36 months of age. They were compared with one another and with age (but not socioeconomically) matched controls. While no differences were discerned between the groups identified according to presence or absence of early maltreatment, the group with early maltreatment compared to age matched controls showed less sufficiency and more deficiency in each domain of conscience functioning. The group without early maltreatment compared to age matched controls showed less sufficiency and more deficiency in some domains but no differences in others, suggesting more preservation of conscience functions when the child is spared from early maltreatment (Galvin et al., 1996).

Neurobiologic Sequelae

Consideration of neurobiologic processes in adult PTSD suggest similar processes in childhood maltreatment. Vietnam veterans with PTSD excrete elevated concentrations of urinary epinephrine, norepinephrine (NE), and dopamine compared to controls (Kosten, Mason, Giller, Ostroff, & Harkness, 1987; Yehuda, Southwick, Giller, Ma, & Mason, 1992). Adults with PTSD also have lower urinary free cortisol compared to adults with major depressive disorders (Mason, Giller, Kosten, Ostroff, & Podd, 1986) and to controls (Yehu-

da, Southwick, & Nussbaum, 1990), blunted adrenocorticotrophic hormone (ACTH) response to corticotropin releasing factor (CRF) (Smith, Davidson, & Ritchie, 1989), higher urinary NE/cortisol ratios (Mason, Giller, Kosten, & Harkness, 1988), and increased lymphocyte glucocorticoid receptor number compared to controls (Yehuda, Lowry, Southwick, Shaffer, & Giller, 1991). Enhanced suppression of cortisol following dexamethasone and administration has also been found in PTSD (Yehuda et al., 1993). Strong evidence suggests that NE, dopaminergic, opiate and hypothalamic-pituitary-adrenal axis (HPA) neuronal systems and the locus coeruleus (LC), amygdala, hypothalamus, hippocampus, and prefrontal cortex are involved in PTSD. Moreover, sophisticated gene-environment interactions are implicated in proposals to account for symptoms associated with chronic PTSD (Charney, Deutch, Krystal, Southwick, & Davis, 1993).

A theoretical model describing the biological transduction of stress into depression has been articulated by Post (1992), who proposed a detailed mechanism of how psychosocial stress associated with initial episodes of affective disorder may sensitize an individual to further episodes, some of which may occur spontaneously. The initial experience kindles neurobiological changes encoded at the level of gene expression. Neuronal transmission sets into motion intracellular changes at the level of gene transcription; transcription factors (e.g., proto-oncogene, c-fos) bind at DNA sites and induce mRNAs for other substances exerting even longer-range effects. Enduring changes in neurotransmitters, receptors and peptides may be the biochemical and anatomical basis for synaptic adaptions and memory that can last indefinitely.

Among many hypotheses about imbalances occurring in the catecholamines, one developed to explain conduct disorder known as Quay's Hypothesis has figured prominently in reviews (Rogeness, Javors, & Pliszka, 1992; also see Quay, 1993; Rogeness, 1994). In brief, primary brain systems are identified. These include the Behavioral Inhibition System (BIS) and the Reward or Behavioral Facilitatory System (BFS). The BIS acts as a comparator and inhibitor of behavior. It responds to nonreward, punishment, and uncertainty. The Behavioral Facilitatory System (BFS) is action without restraint (examples: extroversion, sexual behavior, aggressive behavior) and mobilizes behavior so that active engagement occurs. Quay's Hypothesis posits that severe and persistent undersocialized conduct disorder has its biological foundations in an imbalance between the BIS mediated by NE and serotonergic neuronal pathways and BFS mediated by dopaminergic pathways.

NE is thought to play an important role in the modulation of behavior and even in the internalization of values (Rogeness et al., 1992). The central NE system is one of the first neurotransmitter systems to develop and so may be especially vulnerable during early life (Coyle, 1987). Important areas of central NE activity are the LC, the lateral tegmental areas and (along with serotonin), the Papez Loop, identified as part of the BIS in Quay's Hypothesis (Quay, 1988; Quay, Routh, & Shapiro, 1987). Components of the BFS are thought to be integrated in the mesolimbic dopamine system. The relative strength of the BFS (dopaminergic system) and BIS (NE/serotonergic systems) would theoretically influence this process over time and behavior at a given point in time. Balance is the key word (Quay et al., 1987; Quay, 1988; Rogeness et al., 1992). However, actual studies of dopamine and its metabolite thus far have not demonstrated a difference in subjects with and without conduct disorder. Studies have implicated the NE system. Data are consistent with decreased NE activity being associated with an increase in conduct symptoms. Measures of serotonin function have been consistent with decreased serotonergic function in conduct disorder (Rogeness, et al., 1992).

An understanding of the putative neurobiological factors associated with PTSD, depression, or conduct disorder illuminates—but only indirectly—the neurobiological consequences of maltreatment. For more direct illumination it is necessary to apply our knowledge of the developmental neurobiological factors involved in learning and in stress responses because maltreatment involves both adverse learning processes and psychosocial stressors at the extreme of caregiver casualty. While neglect, physical abuse, and sexual abuse have in common the characteristic of being stressors, either acute or enduring, that trigger stress responses, either circumscribed or prolonged, there may be differential neurobiological sequelae according to the variables of maltreatment. Hence, it is also essential to conduct studies that examine neurobiological factors according to the variables of maltreatment: age at onset, duration, frequency, character, sense of violation, relationship to perpetrator, as well as protective and aggravating factors.

Theoretically, neurobiologic sequelae of maltreatment may involve alterations in receptor numbers, morphological changes in the neuron, modification of the processes of synaptogenesis and synaptic pruning, and even neuronal death. Some forms of psychopathology have been attributed to learning gone awry. For example, Kandel (1983) proposed a molecular explanation for chronic anxiety involving structural changes in both the number and distribution of synaptic vesicles as well as the size and extent of their active zones. He argued that the acquisition of chronic anxiety is a learned process that creates morphological changes (demonstrated in the animal model) altering the functional expression of neural connections. Furthermore, it was proposed that such learning is likely to involve enduring, self-maintaining alterations in gene expressions. More directly relevant to maltreatment, Kandel proposed similar alterations when maltreatment occurs during developmentally critical periods (Kandel, 1985).

Since maltreatment involves acute and/or enduring psychosocial stressors (termed Type I and/or Type II trauma, Terr, 1991), a knowledge of interactive responsive systems in a developmental context is essential in guiding the study of neurobiologic sequelae. The interactive stress responsive systems (Chrousos & Gold, 1992) likely to be involved in maltreatment include neurotransmitter and neuroendocrine (hypothalamic-pituitary-adrenal, thyroid-growth hormone and-gonadal axes) as well as the immune systems. Animal studies and studies of maltreated children have focused on two interactive stress responsive systems: the glucocorticoid and the catecholamine.

Laboratory animal studies have identified receptor changes associated with prolonged exposure to glucocorticoids released in response to stress (Sapolsky, Krey, & McEwen, 1985). Naturalistic studies of primates subordinated in their social hierarchy have demonstrated endocrine alterations (Sapolsky, 1982, 1989) as well as hippocampal damage (Uno, Tarara, Else, Suleman, & Sapolsky, 1990). There is also evidence pertinent to neglect derived from animal models. Nonhuman primates that have experienced abnormal rearing practices have consistently demonstrated emotional and social impairments (Harlow, 1980; Harlow, Dodsworth, & Harlow, 1965; Suomi, 1985, 1991). With regard to biologic sequelae, animal research has demonstrated impairments in the central noradrenergic systems. For example, mother-deprived rhesus infants were found to have lower levels of cerebral spinal fluid NE than mother-reared infants (Kraemer, Ebert, Lake, & McKinney, 1984; Kraemer, Ebert, Schmidt, & McKinney, 1989).

One theoretical account of the consequences of maltreatment is that abusive, neglectful experiences contribute to intrinsic neuropsychiatric vulnerabilities that predispose the child to behavioral problems, inviting more caregiver frustration and more abuse (Lewis et al., 1988). In particular, maltreatment may diminish concentrations in the brain of substances such as serotonin and increase outpouring of dopamine and testosterone, contributing to hypervigilance, fearfulness and paranoia that give rise to violent acts (Lewis, 1992; 1994). De Bellis and Putnam (1994) recently reviewed the state of the field including animal models of uncontrolled and unpredictable stress, the implications of studies in adult PTSD, and the few direct investigations into the neurobiology (or psychobiology) of maltreatment.

Abnormal cortisol levels have been found in sexually abused girls, implicating altered glucocorticoid functions in the hypothalamic pituitary adrenal axis (HPA) (Putnam et al., 1991). Plasma ACTH response to opine corticotropin-releasing hormone (OCRH) is reduced in sexually abused girls compared with control subject (De Bellis et al., 1994). CRH and LC-NE/Sympathetic systems participate in a positive reverbatory feedback loop (Chrousos & Gold, 1992), hence alterations in NE functioning might also be anticipated in sexually abused girls. Findings support the idea that sexually abused girls have higher catecholamine functional activity compared to controls (De Bellis, Lefter, Trickett, & Putnam, 1994). In a study of emotionally disturbed children (Rogeness, 1991), subjects with a history of neglect plus abuse, when compared to subjects without maltreatment, were found to have lower urinary NE.

NE is converted from dopamine by the enzyme Dopamine-beta-hydroxylase (DβH). In fact DβH is used in immunohistochemical studies to locate NE neurons (Charlton, McGadey, Russell, & Neal, 1992; Ginsberg, Hof, Young, & Morrison, 1993). Serum DβH has properties making it a possible marker of early abuse/neglect effects on the NE system (Galvin et al., 1991; Galvin et al., 1995). Serum DβH activity increases particulary in the first 24–36 months of life with little further increase after 72 months of life (Freedman et al., 1972; Weinshilboum, Raymond, Elveback, & Weidman, 1973; Weinshilboum & Axelrod, 1971). Analogous to Post's model of the transduction of stress into depression, genetically determined DβH activity may be modulated by prolonged exposure to glucocorticoids released as part of the stress response.

Environmental adversity occurring at an early age when the DβH enzyme activity is unstable (indicative of vulnerability in the noradrenergic system) may have quite different effects than environmental adversity later in life. In psychiatrically hospitalized boys, there were no differences in DβH activity between maltreated (defined as neglected, physically abused or sexually abused) and nonmaltreated groups—provided age at onset of maltreatment was not considered. However, when age at onset of maltreatment was taken into account, group differences were discerned. The group of boys who had been subjected to maltreatment before 72 months of age had lower serum DβH than groups of boys who had been subjected to maltreatment later on or had not been subjected to maltreatment. Interestingly, among boys who were diagnosed with conduct disorder solitary aggressive type (CDSA), those who were not maltreated at an early age had even lower DβH activity than those who were maltreated at an early age who, in turn, were lower in DβH activity than boys neither maltreated nor diagnosed with CDSA (Galvin et al., 1991, 1995).

Consequently, while low serum DβH is implicated as a neurobiologic marker for the transduction of stress associated with early maltreatment into CDSA, studies to date by no means settle the matter conclusively. Low serum DβH could instead be a biological marker for a genetic trait or maturational delay associated with vulnerabilities to develop CDSA, provided other environmentally adverse conditions such as extremes of caregiver casualty (Sameroff & Chandler, 1975) obtain. In any event, low DβH could mark a trait, either heritable or associated with maturational delay or the sequelae of maltreatment, that comprises the underlying biotype for a phenotype of externalization and impulsiveness. The child may then fail to modulate impulses by internal controls and fail to evince moral emotional responses such as guilt and remorse that have become overvalued by the caregiver(s). The caregiver(s), in spite of their over-determined valuation of certain kinds of moral emotional responses from their child, may nonetheless share more or less the same biotype and phenotype and so be subject generally to low frustration tolerance and lack of internalized control. These caregiver traits interact with inappropriate developmental expectations of the child, thereby compromising the stage salient tasks of parenting, and moving the caregivers to extremes along the continuum of casualty. Depending on the critical period of development the child is in, stressful interactions with the caregiver may further alter the child's biotype in a way that contributes to developmental psychopathology identified on Axis I and/or Axis II.

As pointed out by De Bellis and Putnam (1994), the specificities, if any, of different forms of maltreatment for various neurobiologic systems remain to be explored. We may add that other variables of maltreatment besides age at onset and character or form may be salient in the development of persistent sequelae and therefore deserve exploration. Examples are the presence of forms of caregiver casualty less extreme but more pervasive than abuse or neglect such as harsh and inconsistent or inadequate parenting, the relationship to the perpetrator, the absence of anyone perceived as caring or concerned, or the experience of loss of someone perceived as caring or concerned, all of which shape the meaning of maltreatment experience for the child. Taking a transactional-ecological approach (Cicchetti & Rogosch, 1994), aggravating or potentiating factors can be conceptualized as familial, communal, or societal. Potentiating family features include chronic poverty, domestic violence, unstable marital relationships, parental substance abuse and psychopathology, poor education, unemployment, and parental history of maltreatment. Within the community, potentiators include high levels of violence and crime, poor schools, and impoverished community resources; while in the culture, potentiators include acceptance of violence and failure to sufficiently value the rights of children. Relieving or protective factors may be found in the converse of potentiating factors. The potentiating factors in and of themselves are likely to have neurobiological sequelae mediated by interactive stress responsive systems still poorly understood in the developing child or adolescent.

Psychological and Behavioral Functioning in Child Victims

The psychological and behavioral assessment of maltreated children and their families is broad in focus and encompasses numerous areas of functioning. The reason for this is, quite simply, that virtually every form of child psychopathology has, at one time or another, been obscured in victimized children (The National Research Council, 1993). The range of psychosocial consequences is no doubt related to the numerous influences that either lead to potential adverse developmental outcome or enhance resiliency. Yet, although there is no "syndrome" of child psychopathology unique to child maltreatment (or its subtypes), certain areas of functioning have repeatedly been demonstrated to be compromised. Abused and neglected children are more likely than non-victimized peers to exhibit conduct disorder, oppositional behavior, socialized aggression, attentional problems, anxiety, depression, social withdrawal, and inflexible and maladaptive behaviors. In the case of sexual abuse, in addition to the symptoms of PTSD discussed previously, child victims often display precocious sexual behavior, academic underachievement, social withdrawal, conduct problems, and affective disturbance.

The goals of child assessment, therefore, are twofold. First, because the consequences of child maltreatment are often disruptive and pervasive, it is necessary to identify targets for possible remediation. And second, some difficult-to-manage children may contribute indirectly to the escalation of parent-child conflict through provocative behavior. Recognition of such problems is crucial for treatment planning.

The assessment of childhood psychopathology relies heavily on the report of parents or others involved with the education or care of the child. The Eyberg Child Behavior Inventory (ECBI; Eyberg & Ross, 1978), for example, is comprised of 36 items indicating different forms of behavioral disturbance. Two scales are derived that denote those behaviors the parents find difficult to manage (problem score) and the sum of the occurrence of problem behaviors (intensity). The Child Behavior Checklist (CBCL; Achenbach & Edelbrock, 1983) provides information on social functioning and psychopathology in children. There are forms for parents, teachers, and older children (i.e., Youth Self-Report Form). Similarly, there are separate forms available depending upon age and gender. Normative data are available from both clinic and nonclinic samples to provide a comparison. Scale scores are derived reflecting such areas as school performance, schizoid, hyperactive, anxious, and depressed behavior. Finally, the Vineland Adaptive Behavior Scales-Revised (Sparrow, Balla, & Cicchetti, 1984) is a measure of functional ability in childhood through adulthood. It is administered as an interview to parents or to someone who knows the child well. Information is provided via standardized scores on communication, daily living skills, socialization, and motor skills, among others.

Assessment of Parents

Although there are several factors contributing to maltreatment, often working concurrently, the perpetrator (most often the parent) is the primary focus of clinical attention. It is through intervention with the parent that abuse and neglect will eventually be reduced or eliminated and adequate care of the child enhanced. There are seven broad areas of parental functioning that warrant examination: parenting practices and adequacy of care, social functioning, psychopathology, problem-solving skills, parental knowledge and attitudes, stress, and anger responsivity. Each of these is considered in turn.

Parenting practices and adequacy of care. Because of the private nature of abuse and neglect, indirect methods are needed to examine specific parenting behaviors. In general, there are four strategies that can be used to this end: (1) observation of interactions in the home, (2) observation of simulated interactions in the laboratory or clinic, (3) evaluation of the home environment through observation, and (4) parent interview.

The Home Observation for Measurement of the Environment (HOME; Caldwell & Bradley, 1984) has been utilized in measuring the adequacy of care and stimulation provided to the child by parents. A trained rater enters the home while the child is awake and rates the occurrence or absence of certain situations or family procedures. Items that are not understood by parents are clarified in a brief discussion. There are three versions of the HOME based on age (birth to 3 years old, 3 to 6 years old, and 6 to 10 years old). The number of items range from 42 to 59, depending upon the form used, and a variety of subscales are derived reflecting specific aspects of the home environment (e.g., emotional and verbal responsivity of the parent, organization of physical and temporal environment, warmth and affection, academic stimulation, growth fostering materials, and experiences). The HOME has excellent reliability characteristics and correlates highly with IQ and language development.

The Child Abuse and Neglect Interview Schedule–Revised (CANIS-R; Ammerman, Hersen, & Van Hasselt, 1988) is a semistructured interview that is administered to the parent to derive information about disciplinary practices and related factors. It is approximately 45 minutes in length and is divided into seven sections: demographics, family situations, child care, child behavior problems and disciplinary practices, past history of family violence, sexual abuse, and parent history. An advantage of the CANIS-R is that it yields information about many aspects of maltreatment, including the use of harsh physical punishment, psychological mistreatment, sexual abuse, and child observation of spouse battering.

Project 12-Ways (Lutzker & Rice, 1984) has produced two observation instruments suitable for use with neglectful parents. The Checklist for Living Environments to Assess Neglect (CLEAN; Watson-Perczel, Lutzker, Greene, & McGimpsey, 1988) is used to examine cleanliness in the home. Specific areas in each room are rated according to presence of dirt or organic matter, the number of clothes or linens in contact with the area, and the number of nonclothing items or nonorganic matter touching the area. This measure has excellent reliability characteristics and has been found to be sensitive to changes in cleaning practices following a home cleanliness intervention (Watson-Perczel et al., 1988). Likewise, the Home Accident Prevention Inventory (HAPI; Tertinger, Greene, & Lutzker, 1984) is used to evaluate home safety in neglectful families. A home observer rates the presence or absence of hazardous items involving fire and electrical dangers, suffocation by ingested objects, suffocation by mechanical objects, firearms, and solid and liquid poisons. Both of these measures add considerably to the assessment of neglect.

Social functioning. Social inadequacy is a common feature of child maltreatment. There is evidence to suggest that abusive parents have fewer social contacts and more restricted social networks than their nonabusive peers (Salzinger et al., 1983). Likewise, some abusive parents indicate a dissatisfaction with their social network, independent of its size.

Salzinger et al. (1983) developed an especially thorough structured interview designed to measure the size and nature of abusive parents' social networks. The interview, which lasts from 1 to 1½ hours in duration, evaluates social contacts in the following areas: home subnetwork, close family outside the home, distant family outside the home, close and best personal friends, work connections, school connections, neighbors, organizational connections, other friends or acquaintances, and professional caretakers. The parent is asked about the frequency of social contacts and the interconnectedness among contacts. Data are derived from the interview reflecting size and frequency of contacts, as well as interconnectedness (i.e., insularity). Interrater agreement for the interview is high, ranging from 62 percent to 100 percent.

The Social Provisions Scale (SPS; Russell & Cutrona, 1984) provides an excellent summary of the individual's satisfaction with his or her social support system. It contains 24 items that are endorsed using a 7-point scale reflecting the extent to which the statement expresses their social network (1 = not at all true, 7 = completely true). The SPS examines six areas: attachment, social integration, opportunity for nurturance, reassurance of worth, reliable alliance, and guidance. This measure has been widely used in research on social support in general, and it demonstrates good psychometric properties (Cutrona, 1982). The Interpersonal Support Evaluation List (ISEL; Cohen, Mermelstein, Kamarck, & Hoberman, 1985) also asks the respondent to evaluate adequacy of solid support. It examines the following four constructs: tangible support, appraisal support, self-esteem support, and belonging support.

Psychopathology. One of the most important measures in the parental assessment of maltreatment is the Child Abuse Potential Inventory (CAPI; Milner, 1986). The CAPI is used primarily as a screening instrument in conjunction with other assessment strategies (Milner, 1994). However, it yields valuable information for already identified abusive parents. Specifically, the CAPI is composed of 160 statements that are endorsed by the respondent as true or false. Items reflect a variety of child-related issues and personality characteristics. Scale scores are derived comprising child abuse risk, distress, rigidity, unhappiness, problems with child or self, problems with family, and problems with others. In addition, validity scales are provided (fake-good, fake-bad, random responding) to determine profile accuracy. The CAPI reliably distinguishes between abusive and nonabusive parents (Milner, Gold, & Wimberley, 1986), and displays adequate internal reliability and construct validity characteristics.

There are many psychometrically sound instruments available to assess psychopathology, deviant personality characteristics, and specific psychiatric disorders. In the area of child maltreatment, some of the more commonly used measures are the Minnesota Multiphasic Personality Inventory–2 (MMPI-2; Butcher, Dahlstrom, Graham, Tellegen, & Kraemmer, 1989) the Symptom Checklist-90-Revised (SCL-90-R; Derogatis, 1983), the Beck Depression Inventory (BDI; Beck, Ward, Mendelsohn, Mock, & Erbaugh, 1961), and the State-Trait Anxiety Inventory (STAI; Spielberger, Gorsuch, & Lushene, 1970). The MMPI-2 is most useful as a general screening measure of psychopathology. The SCL-90-R provides information on specific symptomatology that can be used in diagnosing psychiatric disorders. This measure consists of 90 symptoms that are endorsed on a 5-point scale of distress (0 = not at all, 4 = extremely). Standardized scores are yielded on the following scales: somatic, obsessive-compulsive, interpersonal sensitivity, depression, anxiety, hostility, phobia, paranoia, and psychosis.

The BDI is one of the most commonly employed indices of depression. It is comprised of 21 depressive symptoms that are endorsed using a 4-point scale reflecting a hierarchical increase in intensity. Finally, the STAI permits the assessment of state anxiety (how the respondent feels now) and trait anxiety (how the respondent feels generally). For each type of anxiety, the individual completes 20 items listing subjective anxiety symptoms. These are endorsed using a 4-point rating of severity (1 = not at all, 4 = very much so).

Problem-solving skills. Abusive and neglectful parents often display deficits in problem-solving skills, particularly those involving child situations. The Parent Problem-Solving Instrument (PPSI) (Wasik, Bryant, & Fishbein, 1980, cited in Azar, Robinson, Hekimian, & Twentyman, 1984) contains 10 child problem situations. Parents are asked to generate solutions to these problems, and responses are scored for number of items

in which a solution is given, total number of solutions, number of items on which more than one solution is offered, number of solutions in which elaboration occurs, and total number of content categories used. Azar et al. (1984) found deficits in abusive parents when compared with nonabusive parents on this measure.

Hansen, Pallotta, Tishelman, Conaway, and MacMillan (1989) developed a problem-solving assessment measure that examines both child-related and other types of problematic situations. The Parental Problem-Solving Measure (PPSM) subsumes five areas: child behavior and child management, anger and stress control, financial, child care resources, and interpersonal problems. Responses are rated for number and effectiveness of solutions. There is both a 25-item (Hansen et al., 1989) and a 15-item (Smith, Conaway, Smith, & Hansen, 1988) version of the PPSM, both of which have adequate psychometric characteristics (see Hansen & MacMillan, 1990).

Parental knowledge and attitudes. Parental attitudes about child-rearing and knowledge of specific parenting practices and normal child development are crucial assessment components. Such measures assist in identifying particular skills deficits, as well as attributions that facilitate violent responses in parent-child conflict. The Knowledge of Behavioral Principles as Applied to Children (KBPAC; O'Dell, Tarler-Benlolo, & Flynn, 1979) is an excellent measure of parental knowledge of the use of reinforcement, extinction, and punishment. It contains 50 descriptions of problem behaviors in children followed by four possible solutions, one of which is endorsed by the respondent. An advantage of the KBPAC is that it is a rather difficult test, thus allowing for a wide variability in obtained scores.

The Parent Opinion Questionnaire (POQ; Twentyman, Plotkin, Dodge, & Rohrbeck, 1981) is an 80-item instrument measuring parental views of the appropriateness of expectations for child behavior. It yields six subscales: self-care, family responsibility and care of siblings, help and affection to parents, leaving children alone, proper behavior and feelings, and punishment. The Parenting Sense of Competence Scale (PSOCS; Gibaud-Wallston & Wandersman, 1978), on the other hand, taps parental self-esteem and confidence in the parenting role. It consists of 17 items that are endorsed using a 7-point scale (1 = strongly agree, 7= strongly disagree). Factor analysis has identified two categories in this measure: satisfaction and efficacy (Johnston & Mash, 1989). Summary scores are subsequently derived for the total and the two factors.

Stress. Stress has consistently been implicated in child maltreatment (see Straus, 1980). There is some evidence to suggest that parents who engage in abuse and neglect do not necessarily experience more stressful events than their nonmaltreating counterparts. Rather, they perceive these events to be more stressful (Rosenberg & Reppucci, 1983). The assessment of stress is particularly relevant given that abusive and neglectful parents exhibit poor coping skills (Egeland, Breitenbucher, & Rosenberg, 1980).

One of the most useful measures of parental stress is the Parenting Stress Index (PSI; Abidin, 1986). The PSI is a carefully developed and especially comprehensive instrument examining stress related to parenting as well as other sources. It is comprised of 126 items that reflect stress associated with the parent-child relationship, and child, parent, and situational characteristics. Scale scores are derived reflecting total stress, life stress during the past year, child domain (adaptability, acceptability, demandingness, mood, distractibility/hyperactivity, reinforces parent), and parent domain (depression, attachment, restriction of role, sense of competence, social isolation, relationship with spouse, and parent health). Normative percentile rankings are available for comparison.

Measures of overall stress or the occurrence of significant life stressors are helpful adjuncts to examining parenting stress. The PSI contains a life stress subscale, or several instruments drawn from life events research can also be employed. The Schedule of Recent Experience (SRE; Holmes & Rahe, 1967) is one of the most widely used measures of this type. However, numerous other options are available (see Dohrenwend & Dohrenwend, 1981).

Anger responsivity. There is convincing evidence that many abusive parents exhibit high levels of anger reactivity (see Frodi, 1981). It is hypothesized that these parents have difficulty recognizing physiological cues of anger and are more likely to "explode" in response to conflict (Kelly, 1983; Walker et al., 1988). Several measures are available to assess anger responsivity. The Novaco Provocation Inventory (NPI; Novaco, 1975), originally developed for anger-reactive individuals in general, has also been used with abusive parents. It consists of 80 items reflecting a variety of anger-provoking situations. Respondents endorse each item using a 5-point scale indicating level of anger arousal (1 = very little, 5 = very much). Factor analytic studies have consistently found three factors in the NPI: injustice/unfairness, frustration/clumsiness, and physical affronts.

MacMillan, Olson, and Hansen (1988) developed an anger responsivity inventory specifically designed for abusive parents. The MacMillan-Olson-Hansen Anger Control Scale is comprised of 50 child-related problem situations. Each item is endorsed using a 5-point scale reflecting degree of anger evoked. Preliminary research supports the reliability and validity of this measure (MacMillan et al., 1988).

Clinicians can also monitor physiological reactivity directly. Although this approach has almost exclusively been employed for research purposes (due to equipment needs and logistical difficulties), it has some potential for clinical screening. Frodi and her colleagues (Frodi, 1981) have demonstrated that abusive parents exhibit negative physiological reactions to both crying and positive social behaviors in premature infants. Friedrich, Tyler, and Clark (1985) also used measures of skin conductance, heart rate, and finger blood volume to assess abusive parents' reactions to infant cries. Finally, Wolfe, Fairbank, Kelly, and Bradlyn (1983) monitored physiological reactivity in abusive parents who watched videotapes of child behavior transgressions.

INTERVENTION STRATEGIES

A number of issues must be taken into account when treating families involved in child abuse and neglect. Typically, maltreatment is identified by another professional prior to referral to the clinician. Pediatricians, teachers, other family members, or neighbors will most likely have brought the maltreatment to the attention of the police or a child protective service agency. A caseworker is then assigned to the child, and home visits take place in an effort to confirm or disconfirm maltreatment. If it is determined that abuse or neglect has occurred, steps are taken to ensure the safety of the child. This may involve removing the child from the home and arranging temporary foster home placement. In cases of severe maltreatment, criminal charges may be filed against the parent.

By the time the family is referred for treatment, the clinician is faced with several potential impediments to effective therapy. The child may be out of the home, which will make interventions directly involving the child difficult to implement. Also, parents may be court-ordered to participate in treatment and may lack intrinsic motivation to change their behavior. Likewise, the parent may deny that abuse or neglect took place. They may be hostile, defensive, and reluctant to reveal important information. Such features may augur poorly for a positive outcome. As in the case of assessment, logistical limitations may interfere with optimal treatment. Many maltreating families are characterized by disorganization and instability. They may have difficulty accessing transportation or other resources. Thus, intermittent attendance at clinic sessions may become the rule rather than the exception. It is for this reason that home visitation is an important asset of social service interventions. Indeed, home visitation may be an essential feature of effective treatment.

Abusive parents are often reluctant to relinquish controlling parenting practices and violent approaches to discipline. A number of factors contribute to the maintenance of coercive parenting practices and the use of extreme corporal punishment (Wolfe, 1987). A significant portion of abusive parents were themselves maltreated as children (Ammerman & Patz, 1996), although this figure is not as high as was previously thought (Kaufman & Zigler, 1993). Their own violent behavior can be partly attributed to modeling their parents' excessive use of discipline. Furthermore, abusive parents tend to have an accepting attitude toward the use of physical punishment. Finally, they will have experienced short-term "success" with physically punitive approaches in that such methods interrupt the ongoing negative behavior of the child, even if for a brief time period. Kelly (1983) points out that it is unrealistic to expect abusive parents to completely abandon physical punishment as a disciplinary technique. He recommends that strict guidelines be established for how to use physical punishment and under what circumstances it should apply. A single open-handed spanking applied to the buttocks in situations where the child is in danger (e.g., hand near an open flame) may be permitted. Also, parents should understand why punishment is ineffective over the long term (e.g., results are temporary, it does not teach the child alternative behaviors, children acclimate to punishment) as well as acknowledge its negative side effects (e.g., it increases frustration, it is situation specific, the child is likely to become fearful).

Family-Based Interventions

Most authors recommend using a broad-based behavioral intervention with maltreating parents comprised of multiple components targeting a variety of problem areas (Kelly, 1983; Lutzker & Rice, 1984; Walker et al., 1988; Wolfe, Sandler, & Kaufman, 1981). The two most frequently utilized treatments for abusive and neglectful parents are parent training and anger control training. Because child abuse is one aspect of pervasive problems in parenting and the parent-child relationship (Wolfe, 1987), parent training is crucial to enhancing the

quality of interactions between parent and child and reducing the risk of future abusive incidents or neglect. Anger control training is designed to decrease the likelihood of impulsive angry outbursts that might lead to physical abuse. Finally, a number of additional treatments (i.e., marital therapy, social skills training, problem-solving skills training) have been recommended for problem areas thought to play an important role in the development of maltreatment.

Parent Training

Although a variety of parent training programs have been developed for maltreating parents, most are based on Forehand and McMahon's (1981) extensively researched protocol. The goals of parent training with maltreating parents are twofold: (1) teaching parents nonpunitive child management skills that will allow them to control their child's noncompliance, oppositionality, or acting out, and (2) training parents in the use of reinforcement techniques to encourage and enhance appropriate behaviors in their child and improve the overall parent-child relationship.

Prior to learning more effective child management skills, the parent must be able to identify and define those behaviors in need of change. This can be particularly difficult for abusive and neglectful parents, given that their subjective perceptions of their child's behavior frequently are distorted by mood, unrealistic expectations, or isolated negative incidents (Walker et al., 1988). Indeed, several studies have found that abusive parents are more likely to assign negative labels to their child's behavior when compared with their nonabusive counterparts (Larrance & Twentyman, 1983; Wood-Shuman & Cone, 1986). Definitions of target behaviors must be simple and clear. The parent is taught to monitor their occurrence using appropriate scaling techniques (i.e., frequency, interval, or duration) dependent upon the type and quality of the negative behavior. Finally, parents should graph their observations. By teaching the parents to use more objective techniques in describing their child's behavior, subjective biases toward the child's behavior are diminished.

A firm grounding in social learning principles is also necessary in implementing effective child management techniques. These principles provide a rationale for using specific parenting approaches. Important learning concepts include, but are not limited to, the role of: (1) contiguity between the occurrence of behavior and its consequences, (2) shaping, and (3) selection and use of schedules of reinforcement in altering behavior. The clinician should provide relevant examples of these principles to enhance understanding. In addition, several books are available to assist parents in applying learning techniques (e.g., Patterson, 1976). Training includes teaching parents child development processes in an effort to correct the unrealistic expectations for their children held by most maltreating parents. Filmstrips and videotaped vignettes of child behavior can be used in this effort (Wolfe et al., 1981).

One of the most critical features of child management skills is giving commands. Most abusive and neglectful parents are poor at using verbal commands. Typically, they are vague, inconsistent, and use questions (e.g., "When are you going to clean your room?") rather than specific instructions. Parents should institute concise guidelines and rules in dealing with their children. When giving a command, they should provide clear instructions, inform the child of the consequences if he or she is noncompliant, and follow through on appropriate consequences.

Maltreating parents must also learn to use time-out. Indeed, these parents often are inconsistent and incorrectly employ time-out procedures. Behavioral transgressions that warrant time-out should be identified, and a time-out area in the home is then selected. For younger children, a corner is adequate, whereas older children might need a room or similar location. As in all child management approaches, consistent application and contiguity between occurrence of the target behavior and subsequent time-out is critical. Duration of time-out depends upon the child's age and his or her response to the procedure, although 5–10 minutes are usually sufficient. The clinician must emphasize that distractions and diversions should be eliminated if time-out is to be effective.

Attention withdrawal is an extinction procedure that is used to reduce negative behaviors in children. Children in abusive and neglectful families often maintain high rates of aversive behavior as a function of the negative attention they receive from parents (Kelly, 1983). Behavior problems are further exacerbated by the decreased levels of positive attention directed toward children by maltreating parents (Bousha & Twentyman, 1984). Thus, the parent should refrain from providing both verbal and nonverbal attention to less serious behavior problems. Initially, parents will be resistant to ignoring their child's negative behavior. Therefore, a rationale should be presented along with guidelines for when and how to use attention withdrawal. Parents also need to be prepared for an "extinction burst" following implementation of this procedure. Additional methods for controlling negative child behaviors include response cost and overcorrection.

The second component of parent training is to encourage and reinforce positive child behaviors. Indeed, this aspect of training is most likely to lead to long-term improvements in the parent-child relationship (Kelly, 1983) and is particularly important for neglectful parents (Lutzker, Megson, Webb, & Dachman, 1985). As in the management of behavior problems, parents begin this phase by identifying specific target behaviors to be changed. Appropriate reinforcers to be used in conjunction with techniques outlined next are then selected. Reinforcers can be tangible (e.g., candy), social (e.g., praise), or involve an activity (e.g., going to an amusement park). Reinforcers should be appropriate for the child's developmental level and interest. In fact, children can be given a reinforcement menu to select their "favorite" reinforcing stimuli. It is necessary to have several reinforcers available in order to prevent satiation and subsequent loss of reinforcing properties. Verbal praise should *always* accompany the delivery of tangible reinforcers.

Contingency management is the primary technique used to promote positive behaviors in children. Specifically, it involves establishing contingencies under which the child will be reinforced. Those events that are most likely to be problematic (e.g., bedtime, getting ready for school) and most often lead to parental violence should be addressed. A number of schedules of reinforcement can be employed to shape and increase positive and adaptive behaviors at these times. Likewise, token systems can be used and are especially effective with young children. Complicated programs should be avoided, and parents are instructed to monitor progress of the intervention through data collection. Finally, it may be necessary to train maltreating parents how to interact positively and appropriately with their child (Lutzker et al., 1985).

The format of parent training varies widely. Both group (Wolfe et al., 1981) and individual (Walker et al., 1988) programs have been used. Some therapists employ bibliotherapy as part of the training package, while others do not. Virtually all authors recommend home visits to gather assessment information or conduct in-home training to enhance generalization of newly learned skills. Decisions on how to implement parent training will depend on the resources available and the individual family needs.

The procedures to be followed within sessions utilize traditional behavioral training approaches (Twardosz & Nordquist, 1987). These consist of (1) direct instructions, (2) modeling, (3) behavioral rehearsal, and (4) therapist feedback. Direct instructions provide parents with specific guidelines for handling problematic situations. For example, a mother might be taught precisely what to do in a situation in which a child cries continuously. Modeling is used to give the parent a clear example of how to implement the behavioral technique. The clinician enacts the role of the parent and performs the appropriate response. By observing and then practicing the correct behavior, the parent is more likely to utilize it with success in the home environment. Behavioral rehearsal consists of having the parent practice and role-play the correct response in the session. With feedback from the clinician, the parent can enhance recently acquired skills before applying them at home. Finally, weekly homework assignments are given to promote application of skills in the home and to increase generalizability of training.

Anger Control Training

Anger control training is utilized with abusive parents whose violent behavior is related to impulsive angry outbursts. It also is helpful with neglectful parents who are at high risk for engaging in physical abuse. The goals of anger control training consist of teaching the individual to recognize internal and external cues of anger arousal, and subsequently use coping strategies to prevent the occurrence of outbursts that can lead to abuse. Treatment efforts with abusive parents have largely been adapted from the work of Novaco (1975) on anger inoculation with impulsive individuals.

The first step in anger control training is to give the parent a rationale for implementing the intervention. This involves explaining the three dimensions of anger: physiological arousal, generating cognitive labels for events, and behavior. These three modalities interact synergistically to produce an anger response. Prior to beginning treatment, a thorough assessment of anger incidents and their antecedents and consequences is conducted. The Novaco Provocation Inventory is used to identify those situations that elicit anger arousal. Likewise, child behavior problem measures (e.g., Child Behavior Checklist), parenting stress questionnaires (e.g., Parenting Stress Index), and the clinical interview can provide information about specific child-related factors that are associated with violent outbursts. In addition, parents should keep an *Anger Diary* to record anger incidents, events preceding arousal, and subsequent behavior and its consequences. Data from the Anger Diary are used to identify specific problematic situations and to generate scenes for the desensitization component of anger control training.

The second aspect of anger control training is relaxation training. Relaxation serves two purposes for the parent. First, it provides a self-control mechanism for an individual whose problem is primarily related to lack of self-control. Relaxation also permits the parent to reassess a problematic home situation prior to an anger response and choose a more rational solution to the problem (e.g., leave the room, use a technique learned from parent training). The second purpose of relaxation training is to counter emotional arousal associated with anger. This is particularly critical for the desensitization phase. More extensive instructions for implementing relaxation training can be found in Kelly (1983).

Deep-muscle relaxation consists of alternately tensing and relaxing up to 16 muscle groups in order to learn to: (1) distinguish between tense and relaxed muscle states and, (2) obtain a deep state of relaxation in a relatively quick period of time. Relaxation typically is taught in the office in 25 to 30 minute sessions, and practice is facilitated at home through the use of audiotaped exercises. As training progresses, a cue word is added at the end of each session. The subsequent association of the cue word with a relaxed state permits rapid relaxation during times of arousal.

Desensitization, or anger inoculation (Novaco, 1975), involves the presentation of a hierarchy of imaginary scenes that are increasingly anger arousing. At least seven scenes are developed using the Novaco Provocation Inventory and other sources. These scenes should range from those eliciting a low level of anger arousal to ones that are extremely likely to produce an anger response. The procedure consists of having the parent relax while the therapist describes the first scene on the hierarchy. The parent is instructed to imagine himself or herself as calm, relaxed, and coping well in the situation. After 15 seconds, the parent is again asked to relax. After successfully imagining the scene in a calm state, the clinician advances to the next more anger arousing situation. The parent also is instructed to practice desensitization at home.

The third aspect of anger control training is cognitive restructuring. Through the Anger Diary, the parent and clinician will be able to identify self-statements that serve to elicit, maintain, or exacerbate anger responses to frustrating situations. The first step in the cognitive control of anger is to generate a list of more adaptive coping self-statements to counteract the negative ones involved in the anger response. The second step is to train the parent to use *thought stopping*. The parent is instructed to imagine an anger arousing situation, use thought stopping upon generating negative self-statements, and replace them with more adaptive coping thoughts. The clinician should model out loud the appropriate use of thought stopping and thought replacement. At first, the parent should rehearse using the coping statements out loud, followed by covert practice. Homework assignments should be given to provide experience using the procedure at home. Likewise, home visits by the clinician may be necessary to ensure practice and maximize generalization. The parent should be encouraged to use cognitive control of anger in conjunction with relaxation for best results in preventing future violent outbursts.

Additional Interventions

Although parent training and anger control training are considered the primary interventions for maltreating parents, a number of other adjunctive treatments have been utilized with this population (see Kelly, 1983). Because of the complex presentation of abuse and neglect, parent training and anger control training alone may be insufficient to eliminate the risk of future maltreatment incidents. Moreover, even if the immediate likelihood of abuse and neglect is reduced via these interventions, significant family problems or additional difficulties often remain that require intervention. Indeed, in some cases (e.g., drug or alcohol abuse), alternative interventions must be implemented prior to parent training or anger control training if these treatments are to be effective.

The need for adjunctive treatments must be determined on an individual basis through the comprehensive assessment. These interventions may be given by the clinician treating the family, or additional professional assistance may be required. Typically, difficulties in one or more of the following areas will be encountered: (1) social isolation (Salzinger, Kaplan, & Artemyeff, 1983), (2) substance abuse or dependence (Mayer & Black, 1977), (3) marital dysfunction (Campbell, O'Brien, Bickett, & Lutzker, 1983), (4) poverty and/or unemployment (Gelles, 1973), and (5) deficits in problem-solving skills. Although little research is available evaluating specific interventions for these five problem areas in abusive parents, most authors are in agreement about the need to implement remedial programs in families who exhibit problems in these areas (Kelly, 1983; Walker et al., 1988; Wolfe, 1987a).

Numerous reports have found child abusers to be socially isolated and deficient in social support (Salzinger et al., 1983; Straus, 1980). Lack of social support further contributes to the high levels of stress found in the home. Moreover, it has been shown that socially withdrawn or "insular" mothers have fewer difficulties with their children on days in which they have positive interpersonal interactions with friends when contrasted to days of relative social isolation (Wahler, 1980). Several treatment options are available for socially isolated par-

ents, including social skills training, teaching the parent to engage in and foster positive interactions with others, and home visitations by paraprofessionals or community volunteers. Social skills training can be used to teach conversational skills, heterosocial skills, and assertion. Parents can use these newly learned skills, in turn, to expand their social network and decrease isolation. Other maltreating parents may have an adequate social skills repertoire, but are unable to initiate or maintain an adequate level of positive interpersonal interactions with others. In these cases, parents are taught to structure their time in such a way as to ensure a minimum amount of daily social contact. Leisure skills training is especially important for this purpose (Schinke et al., 1986). Finally, some programs have used trained volunteers to visit the homes of child abusers on a regular basis to provide emotional support and frequent social contact (Kempe, 1973). It has been suggested that volunteers from the community are more likely to develop a trusting relationship with maltreating parents than professionals. Although this type of program offers a short-term intervention for socially isolated abusive parents, it does little to address the long-term needs of developing and maintaining an adequate social network.

It has been estimated that up to 38 percent of maltreatment cases involve parental drug and/or alcohol abuse (see Famularo, Stone, Barnum, & Wharton, 1986). Because of the debilitating effects of substance abuse, it is necessary to treat this condition prior to implementing parent training or related interventions (Walker et al., 1988). Treatment for substance abuse typically involves in-patient hospitalization, individual therapy, and self-help groups (e.g., Alcoholics Anonymous).

Marital dysfunction can also play an important role in maltreating families (Campbell et al., 1983). Many of these families engage in physical violence between partners as well as abuse directed toward children. Marital discord may be symptomatic of general family dysfunction, or it may serve to increase the stress and frustration levels that subsequently can lead to an abusive incident. Marital therapy may be a necessary treatment prior to or in conjunction with parent training and anger control training.

Economic hardship, poverty, and unemployment are frequently associated with child abuse and neglect (Gil, 1975). Although socioeconomic disadvantage does not by itself directly lead to child abuse and neglect, it can drastically increase family stress levels and thus contribute to heightened risk for maltreatment. Increased child care demands, constant financial pressures, and job instability further add to stress in the home. Social service agencies are the primary source of help for these families and they are best qualified to intervene and at-tempt to alleviate the short-term economic crises that so often occur in disadvantaged families. The clinician, however, can offer skills-based treatments in order to effect long-term changes and improvements (Kelly, 1983). For example, job-seeking skills can be developed, including how to: (1) locate employment opportunities, (2) prepare an application or resume, (3) arrange an in-terview, and (4) behave during an interview. Further as-sistance for the family includes training in budgeting and economic planning and seeking help in child care.

Many maltreating parents display deficits in prob-lem-solving skills. In fact, their inability to effectively and appropriately manage their child is often indicative of pervasive difficulties in solving everyday problems (Wolfe, 1987b). While parent training is one form of problem-solving skills training, more general skills-based interventions are available (see Meichenbaum, 1977). Such interventions typically emphasize the use of predetermined logical steps in identifying problems and generating possible solutions. The steps consist of rec-ognizing a problematic situation, developing solutions, weighing the relative advantages and disadvantages of each option, choosing the best alternative, and imple-menting the selected strategy. As with other behavioral training approaches, treatment involves use of reading materials, in-session practice and rehearsal, modeling, and homework assignments to enhance generalization.

Child Interventions

As was previously noted, almost no research has been conducted on interventions with the child victim of maltreatment. Such paucity of information is partly re-lated to the fact that no homogeneous clinical syndrome has been identified in abused and neglected children. Rather, the effects of maltreatment are complex and var-ied, encompassing internalizing disorders, externalizing disorders, developmental delays, and social and peer maladjustment (see Ammerman et al., 1986). As a result, comprehensive assessment strategies are needed to identify specific areas requiring treatment. Such an as-sessment should include measures of intelligence, de-velopmental functioning, peer relations, and behavior problems (see Walker et al., 1988).

Despite the lack of an empirical literature to guide the clinician, a number of intervention strategies for mal-treated children have been proposed (Walker et al., 1988). There are three primary treatment approaches: relaxation and stress reduction training, problem-solving skills training, and social skills training. These treat-ments have been shown to be effective with children displaying symptoms similar to those often exhibited by their abused and neglected counterparts. The decision to use one or more of these interventions will depend upon: (1) the age and developmental level of the child, and (2) the specific deficits uncovered in the assessment. The aforementioned treatments can be used indepen-dently or in conjunction with family therapy, psycho-therapy, or parent training for the maltreating parent.

Relaxation and Stress Reduction Training

Many maltreated children report symptoms of anxi-ety and fearfulness (Green, 1983). These problems may interfere with social functioning and academic achieve-ment. For such children, relaxation training may be war-ranted. The clinician should be aware of potential difficulties in implementing relaxation procedures in very young children or children who do not have the req-uisite cognitive abilities for this treatment approach. Whatever the age of the victim, every attempt should be made to involve the child in the relaxation process in order to increase cooperation and likelihood of success (Walker et al., 1988). Moreover, younger children will require more guidance and concrete instructions than their older peers.

There are four types of relaxation strategies: pro-gressive muscle relaxation, breathing techniques, guided imagery, and systematic desensitization. Progressive muscle relaxation consists of alternately tensing and re-laxing major muscle groups. As in relaxation training with adults, the child is instructed to focus on the inter-nal sensations associated with feeling tense and relaxed. Therapist modeling of relaxation steps will help the child learn the procedure. Relaxation sessions are con-ducted in the office, and homework assignments are given to ensure practice and maximize generalization to other settings. In general, progressive muscle relaxation is most appropriate for children eight years and older (Walker et al., 1988). Because the child's attention span will be limited, relaxation sessions should not exceed 15 minutes. Children rarely view an inability to relax as a problem, thus it is difficult to get them to comply with the relaxation protocol. A reinforcement program should be instituted to reward the child for completing relax-ation assignments. When appropriate, parents can be enlisted in monitoring and supervising their child's compliance with homework. Following mastery of the relaxation program, the child should be taught to use his or her relaxation skills in situations that are likely to elicit an anxiety response.

Breathing techniques are less complex than progressive muscle relaxation. In general, this approach involves teaching the child to use diaphragmatic breathing and take deep breaths. The child is instructed to focus on the difference between the relaxing sensations associated with deep breathing and the tension caused by anxiety. Subsequently, the child is trained to use this breathing strategy during times of arousal.

Guided imagery takes advantage of the child's imagination capabilities. Specifically, the child is asked to generate a relaxing and calm-inducing imaginary scene. The clinician should help the child in constructing these images and encourage the child to use all sensory modalities in constructing the scene. Magazines with colorful pictures are helpful or prerecorded audio tapes of scenes can be used (see Lupin, 1981).

Systematic desensitization is used with children who have phobias of particular situations or stimuli. The first step is training the child in progressive muscle relaxation. Following this, a hierarchy of increasingly anxiety-producing stimuli is developed. Desensitization is conducted in the office using imaginary scenes of phobic situations. As each scene is presented, the child is instructed to relax if he or she feels anxious. Subjective ratings of anxiety are used to determine when the child is no longer anxious upon presentation of the scene, at which point the next scene is offered. Alternatively, the same procedure can be conducted in vivo.

Problem-Solving Skills Training

Problem-solving skills training is used with children who are impulsive, aggressive, hyperactive, or display general deficits in problem solving. As these difficulties are frequently found in abused and neglected children (see Ammerman et al., 1986), it has been suggested that remedial approaches emphasizing problem-solving skills would be useful with maltreated populations (Walker et al., 1988). The goal of problem-solving skills training is to teach the child to identify problematic and frustrating situations, generate solutions, and select an appropriate response. There are three primary interventions designed to enhance problem-solving abilities: interpersonal cognitive problem-solving, self-instructional training, and the turtle technique.

Interpersonal cognitive problem-solving teaches the child to utilize specific steps when confronted with problematic situations (Shure & Spivack, 1978). These steps are (1) determine that a problem exists; (2) define the problem; (3) examine the situation from all perspectives; (4) decide if change is within or outside of your control; (5) change your attitude if change is outside of your control; (6) generate solutions if change is within your control; (7) evaluate the utility of possible solutions; (8) choose the best solution and implement it; (9) analyze the effectiveness of the chosen solution; and (10) if it is ineffective, choose the next best option. The therapist should model the use of these steps in situations that are relevant to the child. Role playing is employed in the session, and homework assignments are given to the child to provide practice in the natural environment.

Self-instructional training has been found to be particularly helpful with children who have a short attention span and are impulsive (see Kendall & Braswell, 1985). This approach consists of using self-talk to work through a task or problem (Meichenbaum, 1977). The self-talk "script" involves statements of how to complete the task, maintain a satisfactory pace, focus on the problem, select a response, cope with failures, and self-reward upon successful completion of the task. The therapist first models out loud the use of self-talk in approaching a problem. As the child practices the technique, the therapist provides prompts when needed. These are gradually faded as the child becomes more proficient in problem solving. Finally, the child should slowly decrease the voice level of self-talk to a whisper to promote covert use of the technique. As in other training strategies, homework assignments and practice in the natural environment is critical for generalization of training.

The turtle technique is used to interrupt impulsive behaviors and encourage the use of problem-solving techniques (Schneider & Robin, 1976). The child is instructed to "act like a turtle" when faced with a frustrating and problematic situation. Specifically, they are to "pull in their limbs," lower their heads, and withdraw from the situation. At this point, relaxation skills are used to calm down and problem-solving techniques are employed to generate an appropriate solution.

Social Skills Training

Research consistently has demonstrated social dysfunction in abused and neglected children (see Ammerman et al., 1986). These children are described as aggressive (Engfer & Schneewind, 1982), lacking in social perception and sensitivity (Barahal et al., 1981), and having few friends (Farber & Egeland, 1987). The roots of social dysfunction can be found in infancy, with disruption in the formation of secure mother-infant attachment (Aber & Allen, 1987). As the maltreated child develops, he or she often displays pervasive social deficits in initiating and maintaining relations with peers (Egeland et al., 1983). Having decreased interactions with other children further contributes to specific deficits in social skill. As a result, interventions have been developed designed to: (1) train abused and neglected children in developmentally appropriate social skills, and (2) use age-matched peers to facilitate interactions between abused and nonabused children.

Numerous programs exist to teach social skills to children (see Ross, 1981). These interventions are typically didactic instruction in components of social skills (e.g., gaze, voice level, posture), role-playing, modeling of appropriate social behavior by the therapist or by peers in films, behavioral rehearsal, and therapist feedback. In addition, adults have been used to administer positive reinforcement for socially skilled behavior at home or in the classroom. In general, these approaches have been successful with nonmaltreated children who display deficits in social skill (see Ross, 1981) and may be useful with abused and neglected children.

Other programs have used exposure to more socially skilled peers to treat socially dysfunctional maltreated children (Fantuzzo et al., 1988). This research stems from the successful use of peers to prompt and initiate social interactions with withdrawn children. Specifically, peers are taught how to initiate play and sharing with maltreated children during semistructured time-limited play sessions. Similar interventions have used adults to prompt play activities. Initial findings show that these programs are helpful in increasing prosocial behaviors in abused and neglected children.

Treatment of Sexually Abused Children

The treatment of sexually abused children has spawned a sizable body of literature comprised primarily of clinical anecdote and speculations. Although empirical work in this area has lagged behind (see Finkelhor & Berliner, 1995), it is widely acknowledged that clinicians working with sexually abused children require considerable skill and experience. Treatment must be long-term (see Friedrich, 1991), reflecting the extensive damage to the child's social and emotional development arising from sexual victimization. Finkelhor and Berliner, in their review of the limited empirical literature on treatment evaluations for sexually abused children, conclude that although treatment may be successful in some cases, effect sizes are small and improvement limited. Some types of psychopathology, much as sexualized behavior and aggression, may be especially resistant to treatment. Finally, no particular approach has been found superior to others at this point.

In one of the few well-controlled evaluations of sexual abuse treatment, Cohen and Mannarino (1996) contrasted cognitive-behavior therapy and a nondirective support control condition in 86 sexually abused children between the ages of 3 and 6. Importantly, the cognitive-behavior therapy regimen was altered to address unique issues associated with sexual victimization. Results were quite positive, showing that the 12-week program brought about reductions in behavioral dysfunction and sexualized behavior relative to the control condition. The scientific rigor of this study strengthens the conclusion that cognitive-behavior therapy is an effective treatment for sexually abused pre-schoolers.

Pharmacotherapy

As a corollary to investigations into neurobiologic sequelae, pharmacotherapy of maltreatment in children may proceed rationally based upon what is eventually discovered about acute and prolonged interactive stress responses in the developing hypothalamic-pituitary-adrenal (and other) axes and the developing CNS. The pharmacotherapy of maltreatment is currently governed by the presence of target symptoms that are (1) associated with criteria for Axis I psychiatric diagnoses, and (2) susceptible to medication management. However, indications for pharmacotherapy of target symptoms associated with Axis I psychiatric diagnoses in children and adolescents (whether maltreated or not) are more often probable or conjectural and less often established than is the case for adults.

Aims of pharmacotherapy in PTSD include decreasing intrusions, avoidance and anxious arousal, minimizing impulsivity, improving sleep, treating secondary disorders and facilitating cognitive and behavioral psychotherapies. Symptoms associated with PTSD in adults have been found to respond to tricyclic antidepressants (TCA's) (Davidson et al., 1990; Friedman, 1988). Current practice favors consideration of serotonergic agents for adult depression often associated with PTSD. There is also evidence that fluoxetine confers benefit for adult PTSD per se (Nagy, Morgan, Southwick, & Charney, 1993). Other medications potentially conferring benefit in adult PTSD, suggesting comparable benefits in childhood PTSD, are lithium or carbamazepine for mood stabilization and propranolol or clonidine for reduction of arousal. Propranolol is a beta blocker that ameliorates some childhood PTSD symptoms associated with autonomic hyperarousal (Famularo, Kinscheff, & Fenton, 1988). Some clinical researchers categorize TCA's and propranolol (for autonomic hyperarousal) as initial medications to consider in childhood PTSD for specific symptoms associated with the stage of trauma and comorbid conditions such as ADHD and depression; secondary medications to consider are lithium, clonidine, carbamazepine, MAOI's and benzodiazepines. Cohen, Greenberg, and Garfinkel-Cohen (1994) add anticonvulsants and buspirone to the list of medications to be considered. There is general agreement that in the absence of psychosis, neuroleptics should be avoided (Cohen et al., 1994).

In children, imipramine has been used for a variety of disorders including separation anxiety and depression. By rational extension, imipramine and other TCA's are sometimes used in PTSD, even if criteria for depression are not fully met. Empirical support for the efficacy of antidepressants in childhood and adolescent depression (irrespective of maltreatment experiences) cannot be marshaled from the double-blind, placebo controlled studies conducted thus far (McCracken & Cantwell, 1992; Ryan, 1990). Hence, as recently as 1992, the recommendation for a conservative pharmacotherapy of childhood depression is to begin with TCA's. Use of fluoxetine, bupropion, and clomipramine are confined to those children who have been unresponsive to or intolerant of standard TCA's (McCracken & Cantwell, 1992). A recent review of actual prescribing practices of child psychiatrists documents some use of fluoxetine for depression but is mute on the subject of any emerging trend to select fluoxetine or other selective serotonin reuptake inhibitors (SSRI's) before TCA's as the initial antidepressant (Kaplan, Simms, & Busner, 1994). Without double-blind, placebo controlled studies demonstrating efficacy, the indications for both SSRI's and TCA's in childhood and adolescent depression are probable, in PTSD conjectural. However, with the cumulative evidence of safety and efficacy from open trial studies of fluoxetine in combination with a psychostimulant for ADHD (Barrickman, Noyes, Kuperman, Schumacher, & Verda, 1991; Gammon & Brown, 1993) and for anxiety (Birmaher et al., 1994), as well as double-blind, placebo controlled studies documenting the short-term safety and efficacy of fluoxetine in adolescents with obsessive-compulsive disorder (Riddle et al., 1992) and mutism (Black & Uhde, 1994), one surmises it will become increasingly common for clinicians to use fluoxetine or other serotonergic agents first in treating both depression and PTSD in older children and adolescents. Studies suggest that a lower initial dose and a more gradual titration of fluoxetine in children and adolescents may reduce side effects of irritability and hypomania sometimes seen in children treated with adult doses (Birmaher et al., 1994; Riddle et al., 1991).

ADHD is one of the most common psychiatric diagnoses made in maltreated children (McCleer, Callagan, Henry, & Wallen, 1994). The medications of first choice for ADHD are the psychostimulants. However, there is evidence that the child with ADHD and comorbid anxiety may not respond as well to psychostimulants as the child with ADHD alone (Pliszka, 1989). In cases where there is comorbid anxiety or depression, nonpsychostimulants such as tricyclic antidepressants are sometimes employed in the treatment of ADHD (Green, 1992). Clonidine is a presynaptic alpha-2 adrenergic blocker that may also confer benefit in reducing hyperarousal and nightmares in PTSD. It is sometimes used alone or adjunctively with a psychostimulant in ADHD associated with aggression (Hunt, Capper, & O'Connell, 1990). An important area for research is the relative efficacy of antidepressants (including fluoxetine and other serotonergic agents), clonidine, psychostimulants, and combinations of these agents in the treatment of ADHD symptoms in the maltreated child versus ADHD symptoms in the nonmaltreated child.

Pharmacotherapy of conduct disorder is limited to specific target symptoms such as aggressiveness that occur in the disorder or to comorbid conditions, typically ADHD or depression. There is recent interest in the potential benefit of psychostimulants for aggressiveness, per se (Werry, 1994). Lithium and haloperidol have been shown in double-blind placebo controlled studies to confer benefit in the treatment of aggression in conduct disorder (Campbell et al., 1984). Serotonergic agents such as fluoxetine have appeal on the basis of theories implicating decreased serotonin turnover in disorders involving poorly modulated aggressive impulses (Zubieta & Alessi, 1993). However, at this time, the use of any antidepressant for conduct disorder must be considered conjectural (Ryan, 1990).

The differential pharmacotherapy of aggression and self-injurious behavior should also be kept in mind in managing maltreated children with brain conditions affecting impulse control. In this regard, propranolol, clonidine, and buspirone, as well as serotonergic agents and anticonvulsants, merit consideration (McDougle, Price, & Volkmar, 1994).

CASE ILLUSTRATION

Clinical Presentation

Andrea was 14 years old when the pediatric neurologist referred her to the adolescent psychiatry in-patient unit for further evaluation and treatment. She had recently made several visits to the emergency room for Tourette's Disorder, originally diagnosed at age seven.

Approximately three weeks prior to admission, the bouts she identified as tics had increased in intensity, frequency, and duration. They occurred at home and at school about twice daily and lasted approximately thirty minutes. Andrea described hand-clenching, mouth gaping, head-banging, kicking and arm swinging as well as eye-twitching. Her mother registered the chief complaint as "something's got to be done now about her jerks" and elaborated that at home Andrea's tics were "like Olympic events" during which family members would place pillows around her to protect her as well as themselves. At school the bouts were of sufficient severity that homebound instruction was being discussed. She and her brother (who also had been diagnosed as having Tourette's) were taunted by schoolmates and called "the AIDS kids." In the week prior to hospitalization, Andrea began having lapses in awareness and recollection of what she was doing. In addition, she experienced dizziness, nausea, ringing in her ears, and visual disturbances. She began harboring suicidal thoughts and had tried to cut herself.

Andrea's past medical history was significant for Tourette's disorder, for which she was taking pimozide. Her tics had been fairly typical and were treated initially with haloperidol, which was discontinued because of apparent treatment emergent side effects. Clonidine had also been used. Of these medications, pimozide was considered to be most (but still only partially) effective. Nonetheless, Andrea enjoyed a tic-free period between nine and twelve years old. Then in the year prior to admission, she reported that she was again subject to tics. She has had several neurology clinic visits over a seven-year period but had not had an EEG. There was no history of epilepsy. Her review of systems was remarkable for hives in response to bee stings. She had experienced menarche at age ten.

Developmental History

Andrea was reported to have met developmental milestones at age appropriate times. However, she repeated first grade. At age seven years 10 months, she was evaluated by her school. The evaluation included a WISC-R (VIQ=84, PIQ=104, and FSIQ=92) and WRAT (Reading 74, Spelling 70, and Arithmetic 66). Note was made that she was referred for academic difficulties and was attractive and outgoing. A House-Tree-Person (HTP) drawing was interpreted as showing a calm and relatively stable personality with possible feelings of insecurity, inadequacy, and absence of striving. Other factors indicated enthusiasm and talkativeness. At age nine, she was referred by the pediatric neurologist who had evaluated her for Tourette's to the University Developmental Clinic for further assessment. WISC-R scores were VIQ=84, PIQ=111, and FSIQ=96. The developmental test of Visual Motor Integration yielded an age-equivalent score of 7 years 6 months. WRAT scores were Reading 75, Spelling 76, and Arithmetic 83. A Piers-Harris Self-Concept reflected her view that she was often in trouble at home and that she had difficulty getting work done at school. She also described herself as frequently sick and breaking bones. She harbored fears about harm befalling her parents. A Thematic Apperception Test reflected themes of sadness, illness, accidents and people fighting. The Tasks of Emotional Development Test and an HTP this time were interpreted as reflecting lack of emotional warmth. A learning disability in language was identified. Recommendations were made for a learning disability resource room and speech and language therapy. Also at that time, psychotherapy that had only involved her brother and mother was recommended to include other family members, including Andrea.

Maltreatment History

At admission, Andrea disclosed to her mother that she, at age seven, and her brother, at age nine, had been sexually abused by a fourteen-year-old female baby-sitter over a month period. Following that experience, her mother would frequently inquire if her children had been subjected to any more abuse. One year prior to Andrea's hospitalization, her brother had been caught inappropriately touching a younger niece and a girl from the neighborhood. Neither of these girls' parents contacted police, so Andrea's mother initiated an investigation of her son. Andrea's mother related that she was distressed that nothing resulted from the investigation. At the time of Andrea's admission, her mother expressed persistent concern about her son's sexual impulses toward young girls, which she attributed in part to his Tourette's Disorder, identifying him as subject to "sexual tics." In addition, mother related that a teacher had filed suspicion of child abuse with Child Protective Services (CPS) on Andrea's behalf.

Family History

Andrea's mother was in her early thirties at the time of her daughter's first admission. She had 12 years of education. She described her own father (Andrea's maternal grandfather) as an alcoholic who had sexually and physically abused her, her brother, and her sister. Mother's first husband, Andrea's father, was also alcoholic and abusive, including during the time of her pregnancy. He abandoned the family when Andrea was two weeks old. Mother divorced him when she was twenty. She married her current husband nine years prior to Andrea's hospitalization. He works as a security officer. They have had one child together, six years younger than Andrea, who was described as having behavior problems. Both mother's and step-father's families lived in the same town, and Andrea's maternal grandparents had frequently taken care of Andrea during her childhood. At the time of Andrea's admission they were principally responsible for the care of Andrea's cousin, who was seven years old. They were currently seen by Andrea's parents as unsupportive and Andrea's family had determined to move to get away from them. Another impetus for moving was the death of Andrea's maternal aunt in her home in a fire attributed to arson. After the family move there was another fire in their new apartment for which Andrea's brother was blamed.

Mental Status

Andrea's mental status evaluation at admission revealed a thin girl appearing her stated age, and embarrassed but nonetheless cooperative with the interview. She exhibited some anxiety, no acute distress, and managed to smile at times. While her thought processes were organized and sequential, she endorsed unusual thought contents including illusory experiences such as hearing her mother call her name or hearing a ringing sound to which she would attend and for which she would attempt to identify an external source. In responding to specific questions about posttraumatic stress disorder, she indicated that she was subject to intrusive memories about her molestation experience. She said that while taking haloperidol for her tics, she was subject to visual hallucinations in which "things came out of pictures." Not attributed to medication was a recurrent image of a man and a boy sitting on a corner of her bed. She could not identify these individuals but associated the experience with a sense of uneasiness. She described being frequently fearful and would check her bedroom windows and behind doors. She slept with her light on. She explained that her sleep was disturbed by nightmares in which a man with wires coming out of his skin menaced her after she discovered a dead baby. She indicated that she had been subject to suicidal thoughts and had a vague plan to slash her wrists but had no current desire to follow through because it would hurt her parents. Her fund of knowledge and vocabulary were consonant with low average intellectual functioning. She seemed to recognize her need for help. Her general physical and neurological examinations were unremarkable.

Andrea's initial hospitalization in an acute adolescent psychiatric in-patient unit at the university hospital was three and one half months. While gains were made during that period and reintegration into home and community were attempted, Andrea was thought likely to require longer-term care. Application was made for intermediate-length psychiatric hospitalization at a state hospital also associated with the university medical school's department of psychiatry. Andrea was accepted but placed on a waiting list. A bed did not become available until twelve months later. During the waiting period, there were two and one half months of out-patient treatment in the university child/adolescent psychiatry clinic followed by a second acute hospitalization (same unit) lasting two months followed by seven months of out-patient treatment (same clinic) punctuated by two more but very brief hospitalizations in other community hospitals. She then was treated at the state hospital for eight months and returned for follow-up at the university clinic where she has continued to be seen.

Admission diagnoses:
Axis I: 1. Tourette's Disorder
2. R/O Major Depression
3. R/O Posttraumatic Stress Disorder
Axis II: 1. Developmental Language Disorder
Axis III: 1. R/O seizures
Axis IV: Severe
Axis V: CGAF: 40-45 HGAF: 60-65

Assessment Findings

During the two-year period from her first admission to her discharge from the state hospital, several assessments were conducted.

Neurologic Assessments

At the first hospitalization, pimozide was discontinued to observe her prospectively while free of medication. Tourette's Rating Scales were used throughout the hospitalization. She continued to have episodes of violent thrashing of her arms, head, and legs. An EEG was obtained and showed no epileptiform activity. A rechallenge with haloperidol appeared to effect gradual suppression of her involuntary movements. A correlation was discerned between increased frequency in these bouts as well as disruptive and self-harm behaviors prior to new disclosures regarding maltreatment experiences. Following each new disclosure the bouts decreased in frequency. During her second hospitalization, she experienced periods of decreased awareness, repetitively opening her mouth, which was described by staff "as if [she was] to scream or yawn," forcefully exhaling while clenching both hands, flexing the extremities and bending at the waist. These episodes lasted 6 to 12 minutes. Neurological consultation generated a differential diagnosis of tics, hyperventilation syndrome, partial complex seizures, and pseudo seizures. Of these, the consultant favored hyperventilation syndrome but nonetheless recommended another EEG and a CT scan of the head with contrast. The CT scan was normal; the EEG was abnormal in showing diffuse background slowing but no epileptiform, localizing, or lateralizing features. The abnormality present on the second EEG was attributed to medication effects. A later sleep deprived study was within normal limits. One year after her first admission, she was seen for follow-up in pediatric neurology clinic. Her Tourette's was considered to be under control and it was felt that management of her medication for tics should be conducted by psychiatry. However, the waxing and waning course of her tics since that appraisal has warranted other visits to neurology for adjustments of haloperidol. It continues to be difficult to separate what are tics, perhaps aggravated by stressors at home and school, from what are conversion symptoms.

Self and Parent Assessments

During the first hospitalization, the Child Behavior Checklist (CBCL) was completed by mother and the Youth Self Report (YSR) was completed by Andrea. CBCL broad-band scores were Internalizing T=67 (elevated), Externalizing T=57, and SUM T=68 (elevated). The Somatic Complaints subscale was especially high (T=81). YSR broad-band T scores were INT T=63 (borderline), EXT T=52, and SUM T=62 (borderline). Childhood Depression Inventories (CDI's) were obtained during the second hospitalization. Scores were 20 at admission and 14 two weeks later.

Some of these same self and parent ratings were also obtained one year after the first admission during the state hospitalization. CBCL completed by mother had Internalizing T=95, Externalizing T=79, and SUM T=93. Another CBCL completed by father had Internalizing T=92, Externalizing T=78, and SUM T=92. The YSR yielded scores of Internalizing T=62, Externalizing T=49, and SUM T=61. Beck Depression Inventories were 26 at admission, 18 one month later, and

4 six months later. In addition, both Andrea and her mother completed the Family Environment Scale (FES), the Dimensions of Temperament Scale–Revised (DOTS-R), and the Coddington Life Events Checklist. Andrea completed the Harter's Self Perception Scale and the Sensation Seeking Scale. Mother viewed the family as more supportive but also as more disorganized and conflicted than did Andrea. Andrea's DOTS-R had high points on activity and mood; her mother rated her high on activity but low on mood. On the Life Events Checklist Andrea and her mother were both considerably below the norm in identifying positive events. However, Andrea only identified one negative life event (mother lost her job) compared to her mother who identified sixteen on Andrea's behalf with a total score of 47 (norm=5.46). The Harter's Self Perception Scale indicated that most competence was perceived by Andrea in appearance, job, conduct and self-worth and least competence in scholastics, with intermediate scores on social, athletic and romantic competencies. The Sensation Seeking Scale had the highest T-score (71) on Boredom. The total score was low (49).

Psychological Testing

Psychological evaluation was carried out two months into the first hospitalization and consisted of the MMPI using adolescent norms, Incomplete Sentences, Rorschach, and Symonds Picture Story Test. The psychologist summarized the evaluation as strongly indicative of an underlying thought disorder most consistent with a diagnosis of either schizophrenia or schizophreniform disorder. She was seen as having highly idiosyncratic and unusual, at times bizarre, perceptions of the world around her, as having a tendency to ruminate unproductively and impaired in reality testing under stress. At the time of this testing, she was seen as extremely agitated, anxious, and fearful. She tended to see the world around her as unpredictable and extremely threatening. Her testing suggested she had difficulty both in establishing and maintaining satisfying interpersonal relations, was suspicious in relations and uncomfortable in social situations. In particular, the prognosis for her developing a therapeutic alliance was characterized as extremely guarded. Her defenses tended to be intellectualization and rationalization and, secondarily, acting-out.

Psychological testing conducted at the intermediate length stay hospital consisted of a WAIS-R with scores FSIQ=92, VIQ=86, and PIQ=111. An MMPI revealed somatic concerns, a history of poor social adjustment, difficulty forming and maintaining interpersonal relations and a tendency to disordered and even delusional thinking. There was evidence of depression and anxiety. Projectives revealed themes of violence and abuse, family conflict, poor social skills, and negative affect.

Speech and Language

The Peabody Picture Vocabulary Test-R (form L), Clinical Evaluation of Language Fundamentals–revised, The WORD Test–Adolescent, and the Test of Problem Solving–Adolescent were also administered. Results indicated significant verbal language difficulty affecting both receptive and expressive skills. Specific areas of difficulty include vocabulary/semantics (categorization, synonyms, antonyms, definitions, multiple definitions, analogies, shades of meaning), inferential thinking, problem solving, expressive grammar, and language processing. Recommendations were made that Andrea be seen for speech/language therapy weekly.

Semistructured Interviews

At the intermediate length stay hospital, the following assessments were administered: Diagnostic Interview for Children and Adolescents (DICA-R), which presents questions consonant with DSM III-R Axis I criteria, and The Stilwell Conscience Interview (SCI), which surveys sufficiency and deficiency in five domains of moral development: conceptualization, moral emotional responsiveness, moral attachment, valuation, and moral volition (Stilwell & Galvin, 1985; Stilwell, Galvin & Kopta, 1991; Stilwell, Galvin, Kopta, & Norton, 1994). On the DICA-R adolescent version, Andrea met criteria for Major Depressive Episode, Manic Episode, Dysthymic Disorder, Avoidant Disorder, and Obsessive Compulsive Disorder. On the DICA-R parent version, she met criteria for ADHD, Major Depressive Episode, Dysthymic Disorder and Presence of Psychotic Symptoms. The SCI was interpreted as showing evidence of internalization (she described a little voice or her imagination that warns of impending danger) and moral emotional responses dominated by fearfulness. She thought other people would find it a surprise if she did something good. She described her response to wrongdoing as "curling up in a ball and withdrawing from people." She was aware of reactions in her face and motorically, feelings of guilt and a desire to tell someone. Reparation requires that she tell offended parties and make up for misdeeds. Healing was unsuccessfully attempted through drinking. Her first memory of moral attachment was a weak affirmation from her mother when she was hurt by her grandmother at age

seven. She also recollected her mother's disbelief and accusations of lying when she described her grandfather's abusive behavior when she was eleven. In spite of this demonstration of mistrust, she retained a sense that her moral development was cared about by both parents and her brother through their hugs, affirmations, and shaming statements. In the domain of valuation, salient values pertained to personal safety and to treating others as she would like to be treated. She also identified herself as a future teacher in a helping role. Since being in treatment she had been trying to redefine herself as a good person. In the domain of self-evaluation and autonomy, core goodness was defined in the constricted sense as "not doing anything wrong and attending to personal appearance." Being helpful to animals and people was added. She identified badness with running away, hurting herself, and drinking. While she was being abused she found she had "to go off in another world, leaving her conscience behind." She envisioned moral growth as finding a sense of self-worth.

Treatment Selection and Course

Treatment modalities during the first hospitalization included use of a safe, secured in-patient facility with formal precautions against suicide, escape, self-mutilation, and sexual acting out. One-to-one observation was ordered twice. Restrictive interventions (i.e., seclusion and restraint) were required seven times, roughly corresponding to disclosures of maltreatment. Andrea was included in the behaviorally based adolescent protocol that linked levels of privilege to demonstrated responsible behavior and positive use of therapeutic modalities according to goals and objectives identified in an interdisciplinary master treatment plan. Andrea attended classes on the ward with assignments obtained from her home school. Her treatment plan called for 1:1 talks with nursing staff once per day and evening shift. She engaged in planned activities in occupational therapy. She was involved in adolescent group therapy. Daily individual psychotherapy sessions were conducted by a resident in psychiatry with daily supervision from a child/adolescent psychiatrist. Family work began with the parents, subsequently integrating Andrea. The therapeutic approach was primarily supportive and matter of fact, becoming focused on maltreatment experiences as she disclosed them, and ensuring her and her parents' understanding of legal requirements governing reporting. Therapy incorporated a psychoeducational component that focused on PTSD and Tourette's Syndrome.

Disclosures of Maltreatment During Hospitalization

In addition to her initial allegations of sexual abuse perpetrated by a female baby-sitter when Andrea was seven, as her hospitalization progressed Andrea made other allegations of sexual abuse. As mentioned above, there appeared to be bouts of severe involuntary movements in the periods of time immediately before, followed by amelioration of symptoms after these disclosures were made. Disclosures were not facilitated by hypnotic techniques and were not presented by Andrea as (what are now termed) recently recovered memories. She indicated instead that she was now ready to talk about experiences that had long troubled her. An additional motivation seemed to be a genuine concern for her cousin in the care of her maternal grandparents. She described sexual abuse perpetrated by her maternal grandfather beginning when she was three years and ending when she was eleven, two neighbors when she was nine, and her older brother when she was fourteen. With patient's and parents' knowledge, formal reports of suspected abuse were made to CPS.

A cascade of events followed from reporting suspicion of abuse. This included an investigation of the brother who initially denied but then admitted to sexually abusing Andrea. He was removed from the home and detained at the juvenile detention center before being placed in a residential home in another part of the state where he continues to reside. Detectives interviewed both Andrea and her mother but by the end of the first hospitalization, the investigation of maternal grandfather had not been completed. However, because there was no current involvement of Andrea with him, CPS allowed for her return home once her brother had been removed. Andrea also reported abuse by a peer in school. Contact was made with the school. The name provided by Andrea did not belong to anyone enrolled.

Andrea continued to have the experience of seeing men in her room and to have frightening nightmares. She was already taking haloperidol for tics. Imipramine was added and titrated into therapeutic levels that were associated with sustained clinical improvement. Andrea made advances in her level of privilege, but in the last month of hospitalization lost them when she made an attempt to escape. Shortly afterward, she made the above-mentioned disclosures about being abused by her older brother. Once her brother was removed from the home, her affect improved and Andrea's ambivalence about returning home diminished. She expressed eagerness to resume living with her parents and her younger brother. Her behavior improved markedly, precautions

were worked through and discontinued, and she attained the highest level on the adolescent protocol. She also did well in school. In-hospital visits with family went well and Andrea and her parents made progress in family therapy. She was sent home for an overnight visit and all concerned agreed that it went well. Discharge plans called for continuation of both haloperidol and imipramine, with follow-up of pharmacotherapy by the psychiatrist, home visits by a psychiatric nurse 3×/wk, and continued family therapy with the hospital social worker. Although prognosis appeared to be favorable for a return home, it was decided to allow an application to the intermediate length stay hospital to remain in process, with the understanding that Andrea and her parents could decline the bed if and when it was offered.

During the summer months that followed the hospitalization, Andrea was seen on an out-patient basis. She had episodic tics, took more haloperidol than had actually been prescribed, and developed somnolence, which resolved when the dose was corrected. She had also had some extrapyramidal side effects and these were managed effectively with Cogentin. She requested a decrease in her imipramine and, because she had been on it almost six months, a 25 percent reduction in dose was made. She was seen frequently by the visiting home nurse and continued in family and group therapy. During this time the family was described as subject to "enormous stress" while awaiting the outcome of the investigation of the maternal grandfather, which promised to eventuate in a trial, and her brother's transfer from detention to the residential home. Still another stressor was her return to school.

Her second hospitalization occurred after her mother found notes written by Andrea stating her intention to run away. She denied she had written the notes when her mother confronted her. She had also written notes to a neighborhood boy alleging that her stepfather was beating her. In the letter stating she intended to run away, she expressed her desire to recant the allegations she had made about her brother sexually molesting her and the allegations about her parents beating her. At admission, she related she felt guilty about disrupting her family. She appeared depressed and endorsed increasing sadness more days than not, crying episodes and diminished energy. She denied suicidal ideation, or change in sleep patterns or appetite. During the second hospitalization, she moved beyond making allegations to identify her frustration with, and desire for attention from, her parents. She also acknowledged her ambivalence about testifying against her grandfather in court. An appeal was made to the court to excuse her from making a court appearance. She began to deal with her experience of being ridiculed by peers and her consequent reluctance to attend school. On the other hand, she began flirting with male peers on the ward and received redirection and a warning about this. She was subsequently observed kissing a male peer. She had been encouraged to continue in an adolescent sexual abuse group that she had begun attending earlier in the summer and that met in a different hospital on campus. During one group therapy session she alleged that she had been sexually molested by the peer in question and he had touched her leg under the table. There was a question as to the extent to which this activity had been mutually engaged in. Her allegation of sexual molestation distressed the family and they considered removing her against medical advice. On the other hand, by this time Andrea's stepfather had become extremely apprehensive about the possibility of her making false allegations implicating him in sexual abuse. He perceived his job as being in jeopardy.

Return home seemed even more remote when she disclosed that she had had some pedophilic urges while engaged in baby-sitting. The family decided they were not able to take care of her at home because they were constantly aware of the threat she posed. Reassurances from team members and education regarding sequelae of maltreatment did nothing to alter their perception that authorities would take the position that "children don't lie" when sexual abuse is concerned. Since the state hospitalization was not immediately forthcoming, they explored the possibility of having her made a ward of county welfare. This would then have allowed for placement in a residential home. The treatment team essentially agreed that a period in a structured setting out of the home would be beneficial and supported the parents' efforts to have Andrea designated a Child in Need of Services (CHINS). However, the parents were informed by the welfare caseworker that she would only be designated CHINS if they identified themselves as negligent, thereby rendering themselves vulnerable to legal charges. This was a sufficiently intimidating prospect that the parents abandoned seeking a CHINS. To make matters worse, a transitional program to which the hospital social worker applied on Andrea's behalf in the hopes it would serve until the state hospital bed became available, turned her down. Andrea initially contended with her rejection experiences by resorting to self-injurious behavior. At this time she experienced an exacerbation of abnormal movements, increased nightmares, and more depression. Imipramine was increased and seemed to confer benefit. She began to address and work through her reluctance to enter the state hospital. Efforts were redoubled to

expedite transfer to that facility. However, Andrea, her family, and the treatment team alike were faced with the reality that she had no other disposition but home with whatever out-patient supports could be marshaled until a bed became available. She agreed that she should avoid baby-sitting in the future. After much work in individual and family therapy, Andrea was able to have a successful overnight visit at home. A second visit also went well. Arrangements for follow-up were much as before, except the Visiting Home Nursing Service was no longer available due to lack of funding.

For two months in the autumn of that year, things were fairly quiet. Then, in mid-December, Andrea disclosed to her mother that she was sexually preoccupied with her stepfather as well as her younger brother. She had not done anything but she was finding her urges difficult to resist. She also began picturing members of her family in hell. She became sensitive to noises and engaged in head banging in the car on the way home from church. Haloperidol was increased. Her mother contacted the family therapist and indicated that "it's starting all over again." She indicated that Andrea had not been forthright about her behavior at school. Mother wanted to know what her daughter's status on the waiting list for the state hospital was. It was ascertained that she was now third or fourth, which meant several more months of waiting. Her frustration mounted and she became angry with the family therapist and the psychiatrist because he had not petitioned the court to commit Andrea as a way to expedite access to the state hospital. The parents were put in touch with the State Commission for Protection and Advocacy then involved in a class action suit against the government to provide services such as residential care for the medically indigent. Andrea's inclusion in the suit, as well as her parents' crisis-motivated advocacy (including use of T.V. news media), still did not result in admission to the state hospital. Subsequently, the stepfather called the family therapist and was described as furious because his daughter had become intolerable, his career was at stake, and he doubted the safety of his son. The result was a termination of the relationship with the family therapist.

In another episode one week later, Andrea struck her mother, who was driving. This resulted in an emergency room visit and new demands for rehospitalization. In the opinion of the psychiatry resident on duty that night, the imminent danger had passed and hospitalization was not recommended. The mother contacted the psychiatrist two days later to report that Andrea was now seeing a new individual therapist but the family would like reassignment in the university clinic to a new family therapist. She would also continue to see the psychiatrist for pharmacotherapy. After much discussion with the former family therapist and the prospective new family therapists, it was decided to reassign the case to two experienced clinicians and to maintain pharmacotherapeutic interventions. This division of labor seemed effective for the duration of the waiting period, although it did not avert brief hospitalizations in the community. The third psychiatric hospitalization occurred when she tried to jump out of a car. It lasted less than a week. The fourth psychiatric hospitalization occurred when she had bouts of head banging associated with anger and accompanied by sweating, jerking (including her neck), and clenching her fingers. She reported flashbacks, depression, nightmares about molestation, and urges to molest her younger brother. According to the mother, at this community hospital, the counselor had been markedly uncomfortable with her and kept the door open. Asked if the discomfort stemmed from fear about false allegations, mother replied in disbelief "Yes and she's a woman!" After discharge, Andrea and her family returned to the university out-patient clinic.

Family therapy sessions at this time seemed to confer benefit. Andrea was able to address her jealousy of her younger brother. She wrote letters about her grandfather's molesting her. Her mother expressed concern that this would trigger allegations against other males with whom Andrea came in contact. Mother seemed to eschew responsibility for her children's care but to maintain an expectation that others step in. Andrea began to discuss the disbelief that she encountered when she and her cousins told her that grandfather had molested them. Her grandmother called her a liar. The court hearing was still a month away. Her tics had a waxing and waning course, aggravated by some of the crises described. Mother's negativism about her daughter seemed to subside and the family seemed to be doing better by the time the bed became available.

During the state hospitalization, individual therapy was conducted twice weekly and focused on the abuse, peer relations, and improving how she handled negative affect. She made progress but experienced a setback when her therapist rotated off service. She become isolative, slept through school, and engaged in head banging. She threatened to escape. Confinement to her room was ordered. Individual therapy focused on her anger and projection. She experienced trembling and body shaking associated with situational stresses. She weathered the transition to a new therapist and began working on attaining a higher privilege level. She began attending a community school for half days. She obtained excellent grades and advanced to full-time status. She responsibly held a town pass, the highest level attainable in the hospital. In therapy, she made gains in understanding how her abuse history affected her current relationships (i.e., in being mistrustful, seeing self as bad and being self-punitive). While the case against her grandfather was dismissed, she later received a phone call from him. In that call he admitted to the abuse and apologized. This was seen as very important in helping her relieve the self-blame and in validating her abuse experience with her parents. She was able to make associations between her pedophilic thoughts and her abuse experiences, eventually becoming free from them.

Family therapy was conducted two to four times per month. Many sessions were devoted to parental fears of false allegations but work was also done on other family members' reactions to Andrea's molestation. Home visits went well and she was allowed to supervise her younger brother without incident. She made telephone contact with her older brother and this was reported to have gone well (no details available). By this time he had found a stable placement.

Termination and Follow-Up

The pharmacotherapy that had been used before for PTSD was continued with minor changes according to the blood level of imipramine and metabolite. Haloperidol was discontinued. Andrea was occasionally observed to have motor and vocal tics typical of Tourette's but of mild severity. She relied less on somatic complaints that nonetheless persisted as low-grade symptoms but that she could connect with anxieties.

She participated in group therapy, therapeutic camping, ward government, assertiveness training, and speech and language therapy. At discharge her affect was bright, her thought processes logical, sequential and goal directed. There was no evidence of psychosis. She denied homicidal and suicidal ideation and she was focused on the future, which included joining ROTC and finding a job in which she would work with animals.

Discharge diagnoses were as follows:

Axis I:	1. Posttraumatic Stress Disorder
	2. Major Depression recurrent, without psychotic features, in remission
	3. Tourette's Disorder, mild
Axis II:	1. Expressive and receptive language disorder
	2. Dependent traits
Axis III:	1. Allergy to bee sting
	2. Orthodontic problems
	3. Myopia
Axis IV:	Severity of psychosocial stressors: severe (4)
Axis V:	Current GAF: 68 Highest GAF: 68

Follow-up was arranged with the university clinic. Andrea and her family have continued in individual and family therapy as well as the medication clinic. Seven months following discharge from the intermediate length stay hospital, Andrea was doing satisfactorily, but in the last three months has had some setbacks. She still takes imipramine, the dose adjusted according to plasma level. Haloperidol was resumed for tic suppression. Recently, Andrea has disclosed to her therapist that she was "molested" by a boy at school, although her therapist did not find the description of the encounter sufficiently compelling to suspect abuse. Approximately three months ago, Andrea expressed interest in expanding contact with her brother. According to Andrea's mother, Andrea's brother had decompensated into psychosis at the residential home. He is now denying the molestation of his sister. At the same time, Andrea has indicated to her therapist that she wishes to recant her allegation about her brother. Her mother apparently has encouraged her to do so and has requested material about Andrea to be forwarded to her brother's caseworker. Appointments made to discuss these matters have been late, canceled or, most recently, simply failed. A medication clinic visit remains scheduled for later this month.

SUMMARY

Child abuse and neglect represent major threats to the health and development of children. The modern recognition of child maltreatment occurred in the field of pediatrics, and the pediatric setting remains a critical gateway to identification and treatment. Ideally, services will be provided by a team of health care professionals, including pediatricians, psychologists, psychiatrists, social workers, and nurses.

The sequelae of maltreatment in children are profoundly deleterious and pervasive. Maltreated children, particularly those who are chronically abused or neglected, are likely to evidence physical injury, physiological dysregulation, developmental delays, impaired socialization, and behavioral psychopathology. Although there is no cluster of psychiatric symptoms that is consistently associated with child maltreatment or its subtypes, some form of behavioral dysfunction or psychosocial maladjustment in victims is the rule rather than the exception. Accordingly, assessment strategies are broad in focus and implementation. Measurement of multiple areas of child, parent, and family functioning is the sine qua non of successful assessment. While relatively few instruments have been developed specifically for perpetrators and their victims, several measures have emerged as sensitive and useful indices of problem identification and treatment evaluation. Instrument development remains a research priority in the near future.

Interventions for child maltreatment have only recently been subjected to empirical scrutiny. Behavioral and cognitive-behavioral treatments appear to be somewhat promising and modestly effective, at least for the short term. A recent review of this literature (Oates & Bross, 1995) laments the paucity of research on treatment effectiveness, and points toward the rather disappointing outcomes obtained in studies conducted to date. It is becoming generally acknowledged that chronic maltreatment is extremely difficult to ameliorate over the long term, and that prevention efforts have the greatest likelihood of reducing the incidence of maltreatment and its effects. Only by intervening early in the familial trajectory toward more ingrained and escalating patterns of violence and mistreatment will intervention have a high probability of success.

REFERENCES

Aber, J. L., & Allen, J. P. (1987). Effects of maltreatment on young children's socio-emotional development: An attachment theory perspective. *Developmental Psychology, 23,* 406–414.

Abidin, R. R. (1986). *Parenting stress index* (2nd Edition). Charlottesville, VA: Pediatric Psychology Press.

Achenbach, T., & Edelbrock, C. (1983). *The child behavior checklist–revised.* Burlington, VT: Queen City Printers.

American Humane Association. (1985). *Highlights of official child neglect and abuse reporting 1983.* Denver, CO: Author.

American Psychiatric Association. (1987). *Diagnostic and statistical manual of mental disorders* (3rd Edition, Revised). Washington, D.C.: Author.

American Psychiatric Association. (1994). *Diagnostic and statistical manual of mental disorders* (4th Edition). Washington, D.C.: Author.

Ammerman, R. T. (1990). Etiological models of child maltreatment: A behavioral perspective. *Behavioral Modification, 14,* 230–254.

Ammerman, R. T. (1991). The role of the child in physical abuse: A reappraisal. *Violence and Victims, 6,* 87–101.

Ammerman, R. T., Cassisi, J. E., Hersen, M., & Van Hasselt, V. B. (1986). Consequences of physical abuse and neglect in children. *Clinical Psychology Review, 6,* 291–310.

Ammerman, R. T., & Hersen, M. (Eds.). (1992). *Assessment of family violence: A clinical and legal sourcebook.* New York: John Wiley & Sons.

Ammerman, R. T., Hersen, M., & Van Hasselt, V. B. (1988). *Child Abuse and Neglect Interview Schedule—Revised.* Unpublished measure, Western Pennsylvania School for Blind Children, Pittsburgh, PA.

Ammerman, R. T., & Patz, R. J. (1996). Determinants of child abuse potential: Contribution of parent and child factors. *Journal of Clinical Child Psychology, 25,* 300–307.

Ammerman, R. T., Patz, R. J., & Hersen, M. (1996). *Physically punitive disciplinary practices in mothers: Intergenerational transmission and proximal determinants.* Unpublished manuscript, Medical College of Pennsylvania and Hahnemann University, Pittsburgh.

Ammerman, R. T., Van Hasselt, V. B., & Hersen, M. (1988). Maltreatment in handicapped children: A critical review. *Journal of Family Violence, 3,* 53–72.

Azar, S. T., & Rohrbeck, C. A. (1986). Child abuse and unrealistic expectations: Further validation of the Parent Opinion Questionnaire. *Journal of Consulting and Clinical Psychology, 54,* 867–868.

Azar, S. T., Robinson, D. R., Hekimian, E., & Twentyman, C. T. (1984). Unrealistic expectations and problem-solving ability in maltreating and comparison mothers. *Journal of Consulting and Clinical Psychology, 54,* 687–691.

Barahal, R. M., Waterman, J., & Martin, H. P. (1981). The social cognitive development of abused children. *Journal of Consulting and Clinical Psychology, 49,* 508–516.

Barrickman, L., Noyes, R., Kuperman, S., Schumacher, E., & Verga, M. (1991). Treatment of ADHD with fluoxetine: A preliminary trial. *Journal of the American Academy of Child and Adolescent Psychiatry, 30,* 762–767.

Beck, A. T., Ward, C. H., Mendelsohn, M., Mock, J., & Erbaugh, J. (1961). An inventory for measuring depression. *Archives of General Psychiatry, 4,* 561–571.

Beitchman, J. H., Zucker, K. J., Hood, J. E., DaCosta, G. A., Akman, D., & Cassavia, E. (1992). A review of long-term effects of child sexual abuse. *Child Abuse and Neglect, 16,* 101–118.

Belsky, J. (1993). Etiology of child maltreatment: A development-ecological analysis. *Psychological Bulletin, 114,* 413–434.

Birmaher, B., Waterman, G. S., Ryan, N., Cully, M., Balach, L., Ingram, J., & Brodsky, M. (1994). Fluoxetine for childhood anxiety disorders. *Journal of the American Academy of Child and Adolescent Psychiatry, 33,* 993–999.

Black, B., & Uhde, T. W. (1994). Treatment of elective mutism with fluoxetine: A double-blind, placebo-controlled study. *Journal of the American Academy of Child and Adolescent Psychiatry, 33,* 1000–1006.

Bousha, D. M., & Twentyman, C. T. (1984). Mother-child interactional style in abuse, neglect, and control groups: Naturalistic observations in the home. *Child Development, 93,* 106–114.

Bronfenbrenner, U. (1979). *The ecology of human development.* Cambridge, MA: Harvard University Press.

Browne, D. H. (1986). The role of stress in the commission of subsequent acts of child abuse and neglect. *Journal of Family Violence, 1,* 289–297.

Butcher, J. N., Dahlstrom, W. G., Graham, J. R., Tellegen, A., & Kraemmer, B. (1989). *Minnesota Multiphasic Personality Inventory–(MMPI=2): Manual for administration and scoring.* Minneapolis: University of Minnesota Press.

Caldwell, B., & Bradley, R. (1984). *Home observation for measurement of the environment.* New York: Dorsey Press.

Campbell, R. V., O'Brien, S., Bickett, A. D., & Lutzker, J. R. (1983). In-home parent training, treatment of migraine headaches, and marital counseling as an eco-behavioral approach to prevent child abuse. *Journal of Behavior Therapy and Experimental Psychiatry, 14,* 147–154.

Campbell, M., Small, A. M., Green, W. H., Jennings, S. J., Perry, R., Bennett, W. G., & Anderson, L. (1984). Behavioral efficacy of haloperidol and lithium carbonate. *Archives of General Psychiatry, 41,* 650–656.

Charlton, B. G., McGadey, J., Russell, D. & Neal, D. E. (1992). Noradrenergic innervation of the human adrenal cortex as revealed by the dopamine beta hydroxylase immunochemistry. *Journal of Anatomy, 180,* 501–506.

Charney, D. S., Deutch, A. Y., Krystal, J. H., Southwick, S. M., & Davis, M. (1993). Psychobiologic mechanisms of post-traumatic stress disorder. *Archives of General Psychiatry, 50,* 294–305.

Chrousos, G. P., & Gold, P. W. (1992). The concept of stress and stress system disorders, overview of physical and behavioral homeostasis. *Journal of the American Medical Association, 267,* 1244–1252.

Cicchetti, D., & Rogosch, F. A. (1994). The toll of child maltreatment on the developing child: Insights from developmental psychopathology. *Child and Adolescent Psychiatric Clinics of North America, 3,* 759–776.

Cicchetti, D., & Toth, S. L. (1995). A developmental psychopathology perspective on child abuse and neglect. *Journal of the American Academy of Child and Adolescent Psychiatry, 34,* 541–565.

Cohen, A. J., Greenberg, D. R., & Garfinkel-Cohen, R. (1994). Ambulatory psychiatric treatment of physically abused school-aged children, adolescents and their families. *Child and Adolescent Psychiatric Clinics of North America, 3,* 845–863.

Cohen, J. A., & Mannarino, A. P. (1996). A treatment outcome study for sexually abused preschool children: Initial findings. *Journal of American Academy of Child and Adolescent Psychiatry, 35,* 42–50.

Cohen, S., Mermelstein, R., Kamarck, T., & Hoberman, H. M. (1985). Measuring the functional components of social support. In I. G. Sarason & B. R. Sarason (Eds.), *Social support: Theory, research, and applications* (pp. 73–94). The Hague, Holland: Martinus Nijhoff.

Corse, S. J., Schmid, K., & Trickett, P. K. (1990). Social network characteristics of mothers in abusing and non-abusing families and their relationships to parenting beliefs. *Journal of Community Psychology, 18,* 44–59.

Coyle, J. T. (1987). Biochemical development of the brain: Neurotransmitters and child psychiatry. In C. Popper (Eds.), *Psychiatric pharmacosciences of children and adolescents* (pp. 3–26). Washington, D.C.: American Psychiatric Press.

Cutrona, C. E. (1982). Transition to college: Loneliness and the process of social adjustment. In L. A. Peplau, & D. Perlman (Eds.), *Loneliness: A sourcebook of current research, theory, and therapy.* New York: John Wiley & Sons.

Davidson, J., Kudler, H., Smith, R., Mahorney, S. L., Lipper, S., Hammett, E., Saunders, W. B., & Cavenar, J. O. (1990). Treatment of post-traumatic stress disorder with amitriptyline and placebo. *Archives of General Psychiatry, 47,* 259–266.

De Bellis, M., Lefter, L., Trickett, P., & Putnam, F. (1994). Urinary catecholamine excretion in sexually abused girls. *Journal of the American Academy of Child and Adolescent Psychiatry, 33,* 320–327.

De Bellis, M., & Putnam, F. (1994). The psychobiology of childhood maltreatment. *Child and Adolescent Psychiatric Clinics of North America, 3,* 663–678.

deLissovoy, V. (1979). Toward the definition of "abuse provoking child." *Child Abuse and Neglect, 3,* 341–350.

Derogatis, L. R. (1983). *SCL-90R administration, scoring, and procedure manual.* Baltimore, MD: Clinical Psychometric Research.

Dohrenwend, B. S. & Dohrenwend, B. P. (Eds.). (1981). *Stressful life events and their contexts.* New York: Prodist.

Egeland, B., Breitenbucher, M., & Rosenberg, D. (1980). Prospective study of significance of etiology of child abuse. *Journal of Consulting and Clinical Psychology, 48,* 195–205.

Egeland, B., Sroufe, L. A., & Erickson, M. (1983). The developmental consequences of different patterns of maltreatment. *Child Abuse and Neglect, 7,* 459–469.

Egeland, B., & Brunnquell, D. (1979). An at-risk approach to the study of child abuse. *Journal of the American Academy of Child Psychiatry, 18,* 219–236.

Engfer, A., & Schneewind, K. A. (1982). Causes and consequences of harsh parental punishment: An empirical investigation in a representative sample of 570 German families. *Child Abuse and Neglect, 6,* 129–139.

Eyberg, S. M., & Ross, A. W. (1978). Assessment of child behavior problems. The validation of a new inventory. *Journal of Clinical Child Psychology, 7,* 113–116.

Faller, K. C. (1993). *Child sexual abuse: Intervention and treatment issues.* Washington, D.C.: U.S. Government Printing Office, National Center on Child Abuse and Neglect, U.S. Department of Health and Human Services.

Famularo, R., Kinscherff, R., & Fenton, T. (1992). Psychiatric diagnoses of maltreated children: Preliminary finds. *Journal American Academy of Child and Adolescent Psychiatry, 31,* 863–867.

Famularo, R., Kinscherff, R., & Fenton, T. (1988). Propranolol treatment for childhood post-traumatic stress disorder, acute type. *American Journal of Disabled Child, 142,* 1244–1247.

Famularo, R., Stone, K., Barnum, R., & Wharton, R. (1986). Alcoholism and severe child maltreatment. *American Journal of Orthopsychiatry, 56,* 481–485.

Fantuzzo, J. W., Jurecic, L., Stovall, A., Hightower, A. D., Goins, C., & Schachtel, D. (1988). Effects of adult and peer social initiations on the social behavior of withdrawn, maltreated preschool children. *Journal of Consulting and Clinical Psychology, 56,* 34–39.

Farber, E. A., & Egeland, B. (1987). Invulnerability among abused and neglected children. In E. J. Anthony & B. J. Cohler (Eds.), *The invulnerable child* (pp. 253–288). New York: Guilford.

Finkelhor, D., & Berliner, L. (1995). Research on the treatment of sexually abused children: A review and recommendations. *Journal of the American Academy of Child & Adolescent Psychiatry, 34,* 1408–1423.

Forehand, R. L., & McMahon, R. J. (1981). *Helping the noncompliant child: A clinician's guide to parent training.* New York: Guilford.

Freedman, L. S., Ohuchi, T., Goldstein, M., Axelrod, F., Fish, I., & Dancir, J. (1972). Changes in human serum dopamine beta hydroxylase activity with age. *Nature, 236,* 310–311.

Freidman, M. (1988). Towards a rational pharmacotherapy of PTSD: An interim report. *American Journal of Psychiatry, 145,* 281–285.

Friedrich, W. N. (1991). *Casebook of sexual abuse treatment.* New York: W. W. Norton.

Friedrich, W. N., Tyler, J. D., & Clark, J. A. (1985). Personality and psychophysiological variables in abusive, neglectful, and low-income control mothers. *Journal of Nervous and Mental Disease, 173,* 449–460.

Frodi, A. M. (1981). Contribution of infant characteristics to child abuse. *American Journal of Mental Deficiency, 85,* 341–349.

Gaines, R., Sandgrund, A., Green, A. H., & Power, E. (1978). Etiological factors in child maltreatment: A multivariate study of abusing, neglecting, and normal mothers. *Journal of Abnormal Psychology, 87,* 531–540.

Galvin, M., Shekhar, A., Simon, J., Stilwell, B., Ten Eyck, R., Laite, G., Karwisch, G., & Blix, S. (1991). Low dopamine beta hydroxylase: A biological sequelae of abuse and neglect? *Psychiatry Research, 39,* 1–11.

Galvin, M. R., Stilwell, B. M., Shekhar, A., Kopta, S. M., McKasson, S., & Goldfarb, C. M. (1996). *Maltreatment, dopamine beta hydroxylase and conscience functioning in emotionally disturbed boys.* Unpublished manuscript, Indiana University School of Medicine.

Galvin, M., Ten Eyck, R., Shekhar, A., Stilwell, B., Fineberg, N., Laite, G., & Karwisch, G. (1995). Serum dopamine beta hydroxylase and maltreatment in psychiatrically hospitalized boys. *Child Abuse and Neglect, 19,* 821–832.

Gammon, G. D., & Brown, T. E. (1993). Fluoxetine and methylphenidate in combination for treatment of attention deficit disorder and comorbid depressive disorder. *Journal of Child and Adolescent Psychopharmacology, 3,* 1–10.

Garbarino, J. (1976). A preliminary study of some ecological correlates of child abuse: The impact of socioeconomic stress on mothers. *Child Development, 47,* 178–185.

Garbarino, J., & Crouter, A. (1978). Defining the community context of parent-child relations: The correlates of child maltreatment. *Child Development, 49,* 604–616.

Gaudin, J. (1993). *Child neglect: A guide for intervention.* Washington, D.C.: U.S. Government Printing Office, National Center on Child Abuse and Neglect, U.S. Department of Health and Human Services.

Gelles, R. J. (1973). Child abuse as psychopathology: A sociological critique and reformulation. *American Journal of Orthopsychiatry, 43,* 611–621.

Gibaud-Wallston, J., & Wandersman, L. P. (1978, August). *Development and utility of the Parenting Sense of Competence Scale.* Paper presented at the meeting of the American Psychological Association, Toronto, Canada.

Gil, D. G. (1975). Unraveling child abuse. *American Journal of Orthopsychiatry, 45,* 346–356.

Ginsberg, S. D., Hof., P. R., Young, W. G., & Morrison, J. H. (1993). Noradrenergic innervation of the hypothalamus of rhesus monkeys: Distribution of dopamine beta hydroxylase immunoreactive fibers and quantitative analyses of varicosities in the paraventricular nucleus. *The Journal of Comparative Neurology, 327,* 597–611.

Giovannoni, J. (1989). Definitional issues in child maltreatment. In D. Cicchetti & V. Carlson (Eds.), *Child maltreatment: Theory and research on the causes and consequences of child abuse and neglect* (pp. 3–37). New York: Cambridge University Press.

Gomes-Schwartz, B., Horowitz, J. M., & Cardarelli, A. P. (1990). *Child sexual abuse: The initial effects.* Newbury Park, CA: Sage Publications, Inc.

Green, A. H. (1983). Dimensions of psychological trauma in abused children. *Journal of the American Academy of Child Psychiatry, 22,* 231–237.

Green, A. H. (1992). Nonstimulant drugs in the treatment of attention deficit hyperactivity disorder. *Child and Adolescent Psychiatric Clinics of North America, 1,* 449–465.

Hansen, D. J., & MacMillan, V. M. (1990). Behavioral assessment of child abusive and neglectful families: Recent developments and current issues. *Behavior Modification, 14,* 255–278.

Hansen, D. J., Pallotta, G. M., Tishelman, A. C., Conaway, L. P., & MacMillan, V. M. (1989). Parental problem-solving skills and child behavior problems: A comparison of physically abusive, neglectful, clinic, and community families. *Journal of Family Violence, 4,* 353–368.

Harlow, H. F. (1980). Ethology. In H. I. Kaplan, A. M. Freeman, & B. J. Sadock (Eds.), *Comprehensive textbook of psychiatry* (3rd Edition) (pp. 424–443). Baltimore: Williams and Wilkins.

Harlow, H. F., Dodsworth, R. O., & Harlow, M. K. (1965). Total social isolation in monkeys. *Proceedings of the National Academy of Sciences, 54,* 90–97.

Holmes, T. H., & Rahe, R. (1967). *Schedule of recent experience (SRE).* Seattle, WA: School of Medicine, University of Washington.

Hunt, R. D., Capper, L., & O'Connell, P. (1990). Clonidine in child and adolescent psychiatry. *Journal of Child and Adolescent Psychopharmacology, 1,* 87–102.

Johnson, C. J. (1996). Abuse and neglect of children. In R. E. Behrman, R. M. Kliegman, & A. M. Arvin (Eds.), *Nelson textbook of pediatrics* (15th Edition) (pp. 112–121). Philadelphia: W. B. Saunders.

Johnston, C., & Mash, E. J. (1989). A measure of parenting satisfaction and efficacy. *Journal of Clinical Child Psychology, 18,* 167–175.

Justice, B., & Justice, R. (1979). *The broken taboo.* New York: Human Science Press.

Kadushin, A., & Martin, J. A. (1981). *Child abuse: An interactional event.* New York: Columbia University Press.

Kandel, E. R. (1983). From metapsychology to molecular biology: Exploration into the nature of anxiety. *American Journal of Psychiatry, 140,* 1277–1293.

Kandel, E. R. (1985). Early experience, critical periods, and developmental fine tuning of brain architecture. In E. Kandel & J. Schwartz (Eds.), *Principles of neural science.* New York: Elsevier Science.

Kaplan, S. L., Simms, R. M., & Busner, J. (1994). Prescribing practices of outpatient child psychiatrists. *Journal of the American Academy of Child and Adolescent Psychiatry, 33,* 35–44.

Kaufman, J., & Zigler, E. (1993). The intergenerational transmission of abuse is overstated. In R. J. Gelles & D. R. Leseke (Eds.), *Current controversies on family violence* (pp. 209–221). Newbury Park, CA: Sage Publications, Inc.

Kelly, J. A. (1983). *Treating child abusive families: Intervention based on skills-training principles.* New York: Plenum Press.

Kempe, C. H. (1973). A practical approach to the protection of the abused child and the rehabilitation of the abusing parent. *Pediatrics, 51,* 804–812.

Kendall, P., & Braswell, L. (1985). *Cognitive-behavioral therapy for impulsive children.* New York: Guilford Press.

Kolko, D. J., & Stauffer, J. (1991). Child sexual abuse. In R. T. Ammerman & M. Hersen (Eds.), *Case studies in family violence* (pp. 153–170). New York: Plenum Press.

Kolko, D. J., Kazdin, A. E., Thomas, A. Mc., & Day, B. (1993). Heightened child physical abuse potential: Child, parent, and family dysfunction. *Journal of Interpersonal Violence, 8,* 169–192.

Kosten, T. R., Mason, J. W., Giller, E. L., Ostroff, R. B., & Harkness, L. (1987). Sustained urinary norepinephrine and epinephrine evaluation in post-traumatic stress disorders. *Psychoneuroendocrinology, 12,* 16–20.

Kraemer, G. W., Ebert, M. H., Lake, C. R., & McKinney, W. T. (1984). Hypersensitivity to d-amphetamine several years after early social deprivation in rhesus monkeys. *Psychopharmacology, 82,* 226–271.

Kraemer, G. W., Ebert, M. H., Schmidt, D. E., & McKinney, W. T. (1989). A longitudinal study of the effect of different social rearing conditions on cerebrospinal fluid norepinephrine and biogenic amine metabolites in rhesus monkeys. *Neuropsychopharmacology, 2,* 175–189.

Knutson, J. F. (1995). Psychological characteristics of maltreated children: Putative risk factors and consequences. *Annual Review of Psychology, 46,* 401–431.

Lahey, B. B., Conger, R. D., Atkeson, B. M., & Treiber, F. A. (1984). Parenting behavior and emotional status of physically abusive mothers. *Journal of Consulting and Clinical Psychology, 52,* 1062–1071.

Larrance, D. T., & Twentyman, C. T. (1983). Maternal attributions and child abuse. *Journal of Abnormal Psychology, 92,* 449–457.

Lewis, D. O. (1992). From abuse to violence: Psychophysiological consequences of maltreatment. *Journal American Academy of Child and Adolescent Psychiatry, 31,* 383–391.

Lewis, D. O. (1994). Etiology of aggressive conduct disorders: Neuropsychiatric and family contributions. *Child and Adolescent Psychiatric Clinics of North America, 3,* 303–319.

Lewis, D. O., Lovely, R., Yeager, C., & Femina, D. (1988). Toward a theory of the genesis of violence: A follow up study of delinquents. *Journal American Academy of Child and Adolescent Psychiatry, 28,* 431–436.

Lupin, N. (1981). *The family relaxation and self-control program.* (Vols. 1-2). Houston, TX: Biobehavioral Publishers & Distributors, Inc. (audio tapes).

Lutzker, J. R., & Rice, J. M. (1984). Project 12-Ways: Measuring outcome of a large in-home service for treatment and prevention of child abuse and neglect. *Child Abuse and Neglect, 8,* 519–524.

Lutzker, J. R., Megson, D. A., Webb, M. E., & Dachman, R. S. (1985). Validating and training adult-child interaction skills to professionals and to parents indicated for child abuse and neglect. *Journal of Child and Adolescent Psychotherapy, 2,* 91–104.

MacMillan, V. M., Olson, R. L., & Hansen, D. J. (1988, November). *The development of an anger inventory for use with maltreating parents.* Paper presented at the meeting of the Association for the Advancement of Behavior Therapy, New York.

Mash, E. J., Johnston, C., & Kovitz, K. (1983). A comparison of the mother-child interactions of physically abused and non-abusive children during play and task situations. *Journal of Clinical Child Psychology, 12,* 337–346.

Mason, J. W., Giller, E. L., Kosten, T. R., & Harkness, L. (1988). Elevation of urinary norepinephrine/cortisol ratio in post-traumatic stress disorder patients. *Journal of Nervous and Mental Disease, 176,* 498–502.

Mason, J. W., Giller, E. L., Kosten, T. R., Ostroff, R. B., & Podd, L. (1986). Urinary free cortisol levels in post-traumatic stress disorder patients. *Journal of Nervous and Mental Disease, 174,* 145–149.

Mayer, J., & Black, R. (1977). Child abuse and neglect in families with an alcoholic or opiate addicted parent. *Child Abuse and Neglect, 1,* 85–98.

McCleer, S. V., Callaghan, M., Henry, D., & Wallen, J. (1994). Psychiatric disorders in sexually abused children. *Journal of the American Academy of Child and Adolescent Psychiatry, 33,* 313–319.

McCracken, J. T., & Cantwell, D. P. (1992). Management of child and adolescent mood disorders. *Child and Adolescent Psychiatric Clinics of North America, 1,* 229–255.

McDougle, C. J., Price, L. H., & Volkmar, F. R. (1994). Recent advances in the pharmacotherapy of autism and related conditions. *Child and Adolescent Psychiatric Clinics of North America, 3,* 71–90.

McGee, R. A., Wolfe, D. A., Yuen, S. A., Wilson, S. K., & Carnochan, J. (1995). The measurement of maltreatment: A comparison of approaches. *Child Abuse & Neglect, 19,* 233–249.

Meichenbaum, D. (1977). *Cognitive-behavior modification: An integrative approach.* New York: Plenum Press.

Milner, J. S. (1986). *The child abuse potential inventory manual* (2nd Edition). Webster, NC: Psytec.

Milner, J. S. (1994). Assessing physical child abuse risk: The Child Abuse Potential Inventory. *Clinical Psychology Review, 14,* 547–583.

Milner, J. S., Gold, R. G., & Wimberley, R. C. (1986). Prediction and explanation of child abuse: Cross-validation of the Child Abuse Potential Inventory. *Journal of Consulting and Clinical Psychology, 54,* 865–866.

Mueller, E., & Silverman, N. (1989). Peer relations in maltreated children. In D. Cicchetti & V. Carlson (Eds.), *Child maltreatment: Theory and research on the cause and consequences of child abuse and neglect* (pp. 529–578). New York: Cambridge University Press.

Nagy, L. M., Morgan, C. A., Southwick, S. M., & Charney, D. S. (1993). Open prospective study of fluoxetine for post-traumatic stress disorder. *Journal of Clinical Psychopharmacology, 13,* 107–113.

National Center on Child Abuse and Neglect. (1995). *Child maltreatment 1993: Reports from the states to the National Center on Child Abuse and Neglect.* Washington, D.C.: U.S. Government Printing Office, U.S. Department of Health and Human Services.

National Research Council. (1993). *Understanding child abuse and neglect.* Washington, D.C.: National Academy Press.

Novaco, R. W. (1975). *Anger control: The development and evaluation of an experimental treatment.* Lexington, MA: D. C. Heath.

Oates, R. K., & Bross, D. C. (1995). What have we learned about treating child physical abuse? A literature review of the last decade. *Child Abuse & Neglect, 19,* 463–473.

O'Dell, S. L., Tarler-Benlolo, L., & Flynn, J. M. (1979). An instrument to measure knowledge of behavioral principles as applied to children. *Journal of Behavior Therapy and Experimental Psychiatry, 10,* 29–34.

Oliver, J. E. (1993). Intergenerational transmission of child abuse: Rates, research and clinical implications. *American Journal of Psychiatry, 150,* 1315–1324.

Patterson, G. R. (1976). *Living with children: New methods for parents and teachers* (rev. ed). Champaign, IL: Research Press.

Pliszka, S. R. (1989). Effect of anxiety on cognition, behavior and stimulant response in ADHD. *Journal of the American Academy of Child and Adolescent Psychiatry, 28,* 882–887.

Polansky, N. A., Ammons, P. W., & Gaudin, J. M. (1985). Loneliness and isolation in child neglect. *Social Casework: The Journal of Contemporary Social Work, 66,* 38–47.

Polansky, N. A., Gaudin, J. M., Ammons, P. W., & Davis, K. B. (1985). The psychological ecology of the neglectful mother. *Child Abuse and Neglect, 9,* 265–275.

Post, R. M. (1992). Transduction of psychosocial stress into the neurobiology of recurrent affective disorder. *American Journal of Psychiatry, 149,* 999–1010.

Putnam, F. W., Trickett, P. K., Helmers, K., Susman, E. J., Dorn, L. & Everett, B. (1991, May). Cortisol abnormalities in sexually abused girl. *New Research Program and Abstracts APA, 144th Annual Meeting,* #514, New Orleans.

Quay, H. C. (1993). The psychobiology of undersocialized aggressive conduct disorder: A theoretical perspective. *Development and Psychopathology, 5,* 165–180.

Quay, H. C. (1988). The behavioral reward and inhibition system in childhood behavior disorders. In L. M. Bloomingdale (Ed.), *Attention deficit disorder* (pp. 176–186). New York: Pergamon Press.

Quay, H. C., Routh, D. K., & Shapiro, S. K. (1987). Psychopathology of childhood: From description to validation. *Annual Review of Psychology, 38,* 491–532.

Reid, J. B., Kavanagh, K., & Baldwin, D. V. (1987). Abusive parent's perceptions of child problem behaviors: An example of parental bias. *Journal of Abnormal Child Psychology, 15,* 457–466.

Reid, J. B., Taplin, P., & Loeber, R. (1981). A social interactional approach to the treatment of abusive families.

In R. B. Stuart (Ed.), *Violent behavior: Social learning approaches to prediction, management, and treatment.* New York: Brunner/Mazel, Inc.

Riddle, M. A., Scahill, L., King, R. A., Hardin, M. T., Anderson, G. M., Ort, S. I., Smith, J. C., Leckman, J. F., & Cohen, D. J. (1992). Double-blind, cross-over trial of fluoxetine and placebo in children and adolescents with obsessive compulsive disorder. *Journal of the American Academy of Child and Adolescent Psychiatry, 31,* 1062–1069.

Rogeness, G. A. (1994). Biologic findings in conduct disorder. *Child and Adolescent Psychiatric Clinics of North America, 3,* 271–284.

Rogeness, G. A. (1991). Psychosocial factors and amine systems. *Psychiatry Research,* 215–217.

Rogeness, G. A., Macedo, C. A., Harris, W. R., & Fisher, C. (1986a). Psychopathology in abused or neglected children. *Journal of the American Academy of Child Psychiatry, 25,* 659–665.

Rogeness, G. A., Javors, M. A., & Pliszka, S. R. (1992). Neurochemistry and child and adolescent psychiatry. *Journal American Academy Child and Adolescent Psychiatry, 31,* 765–781.

Rosenberg, M. S., & Repucci, N. D. (1983). Abusive mothers: Perceptions of their own and their children's behavior. *Journal of Consulting and Clinical Psychology, 51,* 674–682.

Ross, A. (1981). *Child behavior therapy.* New York: John Wiley & Sons.

Russel, A. B., & Trainot, C. M. (1984). *Trends in child abuse and neglect: A national perspective.* Denver, CO: American Humane Association.

Russell, D., & Cutrona, C. E. (1984). *The social provisions scale.* Unpublished manuscript, University of Iowa, Iowa City.

Ryan, N. D. (1990). Heterocyclic antidepressants in children and adolescents. *Journal of Child and Adolescent Psychopharmacology, 1,* 21–31.

Sack, W. H., Mason, R., & Higgins, J. E. (1985). The single-parent family and abusive child punishment. *American Journal of Abnormal Psychology, 92,* 68–76.

Salzinger, S., Kaplan, S., & Artemyeff, C. (1983). Mothers' personal social networks and child maltreatment. *Journal of Abnormal Psychology, 92,* 68–76.

Sameroff, A., & Chandler, M. (1975). Reproductive risk and the continuum of caretaking casualty. In F. Horowitz (Ed.), *Review of child development research* (vol. 4). Chicago: University of Chicago Press.

Sapolsky, R. (1989). Hypercortisolism among socially subordinate wild baboons originates at the CNS level. *Archives of General Psychiatry, 46,* 1047–1051.

Sapolsky, R. (1982). The endocrine stress response and social status in the wild baboon. *Hormones and Behavior, 15,* 279–284.

Sapolsky, R., Krey, L., & McEwen, B. (1985). Prolonged glucocorticoid exposure reduces hippocampal neuron number: Implications for aging. *Journal of Neuroscience, 5,* 1221–1227.

Schinke, S. P., Schilling, R. F., Kirkham, M. A., Gilchrist, L. D., Barth, R. P., & Blythe, B. J. (1986). Stress management skills for parents. *Journal of Child and Adolescent Psychotherapy, 3,* 293–298.

Schneider, M., & Robin, A. (1976). The turtle technique: A method for the self-control of impulsive behavior. In J. D. Drumholtz & C. E. Thoresen (Eds.), *Counseling methods* (pp. 157–163). New York: Holt, Rinehart, & Winston, Inc.

Shure, M., & Spivack, G. (1978). *Problem-solving techniques in childrearing.* San Francisco: Jossey-Bass.

Smetana, J. G., & Kelly, M. (1989). Social cognition in maltreated children. In D. Cicchetti & V. Carlson (Eds.), *Child maltreatment: Theory and research on the causes and consequences of child abuse and neglect* (pp. 620–646). New York: Cambridge University Press.

Smith, M. A., Davidson, J., & Ritchie, J. C. (1989). The corticotropin releasing hormone test in patients with post-traumatic stress disorder. *Biological Psychiatry, 26,* 345–355.

Smith, J. M., Conaway, R. L., Smith, G. M., & Hansen, D. J. (1988, November). *Evaluation of a problem-solving measure for use with physically abusive and neglectful parents.* Paper presented at the Association for the Advancement of Behavior Therapy Convention, New York.

Sparrow, S. S., Balla, D. A., & Cicchetti, D. V. (1984). *The vineland adaptive behavior scales* (rev.). Circle Pines, MN: American Guidance Service.

Spielberger, C. D., Gorsuch, R. L., & Lushene, R. E. (1970). *Manual for the state-trait anxiety inventory.* Palo Alto, CA: Consulting Psychologists Press.

Spinetta, J. J., & Rigler, D. (1972). The child abusing parents: A psychological review. *Psychological Bulletin, 77,* 296–304.

Stilwell, B., & Galvin, M. (1985). Conceptualization of conscience in 11–12 year olds. *Journal of the American Academy Child and Adolescent Psychiatry, 24,* 630–636.

Stilwell, B., Galvin, M., & Kopta, S. M. (1991). Conceptualization of conscience in normal children and adolescents, ages 5 to 17. *Journal of the American Academy of Child and Adolescent Psychiatry, 30,* 16–21.

Stilwell, B., Galvin, M., Kopta, S. M., & Norton, J. A. (1994). Moral-emotional responsiveness: Two domains of conscience functioning. *Journal of the American Academy of Child and Adolescent Psychiatry, 33,* 130–139.

Straus, M. A. (1980). Stress and child abuse. In C. H. Kempe and R. E. Helfer (Eds.), *The battered child* (3rd Edition) (pp. 86–102). Chicago: University of Chicago Press.

Straus, M. A., Gelles, R. J., & Steinmentz, S. K. (1980). *Behind closed doors: Violence in the American family.* Garden City, NY: Anchor Books.

Suomi, S. J. (1985). Ethology: Animal models. In H. I. Kaplan, A. M. Freedman, & B. J. Sadock (Eds.), *Comprehensive textbook of psychiatry* (4th edition) (pp. 226–237). Baltimore: Williams and Wilkins.

Suomi, S. J. (1991, October). *Bowlby's attachment theory: Perspectives from studies with nonhuman primates.* Paper presented at the 38th Annual Meeting of the American Academy of Child and Adolescent Psychiatry, San Francisco.

Tertinger, D. A., Greene, B. V., & Lutzker, J. R. (1984). Home safety: Development and validation of one component of an ecobehavioral treatment program for abused and neglected children. *Journal of Applied Behavior Analysis, 17,* 159–174.

Terr, L. C. (1991). Childhood traumas: An outline and overview. *American Journal of Psychiatry 148,* 10–20.

Trickett, P. K., Aber, J. L., Carlson, V., & Cicchetti, D. (1991). Relationship of socioeconomic status to the etiology and developmental sequelae of physical child abuse. *Development Psychology, 27,* 148–158.

Trickett, P. K., & Kuczynski, L. (1986). Children's misbehaviors and parental discipline strategies in abusive and nonabusive families. *Developmental Psychology, 22,* 115–123.

Twardosz, S., & Nordquist, V. M. (1987). Parent training. In M. Hersen & V. B. Van Hasselt (Eds.), *Behavior therapy with children and adolescents: A clinical approach* (pp. 75–105). New York: John Wiley & Sons.

Twentyman, C. T., Plotkin, R., Dodge, D., & Rohrbeck, C.A. (1981, November). *Inappropriate expectations of parents who maltreat their children.* Paper presented at the 15th Annual Convention of the Association for Advancement of Behavior Therapy, Toronto, Canada.

Tzeng, O. C. S., Jackson, J. W., & Karlson, H. C. (1991). *Theories of child abuse and neglect.* New York: Praeger.

Uno, H., Tarara, K. R., Else, J. G., Suleman, M. A., & Sapolsky, R. M. (1990). Hippocampal damage associated with prolonged and fatal stress in primates. *Journal of Neuroscience, 9,* 1705–1711.

Wahler, R. G. (1980). The insular mother: Her problems in parent-child treatment. *Journal of Applied Behavior Analysis, 13,* 207–219.

Walker, C. E., Bonner, B. L., & Kaufman, K. L. (1988). *The physically and sexually abused child: Evaluation and treatment.* New York: Pergamon Press.

Watson-Perczel, M., Lutzker, J. R., Greene, B. F., & McGimpsey, B. J. (1988). Assessment and modification of home cleanliness among families adjuncted for child neglect. *Behavior Modification, 12,* 57–81.

Weinshilboum, R. M., & Axelrod, F. (1971). Reduced plasma dopamine beta hydroxylase in familial dysautonomia. *New England Journal of Medicine, 285,* 938–942.

Weinshilboum, R. M., Raymond, F. A., Elveback, L. R., & Weidman, W. H. (1973). Serum dopamine beta hydroxylase activity: Sibling-sibling correlation. *Science, 181,* 943–945.

Werry, J. S. (1994). Pharmacotherapy of disruptive behavior disorders. *Child and Adolescent Psychiatric Clinics of North America, 3,* 321–341.

Wissow, L. S. (1995). Child Abuse and Neglect. *The New England Journal of Medicine, 332,* 1425–1431.

Wolfe, D. A. (1985). Child abusive parents: An empirical review and analysis. *Psychological Bulletin, 97,* 462–482.

Wolfe, D. A. (1987). *Child abuse: Implications for child development and psychopathology.* Newbury Park, CA: Sage Publications, Inc.

Wolfe, D. A., Sandler, J., & Kaufman, K. (1981). A competency-based parent training program for child abusers. *Journal of Consulting and Clinical Psychology, 49,* 633–640.

Wolfe, D. A., Fairbank, J., Kelly, J. A., & Bradlyn, A. S. (1983). Child abusive parents' physiological responses to stressful and nonstressful behavior in children. *Behavioral Assessment, 5,* 363–371.

Wood-Shuman, S., & Cone, J. D. (1986). Differences in abusive, at-risk for abuse, and control mothers' descriptions of normal child behavior. *Child Abuse and Neglect, 10,* 397–405.

Yehuda, R., Lowry, M. R., Southwick, S. M., Shaffer, D., & Giller, E. L. (1991). Lymphocyte glucocorticoid receptor number in post-traumatic stress disorder. *American Journal of Psychiatry, 148,* 499–504.

Yehuda, R., Southwick, S. M., Giller, E. L., Ma, X., & Mason, J. W. (1992). Urinary catecholamine excretion and severity of post-traumatic stress disorder. *Journal of Nervous and Mental Disease, 180,* 321–325.

Yehuda, R., Southwick, S. M., & Nussbaum, G. (1990). Low urinary cortisol excretion in patients with post-traumatic stress disorder. *Journal of Nervous and Mental Disease, 178,* 336–369.

Yehuda, R., Southwick, S. M. , Krystal, J. H., Bremner, D., Charney, D. S., & Mason, J. W. (1993). Enhanced suppression of cortisol following dexamethasone administration in post-traumatic stress disorder. *American Journal of Psychiatry, 150,* 83–86.

Zubieta, J. K., & Alessi, N. (1993). Is there a role of serotonin in the disruptive behavior disorders? A literature review. *Journal of Child and Adolescent Psychopharmacology, 3,* 11–35.

CHAPTER 4

FAMILY ADAPTATION TO CHILDHOOD DISABILITY AND ILLNESS

Alexandra L. Quittner
Ann M. DiGirolamo

DESCRIPTION OF THE PROBLEM

Significant medical and social advances over the past forty years have dramatically changed the incidence of childhood illness and disability. Several major infectious diseases of childhood have been eradicated through immunization programs, and dramatic medical breakthroughs, such as new drug treatments and gene mapping, now offer hope to children with diseases such as cancer and cystic fibrosis (Silverberg & Lubera, 1987; Welsh et al., 1994). These medical achievements have led to positive effects: disorders that were previously fatal (e.g., leukemia, congenital heart disease) are now survivable, dramatic increases in life span have occurred for certain terminal conditions, and defective genes, such as those for cystic fibrosis, have been identified, to be "corrected" in the future by gene therapy (Crystal, 1992). Some negative effects, however, must also be noted. Because of reduced resources, families are being asked to take on greater responsibility for complex caretaking and medical regimes.

Estimates of the prevalence of children with chronic illnesses and disabilities range from 10 to 14 percent in the general U.S. population, which translates into approximately 7.5 million children and adolescents (Hobbs, Perrin, & Ireys, 1985; Perrin & MacLean, 1988). Of these children, about 75 to 80 percent have relatively mild or moderate conditions while the other 20 to 25 percent are considered to be more functionally impaired (Newacheck, Budetti, & Halfon, 1986). The most common serious chronic conditions are asthma, seizure disorders, diabetes, cerebral palsy, and arthritis (Gortmaker & Sappenfield, 1984). Thus, approximately one million children and adolescents in the U.S. have a severe chronic illness or disability that necessitates ongoing, comprehensive medical care. Indeed, "chronic disorder is becoming an ordinary feature of family life and development; it is no longer an exotic catastrophe" (Cole & Reiss, 1993, p. viii).

The shift away from the treatment of acute illnesses toward more chronic conditions has led to significant changes in the practice of pediatrics, including greater pressures toward specialization, the emergence of developmental pediatricians who specialize in caring for

Preparation of this chapter was supported in part by a FIRST Award (R29-HL47064) and a Research Career Development Award (K04-HL02892) from NIH to the first author. We thank Robert L. Glueckauf and the editors for their helpful comments on an earlier version of this manuscript.

children with disabilities, and the establishment of multidisciplinary teams to address the complex array of children's medical and psychosocial needs (Garrison & McQuiston, 1989; Karoly, 1988). This approach has been termed the "biopsychosocial model" because it encompasses the interactions of biological, social, and psychological factors in assessing and treating chronic illness (Engel, 1977, 1982; Russo & Varni, 1982). The widespread adoption of this model has been reflected in a growing literature on the psychosocial adaptation of children with chronic illnesses and their families.

Chronic conditions differ in several ways from acute illnesses, and these differences have implications for the family's adjustment to the disease (Johnson, 1988). First, the child's medical condition may be "treatable" but not curable, and therefore, both the child and family must manage the demands of the illness over the course of the life span. This places greater responsibility for management of the illness on the parents and child, rather than the physician. Second, treatment of the disease often entails adherence to complex, time-consuming, and often uncomfortable medical regimens (e.g., insulin injections). Because a majority of chronic illnesses are diagnosed fairly early in life (e.g., diabetes, cystic fibrosis), parents typically assume primary responsibility for carrying out these medical routines, in addition to monitoring the child's symptoms and attending regular clinic visits. This places a tremendous burden on parents' time and energy (Drotar, 1992; Quittner, DiGirolamo, Michel, & Eigen, 1992). Finally, caring for a child with a chronic illness is likely to produce alterations in roles and routines that affect *all* members of the family system. Parents may have less time as a couple to engage in social and recreational activities (Quittner, Opipari, Regoli, Jacobsen, & Eigen, 1992), and nondisabled siblings may develop a perception that the child with the disability receives more time and attention from parents (McKeever, 1981; Opipari & Quittner, 1995).

Because of the family's intense involvement, there have been increasing calls for a "family-centered" approach to understanding and treating chronic childhood illness and disability (Drotar, 1992; Wertlieb, 1993). Although this is an important goal, its realization has been impeded by a lack of theory-driven research, limited assessment tools, and research designs that are inadequate for capturing the complexities of family process (Harper, 1991; Quittner, 1992). This chapter will be organized around the critical problems in the field and will offer suggestions for addressing them. Four major areas will be reviewed: (1) conceptual models of family adaptation, (2) estimates of psychosocial risk for children with chronic illnesses, their siblings and parents,

(3) approaches to assessing child and family functioning, and (4) interventions aimed at family-level issues. Key problems that cut across these areas will be discussed, including a lack of attention to measurement issues, the absence of research on fathers of children with disabilities, and inadequate links between research findings and the development of clinical interventions.

It appears that we are at a crossroads—there is both a need to understand how the process of adaptation unfolds and assist families in coping with these challenges, yet the quality of available research on psychosocial issues is largely inadequate for this task. The purpose of the current chapter is threefold: (1) review what is currently known about family adaptation to childhood illness in terms of its conceptualization, assessment, and treatment, (2) pinpoint methodological limitations of prior studies, and (3) highlight advances and innovations that show promise for moving the field forward.

GENERAL MODELS OF FAMILY ADAPTATION

Research on how families adapt to childhood illness has increased dramatically over the past twenty years. Although a complete review of this literature is beyond the scope of this chapter, the central questions addressed by these studies include: How does chronic illness or disability affect the child's psychosocial adjustment? How does the child's illness affect family functioning? How does the family's response to the illness affect the child's ability to cope with day-to-day management of the disease?

Clearly, these questions are inextricably linked and can only be answered by conceptualizing the process of adaptation as one that involves the whole family (Fiese & Sameroff, 1989). Since the early 1980s, several models of family adaptation have been developed to capture this more systemic view. These models have generally drawn upon three major theoretical frameworks: (1) stress and coping theory (Lazarus & Folkman, 1984; Hill, 1958), (2) social-ecological theory (Bronfenbrenner, 1979), and (3) family systems theory (Minuchin, 1974; Olson, Sprenkle, & Russell, 1979). Some models, such as the "Transactional Stress and Coping model" (Thompson, Gustafson, Hamlett, & Spock, 1992), attempt to integrate aspects of several theories. Of these perspectives, stress theory as originally described by Hill (1949) and then further developed by Lazarus and colleagues (1985), has had the greatest impact on models of adaptation to childhood illness and disability. Several current frameworks, such as the Double ABCX model (McCubbin &

Patterson, 1982; Patterson, 1988), the Varni-Wallander Risk and Resistance model (Varni & Wallander, 1988), and Thompson's Transactional model, draw heavily upon stress and coping theory.

Although these models vary somewhat in their emphases, they assume that chronic illness is a major stressor for the family, which can lead to poor mental and physical health outcomes depending on mediating factors, such as the family's attribution of meaning for the event (Patterson, 1988; Reiss, 1981) and the availability of internal and external resources (Thompson et al., 1992). Three major factors appear consistently across these models: one or more measures of stress (e.g., illness severity, life stress, daily hassles), potential mediators of stress (e.g., appraisal processes, social support, family functioning), and outcomes (e.g., psychosocial adjustment, physical health).

Three models will briefly be described. In the Double ABCX model, the child's illness is considered a crisis event that places extra stress and demands on the family. The family's ability to meet these demands and return to a state of balanced functioning is dependent upon the meaning they ascribe to the event and the family resources that are available (e.g., cohesion, effective coping strategies) (Patterson, 1988). Similarly, the Varni-Wallander Risk and Resistance model (Varni & Wallander, 1988) posits that risk factors (e.g., disease severity, life stress, hassles) will increase the probability of adjustment problems (e.g., physical and mental distress) in the family. However, these negative effects may be mediated by resistance factors, such as intrapersonal resources (e.g., temperament), cognitive appraisals and coping behaviors, and social-ecological influences (e.g., cohesion, social support). Finally, Thompson's Transactional model incorporates many of the same variables as the other two, but postulates that different variables in the model may be more or less relevant depending upon the childhood illness being examined (i.e., categorical approach). In contrast, the Varni-Wallander model has typically been tested with children who have a variety of chronic illnesses and disabilities (i.e., noncategorical approach). Table 4.1 presents a general description of the constructs employed in each of these models.

A major impetus for the proliferation of these models is the general finding that although chronic childhood illness places children and families at risk for psychological disorder, its effects are variable, and a majority of families make a successful adaptation (Drotar, 1992). Thus, the most important questions are when, and under what conditions are families most vulnerable to stress? And, if treatment is needed, which interventions are most effective? To the extent that these models aid us in answering these questions, they serve an important purpose. Given

Table 4.1. Family Models: Independent, Mediating, and Outcome Variables

INDEPENDENT VARIABLES	MEDIATING VARIABLES	OUTCOME VARIABLES
Double ABCX Model[a]		
Severity of handicap	Family resources (FES)[b]	Physical and mental health
Life events	Coping strategies	Child's health status
Pile-up of demands and stressors	Meaning of demands	Adherence to medical regimens
Varni-Wallander Model[c]		
Disease severity and functional impairment	Family resources (FES)	Physical and mental health
Life events	Coping strategies	Social functioning
Hassles	Social support	
Disability-specific problems	Mastery and control	
Transactional Stress and Coping Model[d]		
Type of illness and severity	Family functioning (FES)	Mental health
Daily hassles	Coping strategies	
Illness-specific stressors		
Demographic parameters (SES)		

[a]Double ABCX model (McCubbin & Patterson, 1982); extended by Patterson (1988) into the Family Adjustment and Adaptation Response (FAAR).
[b]Family Environment Scale (Moos & Moos, 1981).
[c]Varni and Wallander (1988); Wallander, Varni, et al. (1989).
[d]Thompson, Gustafson, Hamlett, and Spock (1992).

the plethora of studies that have now been conducted using one or more of these models (see Eiser, 1990; Patterson, 1988 for reviews), we are now in a position to examine the data, accumulated *across* these models, to assess the extent to which they have met these goals.

Stress

In most models, the construct of "stress" is considered a key predictor of family adaptation. Despite its prominence across all models, however, it has been given the least empirical attention. Early studies used the presence or absence of a child's illness or disability as a "proxy" measure of stress, without identifying or measuring a particular source of stress (Fife, Norton, & Groom, 1987; Varni, Wicox, & Hanson, 1988). Differences in adaptation were then compared for families who did or did not have a child with a disability, often with equivocal results (Speechley & Noh, 1992). Contemporary studies have generally examined two sources of stress: illness severity as measured by parental perception or medical indicators (e.g., pulmonary functions), and more direct measures of the stressors themselves (e.g., life events, hassles, illness tasks).

In terms of illness severity, the results have been inconsistent, with some studies finding significant relationships between illness severity and maternal adaptation, whereas others have not (Drotar & Bush, 1985). For example, a large cross-sectional study of mothers of children with diverse medical conditions (e.g., asthma, congenital anomalies) found no relationship between an index of caregiving burden completed by health care professionals and maternal psychiatric symptomatology (Jessop, Riessman, & Stein, 1988). However, maternal reports of the child's functional status were significantly correlated with symptomatology, with mothers who perceived their child as less able to perform age-appropriate roles and tasks (e.g., communication, mobility) endorsing more symptoms of depression and anxiety. Similarly, a longitudinal study of 29 early-intervention programs for infants and toddlers with developmental disabilities (e.g, Down syndrome, seizure disorders) indicated that severity of the child's psychomotor impairment and presence of a seizure disorder were the two most powerful predictors of negative effects on family functioning (e.g., parenting stress, family/social strain) over a one-year period (Shonkoff, Hauser-Cram, Krauss, & Upshur, 1992).

In contrast, other studies testing models of family adaptation have failed to find a relationship between illness severity and family functioning. Tests of the Varni-Wallander model, for example, have not found

associations between disease parameters, such as severity of handicap or child's level of functional independence, and mothers' mental and physical adaptation (Wallander et al., 1989; Wallander, Pitt, & Mellins, 1990). These studies have employed fairly large samples of mothers caring for children 2 through 18 years of age, with a variety of chronic illnesses and disabilities (e.g., spina bifida, cerebral palsy). Similarly, illness severity as measured by objective medical criteria was not related to symptoms of psychological distress in mothers of children with cystic fibrosis (CF) or sickle cell disease (Thompson, Gil, Burbach, Keith, & Kinney, 1993; Thompson et al., 1992; Walker, Ford, & Donald, 1987).

The link between severity of a child's disease or disability and measures of family adaptation is neither clear nor direct. Several factors may explain these discrepant results. First, measures of illness severity are not directly tied to the specific tasks and demands to which families must respond (e.g., treatment regimens), and thus, do not adequately reflect the extent of daily stress experienced by families (Drotar, 1992; Quittner, DiGirolamo, et al., 1992). Second, parental *perceptions* of illness severity versus objective, medical indicators show different relationships to psychological distress. As Drotar and Bush (1985) noted, "disease severity based on objective physical criteria may not be as important as personal perceptions of illness in mediating adjustment" (p. 518). The notion that perceptions are more strongly related to psychological distress is a central tenet of stress and coping theory, and has been demonstrated repeatedly in studies that show that it is not the number of negative life events that are predictive of emotional and physical health outcomes, but the individual's *appraisal* or perception of the event (Lazarus & Folkman, 1984).

Although this analysis might persuade researchers to focus on perceptions of illness severity rather than functional or medical indicators, the potential for circularity and confounding of variables poses additional problems. For example, if the mother reports on *both* the child's illness severity and her own symptoms of depression (which is the typical design) there is a greater likelihood that these two variables overlap and are dependent, producing higher correlations by virtue of their shared variance. This is a complex problem that underlies most models of stress and coping (see Lazarus, DeLongis, Folkman, & Gruen, 1985 and Thoits, 1983 for a complete discussion), and may require researchers to decrease their reliance on self-report data, particularly from a single source (i.e., mother) in order to empirically substantiate these models.

More direct measures of stress (e.g., negative life events, daily hassles) have also been incorporated into models of family adaptation to childhood disability and illness (Patterson, 1988). These "psychosocial" stressors have been conceptualized as major or minor life events that compound the stress directly attributable to the child's medical condition or disability. In the Double ABCX model, for example, the extent to which these stressors "pile-up" and present the family with additional demands should be reflected in increased distress (e.g., depression). Some support for this relationship has been found. In an application of this model to parental adjustment to autism, the "pile-up" stress score was related to both observational measures of the quality of parenting and maternal reports of depression (Bristol, 1987). However, it should be noted that this stress score was a summation of *both* a life events measure and a measure of the limitations imposed on the family as a result of the child's disability. Thus, it represented the combined impact of psychosocial and disability-specific stress, rather than an examination of the impact of life stress alone. In a more recent study of parental adaptation to childhood deafness, three different types of stressors (i.e., stressful life events, general parenting stress, and disability-specific stress) were directly compared (Quittner, Glueckauf, & Jackson, 1990). The results were clear: life stress was *not* significantly related to maternal distress; however, general parenting stress was moderately correlated with distress, and illness-specific stressors were the most strongly and consistently associated with these symptoms.

More recent models of family adaptation have attempted to go beyond a count of discrete negative events to include more minor, daily irritations—or hassles (Kanner, Coyne, Schaefer, & Lazarus, 1981). In a study of maternal adaptation to chronic childhood illness (i.e., CF), perceptions of stress regarding daily hassles and illness tasks differentiated mothers who exhibited good versus poor adjustment on a psychological distress measure (Thompson et al., 1992). An association between daily hassles and adaptation was also found in a study of mothers of handicapped children with a variety of disabilities (i.e., spina bifida, cerebral palsy, hearing problems). In this study, post hoc analyses indicated that life stress did not contribute to maternal mental health scores, but hassles and handicap-related problems did (Wallander et al., 1990).

Although measuring daily hassles rather than life events may bring us closer to the day-to-day context, these minor "irritations" (e.g., car honking) are still somewhat removed from the chronic strains and demands faced daily by families caring for a child with a serious illness or disability. These two types of stress—daily hassles and chronic strains—are likely to differ in several ways. First, the effects of severe, chronic stressors (e.g., adhering to treatment regimens for a child with CF) are likely to be more *pervasive*, leading to alterations in several life domains, including marital and work roles, interactions among siblings (Dyson, 1989; Quittner & Opipari, 1994), and relationships with members of the larger social network, such as relatives and friends (Kazak, 1987; Pearlin & Turner, 1987; Quittner et al., 1990). Second, chronic stressors in this context also imply continuation into the future, changing expectations for the accomplishment of normal milestones (e.g., independence as a young adult), and requiring new shifts and adaptations in response to the needs of the child throughout the developmental life cycle (Rolland, 1984). Thus, in terms of its scope and enduring impact, chronic strain related to childhood illness may be distinguished from both major life events and daily hassles.

A promising alternative to the life stress/hassles approach is to study stressors embedded within a specific context. Several investigators have argued that studies of family adaptation should focus on the specific tasks and demands that must be mastered for successful functioning (Drotar, 1992; Meyerowitz, Heinrich, & Schag, 1983; Moos & Tsu, 1977; Quittner, 1992). For childhood illness, specifically, Melamed, Siegel, and Ridley-Johnson (1988) have advocated the assessment of one set of illness-related tasks (e.g., treatment regimens), and a second set of tasks that are relevant for normal development (e.g., peer relations, school attendance). This approach has several advantages in that it: (1) focuses on the *processes* by which families learn to manage the demands of the illness or disability (e.g., how do families develop strategies for increasing adherence to medical routines?); (2) takes into account the developmental and life span goals of the family; (3) provides a natural context for studying *interactions* among family members, thus linking adaptation of the individual to the larger family system (e.g., how do parents teach children about their disability and effective strategies for managing it?); and (4) links studies of family adaptation to the development of interventions that address these problems (Quittner, 1992).

Quittner and colleagues recently applied this task-demands approach in two studies of maternal adaptation to childhood disability (Quittner, 1989, 1992; Quittner et al., 1990). In both studies, several contextual factors were controlled, including time since diagnosis, the developmental stage of the child, and the specific demands of the medical condition. Three groups of mothers were included: 96 mothers of children with severe to profound hearing losses, 106 mothers of children with seizure disorders, and 118 mothers of children without a disability. To facilitate a developmental approach to studying parenting-related stressors, all children were preschool age (i.e., 2 to 5 years of age). In addition, to differentiate this chronic phase of adaptation from the crisis phase of diagnosis, all children had been diagnosed for a minimum of one year (Rolland, 1987).

Two types of parenting stress were assessed in a structured interview in the home: (1) generic parenting tasks relevant for preschool-age children (e.g., bedtime routines, discipline), and (2) parenting tasks specific to each medical condition. For mothers of hearing-impaired children, the problems and tasks included those related to communication (e.g., choice of oral or manual methods), language training, and the reactions of family, friends, and community members. For mothers of children with seizure disorders, stressors were sampled in the areas of medications, obtaining medical care, and education. As can be seen in Table 4.2, the rankings of stress for these various tasks differed substantially across the three groups and supported the need for greater specificity in identifying sources of stress for parents of chronically ill children. Other than general behavior problems, which were ranked highly by all groups, mothers ranked disability-specific problems as most stressful. In addition, we hypothesized that stressors measured *contextually* would be more strongly correlated with maternal distress than more general stress as measured on the Parenting Stress Index (Abidin, 1983). This hypothesis was supported. An average correlation of .40 was found between task-related parenting stress and maternal symptoms across the three groups (correlations with maternal depression were .55 and above), whereas the correlation between general parenting stress and symptoms was only .29.

In sum, there is currently little evidence that stressful life events are strong predictors of family adaptation to childhood illness and disability. This does not suggest that these families do not experience major life stress, but rather that this type of stress is less likely to account for the psychological and physical health risks that have been observed. Instead, stressors that are frequent and chronic in nature appear to be associated with family outcomes. In fact, stressors that are specific to the context of the child's illness or disability, reflecting the tasks and demands that families must cope with on a daily basis, appear to be most strongly related to indices of psychological and physical symptomatology. Fortunately, the identification and explication of these stressors will not only strengthen models of family adaptation, but will provide much needed information about specific targets for intervention (Drotar, 1992).

Mediators of Stress: Family Environment and Social Support

A majority of models of adaptation have included family environment and social-ecological variables as resources that mediate the stress of raising a child with a chronic illness or disability (Kazak, 1989; Moos & Tsu, 1977; Patterson, 1988). A variable is considered a *mediator* if it serves to reduce the direct effect of the stressor on the outcome variable, thereby explaining a significant amount of the variance in this relationship (see Baron & Kenny, 1986; Quittner et al., 1990). Family

Table 4.2. Rankings of Parenting Stressors

RANK	DEAF GROUP	SEIZURE-DISORDER GROUP	COMPARISON GROUP
1	Behavior problems during language training	Safety	Behavior problems at home
2	Behavior problems at home	Behavior problems away from home	Sibling rivalry
3	Communication	Medications	Toilet training
4	Dual role as mother and teacher	Behavior problems at home	Mealtimes
5	Finding a school program	Mealtimes	Behavior problems away from home
6	Crossing the street	Controlling seizures	Bedtimes

Note. Published with permission from "Re-examining research on stress and social support" (pp. 103), by A. L. Quittner, 1992. In A. M. La Greca, J. Wallander, L. Siegel, & C. Walker (Eds.), *Advances in pediatric psychology: Stress and coping with pediatric conditions.* New York: Guilford Press.

resources, such as greater cohesion and adaptability, have been widely tested as mediators of both disease management (e.g., adherence to treatment) and physical and psychological health outcomes for parents (Anderson, Miller, Auslander, & Santiago, 1981; Hauser et al., 1990; Kazak & Meadows, 1989). We will briefly review findings on the role of two of these potential mediating variables: family resources and social support. In order to maintain our focus on the family, this review will be limited to studies examining outcomes for parents rather than target children.

Family Resources

Family resources have been defined as the characteristic ways in which families interact within and outside the family system (Reiss, 1981). A large number of variables have been tested under the rubric of "family environment," including dimensions of family functioning (e.g., cohesion, expressiveness, conflict), family "resources" (e.g., social support, recreational orientation), and organizational features of the family (e.g., reliance on rules and religious values) (Kronenberger & Thompson, 1990; Moos & Moos, 1981). Across several models of family adaptation, the Family Environment Scale (FES; Moos & Moos, 1981) has been one of the most widely used measures of family functioning. In general, higher levels of cohesion and expressiveness and lower levels of conflict on this measure have been *concurrently* associated with fewer symptoms of anxiety and depression in mothers of children with a variety of medical conditions and disabilities (Kronenberger & Thompson, 1992; Timko, Stovel, & Moos, 1992; Wallander et al., 1989). Recent *longitudinal* studies of maternal adaptation to CF and sickle cell disease confirmed a relationship between increased family conflict and poorer adjustment in the CF but not the sickle cell group (Thompson et al., 1994). Although few researchers have included fathers in their investigations, one study of adaptation to juvenile rheumatic disease found that family resources were more predictive of mothers' than fathers' adaptation (Timko et al., 1992).

The other commonly used measure of family functioning is the Family Adaptability and Cohesion Evaluation Scale III (FACES; Olson, Portner, & Lavee, 1985). This measure was derived from the Circumplex Model of Family Relations (Olson, Sprenkle, & Russell, 1979), which identifies optimal levels of cohesion and adaptability as those that are closer to the center (e.g., neither enmeshed nor disengaged). Results with this measure have also generally supported the mediating role of family variables in models of adaptation. A re-

cent study of parents of adolescent cancer survivors (Kazak & Meadows, 1989) indicated that lack of adaptability, in particular, was related to parental distress. A major problem with the use of either of these family resource measures is the potential circularity inherent in parents completing assessment of both family functioning and psychological distress.

Stronger evidence for the role of family variables comes from studies that assess relationships between family functioning and specific physical health outcomes, such as adherence to treatment. In these studies, although the family variables are measured at a global level, the stressful context (e.g., adherence to specific treatment regimens) is well-defined and the outcome variable is typically an objective physical indicator of functioning (e.g., metabolic control for diabetes). Consistent findings indicate that dimensions of family functioning on both the FES and FACES are associated with adherence to treatment regimens for diabetes and CF (Chaney & Peterson, 1989; Hanson, Henggeler, Harris, Burghen, & Moore, 1989; Hauser et al., 1990; Patterson, 1988).

Social Support

In contrast to the strong role the family environment appears to play in models of family adaptation, the beneficial effects of social support are far less clear. What is social support, and how does it function in families who have a child with a chronic illness or disability? There is general agreement that the construct of "social support" includes several components, such as the provision of instrumental aid (e.g., money), information and advice, and emotional support (e.g., love, affirmation) (House, 1981; Sarason, Pierce, & Sarason, 1994). In addition, broad distinctions have been drawn between the structural properties of the social network (e.g., size, density) and the functions the network may provide (e.g., tangible aid, information). Although a large social network may increase the availability of resources and supportive contacts, it may also bring with it added demands and conflicts. In general, it has now been well-established that it is the individual's *perception* of the availability of support, rather than frequency of contact or size of the social network, that is most strongly linked to positive psychological and physical health outcomes (Cohen & Wills, 1985).

Among families of children with chronic illnesses and disabilities, anecdotal reports over the past 20 years have cited concerns that these families are socially isolated (Fewell & Gelb, 1983). Does social support differ in families raising a disabled versus a nondisabled child? To date, conflicting results have been obtained. In one study, mothers of children with spina bifida had smaller social networks, compared to control families, particularly with respect to number of friends. No differences in network characteristics, however, were found in a PKU or retardation group (Kazak & Marvin, 1984; Kazak, Reber, & Carter, 1988). Smaller networks were also found among mothers of hearing-impaired children, who reported significantly fewer family members, relatives, and friends in their networks than mothers of matched hearing children (Quittner et al., 1990).

The results of these studies suggest that smaller networks may be found in some samples of families of handicapped children, but not others. One reason for this may be the visibility of the child's handicap. Both spina bifida and profound deafness are publicly observable (e.g., use of a wheelchair, communication problems), and network members may be reluctant to offer help, or may feel anxious in unfamiliar and stigmatizing situations (Chesler & Barbarin, 1984; Wortman & Lehman, 1985). Note that studies combining medically diverse samples of children (i.e., noncategorical approach) may not detect important differences in social support provision as a function of these variations, and as a result, may draw premature or inaccurate conclusions.

In our study of mothers of hearing-impaired children (Quittner et al., 1990), although their networks were substantially smaller than comparison mothers, no differences were found between the groups in perceptions of support. Analyses of the *providers* of support revealed dramatic differences: mothers of deaf children relied on health care professionals (e.g., home visiting teachers) for both tangible and emotional support, whereas mothers in the nondisabled comparison group had these needs met by family and friends. Thus, it is possible that mothers of deaf children withdrew from relationships with family members and friends that were stressful or unhelpful, but developed new ties with professionals who provided assistance that was relevant to their child's disability. This led to networks that were smaller in *size*, but not in perceived quality of support. These results highlight the importance of measuring a variety of potential sources of support, as well as assessing the *match* between family needs and support providers (Coyne, Ellard, & Smith, 1990; Cutrona & Russell, 1990).

In multivariate models of family adaptation, social support is typically tested as a mediator of stress. These studies are usually correlational in design and predict inverse relationships between ratings of stress and perceived social support. Thus, higher stress levels are associated with decreased perceptions of support which, in turn, are correlated with greater symptoms of psychological distress. This pattern has been substantiated in several studies, including a recent study of mothers of

children with spina bifida (Barakat & Linney, 1992) and parents of children who survived cancer (Speechley & Noh, 1992). We found similar results with mothers of hearing-impaired children, for whom higher levels of both general and disability-specific parenting stress were associated with decreased perceptions that network members could be counted on as confidants and providers of tangible support (Quittner et al., 1990).

Interestingly, we found no evidence that social support "buffered" or protected these mothers from the negative impact of stress. These findings point to the possibility that social support functions differently in chronic as opposed to acute stress situations (e.g., change in jobs), where buffering effects have been more commonly found (Cohen & Wills, 1985). These contexts differ in several ways. First, traumatic or stigmatizing events, such as serious illness or disability, may lead network members to avoid contact or respond in ways that are unhelpful (Barrera, 1988; Wortman & Lehman, 1985). As parents perceive that the response of network members is one of avoidance, their symptoms of anxiety and depression may increase. Alternatively, parents experiencing chronic stress may have engaged in frequent help-seeking behaviors, and thus, have exhausted their resources. Finally, although an increase in support may be helpful for short-term stress (e.g., moving to a new city), a sudden infusion of support in the context of chronic illness may be viewed as intrusive or suggestive of incompetence (Hobfall & Lerman, 1988). Thus, specific features of the stressful context may be critical in determining both how much support is provided and whether such support has buffering effects.

Stronger tests of the effects of social support come from studies of support *interventions*. In Shonkoff's comprehensive study of 29 early-intervention programs for families of disabled infants and toddlers, only modest increases in the size or perceived helpfulness of the social network were found over a one-year period (Shonkoff et al., 1992). Further, these changes in social support were *not* associated with improvements in family functioning, such as decreased parental stress or greater cohesion. In addition, parents ranked participation in a support group as less helpful than most other aspects of the early-intervention program, and mothers who spent the most time participating in a support group also reported the greatest increases in personal and family strain. Whether increased strain resulted from more frequent participation, or whether mothers who were experiencing the greatest strain sought out this experience more often, is unclear.

Similar disappointing effects were reported for a support program to aid mothers of high-risk neonates in the transition from hospital to home (Affleck, Tennen, Rowe, Roscher, & Walker, 1989). At the 6-month follow-up, positive effects of the program were found only for mothers who stated they needed the most support prior to discharge. For mothers who reported the lowest need for support, however, the intervention actually had *negative* effects on maternal sense of competence, perceived control, and responsiveness. As these studies make clear, simply providing more social support to families at risk, while clinically appealing, may be naive and ineffective. We need to know more about *how*, *under what conditions*, and *for whom* social support is likely to be beneficial. The answers are likely to be complex—reflecting a dynamic interplay of individual, contextual, and interactional factors. Unfortunately, cross-sectional studies of family adaptation that rely on global self-report measures are not likely to provide this type of information.

Methodological Limitations and Advances in Family Models of Adaptation

Although considerable progress has been made in developing conceptual frameworks for assessing family adaptation, for the most part, these models are rarely testable in their entirety and do little to reveal the mechanisms or processes that lead to positive or negative outcomes. The constructs included in these models, such as cohesion and social support, are difficult to operationalize, may have a different meaning or significance for families caring for a child with a serious illness, and do not appear to be sensitive to change (Finney & Bonner, 1992; Thompson et al., 1994). For these reasons, they remain primarily heuristic, and do not provide direct links to clinical interventions. Two other limitations are worthy of discussion: the exclusion of fathers from studies of family adaptation and the use of inappropriate units of analysis.

The Absence of Data on Fathers

Although the models reviewed above focused on processes of *family adaptation*, the vast majority of these studies were conducted with mothers (Hauenstein, 1990); only a handful of studies have included fathers (Barbarin, Hughes, & Chesler, 1985; Quittner, DiGirolamo et al., 1992; Shonkoff et al., 1992; Timko et al., 1992). The exclusive reliance on mothers is often justified by results showing that mothers are the primary caregivers for children with chronic illnesses—typically managing

treatment regimens, visits to clinic, and communications with health care professionals (Bristol, Gallagher, & Schopler, 1988; McKeever, 1981; Quittner, Opipari et al., 1992). However, if a fundamental assumption of this research is that families are *systems* in which each member's perceptions, coping strategies, and psychological well-being affect all other members of the system, then it is essential to include key members of the family, such as fathers (Roberts & Wallander, 1992).

Another compelling reason for including fathers is the likelihood that their role within the family differs from mothers, which in turn may affect their perceptions of stress, use of social support, and levels of psychological and physical distress. The results of studies that have included fathers confirm this conclusion. A majority of these studies find that fathers report greater stress in the areas of finances and emotional attachment to the child, and mothers experience greater stress in relation to daily routines and caregiving (Quittner, DiGirolamo et al., 1992; Shonkoff et al., 1992). More symptoms of depression have also been consistently reported by mothers as compared to fathers (Quittner, DiGirolamo et al., 1992; Timko et al., 1992).

Differences between mothers and fathers have also been found in tests of multivariate models of adaptation. In families caring for a child with juvenile rheumatic disease, Timko and colleagues (1992) found that dimensions of family functioning, such as cohesion and reduced conflict, were important longitudinal determinants of maternal but not paternal depression. Most striking were findings showing that the strongest predictor of both mothers' and fathers' emotional and social functioning one year later was the *spouse's* level of dysfunction (e.g., depression). These results are provocative and point to the importance of considering the reciprocal influence of both parents in the system (Fiese & Sameroff, 1989).

In our study of parents of children recently diagnosed with CF, we also found that different variables were related to depression (Quittner, DiGirolamo et al., 1992). As can be seen in Figure 4.1, after controlling for the impact of CF-specific stressors, both marital satisfaction and parental role strain explained significant proportions of the variance in depression for mothers, but not fathers. For fathers, only CF-specific parenting stress (e.g., doing percussion) was significantly associated with depression; marital satisfaction and role strain were not.

Important differences in social roles were revealed in this study, and may have accounted for the differential pattern of adaptation. First, mothers indicated their spouses rarely assisted with medical routines, were often

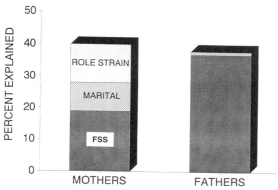

Figure 4.1. Percentage of variance in depression scores accounted for by CF-specific stressors (Family Stress Scale), marital satisfaction, and role strain. Based on hierarchical multiple regression analysis

gone in the evenings, and were not particularly helpful in managing the child's illness. This unequal division of caretaking responsibilities may explain the strong relationship we found between role strain and maternal depression, but the absence of this association for fathers. This study's unique focus on adaptation soon after diagnosis shed light on potentially maladaptive family patterns that emerge within that first year. Early on, mothers and fathers divide caretaking tasks, particularly time spent doing treatment, in such a way that mothers take primary responsibility for the child with the illness. Fathers are viewed as less helpful by mothers, and they themselves readily admit they are less available to assist with child care routines and daily medical regimens. This imbalance of responsibilities appears to be associated with greater strain for mothers and significant symptoms of depression (i.e., 64 percent of mothers scored above a clinical cut-off for depressive symptoms). If these results are replicated in the longitudinal phase of our study, they will have important implications for involving fathers more actively at the point of diagnosis (e.g., teaching fathers to do chest physiotherapy, encouraging both parents to attend clinic appointments).

Another major role difference was noted: all fathers in this study were employed, whereas a minority of mothers worked outside the home (i.e., 31 percent). This emphasis on the parenting role for mothers may have limited their opportunities for intellectual stimulation, social and recreational contacts, and relief from caretaking responsibilities. Consistent with this hypothesis, mothers in this study who worked outside the home reported significantly *lower* levels of role strain and depression than mothers who were unemployed. This fits

with prior results showing that mothers who occupy multiple roles report greater emotional and physical well-being than those with fewer roles (Baruch, Biener, & Barnett, 1987; Walker, Ortiz-Valdez, & Newbrough, 1989). Although rarely incorporated into models of family adaptation, the assessment of role performance and role strain offers a fruitful avenue for examining the impact of chronic illness on all members of the family system (Quittner, 1992; Quittner, DiGirolamo et al., 1992).

Units of Measurement and Analysis

A central problem with a majority of studies of family adaptation is the use of an *individual's* report of a *family-level* construct. In a recent review of health-related studies in family journals, Patterson (1990) found that 80 percent of the studies from 1980 to 1989 relied on a single family member's account of the family group; in most cases, this was some type of self-report questionnaire. This blurring of the distinction between individual and family levels of assessment is problematic because of potential differences in how individuals within the family view the situation (Klein, 1983; Walker, 1985). For example, the same stressful context is likely to affect family members in different ways, and eliciting a "family-level" perception of stress or cohesion by asking one member of the family may not be valid. As Patterson (1990), who has studied family coping for several years notes, "asking the individual how the family copes appears really to measure how the individual copes" (p. 416).

What are the alternatives? One possibility is to calculate a *relational score*, by combining the individual self-reports of several family members (Patterson, 1990). A "family-level" score of cohesion could be created, for example, by adding or multiplying together various family members' reports on this dimension of family functioning. One might question, however, whether a sum of reports from individual family members is the same as an assessment of the family unit (Lewis, Beavers, Gossett, & Phillips, 1976; Reiss, 1981).

A better option may be to directly observe interactions among members of the family unit. The programmatic research of Hauser and colleagues serves as an excellent example of this with families of adolescents with diabetes (Hauser, 1990; Hauser et al., 1990; Hauser et al., 1993). In these studies, families are engaged in a semi-structured interview (Family Life Events Interview adapted from Reiss and Oliveri, 1980) about how a recent major event (e.g, diagnosis of their adolescent's diabetes) has interrupted or changed their activities and interactions as a family. The interviewer specifically probes for four aspects of the family's response: (a) framing of the problem and search for information, (b) approach and handling of the problem, (c) emotional reactions to the event, and (d) their response or resolution of the event (Hauser, 1990). The family interview is audiotaped, transcribed, and then coded by independent raters for the occurrence of various appraisal and coping processes.

Preliminary analyses have revealed significant differences in the family coping patterns of diabetic youngsters versus those with an acute illness. Soon after diagnosis, families of adolescents with diabetes held a shared view of the causes and consequences of the illness, and appeared to take an "upbeat," team-oriented view of the illness when compared to the acute illness families. However, in contrast to this positive tone, they appeared to engage in more avoidance of the illness than the comparison group, reported greater frustration and futility in handling the demands they were facing, and were less likely to seek information (Hauser et al., 1993). Importantly, these researchers do not characterize specific coping strategies a priori as "functional" or "dysfunctional" as is commonly done in coping studies. Instead, their aim is to first identify important patterns of family coping and then conduct systematic, longitudinal studies examining relationships between these patterns and relevant family outcomes. Their transcriptions are also analyzed on a more "molecular" level to determine how family members "constrain" or "enable" one another in their verbal exchanges (Hauser et al., 1990). Although clearly more time-consuming and intensive, this type of research has several advantages in that it: (a) identifies issues and concerns of the family as a unit; (b) assesses interactions and responses of the family directly, rather than through self-report questionnaires; (c) is process-oriented, allowing for identification of bidirectional influences from one family member to another, in "real time" as interactions unfold and in "developmental time" as measured longitudinally; and (d) measures dimensions of family functioning that can be targeted for intervention (e.g., "family coordination"—everyone pitched in and helped with various aspects of treatment).

Summary

In sum, although some progress has been made in identifying key variables associated with adaptation to childhood illness, the family models described above have emphasized *general* concepts such as "stress," "cohesion," and "adaptability," as measured by self-report. Although potentially important, these constructs represent global impressions of the caregiving environment rather than the more proximal, day-to-day influences and transactions that characterize family life (Shonkoff et al., 1992). In general, most families appear to be adapting fairly well on these broad-based measures. However, there is growing evidence that in daily interactions and management of medical routines, these families have significant difficulties (Quittner, DiGirolamo et al., 1992; Shonkoff et al., 1992). It is time to refocus our attention on these more mundane aspects of family life, and on the complexities of family processes as they unfold, in order to develop a more meaningful and clinically relevant understanding of family adaptation to childhood illness.

INCIDENCE AND PREVALENCE

Models of family adaptation to childhood illness become relevant once a significant level of risk for maladjustment has been established. Numerous studies over the past 20 years have assessed the prevalence of psychological and psychiatric disorders in children with chronic physical disorders, and although there have been conflicting results (Tavormina, Kastner, Slater, & Watt, 1976), the weight of the evidence indicates these children are at substantially greater risk than their nondisabled peers (Cadman, Boyle, Szatmari, & Offord, 1987). Fewer studies have examined the level of behavioral and emotional risk for parents and healthy siblings, and the results are not as clear. Across all of these studies, it appears that discrepant results are largely a function of different sampling techniques and measures (see Pless & Nolan, 1991, for a review). In this section we will briefly review evidence on the prevalence of behavioral and emotional disorders in children with chronic illnesses and their families. Two issues must be considered in evaluating this research. First, which study designs are most appropriate and rigorous for this purpose (e.g., epidemiological surveys, controlled clinical comparisons)? And second, is "pathology" the most relevant outcome, or are other functionally-based outcomes, such as school attendance and parental discipline practices, equally important?

PSYCHOLOGICAL RISK FOR CHILDREN WITH CHRONIC ILLNESSES AND DISABILITIES

To date, several large-scale epidemiological studies have been conducted to assess the extent of behavioral and emotional disorders in children with chronic illnesses, including the Isle of Wight studies from England, the Rochester Child Health Studies, and the Ontario Child Health Studies (Breslau, 1985; Cadman et al., 1987; Rutter, Tizard, & Whitmore, 1970). These studies have typically employed clinical ratings of emotional disturbance, parent ratings of behavior problems, and self-report measures of self-concept and self-esteem. Their findings indicate that, in general, children with chronic disorders are twice as likely to have behavioral and emotional disorders as their nondisabled peers. For example, results of the Ontario Child Health Survey, which randomly sampled 3,294 children, indicated that the age and sex-adjusted odds ratio for one or more psychiatric disorders for those with a chronic illness was 2.1 (95 percent confidence interval). These children appeared to be at particular risk for internalizing disorders (e.g., depression, anxiety), social isolation, and lower social competence (Cadman et al., 1987). Although statistical risk does not imply that most children with chronic illnesses have adjustment problems, these figures represent a substantial level of augmented risk, which should be addressed by public policy and the allocation of clinical resources (Drotar, 1992; Perrin & MacLean, 1988).

Additional evidence of elevated risk comes from two recent meta-analytic studies that examined the prevalence of psychological disorders across well-controlled studies published over the past thirty years (Bennett, 1994; Lavigne & Faier-Routman, 1992). Meta-analysis provides a rigorous methodology for examining the reliability of results that have been conducted with limited sample sizes, and yields a measure of the strength and "replicability" of the findings (Hunter & Schmidt, 1990; Glass, McGaw, & Smith, 1981). The study by Lavigne and Faier-Routman (1992), which focused on behavior problems and self-concept, confirmed that children with chronic illnesses are at greater risk for behavior problems, with internalizing disorders more frequently reported than externalizing disorders. The results for self-concept were mixed: the self-concept scores of children with physical disorders were lower than those of healthy children, but these differences did not reach significance in studies using carefully matched comparison groups or normative data. It should also be noted that measures of self-concept and self-esteem have not been as rigorously developed as measures of behavioral and emotional disorders. Children with chronic illnesses also appear to be at slightly greater risk for depression (Bennett, 1994), with a median prevalence rate of 9 percent across the 18 studies that used diagnostic interviews, compared to a prevalence of 1 to 5 percent reported in nondisabled community samples.

In contrast to both the epidemiological and meta-analytic studies, other investigations have found no evidence of elevated risk in children with chronic illnesses (Kellerman et al., 1980; Tavormina et al., 1976). These studies are limited in several ways. First, they have smaller sample sizes than large-scale surveys and thus, have less power to detect differences and are more vulnerable to sampling biases. In addition, subjects for these studies are often recruited from comprehensive pediatric centers where the quality of medical care and service provision may be substantially higher (Perrin & MacLean, 1988). Many of these centers have pediatric psychologists on staff who have sensitized physicians to the risk of behavioral and emotional problems, and have developed preventive approaches to address them.

Nevertheless, the majority of the evidence from well-controlled studies indicates that children with chronic physical disorders *are* at risk for adjustment problems. As Pless and Nolan (1991) noted, "sufficient evidence has accumulated to the point where needless replication and unnecessary revision of previous research is occurring. The main challenge for investigators working in this field has now shifted from establishing the risks associated with chronic illness in general, to that of identifying specific determinants or modifiers of risk" (p. 347). Some progress along these lines has been made in determining which *types* of chronic illness or disability place children at highest risk. Consistent evidence has indicated that children with sensory disorders (e.g., deafness, blindness) and neurological conditions (e.g., seizure disorders) experience more behavioral and emotional disorders than children with other chronic illnesses (e.g., cancer, cystic fibrosis) (Lavigne & Faier-Routman, 1992; Rutter, 1977).

Another issue driving the needless replication of studies on adaptation is the focus on "pathology" to the exclusion of other important dimensions of functioning, such as adherence to treatment, peer relationships, and school attendance (Drotar, 1992; Johnson, 1988; La Greca, 1990; Perrin & MacLean, 1988). This shift away from traditional psychopathology toward a focus on the day-to-day functioning of children with chronic physical disorders fits the recent emphasis in pediatrics on health promotion and prevention, termed the "new morbidity" (Haggerty, 1986; Karoly, 1988). This framework conceptualizes children with chronic illnesses as *normal children responding to an abnormal situation* (Russo & Varni, 1982). There are several advantages to this framework: (a) it normalizes the experience of disability for children and their families, reducing its stigma; (b) it places the process of adaptation within the context of normal developmental change and growth (e.g., establishing independence); and (c) it shifts the focus of analysis from global concepts such as "self-esteem," to the specific tasks that must be mastered by the child and family for successful adaptation. It should be noted that this level of analysis cannot be accomplished using heterogeneous samples of chronically ill and disabled children who are likely to vary on these dimensions (Quittner, DiGirolamo, et al., 1992).

Psychological Risk for Siblings

There is a growing awareness that sibling relationships constitute an important component of the family system (Dunn & Plomin, 1990). Siblings spend a great deal of time together (Csikzentmihalyi & Larson, 1984), and recent studies have suggested that this relationship serves as a model for the development of peer relationships and the resolution of conflict, and is an important source of emotional support throughout the life span (Bedford, 1989; Brody & Stoneman, 1990; Daniels & Plomin, 1985). Finally, sibling relationships appear to be highly influenced by input from parents, and thus, offer a window into the broader interactions within the family system (Brody, Stoneman, & McCoy, 1992; Quittner & Opipari, 1994).

This recognition of the importance of sibling relationships has spurred researchers to examine how "atypical" family contexts (e.g., raising a child with a disability) may affect a sibling's adjustment (Dyson, 1989; McHale & Pawletko, 1992). Growing up with a sibling who is chronically ill or disabled may alter the daily lives of siblings in significant ways: parents may devote less time and attention to the healthy sibling (Crocker, 1981; McHale & Gamble, 1989; Opipari & Quittner, 1995), siblings may be asked to assume more responsibility for household chores and caretaking tasks (Gath, 1974; McHale & Pawletko, 1992), and because of these role changes within the family, siblings may display more behavioral and emotional difficulties (e.g., jealousy, aggression) (Cadman et al., 1988). Tritt and Esses (1988), for example, found that over half of the healthy siblings they interviewed reported that the brother or sister with the chronic illness received special attention from the family, which they resented, and many reported they had greater family responsibilities. In contrast, some studies have suggested that growing up in this family context may have positive effects on siblings, including increased maturity, a greater sense of responsibility, and enhanced perceptions of competence and self-esteem (Cleveland & Miller, 1977).

In terms of risk for psychiatric disorder, the results for siblings parallel those for the child with the illness or disability (Drotar & Crawford, 1985). Controlled studies using validated measures have generally found that these children are at greater risk for adjustment problems, but this risk is dependent upon contextual variables such as the age and gender of the sibling, and the nature of the role changes in the family. For example, Breslau and colleagues (Breslau, Weitzman, & Messenger, 1981) conducted a large-scale survey of siblings (ages 6 to 18) of children with CF, cerebral palsy, and multiple handicaps, and found no differences in risk for serious psychiatric disorder between this sample and a normative one. However, these siblings did score higher than the norm group on subscales measuring Mentation Problems, Fighting, and Delinquency. A more recent study of siblings of children with epilepsy found no evidence of adjustment problems soon after the diagnosis, but did find more behavior problems among children who were older and had been exposed to their sibling's medical condition over a longer period of time (Hoare, 1984).

These results highlight the complexities of assessing "risk" in these families, and point to a number of methodological problems. First, little attention has been given to relevant demographic variables, such as birth order, gender of sibling, age spacing between siblings, and the type of illness or disability. Second, little is known about the role fathers play in these families, which may "compensate" for the extra attention given to the child with the disability. Finally, most studies have examined broad indices of psychological functioning (e.g., depression, self-concept), which shed little light on how the *daily lives* of children growing up in this family context are affected—in either positive or negative ways. What is needed are new methods of data collection (e.g., diaries, observations), and greater attention to how siblings' lives are altered on a daily basis.

A recent study used a diary procedure to assess parental differential treatment in 20 families with a younger child with CF and an older healthy sibling, compared to 20 age-matched control families (Quittner & Opipari, 1994). Parental differential treatment, defined as differences in attention, affection, and discipline directed toward younger versus older children, was measured using both a structured home interview and daily phone diaries. Interestingly, little evidence of differential treatment was found on the interview measures. However, on the diary variables, both quantitative and qualitative differences in parental treatment emerged. Specifically, mothers in the CF group vs. control group spent more individual time with the younger child in play and mealtime activities than with the older, healthy child. Further, the time spent alone with the child with

CF was rated more positively than was the time spent with the older child. The diary data were critical in both revealing differences in the daily living patterns of these families and in pinpointing specific activities in which older siblings were "left out."

Psychological Risk for Parents: Parenting Stress, Marital Satisfaction, and Depression

Parenting Stress

Several studies have assessed whether parents raising a child with a chronic illness or disability report more stress in their parenting role than parents raising a nondisabled child. Two measures are commonly used in these studies: The Parenting Stress Index (PSI; Abidin, 1983) and the Questionnaire on Resources and Stress (QRS; Holroyd, 1974). The PSI has the advantage of providing normative data and a clinical cut-off for determining which scores fall in the "clinical range." Although the evidence is mixed, the majority of studies using the PSI have reported higher levels of parenting stress, particularly on subscales that measure characteristics of the child (e.g., Demandingness, Adaptability). Clinically elevated levels of parenting stress have been reported by parents raising children with autism, deafness, failure to thrive, and cystic fibrosis (Quittner et al., 1990; Quittner, DiGirolamo et al., 1992; Singer, Song, Hill, & Jaffe, 1990; Wolf, Noh, Fisman, & Speechley, 1989). For example, 29 percent of parents of infants with disabilities rated their levels of stress above the clinical cut-off on one of three scales—Demandingness, Adaptability, or Child Mood (Shonkoff et al., 1992). In our study of mothers parenting a child with a profound hearing loss, 65 percent scored at or above the clinical cut-off on child-related subscales compared to 25 percent of mothers in the nondisabled comparison sample (Quittner et al., 1990). This is consistent with studies showing that children with sensory disorders and their families may be at particularly high risk.

A closer examination of studies finding no evidence of elevated stress suggests that although the Total Stress score on the PSI was not substantially higher than the norm, subscales related to managing the child's behavior were above the norm (Goldberg, Morris, Simmons, Fowler, & Levison, 1990; Kazak, Reber, & Snitzer, 1988). Using the total stress score on the PSI is also problematic because it sums across scales measuring stress and emotional distress, confounding these two variables—a problem also found with the QRS.

Marital Satisfaction

What is the impact of chronic childhood illness on a couple's marital relationship? Numerous clinical and anecdotal reports have suggested that the effects are primarily negative, with these couples more likely to report conflict, problems with communication and intimacy, and strains related to childrearing than couples of nondisabled children (Barbarin, Hughes, & Chesler, 1985; Phillips, Bohannon, Gayton, & Friedman, 1985). While some early controlled studies supported this view, reporting greater marital distress and higher rates of divorce in couples with chronically ill versus healthy children (Lansky, Cairns, Hassanein, Wehr, & Lowman, 1978; Tew, Payne, & Laurence, 1974), other later studies reported that the child's illness brought parents closer together (Koocher & O'Malley, 1981).

A prior critique of the literature (Sabbeth & Leventhal, 1984) noted that most studies have used measures with questionable reliability and validity, have failed to use adequate control groups, and have relied almost exclusively on cross-sectional rather than longitudinal designs. More recent studies, relying primarily on the Dyadic Adjustment Scale (DAS; Spanier, 1976), which is considered to be psychometrically sound, continue to report conflicting results (Dalquist et al., 1993; Fife, Norton, & Groom, 1987; Kazak et al., 1988). Several reasons for this discrepancy have been proposed: (1) the DAS is prone to social desirability bias, which may be exacerbated in parents of chronically ill children (Robinson & Anderson, 1983), (2) the DAS does not take into account whether the couple has children, which can significantly lower ratings of marital satisfaction (Belsky, Spanier, & Rovine, 1983), and (3) the cut-off score, based on divorced couples, may be inappropriate for parents of chronically ill children for whom there may be social proscriptions against divorce (Walker, Manion, Cloutier, & Johnson, 1992).

Walker and colleagues recently examined the DAS scores of 158 couples with a chronically ill child (e.g., CF, cancer), to determine whether the usual DAS cut-off score (i.e., 100 or less) was appropriate for this sample, using "need for marital therapy" as the criterion. The results indicated that the usual cut-off score was too low, missing a significant number of parents who were distressed and requesting marital intervention. The authors advocate using a score of 109 to identify couples who are maritally distressed, which is closer to the cut-off score of 107 recommended for assessing marital satisfaction in couples who have children (Bond & McMahon, 1984). The application of a higher cut-off score to the literature cited above results in greater consistency across studies. In fact, the majority of studies report DAS scores that are indicative of significant risk (Kazak et al., 1988; Kronenberger & Thompson, 1992). In our research on 224 mothers of preschool children with profound hearing loss, seizure disorders, and cystic fibrosis, 25 to 37 percent of these samples reported significant marital distress on the DAS using 100 as the cut-off compared to 17 percent of the controls. If the cut-off of 107 is applied, 43 to 63 percent of the chronically ill sample would be considered maritally distressed compared to 22 percent of the controls (Quittner, 1991).

Thus, parents of children with chronic illnesses and disabilities are more likely to experience marital distress than parents of nondisabled children. What is unclear, however, are the reasons for this distress. These could include greater caregiving demands due to medical treatments or the child's physical limitations, inequities in the couple's division of household and childcare responsibilities, and difficulties hiring babysitters to provide parents with weekend relief or time for recreation (Bristol, Gallagher, & Schopler, 1988; Quittner, Opipari et al., 1992). Unfortunately, our present measures of marital satisfaction do not identify specific sources of strain. We must now move beyond "screening" couples for marital difficulties to the harder task of pinpointing the nature of these strains and how they lead to dissatisfaction in a couple's relationship. This would allow development of family interventions aimed at addressing these problems.

Psychological Distress

Considerable attention has focused on the extent to which parents of chronically ill or disabled children experience psychological distress. Most studies have used self-report measures, originally designed as psychiatric screening tools, which assess both physical and emotional symptoms (e.g., headaches, depression). Commonly used measures include the Center for Epidemiological Studies–Depression Scale (CES-D; Radloff, 1977), the Beck Depression Inventory (BDI), and a variant of the Symptom Checklist-90 Revised (Derogatis & Cleary, 1977). As with the other areas of risk reviewed above, although the evidence is mixed, most of these studies document higher levels of emotional symptomatology in these families compared to either matched controls or community samples. This is particularly true for mothers, with whom the vast majority of data has been collected. For example, a large-scale study of mothers caring for children with a variety of physical disorders (e.g., asthma, epilepsy), ages birth to 11 years,

found on average twice the number of symptoms reported by this sample compared to community controls (Jessop, Riessman, & Stein, 1988). Similarly, twice as many mothers (39 percent) of young developmentally disabled (e.g., autism) versus nondisabled children scored above the clinical cut-off for depression on the CES-D (Bristol et al., 1988), and 40 percent of the mothers in our study of severely to profoundly deaf children scored at or above this cut-off compared to 23 percent of the matched controls (Quittner et al., 1990). The findings of these latter two studies are more convincing because comparison groups matched on relevant demographic variables and the child's developmental age, which may influence levels of maternal depression, were included.

In contrast to these results, other investigations have not found significant elevations in symptoms of physical and psychological distress among families of chronically ill or disabled children (Kazak & Meadows, 1989). What factors may account for these discrepant results? One possibility is the child's diagnosis. In general, few consistent findings of psychiatric risk have been found for parents of children with cancer. For example, only 13 percent of the mothers and 8 percent of the fathers of children with various types of cancer reported clinically elevated levels of depression on the BDI (Dahlquist et al., 1993). Childhood cancer may present parents with a different set of challenges than a condition that is chronic and unremitting, such as CF or autism. For childhood cancer, there is typically an intense period of anxiety soon after the diagnosis, followed by several years of aggressive treatment, accompanied by the hope of remission and cure (Kupst et al., 1984). In this case, specific predictions could be made about the periods during which parents might evidence the greatest psychological distress based on the course of the condition and its prognosis (Rolland, 1987). Unfortunately, few studies have been designed to explicitly assess differences in family adaptation in relation to these factors. We recently completed a study of parental adaptation soon after a CF diagnosis was made, and found alarming levels of depressive symptomatology: 64 percent of the mothers and 43 percent of the fathers scored at or above the cut-off on the CES-D (Quittner, DiGirolamo et al., 1992). Based on preliminary analyses of our second and third wave data on these families, these percentages are expected to drop dramatically as families adjust to the diagnosis and its implications.

In addition to considering contextual factors, such as type of illness, phase of the condition, and developmental age, greater attention should be paid to the potential effects of psychological distress on the family as a whole. Recent developmental models (Fiese &

Sameroff, 1989) have advocated the use of an interactional framework to examine how parental distress is likely to influence parent-child interactions that, in turn, may affect the child's behavior. Several studies have clearly documented the negative impact of maternal depression on child behavior (Downey & Coyne, 1990), and this has also been demonstrated in cross-sectional studies of pediatric samples (i.e., cancer, sickle cell disease) in which greater maternal depression was associated with higher levels of child-reported distress (Mulhern, Fairclough, Douglas, & Smith, 1994; Thompson et al., 1994). Parental distress could have a variety of consequences, such as the disruption of parenting practices (e.g., discipline, compliance to treatment), increased marital strain, and differential treatment of other siblings in the family (Hauenstein, 1990; Quittner & Opipari, 1994). Evaluation of these systemic processes requires more complex models of adaptation, longitudinal designs, and measures that capture family processes at an interactional level.

Summary

Overall, the cumulative body of research assessing the physical and psychological impact of chronic illness on children and their families indicates that the risks are real and need to be more systematically addressed. The conflicting results reported across studies appear to be due largely to variations in research designs, sampling procedures, and choice of measures. Although elevated risk for behavioral, social, and emotional difficulties is not synonymous with diagnosed pathology, these adaptational problems are sufficiently serious to warrant the attention of clinicians and researchers in the field.

It is also clear that the field needs to move away from purely descriptive studies comparing families of chronically ill children to controls or normative data. In order to avoid costly and unnecessary replication of this type of research, we must begin to ask questions at a different level of complexity: What are the specific conditions that lead to elevated risk? What processes underlie the family interactions associated with maladaptive behavior (e.g., lack of adherence to treatment) or delays in developmental progress (e.g., adolescent independence)? One of the greatest obstacles to accomplishing this is the paucity of measures that are appropriate for pediatric populations and their family members.

ASSESSMENT APPROACHES

Numerous problems have plagued the assessment of child and family adjustment to chronic illness. First, most standardized measures of child psychopathology were developed with samples of nondisabled children and children being referred for mental health problems, and thus the appropriateness of their use for children with chronic illnesses and disabilities is questionable (La Greca, 1994). The widely used Child Behavior Checklist (Achenbach, 1991), for example, contains items that specifically refer to physical diagnoses (e.g., "asthma," "allergies"), which, if endorsed legitimately by parents, would elevate the child's behavior problem score. Parents may also endorse items that reflect symptoms common to a variety of chronic illnesses ("feels dizzy," "lacks energy"), but which are unrelated in this population to behavioral disturbance. Thus, children with chronic illnesses or disabilities are likely to score higher on the CBCL by virtue of their health status (Perrin, Stein, & Drotar, 1991).

A second problem with checklists, such as the CBCL and the Children's Depression Inventory (Kovacs, 1985), is their lack of sensitivity to behavioral variations within the normal range. As was discussed earlier, the vast majority of children with chronic illnesses do not evidence psychopathology as it has been traditionally defined. However, they are more likely than nondisabled children to experience disruptions in daily functioning, such as school attendance, development of peer relationships, and pubertal development. These disruptions may increase symptoms of anxiety, depression, and social isolation—but not to the extent that the child's score falls within the clinical range. The use of measures that are relatively insensitive to these more minor fluctuations may lead to the loss of potentially valuable information (Mulhern et al., 1994; Perrin et al., 1991).

A third problem with current assessment approaches is the almost exclusive reliance on self-report/checklist measures that purport to assess nearly all aspects of child and family functioning (e.g., stress, social competence, depression). Practical considerations seem to be largely responsible for their overuse, including the short time it takes to administer these questionnaires and the relative ease with which they can be collected from families who have driven long distances to attend a hospital clinic. This allows researchers to increase their sample sizes with a fairly small outlay of resources. Questions must be asked, however, about whether the methods of data collection affect its quality (e.g., specificity, validity), and whether self-report measures are sufficient sources of information given their limited utility. Although an effort is often made to increase the validity of self-report data by having multiple respondents complete the same checklist (mother and father ratings on the

CBCL), this still represents the use of a single assessment technique. A more rigorous approach would include multiple *methods* of assessment (e.g., checklists, diaries, interviews).

Finally, a critical problem with most measures used in pediatric research is their lack of relevance to the population. A majority of assessment tools measure global constructs such as self-esteem, behavioral adjustment, and general social skills. However, if we are interested in how the child negotiates his school environment in terms of taking medications, justifying absences, or explaining symptoms (e.g., coughing in class), then our measures must address these issues. Similar problems have been noted with checklists of family functioning (e.g., FES), which typically yield general indices of cohesion and conflict, but may not reflect ongoing family battles over adherence to treatment (Quittner, Tolbert, Regoli, Orenstein, & Eigen, 1995). The lack of relevant, contextually based measurement has led to confusing and conflicting findings, few direct links between assessment and treatment, and little information about the temporal relationships among variables. It has been the primary stumbling block in efforts to move beyond a descriptive level of research to a deeper understanding of the family processes that lead to successful or unsuccessful adaptation.

The task of developing rigorous measures of family adaptation to childhood illness is a daunting one. Assessment approaches must take into account a variety of contextual factors, including the enormous developmental differences in children from birth through adolescence, a wide range of types of illness and disability, with their accompanying medical regimens and physical limitations, and a myriad of social systems in which the child interacts (e.g., peers, hospital, family). Despite these challenges, several promising approaches have recently emerged. In the following section, we will highlight advances in three areas: (1) the use of diary methods of data collection, (2) the development of role-play measures of coping efficacy, and (3) a system for assessing family-level problems and appropriate treatment strategies.

Diary Methods of Assessment

Diary methods of data collection hold considerable promise for advancing our knowledge of adaptation to childhood illness. They are increasingly being used to assess a wide range of relevant child and family behaviors (e.g., adherence to treatment, parenting practices), and offer several advantages over traditional self-report techniques. First, daily diary procedures allow us to measure, in a reliable and nonreactive manner, an ongoing series of behaviors and activities that would not be accessible through traditional, time-limited in vivo observations (Chamberlain & Reid, 1987). Second, diary methods that include a cued-recall procedure (e.g., evening phone calls to collect the data) decrease the chance that memory or recall difficulties will affect the accuracy of the data being collected. In addition, diary procedures have tremendous flexibility in terms of the types of variables that can be measured, and they can easily be modified to change the focus of assessment (e.g., time spent doing treatment, time spent in recreation). In particular, they lend themselves to the assessment of *family-level* processes since most activities that are reported involve multiple members of the family (Quittner, Opipari et al., 1992). Finally, dairy methods offer the investigator a tool for measuring potentially sensitive behavior patterns (e.g., differential treatment of siblings) in an unobtrusive way (Quittner & Opipari, 1994). Tracking of time spent in various activities throughout the day can yield important and highly accurate estimates of behaviors, such as playtime with a sibling or performance of medical routines, without respondents necessarily being aware of the focus of the study. Although measurement of activity patterns through diary recordings has a long tradition in the rehabilitation psychology field (Margalit, 1984; Rock, Fordyce, Brockway, Bergman, & Spengler, 1984), and has been used for several years to investigate coercive family patterns at the Oregon Social Learning Center (Chamberlain & Reid, 1987), it has rarely been utilized in pediatric research. Two innovative applications of diary methods are described below.

Assessment of Daily Diabetes Management

Johnson and colleagues (Freund, Johnson, Silverstein, & Thomas, 1991; Reynolds, Johnson, & Silverstein, 1990) have recently developed a 24-hour recall interview to assess adherence to the complex tasks associated with diabetes management. The procedure consists of independent telephone interviews with the child with diabetes and one parent. During the phone call, the respondent is asked to recall, in temporal order (from waking in the morning until bedtime), all diabetes-related activities. Thirteen behaviors were identified as important components of diabetes management (e.g., glucose testing, timing of meals, insulin injections) and are coded by the telephone interviewer. Moderate stability estimates have been reported over a 3-month period, and excellent agreement on the occurrence of these behaviors was found both between family members (mother-child) and between trained observers and the child (Freund et al., 1991; Reynolds et al., 1990). The diary data also yielded interesting qualitative information. The 7- to 12-year-olds consistently underestimated their consumption of food and performance of exercise. This has important clinical implications for interventions aimed at teaching children how to more reliably attend to their caloric intake and thus improve their insulin regulation.

Assessment of Daily Activity Patterns

We have recently developed a Daily Phone Diary procedure to track parents and children through their activities and interactions. This procedure entails a phone call in the evening to complete a Daily Activity Log using a cued-recall procedure. Beginning with awakening in the morning, for any activity lasting 5 minutes or longer, respondents are systematically cued to report the following information: type of activity, its duration, who was present, and the quality of that time (positive to negative). We have used this Daily Phone Diary procedure to (1) measure the extent to which parents provide time and attention differentially to siblings, (2) assess the frequency and difficulty of daily problems for school-age and adolescent children with CF, and (3) compare patterns of child care and recreation in families with or without a child with a chronic illness (Quittner, Opipari et al., 1992; Quittner & Opipari, 1994; Quittner et al., 1995). This procedure has yielded high levels of interrater agreement (above 90 percent) and considerable

stability in reports of activities over a 3-week period. Contrary to popular belief, the diary procedure is not overly time-consuming for parents (i.e., 20-minute phone call) and produces a richness of description that is lacking in most other assessment methods. The diary method also provides a "window" into the complex alterations that may occur in the daily lives of families with chronically ill or disabled children. For example, rather than finding that *all* areas of individual and family functioning are negatively affected by a child's illness, we found that the differences in daily life were very specific. As can be seen in Figure 4.2, mothers caring for an infant/toddler with CF have significantly less time for recreational and play activities than mothers of nondisabled children, but in most other areas of daily functioning (e.g., chores, child care) they are quite similar. If relationships between these activity patterns and psychological adjustment are established in future studies, the clinical implications of these data will be clear—families need increased time for recreation (e.g., weekend relief, trained sitters) and assistance in achieving a better "balance" between child care, chores and playtime with their children.

Role-Play Inventory of Situations and Coping Strategies

Research on coping behavior has grown tremendously in recent years because of its importance as an intervening variable in the relationship between stress and adaptation. Coping processes are also important because

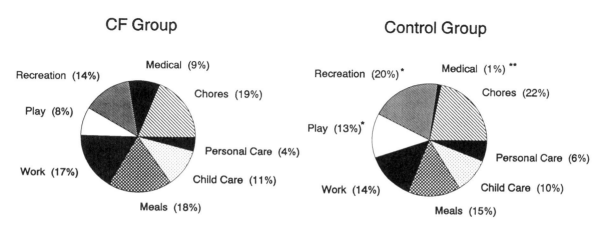

Figure 4.2. Weekday Activity Patterns. Significant based on follow-up ANOVAs (*$p < .05$; **$p < .01$). Published with permission from *Rehabilitation Psychology* (1992), *37*, p. 282.

of their potential amenability to intervention. Despite their prominence in the stress and coping literature, however, we currently have only a limited understanding of how and under what conditions various coping strategies are effective (Menaghan, 1983). Several reasons may account for this limited knowledge, among them confusion and conflict about definitions of coping (e.g., coping styles vs. coping behaviors), and a lack of situational specificity in their assessment. Most studies of coping have asked respondents to consider a recent stressful event and then complete a checklist of the coping strategies they employed. Thus, across subjects, there is no link between the stressful situation they recall and the coping behaviors that are endorsed. In addition, several studies have shown that individuals typically employ several strategies in a single situation, further weakening our understanding of which strategies are or are not effective (Folkman et al., 1986). Finally, most studies have simplified this complex process by developing categories of coping behaviors (i.e., problem-solving vs. emotion-focused), with the explicit assumption that the use of problem-solving strategies will lead to positive outcomes and the use of emotion-focused will lead to poorer outcomes. To date, evidence supporting this claim is inconsistent (Compas, Malcarne, & Fondacaro, 1988; Wertlieb, Weigel, & Feldstein, 1987). Thus, many researchers have begun to question the goal of identifying *generally* effective coping behaviors, noting that the effectiveness of a coping strategy cannot be determined *independently of the context* in which it is used (Stone, Greenberg, Kennedy-Moore, & Newman, 1991).

In an effort to reconceptualize the coping process and its measurement, we have recently conducted a series of studies applying the behavior-analytic model advocated by Goldfried and D'Zurilla (1969) to the assessment and evaluation of coping strategies in children with CF and their parents (Quittner et al., 1995). In this model, competence is defined as the "effectiveness or adequacy with which an individual is capable of responding to the various problematic situations which confront him" (Goldfried & D'Zurilla, 1969; p. 161). Four phases of data collection and analysis were conducted: (1) *Situational Analysis*: a comprehensive survey of the problematic situations encountered by an individual in a particular environment; (2) *Response Enumeration*: a sampling of all possible responses to these situations; (3) *Response Evaluation*: an evaluation of the effectiveness of each coping response by individuals most familiar with the situations (e.g., adolescents with CF, health care professionals); and (4) *Instrument Development*: refinement of the measure and develop-

ment of a detailed scoring manual specifying the criteria for judging the competence of coping responses.

To develop a comprehensive inventory of the problems encountered by adolescents with CF, we conducted home interviews and Daily Phone Diaries with 45 teens (22 boys and 23 girls), 20 parents of adolescents with CF, and 8 health care professionals (e.g., physicians, social workers) (DiGirolamo, Quittner, Regoli, & Jacobsen, 1994). Both CF-specific and normal developmental issues were assessed. A total of 810 problematic situations were elicited from the adolescents themselves, with an additional 236 situations elicited from parents, and 128 elicited from health care professionals. Next, these problematic situations were content-analyzed into a total of 164 non-redundant problem situations across 14 domains (e.g., Medications and Treatment, School, Sexuality). Using this category scheme, two independent raters then re-categorized the problem situations, with an interrater agreement of 87 percent. To select the problem situations that were maximally relevant, a set of criteria was developed based on a problem's frequency and difficulty. Thirty-two situations met the criteria and were subsequently written into role-play vignettes and recorded on audiotape. The following is a sample vignette from the School domain:

"You are sitting in class and you start to cough. It's been a hard day and your cough seems worse than usual. Someone turns to you and asks, 'Are you okay? Are you sick or something?' You feel annoyed by his questions and kind of embarrassed. What would you say or do in this situation?"

The audiotaped role-play vignettes were then presented to the adolescents to assess problem frequency and difficulty, and to elicit their coping responses (Response Enumeration). A set of 38 "expert judges" (e.g., separate sample of teens with CF, parents, and health care professionals) rated the competence of each transcribed response. On the basis of these data, the role-play measure was further refined and a manual was developed for the final set of 25 vignettes (Role-Play Inventory of Situations and Coping Strategies; RISCS). As hypothesized, we have found convergence between our measure of coping efficacy and other assessment devices when the context was "matched" (e.g., competence on the RISCS friend-related problems were correlated with the Empathy and Social Skills subscales of the Social Skills Rating Scales; Gresham & Elliott, 1990). Further, adolescents were clearly competent in responding to problems in some areas, but not others. In sum, this measure holds promise for generating individual profiles of competence for teens with CF and for specifically targeting areas of intervention. Figure 4.3 illustrates the competence of one of the female adolescents with CF in our study; she clearly has areas of both strength and weakness in terms of the coping strategies she employs, depending upon the nature of the problem.

The Family and Disability Assessment System

Although there is consensus among researchers and clinicians that childhood illness and disability affects the family system as a whole, most assessments of family functioning are conducted with individual members of the system. We continue to lack basic information, at the family level, about how specific family interaction patterns, role changes, family beliefs and values influence, or are influenced by, the family member with a chronic illness. To address these issues, we need new approaches that (a) link the *individual* concerns of family members to family and community-level processes, and (b) match the concerns and problems of family members to specific intervention strategies. The direct link between assessment and treatment seems particularly important for moving the field beyond the descriptive level of analysis toward implementation and evaluation of treatment programs.

One promising approach, the Family and Disability Assessment System (FDAS; Glueckauf et al., 1992; Glueckauf, 1993) identifies, at the family-level, the common and difficult problems encountered by family members, *and* "matches" these problems to specific intervention strategies. Several studies now indicate that interventions are more likely to be effective when

matched to the specific context and concerns of the recipients (Taylor & Aspinwall, 1990). The FDAS involves a videotaped interview with all family members to determine the frequency and severity of current concerns, followed by an analysis of each family member's beliefs about the cause of the problem, who is responsible for solving the problem, and steps that have been or could be taken to resolve the problem. Family issues are then analyzed in terms of three fundamental patterns of interaction: repetitive behaviors, roles, and beliefs/values. These three patterns represent an integration of dimensions of family functioning from several schools of family therapy: (1) cognitive-behavioral approach, (2) structural and systemic schools, and (3) psychoeducational counseling (see Glueckauf et al., 1992).

Family issues raised in the interview are then transcribed and coded according to a detailed manual containing definitions of each dimension and specific inclusionary and exclusionary criteria. Based on this assessment, the coding manual (Glueckauf, Webb, & Picha, 1994) specifies intervention strategies that are most likely to be appropriate. For example, if the central problem is judged to be a Repetitive Behavior pattern (e.g., teenager arguing with parents about taking medication), then the therapist should consider an intervention aimed at "breaking" this pattern (e.g., encouraging the teen to "take charge" and design a medication regimen that is acceptable to both teen and parents). In a recent evaluation of this system, substantial agreement was found between independent coders on the content of family problems, and judgments of who was most concerned and involved in the problem. Coders' judgments were also stable across six reliability checks conducted over a period of one year. The investigators are currently evaluating the differential effects of issue-specific (i.e., matching issue and intervention) versus generic psychoeducational counseling in families with an adolescent diagnosed with epilepsy (Glueckauf, 1994). This assessment process is unique in providing family-level data on the specific problems and role changes associated with chronic illness and disability, and provides a theory-based rationale for selecting an appropriate intervention strategy.

INTERVENTION STRATEGIES

Clinical interventions may be broadly divided into prevention and intervention efforts. To date, the greatest area of systematic investigation has been the application of parent training programs to children with disabilities and their parents (Blacher, 1984; Shonkoff et al., 1992). These programs are characterized as

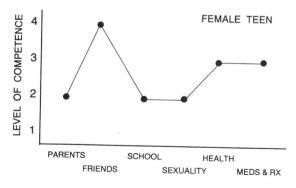

Figure 4.3. Individual profile of the effectiveness of coping strategies employed by an adolescent with CF across several problem domains.

"early interventions," and typically target improvements in both the child's developmental functioning (e.g., motor skills) and the parent's behavior management skills. A meta-analysis of 74 early intervention studies with heterogeneous groups of handicapped children (Casto & Mastropieri, 1986) indicated an overall positive effect for children on standardized cognitive, language, and motor measures. A review of parent training programs also reported positive results (Bailey & Bricker, 1984). The majority of behavioral parent training programs have produced significant gains in parental knowledge and skill. However, these gains are generally restricted to the child behaviors "targeted" in treatment, and only rarely generalize to new or untargeted behaviors.

Despite these generally promising results, programs prior to the 1980s focused primarily on mothers as "teachers" of their children, rather than on the adaptation of the family as a whole. Further, they typically relied on a simplistic deficit model of adaptation—wherein it was assumed that raising a child with a disability inevitably leads to increases in parental stress, marital disintegration, and poor mother-child relationships (Shonkoff et al., 1992). It should be noted that this "deficit" approach has also characterized a great deal of the pediatric psychology research on children with chronic illnesses and their families (Drotar, 1981).

More recent early intervention studies have applied family-centered theoretical frameworks, which focus on empowering parents to participate more actively in decisions related to their children's care and education, and to negotiate the social service system more effectively (Turnbull et al., 1993). An excellent example of applying this family focus can be seen in the Early Intervention Collaborative Study (Shonkoff et al., 1992), which evaluated 29 early-intervention programs using both developmental (e.g., motor skills) and family-oriented (e.g., family environment and support) measures. Although substantial improvements were observed in children across a variety of developmental domains, these gains tended to occur in children with less severe handicaps. In addition, the authors were not able to tie these developmental improvements directly to the effects of the intervention program. Further, changes for family-level variables were more modest and less consistent. Generally, families appeared to be quite stable in their level of functioning, and those who were doing well at the beginning of the study were also doing well at the one-year follow-up. The authors concluded that early-intervention programs should pay greater attention to the more proximal, day-to-day sources of stress for these families (e.g., daily teaching demands).

In the pediatric area, the development and evaluation of family interventions for children with chronic illnesses are strikingly rare. Most studies of family adaptation have been descriptive and comparative in nature, assessing child and family functioning on a wide range of variables. As noted earlier, because of their typically global level of measurement, these models do not lend themselves to clinical interventions. A comprehensive review of the literature revealed less than a handful of family-level interventions. For example, Satin, LaGreca, Zigo, and Skyler (1989) evaluated the effects of a 6-week, family-oriented intervention for adolescents with juvenile diabetes. One innovative component of this intervention was a parent simulation exercise, in which adolescents taught their parents how to manage diabetes and perform various aspects of the treatment regimen (e.g., injections of saline). Families were randomly assigned to either a multifamily psychoeducational intervention, the same multifamily intervention plus parent simulation, or a no-treatment control. Adolescents who participated in the family group plus simulation demonstrated significant improvements in metabolic control compared to the multifamily or control groups. Unfortunately, the effects of the intervention on family functioning were not assessed.

There is clearly a need to develop and evaluate prevention and intervention programs for children with chronic illnesses and their families (LaGreca & Varni, 1993). In order to do that effectively, specific information is required about the needs of families—given the particular disease and developmental context. In addition, few investigators have involved families directly in identifying important targets for treatment or factors that may enhance the acceptability of participating in psychological interventions. Often families of children with chronic illnesses are reluctant to seek psychological treatment because of the possible stigma associated with it (Sabbeth & Stein, 1990). Expert consumers may have a great deal to offer during both the design and implementation phases of program development, including ideas to increase the acceptability and utilization of clinical interventions (Turnbull et al., 1993).

CASE ILLUSTRATION

Clinical Presentation

This case study will attempt to illustrate many of the principles described in the earlier parts of this chapter. The case is a hypothetical account of the Jones family and is based on information from several families seen in an out-patient Hematology/Oncology clinic at a children's hospital. Steven is a four-year-old boy recently diagnosed with Acute Lymphocytic Leukemia (ALL) who lives with his mother, Theresa, his father, Bill, and his six-year-old sister, Julie.

The medical staff in the Hematology/Oncology clinic noticed that Steven was experiencing a great deal of anxiety during medical procedures (e.g., finger sticks), and that Theresa was having difficulty managing his behavioral outbursts in the clinic. They referred the family to the Pediatric Psychology Department to address these issues.

Once the family was referred, the psychologist in the clinic met with Theresa and Steven for an initial assessment session to determine the presenting problems. Bill was also asked to attend this initial session, but was unable to because of work. Based on information from a structured interview with Theresa, the following problems were identified: individual issues for Theresa, marital issues, parenting issues, Steven's reactions to his illness, and Julie's reactions to having a sibling with cancer.

Theresa had a history of emotional problems, including periodic feelings of helplessness, depression, and anxiety when confronted with stressful situations (e.g., financial problems), as well as a tendency to lose her temper and become defensive when dealing with others. The medical staff reported that Theresa was often argumentative, especially in relation to anxiety-provoking issues (e.g., Steven's medical treatment). She wanted immediate answers to her questions, tended to exaggerate the problems she was experiencing, and frequently cried during interactions with the staff. Theresa reported that, because of work commitments, Bill was not very involved in Steven's care, and they had little time to spend alone together. She reported feeling tired and frustrated by Bill's lack of involvement.

In terms of Steven's difficulties, Theresa reported that he was exhibiting frequent temper tantrums and oppositional behavior (e.g., yelling, not minding). He had exhibited behavioral outbursts prior to his diagnosis, but Theresa admitted she had not been consistent in responding to them. She reported that his temper tantrums and oppositionality had increased since his diagnosis, and that she now felt reluctant to discipline him because of his illness. She also noted his fearfulness in new situations and problems separating from her. In particular, he was having difficulty dealing with painful medical procedures, frequent clinic visits, and hospitalizations. For example, he would often cling to his mother and begin to cry as soon as they arrived at the clinic. When it was time for him to have blood drawn, he would stay on his mother's lap and start yelling that he wanted to go home. Theresa mentioned that she felt Steven resented her because she had to bring him into the clinic for medical procedures, such as finger sticks and leg shots.

Steven's older sister, Julie, was also having difficulty adjusting to Steven's illness and treatment—showing signs of feeling left out (e.g., acting out to get attention; fighting frequently with Steven). Theresa said she found it difficult to attend to Steven's medical needs and still find time to spend with her daughter. She noticed that Julie's behavioral outbursts increased when Steven was in the hospital for treatment and both parents were spending a great deal of time at the hospital.

Assessment Findings

In order to obtain more information on the mother's emotional and marital concerns, several questionnaires were administered, including the Brief Symptom Inventory (BSI; Derogatis & Spencer, 1982) and the Dyadic Adjustment Scale (to assess marital discord; DAS; Spanier, 1976). Results from these measures confirmed that the mother was experiencing considerable emotional distress and marital conflict (e.g., scores between the 73rd and 84th percentiles on the Interpersonal Sensitivity, Depression, Anxiety, and Hostility subscales of the BSI; a total score of 95 on the DAS). Based on the assessment results, and the apparent increase in these problems since Steven's diagnosis, Theresa was given a diagnosis of adjustment disorder with mixed anxiety and depressed mood.

To more specifically pinpoint the types of parent-child interactions that were problematic, Steven and his mother participated in a structured behavioral observation. This involved three different phases in which both the parent and child's behavior were recorded while they were sitting at a table in a room with several toys (e.g., puzzles, paper and crayons). The three phases included (1) a child-directed portion, in which the parent was instructed to simply follow the child's lead and not give any commands or instructions, (2) a parent-directed portion, in which the mother initiated a play activity and had the child follow her lead, and (3) a clean-up session, in which both the parent and child tidied up the room. The therapist sat behind a one-way mirror and recorded the occurrence of specific parent and child behaviors. Target parent behaviors included *critical statements* (e.g., "No, that's not the way to do it."), *questions* (e.g., "Do you want to play with this puzzle?"), *indirect commands* with no opportunity to comply (e.g., "Let's put the crayon in the box," followed immediately by the mother putting the crayon away), and *positive behaviors*, such as labeled praise (e.g., "I like it when you sit in your chair and play quietly."). Target child behaviors included *whining*, *yelling*, and *destructive behavior* (e.g., ripping up paper in anger). The mother's responses to the child's behaviors were also recorded.

During the initial behavioral observation, Theresa asked many questions, gave a large proportion of indirect commands, and made several critical, but few positive statements. Steven also had difficulties during this session. He became easily frustrated and whiny, followed by negative outbursts (e.g., yelling and banging a toy on the table), to which his mother responded with a great deal of attention. He rarely complied with Theresa's direct commands, and appeared to "test" the limits in several situations (see Figure 4.4).

In a follow-up session, the mother was asked more directly about Steven's adjustment to his diagnosis. She reported that in addition to exhibiting more frequent oppositional behaviors, he seemed anxious and depressed. The medical staff agreed with these observations. Using a DSM-III-R checklist as part of the interview, Theresa reported that Steven was exhibiting several symptoms of oppositional defiant disorder (e.g., often loses temper, often argues with adults). However, the number, severity, and duration of these symptoms did not meet the criteria for this diagnosis. Instead, Steven was given a primary diagnosis of adjustment disorder with mixed anxiety and depressed mood, and a secondary diagnosis of parent-child relational problem. A single diagnosis did not seem adequate for capturing the complexity of his emotional reactions to his illness and his increase in oppositional behavior. The mother's lack of consistent parenting also appeared to have exacerbated these difficulties.

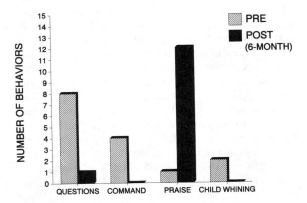

Figure 4.4. Pre-Post evaluations of behaviors targeted in PCIT (Parent-Child Interaction Therapy) intervention.

Treatment Selection and Course

Given the magnitude of these problems, the pediatric psychologist decided that two main types of treatment were necessary. Individual therapy was provided for Theresa by a separate therapist to address her emotional and interpersonal difficulties (e.g., teaching communication skills). Because the father was not willing to be directly involved, marital issues were not addressed at this time.

To address Theresa's difficulty in managing Steven's behavioral problems, Parent-Child Interaction Therapy (Eyberg, 1988; Hembree-Kigin & McNeil, 1995) was conducted with Steven and his mother, and occasionally with Julie. The remainder of the case study will focus on this component of treatment, and on how the therapist addressed some of the specific problems Steven and his sister experienced in relation to the illness and its treatment.

Parent-Child Interaction Therapy (PCIT)

PCIT is a treatment approach for preschool and young school-age children that integrates behavioral and traditional play therapy. It is theoretically consistent with social learning theory and assumes that oppositional behavior is established or maintained by the child's interaction with his or her parents (Eyberg & Boggs, 1989). PCIT involves two main components: (1) Child-Directed-Interaction (CDI), involving play therapy and the development of parenting skills (e.g., describing, reflecting, praising); and (2) Parent-Directed-Interaction (PDI), a combination of play therapy using the above skills and parent discipline training, which focuses on the use of specific commands and follow-through procedures such as Time Out. In this case, PCIT was applied to accomplish the following goals: to establish a more consistent and secure environment at home, to provide Steven with more opportunities for control and decision-making, and to provide structured time for positive parent-child interactions. The skills learned in PCIT were also generalized to the difficult situations Steven encountered in his treatment (e.g., painful procedures, hospitalizations). It was hoped that a combination of positive, relationship-building behaviors learned through play therapy (e.g., praising) and consistent limit setting at home and at clinic would help Steven cope more effectively with the anxiety and distress he experienced in medical situations. Both CDI and PDI were carried out with the therapist behind a one-way mirror, speaking to Theresa through a microphone system. PCIT was carried out first with Theresa and Steven, and then with Julie.

The therapist also worked with Steven to develop alternative ways for him to express his feelings about his illness (i.e., depression, anger), without resorting to oppositional behavior. These suggestions included drawing pictures of what made him anxious or angry, and developing a visual analog that allowed him to let people know how anxious, angry, or sad he was feeling. Various art materials such as play doh, clay, and silly string were used in these sessions. Theresa was encouraged to be receptive to his efforts to communicate in these situations.

Theresa was also given suggestions to facilitate Julie's adjustment to the changes in the family. One option was having a family member stay with Steven for a few hours in the hospital so Theresa could spend time with Julie. Theresa also was encouraged to provide Julie with some special time and attention, maintain open communication with her, and encourage her to share her feelings with her mother. For example, the therapist suggested that Theresa involve Julie in Steven's care by allowing her to visit Steven in the hospital, and encouraging her to draw pictures or make videotapes of herself for him.

Treatment Course

Steven and his mother started with the Child-Directed portion of PCIT, and Theresa picked up the skills fairly quickly. Because Theresa had a tendency to react somewhat defensively to suggestions, the therapist tried to phrase all instructions and feedback in a positive and gentle manner. Theresa was also easily frustrated if things did not go "perfectly," and had trouble applying the communication skills in a flexible manner. However, she seemed to enjoy the structure of the play therapy, and responded well to positive feedback and encouragement. Her sense of frustration decreased over time as she became more skilled and more confident about her own ability to handle difficult child behavior.

Steven started PCIT somewhat hesitantly, preferring to remain on his mother's lap. He initially exhibited numerous temper tantrums to which his mother responded with attention. However, after four or five sessions, Theresa was able to ignore and redirect Steven's behavior. She was also asked not to give any commands during playtime and to follow Steven's lead so he could experience a greater sense of control. In addition, she was supposed to spend five minutes each day in this child-directed "playtime" at home with each of her children.

As treatment progressed, Steven became more outgoing and comfortable in the sessions, and stopped clinging to his mother. The mom's praising and reflecting were then generalized to painful medical procedures, and the "playtime" was carried out during hospital stays. For example, when Steven screamed that he wanted to go home during his leg shot, his mother was told to reply with, "I hear that you want to go home," to praise him for sitting still, and to employ some distraction techniques (e.g., reading a story).

After several weeks of the Child-Directed portion of PCIT, the Parent-Directed discipline portion of therapy was started. Theresa had difficulty following through with Time-Out procedures at first because she felt guilty about setting limits with Steven because of his illness. However, when setting limits was reframed as a way to provide appropriate structure and a safe environment for Steven, Theresa was more willing to follow through.

About once a month, PCIT was also conducted with Theresa and the two children together. In these sessions, Theresa learned to listen and praise each child, as well as exert positive parental control over their behavior. It was clear during earlier sessions that Julie's behavior problems escalated when Theresa was giving attention to Steven. Theresa was asked to ignore these escalations and focus on providing Julie with attention for her positive behaviors. As Theresa began to implement the special "playtime" at home, and include Julie more in Steven's care, Julie's jealous behavior in the structured PCIT sessions decreased, and the children began to play more cooperatively.

Problems Carrying out Interventions

Two major difficulties persisted throughout the course of treatment. The first involved Theresa coming in to the PCIT sessions with an individual crisis to discuss. In order to make sure that both the individual and parenting issues were adequately addressed, clear boundaries were set between Theresa's individual therapy and the PCIT. The therapist acknowledged the mother's feelings of frustration, but encouraged her to speak with her individual therapist about her difficulties.

The second major difficulty was involving the father in treatment. He was busy with his job, often out of town, and was not willing to come in for therapy sessions. To address Bill's time constraints, the therapist offered to call him each week to help him with any difficulties he was having with his children. Bill was also encouraged to observe Theresa when she carried out the play therapy sessions and discipline techniques at home. Theresa was provided with written handouts describing all these procedures and shared them with her husband. As Bill observed some of the changes in the interactions between his wife and his children, he became more interested in reading the handouts and was willing, periodically, to try the special "playtime" with his children. As the two parents became more comfortable with these skills, the number of phone conversations with the therapist decreased.

Termination and Follow-Up

PCIT was terminated at the end of eight months, after a total of 26 sessions. Behavioral observations six months after the beginning of treatment showed a decrease in Theresa's use of questions and critical statements, an increase in her use of labeled praises and specific commands, an increase in child compliance during the sessions, and a decrease in Steven's whining behavior (see Figure 4.4). Theresa also reported that the children were minding better at home, though some sibling rivalry continued. The staff reported positive changes in Steven's behavior—he was clinging much less to his mother during medical procedures, and was more willing to interact with the staff. They also noted that Theresa communicated more effectively with them, and was able to ask questions or express concerns in a more appropriate way, particularly about issues regarding Steven's medical care. She was viewed as less defensive and emotionally upset during clinic visits.

During the last two months, sessions were held bi-weekly instead of weekly. In general, both Steven and Julie were complying with their mother's commands, and their acting-out behaviors had decreased considerably. Normal sibling rivalry continued, and both children exhibited occasional behavioral outbursts, but Theresa was able to set appropriate limits in these situations and refrain from providing negative attention. Both children's behavior problems increased when Steven was in the hospital, but Theresa found that generalizing the special "playtime" and limit-setting procedures to the hospital setting was helpful during these periods. Although Bill was not consistently involved in the playtime and discipline practices, he was supportive of his wife's efforts and tried to participate when he was home. He and Theresa also agreed to find ways that he could spend some individual time with both children, and give Theresa breaks during Steven's hospital stays.

Steven continues to be followed by the Hematology/ Oncology Clinic for his ALL. He has currently finished his treatment protocol and is being seen once a month to check his health status. During these clinic visits, the medical staff also check on the family's psychosocial status by asking questions (e.g., "Are there any new concerns about Steven's behavior?"), and informally observing them in the clinic. If a problem is called to their attention, they encourage the family to contact the staff psychologist or their former therapists. The medical staff also alert the psychologist to any significant changes in Steven's medical status (e.g., relapse). In this way, the team works together with the family to address any problems as soon as they occur. The psychologist also meets with the family periodically during a clinic visit to assess their current psychosocial status and any potential problems. A family-centered approach is crucial to addressing these problems since many of the difficulties associated with adjusting to chronic childhood illness involve changes within the family system and day-to-day routines. Furthermore, early intervention and if possible, prevention, increase the probability that treatment will be effective in dealing with the problems associated with having a child with a chronic illness.

SUMMARY

This chapter critically reviewed research on how children and families adapt to illness and disability. Over the past decade, the most significant growth has been in the development and evaluation of various conceptual models of family adaptation. For several reasons, these models represent important first steps toward increasing our understanding of the adaptation process. First, they have drawn upon widely known theories of stress and coping to select the variables that are likely to be relevant, and have begun the process of testing relationships among them. As such, they have provided useful frameworks for simplifying the complexities of the adaptation process. Second, these models have served to sensitize researchers and clinicians to the potentially negative effects of childhood illness and disability on all members of the family. Although most models have focused on either the child's or parents' adaptation, there have been increasing efforts to incorporate reciprocal relationships between parent-child functioning into these models. Finally, at the conceptual level, these models have offered speculations about the processes by which children and families adapt to the challenges posed by an illness.

Although these models have stimulated tremendous interest in the field and have served as a useful starting point, they have remained largely heuristic, and cannot adequately answer the questions we now need to address: What specific conditions increase a family's risk for adjustment difficulties? What factors mediate the extent of risk? Do interventions lead to improved health outcomes for children and documented benefits for families? The problems with current family models range from the inclusion of so many variables and causal pathways that the models are unwieldy and untestable, to the practicalities of measuring such a large number of variables—which inevitably decreases the rigor of the assessment process.

Perhaps a more serious concern raised in this chapter is the *level* of assessment and analysis that has dominated the literature. Most variables in these models are measured at a global level that provides little information about the specific nature of the stressors faced by children with chronic illnesses and their families, few details about how mediating variables, such as social and family resources, serve to modify this stress, and no delineation of how these processes unfold either on an immediate or long-term time scale. These problems have made it difficult to link the findings from these models to specific interventions. Essentially, these models have provided us with a "snapshot" of the more distal dimensions of the caregiving environment; however, what we need now is an understanding of the dynamics of the environment that is more proximal—the day-to-day influences and transactions that transpire in families raising a child with a disability or illness.

To move toward this more process-oriented approach, new procedures and methods of assessment will be required. For example, questions about how family attitudes and communication patterns influence the child's knowledge of and response to the illness will be best addressed by direct observations of the family, or by paradigms that include *all* family members. Although the difficulties of collecting and analyzing this type of data cannot be underestimated, the work of Hauser and colleagues (Hauser et al., 1993) represents a positive step in this direction. In addition, several promising approaches for assessing daily interactions and events were reviewed in this chapter. Telephone diaries, for example, make use of a technology that is available to most families, and enable the researcher or clinician to examine a wide range of interesting variables in a relatively cost-efficient manner. New technologies on the horizon, such as videophone hook-ups in the home, will allow even greater access to families who live at long-distances from the hospital or in rural areas for interviews, observations, and interventions. These technologies will become increasingly important, not only as we begin to measure more process-level interactions, but as health care and research budgets shrink and limit our ability to provide many of the educational and supportive services pediatric populations and their families have come to rely on.

It is also clear from this review that children with disabilities and their families represent a population that is "at risk" for adjustment difficulties. Two issues are worthy of note. First, on general, broad-based indices of behavioral and emotional functioning, the majority of children and parents are doing quite well. This does not negate the fact, however, that well-controlled, epidemiological studies consistently find that a higher percentage of children with chronic illnesses and their parents are diagnosed with one or more psychological disorders when compared to nondisabled populations. Second, serious questions have been raised in this chapter and elsewhere about the utility of these broad indicators. Although they may be useful for making general comparisons between the incidence of depression or internalizing behavior problems in children with or without disabilities, they tell us nothing about the problems experienced by children with disabilities in their day-to-day lives. In order to intervene effectively, we must know when, developmentally, specific problems are likely to occur (e.g., decreased adherence to treatment in adolescence) and in which settings (e.g., home, school). This information simply cannot be obtained through traditional measures of psychopathology. Similar arguments can be made for the need for this information in order to intervene with parents and siblings.

Finally, in reviewing our current state of knowledge with regard to family adaptation to childhood disability and illness, we were particularly struck by how few controlled studies have been published on clinical interventions. Although systematic interventions have been developed for management of painful medical procedures (Peterson, 1989), and a fair number of intervention studies have addressed issues related to the child's adherence to treatment or development of broader social skills, less than a handful of family intervention studies (other than parent training) could be found (Roberts & Wallander, 1992). Even the recent special issue on "Interventions in Pediatric Psychology" (*Journal of Pediatric Psychology*, Vol. 18, 1993) did not contain a single intervention study focused on family adaptation (La Greca & Varni, 1993). There are several possible reasons for this. First, as this review has attempted to illustrate, we lack the developmental and issue-specific information necessary to design effective family-level interventions. It is hoped that the innovative assessment approaches described in this chapter will ultimately provide this more fine-grained information. Second, pragmatic issues such as time and transportation often prevent families of pediatric populations from accessing programs that would be beneficial.

Creative solutions such as home-visiting therapists, intensive three-day workshops, and the use of technologies may be helpful in overcoming this barrier. Finally, researchers and clinicians need to utilize the expertise of consumers. Families have a tremendous amount to offer in terms of identifying issues that are of greatest importance to them, as well as factors that could increase the acceptance and utilization of clinical interventions.

REFERENCES

Abidin, R. R. (1983). *Parenting Stress Index (PSI)—Manual and administration booklet*. Charlottesville, VA: Pediatric Psychology Press.

Achenbach, T. M. (1991). *Manual for the Child Behavior Checklist/4-18 and 1991 Profile*. Burlington: University of Vermont, Department of Psychiatry.

Affleck, G., Tennen, H., Rowe, J., Roscher, B., & Walker, L. (1989). *Child Development, 60*, 488–501.

Anderson, B. J., Miller, J., Auslander, W., & Santiago, J. (1981). Family characteristics of diabetic adolescents: Relationships to metabolic control. *Diabetes Care, 4*, 586–594.

Bailey, E., & Bricker, D. (1984). The efficacy of early intervention for severely handicapped infants and young children. *Topics in Early Childhood Special Education, 4*, 30–51.

Barakat, L., & Linney, J. (1992). Children with physical handicaps and their mothers: The interrelation of social support, maternal adjustment, and child adjustment. *Journal of Pediatric Psychology, 17*, 725–739.

Barbarin, O., Hughes, D., & Chesler, M. (1985). Stress, coping, and marital functioning among parents of children with cancer. *Journal of Marriage and the Family, 47*, 473–480.

Baron, R. M., & Kenny, D. A. (1986). The moderator-mediator variable distinction in social psychological research: Conceptual, strategic, and statistical considerations. *Journal of Personality and Social Psychology, 51*, 1173–1182.

Barrera, M. (1988). Models of social support and life stress: Beyond the buffering hypothesis. In L. H. Cohen (Ed.), *Life events and psychological functioning: Theoretical and methodological issues* (pp. 211–236). Newbury Park, CA: Sage Publications, Inc.

Baruch, G. K., Biener, L., & Barnett, R. C. (1987). Women and gender in research on work and family stress. *American Psychologist, 42*, 130–136.

Bedford, V. H. (1989). Understanding the value of siblings in old age: A proposed model. *The American Behavioral Scientist, 33*, 33–44.

Belsky, J., Spanier, G. B., & Rovine, M. (1983). Stability and change in marriage across the transition to parenthood. *Journal of Marriage and the Family, 45*, 567–577.

Bennett, D. S. (1994). Depression among children with chronic medical problems: A meta-analysis. *Journal of Pediatric Psychology, 19*, 149–169.

Blacher, J. (1984). *Severely handicapped young children and their families: Research in review*. London: Academic Press.

Bond, C. R. & McMahon, R. J. (1984). Relationships between marital distress and child behavior problems, maternal personal adjustment, maternal personality, and maternal parenting behavior. *Journal of Abnormal Psychology, 93*, 348–351.

Breslau, N. (1985). Psychiatric disorder in children with physical disabilities. *Journal of the American Academy of Child and Adolescent Psychiatry, 24*, 87–94.

Breslau, N., Weitzman, M., & Messenger, K. (1981). Psychologic functioning of siblings of disabled children. *Pediatrics, 67*, 344–353.

Bristol, M. M. (1987). Mothers of children with autism or communication disorders: Successful adaptation and the double ABCX model. *Journal of Autism and Developmental Disorders, 17*, 469–486.

Bristol, M. M., Gallagher, J. J., & Schopler, E. (1988). Mothers and fathers of young developmentally disabled and nondisabled boys: Adaptation and spousal support. *Developmental Psychology, 24*, 441–451.

Brody, G. H. & Stoneman, Z. (1990). Sibling relationships. In I. E. Sigel & G. H. Brody (Eds.), *Methods of family research* (pp. 189–212). Hillsdale, NJ: Erlbaum.

Brody, G. H., Stoneman, Z., & McCoy, K. (1992). Associations of maternal and paternal direct and differential behavior with sibling relationships: Contemporaneous and longitudinal analyses. *Child Development, 63*, 82–92.

Bronfenbrenner, U. (1979). *The ecology of human development*. Cambridge: Harvard University Press.

Cadman, D., Boyle, M., Szatmari, P., & Offord, D. R. (1987). Chronic illness, disability, and mental and social well-being: Findings of the Ontario Child Health Study. *Pediatrics, 79*, 805–813.

Cadman, D., Boyle, M., & Offord, D. R. (1988). The Ontario Child Health study: Social adjustment and mental health of siblings of children with chronic health problems. *Journal of Developmental and Behavioral Pediatrics, 9*, 117–121.

Casto, G., & Mastropieri, M. (1986). The efficacy of early intervention programs: A meta-analysis. *Exceptional Children, 52*, 417–424.

Chamberlain, P., & Reid, J. B. (1987). Parent observation and report of child symptoms. *Behavioral Assessment, 9*, 97–109.

Chaney, J. M., & Peterson, L. (1989). Family variables and disease management in juvenile rheumatoid arthritis. *Journal of Pediatric Psychology, 14*, 389–403.

Chesler, M. A., & Barbarin, O. A. (1984). Difficulties of providing help in a crisis: Relationships between parents of children with cancer and their friends. *Journal of Social Issues, 40*, 113–134.

Cleveland, D. W., & Miller, N. B. (1977). Attitudes and life commitments of older siblings of mentally retarded adults: An exploratory study. *Mental Retardation, 15*, 38–41.

Cohen, S., & Wills, T. A. (1985). Stress, social support, and the buffering hypothesis. *Psychological Bulletin, 98*, 310–357.

Cole, R. E. & Reiss, D. (1993). Introduction. In R. E. Cole & D. Reiss, *How do families cope with chronic illness?* (pp. vii–xiv). Hillsdale, NJ: Lawrence Erlbaum Associates, Inc.

Compas, B., Malcarne, V., & Fondacaro, K. (1988). Coping with stressful events in older children and young adolescents. *Journal of Consulting and Clinical Psychology, 56*, 405–411.

Coyne, J. C., Ellard, J. H., & Smith, D. A. (1990). Social support, interdependence, and the dilemmas of helping. In B. R. Sarason, I. G. Sarason, & G. R. Pierce (Eds.), *Social support: An interactional view* (pp. 129–149). New York: John Wiley & Sons.

Crocker, A. (1981). The involvement of siblings of children with handicaps. In A. Milunsky (Ed.), *Coping with crisis and handicap* (pp. 219–223). New York: Plenum Press.

Crystal, R. G. (1992). Gene therapy strategies for pulmonary disease. *American Journal of Medicine, 92*, 44S–52S.

Csikszentmihalyi, M., & Larson, R. (1984). *Being adolescent: Conflict and growth in the teenage years.* New York: Basic Books.

Cutrona, C. E., & Russell, D. (1990). Type of social support and specific stress: Toward a theory of optimal matching. In B. R. Sarason, I. G. Sarason, & G. R. Pierce (Eds.), *Social support: An interactional view* (pp. 319–366). New York: John Wiley & Sons.

Dahlquist, L. M., Czyzewski, D., Copeland, K. G., Jones, C. L., Taub, E., & Vaughan, J. K. (1993). Parents of children newly diagnosed with cancer: Anxiety, coping, and marital distress. *Journal of Pediatric Psychology, 18*, 365–376.

Daniels, D., & Plomin, R. (1985). Differential experience of siblings in the same family. *Developmental Psychology, 21*, 747–760.

Derogatis, L. R. & Cleary, P. A. (1977). Confirmation of the dimensional structure of the SCL-90: A study in construct validation. *Journal of Clinical Psychology, 33*, 981–989.

Derogatis, L. R., & Spencer, P. M. (1982). *The Brief Symptom Inventory (BSI): Administration, scoring, and procedures manual—I.* Baltimore, MD: Clinical Psychometric Research.

DiGirolamo, A. M., Quittner, A. L., Regoli, M. J., & Jacobsen, J. (1994, April). *Behavioral assessment of coping efficacy: A unique method of measuring coping in adolescents with cystic fibrosis.* Paper presented at the Second Gulf Coast Regional Pediatric Psychology Conference, New Orleans.

Downey, G., & Coyne, J. C. (1990). Children of depressed parents: An integrative review. *Psychological Bulletin, 108*, 50–76.

Drotar, D. (1981). Psychological perspectives in childhood chronic illness. *Journal of Pediatric Psychology, 6*, 211–228.

Drotar, D. (1992). Integrating theory and practice in psychological intervention with families of children with chronic illness. In T. J. Akamatsu, M. A. Stephens, S. E. Hobfall, & J. H. Crowther (Eds.), *Family health psychology* (pp. 175–192). Washington, DC: Hemisphere Publishing.

Drotar, D., & Bush, M. (1985). Mental health issues and services. In N. Hobbs & J. H. Perrin (Eds.), *Issues in the care of children with chronic illness* (pp. 514–550). San Francisco: Jossey-Bass.

Drotar, D., & Crawford, P. (1985). Psychological adaptation of siblings of chronically ill children: Research and practice implications. *Developmental and Behavioral Pediatrics, 6*, 355–362.

Dunn, J., & Plomin, R. (1990). *Separate lives: Why siblings are so different.* New York: Basic Books.

Dyson, L. (1989). Adjustment of siblings of handicapped children: A comparison. *Journal of Pediatric Psychology, 14*, 215–229.

Eiser, C. (1990). Psychological effects of chronic disease. *Journal of Child Psychiatry and Psychology, 31*, 85–98.

Engel, G. L. (1977). The need for a new medical model: A challenge for biomedicine. *Science, 196*, 129–136.

Engel, G. L. (1982). The biopsychosocial model and medical education. *New England Journal of Medicine, 306*, 802–805.

Eyberg, S. M. (1988). Parent-Child Interaction Therapy: Integration of traditional and behavioral concerns. *Child and Family Behavior Therapy, 10*, 33–46.

Eyberg, S. M., & Boggs, S. R. (1989). Parent training for oppositional preschoolers. In C. E. Schaefer & J. M. Briesmeister (Eds.), *Handbook of parent training:*

Parents as cotherapists for children's behavior problems (pp. 105–132). New York: John Wiley & Sons.

Fewell, R. R., & Gelb, S. A. (1983). Parenting moderately handicapped persons. In M. Seligman (Ed.), *The family with a handicapped child: Understanding and treatment* (pp. 175–202). New York: Grune & Stratton.

Fiese, B. H., & Sameroff, A. J. (1989). Family context in pediatric psychology: A transactional perspective. *Journal of Pediatric Psychology, 14*, 293–314.

Fife, B., Norton, J., & Groom, G. (1987). The family's adaptation to childhood leukemia. *Social Science Medicine, 24*, 159–168.

Finney, J. W., & Bonner, M. J. (1992). The influence of behavioural family intervention on the health of chronically ill children. *Behaviour Change, 9*, 157–170.

Folkman, S., Lazarus, R. S., Dunkel-Schetter, C., DeLongis, A., & Gruen, R. J. (1986). The dynamics of a stressful encounter: Cognitive appraisal, coping, and encounter outcomes. *Journal of Personality and Social Psychology, 50*, 992–1003.

Freund, A., Johnson, S. B., Silverstein, J., & Thomas, J. (1991). Assessing daily management of childhood diabetes using 24-hour recall interviews: Reliability and stability. *Health Psychology, 10*, 200–208.

Garrison, W. T., & McQuiston, S. (1989). *Chronic illness during childhood and adolescence: Psychological aspects.* Newbury Park, CA: Sage Publications, Inc.

Gath, A. (1974). Sibling reactions to mental handicap: A comparison of brothers and sisters of mongol children. *Journal of Child Psychology and Psychiatry, 15*, 187–198.

Glass, G. V., McGaw, B., & Smith, M. L. (1981). *Meta-analysis in social research.* Beverly Hills, CA: Sage Publications, Inc.

Glueckauf, R. L. (1993). Use and misuse of assessment in rehabilitation: Getting back to the basics. In R. L. Glueckauf, L. B. Sechrest, G. R. Bond, and E. C. McDonel (Eds.), *Improving assessment in rehabilitation and health* (pp. 135–155). Newbury Park, CA: Sage Publications, Inc.

Glueckauf, R. L., Webb, P. M., Papandria-Long, M., Rasmussen, J. L., Markand, O., & Farlow, M. (1992). The Family and Disability Assessment System: Consistency and accuracy of judgments across coders and measures. *Rehabilitation Psychology, 37*, 291–304.

Glueckauf, R. L., Picha, D., & Webb, P. M. (1994). *The Family and Disability Assessment System Manual.* Indianapolis: Indiana University-Purdue University at Indianapolis.

Goldberg, S., Morris, P., Simmons, R. J., Fowler, R. S., & Levison, H. (1990). Chronic illness in infancy and parenting stress: A comparison of three groups of parents. *Journal of Pediatric Psychology, 15*, 347–358.

Goldfried, M. R., & D'Zurilla, T. J. (1969). A behavior-analytic model for assessing competence. In C. Spielberger (Ed.), *Current Topics in Clinical and Community Psychology*, (pp. 151–195). New York: Academic Press.

Gortmaker, S., & Sappenfield, W. (1984). Chronic childhood disorders: Prevalence and impact. *Pediatric Clinics of North America, 31*, 3–18.

Gresham. F. M., & Elliott, S. N. (1990). *Social Skills Rating System.* Circle Pines, MN: American Guidance Service.

Haggerty, R. J. (1986). The changing nature of pediatrics. In N. A. Krasnegor, J. D. Arasteh, & M. F. Cataldo (Eds.), *Child health behavior: A behavioral pediatrics perspective.* New York: John Wiley & Sons.

Hanson, C. L., Henggeler, S. W., Harris, M., Burghen, G., & Moore, M. (1989). Family system variables and the health status of adolescents with insulin-dependent diabetes mellitus. *Health Psychology, 8*, 239–253.

Harper, D. C. (1991). Paradigms for investigating rehabilitation and adaptation to childhood disability and chronic illness. *Journal of Pediatric Psychology, 16*, 533–542.

Hauenstein, E. (1990). The experience of distress in parents of chronically ill children: Potential or likely outcome? *Journal of Clinical Child Psychology, 19*, 356–364.

Hauser, S. T. (1990). The study of families and chronic illness: Ways of coping and interacting. In G. Brody & I. Sigel (Eds.), *Methods of family research* (pp. 59–86). New York: Plenum Press.

Hauser, S. T., Jacobson, A. M., Lavori, P., Wolfsdorf, J. I., Herskowitz, R. D., Milley, J. E., Bliss, R., Gelfand, E., Wertlieb, D., & Stein, J. (1990). Adherence among children and adolescents with insulin-dependent diabetes mellitus over a four-year longitudinal follow-up: Immediate and long-term linkages with the family milieu. *Journal of Pediatric Psychology, 15*, 527–542.

Hauser, S. T., DiPlacido, J., Jacobson, A. M., Paul, E., Bliss, R., Milley, J., Lavori, P., Vieyra, M. A., Wolfsdorf, J. I., Herskowitz, R. D., Willett, J. B., Cole, C., & Wertlieb, D. (1993). The family and the onset of its youngster's insulin-dependent diabetes: Ways of coping. In R. E. Cole & D. Reiss, *How do families cope with chronic illness?* (pp. 25–55). Hillsdale, NJ: Lawrence Erlbaum Associates, Inc.

Hembree-Kigin, T. L., & McNeil, C. B. (1995). *Parent-Child Interaction Therapy: A step-by-step guide for clinicians.* New York: Plenum Press.

Hill, R. (1949). *Families under stress.* New York: Harper & Row.

Hill, R. (1958). Generic features of families under stress. *Social Casework, 49,* 139–150.

Hoare, P. (1984). Psychiatric disturbance in the families of epileptic children. *Developmental Medicine and Child Neurology, 26,* 14–19.

Hobbs, N., Perrin, J. M., & Ireys, H. T. (1985). *Chronically ill children and their families.* San Francisco: Jossey-Bass.

Hobfoll, S., & Lerman, M. (1988). Personal relationships, personal attributes, and stress resistance: Mothers' reactions to their child's illness. *American Journal of Community Psychology, 16,* 565–589.

Holroyd, J. (1974). The questionnaire on resources and stress: An instrument to measure family response to a handicapped member. *Journal of Community Psychology, 2,* 92–94.

House, J. S. (1981). *Work stress and social support.* Reading, MA: Addison-Wesley.

Hunter, J. E. & Schmidt, F. L. (1990). *Methods of meta-analysis.* Newbury Park: Sage Publications, Inc.

Jessop, D. J., Riessman, C. K., & Stein, R. (1988). Chronic childhood illness and maternal mental health. *Developmental and Behavioral Pediatrics, 9,* 147–156.

Johnson, S. B. (1988). Diabetes mellitus in childhood. In D. K. Routh (Ed.), *Handbook of pediatric psychology* (pp. 9–31). New York: Guilford Press.

Kanner, A. D., Coyne, J. C., Schaefer, C., & Lazarus, R. S. (1981). Comparisons of two models of stress management: Daily hassles and uplifts versus major life events. *Journal of Behavioral Medicine, 4,* 1–39.

Karoly, P. (1988). Child health assessment: Toward a biopsychosocial frame of reference. In P. Karoly (Ed.), *Handbook of child health assessment.* New York: John Wiley & Sons.

Kazak, A. E. (1987). Families with disabled children: Stress and social networks in three samples. *Journal of Abnormal Child Psychology, 15,* 137–146.

Kazak, A. E. (1989). Families of chronically ill children: A systems and social-ecological model of adaptation and challenge. *Journal of Consulting and Clinical Psychology, 57,* 25–30.

Kazak, A. E., & Marvin, R. S. (1984). Differences, difficulties and adaptation: Stress and social networks in families with a handicapped child. *Family Relations, 33,* 66–77.

Kazak, A., & Meadows, A. (1989). Families of young adolescents who have survived cancer: Social-emotional adjustment, adaptability, and social support. *Journal of Pediatric Psychology, 14,* 175–191.

Kazak, A. E., Reber, M., & Carter, A. (1988). Structural and qualitative aspects of social networks in families with young chronically ill children. *Journal of Pediatric Psychology, 13,* 171–182.

Kazak, A. E., Reber, M., & Snitzer, L. (1988). Chronic childhood disease and family functioning: A study of phenylketonuria. *Pediatrics, 81,* 224–230.

Kellerman, J., Zeltzer, L., Ellenberg, L., Dash, J., & Rigler, D. (1980). Psychological effects of illness in adolescence, I. Anxiety, self-esteem, and perception of control. *Journal of Pediatrics, 97,* 126–131.

Klein, D. (1983). Family problem solving and family stress. *Marriage and Family Review, 6,* 39–60.

Koocher, G. P., & O'Malley, J. E. (1981). *The Damocles syndrome: Psychosocial consequences of surviving childhood cancer.* New York: McGraw-Hill.

Kovacs, M. (1985). The Children's Depression Inventory (CDI). *Psychopharmacology Bulletin, 21,* 995–998.

Kronenberger, W. A., & Thompson, R. J. (1990). Dimensions of family functioning in families with chronically ill children: A higher-order factor analysis of the Family Environment Scale. *Journal of Clinical Child Psychology, 19,* 380–388.

Kronenberger, W. A., & Thompson, R. J. (1992). Psychological adaptation of mothers of children with spina bifida: Association with dimensions of social relationships. *Journal of Pediatric Psychology, 17,* 1–14.

Kupst, M. J., Schulman, J. L., Maurer, H., Honig, G., Morgan, E., & Fochtman, D. (1984). Coping with pediatric leukemia: A two-year follow-up. *Journal of Pediatric Psychology, 9,* 149–163.

La Greca, A. M. (1990). Social consequences of pediatric conditions: Fertile area for future investigation and intervention? *Journal of Pediatric Psychology, 15,* 285–307.

La Greca, A. M. (1994). Editorial: Assessment in pediatric psychology: What's a researcher to do? *Journal of Pediatric Psychology, 19,* 283–290.

La Greca, A. M. & Varni, J. W. (1993). Interventions in pediatric psychology: A look toward the future. *Journal of Pediatric Psychology, 18,* 667–680.

Lansky, S., Cairns, N. U., Hassanein, R., Wehr, J., & Lowman, J. T. (1978). Childhood cancer: Parental discord and divorce. *Pediatrics, 62,* 184–188.

Lavigne, J. V., & Faier-Routman, J. (1992). Psychological adjustment to pediatric physical disorders: A meta-analytic review. *Journal of Pediatric Psychology, 17,* 133–157.

Lazarus, R. S., DeLongis, A., Folkman, S., & Gruen, R. (1985). Stress and adaptational outcomes: The problem of confounded measures. *American Psychologist, 40,* 770–779.

Lazarus, R. S., & Folkman, S. (1984). *Stress, appraisal, and coping.* New York: Springer Publishing Company, Inc.

Lewis, J. M., Beavers, W. R., Gossett, J. T., & Phillips, V. A. (1976). *No single thread: Psychosocial health in family systems.* New York: Brunner-Mazel, Inc.

Margalit, M. (1984). Leisure activities of learning disabled children as reflection of their passive life style and prolonged dependency. *Child Psychiatry and Human Development, 15,* 133–141.

McCubbin, H., & Patterson, J. M. (1982). Family adaption to crisis. In H. McCubbin, A. Cuble, & J. Patterson (Eds.), *Family Stress, Coping and Social Support* (pp. 26–47). Springfield, IL: C. Thomas.

McHale, S. M., & Gamble, W. (1989). Sibling relationships of children with disabled and non-disabled brothers and sisters. *Developmental Psychology, 25,* 421–429.

McHale, S. M., & Pawletko, T. M. (1992). Differential treatment of siblings in two family contexts. *Child Development, 63,* 68–81.

McKeever, P. T. (1981). Fathering the chronically ill child. *American Journal of Maternal Child Nursing, 6,* 124–128.

Melamed, B. G., Siegel, L. J., & Ridley-Johnson, R. (1988). Coping behaviors in children facing medical stress. In T. M. Field, P. M. McCabe, & N. Schneiderman (Eds.), *Stress and coping across development* (pp. 109–137). New Jersey: Lawrence Erlbaum Associates, Inc.

Menaghan, E. G. (1983). Individual coping efforts and family studies: Conceptual and methodological issues. *Marriage and Family Review, 6,* 113–135.

Meyerowitz, B. E., Heinrich, R. L., & Schag, C. C. (1983). A competency-based approach to coping with cancer. In T. G. Burish & L. A. Bradley (Eds.), *Coping with chronic disease: Research and applications* (pp. 137–158). New York: Academic Press.

Minuchin, S. (1974). *Families and family therapy.* Cambridge: Harvard University Press.

Moos, R. H. & Tsu, W. D. (1977). The crisis of physical illness. In R. H. Moos (Ed.), *Coping with physical illness.* New York: Plenum Press.

Moos, R. H., & Moos, B. S. (1981). *Family Environment Scale manual.* Palo Alto, CA: Consulting Psychologists Press.

Mulhern, R. K., Fairclough, D., Douglas, S. M., & Smith, B. (1994). Physical distress and depressive symptomatology among children with cancer. *Children's Health Care, 23,* 167–179.

Newacheck, P. W., Budetti, P. P., & Halfon, N. (1986). Trends in activity-limiting chronic conditions among children. *American Journal of Public Health, 76,* 178–184.

Olson, D. H., Sprenkle, D., & Russell, C. (1979). Circumplex model of marital and family systems, I: Cohesion and adaptability dimensions, family types and clinical application. *Family Process, 18,* 3–28.

Olson, D. H., Portner, J., & Lavee, Y. (1985). FACES III: Family adaptability and cohesion evaluation scales. In D. H. Olson, H. I. McCubbin, H. Barnes, A. Larsen, M. Muxen, & M. Wilson (Eds.), *Family inventories: Inventories used in a national survey of families across the life cycle* (pp. 18–42). St. Paul, MN: Family Social Science, University of Minnesota.

Opipari, L. C. & Quittner, A. L. (1995, April). *Effects of differential treatment on sibling and peer relationships.* Paper presented at the Biennial Meeting of the Society for Research in Child Development, Indianapolis.

Patterson, J. M. (1988). Families experiencing stress. *Family Systems Medicine, 6,* 202–237.

Patterson, J. M. (1990). Family and health research in the 1980's: A family scientist's perspective. *Family Systems Medicine, 8,* 421–434.

Pearlin, L. I., & Turner, H. A. (1987). The family as a context of the stress process. In S. V. Kasl & C. L. Copper (Eds.), *Stress and health: Issues in research methodology* (pp. 143–165). New York: John Wiley & Sons.

Perrin, E. C., Stein, R. E., & Drotar, D. (1991). Cautions in using the Child Behavior Checklist: Observations based on research about children with a chronic illness. *Journal of Pediatric Psychology, 16,* 411–422.

Perrin, J. M., & MacLean, W. E. (1988). Children with chronic illness. *The Pediatric Clinics of North America, 35,* 1325–1337.

Peterson, L. (1989). Coping by children undergoing stressful medical procedures: Some conceptual, methodological, and therapeutic issues. *Journal of Consulting and Clinical Psychology, 57,* 380–387.

Phillips, S., Bohannon, W. E., Gayton, W. F., & Friedman, S. B. (1985). Parent interview findings regarding the impact of cystic fibrosis on families. *Journal of Developmental and Behavioral Pediatrics, 6,* 122–127.

Pless, I .B. & Nolan, T. (1991). Revision, replication, and neglect: Research on the maladjustment in chronic illness. *Journal of Child Psychology and Psychiatry, 32,* 347–365.

Quittner, A. L. (1989, August). *Coping with childhood seizures: A comparison of maternal and paternal perceptions of stress and adjustment.* Paper presented at the annual meeting of the American Psychological Association, New Orleans.

Quittner, A. L. (1991). Coping with a hearing impaired child: A model of adjustment to chronic stress. In J. H. Johnson & S. B. Johnson (Eds.), *Advances in Child*

Health Psychology (pp. 206–223). Gainesville, FL: University of Florida Press.

Quittner, A. L. (1992). Re-examining research on stress and social support: The importance of contextual factors. In A. M. La Greca, J. Wallander, L. Siegel, & C. Walker (Eds.), *Advances in pediatric psychology: Stress and coping with pediatric conditions* (pp. 85–115). New York: Guilford Press.

Quittner, A. L., DiGirolamo, A. M., Michel, M., & Eigen, H. (1992). Parental response to cystic fibrosis: A contextual analysis of the diagnosis phase. *Journal of Pediatric Psychology, 17*, 683–704.

Quittner, A. L., Glueckauf, R. L., & Jackson, D. N. (1990). Chronic parenting stress: Moderating vs. mediating effects of social support. *Journal of Personality and Social Psychology, 59*, 1266–1278.

Quittner, A. L., & Opipari, L. C. (1994). Differential treatment of siblings: Interview and diary analyses comparing two family contexts. *Child Development, 65*, 800–814.

Quittner, A. L., Opipari, L. C., Regoli, M. J., Jacobsen, J., & Eigen, H. (1992). The impact of caregiving and role strain on family life: Comparisons between mothers of children with cystic fibrosis and matched controls. *Rehabilitation Psychology, 37*, 289–304.

Quittner, A. L., Tolbert, V. E., Regoli, M. J., Orenstein, D., & Eigen, H. (1995). Development of the Role-Play Inventory of Situations and Coping Strategies (RISCS) for parents of children with cystic fibrosis. Manuscript submitted for publication.

Radloff, L. S. (1977). The CES-D Scale: A self-report depression scale for research in the general population. *Applied Psychological Measurement, 1*, 385–401.

Reiss, D. (1981). *The family's construction of reality*. Cambridge, MA: Harvard University Press.

Reiss, D., & Oliveri, M. E. (1980). Family paradigm and family coping: A proposal for linking the family's intrinsic adaptive capacities to its responses to stress. *Family Relations, 29*, 431–444.

Reynolds, A. L., Johnson, S. B., & Silverstein, J. (1990). Assessing daily diabetes management by 24-hour recall interview: The validity of children's reports. *Journal of Pediatric Psychology, 15*, 493–509.

Roberts, M. C., & Wallander, J. L. (1992). Family issues in pediatric psychology: An overview. In M. C. Roberts & Wallander, J. L. (Eds.), *Family issues in pediatric psychology*. Hillsdale, New Jersey: Lawrence Erlbaum Associates, Inc.

Robinson, E. A., & Anderson, L. L. (1983). Family adjustment, parental attitudes, and social desirability. *Journal of Abnormal Child Psychology, 11*, 247–256.

Rock, D. L., Fordyce, W. E., Brockway, J. A., Bergman, J. J., & Spengler, D. M. (1984). Measuring functional impairment associated with pain: Psychometric analysis of an exploratory scoring protocol for activity pattern indicators. *Archives of Physical Medicine and Rehabilitation, 65*, 295–300.

Rolland, J. S. (1984). Toward a psychosocial topology of chronic and life threatening illness. *Family Systems Medicine, 2*, 245–262.

Rolland, J. S. (1987). Chronic illness and the life cycle: A conceptual framework. *Family Process, 26*, 203–221.

Russo, D. C., & Varni, J. W. (1982). *Behavioral pediatrics: Research and practice*. New York: Plenum Press.

Rutter, M. (1977). Brain damage syndromes in childhood: Concepts and findings. *Journal of Child Psychology and Psychiatry, 18*, 1–21.

Rutter, M., Tizard, J., & Whitmore, K. (1970). *Education, health, and behavior*. London: Longman.

Sabbeth, B. F., & Stein, R. K. (1990). Mental health referral: A weak link in comprehensive care of children with chronic physical illness. *Journal of Developmental and Behavioral Pediatrics, 11*, 73–78.

Sabbeth, B. F., & Leventhal, J. M. (1984). Marital adjustment to chronic childhood illness: A critique of the literature. *Pediatrics, 73*, 762–768.

Sarason, I. G., Pierce, G. R., & Sarason, B. R. (1994). General and specific perceptions of social support. In W. R. Avison & I. H. Gotlib (Eds.), *Stress and mental health: Contemporary issues and prospects for the future* (pp. 151–178). New York: Plenum Press.

Satin, W., La Greca, A. M., Zigo, M. A., & Skyler, J. S. (1989). Diabetes in adolescence: Effects of multifamily group intervention and parent simulation of diabetes. *Journal of Pediatric Psychology, 14*, 259–277.

Shonkoff, J. P., Hauser-Cram, P., Krauss, M. W., & Upshur, C. C. (1992). Development of infants with disabilities and their families: Implications for theory and service delivery. *Monographs of the Society for Research in Child Development*, Serial No. 230.

Silverberg, E., & Lubera, J. (1987). Cancer statistics, 1987. *Ca—A Cancer Journal for Clinicians, 37*, 2–19.

Singer, L. T., Song, L., Hill, B. P., & Jaffe, A. C. (1990). Stress and depression in mothers of failure-to-thrive children. *Journal of Pediatric Psychology, 15*, 711–720.

Spanier, G. B. (1976). Measuring dyadic adjustment: New scales for assessing the quality of marriage and similar dyads. *Journal of Marriage and the Family, 38*, 15–27.

Speechley, K. N. & Noh, S. (1992). Surviving childhood cancer, social support, and parents' psychological adjustment. *Journal of Pediatric Psychology, 17*, 15–31.

Stone, A. A., Greenberg, M. A., Kennedy-Moore, E., &

Newman, M. G. (1991). *Journal of Personality and Social Psychology, 61*, 648–658.

Tavormina, J. B., Kastner, L. S., Slater, P. M., & Watt, S. L. (1976). Chronically ill children—A psychologically and emotionally deviant population? *Journal of Abnormal Child Psychology, 4*, 99–110.

Taylor, S. E., & Aspinwall, L. (1990). Psychosocial aspects of chronic illness. In P. T. Costa & G. R. VandenBos (Eds.) *Psychological aspects of serious illness: Chronic conditions, fatal diseases, and clinical care* (pp. 7–60). Washington, DC: American Psychological Association.

Tew, B., Payne, H., & Laurence, K. M. (1974). Must a family with a handicapped child be a handicapped family? *Developmental Medicine and Child Neurology, 16*, 95–98.

Thoits, P. A. (1983). Multiple identities and psychological well-being: A reformulation and test of the isolation hypothesis. *American Sociological Review, 48*, 174–187.

Thompson, R. J., Gil, K. M., Gustafson, K. E., George, L. K., Keith, B. R., Spock, A., & Kinney, T. R. (1994). Stability and change in the psychological adjustment of mothers of children and adolescents with cystic fibrosis and sickle cell disease. *Journal of Pediatric Psychology, 19*, 171–188.

Thompson, R. J., Gil, K. M., Burbach, D. J., Keith, B. R., & Kinney, T. R. (1993). Psychological adjustment of mothers of children and adolescents with sickle cell disease: The role of stress, coping methods, and family functioning. *Journal of Pediatric Psychology, 18*, 549–560.

Thompson, R. J., Gustafson, K. E., Hamlett, K. W., & Spock, A. (1992). Stress, coping, and family functioning in the psychological adjustment of mothers of children and adolescents with cystic fibrosis. *Journal of Pediatric Psychology, 17*, 573–585.

Timko, C., Stovel, K. W., & Moos, R. H. (1992). Functioning among mothers and fathers of children with juvenile rheumatic disease: A longitudinal study. *Journal of Pediatric Psychology, 17*, 705–724.

Tritt, S. G., & Esses, L. M. (1988). Psychosocial adaptation of siblings of children with chronic medical illnesses. *American Journal of Orthopsychiatry, 58*, 211–220.

Turnbull, A. P., Patterson, J. M., Behr, S. K., Murphy, D. L., Marquis, J. G., & Blue-Banning, M. J. (1993). *Cognitive coping, families, and disability.* Baltimore: Brookes Publishing.

Varni, J. W., & Wallander, J. L. (1988). Pediatric chronic disabilities: Hemophilia and spina bifida as examples. In D. K. Routh (Ed.), *Handbook of pediatric psychology* (pp. 190–221). New York: Guilford Press.

Varni, J. W., Wilcox, K. T., & Hanson, V. (1988). Mediating effects of family social support on child psychological adjustment in juvenile rheumatoid arthritis. *Health Psychology, 7*, 421–431.

Walker, A. (1985). Reconceptualizing family stress. *Journal of Marriage and the Family, 47*, 827–837.

Walker, J. G., Manion, I. G., Cloutier, P. F., & Johnson, S. M. (1992). Measuring marital distress in couples with a chronically ill children: The Dyadic Adjustment Scale. *Journal of Pediatric Psychology, 17*, 345–357.

Walker, L. S., Ford, M. B., & Donald, W. D. (1987). Cystic fibrosis and family stress: Effects of age and severity of illness. *Pediatrics, 79*, 239–245.

Walker, L. S., Ortiz-Valdez, J., & Newbrough, J. R. (1989). The role of maternal employment and depression in the psychological adjustment of chronically ill, mentally retarded, and well children. *Journal of Pediatric Psychology, 14*, 357–370.

Wallander, J. L., Pitt, L. C., & Mellins, C. A. (1990). Child functional independence and maternal psychosocial stress as risk factors threatening adaptation in mothers of physically or sensorially handicapped children. *Journal of Consulting and Clinical Psychology, 58*, 818–824.

Wallander, J. L., Varni, J. W., Babani, L., Banis, H. T., DeHaan, C. B., & Wilcox, K. T. (1989). Disability parameters, chronic strain, and adaptation of physically handicapped children and their mothers. *Journal of Pediatric Psychology, 14*, 23–42.

Welsh, M. J., Smith, A. E., Zabner, J., Rich, D. P., Graham, S. M., Gregory, K. J., Pratt, B. M., & Moscicki, R. A. (1994). Cystic fibrosis gene therapy using an adenovirus vector: In vivo safety and efficacy in nasal epithelium. *Human Gene Therapy, 5*, 209–219.

Wertlieb, D. (1993). Special section editorial: Toward a family-centered pediatric psychology—Challenge and opportunity in the international year of the family. *Journal of Pediatric Psychology, 18*, 541–547.

Wertlieb, D., Weigel, C., & Feldstein, M. (1987). Measuring children's coping. *American Journal of Orthopsychiatry, 57*, 548–560.

Wolf, L. C., Noh, S., Fisman, S. N., & Speechley, M. (1989). Brief report: Psychological effects of parenting stress on parents of autistic children. *Journal of Autism and Developmental Disorders, 19*, 157–166.

Wortman, C., & Lehman, D. (1985). Reactions to victims of life crisis: Support attempts that fail. In I. G. Sarason & B. R. Sarason (Eds.), *Social support: Theory, research, and application* (pp. 463–489). The Hague, The Netherlands: Martinus Nijhoff.

CHAPTER 5

TREATMENT ADHERENCE AND COMPLIANCE

Sharon L. Manne

INTRODUCTION

Non-adherence to pediatric medical regimens is a serious problem confronting medical professionals. Failure to adhere to prescribed medical treatments is a prevalent problem for children with both acute medical problems such as otitis media (Becker, Drachman, & Kirscht, 1972) and chronic illnesses such as diabetes (Wilson & Endres, 1986), asthma (Coutts, Gibson, & Paton, 1992), and juvenile rheumatoid arthritis (Litt & Cuskey, 1980). Estimates of pediatric non-adherence have varied, depending on the disease, the regimen, and the behavior within the regimen being studied. Figures of non-adherence reported in the literature range from a high of 98 percent (Sublett, Pollard, Kadlec, & Karibo, 1979) to a low of 5 percent (Dickey, Mattar, & Chudzik, 1975). The risk of non-compliance may be especially prevalent among children on long-term regimens. Longitudinal studies examining the risk of development of compliance problems in diabetics indicate that, at some point over the first decade of developing diabetes, about half of children will become sufficiently non-compliant to raise medical concerns (Kovacs, Goldston, Obrosky, & Iyengar, 1992). The medical, social, and financial impact of poor adherence is significant. An obvious consequence of failure to comply is that any benefits of therapy are nonexistent, and that money is wasted on medications that are not used. Other negative medical consequences resulting from non-adherence can include emergency room visits associated with non-adherence to asthma regimens (Abduelrhman & Loftus, 1993), and such serious complications as coma, blindness, amputation, and renal disease that may result from persistently negligent self-care in diabetics (Drash & Becker, 1990). Indeed, the primary reason for hospitalization for diabetic ketoacidosis among children is non-compliance (Drash, 1987). Adherence is related to morbidity as well as mortality. For example, asthma is the leading reason for school absenteeism, restricted activity, and bed days and can contribute to family financial problems (Creer, 1979; Parcel, Gilman, Nader, & Bunce, 1979).

With treatment adherence representing such a crucial pediatric health issue, research during the past two decades has focused upon assessment of adherence problems, delineation of reasons for non-compliance, as well as methods of improving compliance. Poor adherence is known to be multiply determined. In the present review, research issues in regimen adherence will be

---

Work on this chapter was supported by a FIRST Award (R29 CA57379) from the National Cancer Institute. I would like to acknowledge the assistance of Caroline Peyser, Deborah Miller, Lobina Kalam, and Amy Eisenberg in the preparation of this work.

reviewed. The first section focuses on the definition and assessment of adherence. The second section focuses on factors associated with compliance problems. Finally, research issues relevant to intervention studies targeted to improving adherence will be discussed.

Because the literature on adherence to pediatric medical regimens is large, this review of research issues will focus mainly on juvenile-onset diabetes and to a lesser extent asthma and other medical regimens. Insulin-dependent diabetes mellitus (IDDM) was chosen because this disease is widely studied with regard to compliance issues and thus knowledge in this area of compliance is most well-developed. In addition, measurement strategies of regimen adherence are more sophisticated and well-validated in this area, thus providing a better basis for the study of correlates of adherence. The diabetes regimen is life-long, highly complex, and requires a substantial degree of behavior change. Thus, it is likely to present difficulty with treatment compliance. Using diabetes as an illustration, critical research issues in treatment adherence will be reviewed.

DEFINING ADHERENCE

Compliance has been generally defined as "the extent to which a person's behavior (in terms of taking medications, following diets, or executing lifestyle changes) coincides with medical advice" (Sackett & Haynes, 1976). For patients with diabetes, traditional management of the more complex form of the disorder, insulin-dependent diabetes, requires that the child follow a complex regimen of diet, exercise, self-monitoring of blood glucose levels, and insulin adjustment and administration to balance insulin need and availability. For children with asthma, the regimen can involve avoiding activities, allergens, and other precipitants that trigger symptoms and require the use of bronchodilators and anti-inflammatory medicines.

Reliable assessment of adherence depends upon a consistent definition of the tasks that are a requirement for "good" adherence. One of the first problems encountered in the literature on adherence is the inconsistency and/or vagueness of medical regimen advice. For some aspects of the diabetic regimen such as exercise, prescriptions may never have been given or were given in a vague manner (Glasgow, Wilson, & McCaul, 1985). For example, patients are typically given general instructions from physicians rather than explicit instructions ("Exercise more and don't eat high-fat foods"). It is difficult to measure compliance when there is no standard of comparison against which the patient's regimen

behaviors can be compared. Some investigators have dealt with this problem by adopting their own standards from consensus standards set forth by organizations such as the American Diabetes Association (e.g, Freund, Johnson, Silverstein, & Thomas, 1991). Other investigators have adopted their own criteria for compliance (e.g., Kovacs et al., 1992), making comparisons across studies difficult.

A second problem with the definition of adherence is that frequently measures only assess whether or not behaviors are performed (yes/no) (Brownlee-Duffeck et al., 1987). However, occurrence/nonoccurrence is frequently not the most accurate means of assessing adherence. Rather, the critical variable associated with long-term health outcome is how *well* the patient or parent performs the desired task or the timing of the task with regard to optimal disease management. For diabetics, whether blood glucose is measured accurately and the proper adjustment in insulin is administered after testing is more important than simply knowing whether a test is performed and insulin is administered. Exercise should be timed in conjunction with insulin levels and blood glucose response to exercise should be assessed. For children with cancer, how well central access line care is performed is more important than whether or not it was performed.

A third problem encountered is that the definition of non-adherence has included behaviors that are not disease-management behaviors and can only be inferentially related to regimen adherence. For example, studies of non-compliance in hemophiliacs have included social-behavior problems and substance abuse as non-compliant behaviors since these problems might affect disease management (Weiss et al., 1991).

A second definitional issue regards the complexity of the medical regimen. Adherence in diabetes, and most other chronic illnesses, consists of a network of behaviors rather than a unidimensional behavior. Performance of diabetes regimen behaviors have consistently been shown to be independent of each other (Johnson, Silverstein, Rosenbloom, Carter, & Cunningham, 1986), and thus performance of one behavior does not necessarily indicate that another aspect of the regimen is being performed.

There are two approaches to defining adherence taken in the literature. The first approach uses global measures of adherence that categorize individuals as "good" or "poor" adherers (e.g., Grey, Genel, & Tamborlane, 1980; Jacobson et al., 1990; Kovacs, Goldston, Obrosky, & Iyengar, 1992; Fehrenbach & Peterson, 1989). There are three main problems with this approach to defining regimen adherence. First, the global approach is insensitive to the behavioral complexity of medical regimens requiring multiple disease-management behaviors, since individual regimen behaviors are not assessed. Psychological correlates of non-adherence to various aspects of the regimen may differ. Second, judgments of adherence across studies using this approach may be made on the basis of different behaviors, and thus comparability across studies is limited. Third, the arbitrary nature of cutoff scores for what constitutes "good" or "poor" adherence limits comparability across studies.

A second approach is to define adherence along a continuum and employ multicomponent measurement of disease management behaviors (e.g., Freund, Johnson, Silverstein, & Thomas, 1991). However, the behaviors measured are often combined together to derive an adherence score, so this approach is problematic for the same reasons outlined above. In addition, the behaviors chosen for study may vary with regard to their therapeutic importance (for example, foot care is probably not as crucial as timely insulin injections). By combining behaviors, this approach also overlooks the behavioral complexity of the medical regimen.

In addition to problems defining the regimen behaviors associated with adherence, many investigators have used indices of health status, typically assays of medication level, as sole indicators of regimen adherence (e.g., Christiaanse, Levine, & Lerner, 1989; Kovacs, Kass, Schnell, Goldston, & Marsh, 1989; Lustman, Griffith, Clouse, & Cryer, 1986). This practice is also extremely common among health care providers, who assume that patients are not adhering if their assays do not fall within the therapeutic range (Clarke, Snyder, & Nowacek, 1985). However, the association between regimen adherence and indices of health status, such as metabolic control in diabetes, is weak (Johnson et al., 1992). Thus, one cannot necessarily infer adherence from measures of health status, and studies defining adherence solely in these terms are problematic.

MEASURING ADHERENCE

There are two common methods used to measure adherence: assessing the performance of disease management behaviors and measuring health status outcomes.

Behavioral Observations

The most obvious measure is the observation of behavioral adherence: Is the patient performing the disease management behaviors, and how accurate is the individual's performance? This assessment strategy uses independent observers to record the performance of regimen behaviors, and thus has the advantage of not being confounded by bias. Observational methods have been used to identify skill deficits, such as ability to test glucose or insulin (Harkavy et al., 1983) or skill in administering insulin injections (Gilbert et al., 1982). With regard to naturalistic observations of regimen behaviors to examine adherence, Reynolds and colleagues (1990) observed children for three days who were participating in a diabetes camp. Insulin injections, exercise, glucose testing, and dietary behaviors were monitored. Other studies have employed parents as observers (Lowe & Lutzker, 1979). Although this strategy can result in more accurate assessment of regimen adherence, measurement reactivity may be an issue. In our own research on children with cancer, we found that when independent observers were present, children who had been rated by parents as non-compliant with hygienic mouth care were more likely to comply when being observed (Manne et al., unpublished data). This strategy is also labor intensive and impractical in many cases, because of the complexity of many chronic disease regimens and the intermittent nature of disease management tasks associated with symptom control in other conditions, such as asthma. For example, it would be difficult and time-consuming to spend 10 to 12 hours per day observing a child to determine when the child takes oral medications.

Parent or Child Reports

Parent and child reports of the performance of regimen behaviors are a common means of assessing adherence (Johnson, Tomer, Cunningham, & Henretta, 1990; Rapoff, Lindsley, & Christophersen, 1985; Wysocki, Green, & Huxtable, 1989). However, these measures have been found to be subject to reporting bias in that compliance is typically overestimated (Gordis, Markowitz, & Lilienfeld, 1969). Parent report is useful as a means of identifying extreme non-compliers since reports of non-compliance have been validated by assay measures (Gordis, Markowitz, & Lilienfeld, 1969). In addition, the timing of parent and child assessments used in most studies is also problematic: regimen adherence may differ on weekdays and weekends. Thus, multiple assessments taken during weekdays and weekends would provide a more accurate assessment. More recently, investigators in the area of juvenile diabetes have attempted to reduce reporting bias in several ways. First, parent reports have been corroborated by an additional family member, such as assessing both the child and parent, and then averaging across reports for most behaviors (Johnson et al., 1986). Results indicate that parent-child agreement is satisfactory, but less concordance was found for children under 9 years and over 15 years of age. Second, child self-report has been compared with behavioral observations of regimen behaviors to test the validity of self-report (Reynolds, Johnson, & Silverstein, 1990). This study found that children were accurate reporters of the occurrence of regimen behaviors and the type and number of units of insulin injected, but that they underestimated diet and exercise behaviors. Third, investigators have assessed specific behaviors over limited time periods (the previous 24-hour period) with the rationale that by limiting the time period assessed and by assessing specific behaviors, accuracy will improve (Johnson et al., 1986). Fourth, parent/child reports taken at multiple times of assessment have been compared with metabolic assay measures taken over the same time period (Johnson et al., 1990), finding that metabolic control was only associated with one self-report measure of adherence to regimen behaviors, calories consumed.

Self-monitoring via daily logs are another method of self-report. Children are asked to record performance of regimen behaviors such as blood glucose testing results (Wilson & Endres, 1986) or number and timing of insulin injections and glucose testing for diabetics (Glasgow, McCaul, & Schafer, 1987), and inhaler use for asthmatics (Zora, Lutz, & Tinkelman, 1989). Parents may be asked to check the child's records for accuracy (Epstein et al., 1981). Although this method can result in more accurate data than self-report ratings, diabetic patients have been known to provide inaccurate reports, including recording lower than actual blood glucose values (Mazze et al., 1984) or reporting blood glucose testing that was not actually performed (Wilson & Endres, 1986).

Physician Report

Physicians or other health care providers have provided estimates of adherence to health care regimens (Pendleton, House, & Parker, 1987; Roth & Caron, 1978). Studies have indicated that physician assessments are inaccurate and tend to overestimate actual adherence (Caron & Roth, 1968). In fact, studies have shown that pediatricians predict oral penicillin compliance with no greater than chance accuracy (Charney et al., 1967). One major reason that physician reports are inaccurate is that their perceptions are typically derived from information obtained by parents and patients and as such are subject to the same reporting bias described

above in addition to the physician's own bias. Also, health providers typically are cognizant of the patient's medication level obtained from assays and their ratings are likely to be influenced by this knowledge.

Medication Measurement and Monitoring Devices

The most commonly used medication measurement strategy is pill counts. This strategy consists of counting the number of pills remaining in a container of prescribed medication. In general, this method is more accurate than physician or patient reports (Caron & Roth, 1968). However, pill counts are subject to manipulation in multiple ways by both parent or child, including removing pills from the container but not taking them or taking the pills at an incorrect time (thus, the right number of pills is taken but they were not taken in the correct dose or at the correct time). Obtaining the pill dispenser from parents in order to make the pill counts can itself constitute a difficult compliance task. Other examples of this strategy include weighing medication canisters, which has been used for asthma inhaler regimens (Zora et al., 1989) or weighing bottles of insulin (Diehl, Bauer, & Sugarek, 1987). Meters with memory have been used to record the time, frequency and result of blood glucose tests in diabetics (Wysocki, Green, & Huxtable, 1989) and inhaler use in asthmatics (Coutts, Gibson, & Paton, 1992). These meters can assess both the timing of behaviors as well as their frequency without depending on patient report. One limitation of such methods is that other important aspects of treatment regimens such as diet or hygienic care are not appropriate for this strategy.

Health Status Outcome

Drug assays are considered the most objective measure of compliance with medications and are the most common method of measuring health status outcome. Assays typically involve collection of blood, urine, or saliva samples and measurement of the presence or concentration of the drug of interest. Such tests are usually conducted on one randomly selected occasion over the course of a short-term regimen or several occasions for long-term regimens. For example, the presence of penicillin prescribed for a short-term regimen can be detected in urine. For patients with asthma, this consists of blood assay or saliva sample of theophylline level, or the addition of a tracer substance to theophylline capsules and urine testing (Dubbert, King, Rapp, Brief, Martin, & Lake, 1985). For cancer, this may consist of blood assay of prednisone level for children prescribed steroids. For most chronic disease regimens, there is no "gold standard" assay measures of compliance. However, in diabetes research, blood assays of average blood glucose measures over the past two or three months, a glycosylated hemoglobin assay, is the "gold standard" used in adherence studies. To a lesser extent, fasting triglycerides and total cholesterol levels, which are used as indices of lipid metabolism, are also employed (Glasgow, August, & Hung, 1981; Johnson et al., 1990). Some investigators have included a measure of albumin excretion rate, which is considered suggestive of early diabetic neuropathy (Wysocki, Hough, Ward, & Green, 1992).

There are several problems with assay measures. First, reliability of assay measures can be influenced by variability in absorption and metabolism of the drug, and by other factors such as stress. For example, in children with cancer, the bioavailability of orally administered chemotherapy agents such as mercaptopurine, thioguanine, and leucovorin, has been shown to be variable (Koren, Solh, Klein, Soldin, & Greenberg, 1989; Lennard & Lilleyman, 1989). A similar problem has been noted for absorption of Theodur when taken with food (Pedersen & Moller-Peterson, 1984). Multiple assessments of drug level at consistent times during each day are recommended. Second, many assays only measure whether the patient is taking the medication (yes/no), not whether they took the complete dose of the medication (Spector, 1985), or took the medication at the appropriate time. Third, assays typically measure the level of the medication for a short period, and thus are not representative of adherence over longer time periods. This issue is particularly critical when patients know the assay will be taken and may alter their regimen behavior to increase compliance to the medication being assessed. Fourth, in diabetes, a critical aspect of desirable adherence is to maintain blood levels in the normal range and avoid hypoglycemic episodes. The glycosylated hemoglobin assay does not assess blood glucose variability, the number of hypoglycemic episodes in the past several months, or the amount of time blood glucose levels were actually in the normal range (Johnson, 1994). Fifth, the timing of assays is critical. The common practice of administering blood assays just prior to or after monthly clinic appointments may positively bias adherence, particularly when patients realize that the assay measure will be taken at this time. Sixth, assays can only measure drug level over a limited period of time because of rapid excretion of the drug from the patient's system. A final problem is that many aspects of medical regimens cannot be assessed by drug assays. Some examples are exercise prescriptions for juvenile diabetics and children with arthritis and central access line care and mouth care for cancer patients.

One issue that complicates the use of assay measures and behavioral adherence is the low correspondence that has been found between these measures. This problem is evident in the diabetes literature, as glycosylated hemoglobin and adherence have not been correlated. Possible reasons for this lack of association are unreliability of self-report measures of adherence, the influence of biological changes in adolescents that obscure the relationship, and the possibility that adherence behaviors are more strongly associated with blood glucose variability than with average glucose levels. Johnson and colleagues (1990) have suggested that some of the problem may be due to inappropriate insulin dose prescriptions; children may be adherent, but overdoses or underdoses may result in problems with metabolic control. They found that more consistent relationships were found with another direct measure, triglyceride levels.

Other health status outcomes can be used as indicators of adherence. Examples include peak flow monitors for asthma that measure the highest amount of air exhaled (Weinstein & Cuskey, 1985), frequency and continuity of patient's use of health care services (Wysocki, Hough, Ward, & Green, 1992), frequency of asthma attacks and emergency room visits for asthmatics, weight loss to assess adherence to diet regimens, and number of school days missed due to illness. Such outcomes may provide unreliable assessments of adherence to regimens because individual differences may influence disease outcome (e.g., metabolism influences weight loss and thus may not reflect dietary compliance; child misses school due to parent physical or emotional problems). In addition, many of the critical health outcomes associated with non-adherence are typically associated with long-term adherence problems and are therefore difficult and costly to undertake.

Summary

In summary, measurement of treatment adherence is a complex issue. Most regimens consist of multiple tasks rather than a single adherence behavior. Few "gold standards" for measurement exist, although a more valid assessment occurs when multiple methods are used. Behavioral observations are preferable, in combination with a measure of permanent product such as a blood assay of medication level. Assessments should include multiple times of assessment and target specific disease-management behaviors assessed over a limited and recent time period (e.g., 24-hour recall interview used by Johnson et al., 1986). However, the correspondence among adherence behaviors and assay measures is weak, at least among juvenile diabetics, making it difficult to determine which is the most "valid" assessment of adherence. Little work has been done on valid and reliable assessment methodologies for treatment regimens other than diabetes, and more attention needs to be given to the development of reliable and valid methods for measuring compliance to asthma, juvenile rheumatoid arthritis, cancer, and other disease regimens.

FACTORS ASSOCIATED WITH TREATMENT ADHERENCE

Multiple psychological, demographic, and medical factors have been examined for their relation to treatment adherence. These factors can be grouped into one of six categories: (a) regimen and illness characteristics, (b) demographic characteristics, (c) psychological correlates, (d) health belief model, (e) behavioral contingencies, and (f) physician and patient/physician relationship characteristics. Initial research efforts focused on sociodemographic characteristics that might predict treatment adherence. However, more recent research has shifted away from this focus toward process variables such as developmental status and the role of the family.

REGIMEN AND ILLNESS CHARACTERISTICS

Complexity of the medical regimen is generally believed to be associated with lower adherence rates. For example, medical regimens for juvenile diabetes and asthma include multiple medications taken at odd times, dietary and/or exercise changes (diabetes), limitations in daily activities (asthma), and blood testing or injections. These are typically more difficult to adhere to than less complex regimens for acute illnesses. For example, the complex dietary prescriptions are particularly difficult for diabetic children and their parents to remember, thereby contributing to adherence problems (Delamater, Smith, Kurtz, & White, 1986). More complicated delivery of medication has been associated with nonadherence. For example, lower levels of adherence have been found when medication for asthma is prescribed as metered-dose aerosol than as a nebulized solution (Smith et al., 1984). Regimen behaviors requiring technical skill also lead to greater non-compliance (although compliance is inadvertent). For example, errors with regard to accurate reading of blood glucose tests (Delamater et al., 1989) and performance of injections (Gonder-Frederick et al., 1988; Harkavy et al., 1983) occur. Parent difficulty with venipuncture and sterile techniques interfere with compliance to factor replacement therapy for children with hemophilia (Sergis-Deavenport & Varni, 1982). Frequency of administration of medication is correlated with poor compliance and improved compliance has been noted when patients are required to use medications less frequently (Tinkelman, Vanderpool, Carroll, Page, & Spangler, 1980). Prescription of more than one medication and multiple doses of medication have been associated with higher non-compliance (Porter, 1969), although Tebbi and colleagues (1986) did not find a significant relationship between compliance to oral medications given to pediatric cancer patients and the number of medications prescribed. Medication recommendations and blood glucose testing are followed more closely than lifestyle changes such as exercise and diet (Glasgow et al., 1987). The association between complexity and compliance by comparing several disease regimens (rating complexity for each disease regimen) has not been investigated.

Disease or regimen characteristics that have been associated with compliance problems include chronicity of the disease or the duration of therapy, the effectiveness of treatment, the severity of side effects from medications, and the intermittent nature of symptomatology. Diabetes is an example of a life-long treatment regimen. Results have indicated that adherence is best at diagnosis (although newly diagnosed patients produce some of their own insulin), and declines over the first year following diagnosis (Jacobson et al., 1987). A longitudinal study by Kovacs and colleagues (1992) suggests that three to four years after diagnosis is a high-risk period for development of adherence problems, although this period of time since disease onset is confounded by the fact that it corresponds with adolescence. Adherence consistently declines over the adolescent years; this finding occurs in diabetes as well as other disease regimens (Kovacs, Goldston, Obrosky, & Iyengar, 1992).

Recent evidence suggests that changes in adherence over time may vary according to the aspect of the disease regimen examined. Johnson and colleagues (1992) assessed diabetics at two timepoints separated by an average of 1.65 years. Injection exhibited the most consistency, with testing frequency, exercise, and diet type exhibiting moderate consistency, and calories consumed exhibiting the lowest across time stability. These results suggest that children on long-term regimens are not extremely consistent in their disease management.

However, compliance with acute problems can also be problematic. Boyd, Covington, Stanaszek, and Coussons (1974) found that patients on acute care regimens prematurely discontinued medications, presumably because symptoms improved.

Perceived effectiveness of the regimen and negative side effects of regimens have also been studied for their association with treatment adherence. Regimens with inconsistent treatment efficacy have been associated with poor adherence. For example, Becker et al. (1978) found that inconsistent effects of theophylline on asthma symptoms were linked with poor adherence. In a related study, Smith, Seale, Lea, Shaw, and Bracs (1986) found that parent doubts about the necessity and safety of medications for asthma were associated with non-adherence. Effectiveness of medications is a particular problem for asthmatics, as a patient may faithfully comply with self-management and still experience attacks (Creer, Wigal, Kotses, & Lewis, 1990).

Regimens that are associated with extremely severe side effects and functional limitations, such as steroid and other oral chemotherapy agents administered to children with cancer, have been shown to be related to problems in treatment compliance (Korsch, Fine, & Negrete, 1978). However, when perception of side effects is more formally assessed (rather than inferred as a reason for non-compliance), inconsistent results are found. For example, Tebbi et al. (1986) did not find that the presence of side effects was associated with compliance problems among children with cancer. In contrast, Manne et al. (1994) found that parent ratings of the severity of treatment side effects and degree of functional limitation was implicated in greater problems in adherence. Because of the difficulty devising a means of comparing disease regimens, studies have not compared several illness regimens to determine whether those involving more severe side effects are associated with compliance problems.

Compliance with medical regimens in which the disease has intermittent periods of symptoms or a gradual course of disability, or variability in symptom severity, such as asthma or chronic bronchitis, may also lead to non-compliance. Children may be less likely to take medication during periods in which they experience few or no symptoms (Creer, 1979).

Demographic Characteristics

Age

The demographic characteristic most commonly associated with treatment adherence is age of the child, which is usually used to assess developmental level. In children with IDDM and asthma, increasing age, particularly adolescence, has been associated with poorer compliance (Christiaanse et al., 1989; Kovacs, Goldston, Obrosky, & Iyengar, 1993; Miller, 1982). Compared with young children, 16- to 19-year-old diabetics administer their injections at less regular times, exercise less frequently, eat too few carbohydrates and too many fats, eat less frequently, and test their glucose levels less often (Delamater et al., 1989; Johnson et al., 1990). However, studies have shown that young diabetics (6 to 8 years) have technical skill deficits such as ability to perform insulin injections and accuracy in glucose testing (Johnson et al., 1982), probably because they have not yet developed the necessary motor skills. Findings from the literature on compliance to other medical regimens such as cancer treatment and renal transplant are conflicting. While some studies indicate that adolescents exhibit more compliance problems than pre-adolescents (Korsch et al., 1978; Smith et al., 1979; Tebbi et al., 1986), other studies have found that very young children have more problems with administration of oral medications (Phipps & DeCuir-Whalley, 1990) or that there are no differences between young children and adolescents (Manne, Lesanics, Meyers, & Redd, 1994). These findings suggest that age differences may vary depending on the treatment regimen under investigation.

Age impacts treatment compliance in several ways. First, age is an indicator of cognitive abilities, generally labelled "developmental status," or the child's ability to comprehend information and perform the required tasks. Older children have developed the cognitive ability to understand their disease in a more complex fashion. For example, adolescents possess higher levels of knowledge about diabetes management (Johnson et al., 1982) and also have been shown to learn more about diabetes management when participating in instructional programs (Harkavy et al., 1983); disease duration has been controlled for in these studies. Studies have shown that 8- to 9-year-old diabetics taught to self-inject insulin were more accurate than were 6 to 7 year olds (Gilbert et al., 1982). Thus, problems with adherence to some aspects of the regimen may reflect developmental abilities to perform the regimen task, but only if the child is responsible for performing the task without parental assistance. One aspect of developmental status is awareness of bodily cues. Adolescents, in comparison to adults, may be less aware of bodily symptoms that indicate the need to take regimen actions. A recent study found that adolescent diabetics are less aware of which symptoms predict hypo- or hyperglycemia than adults (Nurick & Bennett-Johnson, 1991).

Second, age is a reflection of the social-developmental issues typically faced by the child. For adolescents, the need for greater independence may lead to compliance problems, in that the lower level of parental involvement in accomplishing regimen tasks may lead to lower compliance. Reduced parental supervision and need for peer inclusion may be associated with adolescent non-compliance. Another example of developmental issues is the greater attention to physical appearance associated with adolescence. For example, cosmetic side effects from steroids may lead to greater non-compliance to steroids in adolescents with cancer.

Third, the biological changes associated with age may explain some of the lack of correspondence between regimen non-adherence and health outcome measures, at least among diabetics. Adolescents with diabetes exhibit poorer metabolic control (Amiel, Sherwin, Simonson, Lauritano, & Tamborlane, 1986). Although investigators usually attribute this finding to reduced compliance among adolescents, recent findings by Johnson et al. (1992) suggest otherwise. In their study, age remained a predictor of diabetes control even when adherence was placed into a regression model predicting metabolic control, suggesting that some other factor associated with age plays a role in contributing to metabolic control (e.g., biological changes associated with puberty such as increased insulin resistance).

Gender

Findings with regard to gender differences across medical regimens have been inconsistent. While some studies have not documented gender differences (Jacobson et al., 1987; Tebbi et al., 1986; Weinstein & Cuskey, 1985), research in diabetes has shown that girls are more compliant than boys with certain aspects of the diabetes medical regimen, including diet (Lorenz, Christensen, & Pichert, 1985) and accurate urine testing (Harkavy et al., 1983), but that boys are more compliant than girls on injection regularity and exercise frequency (Johnson, Freund, Silverstein, Hansen, & Malone, 1990). Other studies have documented gender differences in metabolic control; boys evidenced better control in a study by Kaar and colleagues (1984). As with age, gender differences may vary across regimen behavior and also with developmental status (e.g., younger boys may exercise more than younger girls, but this difference in regimen behaviors may disappear with age).

Socioeconomic Status and Race

Although many clinicians identify treatment cost and family socioeconomic status as reasons for difficulty in treatment compliance, relatively little is known regarding the empirical relationships between these factors and compliance. Overall, few racial status differences have been found. Race has been associated with theophylline compliance in one study of asthmatics (Christiaanse et al., 1989) but not another (Weinstein & Cuskey, 1985). Obviously, more would be learned by examining correlates of racial status that may account for race differences (e.g., cultural differences in dietary practices, income, metabolic differences). In a study of adults enrolled in a number of medical regimens, Brand et al. (1977) found that self-reported "non-compliers" to medication were from a lower income bracket and that they reported that the cost of the drugs was a barrier to compliance. Again, as with race, studies would most benefit by examining correlates associated with socioeconomic status (e.g., less parent assistance with provision of medical care, parent job difficulties interfering with attendance to clinic appointments for pediatric cancer patients) which might account for the relationship between income and compliance.

Psychological Factors

Individual Factors

Response to Stress. Life stress could influence treatment compliance and health status outcome in all treatment regimens by making it difficult for the child to comply with the demands of the medical regimen. However, the role of stress has only been studied in diabetes. In patients with diabetes, stress might produce disturbances in metabolic control in two ways. First, stress may increase blood glucose secondary to stress hormone release, which is hypothesized to be greater in diabetics because there is little endogenous insulin to offset increased blood glucose. Second, emotional and behavioral stress may interfere with diabetes self-care, which then disrupts metabolic control. The evidence supporting the role of stress in diabetes is equivocal. Studies using experimental stressors have reported inconsistent findings, including the predicted hypergylcemic response (Goetsch, Van Dorsten, Pbert, Ullrich, & Yates, 1987; Goetsch, Wiebe, Veltum, & Van Dorsten, 1990), decreases (Vandenburgh, Sussman, & Titus, 1966), or even no effect (Gilbert, Johnson, Silverstein, & Malone, 1989). Within individuals, the effects of experimental stress appear to be consistent (Gonder-Frederick, Carter, Cox, & Clarke, 1990). These studies are limited by methodological problems such as not controlling for time since the last meal or for last insulin injection. The association between major life event stress and blood glucose has been more consistent. Increased cumulative life stress has been shown to be associated with elevated glycosylated hemoglobin (Barglow, Hatcher, Edidin, & Sloan-Rossiter, 1985; Cox et al., 1984; Wysocki, Hough, Ward, & Green, 1992). There is some evidence that fluctuations in life stress are associated with elevated blood glucose response, at least for some individuals (Halford, Cuddihy, & Mortimer, 1990). A study by Gonder-Frederick et al. (1990) suggests that metabolic state prior to the stress, such as blood glucose and insulin levels, can mediate the diabetic stress response. Recently, a test of the direct versus indirect effect of stress upon blood glucose was conducted by Aikens et al. (1992). Using path analyses, the investigators found evidence to support the direct effect; while variability in daily stress was related to future poor metabolic control, there was no evidence of an indirect effect via regimen adherence. Variability was a more important predictor than average, or "chronic" stress. Hanson and colleagues' (1987b) results were consistent with these data; in their study, the link between stress (total amount, not variability) and metabolic control was not mediated by adolescents' adherence behaviors. The study of stress and metabolic control among adolescents is complicated by the fact that hormonal changes over the adolescent years may influence metabolic indices. The relationship between child stress and adherence to other pediatric medical regimens has not been examined.

Symptom Perception and Self-Regulation. Measurement of symptom perceptions is a critical issue among individuals with chronic diseases. People with chronic illnesses construct representations of their disease and beliefs about certain symptoms that indicate that they must engage in regimen behaviors. For children, these symptom perceptions are formed not only by the child but also by the parent. For example, diabetics believe that certain symptoms indicate that their blood glucose levels are low and act on these perceptions to take actions to raise blood glucose, without testing blood glucose through objective glucometer testing procedures (Gonder-Frederick & Cox, 1986). Although this is not an accurate method of disease management, this method of regimen maintenance is quite common among adolescents and adults and therefore understanding how such decisions are made is critical. Since people vary widely in their ability to accurately estimate blood glucose fluctuations based upon symptoms they believe are indicative of blood glucose elevations or decrements (Gonder-Frederick, Snyder, & Clarke, 1991), treatment errors can result when glucose testing is not conducted to validate perceptions.

Wiebe, Alderfer, Palmer, Lindsay, and Jarrett (1994) examined the role of symptom beliefs in estimation of blood glucose levels and actual glucose levels in adolescents with IDDM. They assessed the role of negative affect (trait anxiety) and attentional focus (internal or external focus) in the self-regulation process. It was hypothesized that people who experienced anxiety would be more internally focused, and thus would more readily detect fluctuations in bodily states. People with low internal focus were predicted to have low accuracy in blood glucose perceptions, whereas subjects with high anxiety would be inaccurate because they overinterpreted non-diabetes related symptoms. Thirty-five adolescents with IDDM completed measures of symptom beliefs, diabetes-specific attentional focus (internal focus would consist of attending to mood and physical symptoms, external focus would consist of recent food intake and last blood glucose reading), and then completed monitoring forms of symptom occurrence (e.g., dry eyes), estimated their blood glucose, and then measured their actual blood glucose level three times daily for two weeks. Metabolic control was also assessed. Results indicated that increased attention to internal cues was associated with greater accuracy in detecting meaningful blood glucose symptoms. Subjects with higher trait anxiety tended to misattribute non-diabetes-related symptoms to blood glucose fluctuations. However, in contrast to predictions, accuracy in blood glucose symptom perception (symptoms which are actually indicative of fluctuations) was not associated with improved blood glucose estimation. However, subjects who both focused on symptoms and experienced high trait anxiety displayed poorer blood glucose control.

These results indicate that diabetics' internal focus and anxiety play a role in symptom perception, but that symptom perception accuracy did not play a role in accuracy in estimation of blood glucose. Rather, both variables appeared to have a direct effect upon metabolic control. This study only begins to elucidate the complex processes whereby self-regulation is conducted. Little attention has been paid to how children and parents make regimen decisions based upon disease symptoms. In diabetes, symptom perception can be validated by measures of blood glucose level, and thus patients can be trained not to rely as much upon symptom perception to make treatment decisions. However, asthmatics do not have a readily available assessment tool and must depend upon symptom monitoring. Thus, studies of self-regulatory processes associated with other chronic diseases such as asthma will be important in understanding how errors in disease management are made.

Self-Efficacy, Temperament, Psychological Problems, and Coping. A number of psychological characteristics have been investigated for their relation to adherence.

These characteristics have fallen into two categories: illness-related and general dispositional characteristics. Few studies have employed disease-related measures. Using a cross-sectional design, Grossman et al. (1987) examined the role of self-efficacy for diabetes, measured as perceptions of personal ability in diabetes situations (e.g., "Figure out my own meals and snacks at home"), in adolescents participating in diabetes summer camp. They found that disease self-efficacy was associated with lower average blood glucose levels (taken from levels recorded in medical charts). McCaul et al. (1987) examined the role of diabetes self-efficacy, assessing separate disease regimen behaviors (insulin, glucose testing, diet, and exercise), as well as measuring two aspects of self-efficacy, expectation that one can perform the behavior and expectation that the behavior would result in positive outcomes, for each regimen behavior. Results supported the role of both aspects of self-efficacy in both concurrent and prospective (6 month) adherence behaviors.

Kuttner, Delamater, and Santiago (1990) studied the relationship between general learned helplessness (not disease-specific), assessed by the Children's Attributional Style Questionnaire, along with level of depressive symptomatology, in metabolic control (three measures over the prior year) and regimen adherence among 10- to 16-year-old children with IDDM. Although learned helplessness and depressive symptoms were not related to regimen adherence, learned helplessness was associated with poorer metabolic control over the prior year (but not with current metabolic control). The mechanism for the relationship between learned helplessness and metabolic control is difficult to entangle. Certainly, learned helplessness could be a response to poor metabolic control, or vice versa. Regimen adherence did not appear to mediate the relationship between the two variables. The authors hypothesized that learned helplessness may be associated with increased stress, which in turn impacts directly upon metabolic control.

The association of temperament to diabetes adherence was examined by Garrison et al. (1990). Using discriminant function analyses, "good" compliers were discriminated from "poor" compliers. Poor compliers were characterized by low attention span, higher general activity level, higher sleep activity level, and lower rhythmicity. Although these findings are intriguing, a rationale for how temperament influences compliance behaviors was not presented.

A number of studies have examined the role of emotional or psychological problems in diabetic treatment adherence and have typically found an association, although most studies have examined metabolic control as the outcome variable rather than regimen adherence. Studies have defined psychological problems in different ways, with measures ranging from self-esteem, behavioral problems, or informal interviews to the formal diagnosis of a psychiatric disorder. Anderson and colleagues (1981) found that well-controlled adolescent diabetics scored higher on total self-concept and on subscales measuring personal happiness and satisfaction, while more poorly-controlled adolescents reported more anxiety. Simonds (1977) also found that diabetic children in poor control (as rated by physician) had more anxiety and depression than a non-diabetic comparison group and had more interpersonal conflicts as assessed by an interview than patients in good control. However, the number of psychiatric diagnoses was not significantly different. Grey et al. (1980) divided 20 children into "maladjusted" and "adjusted" groups using data from a parent interview, and found that maladjusted children had significantly greater 24-hour urinary glucose excretion. In contrast to these studies, Simonds and colleagues' later work (1981) did not find significant associations between blood glucose regulation and self-esteem, anxiety, and locus of control, and did not find evidence of an association.

Findings regarding the role of child psychological adjustment and asthma adherence have been mixed. Christiaanse et al. (1989) found that high levels of child behavior problems, as measured by the Child Behavior Checklist, were associated with non-adherent mean theophylline levels. This variable interacted with family conflict to predict compliance (see Family Factors).

These studies are limited by their cross-sectional methodology; it cannot be determined if, for example, children develop emotional problems in response to a history of poor metabolic control, or if emotional problems impact regimen adherence and/or metabolic control. Because several studies have found that disease outcome is affected while regimen adherence is not, the mechanisms for such processes need to be examined using longitudinal methods.

Several studies have used longitudinal designs to address these questions. Jacobson et al. (1987, 1990) examined child psychological adjustment (defined as a composite of behavior problems, self-esteem, and competence) and three measures of "coping" (locus of control, ego defense mechanisms, and adaptive strength) for their association with health care provider ratings of performance of dietary, metabolic monitoring, and insulin use behaviors among children with IDDM. Locus of control was assessed using a standardized scale, and the other two concepts were rated from interview transcriptions. Psychological measures were administered at the initial assessment and adherence data obtained at the initial assessment, two 9-month follow-ups (Jacobson et al., 1987), and three yearly follow-ups (Jacobson et al., 1990). Results indicated that, after partialling out the effects of age, children with better initial adjustment, more mature defenses, and exhibiting greater adaptive capacity were more likely to remain adherent over the four-year time period. In addition, children with a higher internal locus of control exhibited greater average adherence over the four-year period. Finally, Kovacs et al. (1992) studied a sample of diabetic children for 9 years, to determine the role of self-esteem and psychiatric status in the development of severe non-compliance. Psychiatric status was determined by structured interview, and yearly interviews regarding regimen adherence, rehospitalizations, and metabolic control formed the measure of non-compliance. Although psychiatric status at disease onset was not a risk factor for later non-compliance, later psychiatric disorder was associated with non-compliance. Given the approach to data analyses, directionality between these two variables could not be ascertained.

Hanson, Cigrang et al. (1989) examined the role of coping strategies (categorized into two factors, developing support resources and ventilate feelings/avoidance) in both adherence behaviors and metabolic control among adolescents with IDDM. Results indicated that the use of ventilation and avoidance coping style were negatively related to adherence behaviors, whereas using personal and interpersonal resources (seek support, seek diversions) was not associated with adherence behaviors. Neither coping factor was associated with metabolic control. The authors hypothesize that the use of avoidance coping may lead to minimization and denial of regimen behaviors and use of ventilation may lead to externalizing behavior, which may result in not taking responsibility for adherence behaviors. Although the authors argue that general coping styles may interfere with disease-specific coping (i.e., avoidance by sleeping will lead to lack of exercise), by not assessing disease-specific coping the explanation was not tested. McCaul et al. (1987) measured diabetes-related social skills in adolescents with IDDM by asking subjects how they would respond to situations in which there was social pressure not to adhere to some aspect of the regimen. Their results indicated that social skills were significantly associated with insulin injection, diet, and exercise.

Investigators have proposed that individual psychological characteristics that influence health outcomes in individuals with disease may mediate the link between life stress and metabolic control. Hanson and colleagues (Hanson, Henggeler, & Burghen, 1987a) examined the role of social competence in treatment adherence among adolescents with IDDM. They hypothesized that social competence (along with parental support, which will be discussed later) mediated the negative link between life stress and metabolic control. Using the Perceived Competence Scale for Children and the Social Competence Scale of the Child Behavior Checklist (Achenbach & Edelbrock, 1983), they found that the negative association between stress and metabolic control was significantly buffered by social competence. Under conditions of high stress, adolescents with low social competence had relatively poor metabolic control. In contrast, high levels of stress were not linked with poor metabolic control among adolescents with high social competence. The authors suggest that adolescents with a strong sense of competence are able to cope more effectively in times of stress, although disease-specific coping was not assessed. Aikens et al. (1992) took a similar approach to their examination of the role of individual differences in determining metabolic stress response. They studied "learned resourcefulness," defined by the authors as a "set of behavioral and cognitive skills used to self-regulate internal responses that interfere with behavior including using thoughts to control emotion, applying problem solving strategies, delaying gratification, and self-regulating internal events." Learned resourcefulness was proposed to modify how individuals respond to stress, by modifying stress's effect upon both regimen adherence and metabolic control. Results failed to confirm the model and were in the opposite direction than hypothesized, indicating that learned resourcefulness was directly and positively associated with poorer metabolic control.

Overall, studies suggest that individual psychological variables are associated with adherence to regimens, although more recent evidence suggests that emotional/behavioral problems may play a stronger role in extreme cases of non-compliance, and that some psychological characteristics may mediate the relationship between stress and disease outcome. It appears that, at least among diabetics, individual psychological factors may impact directly upon metabolic control or may function as a mediator between stress and metabolic control rather than influencing metabolic control through the performance of adherence behaviors. Three major problems exist in this literature. First, no conceptual model has been put forth that explains how individual differences might result in compliance problems. Second, many similar characteristics are being assessed across studies, using different instruments and being given different labels. For example, self-efficacy, coping resources and learned resourcefulness may be tapping a similar construct. If investigators were more clear with regard to the concepts being assessed, conclusions based on the results of studies would be more generalizable. Third, findings supporting a mediating role for individual factors between stress and compliance suggest that future research might benefit by examining the mediational influence of individual differences.

Family Factors

The role of parent and family has been the most widely investigated topic with regard to psychological correlates of pediatric treatment adherence, at least in the diabetic population. There is no question that the family plays an important role in management of a child's illness, both psychologically and practically. For young children, parents carry the primary responsibility for the child's medical care. For both young children and adolescents and their families, the pervasive nature of the demands of disease management can drastically alter a family's routine functioning, and the child's compliance requires the cooperation of the whole family. Thus, how the parent and family handle the child and the changes imposed by an illness can impact treatment adherence.

Three approaches have been taken in assessing the role of the family in treatment adherence. First, the role of general family functioning, marital functioning, and parent-child conflict has been examined. The second approach is more disease-specific; family support for disease management behaviors has been investigated. These two approaches will be reviewed separately. Third, the role of parent factors, including parenting stress, problem-solving skills and parenting skills have been explored. The first two areas have focused upon adolescents, as adolescents are generally more responsible for their care and parent-child conflict may influence treatment adherence. The third area has focused on parents of younger children.

The most consistent finding is that family conflict is associated with poor diabetic control. In some research, family functioning has been found to be related to metabolic control, but the most consistent associations have been with adherence behaviors. As outlined by Anderson and Auslander (1980), early studies of family functioning were characterized by a number of methodological problems. These problems include use of subjective judgments of clinicians based on family interviews to measure family functioning, rather than more objective questionnaires or ratings by observers (Koski, Ahlas, & Kumento, 1976; Quint, 1970), lack of

independent assessments of family and health variables (judgments of metabolic control and family functioning are made by the same individual), behavioral adherence and metabolic control are not differentiated, studies were conducted when the measures of metabolic control were less reliable, and finally, the diabetic child's view of family functioning was not taken into account.

Baker, Minuchin, and colleagues (Baker, Minuchin, Milman, Liebman, & Todd, 1975; Minuchin, Rosman, & Baker, 1978; Minuchin et al., 1975) were among the first investigators to more rigorously study family interactions using observational measures of standard family tasks. They identified a group of "psychosomatic" children who were adherent to the medical regimen but continued to have episodes of ketoacidosis. Several interaction patterns were identified that characterized this group of children: (1) psychological overinvolvement or enmeshment between family members, (2) overprotective concern, (3) rigid family interaction patterns, and (4) lack of effective means to resolve family conflicts. After families were taught more flexible strategies for solving conflicts, the ketoacidosis episodes were reduced. Although these children represent an extremely small sample of diabetic children, the concepts are difficult to measure objectively, and the results have not been replicated, the model introduced by Minuchin has had a major influence upon how the family's role is conceptualized by many clinicians and researchers working with children with adherence problems.

Two groups of researchers have measured family functioning using more objective measures, and findings have differed depending upon whether metabolic control or adherence to treatment is being examined. Overall, when the outcome measure is metabolic control, findings are more inconsistent. Anderson et al. (1981) used the Moos Family Environment Scale, administering the scale to both parent and child. Children were categorized into four categories of metabolic control. Results indicated that the child's perception of family cohesion and conflict was associated with diabetic control. Well-controlled adolescents described their families as more supportive and cohesive and less conflictual. These results contradict Minuchin's hypothesis that poor metabolic control is associated with high family cohesion (enmeshment). Parent perceptions of family environment were not associated with metabolic control. In a later study of the role of family environment in metabolic control, the same group of investigators found that maternal perceptions of higher cohesion were associated with better metabolic control but family conflict was not associated with metabolic control (Auslander, Anderson, Bubb, Jung, & Santiago, 1990). Conflicting findings were reported by Schafer, Glasgow, McCaul, and Dreher (1983) who did not find that adolescent ratings of general family functioning as measured by the FES were associated with metabolic control. Hanson, Henggeler, and colleagues (1989) used a different family environment scale, the Family Adaptability and Cohesion Scale, as well as including assessment of marital functioning. Results indicated that good metabolic control was associated with high marital satisfaction and family flexibility (the mean of parent and adolescent ratings was employed for family functioning measure), and marginally associated with family cohesion. The association between family flexibility and control support Minuchin's theory, but the results contrast with Minuchin's findings that family enmeshment is related to poor metabolic control. One interesting set of findings concerned the role of disease duration. Relationships between marital satisfaction, family functioning, and metabolic control were mediated by disease duration. Under conditions of short disease duration, low marital satisfaction was associated with poor metabolic control. Disease duration had similar mediating effects for family rigidity and cohesion. Effects remained the same when child age was taken into account (since age and disease duration are correlated). These findings suggest that family relations may be more strongly linked with metabolic control for children with shorter disease duration.

Longitudinal studies examining the predictive effect of family functioning on metabolic control have also been conducted. One study followed newly diagnosed children with IDDM for six years, measuring both the family functioning variable and glycosylated hemoglobin. Two sets of analyses were conducted: (1) determining family variables assessed at one point in time predicting metabolic control three to four months later, and (2) examining whether family factors and metabolic control covary over the six-year period of time in a meaningful manner. Both sets of analyses failed to reveal an association between family functioning or marital problems and metabolic control. However, the findings are difficult to interpret because the time between assessments varied across subjects and the number of assessments for each varied across subjects. To adjust for these problems, random intercepts regression analysis was used, a unique statistical approach which resulted in data that were difficult to interpret (Kovacs, Kass, Schnell, Goldston, & Marsh, 1989).

Although overall measures of family functioning have not been highly correlated with adherence behavior in cross-sectional studies (Schafer et al., 1983), a four-year longitudinal study indicated that both parent

and adolescent perceptions of increased family support (cohesion) and parent perceptions of family organization at the initial assessment were associated with physician-rated performance of adherence behaviors one year later and average adherence over the next three years. The adolescent's rating of family conflict was strongly related to both one-year and long-term adherence, and parent perceptions of conflict were associated with one-year adherence (Hauser et al., 1990).

Characteristics of the parent-adolescent relationship, rather than the general family environment, has been the focus of several investigations. Parent-child conflict has been examined in more detail in two studies. Bobrow, AvRuskin, and Siller (1985) observed mothers and their diabetic daughters during a discussion of a conflictual issue and coded patterns of interactions associated with self-reported adherence. Interactions were evaluated for multiple characteristics including "assertive," "speculative," and "confrontive" styles. Both mother and daughter were rated on empathy, expressiveness, clarity, and responsibility as well as closeness and conflict. Poorly adherent adolescents made more negative statements that asserted their independence rather than attempting to work out issues with mothers. They were more argumentative. Mothers, in turn, challenged daughters and pointed out discrepancies in daughters' accounts of feelings. In contrast, mothers and more adherent daughters were more likely to ask questions and communicate with greater clarity. Although interesting because interactional patterns are described, these results were limited by their correlational nature, which precludes identification of sequences of behavior. By employing more sophisticated methods to analyze these data (e.g., sequential analyses), these data might result in identification of patterns of interaction.

Wysocki (1993) used a questionnaire measure of parent-adolescent relationship to assess the association between metabolic control and adjustment to diabetes (treatment adherence was one component of this measure but was not assessed separately). Subscales of the parent-adolescent relationship measure included Skill Deficits-Overt Conflicts, a measure of conflict, communication, problem-solving and cohesion, as well as subscales assessing family structure. The adolescent, mother, and father completed the scales. Results indicated that family communication was associated with metabolic control. Given that the factor was comprised of a number of aspects of parent-adolescent communication, it is not known which aspect of this concept was associated with metabolic control. Since adherence was combined with other psychological adjustment measures, conclusions about links with adherence behaviors could not be drawn from these data.

Miller-Johnson et al. (1994) attempted to address methodological concerns about the measurement of adherence by using multiple measures of adherence (nurse, parent, and child ratings as well as daily postcard ratings). Parental warmth, behavioral support, discipline, and conflict were assessed via questionnaires administered to one parent and the child. Both public hospital and private practice patients were included. Results indicated that parent-child conflict predicted both adherence and metabolic control. Warmth as rated by the child and behavioral support as rated by the parent contributed unique variance to parent ratings of adherence in the public hospital sample. The most important finding was the consistent relationship between both parent and child ratings of conflict and measures of diabetes management, reflected in both adherence and metabolic control. The relationship between conflict and metabolic control was not significant when adherence behaviors were entered into the equation, suggesting that the influence is not directly upon metabolic control.

These studies do not provide an explanation as to how general parent-child conflict or other aspects of the parent-child relationship might impact upon disease management or health outcome. Many investigators suggest that global aspects of the relationship translate into how the family behaves specifically with regard to the disease, by either specific conflicts over disease management or a lack of parental support for the child's efforts at diabetes management. Alternately, general family conflict could result in greater stress for the child, which either indirectly affects metabolic control by disrupting disease management or directly impacts metabolic control.

Several studies have examined the role of disease-specific family support and conflict and reported inconsistent findings. Miller-Johnson et al. (1994) included measures of diabetes-specific aspects of the parent-child relationship (diabetes specific warmth, behavioral support, discipline, and conflict). They found that these scales did not provide superior prediction of either adherence or metabolic control over the global family environment scales. Other investigators, however, have compared general family functioning with diabetes-specific family support, and found that the association between diabetes-specific family support ("Praise you for following your diet") and nonsupport ("Nag you about testing your glucose level") and adherence behavior was stronger than the association with the more global measure (Schafer, Glasgow, McCaul, & Dreher, 1983). Other studies have noted a link between diabetes-specific

family behavior, specifically family guidance and control (e.g., "Parent watches while the child tests for sugar" or "Parent writes down the sugar tests") and family warmth/caring and metabolic control (Waller et al., 1986). In contrast, Schafer et al. (1986) found that diabetes-specific family support ("Praise you for following your diet") and nonsupport ("Nag you about testing your glucose level") were both related to better dietary adherence, but neither scale was associated with metabolic control, and Hanson et al. (1987a) reported that parental disease-specific support was related to better treatment adherence but not metabolic control.

Anderson, Auslander, Jung, Miller, and Santiago (1990) examined family sharing of diabetes responsibilities. It was hypothesized that, since disease-management responsibilities are typically transferred from parent to child during the adolescent years, confusion or disagreement between parent and child might be associated with problems in accomplishing disease management tasks. Regimen adherence was defined by a single rating made from an interview with the parent and child, and metabolic control was also measured. Results indicated that children who assumed greater responsibility for regimen-specific tasks were in poorer metabolic control than children who assumed less responsibility, and disagreements between mothers and children in perceptions of who is responsible was a significant predictor of metabolic control. Findings for adherence indicated that mother-rated adherence was higher for mothers and children who each reported that the other member of the dyad was assuming more responsibility for the task, but these parent or child responsibility ratings were not associated with measures of metabolic control. The finding for mother-rated adherence might have been due to the perception among these mothers that a child who is responsible for accomplishing a regimen task actually accomplishes the task. However, the authors do not offer their own possible explanations for this finding or for the lack of an association of the family sharing variable with metabolic control in their discussion of the study results.

Studies of the role of family factors in compliance to other disease regimens have suggested that general family functioning plays a role in compliance. Christiaanse et al. (1989) studied general family functioning (using the Family Environment Scale) in children with asthma, using mean theophylline level as the measure of health status. Results indicated that family environment interacted with child behavior problems to predict compliance; children with the lowest theophylline levels had high family conflict and high levels of behavior problems. Children with only one of these risk factors, or neither risk factor, were less likely to have low mean theophylline levels. Chaney and Peterson (1989) examined general family environment (using the FACES III scale) in parent-rated medication compliance among children with arthritis. In addition, they examined family coping strategies and family life stress. Families whose scores on the FACES were further from the center of the circumplex model of family functioning reported lower levels of medication compliance. That is, families with "optimal" levels of family functioning reported better medication compliance. More family stressful life events were also associated with lower adherence.

Little attention has been given to the impact of parenting skills on treatment compliance in younger children. Fehrenbach and Peterson (1989) examined parent problem-solving skill as well as general family functioning among mothers of young children with phenylketonuria (PKU), using blood level of phenylalanine as the sole compliance measure. Parents engaged in verbal and written problem-solving situations under conditions of high and low time-pressure stress. Responses were rated for quality of problem definition and solution and number of alternative solutions given. Children classified as being in good dietary control (medically acceptable range of blood phenylalanine level) gave higher-quality verbal solutions and gave more verbal alternatives. Written problem-solving solution quality approached significance. Stress influenced compliant and non-compliant parents in the same fashion. In a study conducted on compliance among 3- to 10-year-old children with cancer and their families (Manne, Jacobson, Gorfinkle, Gerstein, & Redd, 1993), nurse-rated compliance problems were associated with general parenting style: children of parents who had a more "supportive" parenting style (were more sensitive to children's input, had a less restrictive attitude toward parenting, and were more nurturant) canceled and delayed fewer appointments, were on time more frequently for appointments, and reported reactions to treatment with less delay. The impact of supportive parenting style was seen among the more functional children. For children with high functional status, a low level of supportive style was associated with significantly more adherence problems. For children with a low functional status, supportive parenting style did not have an impact. These studies suggest that both disease-specific parenting skills and general parenting style may contribute to compliance problems and deserve further investigation.

The role of parenting stress has been addressed in one study (Hauenstein, Marvin, Snyder, & Clarke, 1989). Mothers of children with IDDM completed the Parenting Stress Index, and a measure of glycosylated hemo-globin was taken. Results indicated that parenting stress did not predict metabolic control. However, adherence behaviors were not assessed in this study.

Summary. Methodological problems with studies in this area may account for inconsistencies in the findings across studies. First, family functioning measures assess long-standing patterns, whereas metabolic control measures typically used (HBA1) measures of average glucose level over the past two months. More congruent time frames for measurement might reveal stronger relationships. Second, metabolic control is relied upon as the only assessment of compliance in most of the research in this area. As it is unclear how family environment might directly impact upon metabolic control, future studies need to include behavioral indicators of compliance as well as other possible mediators of the relationship such as stress. Third, family measures used are inconsistent across studies. This problem is particularly problematic for the diabetes-specific family measures given that each measure (e.g., Diabetes Family Behavior Checklist and the Diabetes Specific Behavior Scale) has been used only in one or two studies, and the measures have not been validated. Fourth, adolescents have been the primary focus of the majority of studies, with few studies examining parent-child relationship factors in pre-adolescents. Fifth, only one study employed direct observation of family interactions. Such methodology would elucidate the patterns of parent-child interaction that may result in poor compliance. Sixth, longitudinal studies are needed so that the influence of family environment on adherence can be disaggregated. It seems likely that relationships are reciprocal; that is, family responses both influence adherence behaviors and a poorly adherent adolescent disrupts the family environment. Finally, the role of fathers and other family members is a neglected area of research, and future studies might benefit from including other family members in their assessments. However, the one study that examined the relation between sibling relations and adherence among diabetics did not show evidence of an association (Hanson et al., 1992).

Health Belief Model

One of the few theories that has been put forth to predict behavioral adherence to health care regimens is the Health Belief Model (HBM; Becker & Maiman, 1975). This model was originally developed to explain individuals' compliance with prevention behaviors, but has been applied to chronic disease regimens as well. The model proposes that individuals will comply with regimens if they possess certain "readiness" variables: (a) they perceive themselves as susceptible to the disease, (b) they view the disease as severe, (c) they perceive that the regimen is effective in preventing or controlling disease symptoms, (d) they perceive that barriers to undertaking regimen behaviors are not overwhelming, and (e) cues to action are present to activate the other readiness variables. Many studies have examined the ability of the HBM to predict adherence to health regimens and recommendations (Becker, Drachman, & Kirscht, 1970). In the area of adherence to diabetes regimens in adults, results are mixed. Cerkoney and Hart (1980) examined the five aspects of the HBM and found that perceived susceptibility, cues, and severity of diabetes were associated with separate aspects of the diabetes regimen. Together, these aspects accounted for 50 percent of the variability in adherence as measured by a combination of self-report and direct observational measures. Harris and Linn (1985) found that, while individual HBM variables were associated with adherence, the five aspects of HBM together did not predict adherence among adult diabetics.

Few studies have examined the applicability of this model to pediatric populations. Brownlee-Duffeck et al. (1987) included adolescent diabetics in their study. They also improved assessment of HBM variables by assessing diabetes-specific health beliefs rather than general beliefs. The amount of variance accounted for in metabolic control by the HBM was 20 percent, whereas 52 percent of the variance in self-reported adherence was accounted for by the model. The only individual HBM variable that accounted for a statistically significant amount of variance in self-reported adherence was the perceived cost of adhering. With regard to metabolic control, perceived severity and perceived susceptibility accounted for a significant amount of the variance. However, one finding was contrary to predictions; greater perceived susceptibility to complications was associated with poorer metabolic control. Findings from an older sample of diabetics differed. In this sample, both self-reported adherence and metabolic control were predicted by perceived benefits, while perceived costs were associated with metabolic control. The authors concluded that perceived benefits are more influential among older diabetics, while perceived costs and the negative aspects of the disease (severity, susceptibility) play a more important role for younger diabetics. The authors proposed that the association between perceived susceptibility and metabolic control which was not found for self-reported adherence was explained by the influence of increased anxiety upon metabolic control. However, anxiety would not explain the influence of

perceived severity on metabolic control. They also suggest that the relationship between perceived severity and susceptibility and adherence might have been found if the self-report measures accurately estimated adherence.

Bond, Aiken, and Somerville (1992) examined the role of HBM in younger adolescents (10 to 19 year olds) with diabetes using multiple indicators for all HBM constructs rather than single indicators. A confirmatory factor analysis was conducted to construct a measure of HBM. Due to small sample size, a three-factor solution was derived, labeled perceived Benefits-Costs, perceived Threat, and perceived Cues to action. Cues to action were the most strongly associated with higher self-reported adherence. However, Benefits-Costs were positively associated with adherence. Threat interacted with Benefits-Costs to predict adherence. When perceived Benefits-Costs were low, Threat related positively to compliance. When Benefits-Costs were high, a negative relation to compliance was found. This finding is contrary to predictions from the HBM. With regard to metabolic control, Threat and Cues evidenced an interaction effect. Control was poorest when both Threat and Cues were high, but was best when Threat was low and Cues were high. The authors suggest that the use of threat of negative consequences will not improve adolescents' adherence to diabetes regimens, but that encouraging patients to respond to symptoms (or cues) by undertaking the corrective regimen behaviors is a more effective means of obtaining adherence goals.

These initial studies suggest that the HBM is a promising theoretical model for understanding why some children adhere to regimens whereas other children do not. Some complexity in the relations among the HBM constructs exists, and interactions among variables might provide a more complete understanding of the phenomenon. The constructs in the HBM have not been made developmentally appropriate for young children, as the studies of HBM have been conducted with adolescents. Iannotti and Bush (1993) discussed the development of a Children's Health Belief Model, but did not provide information about measurement of the constructs or examine the model with regard to its relation to chronic disease regimens. Indeed, little is known about children's health beliefs.

Behavioral Contingencies

Negative contingencies or a lack of positive contingencies associated with adherence to regimens may also play a role in non-adherence. In behavioral terms, a behavior is less likely to occur if it is punished and more likely to occur if it is reinforced. Included under this category are regimen behaviors leading to punitive consequences. For diabetics, adherence can result in negative contingencies, such as increased risk of hypo-glycemia or weight gain associated with more intensive insulin regimens (Cox & Gonder-Frederick, 1992). Self-monitoring of blood glucose can act as a negative contingency since the result of testing is an indication that blood glucose is too low or too high, thus suggesting that the patient has not been managing blood glucose level well (Jones, 1990). In addition, regimen adherence does not necessarily lead to better metabolic control (although most health care providers will blame patients' behaviors for poor control). Certainly, when treatment recommendations are incorrect, such as inappropriate doses of insulin, adherence can result in negative consequences such as hypoglycemia and poor metabolic control. Thus, adherence to regimens is not necessarily reinforced and many times can lead to punitive consequences.

Conversely, contingencies may also play a role in reinforcing or punishing non-adherence to medical regimens. An example of negative contingencies for non-adherence are regimens associated with pain or other aversive symptoms, such as juvenile rheumatoid arthritis and diabetes. If the patient does not take pain medication, the symptom will persist. Positive contingencies for non-adherence are illustrated by mouth care performed to prevent mouth sores in children with cancer. If a patient does not perform mouth care when his or her "counts" are low and subsequently does not get mouth sores, then non-adherence is reinforced. One would predict that non-adherence would be more likely to occur the next time the patient's counts are low. Although little work has been conducted to test this hypothesis, behavioral interventions aimed at improving adherence have included self- and parent-reinforcement for performing disease management behaviors (Carney, Schecter, & Davis, 1983; Gross, 1982; Lowe & Lutzker, 1979). In addition, contingencies of adherence and non-adherence can be conceptualized as the costs and benefits of adherence and thus are investigated as components of the Health Belief Model.

Physician-Patient Relationship

As can be easily seen from this review of the literature on adherence, the study of adherence has focused almost exclusively on the child and family. When children and parents do not follow health care recommendations accurately, it is assumed that they are willfully not complying or did not recall instructions given by the health care professional. However, health care providers most

certainly impact adherence. Although some attention has been given to the role of the physician in adult regimen adherence, little attention has been given to this factor as a determinant of pediatric non-adherence.

As was discussed in the introduction of the chapter, the clarity and specificity of physician recommendations is likely to impact adherence (Johnson, 1992). Vague regimen instructions or instructions that are not written down clearly for the patient can lead to inadvertent compliance problems. Indeed, ensuring that patients thoroughly comprehend treatment recommendations and have been given necessary skills to carry out these instructions is a necessity prior to measuring patient compliance to the instructions. Among adult patients, studies have indicated that adherence is lower when physicians do not provide clear recommendations (Armstrong, Glanville, Bailey, & O'Keefe, 1990).

Another physician characteristic that has been investigated is communication style. Hall et al. (1988) found that the doctor's communication style was associated with compliance. Results indicated a trend toward greater expression of positive statements (e.g., reassurance) and refraining from negative statements (e.g., anger) during the medical visit to be related to greater adherence. The role of an associated characteristic, sensitivity to the tone of the patient's communications, has also been examined. DiMatteo et al. (1986) found that physicians' sensitivity to patient voice-tone (e.g., decoding emotion) was related to their patient's compliance to scheduled appointments. Intervention targeting physician communication style and teaching strategies have shown that patient understanding and recall of instructions can be improved (Ley, Bradshaw, Eaves, & Walker, 1973).

Another physician characteristic examined is age, which has not shown consistent relationships with compliance (Cockburn, Gibberd, Reid, & Sanson-Fisher, 1987; DiMatteo et al., 1993; Hurtado, Greenlick & Columbo, 1973). The one study in the literature that included physician gender and ethnic group did not evidence an association with long-term self-reported adherence. However, in that study, physician specialty affected patient adherence, with cardiologists eliciting significantly higher medication adherence and endocrinologists having patients reporting greater dietary adherence (DiMatteo et al., 1993). Physician willingness to answer patient questions and physician global job satisfaction had a positive effect on adherence. Practice characteristics such as number of practice hours per week and appointment planning were also found to have an association of adherence (more practice hours and definite follow-up planning yielded greater adherence).

Patient and parent satisfaction with the physician's professional characteristics and professional competence are factors that have been examined in the pediatric population (Hanson et al., 1987a). Adolescent diabetics who had more favorable attitudes about the doctor's personal characteristics were more adherent, and ratings of professional competence were associated with metabolic control.

Overall, these data suggest that physician characteristics are important variables in determining adult compliance to medical regimens and suggest that this variable should be examined for its role in pediatric regimen adherence.

INTERVENTIONS TO IMPROVE COMPLIANCE

A number of investigators have examined intervention strategies to improve treatment adherence. Most of the studies have targeted children with chronic illnesses. Rather than review the effectiveness of individual strategies to improve compliance separately, intervention studies will be evaluated within disease regimen.

Diabetes

For diabetics, interventions have targeted children's skill in performing regimen tasks and reducing obstacles to compliance. Intervention strategies have typically included the following strategies: reinforcement procedures, visual cues or reminders, education, and modeling of regimen skills. The skills necessary for optimal diabetes self-management include administering injections, conducting blood glucose testing (or urine testing in older studies), and using data from the testing to initiate changes in eating, exercise, and insulin use. In one of the first published studies in this area, Lowe and Lutzker (1979) used a multiple baseline design to test the effects of written instructions (cues) and a point system on a 9-year-old female's performance of foot care, urine tests, and diet. Both interventions were successful in increasing compliance. Several studies have demonstrated that behavioral techniques can be used to improved compliance to urine or blood glucose monitoring. Epstein et al. (1981) instructed both parents and children in insulin adjustment skills, how to decrease intake of simple sugars and saturated fats, how to increase exercise, and stress reduction skills (which included parenting training). Behavioral contracts were negotiated to reward correct glucose measurement and diabetes control. Parents and children were seen separately in a group format. Results

indicated that the proportion of negative urines for children in the intervention group was significantly higher. Glycosylated hemoglobin and serum glucose did not show improvements. A similar program was tested by Schafer, Glasgow, and McCaul (1982), who examined the effect of sequentially introducing self-monitoring, goal setting, and behavioral contracting to three diabetic adolescents. When there were no consistent improvements in adherence, goal setting was added to self-monitoring. Contracts were negotiated between parent and child, and children monitored their own compliance. Two subjects showed marked improvement from pretest to posttest across daily urine tests and blood glucose levels after introduction of goal setting. More recent studies have been able to take advantage of home self-monitoring of blood glucose technology. Carney, Schechter, and Davis (1983) treated three children who were previously non-compliant to blood sugar monitoring. Parents were instructed to praise children for appropriate blood sugar monitoring and were trained to implement a point system with their children, with points awarded for completion of monitoring at the appropriate time and recording of blood glucose values. This program resulted in improved percentage of times glucose tests were conducted in all three children, and improvements were maintained at a four-month follow-up. Hemoglobin A-1C also improved significantly following program implementation.

Teaching children to make appropriate adjustments in insulin dose after conducting glucose testing and administer insulin injections is an important component of regimen adherence. Epstein et al. (1981) included training in insulin adjustment as one of the components of their treatment program for parents and children, although they did not provide details on how the children's self-injecting was assessed at home and if their accuracy in performing the task was assessed. Delamater et al. (1990) taught nine newly diagnosed children how to accurately monitor blood glucose levels and then use the data to make appropriate behavioral changes. Children were also given information to help improve their understanding of blood glucose fluctuations. Parents were instructed in the use of contingent praise for appropriate regimen behaviors. A control group received conventional psychosocial intervention. Follow-up data on blood glucose levels at one and two years indicated that the intervention group had lower glycosylated hemoglobin levels. Episodes of severe hypoglycemia were less frequent in the intervention group. Some indices of adherence (conduction of blood glucose tests, injection-meal timing) evidenced no group differences, while dietary records indicated that intervention group subjects had fewer dietary deviations. A large-scale study targeting improved self-management of blood glucose was undertaken by Anderson et al. (1989). Thirty-five adolescents were taught techniques for self-management that included improving technical skills, effects of puberty on blood glucose control, how to self-monitor blood glucose and make frequent adjustments, understanding how food influences glycemic responses, how to apply glucose monitoring to meal planning, and the effects of exercise on blood glucose. Sessions included both eating and exercising and applying the skills taught. While the control group metabolic control declined over the study period, the intervention group evidenced less of a deterioration in metabolic control. Thus, participation helped prevent the anticipated decline in glucose control. Patient self-report of glucose monitoring, diet and exercise improved in the intervention group.

Gilbert et al. (1982) conducted the only study targeting behavioral skills involved in self-injection. Children were assigned to the experimental group, where they viewed a film involving a peer who was modeling self-injection skills, or to a control group, where they discussed nutrition. All children were taught to self-inject insulin after the film. Of the sample of 28 children, ages 6 to 9 years, the group that showed the greater skill was made up of older girls viewing the modeling film. They performed better than both older girls in the control group and older boys and younger girls viewing the modeling film.

Diet has been included as a component of multicomponent interventions (Lowe & Lutzker, 1979). In their single case study, the patient was given information about the food exchange system, and given "safety rules" for diet (eat at times that coincide with insulin injection). Post-intervention, the subject reported following diet rules 72 percent of the time. Epstein et al. (1981) modified their traffic-light diet for use with diabetic adolescents. The traffic light diet divides foods into Red foods that should be avoided, Yellow foods that should be eaten in moderation, and Green foods that can be eaten with no restriction. The emphasis of the intervention program was to reduce consumption of Red foods. Children received points for staying below the Red food goal. Since the dietary intervention was one aspect of a multicomponent package, the authors did not report data on the children's skill or compliance with the diet program, thus making evaluation difficult.

Exercise is an important component of the management of diabetes, since it can have an effect on blood sugar control. Both Schafer et al. (1982) and Epstein et al. (1981) included exercise as one component of a more general intervention program. Epstein and colleagues' exercise program was quite elaborate, consisting of gradually increasing walking or running distance with a point system corresponding to caloric expenditure. However, specific evaluation of the exercise component was not conducted.

Several studies have targeted methods of coping with obstacles to diabetes management. For adolescents, peer interaction and family "nagging" are particular sources of interference. Interactions with peers can encourage teens not to follow their regimens, or result in teens neglecting their regimens because they want to be more similar to peers or because of increased stress (thereby influencing regimen adherence and metabolic control). Gross (1982) role-played how to handle parent nagging and peer teasing (ignoring), as well as how to handle conflict, with four 10- to 12-year-old diabetic boys as part of a self-management training class. Outcome consisted only of frequency of urine testing, which increased from 9 percent to 74 percent of targeted frequency. Kaplan, Chadwick, and Schimmel (1985) taught 11 adolescents to identify social situations that interfered with regimen behaviors and then instructed them to generate solutions to these situations, and role-play the situations using the solutions they generated. Control group subjects discussed medical information relevant to diabetes. Group comparisons on metabolic control indicated that the social skills group had significantly lower hemoglobin at the four-month follow-up. Group differences in performance of regimen behaviors were not reported. Finally, Gross, Heiman, Shapiro, and Schultz (1983) also compared a social skills training intervention to a no-treatment control group. Unlike Gross (1982), they examined improvements in social skills to ensure that skills increased as a result of training. However, the only dependent measure was metabolic control. Results indicated no differences in metabolic control between the treatment and control groups. An explanation of the conflicting findings of these studies is difficult because changes in adherence behaviors were not assessed in the Gross and Kaplan et al. studies.

Finally, a multifamily group intervention was conducted by Satin, La Greca, Zigo, and Skyler (1989) that targeted improving "self-care." Participants were assigned to one of three conditions: multifamily, multifamily plus parent simulation of diabetes, and control. In the multifamily groups, content consisted of enhancing families' communication about diabetes and their problem-solving skills, and helping families to process issues that arose regarding diabetes management. Role-playing of adaptive solutions to problems was encouraged. In the multifamily plus simulation group, parents pretended to have diabetes and adolescents taught them how to manage their "diabetes." Comparisons of glycosylated hemoglobin at a six-week follow-up indicated that the multifamily plus simulation group demonstrated significant improvements in metabolic control in comparison with the control group subjects. A six-month follow-up evidenced no significant differences. However, an analysis of the subgroup of families participating in a later cycle of groups indicated that both the multifamily group and the multifamily group plus simulation group evidenced improvements in metabolic functioning relative to controls, and the impact was maintained at six-month follow-up. In these subgroups, mothers' self-care ratings also evidenced improvements in comparison with the control group. A detailed assessment of adherence behaviors was not conducted.

As prior studies have found that stress results in metabolic disturbance, researchers have begun to investigate the use of relaxation therapy and biofeedback to prevent the adverse effects of stress-induced increases in sympathetic nervous system activity. Relaxation therapy impacts sympathetic and adrenal cortical activity. Fowler, Budzynski, and VandenBergh (1976) presented a single-case study in which they taught a 20-year-old woman who experienced frequent ketoacidosis in response to physical and emotional stress. Relaxation training consisted of twice daily electomyographic biofeedback (EMG) to the forehead for six months. The training resulted in lowered insulin intake and decreased frequency of ketoacidosis and hospitalization. Rose, Firestone, Heick, and Faught (1983) conducted a multiple-baseline across-subjects design to study the impact of anxiety management training on metabolic control in six adolescents with Type I diabetes. The intervention consisted of seven hours of relaxation training and continued home relaxation practice. One patient was dropped from the study due to instability of blood sugar. For the remaining five subjects, the intervention resulted in lower mean urine glucose percentages on daily tests. Measures of dietary compliance indicated that this aspect of the regimen did not improve.

Asthma

For patients with asthma, interventions can be grouped into two categories: educational and behavioral (Lemanek, 1990). Educational strategies focus on giving parents and children factual information about asthma and the importance of following treatment recommendations. However, empirical examination of the effectiveness of educational programs has not been conducted except as a

component of a larger asthma self-management program, which will be reviewed in a later section.

A variety of behavioral strategies have had beneficial effects on adherence. Successful strategies have included increased medical supervision and support, relaxation training, and self-monitoring. Eney and Goldstein (1976) employed increased medical supervision as an intervention. In the intervention group, physicians monitored theophylline levels. Usual care was provided to the other children. Forty-two percent of those receiving medical supervision reported therapeutic serum theophylline levels, versus 11 percent of children in the usual care group.

Weinstein and Cuskey (1985) employed a combination of behavioral approaches requiring greater physician and parent involvement. This study did not include a control group. Levels of involvement increased when patients did not achieve therapeutic levels of theophylline. Interventions consisted of telephone feedback and reminders of theophylline levels, parent support of asthma regimen compliance, increased parental supervision of medication, and negotiation of parent/child contracts with rewards and contingencies. Results indicated that therapeutic theophylline levels were achieved by 50 percent of families.

Miklich and colleagues (1977) used systematic desensitization techniques with 19 asthmatic children. Children were taught to associate relaxation with imagined anxiety-provoking situations. Records were kept of medications, hospitalizations, symptom reports, and twice daily forced expiratory flow rates. Results indicated that experimental group children differed only with regard to forced expiratory flow rates, and this difference lessened at the five-month follow-up. Overall, few patients evidenced a clinically useful response to the intervention.

Self-monitoring was studied by Baum and Creer (1986), who assigned 16 asthmatic children to one of two conditions: self-monitoring or self-monitoring combined with education and reinforcement. Medication compliance was assessed by serum theophylline levels, pill counts by parents, and self-report measures (peak flow monitor, asthma attacks record). Children assigned to the self-monitoring group were taught how to complete the measures and parents were instructed how to obtain pill counts. The second group of children received self-monitoring training in addition to a two-hour education session on asthma. Children received points weekly for completing self-monitoring data sheets that could be exchanged for McDonald's coupons. Results indicated no differences between groups in outcome measures; both resulted in improved compliance (baseline compliance in this sample was 83 percent, which may have limited improvements across interventions).

The authors reported that children in the combination group performed skills taught to a greater extent (e.g., more likely to try to get away from asthma precipitants).

The most common treatment approaches employed with asthmatics have been general asthma care programs. Numerous, widely-used programs have been developed to teach combinations of education and self-management skills, including the Asthma Care Training Program (Lewis, Rachelefsky, Lewis, de la Sota, & Kaplan, 1984), Living With Asthma (Creer et al., 1988), Open Airways (Clark, Feldman, Evans, Levison, Wasilewski, & Mellins, 1986), and AIRWISE (McNabb, Wilson-Pessano, Hughes, & Scamagas, 1985). Evans and Mellins (1991) and Lemanek et al. (in press) have reviewed common elements of these self-management programs. First, families are provided with information and given a chance to rehearse skills and discuss how to apply these skills. Second, physiological mechanisms underlying asthma, identification of triggers and symptoms, management of symptoms and attacks, and adjustment to living with asthma, are discussed. Third, families are encouraged to be actively involved in the child's asthma care. Finally, increasing compliance with medical regimens is encouraged. These programs have been conducted in the classroom, residential, pediatric outpatient clinic, and community settings. Evaluations of these multicomponent programs indicate that, overall, the programs produce positive changes.

Lewis et al. (1984) conducted a randomized control group study of the Asthma Care Training Program, which consisted of five one-hour weekly sessions. The emphasis of this program is to teach the child how to take charge of the disease. Children are taught to label medications and recognize when to take medications, and parents and children are taught when children need to discuss medication decisions with their parents. Children are also trained in relaxation, how to recognize irritants, and identifying side effects of medications. Results indicated significant changes in self-reported adherence behaviors and reductions in emergency room visits and days of hospitalization at three, six and 12 months after completing the program. However, both groups reported equivalent increases in asthma knowledge.

Fireman, Friday, Gira, Vierthaler, and Michaels (1981) conducted a similar self-management program. A more detailed assessment of asthma symptoms was used, which included a symptom and medication diary, as well as a review of school attendance records, tabulation of emergency room visits and hospitalizations. Results indicated that experimental group subjects reported significantly fewer attacks, fewer wheezing days per month, fewer school days absent, fewer hospitalizations, fewer emergency room visits, and used asthma medications more frequently. Follow-up data were not obtained.

Multiple methodological problems exist in this literature, as outlined by Creer and colleagues in their review of 19 of these programs (Creer, Wigal, Kotses, & Lewis, 1990). These problems include a lack of medical confirmation of an asthma diagnosis and consistent definitions of what defines an asthma "attack," selection of subjects from a dissimilar population with respect to disease severity and not selecting subjects treated medically in a similar manner, failure to include a control group, no assessment of whether self-management skills were actually being used, not controlling for changes in medical treatment that occurs over the course of intervention periods, and not following children for one year so that asthma activity across seasons are assessed.

Hemophilia

For children with hemophilia, prevention of severe bleeding episodes is accomplished by administering the missing clotting factor. Intervention studies have incorporated behavioral strategies into educational programs to train patients and parents in the correct administration of factor replacement. Behavioral techniques that have been successfully employed include modeling of correct procedures, observational learning, behavioral rehearsal of strategies, and corrective feedback and social reinforcement (Sergis-Deavenport & Varni, 1982; 1983). Evidence suggests that they have a long-term impact (Gilbert & Varni, 1988).

Greenan-Fowler, Powell, and Varni (1987) used another behavioral technique, contingency contracting, to increase children's adherence to therapeutic exercises prescribed to children with hemophilia. A three-way contingency contract was signed by parent, child, and therapist. Points were given for session attendance, completing exercise forms, and performance of prescribed exercises. During the treatment phase, adherence averaged 94 percent for the 10 children participating. Six-month follow-up data indicated that average adherence ranged from 81 percent to 90 percent for study participants.

Hemodialysis and Other Disease Regimens

A variety of behavioral strategies have been employed to increase compliance to other medical regimens. Magrab and Papadopoulou (1977) examined the impact of a token economy on adherence to dietary restrictions among children on hemodialysis. Seven in-patients were included in this study, which used weight, potassium level, and BUN as criteria for earning points toward prizes. An ABAB reversal design was used. The contingency system was successful in controlling weight gain, potassium, and BUN levels.

Several studies have examined self-monitoring of disease symptoms or targeted regimen behaviors with mixed results. This strategy appears to be more effective for acute problems such as oral medications for otitis media (Mattar, Markello, & Yaffe, 1975) than chronic illnesses (Epstein et al., 1981). However, La Greca and Ottinger (1979), in a single case study of self-monitoring for increasing adherence to daily hip exercises prescribed for a 12-year-old with cerebral palsy, found that self-monitoring of exercise behavior and reactions and responses to exercising sessions resulted in increases in exercise rates to five to seven times per week. These changes were maintained at three- and six-month follow-ups. There are several problems with the use of self-monitoring as an intervention to increase compliance. First, self-monitoring alone is not likely to result in adherence behavior changes unless the individual uses this information to improve adherence behaviors. Second, monitoring of adherence to regimens is in itself an onerous task for many children and parents, and thus is likely to represent a difficult intervention to implement because of resistance. In another study, McConnell, Biglan, and Severson (1984) added daily telephone calls from a psychologist to a self-monitoring procedure for monitoring adolescent cigarette smoking. Results indicated that subjects receiving phone calls complied significantly more than control subjects in providing saliva samples and recording self-monitoring data.

Killam et al. (1983) used behavioral strategies to improve compliance to diet in children with spina bifida, who are at risk for weight gain due to activity restrictions. Parents of the children were instructed in diet and exercise and the use of behavioral strategies to reinforce adherence to dietary and exercise procedures. Four of the five children evidenced a reduction in percentage overweight at six-month follow-up.

Short-Term Regimens and Common Pediatric Adherence Problems

Lima, Nazarian, Charney, and Lahti (1975) conducted one of the few investigations of the effectiveness of visual cues on adherence. The low income sample of 158 adults and children included 104 children under the age of 12 with a variety of medical problems (e.g., ear infections) on ten-day antibiotic regimens. Two visual cues were used, consisting of a clock printed on the prescription label with appropriate times circled, and a 5×7 inch bright red self-adhering sticker with written instructions to be posted at home. One group of patients was assigned to the control group and received standard care, a second was assigned to the specially marked prescription labels, and the third group received both types of reminders. Results indicated that both reminders resulted in increased compliance and that the children evidenced more drastic increases in adherence than adults. Children in the reminder groups demonstrated 57 percent and 59 percent compliance in comparison with the control group, which had 24 percent compliance at the ninth or tenth day of the regimen.

Two adherence problems that commonly occur across most treatment regimens are difficulty with appointment keeping and difficulty with pill swallowing. Finney et al. (1990) published one of several studies examining the efficacy of reinforcement and reminders upon appointment keeping. Eight children attending a pediatric allergy clinic identified by pediatric allergists as non-adherent participated. A single case reversal design was employed, in which parents and children were told they would receive a coupon that could be exchanged for money for each scheduled appointment they attended (incentive condition). Children also received reminder phone calls prior to scheduled appointments. Appointment keeping increased for three of the five children during the incentive condition for the previously non-adherent children and was maintained for the three previously adherent children. Increases in appointment keeping were not maintained when the incentive condition was discontinued, despite the continuation of reminders. These results suggest that this intervention does not result in treatment gains that are maintained. Other interventions that have been associated with improvements in appointment keeping are fee reductions (Rice & Lutzker, 1984) and cash incentives (Reiss et al., 1976). Educational and reminder strategies have been shown to be less effective than incentive programs for appointment keeping (Frankel & Hovell, 1978). Blount, Dahlquist, Baer, and Wuori (1984) examined the effectiveness of modeling and shaping procedures to teach six children pill-swallowing skills. Results indicated that all subjects were able to swallow pills post-treatment, and that gains were maintained at the three-week and three-month follow ups. Similar results were reported by Sallows (1980) and Funk, Mullins, and Olson (1984).

SUMMARY AND DIRECTIONS FOR FUTURE RESEARCH

Research related to pediatric adherence has continued to grow in the past two decades, although most studies of adherence to chronic disease regimens have been conducted in the last decade. Other than the initial studies of compliance to medication regimens such as otitis media, little attention has been directed toward short-term regimens. In this summary, limitations of the research to date will be reviewed and new areas of study that deserve further attention are proposed.

With regard to assessment of adherence, most studies have targeted insulin-dependent diabetes mellitus. For patients with this illness, a standardized assessment methodology has been developed, which employs multiple methods including self-reports and parent-reports over time-limited periods, as well as direct measures (e.g., biological assays of blood glucose level). Correspondence among self-report methods and the most widely used assay measures is weak, and further examination of the reasons for this poor correspondence is necessary. These methodological advancements have not been made for other disease regimens and should be the focus of future research efforts.

Numerous psychological variables have been examined for their association with treatment adherence. Since adherence is multiply determined, it is impossible for any one study to include all possible factors associated with non-compliance. Thus, the literature is characterized by positive and negative findings for a variety of factors, clouding the "big" picture of non-adherence. With few exceptions, these studies are cross-sectional and thus prediction of the development of adherence problems was not possible. This area suffers from a lack of theoretical basis. There is a clear need to develop models of children's compliance that integrate developmental theories and processes. Promising work on the application of self-regulation theory has been done in the area of diabetes adherence. Children's perceptions of symptoms and what determines whether actions are taken in response to symptom perception is likely to play a role in compliance to other chronic disease regimens, including those for asthma and arthritis. The Health Belief Model has been investigated in several recent studies of adolescents. However, little effort has focused on adapting this model to the developmental level of young children. Studies of symptom perception and HBM suggest that the relationships are not straightforward; the impact of these variables may be mediated by other variables such as anxiety or perceptions of stress. The role of stress in compliance has only been studied in diabetes; little attention has been given to the role of this variable in other chronic diseases. Recent studies have suggested that, at least among juvenile diabetics, stress has a direct effect upon metabolic control rather than indirectly influencing metabolic control through its effects upon adherence behaviors. Further study of the mechanisms whereby stress influences adherence to other disease regimens is needed.

The role of the family, particularly family conflict, appears to be important, at least among adolescent diabetics. However, as with stress, the impact of family conflict appears to be on health outcome (metabolic control) rather than upon the performance of regimen behaviors. The mechanisms for the influence of family conflict upon adherence need further clarification. In addition, studies have relied upon self-report measures, mostly global in nature (e.g., family environment) and have not included observational measures of interaction between parent and child to determine what aspects of the interaction contribute to non-compliance. For adolescent diabetics, one factor that has received little attention is the influence of physiological changes secondary to the onset of puberty. As this factor may explain much of the variance in the higher non-compliance rate among adolescents, taking this variable into account is important.

Although inclusion of both health outcome and adherence behavior measures is preferable from a methodological perspective, interpretation of results becomes complicated when psychological variables are associated with one measure and not another. This problem is particularly salient when the outcome measure associated with psychological variables is the health status measure and not the adherence behavior. This has frequently been the case in diabetes research; psychological variables such as family conflict are more often correlated with metabolic control than adherence behavior. Although many authors attempt to explain such findings by suggesting that family conflict influences stress, which in turn results in metabolic disturbance, the mechanism has not been directly investigated. Some investigators have suggested that the problem arises from validity of the direct measure used, glycosylated hemoglobin.

Several conclusions can be made about the efficacy of interventions to improve compliance. For short-term regimens, simple strategies such as the use of visual cues or supplemental instructions can result in improved compliance. Although incentives are promising with regard to efficacy, improvements in adherence do not appear to be maintained when incentives are withdrawn. For children on long-term medical regimens, the most promising techniques appear to be behavioral procedures (e.g., modeling, reinforcement). These techniques have demonstrated the most efficacy when applied to specific regimen tasks such as administering injections, adherence to diet, and pill swallowing. The application of reinforcing consequences for adherence might be a beneficial component of self-management programs, since consistent self-care is not sufficiently reinforcing in the short run. Teaching children how to accurately monitor and interpret disease symptoms and determine appropriate disease management tasks that should be undertaken are especially promising interventions. In addition, the efficacy of other behavioral techniques, such as time-out or withdrawal of reinforcement for non-compliance, have not been systematically evaluated, although clinicians routinely use such interventions for medically-non-compliant children.

For adolescents, interventions teaching problem-solving skills and parent-adolescent communication also hold promise. One behavioral strategy that does not appear to be effective is self-monitoring used alone. Because most long-term regimens include multiple tasks, multi-component programs that include both behavioral and educational strategies have been shown to be effective. One limitation of such interventions is that the effectiveness of any one component cannot be determined. As many studies use single case designs, future research would benefit from the inclusion of between-subjects designs. Future intervention studies would also benefit from focusing less upon the patient and more upon the provider of medical care. For example, more clear instructions could be provided with regard to regimen prescriptions, better education of necessary skills, and use of fewer medications or alternate means of administering medications (e.g., liquid medications rather than pills, use of central access lines for administration of medications for cancer patients).

REFERENCES

Abduelrhman, E., & Loftus, B. (1993). Childhood asthma: Can admissions be avoided? *Irish Medical Journal, 86*, 22–23.

Achenbach, T., & Edelbrock, C. (1983). *Manual for the Child Behavior Checklist and Revised Child Behavior Profile* (2nd ed). New York: John Wiley & Sons.

Aikens, J., Wallander, J., Bell, D., & Cole, J. (1992). Daily stress variability, learned resourcefulness, regimen adherence and metabolic control in type I diabetes mellitus: Evaluation of a path model. *Journal of Consulting and Clinical Psychology, 60*, 113–118.

Amiel, S., Sherwin, R., Simonson, D., Lauritano, A., & Tamborlane, W. (1986). Impaired insulin action in puberty: A contributing factor to poor glycemic control in adolescents with diabetes. *New England Journal of Medicine, 315*, 215–219.

Anderson, B., Auslander, W., Jung, K., Miller, J. & Santiago, J. (1990). Family sharing of diabetes responsibilities. *Journal of Pediatric Psychology, 15*, 477–492.

Anderson, B., & Auslander, W. (1980). Research on diabetes management and family: A critique. *Diabetes Care, 3*, 696–702.

Anderson, B., Wolf, F., Burkhart, M., Cornell, R., & Bacon, G. (1989). Effects of peer-group intervention on metabolic control of adolescents with IDDM. *Diabetes Care, 12*, 179–183.

Anderson, B., Miller, J., Auslander, W., & Santiago, J. (1981). Family characteristics and diabetic adolescents: Relationship to metabolic control. *Diabetes Care, 4*, 586–594.

Armstrong, D., Glanville, T., Bailey, E., & O'Keefe, G. (1990). Doctor-initiated consultations: A study of communication between general practitioners and patients about the need for reattendance. *British Journal of General Practice, 40*, 241–242.

Auslander, W., Anderson, B., Bubb, J., Jung, K., & Santiago, J. (1990). Risk factors to health in diabetic children: A prospective study from diagnosis. *Health & Social Work*, 133–142.

Baker, L., Minuchin, S., Milman, L., Liebman, R., & Todd, T. (1975). Psychosomatic aspects of juvenile diabetes mellitus: A progress report. *Modern Problems in Paediatrics, 12*, 332–343.

Barglow, P., Hatcher, R., Edidin, D., & Sloan-Rossiter, D. (1984). Stress and metabolic control in diabetes: Psychosomatic evidence and evaluation of methods, *Psychosomatic Medicine, 46*, 127–144.

Baum, D., & Creer, T. (1986). Medication compliance in children with asthma. *Journal of Asthma, 23*, 49–59.

Becker, M. H., Drachman, R. H., & Kirscht, J. P. (1972). Predicting mothers' compliance with pediatric medical regimens. *Journal of Pediatrics, 81*, 843–854.

Becker, M., & Maiman, L. (1975). Sociobehavioral determinants of compliance with health and medical care recommendations. *Medical Care, 13*, 10–23.

Becker, M., Rosenstock, I., Radius, S., Drachman, R., Schuberth, K., & Teets, K. (1978). Compliance with a medical regimen for asthma: A test of the health belief model. *Public Health Reports, 93*, 258–276.

Blount, R., Dahlquist, L., Baer, R., & Wuori, D. (1984). A brief, effective method for teaching children to swallow pills. *Behavior Therapy, 15*, 381–387.

Bobrow, E., AvRuskin, T., & Siller, J. (1985). Mother-daughter interaction and adherence to diabetes regimens. *Diabetes Self-care, 8*, 146–151.

Bond, G., Aiken, L., & Somerville, S. (1992). The health belief model and adolescents with insulin-dependent diabetes mellitus. *Health Psychology, 11*, 190–198.

Boyd, J. R., Covington, T. R., Stanaszek, W. F., & Coussons, R. T. (1974). Drug defaulting part II: Analysis of non-compliance patterns. *American Journal of Hospital Pharmacy, 31*, 485–491.

Brand, F., Smith, R., & Brand, P. (1977). Effect of economic barriers to medical care on patients' noncompliance, *Public Health Reports, 92*, 72–78.

Brownlee-Duffeck, M., Peterson, L., Simonds, J., Goldstein, D., Kilo, C., & Hoette, S. (1987). The role of health beliefs in the regimen adherence and metabolic control of adolescents and adults with diabetes mellitus. *Journal of Consulting and Clinical Psychology, 55*, 139–144.

Carney, R., Schechter, K., & Davis, T. (1983). Improving adherence to blood glucose testing in insulin-dependent diabetic children. *Behavior Therapy, 14*, 247–254.

Caron, H. S., & Roth, H. P. (1968). Patients' cooperation with a medical regimen. *Journal of the American Medical Association, 203*, 120–124.

Cerkoney, K. A., & Hart, L. K. (1980). The relationship between the health belief model and compliance of persons with diabetes mellitus. *Diabetes Care, 3*, 594–598.

Chaney, J., & Peterson, L. (1989). Family variables and disease management in juvenile rheumatoid arthritis. *Journal of Pediatric Psychology, 14*, 389–403.

Charney, E., Bynum, R., Eldridge, D., Frank, D., MacWhinney, J., McNabb, N., Scheiner, A., Sumpter, E., & Iker, H. (1967). How well do patients take oral penicillin? A collaborative study in a private practice. *Pediatrics, 40*, 188–195.

Christiaanse, M. E., Lavigne, J. V., & Lerner, C. V. (1989). Psychosocial aspects of compliance in children and adolescents with asthma. *Journal of Developmental and Behavioral Pediatrics, 10*, 75–80.

Clark, N., Feldman, C., Evans, D., Levison, M., Wasilewski, Y., & Mellins, R. (1986). The impact of health education on frequency and cost of health care use by low income children with asthma. *Journal of Allergy and Clinical Immunology, 78*, 108–114.

Clarke, W. L., Snyder, A. L., & Nowacek, G. (1985). Outpatient pediatric diabetes. *Journal of Chronic Diseases, 38*, 85–90.

Cockburn, J., Gibberd, R., Reid, A., & Sanson-Fisher, R. (1987). Determinants of noncompliance with short term antibiotic regimens. *British Medical Journal, 295*, 814–818.

Coutts, J. A. P., Gibson, N. A., & Paton, J. Y. (1992). Measuring compliance with inhaled medication in asthma. *Archives of Diseases of Children, 67*, 332–333.

Cox, D., & Gonder-Frederick, L. (1992). Major developments in behavioral diabetes research. *Journal of Consulting and Clinical Psychology, 60*, 628–638.

Cox, D., Taylor, A., Nowacek, G., Wilcox, P., Pohl, S., & Guthrowe, T. (1984). The relationship between psychological stress and IDDM blood glucose control: Preliminary investigation. *Health Psychology, 3*, 63–75.

Creer, T. (1979). *Asthma therapy: A behavioral health care system for respiratory disorders.* New York: Springer Publishing Company, Inc.

Creer, T., Backial, M., Burns, K., Leung, P., Marion, R., Miklich, D., Morrill, C., Taplin, P., & Ullman, S. (1988). Living with asthma: I. Genesis and development of a self-management program for childhood asthma. *Journal of Asthma, 25*, 335–362.

Creer, T., Wigal, J., Kotses, H., & Lewis, P. (1990). A critique of 19 self-management programs for childhood asthma: Part II. Comments regarding the scientific merit of the programs, *Pediatric Asthma, Allergy & Immunology, 4*, 41–53.

Delamater, A., Bubb, J., Davis, S., Smith, J., Schmidt, L., White, N., & Santiago, J. (1990). Randomized prospective study of self management training with newly diagnosed diabetic children. *Diabetes Care, 13*, 492–498.

Delamater, A., Davis, S., Bubb, J., Santiago, J., Smith, J., & White, N. (1989). Self monitoring of blood glucose by adolescents with diabetes: Technical skills and utilization of data. *Diabetes Educator, 15*, 56–61.

Delamater, A., Smith, J., Kurtz, S., & White, N. (1986). Dietary skills and adherence in children with type I diabetes mellitus. *Diabetes Educator, 14*, 33–36.

Dickey, F., Mattar, M., & Chudzik, G. (1975). Pharmacist counseling increases drug regimen compliance. *Hospitals, 49*, 85–86.

Diehl, A., Bauer, R., & Sugarek, N. (1987). Correlates of medication compliance in non-insulin dependent diabetes mellitus. *Southern Medical Journal, 80*, 332–335.

DiMatteo, R., Hays, R., & Prince, L. (1986). Relationship of physicians' non-verbal communication skills to patient satisfaction, appointment noncompliance and physician workload. *Health Psychology, 5*, 581–594.

DiMatteo, M., Sherbourne, C., Hays, R., Ordway, L., Kravitz, R., McGlynn, E., Kaplan, S., & Rogers, W. (1993). Physician's characteristics influence patients' adherence to medical treatment: Results from the medical outcomes study. *Health Psychology, 12*, 93–102.

Drash, A. (1987). *Clinical care of the diabetic child.* Chicago: Yearbook Publishers.

Drash, A., & Becker, D. (1990). Behavioral issues in patients with diabetes mellitus, with special emphasis on the child and adolescent. In H. Rifkin & D. Porte, *Ellenberg and Rifkin's diabetes mellitus: Theory and practice* (4th edition) (pp. 205–240). New York: Elsevier Science.

Dubbert, P., King, A., Rapp, S., Brief, D., Martin, J., & Lake, M. (1985). Riboflavin as a tracer of medication compliance. *Journal of Behavioral Medicine, 8,* 287–299.

Eney, R., & Goldstein, E. (1976). Compliance of chronic asthmatics with oral administration of theophylline as measured by serum and salivary levels. *Pediatrics, 57,* 513–517.

Epstein, L., Beck, S., Figueroa, J., Farkas, G., Kazdin, A., Daneman, D., & Becker, D. (1981). The effects of targeting improvements in urine glucose on metabolic control in children with IDDM. *Journal of Applied Behavior Analysis, 14,* 365–375.

Evans, D., & Mellins, R. (1991). Educational programs for children with asthma. *Pediatrician, 18,* 317–323.

Fehrenbach, A., & Peterson, L. (1989). Parental problem-solving skills, stress, and dietary compliance in phenylketonuria. *Journal of Consulting and Clinical Psychology, 57,* 237–241.

Finney, J., Lemanek, K., Brophy, C., & Cataldo, M. (1990). Pediatric appointment keeping: Improving adherence in a primary care allergy clinic. *Journal of Pediatric Psychology, 15,* 571–579.

Fireman, P., Friday, G., Gira, C., Vierthaler, W., & Michaels, L. (1981). Teaching self-management skills to asthmatic children and their parents in an ambulatory care setting. *Pediatrics, 68,* 341–348.

Fowler, J., Budzynski, T., & VandenBergh, R. (1976). Effects of an EMG biofeedback relaxation program on the control of diabetes. *Biofeedback and Self-Regulation, 1,* 105–112.

Frankel, B., & Hovell, M. (1978). Health service appointment keeping: A behavioral and critical review. *Behavior Modification, 2,* 435–464.

Freund, A., Johnson, S. B., Silverstein, J., & Thomas, J. (1991). Assessing daily management of childhood diabetes using 24 hour recall interviews: Reliability and stability. *Health Psychology, 10,* 200–208.

Funk, M., Mullins, L., & Olson, R. (1984). Teaching children to swallow pills: A case study. *Child Health Care, 13,* 20–23.

Garrison, W., Biggs, D., & Williams, K. (1990). Temperament characteristics and clinical outcomes in young children with diabetes mellitus. *Journal of Child Psychology and Psychiatry, 31,* 1079–1088.

Gilbert, B., Johnson, S. B., Silverstein, J., & Malone, J. (1989). Psychological and physiological responses to acute laboratory stressors in IDDM adolescents and nondiabetic controls. *Journal of Pediatric Psychology, 14,* 577–591.

Gilbert, B., Johnson, S. B., Spillar, R., McCullum, M., Silverstein, J., & Rosenbloom, A. (1982). The effects of a peer modeling film on children learning to self-inject insulin. *Behavior Therapy, 13,* 186–193.

Gilbert, A., & Varni, J. (1988). Behavioral treatment for improving adherence to factor replacement therapy by children with hemophilia. *The Journal of Compliance in Health Care, 3,* 67–76.

Glasgow, A., August, G., & Hung, W. (1981). Relationship between control and serum lipids in juvenile-onset diabetes. *Diabetes Care, 4,* 76–80.

Glasgow, R., Wilson, W., & McCaul, K. (1985). Regimen adherence: A problematic concept in diabetes research. *Diabetes Care, 8,* 300–301.

Glasgow, R. E., McCaul, K. D., & Schafer, L. C. (1987). Self-care behaviors and glycemic control in type I diabetes. *Journal of Chronic Diseases, 40,* 399–412.

Goetsch, V., Van Dorsten, B., Pbert, L., Ullrich, I., & Yates, R. (1987, November). *Stress induced blood glucose reactivity in type II diabetes.* Paper presented at the annual meeting of the Association for the Advancement of Behavior Therapy, Boston.

Goetsch, V., Wiebe, D., Veltum, L., & Van Dorsten, B. (1990). Stress and blood glucose in type II diabetes mellitus. *Behaviour Research & Therapy, 28,* 531–537.

Gonder-Frederick, L., Carter, W., Cox, D., & Clarke, W. (1990). Environmental stress and blood glucose change in insulin-dependent diabetes mellitus. *Health Psychology, 9,* 503–515.

Gonder-Frederick, L., & Cox, D. (1986). Behavioral response to perceived hypoglycemic symptoms: A report and some suggestions. *Diabetes Education, 12,* 105–109.

Gonder-Frederick, L., Julian, D., Cox, D., Clarke, W., & Carter, W. (1988). Self measurement of blood glucose. *Diabetes Care, 11,* 579–585.

Gonder-Frederick, L., Snyder, A., & Clarke, W. (1991). Accuracy of blood glucose estimation by children with IDDM and their parents. *Diabetes Care, 14,* 565–570.

Gordis, L., Markowitz, M., & Lilienfeld, A. M. (1969). Why patients don't follow medical advice: A study of children on long-term antistreptococcal prophylaxis. *The Journal of Pediatrics, 75,* 957–968.

Greenan-Fowler, E., Powell, C., & Varni, J. (1987). Behavioral treatment of adherence to therapeutic exercise by children with hemophilia. *Archives of Physical Medicine and Rehabilitation, 68,* 846–849.

Grey, M., Genel, M., & Tamborlane, W. (1980). Psychosocial adjustment of latency-aged diabetics. Determinants and relationship to control. *Pediatrics, 65,* 69–73.

Gross, A. (1982). Self management training and medication compliance in children with diabetes. *Child and Family Behavior Therapy, 4*, 47–55.

Gross, A., Heiman, L., Shapiro, R., & Schultz, R. M. (1983). Children with diabetes: Social skills training and hemoglobin Alc levels. *Behavior Modification, 7*, 151–164.

Halford, W., Cuddihy, S., & Mortimer, R. (1990). Psychological stress and blood glucose regulation in type I diabetic patients. *Health Psychology, 9*, 516–528.

Hall, J., Roter, D., & Katz, N. (1988). Meta-analysis of correlates of provider behavior in medical encounters. *Medical Care, 26*, 1–19.

Hanson, C., Cigrang, J., Harris, M., Carle, D., Ralyea, G., & Burghen, G. (1989). Coping styles in youths with Insulin dependent diabetes mellitus. *Journal of Consulting and Clinical Psychology, 57*, 644–651.

Hanson, C., Henggeler, S., & Burghen, G. (1987a). Model of associations between psychosocial variables and health outcome measures of adolescents with IDDM. *Diabetes Care, 10*, 752–758.

Hanson, C., Henggeler, S., & Burghen, G. (1987b). Social competence and parental support as mediators in the link between stress and metabolic control in adolescents with Insulin dependent diabetes mellitus. *Journal of Consulting and Clinical Psychology, 55*, 529–533.

Hanson, C., Henggeler, S., Harris, M., Burghen, G., & Moore, M. (1989). Family system variables and the health status of adolescents with IDDM. *Health Psychology, 8*, 239–253.

Hanson, C., Henggeler, S., Harris, M., Cigrang, J., Schinkel, A., Rodrigue, J., & Klegges, R. (1992). Contributions of sibling relations to the adaptation of youths with IDDM. *Journal of Consulting and Clinical Psychology, 60*, 104–112.

Harkavy, J., Johnson, S. B., Silverstein, J., Spillar, R., McCallum, M., & Rosenbloom, A. (1983). Who learns what at diabetes summer camp. *Journal of Pediatric Psychology, 8*, 143–154.

Harris, R., & Linn, M. (1985). Health beliefs, compliance, and control of diabetes mellitus. *Southern Medical Journal, 78*, 162–166.

Hauenstein, E., Marvin, R., Snyder, A., & Clarke, W. (1989). Stress in parents of children with diabetes mellitus. *Diabetes Care, 12*, 18–22.

Hauser, S., Jacobsen, A., Lavori, P., Wolfsdorf, J., Herkowitz, R., Milley, J., & Bliss, R. (1990). Adherence among children and adolescents with insulin-dependent diabetes mellitus over a four-year longitudinal follow-up: II. Immediate and long-term linkages with the family milieu. *Journal of Pediatric Psychology, 15*, 527–542.

Hurtado, A., Greenlick, M., & Columbo, T. (1973). Determinants of medical care utilization: Failure to keep appointments. *Medical Care, 11*, 189–198.

Ianotti, R., & Bush, P. (1993). Toward a developmental theory of compliance. In N. Krasnegor, L. Epstein, S. Bennett-Johnson, & S. Yaffe (Eds.), *Developmental aspects of health compliance behavior* (pp. 59–76). Hillsdale, NJ: Lawrence Erlbaum Associates, Inc.

Jacobson, A., Hauser, S., Lavori, P., Wolfsdorf, J., Herskowitz, R., Milley, J., Bliss, R., Gelfand, E., Wertlieb, D., & Stein, J. (1990). Adherence among children and adolescents with Insulin dependent diabetes mellitus over a four-year longitudinal follow-up: I. The influence of patient coping and adjustment. *Journal of Pediatric Psychology, 15*, 511–526.

Jacobson, A., Hauser, S., Wolfsdorf, J., Houlihan, J., Milley, J., Herskowitz, R., Wertlieb, D., & Watt, E. (1987). Psychologic predictors of compliance with recent onset of diabetes. *Journal of Pediatrics, 110*, 805–811.

Johnson, S., Silverstein, J., Rosenbloom, A., Carter, R., & Cunningham, W. (1986). Assessing daily management in childhood diabetes. *Health Psychology, 5*, 545–556.

Johnson, S. B. (1992). Methodological issues in diabetes research. *Diabetes Care, 15*(11).

Johnson, S. B. (1994). Health behaviors and health status: Concepts, methods, and applications. *Journal of Pediatric Psychology, 19*, 129–141.

Johnson, S. B., Freund, A., Silverstein, J., Hansen, C., & Malone, J. (1990). Adherence—Health status relationships in childhood diabetes. *Health Psychology, 9*, 606–631.

Johnson, S. B., Kelly, M., Henretta, J., Cunningham, W., Tomer, A., & Silverstein, J. (1992). A longitudinal analysis of adherence and health status in childhood diabetes. *Journal of Pediatric Psychology, 17*, 537–553.

Johnson, S. B., Pollak, T., Silverstein, J., Rosenbloom, A., Spillar, R., McCallum, M., & Harkavy, J. (1982). Cognitive and behavioral knowledge about insulin-dependent diabetes among children and parents. *Pediatrics, 69*(6), 708–713.

Johnson, S. B., Tomer, A., Cunningham, W., & Henretta, J. (1990). Adherence in childhood diabetes: Results of a confirmatory factor analysis. *Health Psychology, 9*, 493–501.

Jones, P. (1990). Use of a course on self-control behavior techniques to increase adherence to prescribed frequency for self-monitoring blood glucose. *Diabetes Educator, 16*, 296–303.

Kaar, M. L., Akerblom, H. K., Huttunen, N. P., Knip, M., & Sakkinen, K. (1984). Metabolic control in children and adolescents with insulin-dependent diabetes mellitus. *Acta Paediatrica Scandinavia, 73*, 102–108.

Kaplan, R., Chadwick, M., & Schimmel, L., (1985). Social learning intervention to promote metabolic control in type I diabetes mellitus: Pilot experiment results, *Diabetes Care, 8*, 152–155.

Killam, P., Apodaca, L., Mannella, K., & Varni, J. (1983). Behavioral pediatric weight rehabilitation in myelomeningocele: Program description and therapeutic adherence factors. *The American Journal of Maternal Child Nursing, 8*, 280–286.

Koren, G., Solh, H., Klein, J., Soldin, S., & Greenberg, M. (1989). Disposition of oral methotrexate in children with acute lymphoblastic leukemia and its relation to 6-mercaptopurine pharmacokenetics. *Medical & Pediatric Oncology, 17*, 450–454.

Korsch, B., Fine, R., & Negrete, V. (1978). Noncompliance in children with renal transplants, *Pediatrics, 61*, 872–876.

Koski, M., Ahlas, A., & Kumento, A. (1976). A psychosomatic follow-up study of childhood diabetes. *Acta Paedopsychiatrica, 42*, 12–26.

Kovacs, M., Goldston, D., Obrosky, S., & Iyengar, S. (1992). Prevalence and predictors of pervasive noncompliance with medical treatment among youths with Insulin-dependent diabetes mellitus, *Journal of the American Academy of Child and Adolescent Psychiatry, 31*, 1112–1119.

Kovacs, M., Kass, R. E., Schnell, T. M., Goldston, D., & Marsh, J. (1989). Family functioning and metabolic control of school-aged children with insulin dependent diabetes mellitus. *Diabetes Care, 12*, 409–414.

Kuttner, M., Delamater, A., & Santiago, J. (1990). Learned helplessness in diabetic youths. *Journal of Pediatric Psychology, 15*, 581–594.

LaGreca, A., & Ottinger, D. (1979). Self-monitoring and relaxation training in the treatment of medically ordered exercises in a 12-year-old female. *Journal of Pediatric Psychology, 4*, 49–54.

Lemanek, K. (1990). Adherence issues in the medical management of asthma. *Journal of Pediatric Psychology, 15*, 437–458.

Lemanek, K., Trane, S., & Weiner, R. (in press). Asthma. In A. J. Goreczny & M. Hersen (Eds.), *Handbook of pediatric and adolescent health psychology*. Boston: Allyn and Bacon.

Lennard, L., & Lilleyman, J. (1989). Variable mercaptopurine metabolism and treatment outcome in childhood lymphoblastic leukemia. *Journal of Clinical Oncology, 7*, 1816–1823.

Lewis, C., Rachelefsky, G., Lewis, M., de la Sota, A., & Kaplan, M. (1984). A randomized trial of A.C.T. (Asthma Care Training) for kids. *Pediatrics, 74*, 478–486.

Ley, P., Bradshaw, P., Eaves, D., & Walker, C. (1973). A method for increasing patient's recall of information presented by doctors. *Psychology in Medicine, 3*, 217–220.

Lima, J., Nazarian, L., Charney, E., & Lahti, C. (1976). Compliance with short-term antimicrobial therapy: Some techniques that help. *Pediatrics, 57*, 383–386.

Litt, I., & Cuskey, W. (1980). Compliance with medical regimens during adolescence. *Pediatric Clinics of North America, 55*, 3–15.

Lorenz, R., Christensen, N., & Pichert, J. (1985). Diet related knowledge, skill and adherence among children with IDDM. *Pediatrics, 75*, 872–876.

Lowe, K., & Lutzker, J. (1979). Increasing compliance to a medical regimen with a juvenile diabetic. *Behavior Therapy, 10*, 57–64.

Lustman, P., Griffith, L., Clouse, R., & Cryer, P. (1986). Psychiatric illness in diabetes mellitus. *Journal of Nervous and Mental Disease, 174*, 736–748.

Magrab, P., & Papadopoulou, Z. (1977). The effect of a token economy on dietary compliance for children on hemodialysis. *Journal of Applied Behavior Analysis, 10*, 573–578.

Manne, S., Jacobsen, P., Gorfinkle, K., Gerstein, F., & Redd, W. (1993). Treatment adherence difficulties among children with cancer: The role of parenting style. *Journal of Pediatric Psychology, 18*, 47–62.

Manne, S., Lesanics, D., Meyers, P., & Redd, W. (1994). Psychological predictors of pediatric cancer compliance [abstract]. *Annals of Behavioral Medicine, 16*, S188.

Manne, S., Lesanics, D., Meyers, P., Wollner, N., Steinherz, P., & Redd, W. (1994). [Children more compliant when being videotaped]. Unpublished raw data.

Mattar, M., Markello, J., & Yaffee, S. (1975). Pharmaceutic factors affecting pediatric compliance. *Pediatrics, 55*, 101–108.

Mazze, R., Shamoon, H., Pasmantier, R., Lucido, D., Murphy, J., Hartmann, K., Kuykendall, V., & Lopatin, W. (1984). Reliability of blood glucose monitoring by patients with diabetes mellitus. *The American Journal of Medicine, 77*, 211–341.

McCaul, K. D., Glasgow, R. E., & Schafer, L. C. (1987). Diabetes regimen behaviors. *Medical Care, 25*, 868–880.

McConnell, S., Biglan, A., & Severson, H. (1984). Adolescents' compliance with self-monitoring and physiological assessment of smoking in natural environments. *Journal of Behavioral Medicine, 7*, 115–121.

McNabb, W., Wilson-Pessano, S., Hughes, G., & Scamagas, P. (1985). Self-management education of children with asthma: AIRWISE. *American Journal of Public Health, 75*, 1219–1222.

Miklich, D., Renne, C., Creer, T., Alexander, A., Chai, H., Davis, M., Hoffman, A., & Danker-Brown, P. (1977).

The clinical utility of behavior therapy as an adjunctive treatment for asthma. *Journal of Allergy and Clinical Immunology, 60,* 285–294.

Miller, K. (1982). Theophylline compliance in adolescent patients with chronic asthma. *Journal of Adolescent Health Care, 3,* 173–179.

Miller-Johnson, S., Emery, R. E., Marvin, R. S., Clarke, W., Lovinger, R., & Martin M. (1994). Parent child relationships and the management of insulin-dependent diabetes mellitus. *Journal of Consulting and Clinical Psychology, 62,* 603–610.

Minuchin, S., Rosman, B., & Baker, L. (1978). *Psychosomatic families.* Cambridge, MA: Harvard University Press.

Minuchin, S., Baker, L., Rosman, B., Liebman, R., Milman, L., & Todd, T. (1975). A conceptual model of psychosomatic illness in children. *Archives of General Psychiatry, 32,* 1031–1038.

Nurick, M., & Bennett-Johnson, S. (1991). Enhancing blood glucose awareness in adolescents with IDDM. *Diabetes Care, 14,* 1–7.

Parcel, G., Gilman, S., Nader, P., & Bunce, H. (1979). A comparison of absentee rates of elementary school children with asthma and nonasthmatic schoolmates. *Pediatrics, 64,* 878–881.

Pedersen, S., & Moller-Peterson, J. (1984). Erratic absorption of a slow-release theophylline sprinkle product. *Pediatrics, 74,* 534–538.

Pendleton, L., House, W. C., & Parker, L. E. (1987). Physicians' and patients' views of problems of compliance with diabetes regimens. *Public Health Reports, 102,* 21–26.

Phipps, S., & DeCuir-Whalley, S. (1990). Adherence issues in pediatric bone marrow transplantation. *Journal of Pediatric Psychology, 15,* 459–476.

Porter, A. (1969). Drug defaulting in general practice. *British Medical Journal, 1,* 218–222.

Quint, J. (1970). The developing diabetic identity: A study of family influence. In S. Strauss & B. Glaser (Eds.), *Communicating nursing research* (Vol. 3) (pp. 14–32). Boulder, CO: Western Interstate Commission on Higher Education.

Rapoff, M. A., Lindsley, C. B., & Christophersen, E. R. (1985). Parent perceptions of problems experienced by their children in complying with treatments for juvenile rheumatoid arthritis. *Archives of Physical Medicine and Rehabilitation, 66,* 427–429.

Reiss, M., Piotrowski, W., & Bailey, J. (1976). Behavioral community psychology: Encouraging low-income parents to seek dental care for their children. *Journal of Applied Behavior Analysis, 9,* 387–397.

Reynolds, L., Johnson, S. B., & Silverstein, J. (1990). Assessing daily diabetes management by 24 hour recall interview: The validity of children's reports. *Journal of Pediatric Psychology, 15,* 493–509.

Rice, J., & Lutzker, J. (1984). Reducing noncompliance to follow-up appointment keeping at a family practice. *Journal of Applied Behavior Analysis, 17,* 303–311.

Rose, M., Firestone, P., Heick, H., & Faught, A. (1983). The effects of anxiety management training on the control of juvenile diabetes mellitus. *Journal of Behavioral Medicine, 6,* 381–395.

Roth, H., & Caron, H. (1978). Accuracy of doctors' estimates and patients' statements on adherence to the drug regimen. *Clinical Pharmacology and Therapetics, 23,* 361–370.

Sackett, D., & Haynes, R. (1976). (Eds). *Compliance with therapeutic regimens.* Baltimore: The Johns Hopkins University Press.

Sallows, G. (1980). Behavioral treatment of swallowing difficulty. *Journal of Behavioral Therapy and Experimental Psychiatry, 11,* 45–47.

Satin, W., LaGreca, A., Zigo, M., & Skyler, J. (1989). Diabetes in adolescence: Effects of multifamily group intervention and parent simulation of diabetes. *Journal of Pediatric Psychology, 14,* 259–275.

Schafer, L., Glasgow, R., McCaul, K., & Dreher, M. (1983). Adherence to insulin dependent diabetes mellitus regimens: Relationship to psychosocial variables and metabolic control. *Diabetes Care, 6,* 179–185.

Schafer, L., Glasgow, R. & McCaul, K., (1982). Increasing the adherence of diabetic adolescents. *Journal of Behavioral Medicine, 5,* 353–362.

Schafer, L., McCaul, K., & Glasgow, R. (1986). Supportive and unsupportive family behaviors: Relationship to adherence and metabolic control in persons with type I diabetes. *Diabetes Care, 9,* 179–185.

Sergis-Deavenport, E., & Varni, J. (1983). Behavioral assessment and management of adherence to factor replacement therapy in hemophilia. *Journal of Pediatric Psychology, 8,* 367–377.

Sergis-Deavenport, E., & Varni, J. (1982). Behavioral techniques in teaching hemophilia factor replacement procedures to families. *Pediatric Nursing, 8,* 416–419.

Simonds, J. (1977). Psychiatric status of diabetic youth in good and poor controls. *International Journal of Psychiatry in Medicine, 7,* 133–151.

Simonds, J., Goldstein, D., Walker, B., & Rawlings, J. (1981). The relationship between psychological factors and blood glucose regulation in IDDM adolescents. *Diabetes Care, 4,* 610–615.

Smith, N., Seale, J., & Shaw, J. (1984). Medication compliance in children with asthma. *Australian Pediatric Journal, 144,* 119–122.

Smith, N., Seale, J., Ley, P., Shaw, J., & Bracs, P. (1986). Effects of intervention on medication compliance in children with asthma. *Medical Journal of Australia, 144*, 119–122.

Smith, S., Rosen, D., Trueworthy, R., & Lowman, J. (1979). A reliable method of evaluating drug compliance in children with cancer. *Cancer, 43*, 169–173.

Spector, S. (1985). Is your asthmatic really complying? *Annals of Allergy, 55*, 552–556.

Sublett, J. L., Pollard, S. J., Kadlec, G. J., & Karibo, J. M. (1979). Non-compliance in asthmatic children: A study of theophylline levels in a pediatric emergency room population. *Annals of Allergy, 43*, 95–97.

Tebbi, C. K., Cummings, M., Zevon, M. A., Smith, L., Richards, M., & Mallon, J. (1986). Compliance of pediatric and adolescent cancer patients. *Cancer, 58*, 1179–1184.

Tinkelman, D. G., Vanderpool, G. E., Carroll, M. S., Page, E. G., & Spangler, D. L. (1980). Compliance differences following administration of theophylline at six- and twelve-hour intervals. *Annals of Allergy, 44*, 283–286.

Vandenbergh, R., Sussman, K., & Titus, C. (1966). Effects of hypnotically induced acute emotional stress on carbohydrate and lipid metabolism in patients with diabetes mellitus. *Psychosomatic Medicine, 28*, 382–390.

Waller, D., Chipman, J., Hardy, B., Hightower, M., North, A., Williams, S., & Babick, A. (1986). Measuring diabetes-specific family support and its relation to metabolic control. A preliminary report. *Journal of American Academy of Child Psychiatry, 25*, 415–418.

Weinstein, A., & Cuskey, W. (1985). Theophylline compliance in asthmatic children. *Annals of Allergy, 54*, 19.

Weiss, H., Simon, R., Levi, J., Forster, A., Hubbard, M., & Aledort, L. (1991). Compliance in a comprehensive hemophilia center and its implications for home care. *Family Systems Medicine, 9*, 111–120.

Wiebe, D., Alderfer, M., Palmer, S., Lindsay, R., & Jarrett, L. (1994). Behavioral self-regulation in adolescents with type I diabetes: Negative affectivity and blood glucose symptom perception. *Journal of Consulting and Clinical Psychology, 62*, 1204–1212.

Wilson, D., & Endres, R. (1986). Compliance with blood glucose monitoring in children with type 1 diabetes mellitus. *Behavioral Pediatrics, 108*, 1022–1024.

Wysocki, T. (1993). Associations among teen-parent relationships, metabolic control, and adjustment to diabetes in adolescents. *Journal of Pediatric Psychology, 18*, 441–452.

Wysocki, T., Green, L., & Huxtable, K. (1989). Blood glucose monitoring by diabetic adolescents: Compliance and metabolic control. *Health Psychology, 8*, 267–284.

Wysocki, T., Hough, B., Ward, K., & Green, L. (1992). Diabetes mellitus in the transition to adulthood: Adjustment, self-care and health status. *Journal of Developmental and Behavioral Pediatrics, 13*, 194–201.

Zora, J. A., Lutz, C. N., & Tinkelman, D. G. (1989). Assessment of compliance in children using inhaled beta adrenergic agonists. *Annals of Allergy, 62*, 406–409.

CHAPTER 6

FEEDING AND GROWTH DISORDERS

Frances J. Wren
Sally E. Tarbell

DESCRIPTION OF DISORDERS

Introduction

Each child has a genetically determined potential for growth, the fulfillment of which depends on adequate nourishment and the intact hormonal control of the process. Somatic growth is a primary function of the childhood years, and feeding and growth concerns are common. Pediatric assessment of feeding problems is sought by parents of perhaps 25 to 40 percent of children at some point between infancy and the early school years (Maloney & Ruedisueli, 1993) and up to 9 percent of infants and pre-schoolers in primary care may have weight below the third percentile for age (Roberts & Maddux, 1982). As consideration of emotional, behavioral, developmental, and family factors is central to assessment and treatment, this should be one of the most important areas for the collaboration of pediatrician, pediatric psychologist, and pediatric psychiatrist.

Undernourishment may result when adequate food is not offered, is refused, is inefficiently ingested, is not absorbed, or is not normally metabolized. Contributing factors are often multiple and include: physical disease, including structural abnormalities of the feeding apparatus and abnormalities in the neurological or muscular control of the feeding process; poverty; neglect; psychiatric disorders; the aftereffects of traumatic or developmentally abnormal feeding experiences; and factors in the child and/or caregiver that distort the mutually reinforcing social interactions essential for the development of normal feeding skills and behavior.

Disruption of the hormonal control of growth may result from endocrine illness or the administration of exogenous hormone, but it also appears that normal growth hormone secretion can be suppressed in the context of an extremely negative and distorted relationship of the child with a primary caregiver. This condition has been variously called psychosocial dwarfism, psychosocial short stature, or psychosocial growth failure. Children with major depressive disorder may show changes in growth hormone secretion (Ryan et al., 1994), but effects on growth have not been demonstrated clinically.

Community-based studies of failure to thrive and of feeding disorders suggest that underlying physical disease is a factor in only a small minority (Dahl, Eklund, & Sundelin, 1986; Skuse, 1993b), but medical illness and its treatment can contribute to deviations in expected weight gain or growth by increasing nutritional needs, increasing the effort and time needed to ingest adequate nutrients, and by associated malabsorption, nausea, vomiting, appetite suppression, and metabolic abnormalities.

However, the presence of a medical illness does not preclude important psychological and social contributions to growth or feeding problems. For example, children with developmental disabilities, neurological conditions, or structural abnormalities of the feeding apparatus are particularly likely to have unrecognized oral motor dysfunction, which can not only directly affect feeding efficiency, but also disrupt the social interaction with a caregiver essential to the normal development of feeding skills. Medical illness may also lead to prolonged periods of non-oral feeding, depriving an infant of developmentally normal oral stimulation. It may preclude developmentally appropriate self-feeding or may lead to intrusive oral procedures, which may result in the delayed and perhaps permanently arrested emergence of feeding skills, in oral hypersensitivity, and/or in feeding phobias. Conversely, symptoms arising from a mood disorder such as loss of appetite or decreased energy may be inaccurately attributed entirely to a comorbid medical illness. Increased awareness of such interactions has led to a growing consensus that the traditional distinction between organic, non-organic, and mixed failure to thrive is artificial.

Poverty, natural disaster, and endemic food shortages are the most common contributing causes world-wide for failure to make adequate weight gains. It is estimated that 20 percent of Americans under 18 years of age live under the federal poverty line. The figures are higher for younger children (25 percent of those under 6 years old) and for families with parents under 30 years old (42 percent). More children lived in poverty in the United States in 1992 than in any year since 1965 (figures from The Children's Defense Fund, 1994). The possibility that a family is experiencing true physical want must therefore always be considered when a child is failing to make expected weight gains. Pediatric professionals should sensitively pursue this possibility and be aware of federal, state, and local resources for hungry children.

This chapter will take as its principal focus the growth disorders of failure to thrive and psychosocial short stature, and the specific feeding disorders of pica, rumination, and food refusal, selectivity, and phobias. Normal growth and development of normal feeding behavior will be reviewed, as well as commonly occurring deviations that can lead to requests for pediatric medical or psychological/psychiatric intervention.

The classical eating disorders of anorexia and bulimia nervosa and the psychiatric aspects of endocrine disorders are discussed in separate chapters. Although not a primary focus of this chapter, it is worth noting that the most prevalent disorder of growth and weight gain among children in the United States is obesity (Harlan, 1993), and prevalence continues to increase (CDC, 1994; Wolfe, Campbell, Frongillo, Haas, & Melnik, 1994). It has been suggested that decreased physical activity, increased fast food consumption, and increased television viewing may play a role in this social phenomenon (Gortmaker, Dietz, & Cheung, 1990). Longitudinal studies confirm that seriously obese children are highly likely to suffer from obesity and its associated risks as adults (Clarke & Lauer, 1993). The risks of medical complications in childhood are less well defined (Anonymous, Canadian Task Force on the Periodic Health Examination, 1994; Flegal, 1993), but there is emerging evidence of early cardiovascular risk (Shea et al., 1994).

Most studies of treatment for serious pediatric obesity (> 180 percent of ideal body weight) are limited and largely case series based. However, Epstein and colleagues (1990) have reported significant weight control benefits for moderately obese pre-adolescents in a well-controlled ten-year follow-up of a highly structured behavioral medical treatment program that included parental participation. How generalizable these findings are to uncontrolled clinical populations is unclear, but this sort of long-term success contrasts with the generally poor outcome of treatment in adults, providing support for efforts at early intervention.

Normal Growth and the Development of Feeding Skills

Endocrine Control of Growth

As a primary function of the developing organism, somatic growth is influenced by multiple endocrine systems at multiple levels (Van Den Brande & Rappaport, 1993a). The principal "growth axis" is the hypothalamic-growth hormone (GH) axis of which the major factors are growth hormone releasing factor (GRF) and somatostatin (SS) from the hypothalamus (also widely distributed elsewhere), in addition to GH in the anterior pituitary, and somatomedins (or insulin-like growth factors) in the periphery. GH is secreted by the anterior pituitary in a rhythmic, pulsatile manner that is closely linked to sleep and has a distinct circadian pattern. The normal pulsatility and circadian rhythm in GH levels and the many factors that can cause transient variations in its level make the interpretation of tests of GH secretion a task for experts.

Infant and intrauterine growth is primarily dependent on nutrition; hence under one year of age a low growth velocity is likely to be nutritional in origin. Growth hormone receptors are not detectable in the human infant until about 200 days of postnatal life. Even infants with complete GH deficiency have virtually normal growth at birth, and in less profound cases isolated GH deficiency may not declare itself until the end of the first year of life (Brook, 1993), when the clinical picture of true pituitary dwarfism begins to emerge. Hence psychosocial short stature (or "psychosocial dwarfism") is a syndrome of children two years of age and older.

Measurement

To assess growth attention must be paid to the child's attained height and weight, growth curve, genetic potential for growth, and nutritional status. Accurate measurement and interpretation of the data are essential. Standard pediatric and endocrine texts (e.g., Brook, 1993; Tanner, 1990; World Health Organization, 1983) supply more exhaustive discussion of these issues.

A standard pediatric evaluation of growth includes weight, height when standing (or lying in the non-ambulatory), skull circumference and staging of maturity of primary and secondary sex characteristics (Tanner staging). Measurement of skin fold thickness (and/or limb circumferences), sitting height, and bone age, as well as calculation of growth velocity may also be indicated. Ideally, the same person will take the measurements on each visit.

In measuring height the head is held with the outer canthus of the eye in the same horizontal plane as the external auditory meatus and maximum length is obtained by gentle traction applied to the mastoid process (Brook, 1993). Skinfold thickness (obtained using standard skin fold calipers) can aid in the assessment and monitoring of nutritional status. Bone age is a measurement of how nearly growth is complete and can be assessed according to multiple different systems based on skeletal maturity as revealed by X-ray. These systems vary in their clinical practicality and in the validity of their application to normal versus pathological situations, and include the Greulich and Pyle atlas method, the Tanner and Whitehouse rating method, and the Bayley and Pinneau method (Brook, 1993; Tanner, 1990). Delayed bone age is a feature of pituitary dwarfism including psychosocial short stature. Calculation of growth velocity requires at least two measurements that are enough apart in timing that the expectable growth is more than the cumulative error on the two measurements. In childhood this means 3-month intervals at a minimum, but the interval can be less in infancy, where rate of growth is higher (Brook, 1993).

Interpretation of Growth Data

Ideally, growth data should be interpreted in the context of the growth expectations for a given child and the pattern of growth over time. Practically, this usually means that a child's serial growth parameters are first placed on a centile chart based on putative population norms, most typically derived from cross-sectional data. The growth standards conventionally used are the Tanner, Whitehouse, and Takaishi standards (1966) (UK) and the charts of the National Center for Health Statistics (NCHS) (US), which in fact have much similarity. Both these standards are open to criticism and attempts have been made to develop longitudinal (e.g., Berkey, Reed, & Valadian, 1983) and velocity-based standards. Skuse (1993b) has recently reviewed in detail the literature on the limitations of currently used growth standards and the pitfalls related to their interpretation. The recent completion of the third National Health and Nutrition Examination Survey (NHANES III) has shown shifts in the distribution of body weights within the U.S. population (e.g., Center for Disease Control, 1994). Whether and how these should be reflected in modifications of standard growth charts is a subject of debate. The Tanner and NCHS standards also allow calculation of weight for height and some authors have used this criterion to determine the presence of undernourishment, but this method can miss chronic mild to moderate malnutrition. There is no universal agreement as to the best method to define growth failure and undernutrition (Wright, Ashenburg, & Whitaker, 1994).

The normal linear growth curve has three component curves that reflect the developmental differences in the hormonal control of growth: infant, childhood, and pubertal (Karlberg, 1987, 1988). In normal growth and development each component curve "takes off" in turn from the previous curve.

The largely nutrition-dependent growth of infancy is characterized by high, rapidly decelerating growth velocity and a move from predominant dependence on the intra-uterine environment to a growth "channel" in the population in accordance with genetic potential. The correlation between the child's height (length) centile and mid-parental height centile (a clinical marker of the individual child's probable familial genetic endowment for growth) is low at birth, increases through infancy, and becomes stable beyond the age of two years (Brook,

1993). It is common for the percentile rank for a given child for both weight and length to change within the first and second years of life, as the child transitions to a genetically determined growth trajectory (Berkey et al., 1983). This normal variation suggests that defining failure to thrive on the basis of a change in growth percentile alone may lead to overestimates of prevalence (Wright et al., 1991).

Multiple factors affect the interpretation of growth data (Brook, 1993; Skuse, 1993b). Birth weight is inversely related to the rate of growth in both weight and length in infancy. Breast-fed infants are likely to be heavier than bottle-fed infants in the first three months and lighter thereafter through infancy. Infants who are premature or have had intra-uterine growth retardation have distinct growth curves. Excess calories lead to increased length as well as weight. Tall children become and remain tall and become tall adults by growing at a rate consistently greater than their small peers. In childhood the male and female growth rate is virtually identical, but at puberty girls have an earlier, longer, lower peak in growth velocity than boys. The later puberty is the more growth slows; it can be close to zero in late onset puberty.

When growth failure is determined to be present it is also necessary to assess the degree of malnourishment in order to determine the urgency with which intervention is indicated (see the guidelines presented by Frank & Zeisel, 1988).

Normal Development of Feeding Skills

Readers interested in more detailed discussion of this area are referred to specific reviews (Skuse, 1993a; Skuse & Wolke, 1992a; Stevenson & Allaire, 1991). During the first three years of life, the infant and toddler make the transition from the reflex-bound feeding behaviors of the neonate to mature swallowing and chewing behavior by a series of neurodevelopmental stages in which reflexes disappear or are refined and incorporated into more voluntary, learned feeding behaviors (Stevenson & Allaire, 1991). This process is dependent on the anatomical integrity of the multiple structures involved in feeding, neurological maturation, and experiential learning, which is mediated by both social cues and oral sensory feedback, and takes place in a relational context. The development of feeding skills is truly a biopsychosocial process (Stevenson & Allaire, 1991).

Stevenson & Allaire (1991) point out that normal swallowing involves 31 pairs of striated muscles, which are in turn innervated by elements of four cranial nerves. The full-term neonate possesses a series of reflexes related to feeding that are basically under sub-cortical control (summarized by Skuse & Wolke, 1992a). These include the rooting reflex, which involves orienting responses of the head to assist in the location of nutrition; the phasic bite reflex, which involves transient clamping on objects stimulating the front or lateral part of the oral cavity; and the suckle-swallow reflex with a characteristic pattern of bursts of suckling, swallowing, and breathing that is specific to each infant. Suckling or lick-suck involves a backward forward tongue movement with rhythmic compression of the nipple against the upper jaw and hard palate. Over the first six months this progresses to true sucking, a more complex but efficient process involving up and down movement of the body of the tongue with tongue tip elevation and closure of the lips. The efficiency of the coordination of sucking, swallowing, and breathing also increases. When the pharynx is filled, the process of pharyngeal swallowing is initiated reflexively, along with reflex closure of the vocal cords. Respiratory needs will always take priority, so the infant who has cardiorespiratory difficulties will often be a poor feeder. From 6 to 12 months the infant is developing the ability to use the upper lip in clearing a spoon and the tongue, and to close the lip during swallowing (Stevenson & Allaire, 1991). At 24 months the infant, while still needing to bite a cup to maintain jaw stability, can show much of the mature swallow with controlled rotatory jaw movements and tongue lateralization (Skuse & Wolke, 1992a). These phases are variably reflected in the cultural practices of weaning and the offering of food types and consistencies (e.g., liquid food, finger foods).

As in other developmental lines, the presentation of a new challenge, such as a new food or food texture, may produce regression to earlier levels of skill. It has been postulated that within the process of feeding skills development there may be sensitive periods in which the introduction of specific experiences will further optimal development of skills (Skuse, 1993a). For example, at 4 to 6 months virtually any new taste will be accepted, while resistance to novel tastes is normal after the first year, leading to speculation that an overly restricted variety of tastes in the middle of the first year may predispose to later food selectivity problems. Similarly, there is some evidence that when infants are not exposed by 6 to 7 months to solid textures that require chewing, they are likely to have less mature oral-motor skills in the second year of life, with gagging and secondary food refusal. It has also been reported that infants who have not had the opportunity to mouth objects may show failure of the gag reflex to decrease at 6 months of age. Hence infants who are motor disabled and cannot engage in normal hand/mouth play may develop oral hypersensitivity. Conditions affecting the postural stability of the head and neck and fine motor skills can also affect the efficiency of feeding.

It is therefore expectable that children with anatomical abnormalities of the feeding apparatus or abnormalities of its muscular or neurological control may have feeding difficulties reflecting both primary oral motor dysfunction and superimposed delays and deviations in the emergence of feeding skills due to distortions of the normal context for their development. Such infants are at increased risk of failure to make adequate weight gains and, being difficult to feed, of aversive feeding experiences that may further lead to superimposed secondary learned feeding disorders such as food refusal or maladaptive mealtime behaviors.

Failure to Thrive

Diagnostic Criteria

Failure to thrive (FTT) is the persistent failure to make expected weight gains; so defined, it is not a syndrome but a physical sign whose cause is undernourishment whether due to not being fed, to a feeding disorder, or to medical illness (Mayes & Volkmar, 1993; Skuse, 1993b). The use of the term *failure to thrive* is often limited to infants under two years of age, but much of what follows also has relevance to older children. The diagnosis of FTT should be made on anthropometric criteria alone (Frank & Zeisel, 1988; Skuse, 1993b). To thrive appears to imply more than to simply grow (Lancet, 1990). The word reflects the origins of the term in the early clinical observations that recognized that delays in weight gain can be associated with delays in social, cognitive, and motor development and with difficult social and emotional environments. Emphasis on the environment and on the distinction between organic and non-organic FTT has sometimes led to the vague presentation of "social and emotional deprivation" as a "cause" of FTT (Barbero, 1992), obscuring the fact that, despite various and often multiple contributing factors, the final cause of FTT is now held to always be undernourishment (Frank & Zeisel, 1988). Efforts continue to define valid syndromes of FTT, with investigators focusing variously on attachment to caregivers, developmental status, and presence or absence of feeding

disorder (e.g., Chatoor, Dickson, Shaeffer, & Egan, 1985; Woolston, 1985), but this work has not yet produced a well-validated and universally accepted system (Benoit, 1993; Mayes & Volkmar, 1993; Skuse, 1993b). Recent work increasingly emphasizes the importance of the dyadic interaction, of infant characteristics, and of feeding disorders as potential contributors to any case of FTT, whether with or without physical illness. Hence, the suggestion has been made that the phenomenon might be more aptly labeled "failure to make adequate weight gain" (Lancet, 1990), and that it is misleading to pursue the traditional division of cases of FTT into those caused by identifiable physical illness ("organic" FTT) and those caused by social and emotional factors ("nonorganic" FTT) (Frank & Zeisel, 1988; Lancet, 1990; Mayes, 1993; Skuse, 1993b).

If there is now an emerging consensus to define FTT simply as a persistent failure to make expected weight gains, difficulties persist in defining what is "persistent" and what is "expected" with enough precision to identify the point where relatively slow weight gain becomes pathological (Benoit, 1993; Berkey, 1983; Edwards, Halse, Parkin, & Waterson, 1990; Lancet, 1990; Leung & Robson, 1992; Mayes & Volkmar, 1993; Porter & Skuse, 1991; Skuse, 1993b; Wilcox, Nieburg, & Miller, 1989; Wright, Edwards, Halse, & Waterson, 1991). For example, Wright, Ashenburg, and Whitaker (1994) used three common anthropometric methods of defining undernutrition in a population of 258 children referred to a clinic specializing in evaluation of failure to thrive: they found wide variability in whom and how many (75–98 percent) each method categorized as undernourished.

The range of more commonly used screening criteria can be summarized thus:

1. Attained weight below the 5th or 3rd percentile for chronological age or height on population-appropriate growth charts, or
2. Deceleration of the rate of weight gain from birth, or 4–8 weeks after birth (Edwards et al., 1990), to the present as reflected by a decrease by two major percentiles or two standard deviations in attained weight percentile.
3. Persistence of either pattern for a set period. There is no universal agreement as to the length of this period; typically it is somewhere between six weeks and three months.

These criteria can be seen to be imprecise, and in fact when applied to the individual case there are many pitfalls related to their interpretation. They should be viewed as screening guidelines that can help in alerting clinicians to those in whom failure to thrive must be considered. The judgment as to whether a child is failing to meet its own *individual* expectations for weight gain must rest with a pediatric specialist skilled in the interpretation of growth data.

FTT and Developmental Delays and Deviations

Developmental delays and deviations are important associations of FTT. However, given the variations in the definition of FTT used in the literature and the preponderance of clinically referred and hospitalized infants in the published studies it is not possible to make definitive epidemiological statements. Some studies have included developmental delays as an essential part of the definition of FTT, further muddying the literature. Such associations could arise because of pre-existing developmental and temperamental factors that may independently predispose the child to both feeding and other developmental difficulties, direct effects of current malnutrition on infant behavior, and/or possible long-term neurodevelopmental effects of early malnutrition.

Skuse, Reilly, & Wolke (1994) using pure anthropometric criteria in a large population-based study of FTT found that in the second year of life affected infants could be distinguished from normally growing controls on the basis of cognitive and neurodevelopmental status, oral motor competence, and features of the family environment. They have also (Skuse, Pickles, Wolke, & Reilly, 1994) assessed their epidemiological data for support of the concept of a critical period for postnatal growth and mental development during which undernutrition is particularly likely to produce developmental impairment. They sub-divided their sample into an early growth faltering group (onset at less than 6 months) and a late growth faltering group (onset at greater than 6 months). Their data are interpreted as suggesting that early faltering is associated with a worse cognitive and psychomotor outcome although the anthropometric outcome is comparable. Those in the late group in fact had cognitive and motor outcomes comparable to normally growing controls. Potentially confounding psychosocial variables were measured at the same time and included cognitive stimulation. It was concluded that the degree of growth failure appeared to account for up to 37 percent of the variance in developmental outcome, which could be related to the timing, duration, and onset of growth faltering. The early group in fact carried less psychosocial burden. The authors caution that the question of direc-

tion of effects is not fully resolved, as pre-existing unrecognized developmental difficulty might have given rise to the feeding problems and growth failure. The relative importance of these factors therefore has not been disentangled.

FTT and Feeding Disorders

Similar difficulties arise in interpreting the literature on the occurrence of feeding disorders in FTT. It appears likely however that their prevalence is, if anything, underestimated—including the prevalence of frank underlying oral-motor dysfunction. In those studies that have looked at the prevalence of oral-motor dysfunction in groups of otherwise healthy infants with failure to thrive it has been commonly detected, suggesting that even in "non-neurological" populations, discrete, primary feeding difficulties may play a significant role in the development of FTT (Mathisen, Skuse, Wolke, & Reilly, 1989).

Paradoxically, in populations with neurodevelopmental conditions, there may be a particularly strong tendency to overlook the importance of feeding disorders and to ascribe FTT to non-specific effects of the medical condition. However, these are the very populations that are most at risk for disorders of oral-motor function. In a recent study of pre-school children with cerebral palsy and known oral-motor dysfunction, Reilly and Skuse (1992) found a high prevalence of severe feeding difficulties that were largely unknown to the family's medical advisers. Skuse points out that feeding difficulties in cerebral palsy can also be exacerbated by communication difficulties resulting in impaired expression of hunger or food preferences, lack of self-feeding skills, inability to forage, and a high incidence of gastroesophageal reflux. Dahl and Gebre-Medhin (1993) studied the food intake, current feeding situation, and nutritional status of thirty children with cerebral palsy and fourteen with myelomeningocele. Feeding problems, low energy intake, and wasting were frequent among the children with cerebral palsy, particularly those with the dystonic form. Mathisen and colleagues (Mathisen, Reilly, & Skuse, 1992) looked at a group of children with Turner's syndrome and found evidence of a high prevalence of oral motor dysfunction and possible lower gastroesophageal tract difficulties. These findings underline the complexity of this area as children with Turner's syndrome have a distinctive growth curve with short stature that has not been regarded as having a nutritional component.

Growth assessment in premature infants is similarly complex. There is a risk that FTT may be over diagnosed if weight is not corrected for gestational age and account not taken of the distinctive growth curve of prematurity (Skuse, 1993b). On the other hand, prematurity has possible neurological, cardiorespiratory, and gastrointestinal sequelae and may be associated with behavioral disorganization and perhaps prolonged non-oral feeding, creating an increased risk of feeding disorder that may be missed because the infant is simply viewed as having been "born small" (Frank & Zeisel, 1988).

Failure of Older Children to Gain Weight

While the use of the term *failure to thrive* is usually limited to the first two years of life, many of the same factors may be operating when older children fail to make adequate weight gains. The child may be malnourished because of poverty, cognitively or culturally based parental misconceptions as to nutritional needs, or abusive withholding of food. In the pre-school years feeding disorder is likely to be important, and in older children early-onset eating disorder must be considered. There is little information as to the degree of continuity between feeding disorders in early childhood and the eating disorders seen in school-age children and adolescents. However, a proportion of those with eating disorders do retrospectively recall apparent feeding difficulties in earlier childhood (Maloney & Ruedisueli, 1993).

Children will be seen clinically who have neurodevelopmental disorders or who, having survived prematurity or other serious and prolonged early childhood illness, show the persistence of previous feeding difficulties into later childhood. Older children may develop new onset food or swallowing phobia following a choking episode or other traumatic event. Consideration must also be given to emerging psychiatric illness, including early-onset obsessive-compulsive disorder and mood disorder. Obsessive-compulsive disorder has been described as early as in the pre-school years and is often overlooked in pre-adolescent children as the seemingly oppositional battles with parents about self-care and eating regimens may be more apparent than the underlying obsessions or compulsions, often poorly articulated if at all by young children. Anorexia, decreased energy and motivation, decreased enjoyment of food, increased irritability, boredom, and resistance to eating may occur during the course of a depressive episode. Where there is medical co-morbidity these symptoms and the associated failure to make expected weight gains may be inaccurately attributed entirely to the medical illness. Finally,

consideration must be given to endocrine causes of short stature, including psychosocial short stature.

Psychosocial Short Stature

The syndrome of psychosocial short stature (PSS), also known as psychosocial dwarfism, is often confused with the more common clinical sign of failure to thrive. This confusion is reflected by the multitude of existing terms that are either synonymous with PSS (deprivational dwarfism, psychosocial dwarfism, psychosocial growth failure, reversible hyposomatotropinism) or embody overlapping or related concepts such as emotional deprivation, maternal deprivation, and reactive attachment disorder of infancy and early childhood (American Psychiatric Association, DSM-IV, 1994).

Three important criteria distinguish the syndrome of psychosocial short stature from failure to thrive:

1. Psychosocial short stature is primarily a failure to make expected gains in *height or length* as opposed to weight. In contrast, in failure to thrive any decrease in rate of growth in height or length typically occurs late in the course of malnutrition *following* weight loss and is a sign of chronicity (stunting).
2. Psychosocial short stature is primarily, perhaps exclusively, a disorder of *toddlerhood to adolescence* as opposed to infancy and toddlerhood.
3. Psychosocial short stature arises from an *endocrine disturbance* (suppression of normal pulsatile growth hormone [GH] secretion) that appears to be environmentally induced; any endocrine changes seen in FTT are those that arise as a consequence of protein calorie malnutrition. GH levels are usually either normal or increased in malnutrition.

"Mixed" cases are not typical but do occur when a child with PSS is also undernourished: for example, when a caregiver is actually starving a child.

These differences between PSS and FTT make physiological sense in the context of the differences, between the hormonal control of growth in infancy (primarily under nutritional control) and in childhood (growth hormone). Psychosocial short stature was first detected in the investigation of children who appeared to have the endocrinological picture of "pituitary dwarfism," but whose growth failure and apparent GH hormone deficiency were found to be reversible and who typically showed distinctive behaviors (Powell, Brasel, & Blizzard, 1967; Powell, Brasel, Raiti, & Blizzard, 1967).

The subsequent literature on the syndrome, while compelling, has been virtually entirely case report or series based (see reviews in Green, Campbell, & David, 1984; Green, 1986; Green, 1990; Skuse, 1989; Woolston, 1991). PSS has not yet been included in the International Classification of Diseases (World Health Organization, 1992). In the most recent editions of the Diagnostic and Statistical Manual of Mental Disorders (American Psychiatric Association, 1987, 1994), it is mentioned once only, without diagnostic criteria, as a condition to be considered in the differential diagnosis of reactive attachment disorder (Mayes & Volkmar, 1993).

Green's (1990) summary of the picture suggested by the literature is that an inimical psychosocial environment, the most important feature of which is a severely disturbed primary caregiver/child relationship, typically causes endocrine abnormalities, severe growth retardation, behavioral abnormalities, and developmental delays. These features abruptly improve or worsen following changes in a similar direction in the psychosocial environment. He suggests as the "sine qua non" of diagnosis that affected children are inherently capable of normal growth and development, that the cause is an abnormal, inimical social environment, and that growth failure is reversible to a significant degree on removal from the inimical environment. Suggestions for more formal diagnostic criteria have also been developed by Green (1986).

A child with PSS typically has the habitus of a child some years younger ("proportionate stunting"—Skuse, 1989). Underlying this presentation is a slowing in height gain and delay in bone age, with weight for both height and bone age remaining normal (or even increased). Also typical are disturbed eating and, less commonly, drinking behaviors; these include hyperphagia, binging with occasional self-induced vomiting, stealing and hoarding food, driven food seeking as illustrated by reports of eating from garbage pails, and polydypsia with bizarre behaviors such as drinking from toilet bowls. Sleep disorder, which may include night roaming, is commonly reported but details vary (Guilhaume, Benoit, Gourmelen, & Richardet, 1982; Powell & Darragh, 1973; Tormey, Hopwood, & Barratt, 1980). When described, the parental relationship with the affected child is often grossly disturbed, with abuse, neglect, and/or a fixed negative view of the child (Skuse, 1989). A single child in a family may be affected with others being spared. Six of thirteen affected children in a recent case series had been sexually abused (Albanese et al., 1994). Other less specific behavioral and emotional symptoms are variably reported, including enuresis and encopresis; social, cognitive, and language delays; unusual patterns of relatedness; moodiness and irritability; apathy and social withdrawal; elective mutism; pain agnosia; self-injury; cataplexy; aggressiveness and impulsiveness; defiance and antisocial behavior (Blizzard & Bulatovic, 1992; Green, 1986; Guilhaume et al., 1982; Money, Wolfe & Annecillo, 1972; Mouridsen & Nielsen, 1990; Stanhope et al., 1988; Wolff & Money, 1973). Many of these associations may be non-specific effects of abusive or disturbed parent-child relationships rather than being specific to PSS. How much they are reflective of underlying vulnerabilities that make a child susceptible to the condition is unknown.

Although the neuroendocrine disturbance is core to the diagnosis of PSS, the lack of formal studies has produced a limited and inconsistent literature. Green reviewed this literature in 1990. Somatomedin levels were disturbed in all of the 17 reported cases in which they had been measured. They were typically low, in the range usually associated with pituitary dysfunction. Fasting GH on or soon after hospitalization was low in 90 percent of those tested and typically normalized within days of change of environment. GH response to provocative stimulation was blunted soon after hospitalization and before increase in growth rates in 50 percent of those tested; once increase in growth rates occurred it was normal in 95 percent. The isolated reports on nocturnal GH secretion suggest disturbances and decreases in GH secretion during slow wave sleep (Howse et al., 1977; Powell et al., 1973). More recently Albanese and colleagues (1994) have studied GH profiles in eleven prepubertal children with a diagnosis of PSS. On the first day of hospitalization they found a spectrum of abnormalities in spontaneous GH secretion. This GH insufficiency showed reversibility, with significant increase in GH secretion at the end of a three-week stay during which parental access was restricted.

The hallmark of diagnosis is that with removal from the putatively "noxious" environment there is a rapid acceleration in growth rate, which has been reported to be up to a six- to tenfold increase, and a normalization of the endocrine picture; these changes can begin in days and may take months (Green 1986; Skuse, 1989). Removal from the "noxious" environment can be followed by transient hyperkinesis in children who may have previously been apathetic and withdrawn. There may also be an increase in the rate of social and cognitive development, and a decrease in behavioral and emotional symptoms, although this may need, beyond simple removal from home, the development of an appropriate attachment relationship and the provision of a structured, stimulating, age-appropriate environment. One detailed case report documented variations in weight gain and growth, despite equivalent caloric intake, with changes in access to a substitute caregiver favored by the child (Saenger et al., 1977).

Food Refusal, Selectivity and Phobias

Concerns about feeding and weight gain are among the most common reasons for parents of infants and toddlers to seek medical advice. However, it is important to note that much of the clinical research has been with the very small sub-group of infants and children who are referred for specialist evaluation of feeding problems. The most commonly reported difficulties are food refusal and food selectivity or "picky eating" ranging from the child's absolute refusal to take any food or drink by mouth, to refusal of select foods, drinks, textures, or tastes. The challenge for the pediatrician is in distinguishing between, on the one hand, the normal struggles and worries that arise in the course of the development of feeding skills and, on the other, clinically significant feeding disorders. The literature supplies limited help in this area as the prevalence of clinically significant feeding disorders and the boundaries of the pathological are unknown (Harris & Booth, 1992) and the likely longitudinal course of difficulties presenting in infancy and early childhood is unestablished (Maloney, 1993; Skuse, 1993a). Clinically significant disorder is suggested when the problem persists despite simple behavioral and educational intervention by the pediatrician. Clinical concern is also increased when there is associated FTT, behavioral or developmental difficulties in the child, or significant family distress. One epidemiological study used a duration of one month as a guideline for the definition of true feeding disorder in infancy (Dahl & Sundelin, 1986).

Food refusal presents with behaviors ranging from simple turning of the head to avert food intake, to more active tantrums, crying, and escape behaviors. In food selectivity, similar behaviors are observed, but around particular foods only. Food refusal or selectivity can occur with or without food phobias. When a food phobia is present the child will display fear and more classic anxiety symptoms upon presentation of food. This distinction is important because it affects treatment choice. Food phobias have been described most commonly in infants and preschool age children (Archer & Szatmari, 1990; Singer, Nofer, Benson-Szekely, & Brooks, 1991) but can occur at any age.

Food refusal may develop and/or be maintained in a number of different situations including (1) the association of feeding or oral stimulation with aversive experiences (in which case food phobia is particularly likely to be a factor in the observed food refusal); (2) the inadvertent reinforcement of the child's food selectivity or

refusal by excessive caregiver attention; and (3) the absence, typically for medical or developmental reasons, of developmentally normal early feeding experiences.

Children who have been force fed or had other aversive feeding interactions with caregivers may refuse feeding as a means to escape the disagreeable encounter (Archer & Szatmari, 1990; Singer et al., 1991). Children who have experienced or witnessed a choking episode or vomiting may develop a food or swallowing phobia (Singer, Ambuel, Wade, & Jaffe, 1992). Children with gastrointestinal disorders such as gastroesophageal reflux or motility disorders may come to associate eating with unpleasant after events, and thus refuse to eat any foods, or particular foods associated with reflux or vomiting. Children, especially infants, who have been subjected to repeated aversive procedures around their nose and mouth—for example, trauma, wound care, placement and replacement of feeding tubes, or surgical repairs for facial abnormalities such as cleft-palate—may develop food refusal as a learned response to any stimulation around the mouth. Children may develop classically conditioned food aversions, for example, secondary to chemotherapy treatments.

When the child has come to perceive the eating of particular foods as aversive, caregivers may inadvertently maintain the child's avoidant behavior by giving unintended social reinforcement in the form of attention. This is often an important factor in maintaining difficulties that may have arisen for other reasons. "Picky eating," a very common phenomenon in toddlers and preschool children, can likewise be shaped by inadvertent reinforcement of the child's food selections, such as by restricting the diet offered to the child's preferred foods, or by frequent coaxing to eat other foods.

The absence, typically for medical or developmental reasons, of normal early feeding experiences may also contribute to the development of feeding problems. Children diagnosed at birth or in infancy with a medical condition that requires that their nutritional needs be met by non-oral feeding, may have never taken food or drink by mouth. Such children are at risk for extreme resistance to "refeeding" once the need for supplemental feeding has been reduced or eliminated, especially if they receive no compensatory oral-motor stimulation at theorized sensitive periods in early development (Skuse et al., 1994; Stevenson & Allaire, 1991). They may become so sensory defensive that they may refuse even the most superficial encounter with oral stimulation, such as a drop of water on the lips.

Medical disorders in which food refusal is common include gastroesophageal reflux, short-gut syndrome, inflammatory bowel disease, hepatic or pancreatic disease, and oncologic disorders. The health complications of food selectivity, refusal, and phobias can range from minor problems that can be treated simply through dietary supplementation, to major difficulties, including FTT, specific nutritional deficits, extended periods on total parenteral nutrition (TPN), liver failure, and death.

Rumination

This feeding disorder is characterized by the chronic (at least one-month duration) and intentional regurgitation of previously ingested food into the mouth, followed by further chewing and either expelling or reswallowing of the food (American Psychiatric Association, 1994). Rumination is noted most commonly in two populations (1) infants, with onset at approximately six months (Lavigne, Burns, & Colter, 1981; Mestre, Resnick, & Berman, 1983; Sajwaj, Libet, & Agras, 1974; Sauvage, Leddet, Hameury, & Barthelemy, 1985), and (2) the mentally retarded (Mayes et al., 1988; Singh, 1981), with the average age of onset reported to be between five and six years (Mayes, 1992; Mayes et al., 1988). Diagnosis of rumination may be delayed until the medical work up has ruled out gastrointestinal or metabolic abnormalities that may present with chronic vomiting (Mestre et al., 1983). Early psychodynamic formulations of rumination implicated disturbances in the child's personality and in the interactions with caregivers as central to the etiology (Fullerton, 1963; Richmond, Eddy, & Green, 1958). More recent researchers have noted that this disorder occurs not only in those families where there is insufficient stimulation of the infant, but also in children who experience very positive relationships with their caregivers, leading Lavigne and colleagues (1981) to suggest that the population of children who ruminate is not homogeneous with regard to the presence of psychopathology in the family.

Johnston (1993) proposes a subtyping of ruminative disorders to include: (1) organic vomiting, where engagement in ruminative behaviors arises as a function of a medical abnormality, such as gastroesophageal reflux or an abnormal gag reflex; (2) operant vomiting, where vomitus is expelled from the mouth and sometimes "played" with, creating a situation that invites attention and social reinforcement by caregivers; and (3) rumination, where the child intentionally regurgitates, rechews, and reswallows previously ingested food, a self-stimulatory behavior proposed to be maintained by operant contingencies. These differing typologies in turn may suggest different modes of intervention. For a comprehensive discussion of the typology and etiology of ruminative behaviors, see reviews by Johnston (1993) and Mayes et al. (1988).

Potential medical complications from ruminative disorders are significant and include dehydration, electrolyte imbalance, and failure to thrive. The condition can be fatal.

Pica

Pica is the chronic eating of nonnutritive substances. In infants and young children the mouthing and ingestion of nonnutritive substances is part of the normal developmental course up until approximately 36 months. The Diagnostic and Statistical Manual of Mental Disorders, fourth edition (American Psychiatric Association, 1994) requires in its definition of pica that the behavior be developmentally inappropriate, not be a culturally sanctioned practice, and occur for at least one month. The DSM-IV also reports that substances chosen for ingestion vary with age, with infants and young children ingesting substances such as paint and plaster, older children ingesting pebbles, insects, and other items found outdoors, and adolescents dirt or clay. Among the more common forms of pica are pagophagia (ice ingestion), plumbophagia (lead ingestion), and geophagia (clay or soil ingestion). A more comprehensive review of some of the potentially limitless substances used in the practice of pica can be found in Lacey (1993).

Feldman (1986) reviews four possible etiologies for pica, including (1) nutritional, with iron deficiency being cited frequently (2) psychological, with lack of stimulation (Madden, Russo, & Cataldo, 1980) and parent-child interactional difficulties being cited (3) cultural, with pica described as integral to particular cultural traditions and (4) pharmacological, with the individual seeking the pharmacological effects of the substance ingested. There is insufficient research to date to provide definitive support for any of these proposed etiologies or how these factors may interact in the development of pica.

There are potentially significant health risks associated with pica, and these are related to the substance ingested, the dose, and the duration of ingestion. It is especially important to note that greater than 30 percent of children with pica have some evidence of lead poisoning (Feldman, 1986). Lacey (1993) provides a description of substance-dependent risks, including (1) toxicity (if the substance ingested is intrinsically poisonous); (2) infestation by parasites; (3) under and over nourishment; and (4) disorders of the gastrointestinal tract, including altered motility, absorption, obstruction, and perforation.

EPIDEMIOLOGY OF FEEDING AND GROWTH DISORDERS

Failure to Thrive

Until recently, studies of the prevalence and associations of FTT were almost entirely based on clinically referred populations. Failure to thrive has been reported to account for 1–5 percent of admissions to pediatric hospitals (Berwick, 1980; Mitchell & Greenberg, 1980). Over 9 percent of children 4 years of age and younger in primary care have been found to have weight below the third percentile for age (Roberts & Maddux, 1982). Frank and Zeisel (1988) summarized the then-existing epidemiological literature on failure to thrive as suggesting that almost 10 percent of low-income children in primary care have weight or length below the 5th percentile and that 15–30 percent of children brought to inner-city emergency departments for acute care have evidence of "growth deficits." Gender does not appear to be a factor in FTT, but ordinal position may be, with FTT less likely in first-born children.

Skuse and colleagues (Skuse, 1993b; Skuse, Reilly, & Wolke, 1994; Skuse, Pickles, Wolke, & Reilly, 1994), in a large community-based study of FTT, followed full-term, healthy babies with birth weights above the 3rd percentile (standardized for mid-pregnancy weight of mother, gestation, gender, and ordinal position) in a population-derived sample containing 2,510 live births in an ethnically diverse inner-city population of 140,000 in London, England. Infants were defined as failing to thrive when the weight gain trajectory crossed below the third percentile, and persisted below it for at least three months by the end of the first year of life. Using this definition, the investigators (Skuse et al., 1994a) report an annual incidence rate of 3.5 percent in the first year of life in this socioeconomically disadvantaged population. This definition excluded by design cases of "transient" FTT. However, Skuse (1993b) reports that his unpublished data suggests that this group appears similar to "true" persistent FTT in the incidence of intercurrent organic disorders (which had been expected to be higher in the "transient" group) and socially and behaviorally. Although pure anthropometric criteria were used, the investigators report that in the second year the affected infants could also be distinguished from normally growing controls on the basis of cognitive development, neu-

rodevelopment, and competence of feeding skills. Only 20 percent of the identified sample had been referred for investigation. This low level of specialist intervention is consistent with findings in other community-based studies. The prevalence of previously undetected medical conditions in community samples of FTT appears to be low, with the large majority of poorly thriving infants with medical conditions already known to their physicians.

It is likely that the incidence rate of FTT is higher in populations with prematurity and intrauterine growth retardation. Frank (1984) has stated that in clinical studies of children hospitalized with "non-organic" FTT, 10–40 percent have had birth weights below 2500 grams as compared with 7 percent of the general population. Kelleher and colleagues (1993) report that close to 20 percent of a large cohort of low birth weight infants followed longitudinally met case criteria for FTT by 30 months, with a peak incidence of new cases at 8 months of gestation corrected age. FTT was defined as being present when an infant was below the fifth percentile for gestation-corrected age, and had shown a downward percentile shift between assessment visits (which followed a standard schedule with decreasing frequency with age). When the FTT group was compared with the group of infants who met growth expectations, they fared significantly more poorly in health and cognitive outcomes at 3 years of age and in the quality of the home environment. Fewer than 20 percent of affected infants were judged to have contributing organic conditions.

The incidence of abuse and neglect in FTT may have increased but has probably also been overestimated due to the unrepresentative nature of the populations studied most intensively. Indications of possible abuse and neglect are among the reasons that appear to influence pediatricians to refer a child with FTT for specialized assessment, increasing the bias in the referred/hospitalized population. In Skuse's London study (1993b) infants with FTT were six times more likely than their normally thriving peers to appear on child protective registries four years later, but did so at a rate of only 8 percent.

Some, but not all studies (Hutcheson, Black, & Starr, 1993) report difficulties in maternal-child interactions (e.g., Drotar et al., 1990; Polan et al., 1991). Family characteristics found to be associated with children who fail to thrive include fewer family members available for help with child rearing (Bithoney & Newberger, 1987), greater social isolation (Kotelchuck & Newberger, 1983), and more problematic relationships (Drotar & Eckerle, 1989) than families from comparison groups. Multiple studies have reported various associations of FTT, including maternal depression, substance abuse, psychopathology, and mental handicap, family stress including abuse of mothers by partners, and psychosocial adversity. A number of comprehensive recent reviews of the FTT literature exist (Benoit, 1993; Frank & Zeisel, 1988; Lachenmeyer & Davidovicz, 1987; Skuse 1993b).

Psychosocial Short Stature

While psychosocial short stature is viewed as uncommon, there exist no epidemiological studies that test this clinical impression. The existing literature is entirely composed of individual case reports and series of children seen clinically. Children who develop the syndrome are generally of normal weight at birth (Green, 1990; Woolston, 1991) and the syndrome has been reported at all ages from toddlerhood to adolescence. There have also been some reports of cases having a previous history of FTT or feeding problems in infancy.

Food Refusal, Selectivity, and Phobias

Maloney's (1993) review of the literature presents an estimate that pediatric assessment of feeding problems is sought by parents of 25–40 percent of children at some point between infancy and the early school years. Minde and Minde (1986) conclude that the epidemiological literature suggests a 12–34 percent prevalence of feeding problems in pre-school children. However, only 1.4 percent of 3- to 12-month-old infants are referred for specialist evaluation of feeding-related problems. Much of the clinical research is with this small sub-group. Skuse (1994a) presents the clinical impression that many young children with relatively minor feeding problems may go on to develop intractable patterns of behavior with effects on the family and on the child's own health and development if not offered simple, appropriate interventions early on that take into account the normal development of feeding behavior. Skuse (1993a) also suggests that the conditions most likely to present to a pediatrician are food refusal or food selectivity ("picky eating" or "faddiness"). However, epidemiological information about the distribution of specific feeding problems in the community is not easily available, nor is information as to how frequently infants and toddlers with feeding problems will develop growth or other developmental difficulties.

Dahl and colleagues in Sweden (Dahl, Eklund, & Sundelin, 1986; Dahl & Sundelin, 1986, 1992; Dahl,

Rydell, & Sundelin, 1994) have performed one of the few epidemiological studies of infant feeding problems. They diagnosed a clinically significant feeding problem when parents and clinic nurse agreed as to the presence of feeding difficulties that persisted for at least a month and did not respond to simple medical and psychological advice and treatment. Using these criteria, 1.4 percent of infants presenting to ten urban health clinics were judged to have clinically significant feeding problems. The fifty infants so identified were assessed in more detail, including direct observation of meals in the home. The most common problem was refusal to eat (56 percent) followed by colic (18 percent) and vomiting (16 percent). Significant associations were: underweight for age (82 percent); contributing organic disorder (14 percent); difficulties in the mother-child interaction ("refusal to eat" group only); and history of feeding difficulties in the parents' own childhood. Serious and previously undetected illness was found in 6 percent of infants. Forty-six percent were more than one standard deviation and 14 percent more than two standard deviations below the 50th percentile of weight for age. These infants (excluding those with organic illness or prematurity) have now been followed into school age. The onset of "refusal to eat" and of vomiting was associated with a significant downward shift in weight and length curves, and growth impairment was more likely in those who refused all food or all food except breast milk than in those who refused solid food only. At two years of age, 36 percent of the "refusal to eat" group had persisting feeding problems, as had two of the eight children with vomiting. Weight gain remained low in the "refusal to eat" group, while the children with vomiting showed a normal rate of growth and had adequate catch-up growth. At four years of age, 17 of the 24 children with early refusal to eat (71 percent) were reported by the parents to still have feeding problems, and 10 (42 percent) were described as hyperactive. Children with early refusal to eat, when compared with controls, seemed to have an equally good prognosis with respect to health, growth, and development. At school age, 18 of the original "refusal to eat" group were compared with 240 classmates; the study group had significantly more eating problems both at home and at school, but were not different with respect to general behavior, physical health, or growth.

It is likely that not all feeding problems presenting in the pre-school years have been preceded by infant feeding problems of the degree studied by Dahl and her colleagues and summarized above, but the literature does not adequately address this area. Harris and Booth (1992) point out that while the literature does not allow epidemiological conclusions about the growth effects of children's own food selectivity, there are studies in existence that suggest that growth may be affected by limitation of food types by parents due to allergy or to adaptation to a new culture.

Rumination

Rumination appears to be largely a syndrome of infancy and of mental retardation. The published literature, with the exception of some studies examining its prevalence among the institutionalized mentally retarded (6–10 percent), has focused almost entirely on the clinically referred population, often the hospitalized. There has been no study looking at its community prevalence in either population or at the influence of care setting upon its prevalence in the mentally retarded (Johnston, 1993; Mayes, 1992). With these caveats, the currently available literature reports that boys outnumber girls with this disorder, with ratios of 3:1 among infants and 3.7:1 among the mentally retarded (Johnston, 1993), and that prevalence increases with the degree of mental retardation.

Pica

Pica is described most frequently in young children (Kaplan & Sadock, 1985), pregnant women (Hu, 1991), the mentally retarded (Singh, 1981; Winton & Singh, 1983), and among those with cultural beliefs that support its practice. Pica has also been reported to be more prevalent in black children and children from lower socioeconomic groups. Estimates of the community prevalence of pica among children vary widely. Lacey (1993) has pointed out that the population studies that do exist tend to be for specific substances or sub-groups and that even within these there are wide variations. She quotes estimates for the United States that range from 27 percent to 50 percent for black children and 17 percent to 30 percent in white children. These figures include forms of pica that may be substance specific and culture bound. The prevalence of persistent or pervasive childhood pica is even less clear. It is more common in developing countries than developed, in the poor than the affluent, in children than in adults, in more severe mental retardation than in mild. The association with poverty is clinically important as it means that children, already more vulnerable for socioeconomic reasons, may be placed at increased risk of lead poisoning and infestation by parasites.

ASSESSMENT APPROACHES

The literature on the assessment and management of feeding and growth disorders is largely restricted to case studies of children referred for specialized, often in-patient, evaluation, typically with very complex presentations. However, as discussed above, this represents a small sub-group of those children who are seen in pediatric practice with feeding and growth complaints, and this literature uses widely varying definitions of FTT and feeding disorder. Questions persist about its applicability to children presenting to out-patient pediatric settings. Few studies specifically test the reliability and validity of the assessment methods used to evaluate children with feeding problems and their families, therefore the review that follows is based primarily on the reported clinical utility of these methods rather than on studies that have provided empirical validation for their use in this population. With these caveats, it does appear that more children would benefit from referral to a specialized multidisciplinary team than receive the opportunity (Bithoney et al., 1991; O'Brien, Repp, Williams, & Christopherson, 1991; Skuse, 1993a).

The nature of the assessment will necessarily vary with treatment setting. In-patient medical and residential settings provide the best opportunities to conduct a thorough evaluation of the feeding process. The advantages include (1) the opportunity for direct observations of several mealtimes to establish a reliable baseline of the child's feeding behaviors and caregiver-child interactions at mealtime; (2) the provision of intensive treatment intervention under direct supervision of the treatment team; (3) the accurate charting of the response to the feeding interventions; and (4) the capacity to readily modify treatment components. The in-patient setting is available only for the sickest and most impaired children, and in-patient stays in medical settings may fall short of the optimum length of stay for the successful implementation of a feeding program. More commonly, children are seen in out-patient settings where there is more dependence on the caregivers' report. Nonetheless, the model should remain a comprehensive multidisciplinary evaluation that includes mealtime observations. Home-based and school-based evaluations have also been used to better elaborate the environmental factors that may influence the child's feeding problems (Drotar & Crawford, 1987; Werle, Murphy, & Budd, 1993).

The discussion that follows will review aspects of the assessment and management of feeding and growth disorders presenting in standard pediatric out-patient settings, and also discuss their further assessment and

Table 6.1.   Multidisciplinary Assessment and Treatment of Feeding and Growth Disorders

Role of the Pediatrician

1. Review growth data and obtain further growth studies as indicated (e.g. bone age, serial height and weight measurements to establish growth velocity).

2. Screen for major underlying medical conditions or specific organic factors contributing to the child's feeding or growth disorder.

3. Screen for genetic or other dysmorphic syndromes.

4. Refer for specific investigations and specialist consultation as indicated by history and physical examination.

5. Establish the degree of malnutrition, dehydration, deficits of specific nutrients, and the urgency with which nutritional replacement is needed.

6. Consult to and supervise the multidisciplinary team.

Role of the Psychologist and Psychiatrist

1. Screen for psychiatric illness in child or caregiver. Refer for psychiatric treatment as indicated.

2. Assess interactions between child and caregivers related to feeding.

3. Assess the child's developmental level and readiness for a feeding program.

4. Consult on behavioral treatment strategies for feeding.

5. Consult to the family on coping with the demands of a refeeding or behavioral program.

6. Supervise the child's caregivers in the implementation of the feeding program.

Role of the Occupational Therapist

1. Evaluate the child's readiness for feeding by assessing oral structures, reflex development, oral sensitivity and sensory processing, and specific oral-motor functioning, including swallowing, chewing, and respiratory functioning.

2. Assess the child's postural tone and movement patterns related to feeding, and response to handling and positioning.

3. Consult on the optimal positions and equipment for feeding.

4. Consult to the child's caregivers and school to ensure proper implementation of the oral-motor program.

Role of the Nutritionist

1. Nutrition/feeding history, assess medication-nutrient interactions and the impact of any medical conditions on the child's metabolic needs.

2. Evaluate the impact of nutrition on gastrointestinal functioning (e.g., diarrhea, constipation, vomiting).

3. Consult on modification of caloric and fluid intake, food texture progression, introduction of solid foods, formula transition, vitamin/mineral supplementation.

4. Establish the nutritional intake necessary to achieve adequate catch-up growth.

Role of the Social Worker

1. Assess the availability of the social, psychological, and financial resources and supports necessary to undertake a refeeding program and/or behavioral treatment of a feeding disorder.

2. Refer the family to other support services as indicated.

---

management in specialized multi-disciplinary settings. (See Table 6.1.)

Medical Issues

The medical assessment of a child with suspected growth failure or feeding disorder asks four initial questions:

- Is growth failure actually present: Does the attained weight and height, the growth velocity, and the historical patterns of growth meet the expectations for this *individual* child?
- Is a feeding disorder present: Is there evidence of delay or deviation in the development of feeding skills or evidence of a specific feeding disorder?
- Is there a medical illness that accounts for or contributes to the growth failure and/or feeding difficulties?
- Is there evidence of a psychosocial situation, a distortion in caregiver-child interaction, and/or a psy-

chiatric condition in the child or caregiver that may account for or contribute to the growth failure or feeding difficulties?

As has been made clear, it should never be assumed that a case of growth failure has a single cause. In every case all four questions must be considered, though not necessarily aggressively investigated.

Frank and Zeisel (1988) have thoroughly reviewed the principles guiding the medical assessment of infants with FTT. They point out that most medical illness contributing to FTT is readily apparent and that the role of the pediatrician is more commonly the assessment and treatment of malnutrition and its consequences rather than the detection of occult physical disease.

A thorough medical and developmental history and physical examination are essential. Historical items specific to the condition that should not be overlooked include: the parents' nutritional beliefs and knowledge; evidence of deviations or delays in the development of feeding skills; history suggestive of specific feeding problems including pica, rumination, and gastroe-sophageal reflux; the possibility of sleep apnea secondary to enlargement of tonsils and adenoids (an apparent contributing factor in some cases of FTT and behavioral disturbance); evidence of malabsorption or infestation by parasites; history of prematurity, intrauterine growth retardation, or other occasion for neurological insult; severe illness or prolonged non-oral feeding in first three years of life; intrusive oral procedures or other oral- or food-related trauma; social history including the family's access to social, economic, and emotional supports; recent family stresses and changes.

The general physical examination may detect dysmorphisms, evidence of physical abuse, structural abnormality of the feeding apparatus, developmental delays, or occult neurological dysfunction including evidence of oral-motor dysfunction (e.g., excessive gag reflex; drooling; abnormal movements of tongue, mouth, or jaw; presence of abnormal, or persistence of primitive, oral-motor reflexes). Oral-motor dysfunction may not be detectable on routine physical examination, which should be supplemented by specialized occupational therapy evaluation whenever the history suggests that the child is at risk for or has evidence of oral-motor difficulties (see Table 6.1). Reilly and colleagues have developed a Schedule for Oral Motor Assessment (SOMA) in order to objectively rate the oral motor skills of pre-verbal children (Reilly, Skuse, Mathisen, & Wolke, 1995). This instrument, and an abbreviated screening version, has been tested in normal infants and infants with FTT and with cerebral palsy, and is reported to have good reliability and criterion validity (Skuse, Stevenson, Reilly, & Mathisen, 1995). Clinically significant gastroesophageal reflux may also not be readily detectable by history, and specialized imaging and pH studies may be required to make the diagnosis. The caregiver-child interaction should be observed with the caveat that existing difficulties may not be apparent in the context of an office visit.

Much information can be gained by eliciting a careful description of not only the child's diet (usually in consultation with a pediatric nutritionist), but also the feeding process. Dietary content has also been implicated in failure to thrive by several authors (Bithoney & Rathbun, 1983; Pollitt & Thompson, 1977; Whitten, Pettit, & Fischoff, 1969). For example, Smith and Lifshitz's (1994) recent study found that excess fruit juice consumption may displace more nutritionally dense food. A pediatrician's adage that fruit juice is "baby beer" may well apply to some cases of failure to thrive. Nutritional factors may be assessed through a three- to seven-day food record, food frequency checklist, 24-hour recall of foods consumed by the child, and observations of the foods consumed during clinic and home visits. Dietary histories can be unreliable (Whitten et al., 1969), and one indication for a short in-patient stay is to determine whether the child can gain weight when provided with an adequate diet.

Beyond the most basic laboratory screening, investigations should be limited to those specifically indicated by the history and physical findings. Frank and Zeisel (1988) suggest that the basic screen include complete blood count, lead screening, urinalysis and urine culture, PPD, and in genetically at risk populations a sweat test. HIV screening may also be indicated. Where pica is present, the pediatrician must assess for possible nutritional deficits that may be prompting the pica, and for toxicities induced by the pica, notably lead toxicity.

After establishing the presence and likely contributing causes of failure to make adequate weight gains, the pediatrician also assesses the degree and acuity of the condition to determine whether hospitalization and/or non-oral feeding is indicated. The presence and nature of specific nutritional deficits and the nutritional requirements for catch-up growth must also be determined, the latter typically with the input of a pediatric nutritionist (see Table 6.1). It is a rule of thumb that, in malnutrition, weight is affected before height and that when height becomes affected it is a sign of chronicity. Generally the child whose primary difficulty is malnourishment will remain underweight for height; however, in children with chronic malnutrition the picture can appear more proportional, leading to diagnostic confusion, particularly where there is inadequate historical growth data.

Where height is preserved it is unlikely that endocrinological evaluation will be fruitful, but where unexplained small stature as opposed to failure to gain weight appears to be the primary difficulty, endocrinology consultation is indicated. Van Den Brande and Rappaport (1993b) classify causes of small stature as follows: (1) Extremes of normal (determined by gathering a history of parental height and puberty and ruling out family genetic or other dysmorphic syndromes); (2) Primary (e.g., dysmorphic syndromes, disorders of osteochondral development, mucopolysaccharidoses); (3) Secondary (e.g., growth hormone deficiency [including psychosocial short stature], hypothyroidism, Cushing's syndrome, advanced precocious puberty, early hypogonadism [at pubertal age], and central nervous system tumor).

Probable genetic endowment for height can be calculated by determining the mid-parental height, which is the arithmetic mean of the parents' centile heights adjusted for the gender of the child (mothers +12.6 cm for boys; fathers −12.6 cm for girls). This yields within 9 cm a target adult height centile for the child within 95 percent confidence limits (Brook, 1993). Inaccuracies may arise if either parent has an unrecognized or untreated condition which itself causes growth failure or if a parent has endured childhood deprivation sufficient to stunt growth. Where a child shows proportional growth failure with delayed bone age, particularly if other behavioral and family characteristics are observed, the presence of psychosocial short stature may be suspected. It should be remembered that growth hormone suppression in psychosocial short stature may escape detection if growth hormone studies are performed later than the first days of hospitalization or other separation from the usual caretaker. The core to the diagnosis is the demonstration of reversal of endocrine abnormalities and the commencement of catch-up growth on removal from the home environment. Some reports (e.g., Hernandez, Poznanski, Hopwood, & Kelch, 1978) have shown growth lines on long bones, perhaps implying fluctuating environments, sometimes inhibiting and sometimes permitting growth. In some children widened cranial sutures have been noted during catch-up growth, with reports of pseudotumor cerebri in four cases (Tibbles, Vallet, Brown, & Goldbloom, 1972).

Psychological and Psychiatric Issues

Just as the pediatric assessment of feeding and growth disorders is best performed by a multidisciplinary team, the psychological and behavioral assessment of the child requires a multidimensional approach. It follows a patter similar to the medical assessment in that, while it involves screening for the presence of contributing specific psychiatric illness or developmental disorder in parent or child, the most common role for psychiatrist and psychologist lies in explicating, with an eye to the structuring of intervention, the psychological and behavioral mechanisms maintaining the disorder. Where psychiatric disorder is detected in either parent or child it should be appropriately treated, but as is the case where medical illness is detected, its detection should lead neither to the assumption that it is the "cause" of the feeding or growth disorder nor to neglect of specific assessment of the feeding process itself. Maternal depression, for example, is a commonly reported association of feeding and growth disorders. However, its mere detection does not establish whether and how it is contributing to the problem. Is depression undermining efforts to nourish a difficult-to-feed baby? Has depression led to actual neglect? Did the mother's apparent depression develop in response to the stresses of caring for a poorly thriving and perhaps medically ill or developmentally impaired infant or child? Treating maternal depression can be an important step in the successful treatment of a child with FTT or a feeding disorder, but may not be sufficient unless a specific behavioral feeding program is also put in place.

The domains of psychological and psychiatric assessment typically include the child (Benoit, 1993; Drotar, 1989), parents (Benoit, 1993; Drotar & Sturm, 1987; Polan et al., 1991), parent-child interactions, especially at mealtime (Drotar, Eckerle, Satola, Pallotta, & Wyatt, 1990), family functioning and environmental factors (Drotar, 1991, 1994), nutrition (Smith & Lifshitz, 1994) and oral-motor problems (O'Brien, 1991; Ramsay, 1993). Because assessment for the presence of a feeding disorder is integral to the assessment of FTT and vice versa, these issues will be discussed together followed by discussion of some issues of special concern for psychosocial short stature, rumination, and pica. For more in-depth discussions of assessment for particular disorders, the reader is referred to: Green (1986, 1990); Skuse (1989); Woolston (1991) for psychosocial short stature; Benoit (1993), Drotar (1989, 1994) and O'Brien (1991) for failure to thrive; Lavigne (1981), Johnston (1993), and Winton & Singh (1983) for rumination; and Lacey (1993) for pica.

Child Issues

Child characteristics to be evaluated include the child's affect, social responsiveness, developmental level, and cognitive functioning, which can be assessed by observations of the child, especially at mealtimes, as well as through standardized methods, such as the Bayley Scales (Bayley, 1969). Assessment of the infant may also detect evidence of insecure or otherwise distorted attachment to caregivers that may meet criteria for a frank reactive attachment disorder. This condition is characterized by markedly disturbed and developmentally inappropriate social relatedness in most contexts, with abnormally inhibited, ambivalent, or diffuse attachment behavior and evidence of pathogenic care. Such findings may be a marker of serious difficulties in the parent-child relationship, including abuse and neglect.

In older children consideration must be given to the presence of other psychiatric conditions including depressive disorder and obsessive-compulsive disorder. The presence of a distorted body image with dieting, exercising, binge eating, vomiting or purging point to an emerging anorexia nervosa or bulimia. Uncommonly food and eating may become the focus of an emerging psychotic disorder.

Parental Issues

Parental mental illness can be viewed, like socioeconomic deprivation and medical illness, as another factor that may facilitate the emergence of feeding or growth disorders in the vulnerable child. Parental mood or anxiety disorder may distort the parents' view of interactions with the child, leading them to ignore or over-interpret hunger or feeding cues from the child. Mood and anxiety disorders may also impair the parents' energy, resilience, sense of purpose, and organizational abilities, making it difficult to meet the unrelenting demands of caring for a young child. Parental substance abuse, cognitive impairment, or major mental illness may have similar effects. Personality disorder may lead to such distortion of interpersonal relationships that a parent may attribute adult motives to a young child and view normal events (such as a toddler's rejection of a new food) as personal attacks or evidence of badness or recalcitrance. Parental eating disorder may distort understanding of the child or infant's nutritional needs and demands.

Psychiatric evaluation may also elicit a history of significant past experiences, such as abuse or coercive feeding in the parents' own childhood, that may contribute to difficulties in meeting the interactive demands of the feeding process (Fraiberg, Adelson, & Shapiro, 1975).

Family functioning may be assessed through clinical interview and by the use of standardized instruments such as the Family Environment Scale (Moos & Moos, 1986), and the Parenting Stress Index (Abidin, 1985). An interview with the parents will also provide information on the availability of social support, and allow for the gathering of pertinent information about the family's composition and financial circumstances, cultural practices or routines around meals, and the parents' relationship (Bithoney & Newberger, 1987; Drotar & Eckerle, 1989; Drotar & Sturm, 1987).

In summary, the psychiatric assessment must not only establish whether or not a parental psychiatric disorder exists, but also (1) whether there is evidence that it is contributing to the feeding or growth disorder and by which mechanisms; (2) whether there are characteristics of the parent in interaction with the child that may not be due to psychiatric disorder but that may be contributing to the problem; and (3) whether the parent has the psychological, cognitive, and social resources to cope with a refeeding program and/or the behavioral treatment of a feeding disorder.

The Feeding Process and Parent/Child Interaction

Central to the assessment of the feeding process are a detailed history and direct observations of the child during feeding. The history should address oral trauma, coercive feeding experiences and opportunities for developmentally normal feeding experiences. This is supplemented by the oral-motor evaluation, which determines the probable role of oral-pharyngeal development and structures in the display of the problem behavior and the level of development of the child's feeding skills. Baseline observations for several mealtimes typically precede intervention (Luiselli, Evans, & Boyce, 1985; Singer, Ambuel, Wade, & Jaffe, 1992). The incidence of the problem behavior(s), such as food refusal, at baseline may be recorded by a simple log that also notes the incidence of appropriate feeding behaviors, as well as the interactions of the child with caregivers. It is often useful to exclude the child's caregivers from at least one baseline mealtime observation, in order to determine if any interactional problems around feeding are specific to the child's caregivers. Examples of behavioral logs, including how different feeding behaviors and child-caregiver interactions have been defined and recorded, can be found in Ginsberg (1988), Handen, Mandell, and Russo (1986), O'Brien et al., (1991), Riordan et al., (1984), and Singer et al., (1991).

Difficulties in maternal-child interactions described when some cases of FTT were compared with normally growing controls include (1) increased display of negative affect during feeding, and decreased display of positive affect in both feeding and non-feeding situations (Polan et al., 1991); and (2) generalized deficits in social behavior for mothers of children with "nonorganic" FTT in non-feeding situations, and the arbitrary termination of their child's mealtime (Drotar et al., 1990). Interactions between caregiver and child can further be assessed by standardized instruments such as the Behaviors of Eating and Activity for Children's Health Evaluation System (BEACHES) (McKenzie et al., 1991), and the Children's Eating Behavior Inventory (Archer, Rosenbaum, & Streiner, 1991).

Issues Specific to the Assessment of Psychosocial Short Stature

The diagnosis of psychosocial short stature is dependent on the demonstration of the reversibility of its features out of the home environment. The initial evaluation should take place in an in-patient setting where, besides documenting endocrine and behavioral changes and catch-up growth, interactions between parent and child can be observed, as well as the behavior of the child in the absence of the parents. Evidence of disturbed eating behavior and sleep disorder should be sought by history and observation. Formal psychiatric and developmental evaluation of the child may yield evidence of any of the wide range of other symptoms and delays that have been reported. Sensitive interviewing of the child about sleeping, eating, disciplinary, and other routines at home may yield important information about the home environment and the child's treatment by caretakers. This information should be supplemented by information gathered, not only from parents, but from schools, relatives, siblings, and others who may have knowledge of the child's home environment and of the child 's behaviors. Ideally a home visit should also take place to gather direct knowledge of the child's physical environment.

Obtaining the information needed may not be possible without involving child protective services. Indeed, as the current understanding of PSS is that an extreme distortion in the parent-child relationship results in direct physical and emotional harm to the child, the making of the diagnosis is an indication for doing so. The same applies in the situation where the diagnosis is strongly suspected but parents are unwilling to complete the evaluation. As PSS is often misunderstood, even by those with medical training, it may be necessary for the involved medical and mental health professionals to educate the non-medical personnel in child protective services about the nature and implications of the diagnosis. The management of PSS can become charged and difficult, often requiring the removal of the child from the home. It is therefore particularly important that the multidisciplinary team work tightly together from the point of assessment. The team should at minimum be comprised of endocrinology, psychiatry, social work, and primary pediatric care.

Much care has already been given to distinguishing between FTT and PSS, but the existing widespread confusion means that the following point cannot be made too strongly: Our current understanding implies that the diagnosis of PSS (reversible suppression of GH secretion in a child two years old or older) is reflective of a seriously disturbed parent-child relationship and is an indication for the involvement of child protective services; FTT (malnourishment resulting in inadequate weight gain) **may** be associated with child abuse and neglect and with distortions in the parent-child interaction, but this is by no means universal and must not be considered as being automatically implied by the diagnosis.

Issues Specific to the Assessment of Rumination

Observations of children who ruminate reveal what amounts to a developmental progression of skills. These range from overt, highly visible displays during which the child uses fingers to stimulate the gag reflex or positions the body to facilitate regurgitation, to more covert strategies where facilitative movements are absent and rumination can only be detected by observation of bulging of the cheeks and of chewing outside of mealtimes (Johnston, 1993). Johnston (1993) also notes that while there is significant variation between individuals in the topography of ruminative behavior, there tends to be consistency in how it presents in each individual child, providing a framework for behavioral assessment techniques. Humphrey, Mayes, Bixler, and Good (1989) assessed the topology of rumination in a retarded child and found the frequency to vary with the child's activities (less rumination during school hours and when receiving individual attention), and to increase immediately after meals and over the course of the day. Johnston (1993) describes a decrease in ruminative behaviors with environmental stimulation after meals, and also notes that characteristics of the food consumed, such as its texture, taste, and caloric density, may influence the frequency of rumination. Mealtime observations of caregiver and child should also be conducted in order to evaluate whether disturbed interactions contribute to the maintenance of the ruminative behavior. However, as noted previously, ruminative behaviors can occur without evidence of pathology in the parent or child (Johnston, 1993; Lavigne et al., 1981).

Issues Specific to the Assessment of Pica

It can be difficult to gather direct observations of pica as it may occur sporadically and during periods of decreased supervision. Parents may not report their child's pica due to concerns about its social acceptability. The reader is referred to Lacey (1993) for a discussion of how the clinician may optimally elicit a child's pica history from parents. Often, the diagnosis follows the medical detection of high blood lead levels (Madden et al., 1980) or intestinal problems (Singh, 1981). Pica may have its own temporal course, typically occurring more often during periods of decreased stimulation (Madden et al., 1980), and at times of the day other than mealtimes. These topographical features need to be taken into account when planning baseline observations.

Visits to the child's home or school may help in determining any environmental and interactional factors that prompt or maintain its occurrence.

TREATMENT STRATEGIES

Treatment, like assessment, may be best provided by a multidisciplinary team (Bithoney et al., 1991). Ideally, whether in an in-patient or out-patient setting, the individual members of the team conduct their own evaluations of the child and then meet as a group to identify the treatment goals and the members of the team who will be primarily responsible for implementing the treatment plan and monitoring its progress.

Treating professionals must be aware that for parents, who form part of the treatment team, their intervention may be emotionally charged. Parents whose child is failing to grow or refusing food typically experience feelings of failure as caregivers, and may become angry and defensive, especially if they feel that their perspective on the problem is not being taken into account. Parents need to understand the team's multidimensional approach and the importance of their own input to the child's rehabilitation. Parents will be actively involved in implementing a refeeding and/or behavioral feeding program. It is essential to gain their cooperation, to anticipate difficulties they may face, and to provide them with ongoing support, particularly if the family situation is chaotic. Telephone contacts, frequent outpatient follow-up, and referral for treatment of parental psychopathology may all be useful. Home or school visits, if feasible, allow the team the opportunity to consult with and directly supervise the caregivers in the child's natural environment. The same principles apply when care is being given by institutional staff. When the required level of attentiveness is not available from the parents, treatment may be best implemented initially in an in-patient setting (Linscheid & Rasnake, 1985).

Overview of Medical Management

Failure to Thrive

For the large majority of infants with FTT, the major role for the pediatrician is in the assessment and treatment of malnutrition and its consequences rather than in the detection of occult organic disease (Frank & Zeisel, 1988). Generic issues that confront the pediatrician include: on-going monitoring for degree of malnutrition

and the rate of catch-up growth; determining when safety demands that an infant should be managed in an inpatient setting or with non-oral supplementary feeds; giving instructions for nutritional replacement adapted to any special medical needs of the child and adequate not just for current needs but also for catch-up growth; detecting and treating associated deficiencies of specific nutrients such as iron and zinc; detecting and treating lead toxicity if present; continuing to monitor for evidence of physical abuse (for further discussion see Frank & Zeisel, 1988). When an infant fails to respond adequately to treatment the pediatrician should assess for and treat aggressively any intercurrent infection. A vicious cycle can develop with malnutrition causing apathy and anorexia, as well as impairing immune status and causing increased infection. Structural or neurological abnormalities of the feeding apparatus or disordered feeding skills also increase the risks of aspiration.

The typical family with an FTT child carries many burdens—ranging from medical illness in the child to socioeconomic deprivation—that will have already strained the family's abilities to remain organized and effective. The treatment of FTT introduces new organizational, financial, and emotional demands. In this context it is vital that the family be offered a clear pediatric treatment plan that includes explicit guidelines as to expectations for weight gain, the plan to meet nutritional requirements, and the safety parameters, all expressed in terms of easily understandable weight or feeding goals. Ideally this should be in written form and include a pre-established schedule for follow up pediatric visits which should be with the same person on each visit and which, as well as monitoring of nutritional status, should include review of the treatment plan and an opportunity to discuss any practical or financial difficulties presented by its implementation.

When an infant is treated by a specialized multidisciplinary team, the role of the pediatrician as team leader and the routes of communication are clear. Where such a service is not available treatment may be shared by professionals in different disciplines and settings and it will require extra effort to maintain the coordinating role of the pediatrician. However, it is essential that the pediatrician, as holder of the key medical information and refeeding goals, should be in a position to communicate this information authoritatively to the other members of the treatment team, including the child's caregivers. Clear pediatric leadership in this manner greatly simplifies the task of mental health and other involved professionals, as what has to be achieved and the point where more intensive intervention (usually hospitalization) is indicated will be explicit. Other professionals can focus on the task of helping the family to organize for and master the necessary challenges.

Psychosocial Short Stature

The child with PSS must be followed to ensure that catch-up growth is in fact occurring in their current environment. The literature to date suggests that growth can normalize in situations that do not produce emotional and developmental improvement, but that emotional and developmental improvement will not occur unless the new environment is at least satisfactory enough to allow resolution of growth suppression. The situation requires close monitoring. For example, Powell, Brasel, Raiti, and Blizzard (1967) describe a child who had returned to an apparently normal growth rate at home but who still showed catch-up growth when hospitalized. Hopwood & Becker (1979) report a child who showed recurrence of growth delay when a sibling joined them in foster care. Infestation by parasites and lead toxicity arising from distorted eating behavior must be treated. Attempts to treat the disorder with exogenous growth hormone have not been successful.

Food Refusal, Selectivity, and Phobia

Where an infant or child has oral-motor dysfunction and/or a persistent, clinically significant feeding disorder specialized treatment will be indicated. However, as we have reviewed, the pediatrician must distinguish those children in whom specialized referral is indicated from many infants and pre-school children who will present because their caregivers have concerns about "faddiness" and food refusal. Where office management is indicated, the pediatrician counsels the family in the use of basic behavioral principles grounded in an understanding of the normal development of feeding skills. The pediatrician ensures that the caregivers' expectations are developmentally realistic. For example, feeding for a toddler may become aversive because the parents are expecting "table manners" or that the child will be capable of sitting through a long, adult family meal. The pediatrician ensures the infant or child is being offered developmentally appropriate feeding experiences; for example, the unpressured presentation of small amounts of new foods to the normally "neophobic" toddler. The parents are then instructed in the techniques of ignoring the negative behavior in the affected child and of rewarding desired behavior in the child, siblings and peers

by matter of fact positive attention. Good practical reviews of this area exist (Harris & Booth, 1992; Skuse & Wolke, 1992b; Skuse, 1993a).

Finally, the pediatrician can play a preventive role in those situations in which an infant or young child is prescribed prolonged non-oral feeding by ensuring the provision of non-nutritive sucking or mock oral feeds during tube feeds, which may help foster the development of more normal feeding skills (e.g., Lloyd, Pursall, & Emery, 1981).

Pica

Medical screening to evaluate possible nutritional deficits that may be prompting pica, or toxicity or infestation induced by pica, should be performed before psychological or behavioral treatments are instituted. Other appropriate treatment interventions should be initiated (e.g., nutritional intervention for iron deficiency, chelation therapy for lead poisoning). The pediatrician should monitor for recurrence of these syndromes, which may indicate recurrence or incomplete resolution of pica.

Rumination

As well as managing underlying medical conditions, including gastrointestinal reflux, the pediatrician must assess and correct nutritional status and fluid and electrolyte imbalance. When life-threatening rumination continues despite appropriate behavioral intervention, it may be necessary to proceed to surgical correction of gastroesophageal reflux, if present, before weight gain occurs (Herbst, 1992).

Psychological and Behavioral Treatments

In this section we focus on the treatment of those infants and children whose feeding and growth difficulties are sufficiently severe to warrant specialized psychological and behavioral intervention.

Issues Specific to the Treatment of Failure to Thrive

If failure to thrive is understood as a symptom with many and varied contributing causes, it should come as no surprise that the psychological treatment literature describes multiple treatment modalities with mixed and inconsistent results. There have been few studies that assess the relative efficacy of approaches to FTT. Drotar and colleagues (1985) found that short-term advocacy, family intervention, and parent-child intervention each produced comparable outcomes with regard to the child's physical growth, nutritional status, and psychological functioning. Bithoney and colleagues (1991) found that a multidisciplinary team dedicated to the treatment of FTT effected better outcomes than treatment by pediatricians who did not specialize in the treatment of FTT. It has also been reported that whatever the role of organic factors in the development of a given case of FTT, the treatment program to which the child can respond may be quite similar (Bithoney et al., 1989).

Typically, treatment programs described in the literature combine a variety of interventions introduced concomitantly or sequentially, often including family therapy, individual psychotherapy for the primary caregiver, involvement of social service agencies, and behavioral feeding programs. When there is primary oral-motor dysfunction, or delays or deviations in feeding skill development, behavioral treatment will need to be supplemented by a specific occupational therapy program aimed at increasing oral-motor efficiency. Treatment of FTT is demanding. The family must obtain the extra food needed for catch-up growth, must attend more frequent medical and perhaps other appointments, and provide calm, distraction-free feeding times that may initially need to be of increased frequency (Lachenmeyer & Davidovicz, 1987). It is likely that meal times are already charged experiences and the child may be particularly difficult to feed, whether due to a primary difficulty (such as oral-motor dysfunction or cardiorespiratory illness) or a secondary difficulty (such as food aversion or refusal arising from previous negative feeding interactions or apathy and irritability arising from malnutrition). The importance of involving the child's parents in the treatment of FTT is emphasized by Drotar & Sturm (1994), who describe the use of parent training, including instruction in the behavioral management of feeding problems and nutritional education. Bithoney (1991) provides specific examples of how a multidisciplinary team dedicated to the treatment of FTT intervenes.

The practical clinical application of this literature is simplified if the principles outlined in the discussion of assessment are recalled. The treatment plan devised for a given child should combine interventions that explicitly target the specific factors shown during assessment to be impeding successful nourishment. For example, for children with feeding skill deficits or maladaptive mealtime behaviors, a number of behavioral treatment strategies

using classical and operant-based methods have been used effectively. The specific approaches to food refusal described below may be applicable. Where parental psychopathology is undermining the refeeding program, treatment of the parent is indicated, especially for maternal affective and personality disorders (Benoit, 1993), with psychotherapy and psychopharmacological intervention where appropriate. Interventions aimed at improving the quality of the parent-infant relationship may also be indicated (Drotar & Sturm, 1994). Fraiberg and colleagues (1975), in classic contributions to the literature, have eloquently described their work with parents whose ability to care appropriately for their infants is impeded by their own childhood experiences (Fraiberg, Adelson, & Shapiro, 1975; Fraiberg, 1980). Family interventions may also focus on factors that are known to be associated with FTT, such as financial difficulties, substance abuse, social supports, and family conflict (Drotar & Sturm, 1994).

Issues Specific to the Treatment of Psychosocial Short Stature

The primary treatment of PSS is placement in an alternative setting that provides a structured, stimulating, age-appropriate environment and the opportunity to form appropriate attachment relationships (Green, 1986). Generally, it is very difficult to engage the family of origin in treatment and there are few reports of successful catch-up growth and emotional and developmental improvement at home. It should, however, be remembered that this literature is entirely case report based. There exist a number of case reports and series that show, with placement out of the home, dramatic gains in catch-up growth, feeding behavior, sleep, emotional and developmental status, and measured IQ (reviewed by Green, 1986). Emotional and developmental improvement can be expected to be limited unless the new placement is at least satisfactory enough to produce catch-up growth, but growth can occur in settings that are not optimal for other developmental improvements (Hopwood & Becker, 1979). While the pediatrician is monitoring the appropriateness of the placement by following the child's somatic growth, the mental health team does so by monitoring the child's developmental and emotional status. The child is likely to benefit from individual psychotherapy focusing on the mastering of past experiences and adaptation to the new environment. Family intervention in the new home, including education of the foster parents, may help ensure an optimal environment for the child. Specialized school placement, learning support, speech, and other developmental therapies may be indicated on the basis of the developmental evaluation. Where an attempt is made to treat a child with PSS in the original home, all of the above are required along with intensive and closely monitored family intervention, which should include attention to the parents own treatment needs and, ideally, in home treatment. Ongoing monitoring by child protective services is appropriate and may help ensure the family's continued involvement in treatment.

Issues Specific to the Treatment of Food Refusal, Selectivity, and Phobias

The core of treatment for feeding disorders is a carefully designed behavioral program.

The "A-B-C" (i.e., antecedent-behavior-consequences) model works well to develop a baseline log of the child's feeding problems and to determine which interventions need to occur. The child's feeding difficulties may be the result of a skills deficit, in which case a behavioral shaping program might be considered in conjunction with input from occupational therapy. They may be related to antecedents to feeding, suggesting a classically conditioned behavior problem, or to the consequences of the child's feeding behaviors, suggesting operant learning. These different learning paradigms suggest different primary modes of intervention. Any of the methods described below may not work optimally for a given child at a given time, and reanalysis of the problem behavior may be needed to refine and revise the plan. For example, the child may become frustrated if the program advances too quickly or bored if the program advances too slowly, indicating the need to change the pace of the shaping process. Training across settings will facilitate generalization of the skills learned in clinical settings to the child's home and/or school (Drotar & Crawford, 1987; Werle et al., 1993). It is also important to assess the family's willingness and ability to implement the program.

The most commonly considered specific techniques are:

1. *Reinforcement procedures* (material or social rewards for the occurrence of desired behavior): These work best to increase a low-frequency behavior or develop a new behavior (e.g., transitioning from fluids to solids), or to generalize a behavior to a new setting (e.g., home or school). The child may become satiated on a particular reinforcer, in which case a reinforcer menu may be needed. Reinforcement procedures are also commonly used together with punishment, extinction, and time-out strategies to help shape appropriate behaviors to fill the "behavior vacuum" left by the behavior targeted for elimination.

2. *Extinction procedures* (withdrawal of whatever is reinforcing the undesirable behavior): The targeted behavior often becomes more frequent in response to the initial withdrawal of reinforcement ("extinction burst"). This is a high-risk period, because parents may assume that the intervention is only making matters worse and may give up the program. Parents should be forewarned that they should expect to see some increase in frequency before they see improvement. They can be told that an extinction burst is evidence that the program is accurately targeting the undesirable behavior. Extinction procedures gradually reduce the undesirable behavior.

3. *Time-out from positive reinforcement:* The caregiver may simply need to avert his or her gaze from the child for a short period after the problem behavior occurs. For older children with significant behavioral problems at mealtime, a more traditional time-out may be needed, with the child placed in a setting of low stimulation for a fixed period of time.

4. *Punishment:* This is used most often when the behavior presents a significant danger to the child and needs to be quickly suppressed (e.g., squirting of pepper sauce into the mouth of a child when rumination is detected). Caregivers are often reluctant to use such highly aversive techniques and there may be a risk of adverse emotional consequences for the child. There is also the risk of inadvertently creating a learned negative association to environmental stimuli that are present when the punishment is being delivered (e.g., the children may come to associate preparation for feeding with the punishment, and develop a conditioned aversion to the process).

Where a phobia is present, as indicated by the development of fear and distress before a meal has begun, a desensitization procedure is indicated (Archer & Szatmari, 1990; Johnson & Babbitt, 1993). Specific antecedents inducing fear or food refusal may be identified, such as being fed in the room where aversive procedures have been performed. Alternatively the intervention may need to focus on the consequences of the targeted behavior (e.g., excess attention paid to non-eating behaviors, such as rewarding food refusal by coaxing the child to eat) (Linsheid, Tarnowski, Rasnake, & Brams, 1987; Luiselli et al., 1985).

It is also useful to consider combination of strategies. One study of the treatment of food refusal combined strategies focused on both antecedents (increasing specific feeding-related prompts to the child), and consequences (offering positive reinforcement for the child's attempts with non-preferred foods), and was successful in improving the caregiver's behaviors during mealtime (Werle et al., 1993). A combined antecedent/consequent treatment approach has also been used for food phobia through the addition of positive reinforcement for progress with a desensitization program (Singer et al., 1992). Linsheid and colleagues (1987) successfully treated food refusal in a six-year-old child with short-gut syndrome by combining a variety of contingency management procedures, including limiting mealtime, a "hero badge" upon meeting the criterion amount specified for a meal (which in turn served as a discriminative stimulus for staff to offer praise for mealtime success), a token system, contingent attention for desirable mealtime behaviors, and removal of attention for those that were undesirable.

Issues Specific to the Treatment of Rumination

Behavioral strategies for rumination have progressed from a predominant use of punishment to combinations of punishment and less aversive techniques. Punishment strategies reported include the use of electric shock (Lang & Melamed, 1969; Linsheid & Cunningham, 1977), and the squirting of bitter fruit juices or a pepper sauce into the child's mouth upon the occurrence of ruminative behavior (Glasscock, Friman, O'Brien, & Christopherson, 1986; Mestre et al., 1983; Sajwaj et al., 1974). Less aversive techniques have included overcorrection (i.e., the forced practice of an alternative behavior) (Azrin & Wesolowski, 1975; Duker & Seys, 1977), verbal reprimands (Lavigne, 1981; Wright, 1978), differential reinforcement of other (non-ruminative) behaviors, (Daniel, 1982; O'Neil et al., 1979), and the use of social contingencies to reinforce appropriate behaviors (Lavigne, Burns, & Cotter, 1981).

While behavioral methods generally have been reported to be successful in reducing the frequency of rumination, there are methodological concerns. For example, the frequent use of multiple behavioral strategies concurrently makes it difficult to determine which strategies are the most potent for effecting change. Additionally, as most studies have had small numbers of subjects, and as only a few studies have included long-term follow-up, it is difficult to predict which techniques will be most effective for the individual child and how long the effect will last. There are also ethical barriers to the use of the punishment techniques that characterize

the earlier literature, which usually were employed only after all other methods of treatment had failed. Lavigne and colleagues (1981) emphasize social reinforcement strategies to modify rumination, especially for those cases where there is little evidence of disturbances in the caregiver-child relationship. For a more in-depth analysis of the various behavioral strategies used to manage rumination, the reader is referred to Lavigne et al. (1981), Johnston (1993), and Winton & Singh (1983a).

Psychodynamic treatment has also been used to treat rumination, but it has been criticized on the grounds that it assumes psychopathology in the child, mother, or their interactions that other studies have shown may well not be universally present (Lavigne et al., 1981), and involves a very labor-intensive treatment regimen that is lengthy and costly to implement.

Issues Specific to the Treatment of Pica

Most studies of the treatment of pica have used behavioral strategies, usually combining several interventions, and have involved small numbers of subjects, many of whom are mentally retarded. Madden and colleagues (1980) used discrimination training (i.e., teaching the child the difference between edible and inedible items), DRO, and overcorrection. Winton and Singh (1983b) used response contingent physical restraint and verbal reprimand. Winton and Singh (1983b) found physical restraint of very short (ten seconds) duration to be effective by itself, and to be more easily implemented and to require less time than more complex multi-component interventions. Overcorrection has also been used by itself (Foxx & Martin, 1975; Mulick, Barbour, Schroeder, & Rojahn, 1980). Environmental manipulations to manage pica have been suggested by Madden and colleagues (1980), who assessed the relationship between mouthing behavior and different environmental conditions for three young children. They found that mouthing was related to the relative richness of the environment, occurring less frequently in the presence of activities, toys, and adult and child contact.

Pharmacological Treatments

The specific role of psychopharmacology in the treatment of feeding and growth disorders is limited to treating specific underlying psychiatric disorders where present. Where mood or anxiety disorder (notably obsessive-compulsive disorder) is playing a role, pharmacologic treatment may be indicated, particularly if the child does not respond to appropriate psychological intervention. When psychopharmacologic agents are used, careful attention must be paid to monitoring for effects on appetite. The current status of pediatric psychopharmacology has been extensively reviewed (Riddle, 1995).

CASE ILLUSTRATIONS

The cases that follow are included for purposes of illustration. They may represent condensations of more than one case history.

Case 1: Ann, a 24 Month Old with Poor Oral Intake

Clinical Presentation

Ann, 24 months old with global developmental delay and no expressive speech, was referred by her Early Intervention Program for evaluation of disinterest in eating which worsened after the birth of a sibling four months previously. She was accompanied to the feeding clinic by her parents and a staff person from the Early Intervention Program.

Assessment Findings

Ann was judged to be at high risk for oral-motor dysfunction and delay or deviation in the development of feeding skills. Assessment needed to determine whether either factors in the interaction with her caregivers or the emergence of a food phobia were playing a role in her food refusal, particularly in its recent exacerbation. Further, the development of a physical disease affecting appetite had to be considered. Nutritional evaluation revealed an intake of 650–850 calories per day, which was below the RDA of 1000–1100 calories for this patient. Ann's height and weight were at the tenth percentile. Meal times were reported to last 40–60 minutes. Oral-motor evaluation revealed that she had not yet developed two-year-old feeding skills, such as active cheek motion during chewing and swallowing, and the ability to take 2 or 3 sips of liquid at one time. Behaviorally she was observed to be very restless and easily distracted. She picked at a peanut butter and jelly sandwich, but readily consumed Cheerios. She was observed to receive significantly more attention from her mother for food refusal and non-feeding behaviors (e.g., refusing to sit in her chair), than she did for appropriate food intake. Medical evaluation ruled out significant physical causes for her feeding disorder.

Diagnoses: Food Refusal, with underlying developmental delay in the emergence of oral-motor feeding skills, and with possible emerging FTT. Consequences of food refusal play a significant role in maintaining the behavior.

Treatment Selection and Course

The feeding program for Ann consisted of:

1. Nutritional recommendations to increase the caloric density of the food presented.
2. Institution and supervision of an oral-motor program to be implemented by Ann's parents and the Early Intervention Program's staff.
3. Behavioral recommendations included use of a favored food, Cheerios, as a reinforcer for her intake of other nutritionally and calorically dense foods, while limiting Ann's access to the Cheerios at other times to increase their potency as a reinforcer; decreasing mealtime distractions; reinforcing appropriate eating with social praise and nonverbal encouragers (clapping, smiles etc.); withdrawal of attention for non-eating behavior by averting gaze; limiting meals to approximately 30 minutes; and mother spending extra time playing with Ann (approximately 15 minutes) after meals as a reward for good eating.
4. Follow-up visits with the clinic staff approximately every three weeks with phone contact as indicated between visits.

Termination and Follow-Up

Six months after the initiation of treatment, Ann's eating behavior showed significant improvement. Her weight and height had increased to the 25th percentile. She ate a broader variety of foods, including foods that were calorically and nutritionally dense. Oral-motor skill development was evident, with more mature chewing and drinking skills. She showed an increased interest in eating, while her parents showed increased attention to appropriate eating behavior. Ann was seen on a monthly basis for follow-up and for modification of the treatment plan to accommodate her increased behavioral and oral-motor competencies.

Case 2: Eric, a 9 Year Old with Small Stature

Clinical Presentation

Eric presented as a nine-year-old boy who was small for his age. His maternal grandmother sought psychiatric assessment because of her concerns about unusual eating behavior, including drinking from toilet bowls, food hoarding, and what she viewed as an abnormally voracious appetite. Eric had received only intermittent pediatric care and had lived alternately with his mother, who was reported to now be out of state in an unknown location and to have unspecified major mental illness complicated by drug and alcohol use, and with his maternal grandparents. His grandparents reported being concerned about Eric, but viewed him as in need of firm discipline and of food restriction because of his abnormal eating and what they viewed as emerging obesity. They experienced his eating behavior as so uncontrollable that they initially wanted him to be hospitalized.

Assessment Findings

The possibility of emerging endocrine or neurological disorder affecting eating behavior and growth was considered. Although Eric's grandmother's primary complaints included excessive eating, he exhibited behaviors that are frequent features of PSS. Possibilities also included obsessive-compulsive disorder with food-centered compulsions, atypical eating disorder with early equivalents of binge eating, unrecognized developmental disorder, and distorted perceptions of the child by his caregivers with associated risk of abuse or misguided withholding of food.

Eric's height was beneath the 5th percentile for age, putting him at the 50th percentile for age 6 years, consistent with his bone age. His weight was at the 75th percentile for his height. There was no physical evidence of abuse. Records gathered from intermittent visits to the hospital's walk-in clinic showed that his birth weight had been 8 lbs and that he appeared to have followed the 40th percentile for weight and height until age four years. His grandmother recalled that at around that time her daughter's mental illness and drug problem had deteriorated and she had begun to make frequent moves in and out of state, sometimes with and sometimes without Eric. Eric's school teacher was contacted by phone. She saw him as a quiet, sad boy whose behavior was not a problem. He had few friends and achieved passing grades, but

often did not turn in homework. Eric presented as a serious, guarded boy who was reluctant to discuss his home life and denied any sadness, worries, or fears. He described himself as "a bad boy" and "too hungry."

Treatment Selection and Course

Plans were made to admit Eric to the hospital for endocrine and neurological assessment in consultation with psychiatry and social work. Eric's grandmother abruptly changed her mind, declining further assessment and announcing her intention to move out of state. Child protective agencies were unwilling to accept as sufficient evidence for their intervention the medical team's serious concerns, supplemented by explanation of the implications of PSS.

Termination and Follow-Up

Further attempts to contact the family met with no response. Eric's status and whereabouts are unknown. This concerning and unsuccessful case is included to illustrate the typical difficulties that arise in the assessment of children with possible PSS.

Case 3: Mary W., a 9-Year-Old Girl with a History of Prematurity and Current Food Selectivity and Low Weight

Clinical Presentation

Mary's parents sought psychiatric assessment for her because of their concerns about her chronic low weight and very limited food repertoire. Mary had not accepted a new food type for the previous four years. When presented with a food she did not favor, Mary would become anxious and avoidant. Attempts at trying new foods generally resulted in "temper tantrums." Mary's parents agreed that they had differed in their attempts to introduce new foods to Mary and that this had caused conflict between them. Her mother did not like to "force her" to try to eat new foods, while her father reported that he had at times tried to put food in Mary's mouth and let her sit until she ate it. Mary also had a severe articulation disorder for which she had received long-term speech therapy. With some support for math and reading she did well academically in a mainstream third grade classroom. She received regular pediatric care and was in good general health.

Assessment Findings

Mary's anxious, avoidant behavior raised the possibility of food phobia, while her articulation disorder suggested that she might have oral-motor difficulties. Family struggles about her eating may have played a possible role in maintaining her symptoms. Although her symptoms were long-standing, obsessive-compulsive disorder and early-onset anorexia nervosa were part of the differential diagnosis.

History revealed that Mary was born at 26 weeks gestation and spent the first 6 months of her life in the neonatal intensive care unit. Her postnatal course was complicated by intracranial hemorrhage, bronchopulmonary dysplasia, and necrotizing enterocolitis. For the first three months of her life she was on a respirator and was fed by nasogastric tube. After being discharged home at six months of age she was initially entirely bottle fed, but due to extreme feeding difficulties a gastrostomy was soon performed and remained in place until she was 3 years old. Her parents recalled that during those early years she required prolonged, daily "breathing treatments," vomited often after eating, and was on multiple medications.

Salient points on interview were severe articulation problems that made her speech difficult to understand. She was somewhat preoccupied with the idea of having to try new foods and reported a fearful aversion to them. Mary's height was just at the third percentile for age; her weight was well below the third percentile, as was her weight for height.

Nutritional assessment confirmed that Mary was undernourished and revealed that she limited her food intake to some breads, cheese and crackers, cookies, chocolate, ice cream, french fries, and fried foods. She would only drink milk or water and would not drink juice or pop. She would eat neither vegetables nor fruit.

When a meal was observed it was noted that Mary had difficulty chewing her food, moved her mouth excessively while chewing, and appeared to have difficulty manipulating food and keeping food in her mouth. Formal occupational therapy evaluation of feeding skills revealed both oral hypersensitivity and oral-motor dyskinesis.

Diagnoses: Mary had significant oral-motor dysfunction with resultant feeding skills disorder that was complicated by oral hypersensitivity that could be a sequela of her abnormal early feeding experiences. Superimposed on this she had developed a food phobia (new foods) that seemed exacerbated by intermittent attempts to force her to eat feared foods. Her food refusal had resulted in clinically significant undernourishment.

Treatment Selection and Course

1. Ongoing nutritional consultation was sought to identify reasonable goals for nutritional replacement for Mary and to guide the family and the psychologist in the shaping of Mary's food selections to meet her nutritional needs.
2. Mary embarked on a program of oral-motor exercises under the supervision of an occupational therapist and in collaboration with her speech therapist. The occupational therapist also worked to educate Mary and her family as to which foods and textures would present specific practical problems for her given her oral-motor difficulties.
3. Recommendations from the behavioral psychologist included developing a reward system to increase the amount and range of food that Mary would eat, systematic desensitization, and parent training in behavioral techniques, including withdrawal of attention for food refusal. The psychologist took primary responsibility for the systematic desensitization and parent training aspects of the program and supervised the development and implementation of the reward system. In the course of developing a hierarchy of feared foods and food textures for desensitization, Mary and the psychologist incorporated her emerging understanding of those food types and textures likely to present particular physical challenges to her.

Mary's reward system is briefly summarized.

   i. Mary along with her parents ranked the foods/beverages normally consumed in the household at least once every two weeks, with a sample included in the following table:

Mary <u>will</u> eat	Mary <u>might</u> eat	Mary <u>won't</u> eat
peanut butter	apple	banana
waffle	fruit yogurt	soda pop
crackers		
milk		

   ii. Points were assigned to foods/beverages as follows:

Mary will eat = 1 point; Mary might eat = 2 points; Mary won't eat = 3 points

iii. By keeping food records Mary and her parents calculated how many points Mary generally earned in a day (10 points) and set a weekly goal to earn 13 points on 5 out of 7 days in the week.

iv. Mary, with her parents, chose a daily reward (e.g., special time reading, playing catch, going over homework with Dad; staying up for 15 extra minutes at bed time; having choice over one television show that evening) and weekly rewards (e.g., having mom take Mary to a movie of her choice; going to a video arcade for 30 minutes) to correspond with the daily and weekly goals. As her mother usually spent time every day reading with Mary, this was not used as a reward. Mary and her parent signed a written contract outlining the plan.

v. During the course of treatment the psychologist worked with Mary and her family to modify the plan on the basis of her progress.

Termination and Follow-Up

Tension around eating in Mary's family quickly decreased after the initial evaluation. Mary's parents, confirmed in their long-held impression that "something was wrong," were very quickly able to work competently together around her treatment program. Six months after assessment Mary's weight and height were approaching the tenth percentile for age. Her food repertoire had greatly widened and was felt to meet her nutritional needs. She remained cautious about new foods but had become her own "expert" on food types and textures and attempted or rejected new foods on the basis of whether they were likely to be "easy" or "hard" for her. Although oral-motor difficulties persisted, the occupational therapist rated her oral-motor competence as somewhat improved. Mary and her parents now felt comfortable in managing her program alone. They requested "booster sessions" with the psychologist every two months.

SUMMARY

Although each can occur alone, feeding and growth disorders are intimately intertwined, and the detection of one should lead to assessment for the other. The rapid growth of infancy has to be achieved at the very time when feeding skills are developing. This complex biopsychosocial process is under the influence of multiple factors within the child, the parent, and the interaction between them, including the structural and functional intactness of the feeding apparatus. A very wide range of factors can contribute to the development of clinically significant feeding disorder, which often becomes the final mediating factor in the development of FTT.

For neither growth nor feeding disorders is there universal agreement as to the boundaries of the pathological. Feeding concerns are among the most common complaints in primary care pediatrics, yet there is little research as to their future implications for the health and development of child and family. Further, while some commonly used guidelines (notably percentile crossing in infancy) appear to overestimate the prevalence of FTT when applied in epidemiological studies, infants and toddlers in primary care with bona fide FTT appear to be under-identified and under-referred. Similarly, the presence of feeding disorder in FTT, with or without clear-cut medical illness, is probably under-identified, as is the presence of oral-motor dysfunction. It is unclear how confidently information gained from the study of FTT and feeding disorders in hospital and in specialized clinic settings can be applied to children in primary care and in the community.

Despite attempts to develop valid subtypes of FTT, it remains no more than an anthropometrically defined clinical sign (failure to gain adequate weight) with commonly reported associations. Nor is the simplistic division of feeding and growth disorders into those that are "explained" and "not explained" by organic factors supported by current research. It is the role of the professionals involved in assessment and treatment to identify the *specific* factors that are causing undernourishment. It is not valid to broadly attribute FTT to non-specific effects of family dysfunction, disordered parent-child relationships, medical illness or developmental disorder, although all are common associations of the finding. Similarly, while the treatment plan may involve intervention in many domains, the core goal is the implementation of an adequate feeding program with *specific* behavioral goals and, where indicated, occupational therapy treatment for oral-motor dysfunction. For these reasons FTT and persistent feeding disorders may be best assessed and treated by a multidisciplinary team that has access to specialist consultation and can coordinate diagnostic formulation and intervention in the medical, developmental, psychiatric, nutritional, occupational therapy, and social domains.

The most common specific feeding disorders are food refusal (either general or selective), rumination, and pica. Baseline assessment establishes whether the problem behavior is due to skills deficit, is being maintained by its antecedents (including whether a specific phobia is present), and or by its consequences. Successful treatment requires the design of a behavioral strategy using interventions, often in combination, that accurately target the factors so identified.

The term FTT is usually reserved to the first two years of life, and feeding disorders are most common in infancy and the pre-school years. Eating problems and failure to gain adequate weight in older children may sometimes be the continuation of problems that have developed earlier in life but can also arise de novo. Among the important considerations is the emergence of psychiatric disorder, most specifically early-onset eating disorder, mood disorder and anxiety disorder, including phobias and obsessive-compulsive disorder.

While typically viewed in the context of feeding and growth disorders, PSS is a distinct disorder with very different implications. Although eating symptoms are commonly seen (a bizarre complex that includes food seeking, hoarding, hyperphagia, eating and drinking of non-food items, and occasionally polydypsia), PSS is not a disorder of undernutrition. It is a failure to grow in height that arises from a reversible suppression of pulsatile growth hormone secretion that appears to be induced by a "noxious" parent-child relationship. Weight for height is typically normal and bone age is delayed. A seriously distorted parent-child relationship is the rule. Abuse and neglect appear to be common. Treatment without removal from the home is unlikely to be successful.

Confronted with the many families who will present seeking consultation about feeding and growth concerns, the pediatrician faces the task of identifying not only contributing medical illness, but also those children who are undernourished, appear to have a specific disorder such as food phobia or rumination, whose family situation requires intervention, and who may have developmental or emerging psychiatric disorder. For the likely majority of children who do not fit that description, education and counseling by the pediatrician based on solid behavioral and developmental principles is the first line of intervention, with referral for specialized evaluation reserved for those who do not respond to first line treatment.

REFERENCES

Abidin, R. R. (1985). *Parenting Stress Index.* University of VA: Pediatric Psychology Press.

Albanese, A., Hamill, G., Jones, J., Skuse, D., Matthews, D. R., & Stanhope, R. (1994). Reversibility of physiological growth hormone secretion in children with psychosocial dwarfism. *Clinical Endocrinology, 40,* 687–692.

American Psychiatric Association. (1987). *Diagnostic and statistical manual of mental disorders, Third edition, revised.* Washington, D.C.: American Psychiatric Association Press.

American Psychiatric Association. (1994). *Diagnostic and statistical manual of mental disorders, Fourth edition.* Washington, D.C.: American Psychiatric Association Press.

Anonymous. (1990). Failure to thrive revisited [see comments]. [Editorial]. *Lancet, 336,* 662–663.

Anonymous. (1994). Periodic health examination, 1994 update: 1. Obesity in childhood. Canadian Task Force on the Periodic Health Examination. [Review]. *Canadian Medical Association Journal, 150(6),* 871–879.

Archer, L. A., Rosenbaum, P. L., & Streiner, D. L. (1991). The Children's Eating Behavior Inventory: Reliability and validity results. *Journal of Pediatric Psychology, 16,* 629–642.

Archer, L. A. & Szatmari, P. (1990). Assessment and treatment of food aversion in a four year old boy: A multidimensional approach. *Canadian Journal of Psychiatry, 35,* 501–505.

Barbero, G. J. (1992). Failure to Thrive. In R. E. Behrman & V. C. Vaughan (Eds.), *Nelson textbook of pediatrics, fourteenth edition* (pp. 214–215). Philadelphia, PA: W. B. Saunders.

Bayley, N. (1969). *Bayley Scales of Infant Development.* New York: The Psychological Corporation.

Benoit, D. (1993). Failure to thrive and feeding disorders. In C. H. Zeanah (Ed.), *Handbook of infant mental health* (pp. 317–331). New York: The Guilford Press.

Berkey, C. S., Reed, R. B., & Valadian, I. (1983). Longitudinal growth standards for preschool children. *Annals of Human Biology, 10,* 57–67.

Berwick, D. M., Nonorganic failure to thrive. (1980). *Pediatrics in Review, 1,* 265–270.

Bithoney, W. G., McJunkin, J., Michalek, J., Egan, H., Snyder, J., & Munier, A. (1989). Prospective evaluation of weight gain in both nonorganic and organic failure to thrive children: An outpatient trial of a multi-disciplinary team strategy. *Journal of Developmental and Behavioral Pediatrics, 10,* 27–31.

Bithoney, W. G., McJunkin, J., Michalek, J., Snyder, J., Egan, H., & Epstein, D. (1991). The effect of a multi-disciplinary team approach on weight gain in nonorganic failure-to-thrive children. *Journal of Developmental and Behavioral Pediatrics, 12,* 254–258.

Bithoney, W. G. & Newberger, E. H. (1987). Child and family attributes of failure to thrive. *Journal of Developmental and Behavioral Pediatrics, 8,* 32–36.

Bithoney, W. G. & Rathbun, J. M. (1983). Failure to thrive. In M. D. Levine, W. B. Carey, A. C. Crocker, & R. T.

Gross (Eds.), *Developmental behavioral pediatrics* (pp. 557–572). Philadelphia: W. B. Saunders.

Blizzard, R. M., & Bulatovic, A. (1992). Psychosocial short stature: A syndrome with many variables. [Review]. *Baillieres Clinical Endocrinology & Metabolism, 6(3)*,687–712.

Brook, C. G. D. (1993). Growth. In C. G. D. Brook, *A guide to the practice of pediatric endocrinology.* (pp. 18–54). Cambridge: Cambridge University Press.

Center for Disease Control. (1994). Prevalence of overweight among adolescents—United States, 1988–1991. *MMWR, Morbidity and Mortality Weekly Report, 43(44)*, 818–821.

Chatoor, I., Dickson, L., Schaeffer, S., & Egan, J. (1985). A developmental classification of feeding disorders associated with failure to thrive: Diagnosis and treatment. In D. Drotar (Ed.), *New directions in failure to thrive: Implications for research and practice* (pp. 235–258). New York: Plenum Press.

Children's Defense Fund. (1994). *Wasting America's future: The Children's Defense Fund report on the costs of child poverty.* Boston: Beacon Press.

Clarke, W. R., & Lauer, R. M. (1993). Does childhood obesity track into adulthood? *Critical Reviews in Food Science & Nutrition, 33(4–5)*, 423–430.

Dahl, M., Eklund, D., & Sundelin, C. (1986). Early feeding problems in an affluent society—Determinants. *Acta Paediatrica. 75*, 380.

Dahl, M., & Sundelin, C. (1986). Early feeding problems in an affluent society—Clinical signs. *Acta Paediatrica. 75*, 370.

Dahl, M., & Sundelin, C. (1992). Feeding problems in an affluent society. Follow-up at four years of age in children with early refusal to eat. *Acta Paediatrica. 81(8)*, 575–579.

Dahl, M., & Gebre-Medhin, M. (1993). Feeding and nutritional problems in children with cerebral palsy and myelomeningocoele. *Acta Paediatrica. 82(10)*, 816–820.

Dahl, M., Rydell, A. M., & Sundelin, C. (1994). Children with early refusal to eat: Follow-up during primary school. *Acta Paediatrica. 83(1)*, 54–58.

Daniel, W. H. (1982). Management of chronic rumination with a contingent exercise procedure employing topographically dissimilar behavior. *Behavior Therapy and Experimental Psychiatry, 13*, 149–152.

Drotar, D. (1989). Behavioral diagnosis in nonorganic failure-to-thrive: A critique and suggested approach to psychological assessment. *Developmental and Behavioral Pediatrics, 10*, 48–55.

Drotar, D. (1991). The family context of nonorganic failure to thrive. *American Journal of Orthopsychiatry, 61*, 23–34.

Drotar, D., & Crawford, P. (1987). Using home observations in the clinical assessment of children. *Journal of Clinical Child Psychology, 16*, 342–349.

Drotar, D., & Eckerle, D. (1989). The family environment in nonorganic failure to thrive: A controlled study. *Journal of Pediatric Psychology, 14*, 245–257.

Drotar, D., Eckerle, D., Satola, J., Pallotta, J., & Wyatt, B. (1990). Maternal interactional behavior with nonorganic failure-to-thrive infants: A case comparison study. *Child Abuse and Neglect, 14*, 41–51.

Drotar, D., Malone, C. A., Devost, L., Brickell, C., Mantz-Clumpner, C., Negray, J., Wallace, M., Woychik, J., Wyatt, B., Eckerle, D., Bush, M., Finlon, M. A., El-Amin, D., Nowak, M., Satola, J., & Pallotta, J. (1985). Early preventive interventions in failure to thrive: Methods and early outcome. In D. Drotar (Ed.), *New directions in failure to thrive: Implications for research and practice* (pp. 119–138). New York: Plenum Press.

Drotar, D., & Sturm, L. (1987). Paternal influences in non-organic failure to thrive: Implications for psychosocial management. *Infant Mental Health Journal, 8*, 37–50.

Drotar, D., & Sturm, L. (1994). Failure to thrive. In R. A. Olson, L. L. Mullins, J. B. Gillman, & J. M. Chaney (Eds.), *The sourcebook of pediatric psychology* (pp. 26–41). Boston: Allyn & Bacon.

Edwards, A. G., Halse, P. C., Parkin, J. M., & Waterston, A. J. (1990). Recognising failure to thrive in early childhood [see comments]. *Archives of Disease in Childhood, 65*, 1263–1265. (See comments Porter 1991.)

Epstein, L. H., Valoski, A., Wing, R. R., & McCurley, J. (1990). Ten-year follow-up of behavioral, family-based treatment for obese children [see comments]. *JAMA, 264(19)*, 2519–2523.

Feldman, M. D. (1986). Pica: Current perspectives. *Psychosomatics, 27*, 519–523.

Flegal, K. M. (1993). Defining obesity in children and adolescents: Epidemiologic approaches. [Review]. *Critical Reviews in Food Science & Nutrition, 33(4–5)*, 307–312.

Foxx, R. M., & Martin, E. F. (1975). Treatment of scavenging behavior (coprophagy and pica) by overcorrection. *Behavior Research and Therapy, 13*, 153–162.

Fraiberg, S., Adelson, E., & Shapiro, V. (1975). Ghosts in the nursery. *Journal of the American Academy of Child and Adolescent Psychiatry, 14*, 387–421.

Fraiberg, S. (Ed.). (1980). *Clinical studies in infant mental health: The first year of life.* New York: Basic Books.

Frank, D. A. (1984). Biologic risk factors in "non-organic" failure to thrive: Diagnostic and research implications. In D. Drotar (Ed.), *New directions in failure to thrive: Implications for research and practice* (pp. 17–26). New York: Plenum Press.

Frank, D. A. & Zeisel, S. H. (1988). Failure to thrive. *Pediatric Clinics of North America, 35,* 1187–1205.

Fullerton, D. T. (1963). Infantile rumination: A case report. *Archives of General Psychiatry, 9,* 592–600.

Ginsberg, A. J. (1988). Feeding disorders in the developmentally disabled population. In D. C. Russo & J. H. Kedesky (Eds.), *Behavioral medicine with the developmentally disabled* (pp. 21–41). New York: Plenum.

Glasscock, S. G., Friman, P. C., O'Brien, S., & Christopherson, E. R. (1986). Varied citrus treatment of ruminant gagging in a teenager with Batten's disease. *Behavior Therapy and Experimental Psychiatry, 17,* 129–133.

Goldson, E. (1989). Neurological aspects of failure to thrive. *Developmental Medicine and Child Neurology, 31(6),* 821–826.

Gortmaker, S. L., Dietz, W. H. Jr., & Cheung, L. W. (1990). Inactivity, diet, and the fattening of America. *Journal of the American Dietetic Association, 90(9),* 1247–1252, 1255.

Green, W. H. (1986). Psychosocial dwarfism: Psychological and etiological considerations. In B. Lahey & L. Kazdin (Eds.), *Advances in clinical child psychology* (pp. 245–278). New York: Plenum.

Green, W. H. (1990). A theoretical model for classic psychosocial dwarfism (psychosocially determined short stature). In C. S. Holmes (Ed.), *Psychoneuroendocrinology: Brain, behavior and hormonal interactions,* (pp. 92–112). New York: Springer-Verlag.

Green, W. H., Campbell, M., & David, R. (1984). Psychosocial dwarfism: A critical review of the evidence. *Journal of the American Academy of Child Psychiatry 23,* 39–48.

Guilhaume, A., Benoit, O., Gourmelen, M., & Richardet, J. M. (1982). Relationship between sleep stage IV deficit and reversible HGH deficiency in psychosocial dwarfism. *Pediatric Research, 16(4 Pt 1),* 299–303.

Handen, B. L., Mandell, F., & Russo, D. C. (1986). Feeding induction in children who refuse to eat. *American Journal of Diseases of Children, 140,* 52–54.

Harlan, W. R. (1993). Epidemiology of childhood obesity. A national perspective. [Review]. *Annals of the New York Academy of Science, 699,* 1–5.

Harris G., & Booth I. W. (1992). The nature and management of eating problems in pre-school children. In P. J. Cooper & A. Stein (Ed.), *Monographs in clinical pediatrics, 5: Feeding problems and eating disorders in children and adolescents* (pp. 61–84). Chur, Switzerland: Harwood Academic Publishers.

Herbst, J. J. (1992). Disorders of the esophagus. In R. E. Behrman & V. C. Vaughan (Eds.), *Nelson textbook of pediatrics, fourteenth edition* (pp. 941–947). Philadelphia: W. B. Saunders.

Hernandez, R. J., Poznanski, A. K., Hopwood, N. J., & Kelch, R. P. (1978). Incidence of growth lines in psychosocial dwarfs and idiopathic hypopituitarism. *American Journal of Roentgenology, 131,* 477–479.

Hopwood, N. J., & Becker, D. J. (1979). Psychosocial dwarfism: Detection, evaluation and management. In A. W. Franklin (Ed.), *Child abuse and neglect (Vol. 3)* (pp. 439–447). London: Pergamon Press.

Howse, P. M., Rayner, P. H. W., Williams, J. W., Rudd, B. T., Bertrande, P. V., Thompson, C. R. S., & Jones, L. A. (1977). Nyctohemeral secretion of growth hormone in normal children of short stature and in children with hypopituitarism and intrauterine growth retardation. *Clinical Endocrinology, 6,* 347–359.

Humphrey, F. J., Mayes, S. D., Bixler, E. O., & Good, C. (1989). Variables associated with frequency of rumination in a boy with profound retardation. *Journal of Autism and Developmental Disorders, 19,* 435–447.

Hutcheson, J. J., Black, M. M., & Starr, R. H. (1993). Developmental differences in interactional characteristics of mothers and their children with failure to thrive. *Journal of Pediatric Psychology, 18,* 453–466.

Johnson, C. R., & Babbitt, R. L. (1993). Antecedent manipulation in the treatment of primary solid food refusal. *Behavior Modification, 17,* 510–521.

Johnston, J. M. (1993). Phenomenology and treatment of rumination. *Child and Adolescent Psychiatry Clinics of North America, 2,* 93–107.

Kaplan, H. I., & Sadock, B. J. (Eds.) (1985). *Comprehensive textbook of psychiatry, 4th ed.* (pp. 1734–1735). Baltimore: Williams & Wilkins.

Karlberg, J. (1987). On the modelling of human growth. *Statistics in Medicine, 6,* 185–192.

Karlberg, J., & Albertsson Wikland, K. (1988). Infancy growth pattern related to growth hormone deficiency. *Acta Paediatrica Scandinavica, 77,* 385–391.

Kelleher, K. J., Casey, P. H., Bradley, R. H., Pope, S. K., Whiteside, L., Barrett, K. W., Swanson, M. E., & Kirby, R. S. (1993). Risk factors and outcomes for failure to thrive in low birth weight preterm infants [published erratum appears in Pediatrics 1993, 92(1):190]. *Pediatrics, 91(5),* 941–948.

Kotelchuck, M., & Newberger, E. H. (1983). Failure to thrive: A controlled study of familial characteristics. *Journal of the American Academy of Child and Adolescent Psychiatry, 22,* 322–328.

Lacey, E. P. (1993). Phenomenology of pica. *Child and Adolescent Psychiatry Clinics of North America, 2,* 75–91.

Lachenmeyer, J. R, & Davidovicz, H. (1987). Failure to thrive: A critical review. In B. Lahey & L. Kazdin (Eds.), *Advances in Clinical Child Psychology* (pp. 335–358). New York: Plenum.

Lang, P. J., & Melamed, B. G. (1969). Avoidance conditioning therapy of an infant with chronic ruminative vomiting. *Journal of Abnormal Psychology, 74,* 1–8.

Lavigne, J. V., Burns, W. J., & Cotter, P. D. (1981). Rumination in infancy: Recent behavioral approaches. *International Journal of Eating Disorders, 1,* 70–82.

Leung, A. K., & Robson, W. L. (1992). Failure to thrive—or physiologic adjustment to growth? [letter; comment]. *Journal of Pediatrics, 120,* 497–498.

Linscheid, T. R., & Cunningham, C. E. (1977). A controlled demonstration of the effectiveness of electric shock in the elimination of chronic infant rumination. *Journal of Applied Behavior Analysis, 10,* 500.

Linscheid, T. R., & Rasnake, L. K. (1985). Behavioral approaches to the treatment of failure to thrive. In D. Drotar (Ed.), *New directions in failure to thrive: Implications for research and practice* (pp. 279–294). New York: Plenum Press.

Linscheid, T. R., Tarnowski, K. J., Rasnake, L. K., & Brams, J. S. (1987). Behavioral treatment of food refusal in a child with short-gut syndrome. *Journal of Pediatric Psychology, 12,* 451–459.

Lloyd, B., Pursall, E., & Emery, J. (1981). Hospital morbidity pattern in children under 1 year of age born in Sheffield 1975–6. *Archives of Disease in Childhood, 56,* 36.

Luiselli, J. K., Evans, T. P., & Boyce, D. A. (1985). Contingency management of food selectivity and oppositional eating in a multiply handicapped child. *Journal of Clinical Child Psychology, 14,* 153–156.

Madden, N. A., Russo, D. C., & Cataldo, M. F. (1980). Environmental influences on mouthing in children with lead intoxication. *Journal of Pediatric Psychology, 5,* 207–216.

Maloney, M. J., & Ruedisueli, G. (1993). The epidemiology of eating problems in non-referred children and adolescents. *Eating and Growth Disorders: Child and Adolescent Psychiatric Clinics of North America, 2,* 1–14.

Mathisen, B., Skuse, D., Wolke, D., & Reilly, S. (1989). Oral-motor dysfunction and failure to thrive among inner-city infants. *Developmental Medicine & Child Neurology. 31(3),* 293–302.

Mathisen, B., Reilly, S., & Skuse, D. (1992). Oral-motor dysfunction and feeding disorders of infants with Turner syndrome. *Developmental Medicine & Child Neurology, 34(2),* 141–149.

Mayes, L. C., & Volkmar, F. R. (1993). Nosology of eating and growth disorders in early childhood. In J. L. Woolston (Ed.), *Eating and growth disorders: Child and adolescent Psychiatric Clinics of North America, 2,* 15–35.

Mayes, S. D. (1992). Rumination disorder: Diagnosis, complications, mediating variables, and treatment. In B. B. Lahey & A. E. Kazdin (Eds.), *Advances in clinical child psychology* (Vol. 14, pp. 223–261). New York: Plenum.

Mayes, S. D., Humphrey, F. J., Handford, H. A., & Mitchell, J. F. (1988). Rumination disorder: Differential diagnosis. *Journal of the American Academy of Child and Adolescent Psychiatry, 27,* 300–302.

McKenzie, T. L., Sallis, J. F., Nader, P. R., Patterson, T. L., Elder, J. P., Berry, C. C., Ruff, J. W., Atkins, C. J., Buono, M. J., & Nelson, J. A. (1991). Beaches: An observational system for assessing children's eating and physical activity behaviors and associated events. *Journal of Applied Behavior Analysis, 24,* 141–151.

Mestre, J. R., Resnick, R. J., & Berman, W. F. (1983). Behavior modification in the treatment of rumination. *Clinical Pediatrics, 22,* 488–491.

Minde, K., & Minde, R. (1986). *Infant psychiatry: An introductory text.* London: Sage.

Mitchell, W. G., & Greenberg, R. (1980). Failure to thrive: A study in a primary care setting. *Pediatrics, 65(5),* 971–977.

Money, J., Wolff, G., & Annecillo, C. (1972). Pain agnosia and self-injury in the syndrome of reversible somatotropin deficiency (psychosocial dwarfism). *Journal of Autism & Childhood Schizophrenia, 2(2),* 127–139

Moos, R., & Moos, B. (1986). *The Family Environment Scale Manual,* 2nd ed. Palo Alto, CA: Consulting Psychologists Press.

Mouridsen, S. E., & Nielsen, S. (1990). Reversible somatotropin deficiency (psychosocial dwarfism) presenting as conduct disorder and growth hormone deficiency. *Developmental Medicine and Child Neurology, 32(12),* 1093–1098.

Mulick, J. A., Barbour, R., Schroeder, S. R., & Rojahn, J. (1980). Overcorrection of pica in two profoundly retarded adults: Analysis of setting effects, stimulus, and response generalization. *Applied Research in Mental Retardation, 1,* 241–252.

O'Brien, S. O., Repp, A. C., Williams, G. E., & Christopherson, E. R. (1991). Pediatric feeding disorders. *Behavior Modification, 15,* 419–443.

O'Neil, P. M., White, J. L., King, C. R., & Carek, D. J. (1979). Controlling childhood rumination through differential reinforcement of other behavior. *Behavior Modification, 3,* 355–372.

Polan, H. J., Kaplan, M., Kessler, D., Schindeldecker, R., Newmark, M., Stern, D. N., & Ward, M. J. (1991). Psychopathology in mothers of children with failure-to-thrive. *Infant Mental Health Journal, 12,* 55–64.

Pollitt, E., & Thompson, C. (1977). Protein-calorie malnutrition and behavior: A view from psychology. In R. J. Wurtman & J. J. Wurtman (Eds.), *Nutrition and the brain, Vol. 2: Control of feeding behavior and biology of the brain in protein-calorie malnutrition.* New York: Raven Press.

Porter, B., & Skuse, D. (1991). When does slow weight gain become "failure to thrive"? [letter; comment]. *Archives of Disease in Childhood, 66,* 905–906.

Powell, G. F., Brasel, J. A. & Blizzard, R. M. (1967). Emotional deprivation and growth retardation simulating idiopathic hypopituitarism. I. Clinical evaluation of the syndrome. *New England Journal of Medicine, 8;276(23),* 1271–1278.

Powell, G. F., Brasel, J. A., Raiti, S., & Blizzard, R. M. (1967). Emotional deprivation and growth retardation simulating idiopathic hypopituitarism. II. Endocrinologic evaluation of the syndrome. *New England Journal of Medicine, 8;276(23),* 1279–1283.

Powell, G. F., Hopwood, N. J., & Barratt, E. S. (1973). Growth hormone studies before and during catch-up growth in a child with emotional deprivation and short stature. *Journal of Clinical Endocrinology and Metabolism, 37(5),* 674–679.

Ramsay, M., Gisel, E. G., & Boutry, M. (1993). Nonorganic failure to thrive: Growth failure secondary to feeding-skills disorder. *Developmental Medicine and Child Neurology, 35,* 285–297.

Reilly, S., & Skuse, D. (1992). Characteristics and management of feeding problems of young children with cerebral palsy. *Developmental Medicine & Child Neurology, 34(5),* 379–388.

Reilly, S., Skuse, D., Mathisen, B., & Wolke, D. (1995). The objective rating of oral-motor skills during feeding. *Dysphagia, 10 (3),* 177–191.

Richmond, J. B., Eddy, E., & Green, M. (1958). Rumination: A psychiatric syndrome of infancy. *Pediatrics, 22,* 49–54.

Riddle, M. A. (Ed.). (1995). Pediatric psychopharmacology I & II. *Child and Adolescent Psychiatric Clinics of North America, 2 (1 & 2).*

Riordan, M. M., Iwata, B. A., Finney, J. W., Wohl, M. K., & Stanley, A. E. (1984). Behavioral assessment and treatment of chronic food refusal in handicapped children. *Journal of Applied Behavior Analysis, 17,* 327–341.

Roberts, M. C., & Maddux, J. E. (1982). A psychosocial conceptualization of non-organic failure to thrive. *Journal of Clinical Child Psychology, 11(3),* 216–223.

Ryan, N. D., Dahl, R. E., Birmaher, B., Williamson, D. E., Iyengar, S., Nelson, B., Puig-Antich, J., Perel, J. M. (1994). Stimulatory tests of growth hormone secretion in prepubertal major depression: Depressed versus normal children. *Journal of the American Academy of Child & Adolescent Psychiatry, 33(6),* 824–833.

Saenger, P., Levine, L. S., Wiedemann, E., Schwartz, E., Korth-Schutz, S., Pareira, J., Heinig, B., & New, M. I. (1977). Somatomedin and growth hormone in psychosocial dwarfism. *Padiatrie und Padologie—Supplementum, (5),* 1–12.

Sajwaj, T., Libet, J., & Agras, S. (1974). Lemon-juice therapy: The control of life threatening rumination in a six-month-old infant. *Journal of Applied Behavior Analysis, 7,* 557–563.

Sauvage, D., Leddet, I., Hameury, L., & Barthelemy, C. (1985). Infantile rumination, Diagnosis and follow-up study of twenty cases. *American Academy of Child and Adolescent Psychiatry, 24,* 197–203.

Shea, S., Basch, C. E., Gutin, B., Stein, A. D., Contento, I. R., Irigoyen, M., & Zybert, P. (1994). The rate of increase in blood pressure in children 5 years of age is related to changes in aerobic fitness and body mass index. *Pediatrics, 94,* 465–470.

Singer, L. T., Ambuel, B., Wade, S., & Jaffe, A. (1992). Cognitive-behavioral treatment of health-impairing food phobias in children. *Journal of the American Academy of Child and Adolescent Psychiatry, 31,* 847–852.

Singer, L. T., Nofer, J. A., Benson-Szekely, L. J., & Brooks, L. J. (1991). Behavioral assessment and management of food refusal in children with cystic fibrosis. *Developmental and Behavioral Pediatrics, 12,* 115–120.

Singh, N. N. (1981). Rumination. In N. R. Ellis (Ed.), *International review of research in mental retardation* (Vol. 10, pp. 139–177). New York: Academic Press.

Skuse, D. (1989). Emotional abuse and delay in growth. *British Medical Journal, 299, 8 ,* 113–115.

Skuse, D. (1993a). Identification and management of problem eaters. *Archives of Diseases in Children, 69,* 604–608.

Skuse, D. (1993b). Epidemiologic and definitional issues in failure to thrive. In J. L. Woolston, (Ed.), *Eating and Growth Disorders: Child and Adolescent Psychiatric Clinics of North America, 2,* 37–59.

Skuse, D., & Wolke, D. (1992a). The nature and consequences of feeding problems in infancy. In P. J. Cooper & A. Stein (Ed.), *Monographs in clinical pediatrics, 5: Feeding problems and eating disorders in children and adolescents* (pp. 1–25). Chur, Switzerland: Harwood Academic Publishers.

Skuse, D., & Wolke, D. (1992b). The management of infant feeding problems. In P. J. Cooper & A. Stein (Ed.), *Monographs in clinical pediatrics, 5: Feeding problems and eating disorders in children and adolescents* (pp. 27–59). Chur, Switzerland: Harwood Academic Publishers.

Skuse, D., Reilly, S., & Wolke, D. (1994). Psychosocial adversity and growth during infancy. *European Journal of Clinical Nutrition, 48(1)*, S113–30.

Skuse, D., Pickles, A., Wolke, D., & Reilly, S. (1994). Postnatal growth and mental development: Evidence for a "sensitive period." *Journal of Child Psychology & Psychiatry & Allied Disciplines, 35(3)*, 521–545.

Skuse, D., Stevenson, J., Reilly, S., & Mathisen, B. (1995). Schedule for oral-motor assessment (SOMA): Methods of validation. *Dysphagia, 10 (3)*, 192–202.

Smith, M. M., & Lifshitz, F. (1994). Excess fruit juice consumption as a contributing factor to nonorganic failure to thrive. *Pediatrics, 93*, 438–443.

Stanhope, R., Adlard, P., Hamill, G., Jones, J., Skuse, D., & Preece, M. A. (1988). Physiological growth hormone (GH) secretion during the recovery from psychosocial dwarfism: A case report. *Clinical Endocrinology, 28(4)*, 335–339.

Stevenson, R. D., & Allaire, J. H. (1991). The development of normal feeding and swallowing. *Pediatric Clinics of North America, 38*, 1439–1453.

Tanner, J. M., Whitehouse, R. H., & Takaishi, M. (1966). Standards from birth to maturity for height, weight, height velocity and weight velocity; British children 1965, part I. *Archives of Disease in Childhood, 41*, 454–471.

Tanner, J. M. (1990). *Foetus into man: Physical growth from conception to maturity. (Rev. and enl. ed.).* Cambridge, Mass.: Harvard University Press.

Tibbles, J. A. R., Vallet, H. L., Brown, B. St. J., & Goldbloom, R. B. (1972). Pseudotumor cerebri and deprivational dwarfism. *Developmental Medicine and Child Neurology, 14*, 322–331.

Tormey, W. P., & Darragh, A. S. (1980). Increased slow wave sleep in a hypopituitary dwarf. *Postgraduate Medical Journal, 56(652)*, 110–111

Van Den Brande, J. L., & Rappaport, R. (1993a). Postnatal growth and its endocrine regulation. In J. Bertrand, R. Rappaport & P. C. Sizonenko (Eds.), *Pediatric endocrinology: Physiology, pathophysiology and clinical aspects* (pp. 154–174). Baltimore: Williams & Wilkins.

Van Den Brande, J. L., & Rappaport, R., (1993b). Normal and abnormal growth. In J. Bertrand, R. Rappaport & P. C. Sizonenko (Eds.), *Pediatric endocrinology: Physiology, pathophysiology and clinical aspects.* (pp. 185–207). Baltimore: Williams & Wilkins.

Werle, M. A., Murphy, T. B., & Budd, K. S. (1993). Treating chronic refusal in young children: Home-based parent training. *Journal of Applied Behavior Analysis, 26*, 421–433.

Whitten C. F., Pettit, M. G., & Fischoff, J. (1969). Evidence that growth failure from maternal deprivation is secondary to undereating. *Journal of the American Medical Association, 209*, 1675–1682.

Wilcox, W. D., Nieburg, P., & Miller, D. S. (1989). Failure to thrive: A continuing problem of definition. *Clin Pediatr, 28*, 391–394.

Winton, A. S. W., & Singh, N. N. (1983a). Rumination in pediatric populations: A behavioral analysis. *Journal of the American Academy of Child Psychiatry, 22*, 269–275.

Winton, A. S. W., & Singh, N. N. (1983b). Suppression of pica using brief-duration physical restraint. *Journal of Mental Deficiency Research, 27*, 93–103.

Wolfe, W. S., Campbell, C. C., Frongillo, E. A. Jr., Haas, J. D., & Melnik, T. A. (1994). Overweight schoolchildren in New York State: prevalence and characteristics. *American Journal of Public Health, 84(5)*, 807–13.

Wolff, G., & Money, J. (1973). Relationship between sleep and growth in patients with reversible somatotropin deficiency (psychosocial dwarfism). *Psychological Medicine, 3(1)*, 18–27.

Woolston, J. L. (1985). Diagnostic classification: The current challenge in failure to thrive syndrome research. In D. Drotar (Ed.), *New directions in failure to thrive: Implications for research and practice* (pp. 225–234). New York: Plenum Press.

Woolston, J. L. (1991). Psychosocial dwarfism. In J. L. Woolston (Ed.), *Eating and growth disorders in infants and children.* (pp. 37–42). Newbury Park, CA: Sage.

World Health Organization. (1983). *Measuring changes in nutritional status.* Geneva, Switzerland: World Health Organization.

World Health Organization. (1992). *ICD-10: International statistical classification of diseases and related health problems: Tenth revision.* Geneva: World Health Organization.

Wright, C. M., Edwards, A. G., Halse, P. C., & Waterston, A. J. (1991). Weight and failure to thrive in infancy [letter]. *Lancet, 337*, 365–366.

Wright, J. A., Ashenburg, C. A., & Whitaker, R. C. (1994). Comparison of methods to categorize undernutrition in children. *Journal of Pediatrics, 124 (6)*, 944–946.

CHAPTER 7

TRAUMATIC BRAIN INJURY

Jacques Donders
Andrea Kuldanek

DESCRIPTION OF DISORDERS

Children may experience trauma of various etiologies, including physical and sexual abuse (Knutson, 1988), bereavement (Van Eerdewegh, Clayton, & Van Eerdewegh, 1985), environmental and psychosocial catastrophes (Webb, 1991), and so on. Because these nonmedical sources of trauma have been described elsewhere in detail, this chapter will focus on the most common form of medical trauma in children, traumatic brain injury (TBI). In particular, neuropsychological and psychiatric aspects of pediatric TBI will be emphasized.

Injury Variables

TBI occurs when the head is subjected to acute mechanical forces that cause physical damage to the brain or alteration in physiologic brain function. Pediatric TBI results most commonly from accelerating or decelerating forces to the skull, with resultant disruptions of underlying brain matter. Such forces may occur in a translational or linear fashion and may cause focal damage such as fractures, focal brain contusions, and subarachnoid hemorrhage (Duhaime et al., 1992; Pang, 1985). Severe TBI generally occurs through a combination of translational and rotational forces, with the rotation causing significant brain deformation and shear strain, leading to diffuse cerebral edema, multiple cortical contusions, and diffuse axonal injury. These injuries are considered the primary or direct lesion to the brain

and usually result in some degree of cell disruption or irreversible cellular destruction (Ghajar & Hariri, 1992; Noah, Hahn, Rubenstein, & Aronyk, 1992).

The moderately to severely injured brain is also vulnerable to secondary or indirect injury arising from disrupted cerebral circulation. Brain metabolism is oxygen-dependent and, with impaired perfusion, acidosis rapidly occurs, altering cellular membrane function and allowing calcium influx, which causes further cellular loss. With resumption of circulation, there may be additional injury caused by an oxygen glut that leads to excessive production of oxygen free radicals. These can cause further cell damage and alteration in brain metabolic processes.

Many studies have commented on differences between children and adults in the manifestations of TBI. Children may have fewer focal mass lesions, and more frequent diffuse brain swelling and/or white matter shearing than adults (Goldstein & Levin, 1987; Oddy, 1993). A prospective study of nearly 9,000 individuals with TBI also noted variability in severity and mortality rates in relation to age (Luerssen, Klauber, & Marshall, 1988). Peak mortality rates were noted in the under two-year-old age group and in the 15 to 24-year-old age group. Differences were also noted in the frequency of severe TBI, with 5.6 percent of the children having severe injuries as compared to 12.1 percent of the adult population.

Observation of differences in severity and mortality have led to the common misperception that children have generally better functional recovery than adults. This has not been supported by recent research. In fact, there is mounting evidence that children may have less favorable long-term functional outcomes than some adults, and that very young children are at greater risk for long-term impairment than older children (Capruso & Levin, 1992; Goldstein & Levin, 1985; Oddy, 1993).

It has been well established that TBI in children is often associated with a variety of cognitive and behavioral deficits, and that the extent of these deficits is directly related to levels of injury severity (Dalby & Obrzut, 1991; Oddy, 1993; Telzrow, 1987). Severely injured children often continue to exhibit significant cognitive problems several years after injury, whereas mild TBI most often produces few (if any) clinically significant long-term cognitive sequelae (Fay et al., 1993; Fay et al., 1994).

The most reliable and valid indicator of injury severity in children with TBI is the duration of impaired consciousness, often defined as the time until the child demonstrates a meaningful response to verbal commands (Knights et al., 1991). Other measures, such as the Glasgow Coma Scale (Teasdale & Jennett, 1974) and the length of post-traumatic amnesia, have also been used in the evaluation of the relationship between injury severity and outcome. However, results from such studies have been less consistent, most likely because these measures were more geared for use with adults and/or tend to be more labile in pediatric populations (Goldstein & Levin, 1985).

Cognitive Sequelae of TBI

Various cognitive deficits after relatively severe pediatric TBI have been described. With regard to psychometric intelligence, children with TBI often demonstrate greater and more persistent decrements in Performance IQ than in Verbal IQ (Chadwick, Rutter, Brown, Shaffer, & Traub, 1981; Chadwick, Rutter, Shaffer, & Shrout, 1981; Winogron, Knights, & Bawden, 1984). Deficits in memory and attention are among the most significant and pervasive cognitive sequelae of pediatric TBI (Bassett & Slater, 1990; Donders, 1993b; Kaufman, Fletcher, Levin, Miner, & Ewing-Cobbs, 1993; Levin, Eisenberg, Wigg, & Kobayashi, 1982). Furthermore, these children often display deficits on tasks that emphasize speed of performance, especially when a motor component is involved (Bawden, Knights, & Winogron, 1985; Chadwick, Rutter, Shaffer et al., 1981). Linguistic deficits are less pervasive, although persistent deficits in expressive language abilities and especially

written expression may occur (Ewing-Cobbs, Levin, Eisenberg, & Fletcher, 1987; Ewing-Cobbs, Miner, Fletcher, & Levin, 1989; Jordan & Murdoch, 1990).

Because the cognitive sequelae that are associated with (especially severe) TBI can seriously interfere with the child's ability to learn and remember new information, it is not surprising that poor academic achievement and need for special education support are common (Cooley & Singer, 1991; Donders, 1994; Savage & Wolcott, 1994). However, evaluation of cognitive and academic outcomes must always be considered within the context of the child's premorbid level of functioning (Donders, 1993c; Goldstein & Levin, 1985). Furthermore, it is crucial to take a developmental perspective with regard to cognitive and academic outcomes of pediatric TBI (Fletcher & Levin, 1988; Lehr, 1990). An early injury may be particularly disruptive to skills that are still in stages of rapid development (Fletcher, Miner, & Ewing-Cobbs, 1987). Furthermore, the effects of an early injury on higher levels of problem solving may not become apparent until several years after injury, when the multitude and complexity of academic demands increase and/or when specifically injured cerebral substrates would otherwise mature (Rourke, Bakker, Fisk, & Strang, 1983). A tangible example of this is the late emergence of difficulties in conceptual learning and adaptive problem solving in a recent three-year prospective study of children with TBI (Fay et al., 1994). The frequent presence of diffuse white matter lesions may put children with TBI at particular risk for such delayed effects (Rourke, 1988).

Psychiatric Sequelae

Behavioral and adjustment deficits are also common after pediatric TBI, but this is not associated with a single or characteristic pattern of disruption (Deaton & Waaland, 1994; Parmelee, 1989). There is fairly consistent evidence that severe TBI in children is associated with an increase in psychiatric symptoms (Brown, Chadwick, Shaffer, Rutter, & Traub, 1981; Fletcher, Ewing-Cobbs, Miner, Levin, & Eisenberg, 1990; Knights et al., 1991; Papero, Prigatano, Snyder, & Johnson, 1993; Pettersen, 1991). Symptoms may include behavioral disinhibition, irritability, impaired interpersonal pragmatics, and/or deficient sensitivity to facial expression and contextual cues. As with cognitive issues, these psychiatric sequelae may sometimes only become manifest relatively late (sometimes years) after injury, when the child reaches a stage of development with different social and emotional demands (Oddy, 1993). Furthermore, behavioral sequelae may overlap with cognitive sequelae, as evidenced by the fact that even preschool-aged children with TBI have an increased risk for later behavioral disorder sufficient to interfere with subsequent school performance (Michaud, Rivara, Jaffe, Fay, & Dailey, 1993).

There is some controversy about the extent to which psychiatric problems represent "true" sequelae of TBI or are simply pre-existing conditions. There is no evidence that premorbid behavioral or psychosocial factors play a major role in relatively severe pediatric TBI (Donders, 1992a). However, some authors (e.g., Brown et al., 1981; Fletcher et al., 1990) have provided persuasive evidence to suggest that reports of psychiatric changes after mild TBI may be largely due to pre-existing difficulties in the vast majority of cases. At the same time, even in a carefully screened sample without premorbid deficits, there may be a subset of children with mild TBI that demonstrates behavior problems post injury that were not observed prior to injury (Asarnow, Satz, Light, Lewis, & Neumann, 1991).

What exactly determines why some children with TBI develop psychiatric problems whereas others do not remains a matter of speculation. Injury severity clearly plays an important role, as children with severe injuries have been reported to exhibit more significant deficits and declines in behavioral adjustment, social competence, and general adaptation, than children with mild or moderate injuries (Asarnow et al., 1991; Brown et al., 1981; Fletcher et al., 1990; Perrott, Taylor, & Montes, 1991). At the same time, pre-injury child and family functioning play at least a moderating role. For example, child adjustment one year after injury appears to be better in families that are very cohesive and not overly controlling (Rivara et al., 1993). It has even been suggested that pre-injury family functioning may be a greater determinant of child behavioral outcome after TBI than injury severity (Rivara et al., 1994). This would be consistent with the results of studies of children with various chronic illnesses. These have also suggested that coping styles and family resources may be more predictive of psychological adjustment than is the physical severity of the condition (Donders, Rourke, & Canady, 1992; Murch & Cohen, 1989; Varni, Wilcox, & Hansen, 1988; Wallander & Varni, 1989).

Direct organic sequelae of TBI are most commonly expressed in what has been labeled a "frontal lobe syndrome," which may include disinhibition, lack of judgment or foresight, and moods that can range from apathy to euphoria (Gerring, 1986). DSM-IV (American Psychiatric Association, 1994) allows a diagnosis of personality change due to TBI under those circumstances. It should be noted, however, that this would require a duration of symptoms of at least one year and that there must be conclusive evidence to suggest a direct physiological consequence of the TBI.

Cognitive sequelae of TBI can be coded as a cognitive disorder not otherwise specified. This represents an important improvement over previously used categories such as delirium or dementia, neither of which characterized accurately the nature and scope of cognitive impairment of TBI in children. DSM-IV also includes proposed research criteria for postconcussional disorder. These criteria may facilitate more accurate diagnosis and professional communication, especially in cases with relatively less severe TBI (Brown, Fann, & Grant, 1994).

Impairments of interpersonal pragmatic skills are common after severe TBI. These can be manifested as a relational problem involving peers or siblings. When there are no significant premorbid psychiatric conditions or environmental adversities, clear conduct disorder or oppositional-defiant disorder are relatively uncommon as new problems. More typical are emotional and behavioral reactions to perceived deficits, social isolation, and other losses. These are often manifested as adjustment reactions, which may also become chronic. Other possible, though less frequent, diagnoses include, but are not limited to, mood disorders, bereavement, posttraumatic stress disorder, and psychotic disorder due to TBI. Other examples of entities that comprise the broad range of psychiatric conditions that can be found after TBI in children have been described by Gerring (1986), Parker (1994), and Parmelee (1989).

The diagnosis of the exact nature of the psychiatric condition of the child with TBI may, however, be confounded by a variety of factors. First of all, the same level of apparent injury severity may have different risks for delayed complications, depending on the age of the child and mechanism of injury (Goldstein & Levin, 1987). Second, the behavioral and cognitive sequelae of TBI are not specific to this condition. For example, impairments of impulse control and sustained attention can also be found in children with attention-deficit/hyperactivity disorder. Finally, many children with TBI either lack insight into their own deficits or may not be able to modulate their emotional reactions in the same manner as uninjured children. For this reason, apparent emotional reactions (or lack thereof) may appear out of context or out of proportion. Caution must be exercised not to mistake this for indifference, deliberate symptom magnification, or psychosis.

Other Sequelae

Children surviving TBI may continue to experience a variety of physical symptoms and impairments. Children recovering from mild TBI may experience vomiting, headache, irritability, and sleep disturbance for several weeks following the injury (Luerssen, 1991). With severe TBI, there tend to be prolonged difficulties that are related not only to severity of the brain injury, but also to the associated extracranial injuries that are often seen in this population as a result of a high incidence of traffic-related accidents (DiScala, Osberg, Gans, Chin, & Grant, 1991). These children may require additional weeks or months to recover from orthopedic and soft tissue injuries.

Children with severe TBI may require initial monitoring for complications such as hydrocephalus, meningitis, and respiratory system infections, as well as ongoing medical management for seizure disorders, nutritional recovery, and endocrine dysfunction (Edwards & Clark, 1986; Humphreys, 1991; Jaffe & Hays, 1986; Lau & Kenna, 1986). They may experience changes in sensory organ function, affecting vestibular function and hearing, oculomotor control and vision, and olfactory sense (Cockrell & Gregory, 1992; Healy, 1982; Kaye & Herskowitz, 1986; Sabates, Gonce, & Farris, 1991). There may also be significant alteration in motor function such as weakness, dystonia, spasticity, or apraxia due to upper motor neuron deficits or peripheral nerve injury (Jaffe & Hays, 1986; Humphreys, 1991). All these combined symptoms and impairments can affect mobility and self-care ability, causing significant changes in the child's functional independence that may further interact with cognitive or psychiatric sequelae.

EPIDEMIOLOGY

Consideration of epidemiologic factors in childhood trauma is useful in providing information regarding risk factors, such as who is at most risk for injury and what are the circumstances that commonly lead to injury. This information is helpful in understanding age-specific risk factors and in formulating effective prevention strategies. Information regarding the frequency and severity of injuries is important for rational planning of efficient, cost-effective services. Lastly, epidemiologic monitoring over time can provide information regarding the effectiveness of injury prevention strategies.

Traumatic injuries are the most common cause of childhood disease, disability, and death (Berger, 1981;

Rivara, Bergman, LoGerfo, & Weiss, 1982). Among children between birth and 19 years of age, the highest rates of death and of severe TBI occur as a result of injuries sustained in motor vehicle accidents, with 33 percent of these injuries occurring to occupants and 8 percent to pedestrians (Rodriguez & Brown, 1990). Homicide, accounting for 12.8 percent, is the second most frequent cause of pediatric injury death, followed by suicide (9.6 percent), drownings (9.2 percent), fire and burn injuries (7.2 percent), and falls (1.4 percent).

Approximately 30 percent of all childhood injury deaths arise from a brain injury, making TBI a very important category for further exploration. The incidence of mortality from TBI in the birth to 19-year-old age group is estimated at 10 per 100,000 cases per year (Kraus, Rock, & Hemyari, 1990; Rodriguez & Brown, 1990). Mortality rates ranging from 33 percent (Michaud, Rivara, Grady, & Reay, 1992) to 59 percent (Kraus et al., 1990) have been reported among individuals with severe brain injuries.

Variability in the reported frequency of pediatric TBI is noted in the literature (Kalsbeek, McLaurin, Harris, & Miller, 1980; Klauber, Barrett-Connor, Marshall, & Bowers, 1981; Kraus et al., 1990). Many studies cite the frequency of head injury rather than brain injury and may include cases of craniofacial injury in which there is no evidence of brain injury. Variability is also noted due to the exclusion in some studies of those dead at the scene of the accident or on arrival at the treatment facility. One study, including pre-hospital and hospital deaths, of the brain injury incidence for birth to 19-year-old persons in San Diego County in 1981, cites incidence rates of TBI of 185 per 100,000 for those under 15 years of age and 294 per 100,000 in the 15 to 19-year-old age group (Kraus et al., 1990).

Brain injuries are commonly classified as mild, moderate, and severe. This distinction is generally based on the Glasgow Coma Scale (GCS) score noted at the time of admission to the hospital or emergency department (Michaud et al., 1992; Teasdale & Jennett, 1974). The GCS is a standardized assessment measure that is widely used with pediatric and adult brain injury victims. It is based upon the best motor, verbal, and eye-opening responses, with the lowest score being 3 and the highest score being 15. Patients with a GCS score of less than 9 are considered to be in coma and to have a severe brain injury. Those with scores ranging from 9 to 12 are classified as moderate injuries. Individuals with GCS scores from 13 to 15 are considered to have mild injuries, unless there is evidence of an intracranial mass lesion (such cases are typically considered to be moderate injuries).

A number of factors are important to consider in using the GCS to estimate injury severity. This assessment tool was initially developed for conversant adults. Therefore, reliability may be compromised in young children (especially those who are not yet verbal) and in all patients who are intubated and cannot speak. There may also be compromised reliability related to "best" motor responses in individuals with focal motor deficits arising from spinal cord or peripheral nerve injuries.

The majority of TBI cases (82–88 percent) are classified as mild, but it is estimated that about 29,000 individuals in the birth to 19-year-old age group incur permanent disability from TBI each year, typically due to moderate or severe TBI (DiScala et al., 1991; Kraus et al., 1990). Annual incidence estimates of TBI range from 180 per 100,000 to 295 per 100,000, with an age-adjusted rate for males of 270 per 100,000 and for females of 116 per 100,000, and a peak rate during the years of 15 through 19 for both sexes (Annegers, Grabow, Kurland, & Laws, 1980; Klauber et al., 1981; Kraus, Fife, Cox, Ramstein, & Conroy, 1986; Rivara & Mueller, 1986). Rates for males are about 1.3 to 2.0 times greater than those for females at all ages, which may reflect differences in behavior as well as differences in exposure to hazards (Rivara, 1994).

The mechanism of injury varies with age and also affects the severity of injury (DiScala et al., 1991). Falls are the single largest cause of injury, and tend to occur most often in infants and young children in the home setting and result most often in mild TBI. Injuries to the 5- to 9-year-old child tend to be equally divided among motor vehicle accidents, falls, and sport and recreational activities. Young adolescents in the 10- to 14-year-old age group become injured most frequently during recreational activities, followed by motor vehicle injuries and falls. Older adolescents in the 15- to 19-year-old age range are most frequently injured in motor vehicle accidents.

Nearly one half of all pediatric TBI cases arise from a motor vehicle accident involving either drivers, occupants, pedestrians or cyclists, but this proportion is much higher among children with severe TBI (DiScala et al., 1991). Traffic-related TBI is more likely to be serious and to be accompanied by extra-cranial injuries. Use of alcohol is a factor noted in the older adolescents' traffic-related injuries. One study noted a measurable blood alcohol concentration in 51 percent of older adolescents and young adults tested, with 40 percent of tested individuals having levels above the legal limit for driving (Kraus et al., 1990).

Assaults are a frequent mechanism of injury in two age groups at the extremes of the pediatric age spectrum: infants and older adolescents. Assaults are the most frequent cause of severe TBI or death in the first year of life, with one author citing nearly 40 deaths per 100,000 children per year (Bruce, 1990). Infants incurring "shaken impact syndrome" commonly have subdural hemorrhage, evidence of diffuse axonal injury, and retinal hemorrhages (Duhaime et al., 1992). Older adolescents and young adults are experiencing increasing exposure to homicide and assault (Christoffel, 1992; Levy, 1993; Rodriguez & Brown, 1990). African American and Hispanic young males are most frequently affected. Youths from large urban areas are more likely to be exposed through gang and drug involvement, whereas youths from smaller towns and urban areas are more likely to be injured in the home by an unsecured firearm.

A number of intrinsic factors have been reported to place children at a higher risk for injury (Berger, 1981; Bijur, Stewart-Brown, & Butler, 1986). These include behavioral characteristics such as aggression, impulsivity, overactivity, and risk-taking; cognitive characteristics such as poor judgment and problem-solving ability; and differences in perceptual-motor skills and coordination. However, other investigations have not found an association between such premorbid characteristics and pediatric head injury (Klonoff, Low, & Clark, 1977). It should be noted that these traits are all seen to a variable extent in the general pediatric population. Several studies have raised the possibility that there may be a higher rate of these characteristics in children who sustain mild TBI, but not necessarily in children who sustain severe TBI (Brown et al., 1981; Donders, 1992; Rutter, Chadwick, Shaffer, & Brown, 1981; Fletcher et al., 1990). It is also possible that such characteristics may predispose children with mild TBI to incur a repeat injury.

The importance of prevention of pediatric TBI has been stressed by most authors reviewing epidemiologic factors (Berger, 1981; Kraus et al., 1990; Michaud, Duhaime, & Batshaw, 1993; Rivara, 1990, 1994; Rodriguez & Brown, 1990). Advances in pediatric trauma, rescue services, and acute care management have been beneficial in improving the outcome of pediatric brain injury victims. However, it should be noted that over two-thirds of children who die of TBI still do so at the scene of the accident or before arriving at the hospital (Kraus et al., 1990; Rivara, 1994).

Seatbelts and child restraint devices have been shown to reduce motor vehicle occupant death and injury (Decker, Dewey, Hutcheson, & Schaffner, 1984; Margolis, Wagenaar, & Liu, 1988). Helmets for bicycle and motorcycle riding have also been shown to reduce head injury and death (Thompson et al., 1989). Many states have legislated mandatory use of restraint or protective devices. Unfortunately, such devices are not always used appropriately or consistently. The National Pediatric Trauma Registry of April, 1994 notes restraint use in only 28 percent of motor vehicle victims, 1.4 percent of bicycle injuries, and 32 percent of motorcycle injuries.

Other preventive measures could include the use of helmets and safety equipment for rollerblading, skateboarding and horseback riding. TBI due to falls in young children might be prevented by eliminating baby walkers, by providing protective bars for elevated windows, and by limiting the height of playground equipment and using impact absorbing surface materials. Recommendations to reduce adolescent exposure to motor vehicle injuries could include increasing the licensure age and establishing and enforcing penalties for teenagers driving at lower blood alcohol concentrations than is accepted in adults (Michaud, Duhaime, & Batshaw, 1993). Restricting gun access may contribute to reducing firearm injuries. More emphasis also needs to be placed on the need to educate parents regarding injury risk for various age groups, and on the need to provide preventive parenting classes as a means to reduce child abuse.

ASSESSMENT APPROACHES

Medical Issues

Outcome of TBI varies in relationship to not only injury severity but also timeliness and appropriateness of initial medical management. Currently, there is no way to reverse the cell loss arising from direct impact forces occurring at the time of injury. There are, however, strategies that can be helpful in ameliorating secondary injuries, provided that these strategies are applied in a timely fashion.

Initial medical assessment following TBI may occur in the Emergency Department of a hospital or, as is more often the case with severe TBI, at the scene of the accident. A survey to evaluate the adequacy of the child's airway, ventilation, and circulation is typically initiated first. Treatment at this stage is directed toward preventing or correcting systemic hypotension and hypoxia, and may involve airway intubation, assisted ventilation, and resuscitation measures to restore adequate circulation. Children injured in motor vehicle accidents often incur multi-system injuries and may require prompt attention to life-threatening chest and abdominal injuries to allow adequate ventilation and maintenance of vascular volume.

The secondary survey involves a systemic physical assessment to evaluate the extent of injuries. Assessment for neurotrauma includes evaluation of level of consciousness; assessment of cranial nerve function for pupillary, corneal, gag, and cough reflexes; and a screening of sensory and motor functions. This assessment is not only important to describe the child's current status but also because some symptoms, such as pupillary abnormalities, are known to be associated with poor long-term outcome.

Computerized tomography (CT) scan of the brain should generally be performed on any child with a history of altered or depressed consciousness, to evaluate for intracranial lesions. Magnetic resonance imaging (MRI) has more precise resolution than the CT scan but is less cost-efficient, and may not be warranted in all cases. However, cervical spine radiographs are generally obtained to explore the possibility of an associated spinal cord injury.

Lesions identifiable by CT or MRI scan include skull and facial fractures, evidence of diffuse axonal injury and cerebral edema, as well as epidural, subdural, subarachnoid, parenchymal, and intra-ventricular hemorrhages. Some of these lesions may not be identifiable on initial CT/MRI scan but can become more apparent after 48–72 hours, which is why repeat scans are often indicated.

In general, intracranial lesions warranting surgical intervention occur less frequently in children than in adults (Luerssen, 1991). However, surgery is indicated for a child with an expanding epidural hematoma or with a subdural hematoma producing a significant cerebral midline shift (Ghajar & Hariri, 1992). Surgery may also be indicated for children with significantly depressed skull fractures, in order to achieve fracture elevation and repair of the underlying tear in the dura mater.

Psychological and Psychiatric Issues

Because of the multitude of cognitive and psychiatric deficits that may result from pediatric TBI, a comprehensive neuropsychological evaluation is often desirable. This involves an empirical and quantitative analysis of the child's cognitive and behavioral strengths and weaknesses, using psychometric instruments. Such an evaluation is conventionally deferred until the child is medically stable and has emerged from post-traumatic amnesia. The latter can be assessed in various ways, including the Children's Orientation and Amnesia Test (Ewing-Cobbs et al., 1984; Ewing-Cobbs, Levin,

Fletcher, Miner, & Eisenberg, 1989) or other procedures aimed at addressing levels of orientation, retrospective memory, and prospective memory (Ruijs, Keyser, & Gabreels, 1992). Because the child's clinical presentation often continues to change rapidly within the first few weeks post-injury, it may also be advisable to postpone a comprehensive neuropsychological assessment until the child is at least four to six weeks post-injury.

It is not the aim of this chapter to discuss in detail all the various psychometric instruments that can be utilized within the context of neuropsychological assessment. Such comprehensive descriptions are readily available elsewhere (e.g., Begali, 1992; Rourke, Fisk, & Strang, 1986; Spreen & Strauss, 1991; Teeter, 1986; Tramontana & Hooper, 1998). It is also not our intent to endorse one particular test battery as preferable to other instruments or procedures. Instead, some general considerations with regard to the neuropsychological assessment of children with TBI will be emphasized.

Psychometric Issues

Psychometric test results in children with TBI always need to be considered within the context of premorbid status, family characteristics, and moderator variables such as social/cultural, environmental, and motivational factors (Fletcher & Taylor, 1984; Goldstein & Levin, 1985; Lehr, 1990). A child who has a premorbid history of learning disability, comes from a home where English is not the primary spoken language, or has parents that have a psychiatric history has an increased likelihood of poor performances on neuropsychological tests, regardless of the severity of the incurred TBI.

Although many neuropsychological assessment procedures were initially developed to determine the likelihood and possible localization of brain damage (e.g., Reitan & Wolfson, 1992), this is hardly an important issue with most severely injured children. There is typically no question about whether a child who has been in coma for more than 24 hours has brain damage or not, and most injuries tend to be fairly diffuse or multifocal (Fletcher & Levin, 1988; Goldstein & Levin, 1987; Oddy, 1993). Furthermore, recent advances in neuro-imaging have substantially reduced the need for reliance on psychometric data to localize brain impairment. Advances have, however, recently been made in relating neuropsychological test scores to MRI findings, specifically in attempts at evaluating the impact of predominantly frontal lesions on cognitive performance (e.g., Levin, Culhane et al., 1994).

Originally, neuropsychological assessment developed from a deficit approach, focusing primarily on areas of impairment. Recent reviews of the most common cognitive sequelae of TBI in children (e.g., Dalby & Obrzut, 1991; Oddy, 1993) often follow this model, typically describing impairments in more or less arbitrarily defined areas. However, TBI does not result in a unitary cognitive syndrome in children and it is crucial that children with TBI not be considered as a homogeneous group (Johnson, 1992). There is evidence that subtypes of particular patterns of impairment may be present in this population, and that these may be related to factors such as injury severity and injury location, as well as premorbid variables (Donders, 1993c; Levin, Culhane et al., 1994).

Thorough awareness of the range of cognitive sequelae of TBI is important for the clinician. However, it must be realized that recognition of the child's neurocognitive strengths may be just as important as documentation of its deficits (Lehr, 1990; Rourke, Fisk, & Strang, 1986). Additional consideration of characteristics such as test-taking attitudes, self-monitoring behaviors, and reactions to failure are important when determining the intervention techniques that will most likely facilitate the child's performance and rehabilitation (Begali, 1994). Additional real-life contextual observations are also desirable when possible (Ylvisaker, Hartwick, Ross, & Nussbaum, 1994). This is because the structured setting of a one-to-one environment with few distractors (which is the standard for most neuropsychological assessments) may actually mask some of the child's deficits that would be more evident in a classroom or community milieu. Of course, it may not always be feasible to obtain such observations (e.g., if the child comes in for an outpatient assessment and travels from a remote area). At the very least, the examiner should then obtain a thorough family history, obtain up-to-date school records, and interview parents about the child's behavior in nonstructured settings.

It is also crucial that neuropsychological assessment be performed with a thorough understanding of federal and state guidelines regarding special education eligibility. Prior to the passage of Public Law 94–142 in 1975, children with TBI often received no special education support at all. Subsequently, some children with TBI were able to receive services under the "Otherwise Health Impaired" qualification. However, this did not necessarily mean that their specific needs were being met (Cooley & Singer, 1991; Rosen & Gerring, 1986). The inclusion of TBI as one of 13 educational disabilities under the Individuals with Disabilities Education Act in 1991 has provided federal guidelines and requirements for service delivery to children with TBI. However, individual states have varied widely in their modifications of the definition of TBI under these guidelines, and in their implementation of specific programs. Neuropsychological assessment needs to provide data to facilitate determination of eligibility for special education support under the most recent state rules.

The evaluation of cognitive sequelae of TBI in children also needs to account for some of the general shortcomings of pediatric neuropsychological assessment procedures. There is a tendency to take tests that were developed for adults and apply them (sometimes in abbreviated form) to children, but this is not consistently done with proper consideration of issues of task difficulty and differences in measurement characteristics (Fletcher & Taylor, 1984). In the context of recent evidence implicating the frontal lobes in some of the problem-solving and memory deficits in children with TBI (e.g., Levin, Culhane et al., 1994; Levin, Mendelsohn et al., 1994), it is also of concern that relatively few well-normed psychometric measures exist that have demonstrated selective sensitivity to frontal lobe dysfunction in children (Mateer & Williams, 1991; Welsh & Pennington, 1988).

Adequate norms and acceptable levels of reliability are lacking for at least some common neuropsychological tests (Spreen & Strauss, 1991). The Halstead-Reitan Neuropsychological Test Battery for Older Children (Reitan & Wolfson, 1992) and the Reitan-Indiana Neuropsychological Test Battery for Young Children (Reitan & Wolfson, 1994) are probably the best researched and validated comprehensive pediatric assessment batteries. However, reliability estimates for the measures included in these batteries range from satisfactory on some tasks, such as the Finger Tapping Test and the Target Test, to very problematic for some other instruments, including the Speech Sounds Perception Test and some of the scores obtained from the Tactual Performance Test (Brown, Rourke, & Cicchetti, 1989; Leckliter, Forster, Klonoff, & Knights, 1992). Furthermore, there are still few neuropsychological instruments for the assessment of infants and preschoolers (Hooper, 1991).

Notwithstanding all of these cautions and reservations, neuropsychological assessment can provide a wealth of information to facilitate service delivery to children with TBI. It is crucial that the examiner be familiar with developmental issues pertaining to cognition, psychopathology, and brain-behavior relationships. Professional organizations such as Division 40—Neuropsychology—of the American Psychological Association (Division 40, 1989) and the National Academy of Neuropsychology (Puente, 1994) have recently provided explicit definitions of the credentials required for individuals to claim expertise in clinical neuropsychology. There is no clearer evidence of competence in this field than the Diplomate in Clinical Neuropsychology from the American Board of Professional Psychology.

General Measures

Most neuropsychological assessments include general measures of psychometric intelligence and academic achievement. These tests are administered because (a) it is conventional to so, (b) this type of information is typically familiar to school professionals, and (c) a sizable body of research has documented the short- and long-term effects of TBI on such measures. The most recently standardized and normed intelligence test that is applicable to a fairly wide pediatric age range is the Wechsler Intelligence Test for Children–Third Edition (WISC-III; Wechsler, 1991). This instrument has excellent psychometric properties (Kaufman, 1993) and also has the advantage that it was normed on the same population that was used for the Wechsler Individual Achievement Test (WIAT; Weschler, 1992), one of the most comprehensive measures of academic achievement. This allows for direct comparisons of obtained results on both tests (Flanagan & Alfonso, 1993a, 1993b).

Several other measures of academic achievement and psychometric intelligence are available (see Begali, 1992 and Sattler, 1992 for reviews). However, care should be taken to avoid uncritical acceptance of claims of neuropsychological foundations of some of these tests in the absence of research demonstrating strong and consistent links between test performance and specific brain or injury characteristics (Donders, 1992b). It has even been suggested that some of these other tests are misguided to the point that one is better off using the WISC-III, despite the fact that even that instrument is not without its limitations (Sternberg, 1993).

The WISC-III departs from exclusive reliance on IQ scores, and offers a multi-factorial approach. However, there is still considerable controversy over the validity of this factor structure (Carroll, 1993; Little, 1992; Naglieri, 1993; Roid, Prifitera, & Weiss, 1993; Sattler, 1993). Concern has also been expressed about the fact that the WISC-III has failed to incorporate recent developments in cognitive psychology, or to provide a foundation for treatment validity (Little, 1992; Sternberg, 1993).

When assessing children with TBI, it is important to avoid exclusive reliance on measures of psychometric intelligence and/or academic achievement, however useful these may be. Such instruments assess to a great extent skills that were relatively overlearned prior to the injury and do not necessarily sample a sufficiently broad range of skills, particularly regarding new learning (Telzrow, 1987). Therefore, additional inclusion of measures of speeded performance, attention and memory, and problem solving need to be included in neuropsychological evaluations of children with TBI (Begali, 1994; Ewing-Cobbs & Fletcher, 1987; Goldstein & Levin, 1985; Johnson, 1992; Ylvisaker, Hartwick, Ross, & Nussbaum, 1994).

Specific Neuropsychological Procedures

There have been significant advances in recent years with regard to the standardization and norming of specific pediatric neuropsychological measures. Significantly improved age-based norms have become available for measures of concept formation, novel problem solving, and cognitive flexibility, including the Wisconsin Card Sorting Test (WCST; Heaton, Chelune, Talley, Kay, & Curtiss, 1993) and the Children's Category Test (CCT; Boll, 1993). Comprehensive batteries for the assessment of attention and memory have also become available, including the California Verbal Learning Test–Children's Version (CVLT-C; Delis, Kramer, Kaplan, & Ober, 1994), the Test of Memory and Learning (TOMAL; Reynolds & Bigler, 1994), and the Wide Range Assessment of Memory and Learning (WRAML; Sheslow & Adams, 1990). With many of these newer measures, however, further research is needed with regard to issues such as sensitivity to cerebral impairment, and the validity of the proposed indices or scales. For example, considerable reservations have already been raised about the proposed factor structure of the WRAML (Burton, Mittenberg, & Burton, 1993; Gioia, 1991). It always behooves neuropsychologists to heed Anastasi's (1988) caution against simply accepting a test's name as a true index of what it really measures.

Measures of Behavior, Adjustment, and Personality

Assessment of emotional and behavioral adjustment through appropriately standardized and normed instruments is an important component of any pediatric neuropsychological evaluation, and is particularly essential in the determination of sequelae of TBI, given the high risk for deficits in adaptive behavior after relatively severe TBI. As much as possible, the examiner should obtain information from multiple sources, such as parents and teachers, and (especially with older children) from the child. Various instruments are available that offer formats for parent-, teacher-, and self-reports, including

the Behavior Assessment System for Children (Reynolds & Kamphaus, 1992) and the Child Behavior Checklist and derivatives developed by Achenbach (1991a, 1991b, 1991c). Some of these instruments have also been used to evaluate premorbid adjustment in children with TBI (Donders, 1992a; Fletcher et al., 1990; Pelco, Sawyer, Duffield, Prior, & Kinsella, 1992).

In terms of a more comprehensive evaluation of specific dimensions of a child's personality, the parent questionnaire with the best demonstrated psychometric properties is probably the Personality Inventory for Children–Revised (Lachar, 1982; Wirt, Lachar, Klinedinst, & Seat, 1984). Some of the scales on this instrument, though, can be inflated by lack of independence due to orthopedic or other physical but non-cerebral sequelae of TBI. The Vineland Adaptive Behavior Scales (Sparrow, Balla, & Cicchetti, 1984) offer a psychometrically sound method of obtaining detailed information about various aspects of children's personal and social adaptive functioning in daily living, using the technique of a semi-structured interview with the primary caretaker. The recent addition of the Minnesota Multiphasic Personality Inventory–Adolescent (Butcher et al., 1992) to the assessment pool is promising because it allows for a much more in-depth evaluation of psychopathology on the basis of self-report by the child. However, this instrument can only be applied with older children and also requires further validation for use with neurologically impaired subjects.

Finally, recent research (e.g., Rivara et al., 1993, 1994) has suggested that formal assessment of family dynamics may be an important factor to consider in the evaluation of outcome of pediatric TBI. Various instruments are available in the literature (see Bishop & Miller, 1988 for a review), of which the Family Assessment Device (Epstein, Baldwin, & Bishop, 1983) appears to have the most acceptable psychometric properties.

TREATMENT STRATEGIES

Overview of Medical Management

Following initial medical assessment, children who demonstrate alteration in level of consciousness require close (at least overnight) observation of signs of neurological deterioration. Access to an intensive care unit capable of managing pediatric patients is desirable. Children in coma (GCS<9) require careful management of cardiopulmonary function, fluid and electrolyte balance, and nutrition. They must be monitored closely for changes in neurological function and for complications such as infections and coagulopathies (disorders of blood clotting mechanisms), or for changes in fluid and electrolyte metabolism associated with hypothalamic/pituitary axis dysfunction.

Children in coma often have an intracranial pressure (ICP) monitor placed to facilitate monitoring and timely management of intracranial hypertension. ICP, along with mean arterial pressure, is also used to indirectly monitor cerebral perfusion pressure, which provides an indication of brain oxygen and nutrient supply (Noah et al., 1992). Intracranial hypertension can be managed by various interventions, including sedation, hyperventilation, and osmotic diuresis with agents such as Manitol and high-dose barbiturates to reduce brain metabolic demand. Use of prophylactic anticonvulsant medication is no longer universally accepted. However, management of early post-traumatic seizures is important in order to reduce the likelihood of hypoxia or hypercarbia.

Children who survive severe TBI generally experience a variety of functional impairments related to the brain injury itself as well as to associated extracranial injuries. Recovery potential for children with multiple impairments is often enhanced through rehabilitative services provided by a team of pediatric therapists. In rehabilitation facilities, an interdisciplinary team approach under the management of a physician familiar with medical and rehabilitation concerns of children is desirable. Services can be provided conjointly by various professionals, including representatives from the fields of psychology, psychiatry, occupational therapy, physical therapy, speech and language pathology, social work, recreation therapy, educational services, and rehabilitation nursing.

The rehabilitation process incorporates a number of key components. Assessment of the neurological, physical, and psychological factors contributing to the functional impairments allows the rehabilitation team to develop strategies to facilitate recovery (Jaffe & Hays, 1986). Therapy strategies need to be designed to accommodate the child's developmental level and interests. Medical problems such as seizure disorders, nutritional problems, visual disturbances, and orthopedic and soft tissue injuries need to be identified and appropriately managed. Preventive measures must be taken to avoid secondary problems such as orthopedic deformities, pressure injuries to the skin, and infections, all of which may lead to further functional impairment. The child also needs ongoing monitoring for evolving neu-

rologic complications such as hydrocephalus, emergence of a post-traumatic seizure disorder, or endocrine problems associated with hypopituitarism. Education of the family and the child regarding the rehabilitation process should be given strong emphasis. Family members should be encouraged to actively participate in the child's rehabilitation program.

Generally, the most rapid phase of recovery from TBI occurs within the first 3 months following injury. It is essential to coordinate, from the beginning, rehabilitative and academic services into a format that facilitates the child's optimum physical and cognitive recovery, while also allowing the child to comfortably resume family and social activities. Following this phase of rapid recovery, however, many children with severe TBI may be left with various disabling physical, cognitive, or behavioral conditions, some of which may have a significant impact on development. Long-term follow-up services by a pediatric interdisciplinary clinic are therefore often indicated.

Psychological and Behavioral Treatments

Intervention techniques vary with the level of recovery of the child with TBI. Early on in this process, it is not unusual to encounter agitated behavior, which can best be managed by reduction of the level of stimulation. As progress continues, impulsiveness, disinhibition, decreased frustration tolerance, reduced motivation, lack of initiative, and other psychiatric problems may emerge, but there is no one unvarying picture of behavioral deficit (Lehr, 1990). In this section, we will review behavioral management interventions, psychotherapeutic approaches, and the treatment of cognitive deficits.

Behavioral Management

Comprehensive descriptions of behavioral management issues (Gelfand & Hartmann, 1984; Kazdin, 1984), and descriptions of applications with children with TBI (Cockrell, Chase, & Cobb, 1990; Deaton, 1994; Divack, Herrie, & Scott, 1985; Jacobs, 1991) are readily available in the literature. Only some general guidelines related to behavioral management issues with children with TBI will be reviewed here.

It is usually a good idea to start with the selection of a specific target undesirable behavior, as well as a specific target desirable behavior. These behaviors should be clearly defined and measurable, and baseline levels of frequency should be obtained. There must be agreement among all parties involved (e.g., parents, teachers, and therapists) regarding priorities and intervention methods. The goal is to reduce the frequency of the undesirable behavior while at the same time increasing the frequency of the desirable behavior. As a rule of thumb, this should be done with the least intrusive procedures that are effective. Restrictive or aversive procedures should be used only as a last resort, after all other measures have failed.

Behavior problems can be defined heuristically in terms of an A-B-C approach that clearly describes the Behavior, the Antecedents, and the Consequences (Karoly, 1980). Antecedents pertain to variables that occur prior to the specific behavior in question: who was present, what happened that might elicit the behavior, and what is the temporal course? Consequences include environmental reactions to the behavior, which can range from neutral (i.e., no reaction, such as in ignoring), to rewarding, to punitive. Most behavioral management strategies involve attempts at modifying the child's behavior by means of structured control over both the antecedents and the consequences.

Antecedents that commonly elicit behavioral difficulties in children with TBI include excessive amounts of stimulation and unanticipated changes in the child's routine. Reducing the amount of stimulation (e.g., working in smaller groups or quieter rooms), or carefully explaining the nature of and reasons for changes before they occur, are examples of manipulating such antecedents.

Consequences can be divided into strengtheners (those interventions that make it more likely that the behavior will occur again) and weakeners (those interventions that make it less likely that the behavior will occur again). It is important to use consequences that are practical. For example, leaving the room is not a feasible consequence in response to swearing for a child who has severe balance problems and who is attempting to stand up. Consequences that inadvertently work as strengtheners and thereby maintain the behavior in question should be eliminated (e.g., overly emotional reactions may be reinforcing to children seeking attention). It is important to realize that a consequence that is meant to be punitive may in fact be rewarding. For example, dismissing a child from therapy or class in response to swearing may give the child exactly what he/she wants (i.e., an escape from a frustrating situation), making it more likely that the same behavior will occur in the future. Consequences must also be meaningful to the child. For example, an adolescent may not be motivated to work for candy but may react well to an approach that makes T.V. privileges contingent upon cooperation with treatment. With all

consequences, it is crucial that these follow the behavior immediately and consistently. Some of the major reasons why behavioral management programs can fail include time delays between the behavior and the consequence, and lack of consistency in responding to the behavior.

For children with TBI, it is particularly important to avoid complex behavioral management programs. Lack of structure and specificity are likely to doom any well-intended behavioral intervention. Due to the frequency of cognitive deficits, the program should be kept simple and concrete. Preferably, the child should be able to restate the contingencies in his or her own words. The use of a simple written checklist or outline can be very helpful with children with memory deficits. With higher levels of functioning, behavioral contracts, token economy, and other more sophisticated interventions can also be utilized (Mateer & Ruff, 1990; Wood, 1990).

Psychotherapeutic Interventions

There is no one particular psychotherapeutic approach that is indicated exclusively for use with children with TBI. Specific interventions may depend on the level of child development, the cultural background of the family, and the family life cycle stage that is interrupted by TBI (Williams & Savage, 1991). Because of cognitive deficits, it may be advisable to use a somewhat more directive and concrete approach, as opposed to an abstract or insight-oriented approach, in individual therapy with children with TBI (Donders, 1993a). However, some strategies that have been successfully applied with children with hyperactive, impulsive, or aggressive behaviors, such as cognitive behavior modification through self-instruction training (Meichenbaum & Genest, 1980), may also be applicable for children with higher levels of cognitive functioning.

It is also not unusual to see the need for psychotherapeutic intervention increase with time (especially with severely injured children), because of the cumulative effects of various deficits and consequences of which the child is becoming increasingly aware (Lehr, 1990). Similarly, the nature of the relationship between levels of injury severity and disability on the one hand, and parental distress on the other, may also change over time (Livingston & Brooks, 1988).

The method of intervention will also depend to a great extent on a detailed analysis of the degree to which and the reasons why the child presents with psychiatric problems. It has been suggested that there are at least six ways TBI and psychiatric symptoms in children may be related functionally (Asarnow et al., 1991): (a) the problem antedated the TBI; (b) the TBI exacerbated a preexisting problem; (c) the problem is a direct consequence of brain damage secondary to TBI; (d) the problem is an immediate secondary effect (e.g., an emotional response to the psychosocial trauma of the accident); (e) the problem is a long-term secondary effect; and (f) the problem is caused by factors other than the TBI. This classification is consistent with the framework suggested by Lewis (1991) for tailoring the therapy process to the presenting problem.

The differentiation of these various possible relationships between TBI and psychiatric disorder starts with a thorough review of child and family history. This review should include exploration of any premorbid psychiatric conditions in the child because these are known to have strong predictive power with regard to post-traumatic psychiatric status (Gerring, 1986). This review can be accomplished by means of parent interview and review of premorbid school and medical records. Furthermore, consideration must be given to a variety of other possible contributing factors, including the premorbid psychosocial adjustment of the family, the prevalence of psychiatric conditions in biological relatives, and additional psychosocial and environmental stressors that are unrelated to TBI (e.g., longstanding financial problems, or recent death of a loved one). The parental reaction to the injury, and any associated primary or secondary gain issues with either the child or the parent, must also be considered. For example, some parents may be overprotective and this may lead to learned helplessness or dependence. In cases where litigation is involved, the family may also stand to gain significant financial incentives if the child continues to appear impaired. Finally, children may (intentionally or subconsciously) use their TBI as an "excuse" to avoid increasing environmental demands or social responsibilities.

As a general rule, new psychiatric disorders are less likely with unremarkable preinjury child and family functioning, and more likely with increasing severity of injury and psychosocial adversity in the child's home and environment (Brown et al., 1981). Laboratory evidence for involvement of the frontal lobes and/or the hypothalamic/pituitary axis increases the likelihood for a direct organic contribution of TBI to the psychiatric condition (Parker, 1994). Furthermore, one must consider the amount of congruence between injury severity and behavioral dysfunction. A severe psychiatric disorder would be out of proportion with a TBI characterized by minimal loss of consciousness and negative CT/MRI findings. In such cases, premorbid issues and secondary effects, as well as unrelated contributing factors, may be more likely candidates regarding causation. Secondary effects, such as emotional reactions to perceived deficits and losses, may also occur at a later point in time, particularly with advanced cognitive recovery.

If it can be determined that there was a pre-existing condition, it is often helpful to determine if it had ever been treated successfully. For example, if a premorbid attention-deficit/hyperactivity disorder had been managed effectively with stimulant medication, consideration may be given to utilizing this method of intervention again after injury (provided that there are no additional factors to suggest an increased risk for seizures). Attempts must also be made to alleviate non-TBI contributing factors whenever possible. For example, if there are unresolved issues related to premorbid physical or sexual abuse, it may be necessary to address these formally through individual or family therapy, especially in children with decreased physical independence who may experience greater sense of vulnerability. Direct organic sequelae of TBI may require a combination of medical and behavioral management approaches. Secondary emotional reactions often require psychotherapeutic intervention.

Very often, family members (including parents as well as siblings) are in need of psychotherapeutic support after pediatric TBI (Brooks, 1984; Lehr, 1990; Waaland, 1990). Significant levels of distress have been reported among parents of children with TBI, and there is some indication that this may be related at least in part to the coping strategies of parents (Kay & Cavallo, 1991; Livingston, 1987; Novack, Bergquist, Bennett, & Bouvier, 1991). It has even been suggested that the family's reaction may contribute to the persistence of behavioral change in children with severe TBI (Hartman, 1987). Interventions may include general support, education, and advocacy, as well as specific family therapy, to deal with issues such as grief and loss. Assistance in the management of behavioral problems is also appropriate with many families.

Rehabilitation of Cognitive Deficits

Remediation of cognitive sequeale of pediatric TBI is an area of great controversy. Although much has been written about cognitive rehabilitation techniques that can be used with adults (Harrell, Parente, Bellingrath, & Liscia, 1992; Kreutzer & Wehman, 1991; Parente & Anderson-Parente, 1991) as well as children (Routh, 1987; Ylvisaker, Szerkes, Hartwick, & Tworek, 1994), this is a subdomain of TBI rehabilitation where the industry appears to have proceeded faster than the science (Putnam & Adams, 1992).

Much of the controversy pertains to the limited and often inconsistent evidence for the efficacy of many cognitive rehabilitation interventions (Benedict, 1989; Ruff, Niemann, Troster, & Mateer, 1990; Schacter & Glisky, 1986). Well-controlled outcome research studies (as opposed to ancecdotal reports on highly selective cases) of cognitive rehabilitation with children with TBI in particular are quite scarce. The few studies that have been done (e.g., Light et al., 1987) have typically involved small numbers of patients that were not randomly assigned to treatment. Gordon, Hibbard, and Kreutzer (1989) have summarized other problems with studies of the efficacy of cognitive rehabilitation in general, including the lack of theory-driven research and controlled group comparisons.

In the adult literature, there are some emergent efforts employing alternative methods to the most common cognitve remediation techniques. For example, Kirsch, Levine, Fallon-Krueger, and Jaros (1987) have described ways to use computers as an orthotic device to increase functional skills. Furthermore, in an excellent, well-controlled study, Berg, Koning-Haanstra, and Deelman (1991) demonstrated that compensatory strategy training yielded superior long-term effects on memory performance as compared to repetitive drill training or no treatment. Studies such as these are encouraging with regard to the possibility of effective cognitive rehabilitation, but more research with children with TBI is clearly needed.

Close collaboration between psychologists, psychiatrists, and other professionals within the child's home school district is crucial to facilitate optimal rehabilitation of cognitive deficits after pediatric TBI. Helpful concrete guidelines in this respect have been suggested by Ylvisaker, Hartwick, and Stevens (1991), emphasizing a continuing and interactive process that starts at the time of hospital admission and that proceeds with follow-up after discharge. An excellent review of pragmatic issues pertaining to planning, implementing, and evaluating the school re-integration process for children with TBI has been provided by Blosser and DePompei (1994). Specific considerations in the context of the recent amendments to Public Law 94-142 (which mandates special education services for children with TBI) may include a need to write Individual Education Plans for shorter periods of time, with more frequent review (Cohen, 1991), and to move away from categorical service delivery and toward a service-needs model (Cooley & Singer, 1991).

Pharmacological Treatments

Pharmacological interventions need to be considered carefully in the management of children recovering from TBI. Various drugs have the potential to blunt cognition and to slow the pace of recovery. In recent years, there has been increasing attention devoted to the use of psychopharmaceutical agents to affect central nervous system (CNS) neurotransmitter systems in order to facilitate improvement in cognitive skills, mood, or behavior. Unfortunately, there has been a paucity of organized research to provide a rational approach to pharmacological interventions in the TBI population, especially for children. This has resulted in a tendency in many rehabilitation settings to favor traditional therapeutic intervention and environmental manipulation over pharmacological measures. There has also been a reluctance to study the effects of various agents in young children, due to concerns about drug effects on developing organ systems and/or litigation concerns, leaving significantly fewer options for treatment in this group.

Pharmacological strategies have been considered in the adult TBI population to deal with a variety of problems, including low arousal, aggression, affective disorders, frontal lobe syndromes, atypical seizure disorders, and an assortment of miscellaneous conditions (Cope, 1994). Treatment strategies have been based to some extent on merging knowledge regarding derangements of CNS neurotransmitter function following TBI and information from studies of pharmacological interventions in other disorders such as attention-deficit/hyperactivity disorder, dementia of the Alzheimer type, and Parkinson's disease (Wroblewski & Glenn, 1994). Pharmacological intervention has also been based on accumulated individual clinical experience and individual case reports in the literature. There has been little information published regarding controlled trials of neuropharmacological intervention in the adult TBI population (Whyte, 1994) and there is even less available on pediatric samples.

In general, the practice in many rehabilitation settings is to use pharmacological interventions as a last resort measure when other therapeutic techniques have failed to yield the desired outcome. Negative attitudes toward use of psychopharmacological agents are based on several concerns. These agents tend to have complex effects and oftentimes significant negative side effects. There is inadequate information regarding their efficacy (especially with young children) and their potential for negative effect on long-term recovery. Lastly, there may be a lack of familiarity with the use of psychopharmacological agents among physicians working with TBI patients.

Cope (1994) has proposed consideration of three phases of treatment to provide a structured approach to psychopharmacological intervention, and to deal with the concerns regarding these agents interfering with potential recovery. The first or emergent phase takes place immediately post injury when the goal of intervention is to promote survival and recovery of neuronal structures. A number of measures to prevent secondary neuronal loss are under investigation, including calcium entry blockade, free radical blockade, and facilitation of free radical degradation (Boyeson & Harmon, 1994).

The second phase is the acute or active recovery phase. This period occurs when the patient is medically stable and able to benefit from active rehabilitative intervention. During this period, pharmacological intervention can be utilized to manage problems such as destructive behaviors, affective disorders, and cognitive deficits. Cassidy (1994) provides concrete guidelines regarding drugs of choice for specific conditions after TBI, such as carbamazepine for organic mania, selective serotonin-reuptake inhibitors (e.g., fluoxetine, paroxetine, or setraline) for organic depression, and amytriptyline for secondary aggressive disorder. There is also an emerging literature regarding the use of classic stimulants such as dextroamphetamine, methylphenidate, and pemoline in the treatment of arousal and attention disorders after TBI (Evans, Gualtieri, & Patterson, 1987; Gualtieri, 1988; Wroblewski & Glenn, 1994). Psychopharmacological intervention has also been suggested as a means to improve the rate of recovery (Boyeson & Harmon, 1994), but this is an issue that has yet to receive systematic exploration in a pediatric population with TBI.

The third phase of possible psychopharmacological intervention is the chronic or fixed deficit phase. This period occurs when there is little discernible ongoing recovery or minimal expectation for functional gain. Cope (1994) suggests that more aggressive psychopharmacological intervention strategies than are currently the standard of practice are indicated at this stage for the residual cognitive, affective, and behavioral deficits. Increased understanding of the role of acetylcholine in memory processes, the association of dopamine and norepinephrine with general arousal and alertness, and the effect of serotonin on pain, aggression, and mood, may encourage strategies in the future to affect CNS neurotransmitter function in the long-term care of patients with TBI.

There are several underlying principles to consider in formulating a rational psychopharmacological approach to disorders of cognition, mood, or behavior. It is important to have an understanding about the nature of the injury and the pathological changes incurred (Cassidy, 1994). For example, both diffuse axonal injury and hypoxic/ischemic injury affect neurotransmitter functioning. It is also necessary to search for underlying central nervous system complications such as infections, hydrocephalus, seizure disorders, and systemic problems such as endocrine disregulation, or fluid and electrolyte imbalance. Many medications have potential adverse CNS side effects, particularly of an anticholinergic nature, that may directly impede attention and memory (Silver & Yudofsky, 1994). Medications should be routinely reviewed for efficacy, appropriate dosage, and adverse effects. Patients with TBI are especially sensitive to such side effects (particularly involving cognitive and behavioral functions) and therefore medications should be introduced at low doses and increased only slowly. Furthermore, psychopharmacological interventions should never take place in isolation, but should instead be coordinated with other therapeutic and rehabilitative strategies (e.g., behavioral management) to facilitate optimal results.

A few specific applications of psychopharmacology in the management of TBI deserve special consideration. We will briefly review issues pertaining to the management of arousal and attention, as well as destructive behavior.

Strategies for management of deficits in arousal, attention, and memory have been developed based on information obtained from pharmacological interventions in children with attention-deficit/hyperactivity disorder (ADHD). Stimulants such as dextroamphetamine, methylphenidate, and pemoline have been known to improve attention and related functions in the ADHD population. The therapeutic effect of these agents is postulated to occur through modulation or enhancement of dopaminergic neurotransmission to rostral brain structures (Gualtieri, 1988). Their use may be considered for individuals with TBI with deficits related to frontal lobe injuries (Wrobleski & Glenn, 1994). Aside from the classic CNS stimulants, other medications used in children to affect arousal and attention have included imipramine and amantadine. Additional dopamine- or norepinepherine-enhancing agents that may affect arousal and attention include levodopa-carbidopa, bromocriptine, selegiline, and trycyclic antidepressants. Serotonin specific reuptake inhibitors may also influence arousal and attention. Many of these agents, however, have not been evaluated for use with children.

Destructive or violent behavior can be a challenge to manage, particularly in the older child or adolescent. This may present as a transient delirium early in the process of recovery. Children recovering from severe TBI generally present with altered levels of consciousness, global cognitive impairment, significantly increased or decreased psychomotor activity, and a disordered sleep-wake cycle. Once underlying medical complications or drug side effects have been eliminated as factors, medication management may be indicated for those children who present a danger to self or to others, or who become increasingly agitated with physical restraint. Low dose haloperidol given intravenously or by bolus continuous drip has been recommended for adults because fewer extrapyramidal side effects are reported associated with this route than when it is administered orally (Cassidy, 1994). Low-dose lorazepam has also been recommended as an adjunct to haloperidol and may allow reduction in the dose of haloperidol. One has to wonder, however, at the challenge of maintaining intravenous access in a restless and confused patient. The importance of attempting to gradually withdraw medications once delirium or post-traumatic amnesia clear cannot be overstated.

Destructive behavior may also be associated with depression or psychosis, in which case an antidepressant or neuroleptic medication may be helpful. Episodic non-directed aggression can be a manifestation of a partial complex seizure disorder. An EEG may show frontal and temporal slow wave activity or sharp discharges, in which case an anticonvulsant such as carbamazepine, valproate, or clonazepam may be beneficial. Organic aggressive syndromes can occur, characterized by reactive, non-purposeful, explosive behaviors. Medications suggested for this disorder include oral haloperidol, amantadine, trazodone and buspirone (which also have serotonergic effects), propranolol, and amitriptyline (Cassidy, 1994). However, trazodone and buspirone have not been evaluated for use in children, and amitriptyline is typically not recommended for children under twelve years of age.

CASE ILLUSTRATION

The following case is presented to illustrate the various assessment and treatment issues that were discussed above, as well as to demonstrate the importance of a long-term developmental perspective with regard to pediatric TBI. All information is based on a real case from the authors' practice. Informed written consent was obtained from the parents to use these data, but names and other non-crucial identifying information have been altered to protect confidentiality. Because this case represents a child who is now several years post injury, some of the assessment instruments represent older versions of currently available measures.

Clinical Presentation

Ann was struck as a pedestrian by a car at the age of 10 years. There was immediate loss of consciousness. In the emergency room, she was unresponsive to pain, but both pupils were midpoint and equally reactive to light. Initial GCS score was 7 (severe range). Head CT scan revealed a minimally depressed occipital skull fracture, small intra-ventricular hemorrhage, and diffuse edema. There were no long bone fractures or abdominal injuries. Ann had two tonic-clonic seizures within the first 24 hours after injury. She was initially managed with mannitol, dexamethasone, phenobarbital, phenytoin, and intra-cranial pressure monitoring. No neurosurgical interventions were required. Spontaneous eye opening was observed within five days after injury, and she reacted to verbal commands on the sixth day. Acute care was complicated by high fevers, presumably due to sinusitis, which were treated successfully with antibiotics. Two weeks after injury, Ann was transferred to an in-patient pediatric rehabilitation unit, where she remained four weeks and received intensive interdisciplinary treatment. After discharge to her parents' home, she entered an out-patient transitional pediatric day treatment program, which she attended for eight weeks. During that time, a gradual return to her home school district (with special education support) was initiated.

Assessment Findings

School records reflected that Ann had premorbidly just completed the fourth grade, with average to high-average grades and average national percentile scores on a standardized achievement test. She had never been retained, nor had she had any special education support prior to her accident. Premorbid medical history was non-contributory. A standardized questionnaire with regard to Ann's premorbid adjustment (Achenbach & Edelbrock, 1986) could not be completed by Ann's new teacher because she did not know her well enough, and Ann's previous teacher was not available.

A significant element in the family history was the divorce of the biological parents five years prior to the injury. In addition, an older sibling had a long-standing history of ADHD. The responses of the mother to a standardized and age-normed questionnaire with regard to

Ann's premorbid adjustment (Achenbach & Edelbrock, 1983), completed at the time of admission to the rehabilitation unit, were not suggestive of any long-standing behavioral or psychosocial deficits. Thus, although premorbid family history had been complicated, Ann had not demonstrated significant academic or adjustment difficulties prior to her TBI.

Initial neuropsychological evaluation was completed one week after Ann emerged from post-traumatic amnesia (about five weeks post injury). Follow-up neuropsychological assessment was completed one year later. The results from these assessments are presented in Table 7.1. For purposes of convenience, scores from the Wechsler Intelligence Scale for Children–Revised (WISC-R; Wechsler, 1974) and from the Kaufman Test of Educational Achievement (KTEA; Kaufman & Kaufman, 1985) are presented in the conventional manner ($M=100$; $SD=15$). All other scores, including those from the Denman Neuropsychology Memory Scale (DENMAN; Denman, 1984), the Halstead Category Test (HCT; Reitan & Wolfson, 1992), and the Tactual Performance Test (TPT; Reitan & Wolfson, 1992) were converted to T-scores ($M=50$, $SD=10$) on the basis of age-based norms for each test. All scores in Table 7.1 were constructed such that higher values reflected better performance.

Inspection of Table 7.1 reveals that Ann's levels of psychometric intelligence (as assessed with the WISC-R) were at first in the low-average range, which most likely reflected a decline from her documented premorbid functioning. Verbal IQ demonstrated much progression within one year, but Performance IQ remained relatively depressed. This is a common finding in children with TBI (Chadwick et al., 1981a, 1981b; Winogron et al., 1984). Academic achievement test scores (KTEA) were within normal limits on both occasions, which again is not uncommon after traumatic brain injury because such tests measure primarily overlearned skills (Telzrow, 1987). In contrast, Ann demonstrated on both assessments significant deficits on tasks pertaining to recall of new (especially nonverbal) information (DENMAN), novel reasoning (HCT), and sensori-motor performance (especially with the dominant left hand; TPT). This pattern of findings is suggestive of persistent significant cerebral dysfunction (possibly with relatively greater posterior right-hemisphere involvement due to contre-coup injury) and may represent an increased risk for long-term deficits in cognitive and adaptive abilities (Rourke, 1988).

Parent-, teacher-, and self-report versions of standardized rating scales (Achenbach & Edelbrock, 1983, 1986, 1987) were administered at the time of the repeat neuropsychological evaluation to ascertain behavioral, emotional, and adjustment deficits. These findings (again expressed as T-scores; $M=50$, $SD=10$) are presented in Table 7.2. For purposes of comparison, initial

Table 7.1. Neuropsychological Test Performance on Initial Evaluation (Five Weeks Post Injury) and Repeat Evaluation (15 Months Post Injury).

TEST	MEASUREMENTS OBTAINED	INITIAL	REPEAT
WISC-R	Verbal IQ	86	113
	Performance IQ	82	101
KTEA	Reading Comprehension	104	105
	Mathematics Computation	105	111
DENMAN	Immediate Recall; Story	47	53
DENMAN	45-Minute Delayed Recall; Story	37	50
DENMAN	Immediate Recall; Figure	—	20
DENMAN	45-Minute Delayed Recall; Figure	—	20
HCT	Problem Solving (Total Errors)	16	34
TPT	Tactile-Motor Skills (Left Hand)	42	37
TPT	Tactile-Motor Skills (Right Hand)	54	57
TPT	Tactile-Motor Skills (Both Hands)	35	37
TPT	Tactile-Motor Skills (Memory)	30	34
TPT	Tactile-Motor Skills (Location)	40	36

Note: Higher scores reflect better performance on all tasks.

Table 7.2. Results of Various Child Behavior Rating Scales Regarding Patient Status Premorbidly and at Repeat Neuropsychological Evaluation (15 Months Post Injury).

	PREMORBID (PARENT)	15 MONTHS (PARENT)	15 MONTHS (TEACHER)	15 MONTHS (PATIENT)
Total Competence[a]	51	25	31	48
Total Problems[b]	47	72	73	47
Internalizing[b]	46	70	58	33
Externalizing[b]	47	73	74	39

[a]Higher scores reflect better adjustment.
[b]Higher scores reflect poorer adjustment.

ratings from the mother with regard to Ann's premorbid adjustment (obtained at the time of admission to the in-patient rehabilitation unit) are also provided.

Inspection of Table 7.2 reveals that both the mother and the school teacher identified significant behavioral and social adjustment deficits more than one year post-injury, whereas such concerns had not been reported prior to injury. Importantly, Ann appeared to be oblivious to these deficits, as she rated herself as unremarkable in all areas. This represents an important lack of deficit awareness.

Treatment Selection and Course

When Ann was admitted to the in-patient rehabilitation unit, her home school district was notified and school materials (including work books used in the fifth grade) were obtained. One week prior to discharge, a meeting between her parents, hospital treatment staff, and professionals from her school was arranged to discuss her discharge status, likely further progress, and special education needs. It was mutually agreed upon that Ann would initially start classroom services through an out-patient pediatric transition program, followed by a gradual part-time return to her home school. Eligibility for special education services under the qualification of Otherwise Health Impaired was also mutually determined.

Behavioral management interventions (including time-out in response to inappropriate behaviors and a token economy system to earn off-unit recreation privileges) were initiated during Ann's hospitalization at the in-patient rehabilitation unit to deal with outbursts of angry frustration. Over the course of three weeks, these interventions were very successful in reducing the frequency of outbursts to less than three times per week (as compared to more than three times per day at the beginning of treatment).

Additional interventions during Ann's in-patient rehabilitation included participation in a peer play group, which focused on interpersonal skills such as sharing, turn-taking, and pragmatic language behaviors. Moderate improvement in self-monitoring of behavior was noted over the course of six sessions, although Ann remained cue-dependent in many areas.

Supportive individual psychotherapy had been initiated with Ann prior to the repeat neuropsychological evaluation, but had not been very successful. The format was then switched to a group format, which facilitated direct feedback from peers with regard to Ann's behavior. This was combined with enrollment in community-based peer group recreational activities under supervision of an adult. These interventions were relatively more successful over the course of six months.

Termination and Follow-Up

Ann is now more than four years post injury. She is enrolled full-time in the tenth grade where she receives one hour of resource room per day to work on study skills, but is mainstreamed for all other academic activities. Because of a recent increase in awareness on Ann's part of her interpersonal isolation, and associated reactive distress, counseling services are now again provided on a monthly basis. She continues to be followed in an out-patient pediatric brain injury clinic on a yearly basis.

SUMMARY

TBI in children can lead to a variety of cognitive and behavioral sequelae. Deficits in attention, memory, and speed of processing are among the most common cognitive consequences, whereas behavioral disinhibition and impaired social pragmatics are among the most frequent psychiatric difficulties. However, no unique or invariant syndrome of TBI sequelae exists. Severity of TBI (most reliably expressed as the duration of coma) is one of the most significant factors affecting recovery, although other variables such as pre-injury level of functioning and family dynamics also play an important role. Children may have better survival than adults with similar injuries, but the notion that children generally have better functional recovery than adults is a misconception that is unsupported by recent research. Furthermore, TBI in children needs to be understood from a developmental perspective. Many children who sustain a severe TBI at an early age may initially appear to recover fairly well but often will display more significant deficits in novel learning and adaptive behavior when they grow older.

There have been significant developments in clinical assessment in recent years that directly impact the population of children who sustain TBI. Neuro-imaging techniques (especially MRI) have allowed increasingly specific characterizations of the cerebral changes after TBI. Standardization and norms of neuropsychological assessment instruments have been improved tremendously, allowing for more accurate definition of the child's cognitive strengths and weaknesses. There are now federal guidelines mandating special education service delivery to children with TBI. Preventive measures such as seatbelts and bicycle helmets have also had an impact on the incidence of pediatric TBI.

At the same time, much remains to be done to improve the level of understanding of sequelae of pediatric TBI, as well as management of its consequences. Prevention strategies are only in their infancy and could be expanded to other domains, such as restricting gun access for children, and teaching parenting skills to those individuals at risk for child abuse. In the area of medical management, there is considerable need for further investigation of neuropharmacological strategies to prevent secondary neuronal loss, to facilitate early recovery, and to address persistent deficits affecting cognition, affect, and behavior. There is also a need to further explore the effects of currently available medications on children. The efficacy of post-acute rehabilitative and academic strategies, particularly in the area of cognitive deficits, needs to be demonstrated more clearly and more consistently.

Further research with regard to the sequelae of pediatric TBI could greatly benefit from inclusion of some of the following strategies. Multivariate statistical approaches need to be applied to identify the additive and interactive effects of various premorbid, injury, and post-injury variables. There is also a need for longitudinal investigations of children with TBI and controls, particularly in the context of furthering our understanding of the developmental implications of TBI. Recent studies that have included case-controlled cohorts (Fay et al., 1994) and the application of individual growth curve analysis (Thompson et al., 1994) are examples of carefully designed and well-analyzed investigations that address these issues.

Additional research could further delineate possible subtypes of TBI sequelae and how these relate to premorbid status, injury characteristics, and outcome (Donders, 1993c). Functional brain imaging techniques, such as single photon emission computed tomography, have promising research applications, especially since these may have a stronger relationship to patterns of neuropsychological impairment than structural changes on CT or MRI scan (Levin, 1993).

The management and study of pediatric TBI require specific pediatric expertise from both the clinician and the scientific investigator. The clinical application of a developmental perspective that incorporates replicated findings of carefully designed research may benefit not only our understanding of pediatric TBI but also our impact on its outcome.

REFERENCES

Achenbach, T. M. (1991a). *Manual for the Child Behavior Checklist and 1991 Profile.* Burlington, VT: University of Vermont.

Achenbach, T. M. (1991b). *Manual for the Teacher's Report Form and 1991 Profile.* Burlington, VT: University of Vermont.

Achenbach, T. M. (1991c). *Manual for the Youth Self Report Form and 1991 Profile.* Burlington, VT: University of Vermont.

Achenbach, T. M., & Edelbrock, C. (1983). *Manual for the Child Behavior Checklist and Revised Child Behavior Profile.* Burlington, VT: University of Vermont.

Achenbach, T. M., & Edelbrock, C. (1986). *Manual for the Teacher's Report Form and Teacher Version of the Child Behavior Profile.* Burlington, VT: University of Vermont.

Achenbach, T. M., & Edelbrock, C. (1987). *Manual for the Youth Self Report and Profile.* Burlington, VT: University of Vermont.

American Psychiatric Association. (1994). *Diagnostic and statistical manual of mental disorders (fourth edition).* Washington, D.C.: American Psychiatric Association.

Anastasi, A. (1988). *Psychological testing* (6th ed.). New York: MacMillan.

Annegers, J. F., Grabow, J. D., Kurland, L. T., & Laws, E. R. (1980). The incidence, causes, and secular trends of head trauma in Olmsted County, Minnesota, 1935–1974. *Neurology, 30,* 912–919.

Asarnow, R. F., Satz, P., Light, R., Lewis, R., & Neumann, R. (1991). Behavior problems and adaptive functioning in children with mild and severe closed head injury. *Journal of Pediatric Psychology, 16,* 543–555.

Bassett, S. S., & Slater, E. J. (1990). Neuropsychological functioning adolescents sustaining mild closed head injury. *Journal of Pediatric Psychology, 15,* 225–236.

Bawden, H. N., Knights, R. M., & Winogron, H. W. (1985). Speeded performance following head injury in children. *Journal of Clinical and Experimental Neuropsychology, 7,* 39–54.

Begali, V. (1992). *Head injury in children and adolescents: A resource and review for school and allied professionals* (2nd ed.). Brandon, VT: Clinical Psychology Publishing Company.

Begali, V. (1994). The role of the school psychologist. In R. C. Savage & G. F. Wolcott (Eds.), *Educational dimensions of acquired brain injury* (pp. 453–473). Austin, TX: PRO-ED.

Benedict, R. H. B. (1989). The effectiveness of cognitive remediation strategies for victims of traumatic head injury: A review of the literature. *Clinical Psychology Review, 9,* 605–626.

Berg, I. J., Koning-Haanstra, M., & Deelman, B. G. (1991). Long-term effects of memory rehabilitation: A controlled study. *Neuropsychological Rehabilitation, 1,* 97–111.

Berger, L. R. (1981). Childhood injuries: Recognition and prevention. *Current Problems in Pediatrics, 12,* 2–58.

Bijur, P. E., Stewart-Brown, S., & Butler, N. (1986). Child behavior and accidental injury in 11,966 preschool children. *American Journal of Diseases of Children, 140,* 487–492.

Bishop, D. S., & Miller, I. W. (1988). Traumatic brain injury: Empirical family assessment techniques. *Journal of Head Trauma Rehabilitation, 3,* 16–30.

Blosser, J. L., & DePompei, R. (1994). Creating an effective classroom environment. In R. C. Savage & G. F. Wolcott (Eds.), *Educational dimensions of acquired brain injury* (pp. 393–451). Austin, TX: PRO-ED.

Boll, T. (1993). *Children's Category Test Manual.* San Antonio, TX: Psychological Corporation.

Boyeson, M. G., & Harmon, R. L. (1994). Acute and postacute drug-induced effects on rate of behavioral recovery after brain injury. *Journal of Head Trauma Rehabilitation, 9,* 78–90.

Brooks, D. N. (1984). *Closed head injury: Psychological, social, and family consequences.* Oxford, England: Oxford University Press.

Brown, G. W., Chadwick, O., Shaffer, D., Rutter, M., & Traub, M. (1981). A prospective study of children with head injuries: III. Psychiatric sequelae. *Psychological Medicine, 11,* 63–78.

Brown, S. J., Fann, J. R., & Grant, I. (1994). Postconcussional disorder: Time to acknowledge a common source of neurobehavioral morbidity. *Journal of Neuropsychiatry and Clinical Neurosciences, 6,* 15–22.

Brown, S. J., Rourke, B. P., & Cicchetti, D. V. (1989). Reliability of tests and measures used in the neuropsychological assessment of children. *The Clinical Neuropsychologist, 3,* 353–368.

Bruce, D. A. (1990). Head injuries in the pediatric population. *Current Problems in Pediatrics, 20,* 65–106.

Burton, D. B., Mittenberg, W., & Burton, C. A. (1993, February). *A structural equation analysis of the Wide Range Assessment of Memory and Learning in the standardization sample.* Paper presented at the meeting of the International Neuropsychological Society, Galveston, TX.

Butcher, J. N., Williams, C. L., Graham, J. R., Archer, R. P., Tellegen, A., Ben-Porath, Y. S., & Kaemmer, B. (1992). *Multiphasic Personality Inventory–Adolescent Manual.* Minneapolis, MN: University of Minnesota Press.

Capruso, D. X., & Levin, H. S. (1992). Cognitive impairment following closed head injury. *Neurologic Clinics, 10,* 879–893.

Carroll, J. B. (1993). What abilities are measured by the WISC-III? In B. A. Bracken (Ed.), *Wechsler Intelligence Scale for Children: Third Edition* (pp. 134–143). Brandon, VT: Clinical Psychology Publishing Press.

Cassidy, J. W. (1994). Neuropharmacological management of destructive behavior after traumatic brain injury. *Journal of Head Trauma Rehabilitation, 9,* 43–60.

Chadwick, O., Rutter, M., Brown, G., Shaffer, D., & Traub, M. (1981). A prospective study of children with head injuries: II. Cognitive sequelae. *Psychological Medicine, 11,* 49–61.

Chadwick, O., Rutter, M., Shaffer, D., & Shrout, P. E. (1981). A prospective study of children with head injuries: IV. Specific cognitive deficits. *Journal of Clinical Neuropsychology, 3,* 101–120.

Christoffel, K. K. (1992). Pediatric firearm injuries: Time to target a growing population. *Pediatric Annals, 21,* 430–436.

Cockrell, J. L., Chase, J., & Cobb, E. (1990). Rehabilitation of children with traumatic brain injury: Coma to community. In J. S. Kreutzer & P. Wehman (Eds.), *Community integration following traumatic brain injury* (pp. 287–300). Baltimore: Paul H. Brookes Publishing Company.

Cockrell, J. L., & Gregory, S. (1992). Audiological deficits in brain injured children and adolescents. *Brain Injury, 6*, 261–266.

Cohen, S. B. (1991). Adapting educational programs for students with head injuries. *Journal of Head Trauma Rehabilitation, 6*, 56–63.

Cooley, E., & Singer, G. (1991). On serving students with head injuries: Are we reinventing a wheel that doesn't roll? *Journal of Head Trauma Rehabilitation, 6*, 47–55.

Cope, D. N. (1994). An integration of psychopharmacological and rehabilitation approaches to traumatic brain injury rehabilitation. *Journal of Head Trauma Rehabilitation, 9*, 1–18.

Dalby, P. R., & Obrzut, H. E. (1991). Epidemiological characteristics and sequelae of closed head-injured children: A review. *Developmental Neuropsychology, 7*, 35–68.

Deaton, A. V. (1994). Changing the behaviors of students with acquired brain injuries. In R. C. Savage & G. F. Wolcott (Eds.), *Educational dimensions of acquired brain injury* (pp. 257–275). Austin, TX: PRO-ED.

Deaton, A. V., & Waaland, P. (1994). Psychosocial effects of acquired brain injury. In R. C. Savage & G. F. Wolcott (Eds.), *Educational dimensions of acquired brain injury* (pp. 239–255). Austin, TX: PRO-ED.

Decker, M. D., Dewey, M. J., Hutcheson, R. H., & Schaffner, W. (1984). The use and efficacy of child restraint devices; the Tennessee experience 1982 & 1983. *Journal of the American Medical Association, 252*, 2571–2575.

Delis, D. C., Kramer, J. H., Kaplan, E., & Ober, B. A. (1994). *California Verbal Learning Test–Children's Version Manual.* San Antonio, TX: Psychological Corporation.

Denman, S. B. (1984). *Manual: Denman Neuropsychology Memory Scale.* Charleston, SC: Author.

DiScala, C., Osberg, J. S., Gans, B., Chin, L. J., & Grant, C. C. (1991). Children with traumatic head injury: Morbidity and postacute treatment. *Archives of Physical Medicine and Rehabilitation, 72*, 662–666.

Divack, J. A., Herrie, J., & Scott, M. B. (1985). Behavior management. In M. Ylvisaker (Ed.), *Head injury rehabilitation: Children and adolescents* (pp. 347–360). Austin, TX: PRO-ED.

Division 40. (1989). Definition of a clinical neuropsychologist. *The Clinical Neuropsychologist, 3*, 22.

Donders, J. (1992a). Premorbid behavioral and psychosocial adjustment of children with traumatic brain injury. *Journal of Abnormal Child Psychology, 20*, 233–246.

Donders, J. (1992b). Validity of the Kaufman Assessment Battery for children when employed with children with traumatic brain injury. *Journal of Clinical Psychology, 48*, 225–230.

Donders, J. (1993a). Bereavement and mourning in pediatric rehabilitation settings. *Death Studies, 17*, 517–527.

Donders, J. (1993b). Memory functioning after traumatic brain injury in children. *Brain Injury, 7*, 431–437.

Donders, J. (1993c). WISC-R subtest patterns in children with traumatic brain injury. *The Clinical Neuropsychologist, 7*, 430–442.

Donders, J. (1994). Academic placement after traumatic brain injury. *Journal of School Psychology, 32*, 53–65.

Donders, J., Rourke, B. P., & Canady, A. I. (1992). Emotional adjustment of children with hydrocephalus and of their parents. *Journal of Child Neurology, 7*, 375–380.

Duhaime, A. C., Alario, A. J., Lewander, W. J., Schut, L., Sutton, L. N., Seidl, T. S., Nudelman, S., Buddenz, D., Hertle, R., Tsiaras, W., & Loporchio, S. (1992). Head injury in very young children: Mechanisms, injury types, and ophthalmologic findings in 100 hospitalized patients younger than 2 years of age. *Pediatrics, 90*, 179–185.

Edwards, O. M., & Clark, D. A. (1986). Post-traumatic hypopituitarism. Six cases and a review of the literature. *Medicine, 54*, 281–290.

Epstein, N., Baldwin, L., & Bishop, D. (1983). The McMaster Family Assessment Device. *Journal of Marital and Family Therapy, 9*, 171–180.

Evans, R. W., Gualtieri, C. T., & Patterson, D. R. (1987). Treatment of closed head injury with psychostimulant drugs: A controlled case study and appropriate evaluation procedure. *Journal of Nervous and Mental Disorders, 175*, 106–110.

Ewing-Cobbs, L., & Fletcher, J. M. (1987). Neuropsychological assessment of head injury in children (1987). *Journal of Learning Disabilities, 20*, 526–535.

Ewing-Cobbs, L., Levin, H. S., Eisenberg, H. M., & Fletcher, J. M. (1987). Language functions following closed head injury in children and adolescents. *Journal of Clinical and Experimental Neuropsychology, 9*, 575–592.

Ewing-Cobbs, L., Levin, H. S., Fletcher, J. M., McLaughlin, E. J., McNeely, D., Ewert, J., & Francis, D. (1984, February). *Assessment of post-traumatic amnesia in head injured children.* Paper presented at the meeting of the International Neuropsychological Society, Houston, TX.

Ewing-Cobbs, L., Levin, H. S., Fletcher, J. M., Miner, M. E., & Eisenberg, H. M. (1989, February). *Post-traumatic amnesia in children: Assessment and outcome.* Paper presented at the meeting of the International Neuropsychological Society, Vancouver, BC.

Ewing-Cobbs, L., Miner, M. E., Fletcher, J. M., & Levin, H. S. (1989). Intellectual, motor, and language sequelae following closed head injury in infants and preschoolers. *Journal of Pediatric Psychology, 14,* 531–547.

Fay, G. C., Jaffe, K. M., Polissar, N. L., Liao, S., Martin, K. M., Shutlleff, H. A., Rivara, J. B., & Winn, H. R. (1993). Mild pediatric traumatic brain injury: A cohort study. *Archives of Physical Medicine and Rehabilitation, 74,* 895–901.

Fay, G. C., Jaffe, K. M., Polissar, N. L., Liao, S., Rivara, J. B., & Martin, K. M. (1994). Outcome of pediatric traumatic brain injury at three years: A cohort study. *Archives of Physical Medicine and Rehabilitation, 75,* 733–741.

Flanagan, D. P., & Alfonso, V. C. (1993a). Differences required for significance between Wechsler Verbal and Performance IQs and WIAT subtests and composites: The predicted-achievement method. *Psychology in the Schools, 30,* 125–132.

Flanagan, D. P., & Alfonso, V. C. (1993b). WIAT subtest and composite predicted-achievement values based on WISC-III Verbal and Performance IQs. *Psychology in the Schools, 30,* 310–320.

Fletcher, J. M., Ewing-Cobbs, L., Miner, M. E., Levin, H. S., & Eisenberg, H. M. (1990). Behavioral changes after closed head injury in children. *Journal of Consulting and Clinical Psychology, 58,* 93–98.

Fletcher, J. M., & Levin, H. S. (1988). Neurobehavioral effects of brain injury in children. In D. K. Routh (Ed.), *Handbook of pediatric psychology* (pp. 258–295). New York: Guilford Press.

Fletcher, J. M., Miner, M. E., & Ewing-Cobbs, L. (1987). Age and recovery from head injury in children: Developmental issues. In H. S. Levin, H. M. Eisenberg, & J. Grafman (Eds.), *Neurobehavioral recovery from head injury* (pp. 279–291). New York: Oxford.

Fletcher, J. M., & Taylor, H. G. (1984). Neuropsychological approaches to children: Towards a developmental neuropsychology. *Journal of Clinical Neuropsychology, 6,* 24–37.

Gelfand, D. M., & Hartmann, D. P. (1984). *Child behavior analysis and therapy.* New York: Pergamon Press.

Gerring, J. P. (1986). Psychiatric sequelae of severe closed head injury. *Pediatrics in Review, 8,* 115–121.

Ghajar, J., & Hariri, R. (1992). Management of pediatric head injury. *Pediatric Emergency Medicine, 39,* 1093–1125.

Gioia, G. A. (1991, February). *Re-analysis of the factor structure of the Wide Range Assessment of Memory and Learning: Implications for clinical interpretation.* Paper presented at the meeting of the International Neuropsychological Society, San Antonio, TX.

Goldstein, F. C., & Levin, H. S. (1985). Intellectual and academic outcome following closed head injury in children and adolescents: Research strategies and empirical findings. *Developmental Neuropsychology, 1,* 195–214.

Goldstein, F. C., & Levin, H. S. (1987). Epidemiology of pediatric closed head injury: Incidence, clinical characteristics, and risk factors. *Journal of Learning Disabilities, 20,* 518–525.

Gordon, W. A., Hibbard, M. R., & Kreutzer, J. S. (1989). Cognitive remediation: Issues in research and practice. *Journal of Head Trauma Rehabilitation, 4,* 76–84.

Gualtieri, C. T. (1988). Pharmacotherapy and the neurobehavioral sequelae of traumatic brain injury. *Brain Injury, 2,* 101–129.

Harrell, M., Parente, F., Bellingrath, E. G., & Lisicia, K. A. (1992). *Cognitive rehabilitation of memory: A practical guide.* Gaithersburg, MD: Aspen Publishers.

Hartman, S. (1987). Patterns of change in families following severe head injuries in children. *Australia and New Zealand Journal of Family Therapy, 8,* 125–130.

Healy, G. (1982). Current concepts in otolaryngology: Hearing loss and vertigo secondary to head injury. *Medical Intelligence, 306,* 1029–1031.

Heaton, R. K., Chelune, G. J., Talley, J. L., Kay, G. C., & Curtiss, G. (1993). *Wisconsin Card Sorting Test Manual: Revised and expanded.* Odessa, FL: Psychological Assessment Resources.

Hooper, S. R. (1991). Neuropsychological assessment of the preschool child: Issues and procedures. In B. A. Bracken (Ed.), *The psychoeducational assessment of preschool children* (2nd ed.; pp. 465–485). Boston: Allyn & Bacon.

Humphreys, R. P. (1991). Complications of pediatric head injury. *Pediatric Neurosurgery, 17,* 274–278.

Jacobs, H. E. (1991). Family and behavioral issues. In J. M. Williams & T. Kay (Eds.), *Head injury: A family matter* (pp. 239–251). Baltimore: Paul H. Brookes.

Jaffe, K. M., & Hays, R. M. (1986). Pediatric head injury: Rehabilitative medical management. *Journal of Head Trauma Rehabilitation, 1,* 30–40.

Johnson, D. A. (1992). Head injured children and education: A need for greater delineation and understanding. *British Journal of Educational Psychology, 62,* 404–409.

Jordan, F. M., & Murdoch, B. E. (1990). Linguistic status following closed head injury in children: A follow-up study. *Brain Injury, 4,* 147–154.

Kalsbeek, W. D., McLaurin, R. L., Harris, B. S. H., & Miller, J. D. (1980). The national head injury and spinal cord survey: Major findings. *Journal of Neurosurgery, 53,* 519–531.

Karoly, P. (1980). Operant methods. In F. H. Kanfer & A. P. Goldstein (Eds.), *Helping people change* (pp. 210–247). New York: Pergamon Press.

Kaufman, A. S. (1993). King WISC the third assumes the throne. *Journal of School Psychology, 31,* 345–354.

Kaufman, A. S., & Kaufman, N. L. (1985). *Kaufman Test of Educational Achievement Comprehensive Form Manual.* Circle Pines, MN: American Guidance Service.

Kaufman, P. M., Fletcher, J. M., Levin, H. S., Miner, M. E., & Ewing-Cobbs, L. (1993). Attentional disturbance after pediatric closed head injury. *Journal of Child Neurology, 8,* 348–353.

Kay, T., & Cavallo, M. M. (1991). Evolutions: Research and clinical perspectives on families. In J. M. Williams & T. Kay (Eds.), *Head injury: A family matter* (pp. 121–150). Baltimore: Paul H. Brookes.

Kaye, E., & Herskowitz, J. (1986). Transient post traumatic cortical blindness: Brief versus prolonged syndromes in childhood. *Journal of Child Neurology, 1,* 206–210.

Kazdin, A. E. (1984). *Behavior modification in applied settings.* Homewood, IL: Dorsey.

Kirsch, N. L., Levine, S. P., Fallon-Krueger, M., & Jaros, L. A. (1987). The microcomputer as an "orthotic" device for patients with cognitive deficits. *Journal of Head Trauma Rehabilitation, 2,* 77–86.

Klauber, M. R., Barrett-Connor, E., Marshall, L. F., & Bowers, S. A. (1981). The epidemiology of head injury. *American Journal of Epidemiology, 113,* 500–509.

Klonoff, H., Low, M. D., & Clark, C. (1977). Head injuries in children: A prospective five year follow-up. *Journal of Neurology, Neurosurgery & Psychiatry, 40,* 1211–1219.

Knights, R. M., Ivan, L. P., Venturey, E. C. G., Bentivoglio, C., Stoddart, C., Winogron, H. W., & Bawden, H. N. (1991). The effects of head injury in children on neuropsychological and behavioral functioning. *Brain Injury, 5,* 339–351.

Kraus, J. F., Fife, D., Cox, P., Ramstein, K., & Conroy, C. (1986). Incidence, severity, and external causes of pediatric brain injury. *American Journal of Diseases of Children, 140,* 687–693.

Kraus, J. F., Rock, A., & Hemyari, P. (1990). Brain injuries among infants, children, adolescents, and young adults. *American Journal of Diseases of Children, 144,* 684–691.

Knutson, J. F. (1988). Physical and sexual abuse of children. In D. K. Routh (Ed.), *Handbook of pediatric psychology* (pp. 32–70). New York: Guilford Press.

Kreutzer, J. S., & Wehman, P. H. (1991). *Cognitive rehabilitation for persons with traumatic brain injury: A functional approach.* Baltimore: Paul H. Brookes.

Lachar, D. (1982). *Personality Inventory for Children (PIC): Revised format supplement.* Los Angeles: Western Psychological Services.

Lau, Y. L., & Kenna, A. P. (1986). Post traumatic meningitis in children. *Injury: The British Journal of Accident Surgery, 17,* 407–409.

Leckliter, I. N., Forster, A. A., Klonoff, H., & Knights, R. M. (1992). A review of reference group data from normal children for the Halstead-Reitan neuropsychological test battery for older children. *The Clinical Neuropsychologist, 6,* 201–229.

Lehr, E. (1990). *Psychological management of traumatic brain injuries in children and adolescents.* Rockville, MD: Aspen Publishers.

Levin, H. S. (1993). Head trauma. *Current Opinion in Neurology, 6,* 841–846.

Levin, H. S., Culhane, K. A., Fletcher, J. M., Mendelsohn, D. B., Lilly, M. A., Harward, H., Chapman, S. B., Bruce, D. A., Bertolino-Kusnerik, L., & Eisenberg, H. M. (1994). Dissociation between delayed attention and memory after pediatric head injury: Relationship to MRI findings. *Journal of Child Neurology, 9,* 81–89.

Levin, H. S., Eisenberg, H. M., Wigg, N. R., & Kobayashi, K. (1982). Memory and intellectual ability after head injury in children and adolescents. *Neurosurgery, 11,* 668–673.

Levin, H. S., Mendelsohn, D., Lilly, M. A., Fletcher, J. M., Culhane, K. A., Chapman, S. B., Harward, H., Kusnerik, L., Bruce, D., & Eisenberg, H. M. (1994, February). *Tower of London performance in relation to MRI in children following closed head injury.* Paper presented at the meeting of the International Neuropsychological Society, Cincinnati, OH.

Levy, M., Masri, L. S., Levy, K. M., Johnson, F. L., Martin-Thompson, E., Couldwell, W. T., McComb, J. G., Weiss, M. H., & Apuzzo, M. L. J. (1993). Penetrating craniocerebral injury resultant from gunshot wounds: Gang and related injury in children and adolescents. *Neurosurgery, 33,* 1018–1025.

Lewis, L. (1991). A framework for developing a psychotherapy treatment plan with brain-injured patients. *Journal of Head Trauma Rehabilitation, 6,* 22–29.

Light, R., Neumann, E., Lewis, R., Morecki-Oberg, C., Asarnow, R., & Satz, P. (1987). An evaluation of a neuropsychologically based reeducation project for the head-injured child. *Journal of Head Trauma Rehabilitation, 2,* 11–25.

Little, S. G. (1992). The WISC-III: Everything old is new again. *School Psychology Quarterly, 7,* 136–142.

Livingston, M. G. (1987). Head injury: The relative's response. *Brain Injury, 1,* 33–39.

Livingston, M. G., & Brooks, D. N. (1988). The burden on families of the brain injured: A review. *Journal of Head Trauma Rehabilitation, 4,* 6–15.

Luerssen, T. G. (1991). Head injuries in children. *Neurosurgery Clinics of North America, 2,* 399–410.

Luerssen, T. G., Klauber, M. R., & Marshall, L. F. (1988). Outcome from head injury related to patient's age. *Journal of Neurosurgery, 68,* 409–416.

Margolis, L. H., Wagenaar, A. C., & Liu, W. (1988). The effects of mandatory child restraint law on injuries requiring hospitalization. *American Journal of Diseases of Children, 142,* 1099–1103.

Mateer, C. A., & Ruff, R. M. (1990). Effectiveness of behavioral management procedures in the rehabilitation of head-injured patients. In R. L. Wood (Ed.), *Neurobehavioral sequelae of traumatic brain injury* (pp. 277–304). New York: Taylor & Francis.

Mateer, C. A., & Williams, D. (1991). Effects of frontal lobe injury in childhood. *Developmental Neuropsychology, 7,* 359–376.

Meichenbaum, D., & Genest, M. (1980). Cognitive behavior modification: An integration of cognitive and behavioral methods. In F. H. Kanfer & A. P. Goldstein (Eds.), *Helping people change* (pp. 390–422). New York: Pergamon Press.

Michaud, L. J., Duhaime, A. C., & Batshaw, M. L. (1993). Traumatic brain injury in children. *Pediatric Clinics of North America, 40,* 553–565.

Michaud, L. J., Rivara, F. P., Jaffe, K. M., Fay, G. F., & Dailey, J. L. (1993). Traumatic brain injury as a risk factor for behavioral disorders in children. *Archives of Physical Medicine and Rehabilitation, 74,* 368–375.

Michaud, L. J., Rivara, F. P., Grady, M. S., & Reay, D. T. (1992). Predictors of survival and severity of disability after severe brain injury in children. *Neurosurgery, 31,* 254–264.

Murch, R. L., & Cohen, L. H. (1989). Relationships among life stress, perceived family environment, and the psychological distress of spina bifida adolescents. *Journal of Pediatric Psychology, 14,* 193–214.

Naglieri, J. A. (1993). Pairwise and ipsative comparisons of WISC-III IQ and Index scores. *Psychological Assessment, 5,* 113–116.

National Pediatric Trauma Registry. (1994). *Pediatric Trauma Registry—Phase 2.* Washington, DC: National Institute on Disability and Rehabilitation Research.

Noah, Z. L., Hahn, Y. S., Rubenstein, J. S., & Aronyk, K. (1992). Management of the child with severe brain injury. *Critical Care Clinics, 8,* 59–77.

Novack, T. A., Bergquist, T. F., Bennett, G., & Gouvier, W. D. (1991). Primary caregiver distress following severe head injury. *Journal of Head Trauma Rehabilitation, 6,* 69–77.

Oddy, M. (1993). Head injury during childhood. *Neuropsychological Rehabilitation, 3,* 301–320.

Pang, D. (1985). Pathophysiologic correlates of neurobehavioral syndromes following closed head injury. In M. Ylvisaker (Ed.), *Head injury rehabilitation: Children and adolescents* (pp. 3–70). Austin, TX: PRO-ED.

Papero, P. H., Prigatano, G. P., Snyder, H. M., & Johnson, D. L. (1993). Children's adaptive behavioural competence after head injury. *Neuropsychological Rehabilitation, 3,* 321–340.

Parente, R., & Anderson-Parente, J. (1991). *Retraining memory: Techniques and applications.* Houston, TX: CSY Publishing.

Parker, R. S. (1994). Neurobehavioral outcome of children's mild traumatic brain injury. *Seminars in Neurology, 14,* 67–73.

Parmelee, D. X. (1989). Neuropsychiatric sequelae of traumatic brain injury in children and adolescents. *Psychiatric Medicine, 7,* 11–16.

Pelco, L., Sawyer, M., Duffield, G., Prior, M., & Kinsella, G. (1992). Premorbid emotional and behavioural adjustment in children with mild head injuries. *Brain Injury, 6,* 29–37.

Perrott, S. B., Taylor, H. G., & Montes, J. L. (1991). Neuropsychological sequelae, familial stress, and environmental adaptation following pediatric head injury. *Developmental Neuropsychology, 7,* 69–86.

Pettersen, L. (1991). Sensitivity to emotional cues and social behavior in children and adolescents after head injury. *Perceptual and Motor Skills, 73,* 1139–1150.

Puente, A. E. (1994). Billing recommendations and CPT codes for neuropsychological assessment. *Bulletin of the National Academy of Neuropsychology, 11,* 14–15.

Putnam, S. H., & Adams, K. M. (1992). Regression-based prediction of long-term outcome following multidisciplinary rehabilitation for traumatic brain injury. *The Clinical Neuropsychologist, 6,* 383–405.

Reitan, R. M., & Wolfson, D. (1992). *Neuropsychological evaluation of older children.* South Tucson, AZ: Neuropsychology Press.

Reitan, R. M., & Wolfson, D. (1994). *Neuropsychological evaluation of young children.* South Tucson, AZ: Neuropsychology Press.

Reynolds, C. R., & Bigler, E. D. (1994). *Test of Memory and Learning Examiner's Manual.* Austin, TX: PRO-ED.

Reynolds, C. R., & Kamphaus, R. W. (1992). *Behavior Assessment System for Children Manual.* Circle Pines, MN: American Guidance Service.

Rivara, F. P. (1990). Child pedestrian injuries in the United States: Current status of the problem, potential interventions, and future research needs. *American Journal of Diseases of Children, 144,* 692–696.

Rivara, F. P. (1994). Epidemiology and prevention of pediatric traumatic brain injury. *Pediatric Annals, 23,* 12–17.

Rivara, F. P., Bergman, A. B., LoGerfo, J. P., & Weiss, N. S. (1982). Epidemiology of childhood injuries, II: Sex differences in injury rates. *American Journal of Diseases of Children, 136,* 502–506.

Rivara, J. B., Jaffe, K. M., Fay, G. C., Polissar, N. L., Martin, K. M., Shurtleff, H. A., & Liao, S. (1993). Family functioning and injury severity as predictors of child functioning one year following traumatic brain injury. *Archives of Physical Medicine and Rehabilitation, 74,* 1047–1055.

Rivara, J. B., Jaffe, K. M., Polissar, N. L., Fay, G. C., Martin, K. M., Shurtleff, H. A., & Liao, S. (1994). Family functioning and children's academic performance and behavior problems in the year following traumatic brain injury. *Archives of Physical Medicine and Rehabilitation, 75,* 369–379.

Rivara, F. P., & Mueller, B. A. (1986). The epidemiology and prevention of pediatric head injury. *Journal of Head Trauma Rehabilitation, 1,* 7–15.

Rodriguez, J. G., & Brown, S. T. (1990). Childhood injuries in the United States. *American Journal of Diseases of Children, 144,* 627–646.

Roid, G. H., Prifitera, A., & Weiss, L. G. (1993). Replication of the WISC-III factor structure in an independent sample. In B. A. Bracken (Ed.), *Wechsler Intelligence Scale for Children: Third Edition* (pp. 6–21). Brandon, VT: Clinical Psychology Publishing Company.

Rosen, C. D., & Gerring, J. P. (1986). *Head trauma: Educational reintegration.* San Diego, CA: College Hill.

Rourke, B. P. (1988). The syndrome of nonverbal learning disabilities: Developmental manifestations in neurological disease, disorder, and dysfunction. *The Clinical Neuropsychologist, 2,* 293–330.

Rourke, B. P., Bakker, D. J., Fisk, J. L., & Strang, J. D. (1983). *Child neuropsychology: An introduction to theory, research, and clinical practice.* New York: Guilford Press.

Rourke, B. P., Fisk, J. L., & Strang, J. D. (1986). *Neuropsychological assessment of children: A treatment-oriented approach.* New York: Guilford Press.

Routh, D. K. (1987). Cognitive rehabilitation for children with head injury, learning disability, and mental retardation. *Cognitive Rehabilitation, 5,* 16–21.

Ruff, R. M., Niemann, H., Troster, A. I., & Mateer, C. (1990). Effectiveness of behavioral management in rehabilitation: Cognitive procedures. In R. L. Wood (Ed.), *Neurobehavioral sequelae of traumatic brain injury* (pp. 305–334). New York: Taylor & Francis.

Ruijs, M. B. M., Keyser, A., & Gabreels, F. J. M. (1992). Assessment of post-traumatic amnesia in young children. *Developmental Medicine and Child Neurology, 34,* 885–892.

Rutter, M., Chadwick, O., Shaffer, D., & Brown, G. (1980). A prospective study of children with head injuries: I. Design and methods. *Psychological Medicine, 10,* 633–645.

Sabates, N. R. Gonce, M. A., & Farris, B. K. (1991). Neuro-ophthalmological findings in closed head trauma. *Journal of Clinical Neuro-Ophthalmology, 11,* 273–277.

Sattler, J. M. (1992). *Assessment of children—Revised and updated* (3rd edition). San Diego, CA: Author.

Savage, R. C., & Wolcott, G. F. (1994). *Educational dimensions of acquired brain injury.* Austin, TX: PRO-ED.

Schacter, D. L., & Glisky, E. L. (1986). Memory remediation: Restoration, alleviation, and the acquisition of domain-specific knowledge. In B. P. Uzzell & Y. Gross (Eds.), *Clinical neuropsychology of intervention* (pp. 257–282). Boston: Martinus Nijhoff.

Sheslow, D., & Adams, W. (1990). *Wide Range Assessment of Memory and Learning Administration Manual.* Los Angeles: Western Psychological Services.

Silver, J. M., & Yudofsky, S. C. (1994). Psychopharmacological approaches to the patient with affective and psychotic features. *Journal of Head Trauma Rehabilitation, 9,* 61–77.

Sparrow, S. S., Balla, D. A., & Cicchetti, D. V. (1984). *Vineland Adaptive Behavior Scales.* Circle Pines, MN: American Guidance Service.

Spreen, O., & Strauss, E. (1991). *A compendium of neuropsychological tests: Administration, norms, and commentary.* New York: Oxford University Press.

Sternberg, R. J. (1993). Rocky's back again: A review of the WISC-III. In B. A. Bracken (Ed.), *Wechsler Intelligence Scale for Children: Third Edition* (pp. 161–164). Brandon, VT: Clinical Psychology Publishing Company.

Teasdale, G., & Jennett, B. (1974). Assessment of coma and impaired consciousness: A practical scale. *Lancet, 2,* 81–84.

Teeter, P. A. (1986). Standard neuropsychological batteries for children. In J. E. Obrzut & G. W. Hynd (Eds.), *Child neuropsychology: Volume 2, Clinical practice* (pp. 187–227). San Diego: Academic Press.

Telzrow, C. F. (1987). Management of academic and educational problems in head injury. *Journal of Learning Disabilities, 20,* 536–545.

Thompson, N. M., Francis, D. J., Stuebing, K. K., Fletcher, J. M., Ewing-Cobbs, L., Miner, M. E., Levin, H. S., & Eisenberg, H. M. (1994). Motor, visual-spatial, and somatosensory skills after closed head injury in children and adolescents: A study of change. *Neuropsychology, 8,* 333–342.

Thompson, R. S., Rivara, F. P., & Thompson, D. C. (1989). A case control study of the effectiveness of bicycle safety helmets. *New England Journal of Medicine, 320,* 1361–1367.

Tramontana, M. G., & Hooper, S. R. (1988). *Assessment issues in child neuropsychology.* New York: Plenum Press.

Van Eerdewegh, M. M., Clayton, P. J., & Van Eerdewegh, P. (1985). The bereaved child: Variables influencing early psychopathology. *British Journal of Psychiatry, 147,* 188–194.

Varni, J. W., Wilcox, K. T., & Hanson, V. (1988). Mediating effects of family social support on child psychological adjustment in juvenile rheumatoid arthritis. *Health Psychology, 7,* 421–431.

Waaland, P. K. (1990). Family response to childhood traumatic brain injury. In J. S. Kreutzer & P. Wehman (Eds.), *Community integration following traumatic brain injury* (pp. 225–247). Baltimore: Paul H. Brookes.

Wallander, J. L., & Varni, J. W. (1989). Social support and adjustment in chronically handicapped and ill children. *American Journal of Community Psychology, 17,* 185–201.

Webb, N. B. (1991). *Play therapy with children in crisis.* New York: Guilford Press.

Wechsler, D. (1974). *Wechsler Intelligence Scale for Children–Revised Manual.* San Antonio, TX: Psychological Corporation.

Wechsler, D. (1991). *Wechsler Intelligence Scale for Children–Third Edition Manual.* San Antonio, TX: Psychological Corporation.

Wechsler, D. (1992). *Wechsler Individual Achievement Test Manual.* San Antonio, TX: Psychological Corporation.

Welsh, M. C., & Pennington, B. F. (1988). Assessing frontal lobe functioning in children: Views from developmental psychology. *Developmental Neuropsychology, 4,* 199–230.

Whyte, J. (1994). Toward rational psychopharmacological treatment: Integrating research and clinical practice. *Journal of Head Trauma Rehabilitation, 9,* 91–103.

Williams, J. M., & Savage, R. C. (1991). Family, culture, and child development. In J. M. Williams & T. Kay (Eds.), *Head injury: A family matter* (pp. 219–238). Baltimore: Paul H. Brookes.

Winogron, H. W., Knights, R. M., & Bawden, H. N. (1984). Neuropsychological deficits following head injury in children. *Journal of Clinical Neuropsychology, 6,* 269–286.

Wirt, R. D., Lachar, D., Klinedinst, J. K., & Seat, P. D. (1984). *Multidimensional description of child personality: A manual for the Personality Inventory for Children–Revised.* Los Angeles: Western Psychological Services.

Wood, R. L. (1990). Conditioning procedures in brain injury rehabilitation. In R. L. Wood (Ed.), *Neurobehavioral sequelae of traumatic brain injury* (pp. 153–193). New York: Taylor & Francis.

Wrobleski, B. A., & Glenn, M. B. (1994). Pharmacological treatment of arousal and cognitive deficits. *Journal of Head Trauma Rehabilitation, 9,* 19–42.

Ylvisaker, M., Hartwick, P., Ross, B., & Nussbaum, N. (1994). Cognitive assessment. In R. C. Savage & G. F. Wolcott (Eds.), *Educational dimensions of acquired brain injury* (pp. 69–119). Austin, TX: PRO-ED.

Ylvisaker, M., Hartwick, P., & Stevens, M. (1991). School re-entry following head injury: Managing the transition from hospital to school. *Journal of Head Trauma Rehabilitation, 6,* 10–22.

Ylvisaker, M., Szerkes, S., Hartwick, P., & Tworek, T. (1992). Cognitive intervention. In R. C. Savage & G. F. Wolcott (Eds.), *Educational dimensions of acquired brain injury* (pp. 121–184). Austin, TX: PRO-ED.

CHAPTER 8

BURNS

David S. Chedekel
Lisa P. Rizzone
Alia Y. Antoon

DESCRIPTION OF DISORDERS

Burn trauma is a multisystemic condition requiring intense physical care, rigorous rehabilitation, and psychological adaptation to immediate and long-term life changes. Most often, treatment does not end after the initial hospitalization. Instead, as the child matures, repeated admissions for reconstructive surgery and clinic visits are required for proper healing and physical management. Psychologically, stress from the initial burn injury and subsequent frequent hospital visits may contribute to the development of emotional disorders (Kravitz et al., 1993; Stoddard, Norman, & Murphy, 1989; Stoddard, Stroud, & Murphy, 1992).

The care of a child who has been burned has become more advanced, resulting in decreased mortality. Physiologically, aggressive treatment of burns minimizes subsequent localized and systemic infections. Early excision of devitalized tissue is performed during the first three to five days of hospitalization. Advantages to this method are increased survival rate for burns greater than 40–60 percent total body surface area (TBSA), shorter hospital visits, and less pain during dressing changes.

Eschar excision with prompt wound closure is an effective method in reducing mortality in major burns (Sheridan, Tompkins, & Burke, 1994; Tompkins et al., 1988). The number of excisions necessary and type of wound closure used depends upon the size of the burn injury (see Table 8.1). Small burns require only one stage of excision with autographs as the method of closure, while larger burns involve multiple excisions and grafting depending upon severity.

There are four stages of burn treatment relating to medical management: prophlaxis, acute care and resuscitation, reconstruction and rehabilitation, and pain relief and psychosocial adjustment (Herrin & Antoon, 1996). Prevention of burn injuries through education as well as the knowledge of limiting the extent of trauma through methods of extinction are essential.

During the initial acute phase, resuscitation is important for preventing burn shock (Antoon, 1996; Herrin & Antoon, 1996). Interstitial edema may develop, with children gaining up to 20 percent above their pre-burn weight. At Shriners Burns Institute, Boston, Parkland Formula infused with 4 cc's Ringer's Lactate per kilogram body weight per percent surface area burned has been found to be an effective method of initiating resuscitation for the first 24 hours. Half of this is given in the first 8 hours from the time of the burn. Continuous reassessment of resuscitation is done through measurement of urine output, hematocrit and protein levels, blood gases, and vital signs. Stabilization of acid-base balances, vital signs, and mental status indicates an adequate amount of fluid resuscitation.

Reconstructive surgery provides not only wound closure to prevent bacterial infection but also enhances

Table 8.1. Severity of Burn with Required Excision and Grafting for Wound Closure

	EXTENT OF INJURY	PROCEDURES REQUIRED FOR EXCISION	METHOD OF CLOSURE	AVAILABILITY OF DONOR SITES	USE OF ALLOGRAFT FOR PROMPT PHYSIOLOGICAL WOUND CLOSURE AND DELAYED AUTOGRAFT CLOSURE
Small burns	0–19% BSA	One stage	Autograft, sheet or mesh	Adequate	None
Moderate burns	20–49% BSA	Multiple stages; usually every other day	Autograft sheet or mesh for special areas	Adequate	None
Severe burns	50–79% BSA	Multiple stages; usually every other day	Autograft mesh supplemented with temporary allograft (sheet); replaced with autograft (mesh)	Special sites needed; usually scalp and feet.	Allograft removed 2–3 days before rejection. Replace with autograft from reharvested donor site
Massive burns	80–95% BSA	Multiple stages; usually every other day	Autograft mesh supplemented with temporary allograft (sheet); replaced with autograft (mesh)	Special sites needed; usually scalp and feet	Allograft removed 2–3 days before rejection. Replace with autograft from reharvested donor site— cultured cells used when available

functional and cosmetic results. Occupational and physical therapy begins upon admission, continuing throughout hospitalization to maintain muscle tone and flexibility. Positioning and splinting are essential methods of treatment in acute burns for limiting the extent of contraction with exercises to increase range of motion (Flynn & Gunter, 1990).

Pain is experienced both physically and emotionally. Physically, pain is present throughout hospitalization but is more intense during the acute period. Factors relating to pain levels are depth of burn, age, phase of healing, level of emotional and cognitive development, pain threshold, analgesia, culture, and efficiency of the burn team (Herrin & Antoon, 1996). For most burn victims, dressing changes are extremely painful and require some form of pain control, either drug treatment, relaxation techniques, or hypnosis. In many instances a combination of techniques can be utilized for effective results. The use of patient controlled analgesic (PCA) can be very effective because it helps children psychologically by giving them a sense of control.

Emotionally, fear and anxiety may be exhibited in combination with physical pain. Issues of survival, recovery, ability to regain some level of pre-burn functioning, and acceptance of oneself challenge psychological resources. Indirectly, parents suffer emotionally along with their child through feelings of guilt and helplessness. Support for the entire family is essential to enhance better understanding of physical and psychological adaptation to burn trauma.

Types of burn traumas are scalds, contact, flame, chemical, electrical, inhalation injury, and abuse. Within the category of scald burns, there are two types: spill and immersion. Spill scalds usually occur when hot liquid splashes onto the child from a high place (e.g., stove or counter). Burns from immersions tend to be deeper due to a longer duration of time in hot liquid. The victim's inability to escape the burning agent, whether from panic or abuse, usually makes it possible for these burns to occur.

Electrical burns are also of two categories. Minor burns usually occur when a child bites on an electrical cord, resulting in localized burn trauma to the mouth. Major electrical burns are more serious due to deep muscle involvement, a mortality rate of 3–15 percent, and a high morbidity rate involving possible limb amputations. High-tension wires containing more than 1000 volts and other high-voltage equipment such as railroads and power stations are the usual electrical agent for these burns.

Another form of injury is self-inflicted burns that are meant to result in death. Though this method of suicide is uncommon in this country, self-immolation does occur in both pediatric and adult populations. For example, Hammond, Ward, and Pereira (1988) indicated that health issues were the predominant motivator for self-harm through burning in Latin women, more than any other life stressors. The authors also report other studies indicating a pre-existing emotional disturbance that contributed to suicide attempts through self-immolation.

In pediatrics, self-immolation is present more often in adolescents than in young children (Stoddard, 1993). Emotional disturbances may go unnoticed until some attention is given after the burn injury. Suicide attempts through burning suggests a high risk for psychological problems post-burn in comparison to children and adolescents burned by other methods. Unsuccessful suicide attempts leave the adolescent not only with the initial stressors, but also with additional issues of guilt, scarring, and adaptation to an altered life style

Other disorders that can result in burn trauma but do not originate from intentional self-harm are careless, risk-taking behavior. Child psychosis, hyperactivity, conduct disorder, and attention deficit/hyperactivity disorder may contribute to physical trauma due to the child's limited self-control and insight into potentially dangerous acts (Herman, 1991). Family discord along with absent parents can be factors relating to the child's performing potentially dangerous behaviors. Even though burns acquired secondary to pre-morbid dysfunctional behavior do not constitute the majority of burn cases, coping with hospitalization, treatment, and aftercare are affected by the presence of psychiatric disorders, requiring attention to treatment plans and education for both child and staff.

Physical recovery from a burn injury is a slow process, with the child usually having more than one operation and enduring painful treatment procedures. Simultaneous to this, the child is attempting to cope with not only the traumatic event but also subsequent hospitalizations. Three phases of adaptation have been identified in regard to psychological adjustment during

initial admission. These are the acute, intermediate, and rehabilitative phases (Stoddard, Chedekel, & Cahners, 1990).

Medical and operative procedures are the predominant factors in stabilization during the acute phase. Monitors, IV tubes, intubation and respiration equipment, and surgical procedures are the focus during initial recovery. Isolation in a bacteria-controlled nursing unit (BCNU) or side-room contribute to feelings of loneliness and separation from family. Frequently, sleep disturbances, feelings of helplessness, fear of the unexpected, and anxiety are experienced along with confusion and disorientation. Delirium may sometimes occur with severe burns. Physically surviving the burn trauma is the most important aspect at this phase. However, emotional flooding of unfamiliar sights, sounds, and experiences are usually overwhelming during this initial adjustment period.

The intermediate phase is identified by stabilization of medical status with an increase in environmental awareness. Rehabilitative procedures predominate over grafting as a means to strengthen muscles and increase mobility while healing. Exercises performed in physical and occupational therapy can be painful, resulting in resistance by the child to therapy. Baths and dressing changes can be traumatizing for children who must view the extent of their burns and endure considerable physical pain (Ravenscroft, 1982).

Perceptions of punishment related to the burn injury and subsequent medical treatment are often expressed as anger toward the staff or family (Cooper & Thomas, 1988). Feelings of abandonment are usually the underlying issues, with the child perceiving his/her parents as not being in control and unable to give protection. In an attempt to regain control, behavior problems such as eating disturbances are frequently observed. Allowing the child to make choices is important for reinstating a sense of mastery and independence.

The third phase of hospitalization is rehabilitation, during which total wound healing, improved physical strength and flexibility, greater involvement in physical therapy and dressing changes by both child and parent, and preparation for discharge are observed. Issues of acceptance by peers and society create anxiety related to rejection or isolation from other people. In addition to discussing fears and coping methods, a social worker or hospital teacher will go to the child's school to explain facts about burns and required dressing garments that are worn. This helps make the transition back into school easier for both the child and classmates.

Each of these three phases do not occur in a separate, time-limited formation. Rather, overlap is evident, with every child experiencing each phase at various rates according to percent burn, age, cognitive level, and adaptation styles. Another factor that affects the process of phase adjustment is length of hospitalization. Small burns need only brief stays of possibly three to seven days, if no complications develop. Thus, all three phases may not be experienced as they would if hospitalization were longer in duration.

Sudden changes in lifestyle are forced upon a child and the family as a result of the burn injury. Adaptation to a frightening hospital environment, separation from home, possible loss of possessions or family members through death, and adjustment to an altered body image are immediate issues that are faced early in treatment. All of these issues create anxiety not only for the child but also for the entire family. Providing support and education for the family regarding their own reactions toward physical trauma is necessary to enable parents to feel less helpless. In turn, the child also receives the continued support needed from his/her parents.

EPIDEMIOLOGY

Burn injuries are a major factor in pediatric hospitalization and are the second leading cause of accidental death (Herrin & Antoon, 1996; Snyder & Saieh, 1987). Legislation has reduced temperature in hot water heaters to 120 degrees Fahrenheit, produced flame retardant childrens' sleepwear, and installed smoke detectors in homes and buildings. However, 2 million people receive medical attention yearly for burns with 100,000 being hospitalized (Antoon, 1996). Thirty to forty percent of those admitted are under age 15, with a mean age of 32 months.

Scald burns are the most commonly reported burn injury and account for 85 percent of pediatric admissions. Most children who receive scald burns tend to be younger than 4 years (Feldman, Schaller, Feldman, & McMillon, 1978; Jay, Bartlett, Danet, & Allyn, 1977). Simon and Baron (1994) reported various types of burns in children younger than 5 years, with 64 percent being scalds, 20 percent contact, and 16 percent flame, chemical, electrical, or flash injuries. Scalds and contact injuries are identified as the major cause of burn trauma during ages 6 months to 2 years.

Thirteen percent of burn injuries are caused by flame accidents (Antoon, 1996). These burns tend to occur in preschool and older children whose interest in the surroundings precedes caution (e.g., match play). Electrical and chemical burns are not as commonly seen but do make up a small percentage of in-patient admissions.

Another type of injury that is frequently seen yearly is that sustained from fireworks. McCauley and colleagues (1991) reported that the Consumer Product and Safety Commission identified 11,400 firework injuries requiring treatment in 1981. Forty-five percent of those burns were experienced by children 14 years and younger, with only 8.8 percent requiring hospitalization. Episodes where firecrackers explode in close proximity to the child tend to occur when there is no initial blast and the child picks up the firework to investigate it.

Burn injuries resulting from child abuse account for 15 percent of pediatric burn admissions (Bernstein, 1990). Mortality rates for abused children are approximately 30 percent as compared to a 2 percent death rate in nonabused children (Purdue, Hunt, & Prescott, 1988). Scalding from immersion in hot water, contact injuries from pressing against flat heated surfaces or cigarettes, and deliberate ignition of clothing are frequent methods of abuse. Disrupted family units, high stress, and pre-existing emotional disorders are major contributors in abuse cases.

Inability to cope with childrens' behavioral problems and constant demands of developmental needs puts the child at risk when family stability is lacking. Ages 13–24 months tend to be the most susceptible period for child abuse to occur (Hight, Bakalar, & Lloyd, 1979). Examination of abuse in a burned child is important in distinguishing accidental from deliberate injury, thus allowing for proper treatment.

ASSESSMENT APPROACHES

Medical Issues

Initial physical examination assesses burn severity to determine whether hospitalization is required. Burns of first and second degree that are under 10 percent TBSA are treated on an out-patient basis unless there is suspicion of child abuse. Criteria for pediatric hospitalization are burns greater than 15 percent TBSA, all inhalation injuries, high-tension electrical burns, suspicion of neglect or abuse, and inadequate home environment.

A burned child during evaluation should be approached as a multiple trauma victim due to possible additional injuries. Evaluation and securing of the airway should be performed prior to assessment of breathing, presence of hypovolemia, and level of consciousness. The child is completely undressed for adequate evaluation of extent of injury. Complete medical history, vital signs, physical examination with laboratory and radiographic tests, if required, are obtained.

Details of the burn incident, burn agent (e.g., liquid, chemical, flame), and whether the accident occurred in an enclosed area, if smoke inhalation trauma is present, are recorded from family members or emergency technicians. Past surgical procedures, present use of medications and allergies, last tetanus injection, and what time the child ate last are additional important factors for complete assessment.

Estimation of percent and depth of burn provides information not only about extent of injury but also the amount of fluid required for resuscitation. A body surface area chart is necessary in determining the percent of burn according to the child's age and body proportions. The chart used at our institution (Shriners Burns, Boston) displays percentages for calculation depending upon age, with corresponding pattern-coded percent of burn degree (see Figure 8.1). Method of calculation by the rule of nines may be used with children over age 14 or as an estimate before arrival at a burn center.

The depth of a burn is described as either first, second, or third degree. Table 8.2 outlines cause, depth, appearance, and level of pain for each degree. Length of

Table 8.2. Characteristics of Burn Depth

FIRST DEGREE	
CAUSE:	Flash, flame, ultraviolet (sunlight).
SURFACE APPEARANCE:	Dry, no blisters. No or minimal edema.
COLOR:	Eythematous.
PAIN LEVEL:	Painful.
HISTOLOGIC DEPTH:	Epidermal layers only.
HEALING TIME:	Two to five days with peeling, no scarring.
	May have discoloration.
SECOND DEGREE—PARTIAL THICKNESS	
CAUSE:	Contact with hot liquids or solids.
	Flame to clothing.
	Direct flame chemical.
SURFACE APPEARANCE:	Moist blebs, blisters.
COLOR:	Mottled white to pink to cherry red.
PAIN LEVEL:	Very painful.
HISTOLOGIC DEPTH:	Epidermis, papillary and reticular layers of dermis.
	May include fat domes of subcutaneous layer.
HEALING TIME:	Superficial: Five to twenty-one days with no grafting.
	Deep partial: With no infection, twenty-one to thirty-five days. If infected, converts to full thickness.
THIRD DEGREE—FULL THICKNESS	
CAUSE:	Contact with hot liquids or solids. Flame, chemical, electrical.
SURFACE APPEARANCE:	Dry with leathery eschar until debridement.
	Charred blood vessels visible under eschar.
COLOR:	Mixed white, waxy pearly. Dark khaki, mahogany.
	Charred.
PAIN LEVEL:	Little or no pain. Hair pulls out easily.
HISTOLOGIC DEPTH:	Epidermal and dermal layers.
HEALING TIME:	Heal after full grafting.

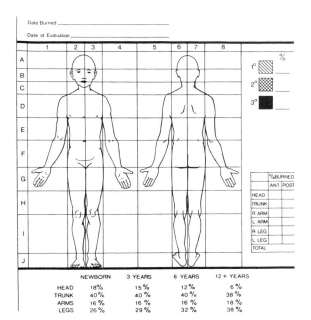

Figure 8.1. Sample burn chart used to indicate percent and degree of burn according to age

hospitalization depends upon burn depth, as well as absence of infection. Fourth-degree burns may exist in severely burned children, resulting in destruction of skin, subcutaneous tissue, and bone with an appearance resembling that of a third-degree burn.

Psychological and Psychiatric Issues

Physical pain is the most constant symptom all burned children experience. During the healing process of an acute burn, medical treatment such as dressing changes or physical therapy produce extreme pain as limbs are mobilized. Pain has been identified as the primary reason for consultation in burn patients of various ages (Bastani, Baskin, & Wiebelhaus, 1992). Not only has physical pain been associated with recovery, but pain also acts as a barrier to human contact. Infants and young children who are reassured when held must be handled with special care due to the production of pain upon touch. This, in turn, results in emotional distress through the sense of hurt, rejection, and aloneness if physical handling is impossible.

Coping with pain is exhibited according to the child's developmental stage. An infant reacts to pain by withdrawing, being irritable, and having disturbances in appetite and sleep. Preschool-age children regress, become increasingly needy, have nightmares, and are highly anxious (Stoddard, 1982). Latency-age children may exhibit hyperactivity, nightmares, and regression, as well as demandingness, depression, or anxiety. Symptoms of depression and anxiety may also be displayed during adolescence, in addition to either verbal or physical aggression.

Anticipation and occurrence of pain can result in anxiety that in turn affects the amount of physical discomfort. Children often become panicky prior to procedures when anticipatory anxiety is at its highest. Fear of dismemberment, bleeding, the amount of expected pain, and viewing the extent of one's burn contributes to overwhelming anxiety. There are times when anxiety is more intense than the actual pain level. The combination of fear with expectation of discomfort can intensify anxiety beyond the point of tolerance.

Anxiety and pain levels can be assessed through subjective scales ranging from 0 to 10: 0 being absence of pain/anxiety and 10 being the maximum amount of pain/anxiety. These scales help identify the intensity of pain/anxiety during specific procedures or at rest. Comparison of decreased levels of anxiety and pain can be monitored efficiently throughout the child's hospital stay by obtaining scores periodically.

Mental status assessment of an acutely burned child is generally not done in the emergency room or upon admission. Evaluation occurs once the child is physically stable and able to interact with the environment. There are exceptions in which psychiatric consultation is re-quired during the acute burn phase, such as when the child is agitated and hallucinating due to delirium. Mental status examination is required to determine degree of disorientation, type of hallucination, presence of sleep disturbance, and reassurance of safety for the child as well as for staff. Common symptoms of delirium are visual hallucinations, anxiety, confusion, insomnia, and agitation (Stoddard & Wilens, 1990).

Early intervention is also needed if the child is in a bacteria-controlled nursing unit (BCNU). This is a specialized unit used for burns over 30 percent TBSA that regulates air temperature and humidity and protects against cross-contamination of bacterial agents. All senses are dulled by the thick plastic enclosure that surrounds the bed completely. Vision is slightly distorted, with auditory stimulation diminished, resulting in staff needing to speak louder in order to communicate. The sense of touch is virtually absent due to the need to use long, plastic, sterile gloves, which prevent any contact with skin.

Regarding a child who is alert in the BCNU, orientation to time, person, and place, sleep disturbance, and level of anxiety are important factors to assess. Typically, it is difficult to differentiate night and day due to the absence of windows on the acute ward, so informing a child who is disoriented to time and day is important. Amount of eye contact made by the child is an indicator of interpersonal withdrawal. An increased awareness of the environment (i.e., hypervigilance), with the child observing any movement, may indicate intense anxiety or fear of the unknown. Often a sense of isolation and separation occurs, with children feeling as if they are in another world far from others.

Assessment of a child in the BCNU who is alert but unable to speak due to intubation or other medical reasons requires simple, concrete, yes/no questions that can be answered by nodding the head. For example, questions like "Do you know where you are?"; "Are you in pain?"; "Are you scared?"; "Are you having nightmares?" can provide information regarding the child's status in addition to initiating communication. Maintaining verbal contact and providing support helps lessen feelings of isolation while reassuring the child that he/she is cared for.

The acute phase of hospitalization is the most intense period of adjustment due to unfamiliar sights and sounds, possible containment in the BCNU, and aggressive medical treatment. Multiple surgical procedures create intense anxiety about dying and survival. Fear of abandonment related to separation from family and fear of being subjected to invasive medical techniques are expressed through panic, nightmares, and depressive symptoms. An initial psychological assessment during the acute phase can provide a baseline from which to compare progress.

Increased involvement in psychotherapy, with less surgical procedures required, occurs during the intermediate phase. Expression of anger and loss of control are predominant issues. Depending upon the event of limb or digit loss, relearning basic activities (e.g., grasping, tying shoe laces, and holding utensils) can be frustrating, often with the child feeling like a failure. Regression in behavioral or verbal skills reflects a sense of helplessness secondary to loss of independence. It is critical for family members to communicate acceptance of the child and to encourage effective coping. Early involvement of parents in the care of their child re-establishes the parent as an active rather than a passive participant.

Total concentration on strengthening muscles and increasing self-care is obtained during the rehabilitative phase. Surgical procedures are complete with treatment focusing on physical and occupational therapy. Anxiety tends to be related to impending discharge rather than to surgical operations and dressing changes. Symptoms of panic, insomnia, or depression may occur. Referral for out-patient treatment either on clinic visits or to a private clinician should be considered if psychiatric symptoms continue to interfere with overall adaptation.

Coping with burn injuries depends on personality style, skill level, and developmental level. For each period of maturation, certain developmental issues predominate and become the focal point of stress during hospitalization. Evaluation should note the particular developmental need in relation to any presenting symptoms or disorder that may be evident. Initial evaluation is important to obtain a baseline with which to compare future observations. Children should be followed throughout their admission due to the continuous adjustment issues that occur at each stage of hospitalization.

For an infant, interaction with other people and environmental stimulation promote healthy development. The sense of being loved and comforted is most often derived through being held or rocked, both of which are soothing experiences for the baby. A burn injury disrupts this developmental pattern primarily because pain now occurs where once physical contact provided security. This produces a sense of loss, for both the infant and primary caretaker, with new techniques of being held needing to be learned to promote the sense of security while minimizing discomfort.

Important indicators of adaptation during this age are level of environmental awareness, eye contact, facial ex-

pressions, and cooing. Interest in the surrounding environment pertains to the infant reaching for objects, tracking objects, observing staff approaching the crib, and crawling. Reaching and crawling are limited by the area of burn plus the amount of bandages. Direct eye contact with some interest in objects through tracking can be seen, and verbal sounds and cooing can be detected. Once the child is familiar with the staff, smiles and signs of recognition can evolve as security increases.

Withdrawal, apathy, avoidance of eye contact, and inability to be comforted can be responses to pain as well as emotional distress. Depressed infants appear weak, with blank facial expressions, and are unresponsive to any interaction. Regression may be exemplified in the behavior of an infant who was crawling prior to the injury but who remains inactive after receiving a scald burn to the chest and shoulder area. Infants who present with consistent depressive symptoms throughout admission and who remain quiet or passive during painful procedures should be re-assessed for abuse. Typically, crying from absolute fright is observed, with some pulling away to protect themselves. Absence of responsiveness and the pattern of burn trauma should be two key indicators when suspecting abuse.

During the toddler and early childhood stages, separation and stranger anxiety are the predominant issue. At this time, being apart from the security of home creates a sense of abandonment for the child left behind in the care of strangers. Some children at this age perceive hospitalization as a form of punishment for previous wrongdoings. Lack of parental presence, coupled with feelings of abandonment, create tremendous anxiety and emotional distress.

Excessive clinging to staff occurs as a means of regaining security. Regression is very common; for example, a four-year-old might lose sphincter control, resulting in the need for diapers. Sleep disturbances occur with nightmares and frightening memories of the burn trauma interrupting the sleep cycle. Irritability and moodiness emerge from a sense of insecurity as the child attempts to deal with pain, anger, and anxiety. These symptoms are normal for a burned child to exhibit, but the frequency at which these behaviors occur typically diminishes as discharge approaches.

Acting out in an attempt to gain control is mostly observed in school-age children. A common issue for which consultation is required occurs with eating disturbances in which the child eats minimally or nothing at all. Given that there are very few situations that provide the child with an opportunity to make a decision, eating is one of the few activities that are within the child's power to accept or decline. This, however, can be a serious matter and should be addressed quickly due to the importance of nutrition for the proper healing of wounds.

Among this age group, body image is usually developed, with the concept of self being clearly formulated (Stoddard, 1982). Alteration in self-image through deep scarring or loss of digit or limb creates intense emotional stress that can be experienced through depression, anger, or acting out behaviors. Grieving the loss of self-identity is a necessary process prior to accepting a new body image.

Regression is also common for children in this age range. Two types of regression are verbal and behavioral. Verbal regression is often observed when "baby-talk" is produced by a child who is capable of communicating effectively for his or her age. Bilingual children will converse in the language spoken at home even though English may be known. Both types of regression can provide safety for the child faced with a frightening, uncontrollable situation. As hospitalization progresses and wounds begin healing, regression typically decreases with the return of age-appropriate language.

Behaviorally, children regress by becoming overly dependent, irritable, or having temper tantrums. This may originate from feelings of helplessness regarding loss of previous independence and lack of security. For young children who are toilet trained, need to use diapers is a common occurrence when regression is experienced. Generally, loss of control often results in the child releasing anger behaviorally while attempting to master overwhelming, painful situations.

Adolescence is a difficult period of growth for many teen-agers generally. Independence, peer acceptance, decisions about future goals, and acceptance of oneself are the primary issues faced by adolescents. When assessing either acute or reconstructive burned teenagers, withdrawal, lack of interest, and other signs of depression should be assessed. Interruption of lifestyle due to a major burn trauma severely alters future prospects, with much encouragement and determination needed to regain hope. Lack of motivation and hopelessness may lead to suicidal ideation. Absence of a supportive family or friends deepens issues of rejection resulting either from pre-burn stressors or from the burn injury itself.

Normally, teenagers are concerned with physical appearance and acceptance by peers. Fear of rejection is a major factor related to isolation, withdrawal, and poor self-image problems. Cahners (1992) notes that women (ages 16 to 30) experiencing burns in the breast area

struggle with issues of acceptance, trust, and self-identity. Depression over scar tissue and anxiety about dating men were important concerns mostly for the teenage participants compared with the older women who had developed a positive attitude toward themselves and their interaction with others. Even when they were burned as a young child, the curiosity of peers about the reason for scarring can be particularly difficult for adolescents who strive to affiliate with others (Willis-Helmich, 1992).

Even though age-specific issues occur at various developmental stages, common psychiatric problems that can occur at any age are depression, regression, anxiety, aggression, and body-image disorders (Long & Cope, 1961; Stoddard, 1982). Post-traumatic stress disorder (PTSD) has been identified as most prevalent soon after the burn trauma as well as years afterwards (Stoddard, Norman, & Murphy, 1989). Symptoms include irritability, nightmares, flashbacks, avoidance of objects triggering the burn event, and extreme anxiety. Although most burned children exhibit these problems, the combination and duration of symptoms are important indicators of the disorder.

When a child is exhibiting consistent behavior problems and there is possibly a pre-existing psychiatric disorder prior to the burn trauma, psychological testing is helpful to obtain a more complete assessment. With regards to co-morbidity, children with premorbid phobias, childhood asthma, panic attacks, and generalized anxiety disorders tend to be pre-conditioned to experience heightened symptoms of anxiety or stress. When symptoms become so severe that the child is completely distressed, evaluation for medication is required to provide relief and reduce tension.

Other pre-burn disorders, such as conduct disorder or substance abuse, need attention because possible family dysfunction or depression places the child at greater risk for continued psychiatric disturbance and a more difficult adjustment period. Awareness of pre-burn activities, hobbies, and interpersonal relationships is important to develop a complete characterological report with which to plan effective interventions.

Consultation with other health care professionals such as ophthalmologists or speech/language specialists is useful when a deficit in these areas is in question. The possibility of developmental delay or physiological problems is important to identify in order to assess the level of functioning and any additional intervention needed. It is critical that the staff work as a cohesive multidisciplinary team in which all aspects of child care can be addressed, with interventions implemented accordingly.

TREATMENT STRATEGIES

Overview of Medical Management

Medical treatment of burns requires a multidisciplinary approach involving surgeons, pediatricians, pediatric anesthesiologists, physical and occupational therapists, and nutritionists. As discussed earlier, fluid resuscitation begins within the first 24 hours post-burn in order to re-establish metabolic homeostasis. Also, during the first 2 or 3 days, actual depth of burn is declared, allowing for either method of topical antimicrobial treatment or grafting for wound closure. In our practice, all acutely burned children receive during the first 5 days prophylactic penicillin treatment to prevent betahemolytic streptococcal infection. In cases where the child is allergic to penicillin, erythromycin is used as a substitute.

The use of topical antimicrobial agents provides a delay in wound infection. There are four types most often used: silver sulfadiazine, mafenide acetate, 0.5% silver nitrate, and providone solution. Table 8.3 explains the advantages and disadvantages of these topical antibacterial agents. Each have their own specific qualities in relation to presence of pain and absorption/penetration rate.

Wound closure not only promotes healing but also reduces wound infection, and decreases loss of electrolytes, proteins, and fluids. Reduction in pain is achieved with closure by limiting the exposure of open wound to air currents. Grafting occurs in temporary and final phases. Human allografts provide temporary coverage and reduces bacterial growth until replaced with autografts. The ability of human allografts to vascularize is an important feature in favor of their use. Two other temporary bacterial wound coverings are porcine xenograft and synthetic bilaminade biobrane. For final closure, reharvested autografts are needed for permanent closure.

Biological dressings used in wound closure serve two very important functions. First, preventing bacteria from entering lessens chances of infection. Second, while acting as a physiological barrier, epithelialization will occur, resulting in the wound remaining clean with minimal amounts of pain.

Recovering from a burn involves a great amount of energy, which often creates physiological stress. High energy expenditure requires various techniques of stress reduction, such as sufficient covering of the child during transport, controlling room temperature around 28–33 degrees centigrade, and adequate use of analgesics. Caloric intake is essential in replacing nutritional demands required for regaining homeostasis and proper wound healing. The main objective in providing calories is to lower metabolic stress in order to maintain an acceptable body weight. Proper growth in children is essential, with multivitamins provided to ensure nutritional balance.

In addition to surgery, grafting, and daily dressing changes, physical therapy is an essential aspect of medical management. Exercises performed according to the physical ability of the child are required for range of motion, maintaining muscle tone, and minimizing the occurrence of joint contractures. Splints are fitted early in treatment to prevent shortening of muscles, resulting in possible deformity.

The completion of wound coverage depends upon the severity of the burn as well as the acceptance of the

Table 8.3. Features of Topical Antibacterial Agents

	ADVANTAGE	DISADVANTAGE
Silver Nitrate	Painless Wide spectrum No resistant strains No sensitivity	Poor penetration Electrolyte changes Potentially messy Immobility from dressings
Mafenide	Active penetration Easy to use Allows mobilization	Systemic effects Pain Some sensitivity
Silver sulfadiazine	Painless Sensitivity infrequent Wide spectrum Minimal inactivation	Intermediate penetration Supplemental Rx required
Providone	Minimal pain Allows mobilization Wide spectrum	Possible inactivation by wound exudate

graft by the wound site. Medical intervention begins as early as possible in order to promote a healthy outcome with minimal chances of infection. Careful excision of any eschar formation is essential in maintaining clean burn wounds.

Psychological and Behavioral Treatments

There are clear variations in treatment and management of children's emotional well-being as they go from acute to intermediate and then to reconstructive or rehabilitative phases of hospitalization. The psychological issues that confront the child and family during each phase vary, thus requiring flexibility in the type of intervention used.

The acute burn victim is faced with the greatest challenge of all: surviving the burn injury. Many fears related to pain, death, and dismemberment are verbalized, with the child needing constant explanation of procedures and reassurance that whatever emotions they feel are normal. Because most acutely burned children are bed-ridden during the acute phase, therapy is provided individually at bedside. The length of therapy depends upon the child's tolerance level, with some being capable of talking for only ten minutes due to pain, sleepiness, or inability to address pertinent issues when feeling weak or depressed.

Pain control is a major factor that has a direct influence on the child's temperament and behavior. In addition to psychopharmacological interventions, being read a story, listening to the radio, or watching a television program can be relaxing methods to decrease stress (Stoddard, 1990). Another form of relaxation that is used at our institution is mental imagery, through which the child imagines a pleasant environment, resulting in a relaxed state. This method also gives the child a form of control over both pain and anxiety associated with painful medical procedures.

Hypnosis can also be effective in managing intense fears as well as relieving pain associated with medical procedures and recovery. Zeltzer, Jay, and Fisher (1989) reported studies identifying hypnosis as a beneficial technique in reducing anxiety and physical pain in children undergoing bone marrow aspirations and lumbar punctures. Hypnosis involving fantasy and imagery was also found to be more effective in reducing intense anxiety and pain in children experiencing cancer treatment as compared with nonhypnotic techniques (Zeltzer & LeBaron, 1982).

The acute burn phase is not only stressful for the burned child but also for the family. Issues of guilt and survival tend to make parents more vulnerable to stress. Emotional support is important for parents to begin the process of grieving the loss of their previously healthy, unburned child and come to understand the care needed for their child's recovery. Parents also experience fear and can exhibit symptoms of post-traumatic stress, which can further interfere with their feeling competent in protecting and caring for their child (Rizzone, Stoddard, Murphy, & Kruger, 1994).

Cahners and Kartiganer (1990) describe how parents must adapt to each phase of their child's treatment. Overwhelming feelings of helplessness and the threat of losing one's child produce great insecurity. However, as the child's condition improves and parents become more involved in treatment, more confidence in caring for their child is gained. One study reported how parent participation in the care of their burned child while hospitalized enhances the parent's understanding of burns and coping skills (George & Hancock, 1993). Supportive group therapy is essential for parents to share similar feelings and obtain support while adjusting to their child's trauma.

Increased involvement in psychotherapy is done during the intermediate phase when the child is more alert and active. Play therapy sessions are conducted either individually or in a group setting. When placed in a hospital setting, any type of activity that simulates the preburn environment is extremely useful. Young children often spend time in the playroom exploring toys and becoming involved in recreational activities when not in medical or psychiatric therapy. In individual play therapy, the children are provided with an opportunity to release intense feelings of anger, loss, or grief and work through other issues relating to the burn. Play therapy can help children become less inhibited by their emotions and more active in mastering their fears in a therapeutic environment (Mahoney, 1990).

Group therapy provides children with the opportunity not only to share experiences but also to receive support from others who are experiencing similar losses or feelings. In addition to being a supportive environment, children may encourage each other to achieve independence. For example, if a child has lost two or three digits on each hand, another child may help develop a method of holding scissors to cut paper. Resistance to therapy may evolve in some children if they are frightened by other patients' deformities or wary of confronting the implications of their injuries.

Loss of control is a common issue that is frequently addressed during the intermediate phase of intervention.

When hospitalized for a burn, regression occurs in the form of less independence, with staff taking total charge of all activities. Eating disturbances can be a major problem and should be addressed quickly. Proper nutrition is essential for rapid healing of wounds, ensuring the body's acceptance of grafts, and to produce energy required for physical or occupational therapy. When children refuse to eat or intake is minimal, tube-feedings are utilized to provide adequate amounts of calories and nutrition. One method that helps children increase their intake is having special foods prepared and brought from home, especially if the child is from another culture or ethnic group. This allows children to maintain some continuity of their lifestyle, in addition to making meals pleasurable instead of a struggle.

Another technique for increasing nutritional intake is for the child to select what to eat and what snacks are desired. The more choices available for children, the more independently they behave with less likelihood of regression. Having an active role in decision making may also be provided during dressing changes where very few choices are available. By deciding which limb's or body area's dressing will be changed, and by having the child actually help, the child can maintain some control over his or her treatment and care. By obtaining an active role, decreased helplessness is experienced and a greater sense of accomplishment in mastering painful physical trauma is achieved.

For adolescents, as well as younger children, the intermediate phase of treatment is a time to reflect upon their experiences and to explore and identify effective coping methods to be used following discharge. Surviving a burn is traumatic, often involving feelings of guilt (regardless of the actual amount of responsibility for the injury), concerns over extent of recovery, and worries about changes in lifestyle upon the return home. Group therapy is important to provide a safe, contained environment in which to initiate and process feelings involving the burn, survival, and adjustment.

The reconstructive phase prepares children for discharge. Continued involvement in treatment is evident by learning about special garments that should be worn (e.g., compression masks, soft foam conformers, Elastomer inserts, and breast conformers, all of which are garments used to decrease scarring and enhance cosmetic outcomes) (Flynn & Gunter, 1990). Choices regarding type of reconstructive surgery allows the child to discuss what operation would be most useful for increasing bodily function and appearance.

In addition to supportive therapy provided during hospitalization, behavioral checklists have been found to be a useful tool for assessing behavior changes. Blakeney and colleagues (1993) reported that parents identified more problems with their children through the Child Behavioral Checklist (CBCL) as compared with teacher's report and child self-reporters. The CBCL assists in determining problems in child development and behavior. However, observational data are insufficient to assess problem areas that may otherwise be overlooked. Holaday and Blakeney (1994) described how the CBCL is limited in identifying emotional disturbances, whereas projective tests, such as the Rorschach, reveal internal distress. A battery of psychological tests, in addition to structured interviews, can provide a global assessment of the child's emotional functioning and adjustment to the burn trauma.

Referral for out-patient psychotherapy is equally important for both the child and family to continue to receive support after recovery. Although some children adapt more readily and may not require a referral, post-burn depression, anxiety, and adjustment disorders can interfere with effective adaptation back into school and home life for most patients. Assessment for suicidality in depressed children is essential, and referral to an outpatient therapist should be made if there are any suspicions of the child being at risk.

Pharmacological Treatments

Medications have an important role in the medical and psychiatric care of burned children. Amount of pain experienced by each child varies with percent burn, depth of burn, individual pain threshold, and emotional factors. Treating adolescents with pain medication may become problematic due to cautiousness about possible addiction, potentially resulting in undermedication. This should be monitored closely so that proper doses can be administered to relieve pain symptoms. Methods of pain management are provided during and in between specific medical procedures.

What has been found helpful in controlling pain at our hospital is oral morphine sulphate immediate release (MSIR) given consistently at 0.3–0.6 mg/kg every 4–6 hours until the wound is covered. Utilization of patient controlled analgesia (PCA) is provided for older children every 2 hours with morphine sulphate IV bolus at 0.05–0.1 mg/kg. For pain control involving a procedure (e.g., debridement and dressing changes), 0.3–0.6 mg/kg of MSIR is given orally 1/2 hour prior to procedures, with 0.05–0.1 mg/kg of morphine IV bolus administered immediately before the procedure (Antoon, 1996; Herrin & Antoon, 1996).

Often prior to and during dressing changes or physical therapy sessions, children are anxious and frightened.

Lorazepam (Ativan) 0.01–0.05 mg/kg (Stoddard, Chedekel, & Cahners, 1990) may be provided prior to a procedure for reducing symptoms of anxiety. For some children, clonazepam (Klonopin) has been beneficial due to the longer-acting potency, as well as the pain reducing qualities that medication contains (Stoddard, 1990).

Antipsychotic medications are useful in treating delirium and agitation. In conjunction with these medications, anti-Parkinsonian drugs such as Cogentin (benztropine mesylate) reduce the risk of side-effects. Stoddard, Chedekel, and Cahners (1990) reported that IV haloperidol (Haldol) at 0.02–0.05 mg/kg every 30 minutes is beneficial when attempting to restore stabilization. This may be continued for one to two days prior to tapering. Antidepressants are usually not used with acute burn children due to metabolic and cardiovascular complications. However, once the child is physically stable and in the later phases of treatment, antidepressants are beneficial in relieving depression (Stoddard, 1990).

CASE ILLUSTRATION

Clinical Presentation

Peter Y. was a 5-year-old white male admitted to Shriners Burns Institute with severe burns resulting from a house fire. His total body surface area burn was 60 percent with injuries involving his face, trunk, arms, hands, and legs. Peter's father was also severely burned and hospitalized in their state of residence. Mrs. Y. traveled to both hospitals in attempts to equally divide her time and support between her husband and son.

Peter appeared to be of average height and weight for his age. No pre-burn behavioral or emotional problems were reported by his mother. Also, Peter was in good physical health prior to the burn accident. Due to the severity of his burn injuries, the 4th and 5th digits on his left hand as well as his big toe on his left foot were amputated. Mobility was restricted, resulting in Peter using a go-cart to maneuver around the hospital.

Initial psychological consultation did not occur until one month after admission. During that first month, Peter underwent surgeries for wound grafting and was too ill to begin addressing emotional issues. Medical staff reported that Peter appeared sad and minimally verbal, particularly in his mother's absence. Though not verbally expressed, fear relating to missing digits on his

hand was noticed by staff. Depressed affect, body-image issues, and anxiety were the reasons for consultation.

Assessment Findings

Upon approach, Peter presented as a quiet, withdrawn child who observed his environment carefully. Though cautious of the therapist (LPR), interest in the bag of toys soon helped lessen any anxiety related to possibly receiving medical treatment. The presence of GI Joe figures stimulated Peter to talk of his own toy missiles and GI maneuvers that he creates. This interaction with Peter resulted in a brief discussion of how difficult it was to only have one hand with which to manipulate objects.

Affect was sad, and Peter made little eye-contact. This sadness was associated with the loss of previous physical function and of his mother's being away. Though minimally verbal, Peter acknowledged concern for his mother's return and how lonely he felt when she was not with him. Psychomotor retardation was present, with Peter making deliberate gestures when showing his toys. This could have been a result of pain associated with movement, as well as a symptom of depression. Periodically, Peter would touch his forehead and chest area to feel any bandages or flaking skin. Though concerned over body image, Peter did not discuss his feelings but remained silent and withdrawn.

Initial assessment found Peter to be a cautious child who exhibited symptoms of depression. Concern regarding the body image was revealed behaviorally rather than verbally at that session. Separation from his mother, who had been supportive, also contributed to Peter's withdrawn, sad disposition. Additional sessions were required to continue assessment of adaptation, as well as to build trust.

Treatment Selection and Course

Play therapy was initially conducted at bedside until Peter was physically able to move around in a go-cart. At that time, individual sessions continued at bedside or off the unit. Group play therapy was also attended by Peter later in his hospitalization. Throughout his inpatient stay, issues of altered body image were of concern for Peter, who frequently observed his hand. Discussion of physical losses was limited to his only saying a few words before withdrawing into himself. Avoidance occurred often and was demonstrated by minimal eye contact, remaining nonverbal, or looking away whenever feeling sad. This defense appeared to be the most effective method of minimizing emotional pain.

Depression episodes and avoidance of issues are common reactions during the initial phase of burn care. One strength that Peter had was his interest in play and in other people. Playing in the unit's playroom allowed for fun in a non-medical environment. Brighter affect with involvement in play activities could be observed in Peter, who otherwise separated himself from others when anxious or sad.

Peter stayed on the acute (ICU) burn unit for 1½ months before moving onto the reconstructive burn unit within Shriners Burns Hospital. Prior to his transfer, Peter began to exhibit anger by yelling at staff during dressing changes. Aggression was also released in play sessions through banging objects or knocking down blocks. Though remaining minimally verbal as to the issues behind his anger, aggression seemed to have been related to body image and physical limitations.

The intermediate phase of Peter's burn treatment overlapped between his later period on the acute ward and transfer onto the reconstructive unit. Physical therapy and dressing changes were the predominant methods of medical treatment during this phase. When not in individual or group therapy, Peter enjoyed free time in the playroom with other burn patients.

Depression relating to forced adaptation to hospitalization continued as noted by irritability, sad affect, and decreased appetite. His wish to leave the hospital was expressed through frustration and anger whenever the playroom was closed or there was a delay in engaging in an activity. In play therapy, Peter verbalized more anger and disappointment about his burns and the need to endure continued rehabilitative treatment.

As is often seen in a burn population, control issues emerged in the form of diminished food intake. Peter eventually refused any food. The possibility of tube feedings as a means of obtaining nourishment had no effect on his voluntary food intake. This struggle symbolized Peter's frustration and anger over loss of autonomy and control over the situation occurring in his life. Though the depression was diminishing slightly, his sadness contributed to a loss of appetite. Tube feedings were never required for Peter; he resumed eating very gradually on his own and with the encouragement of his mother.

Avoidance of painful issues remained a prominent defense mechanism. However, certain environmental objects acted as stimuli that elicited feelings related to the fire. For example, upon receiving a card picturing a teddy bear and blanket on a red background, Peter proceeded to talk about a blanket that was lost when the house burned. Other material losses were discussed, with Peter expressing sadness and grief. The process of grieving was very important for Peter, who had experienced multiple losses ranging from material to emotional separation, to physical losses of digits and appearance.

Termination and Follow-Up

The progression from the intermediate to rehabilitative phases prior to discharge was not clearly defined in Peter's case. As discharge approached, his depression was improved, yet irritability, sadness, and anger were still evident. Appetite had increased but methods of control were exhibited beyond nutritional intake to resisting physical therapy exercises. Recent life losses were the main theme of therapy sessions, with overwhelming feelings expressed through anger and frustration.

Throughout Peter's hospitalization, Mrs. Y. visited routinely and always informed her son of necessary three- or four-day absences to visit her husband. Anxiety and frustration were also expressed by Mrs. Y., who took the opportunity to receive support from social services and the psychiatry department. She involved herself in Peter's physical recovery as well as his emotional adaptation to the burns. Mrs. Y.'s ability to maintain as much of her parental role as possible was beneficial to both her and Peter as they tried to maintain family unity.

Upon discharge, Peter was to be transferred to the hospital where his father was staying. Affect at that time was bright, with Peter being excited at seeing his father and the family coming closer together. A referral for psychotherapy was made in order that the process of adjustment and grieving be continued with support.

One important aspect that must be stressed is that the process of emotional adaptation is lengthy, with many phases that may extend beyond discharge. For Peter, increased verbalization and expression of anger were beginning to evolve slowly as his hospitalization progressed. Follow-up at Shriners Burns occurred with Peter's second admission for reconstructive surgery.

SUMMARY

At the Shriners Burns Institute, Boston, our work with burn victims has been effective for numerous reasons that have been outlined in this chapter. However, two key factors that contribute to the overall success of treatment must be addressed. One is the family-centered care approach in which the parents and families of the burned child are also seen as victims. Thus, it is clear that they must also be the recipients of various services during the ongoing treatment process. It is also crucial that they become part of the treatment itself. Not only are parents encouraged to express their feelings and concerns, but they are also provided with opportunities to maintain close and ongoing contact with their child throughout all phases of treatment.

As early as possible, parents are provided with opportunities to learn about the care of their child and to participate in this process to the best of their ability. Encouragement to take an active, caregiving role lessens the passivity and helplessness many parents experience. We have found this provides parents and families with a sense of focus rather than forcing them to be bystanders, which only contributes to increased anxiety and often depression.

The team approach has proven to be an enormously effective but also stressful method of administering care. It is obvious that there is a tremendous amount of gratification involved in this type of work, yet those who provide burn care often feel a sense of isolation and alienation from their peers. Other professionals may be very supportive and acknowledge the importance of what has been done by medical professionals providing burn care, and yet it is not something that they generally want to discuss in any detail.

For the medical team providing burn care, the work can be frustrating and at times overwhelming. Periodically, staff may become irritable and depressed and question the value of what they are doing. It is one more reason why mental health professionals are important to the burn unit. Providing opportunities for staff to discuss their feelings is equally as important as addressing the concerns of the children and their families. This type of input has been proven to be effective both on an individual as well as a group basis.

Work on a burn unit also presents staff with numerous ethical dilemmas. When confronted with severe burns, staff often question the value of what they are doing. That is, if this child's life is saved, what will the child's quality of life be like? Medical staff are trained to save lives, and yet it is often hard to justify the end result when it seems likely that a child must spend the rest of his or her life faced with uncertainties because of disfigurement and the ongoing surgical procedures that may be necessary as the years go by. However, it is encouraging to know that in examining long-term adaptation and adjustment in burn victims, the indications are that a greater proportion of burned children with extensive injuries do quite well as they progress in their lives.

Although many children are able to proceed with their life plans, it has also been evident that others need ongoing psychotherapeutic intervention to help them cope with the many issues that confront them. Often their families are in need of similar support. It is difficult to determine exactly at what point children finally come to terms with the trauma of being burned, as well as when they can cope and function effectively without additional support services. What is known is that the greater the level of stability in the individual's life and the more effective the supports available to them, the more likely they will go forward and lead productive, meaningful lives.

REFERENCES

Antoon, A. Y. (1996). Burns. In F. D. Burg, J. R. Ingelfinger, E. K. Wald, & R. A. Polin (Eds.), *Current pediatric therapy*. Philadelphia: W. B. Saunders Company.

Bastani, J. B., Baskins, M. A., & Wiebelhaus, P. (1992). Psychiatric referral pattern in a burn center. *Journal of Burn Care and Rehabilitation, 13,* 709–712.

Bernstein, N. R. (1990). Burns: an overview. In M. S. Jellinek & D. B. Herzog (Eds.), *Psychiatric aspects of general hospital pediatrics* (pp. 235–237). Chicago: Year Book Medical Publishers.

Blakeney, P., Meyer, W., Moore, P., Broemeling, L., Hunt, R., Robson, M., & Herndon, D. (1993). Social competence and behavioral problems of pediatric survivors of burns. *Journal of Burn Care and Rehabilitation, 14,* 65–72.

Cahners, S. S. (1992). Young women with breast burns: A self-help "group by mail." *Journal of Burn Care and Rehabilitation, 13,* 44–47.

Cahners, S. S. & Kartiganer, P. P. (1990). The social worker and the family: A long-term relationship in burn care. In J. A. Martyn (Ed.), *Acute management of the burned patient* (pp. 306–319). Philadelphia: W. B. Saunders Company.

Cooper, M. K., & Thomas, C. M. (1988). Psychosocial care of the severely burned child. In H. F. Carvajal & D. H. Parks (Eds.), *Burns in childhood: Pediatric burn management* (pp. 345–362). Chicago: Year Book Medical Publishers.

Feldman, K. W., Schaller, R. T., Feldman, J. A., & McMillon, M. (1978). Tap water scald burns in children. *Pediatrics, 62,* 1–7.

Flynn, A. E., & Gunter, L. L. (1990). Rehabilitation of the burn patient. In J. A. J. Martyn (Ed.), *Acute management of the burned patient* (pp. 320–332). Philadelphia: W. B. Saunders Company.

George, A., & Hancock, J. (1993). Reducing pediatric burn pain with parent participation. *Journal of Burn Care and Rehabilitation, 14,* 104–107.

Hammond, J. S., Ward, C. G., & Pereira, E. (1988). Self-inflicted burns. *Journal of Burn Care and Rehabilitation, 9,* 178–179.

Herman, S. P. (1991). The burned child. In M. Lewis (Ed.), *Child and adolescent psychiatry* (pp. 1004–1009). Baltimore: Williams & Wilkins.

Herrin, J. T., & Antoon, A. Y. (1996). Burn injuries. In R. E. Behrman, R. M. Kliegman, & A. M. Arvin (Eds.), W. E. Nelson (Sr. Ed.), *Nelson Textbook of Pediatrics, 15th edition* (pp. 270–277). Philadelphia: W. B. Saunders Company.

Hight, D. W., Bakalar, H. R., & Lloyd, J. R. (1979). Inflicted burns in children. *Journal of American Medical Association, 242,* 517–520.

Holaday, M., & Blakeney, P. (1994). A comparison of psychologic functioning in children and adolescents with severe burns on the Rorschach and the Child Behavior Checklist. *Journal of Burn Care and Rehabilitation, 15,* 412–415.

Jay, K. M., Bartlett, R. H., Danet, R., & Allyn, P. A. (1977). Burn epidemiology: A basis for burn prevention. *The Journal of Trauma, 17,* 943–947.

Kravitz, M., McCoy, B. J., Tomkins, D. M., Daly, W., Mulligan, J., McCauley, R. L., Robson, M. C., & Herndon, D. N. (1993). Sleep disorders in children after burn injury. *The Journal of Burn Care and Rehabilitation, 14,* 83–90.

Long, R. T., & Cope O. (1961). Emotional problems of burned children. *The New England Journal of Medicine, 264,* 1121–1127.

Mahoney, N. B. (1990). Restoration of play in a severely burned three-year-old child. *Journal of Burn Care and Rehabilitation, 11,* 57–63.

McCauley, R. L., Stenberg, B. A., Rutan, R. L., Ronson, M. C., Heggers, J. P., & Herndon, D. N. (1991). Class C firework injuries in a pediatric population. *The Journal of Trauma, 31,* 389–391.

Purdue, G. F., Hunt, J. L., & Prescott, P. R. (1988). Child abuse by burning—An index of suspicion. *The Journal of Trauma, 28,* 221–224.

Ravenscroft, K., (1982). The burn unit. *Psychiatric Clinics of North America, 5,* 419–432.

Rizzone, L. P., Stoddard, F. J., Murphy, J. M., & Kruger, L. J. (1994). Posttraumatic stress disorder in mothers of children and adolescents with burns. *Journal of Burn Care and Rehabilitation, 15,* 158–163.

Sheridan, R. L., Tompkins, R. G., & Burke, J. F. (1994). Management of burn wounds with prompt excision and immediate closure. *Journal of Intensive Care Medicine, 9,* 6–19.

Simon, P. A., & Baron, R. C. (1994). Age as a risk factor for burn injury requiring hospitalization during early childhood. *Archives of Pediatric and Adolescent Medicine, 148,* 394–397.

Synder, C. C., & Saieh, T. A. (1987). Burn injuries in children. In V. C. Kelly (Ed.), *Practice of pediatrics* (pp. 1–13). Philadelphia: Harper & Row.

Stoddard, F. J. (1982). Coping with pain: A developmental approach to treatment of burned children. *American Journal of Psychiatry, 139,* 736–740.

Stoddard, F. J. (1990). Psychiatric management of the burned patient. In J. A. J. Martyn (Ed.), *Acute management of the burned patient* (pp. 256–272). Philadelphia: W. B. Saunders Company.

Stoddard, F. J. (1993). A psychiatric perspective on self-inflicted burns. *Journal of Burn Care and Rehabilitation, 14,* 480–482.

Stoddard, F. J., Chedekel, D. S., & Cahners, S. S. (1990). Burns. In M. S. Jellinek & D. B. Herzog (Eds.), *Psychiatric aspects of general hospital pediatrics* (pp. 238–246). Chicago: Year Book Medical Publishers.

Stoddard, F. J., Norman D. K., & Murphy, J. M. (1989). A diagnostic outcome study of children and adolescents with severe burns. *The Journal of Trauma, 29,* 471–477.

Stoddard, F. J., Stroud, L., & Murphy, J. M. (1992). Depression in children after recovery from severe burns. *The Journal of Burn Care and Rehabilitation, 13,* 340–347.

Stoddard, F. J., & Wilens, T. E. (1990). Delirium. In M. S. Jellinek & D. B. Herzog (Eds.), *Psychiatric aspects of general hospital pediatrics* (pp. 254–259). Chicago: Year Book Medical Publishers.

Tompkins, R. G., Remensnyder, J. P., Burke, J. F., Tompkins, D. M., Hilton, J. F., Schoenfield, D. A., Behringer, G. E., Bondoc, C. C., Brigs, S. E., & Quinby, W. C. (1988). Significant reduction in mortality for children with burn injuries through the use of prompt eschar excision. *Annals of Surgery, 208,* 577–585.

Willis-Helmich, J. J. (1992). Reclaiming body image: The hidden burn. *Journal of Burn Care and Rehabilitation, 13,* 64–67.

Zeltzer, L. K., Jay, S. M., & Fisher, D. M. (1989). The management of pain associated with pediatric procedures. *Pediatric Clinics of North America, 36,* 941–964.

Zelter, L., & LeBaron, S. (1982). Hypnosis and nonhypnotic techniques for reduction of pain and anxiety during painful procedures in children and adolescents with cancer. *The Journal of Pediatrics, 101,* 1032–1035.

CHAPTER 9

GASTROINTESTINAL DISORDERS

Ingemar Engström
Bo L. Lindquist

DESCRIPTION OF DISORDERS

The clinical spectrum of disorders in pediatric gastroenterology is significantly different from that encountered in adult gastroenterology. Besides the fact that different disorders predominate in pediatric gastroenterology, the clinical manifestations of disorders common to both pediatric and adult gastroenterology may be different as well.

Pediatric gastrointestinal disorders frequently affect both somatic and psychological development. Such disorders may result in retardation of physical growth, particularly during periods of disease activity. However, through infancy, childhood and adolescence, human life is a process not just of physical growth, but also of integrated and complex maturation. Clinical pediatrics is based on the fact and the conceptualization that children are not just miniature adults. Their susceptibility to diseases and their responses are conditioned by the stage of maturation and a range of developmental processes (Walker, Durie, Hamilton, Walker-Smith, & Watkins, 1991). These considerations must be emphasized in pediatric gastroenterology, and the clinical follow-up must be focused on supervising somatic and psychological development, as well as physical growth and nutritional issues.

Regarding the impact of gastrointestinal disease in young patients, it might seem surprising that most young patients are extraordinarily resilient, in spite of their apparent vulnerability and dependence. However, certain gastroenterologic diseases are particularly hazardous to infants and children. For example, systemic dehydration and electrolyte imbalance due to diarrhea are much more likely to occur in infancy than in adulthood because of relative lack of reserves of the immature gut, immaturity of renal compensatory capacity, and the fundamental needs for adequate fluid intake.

Pediatric gastroenterology is rapidly emerging as a specialized medical field based on an expansion of knowledge of the developmental characteristics of the gastrointestinal system and the evolution of new technology for investigating young patients, including infants with low birth weight.

Table 9.1 depicts the main groups of disorders seen in pediatric gastroenterology.

From a global point of view, various infections affecting the gastrointestinal tract are by far the most common gastrointestinal disorders, both in developed and developing countries. A survey conducted by the Program for Control of Diarrheal Diseases (Lebenthal, 1984) has indicated that in 1980, 1 billion episodes of acute diarrhea occurred in children below 5 years of age. In addition 4 to 5 million deaths per year occurred in children less than 5 years old in underdeveloped and developing countries (Snyder & Merson, 1982). A significant number of these episodes also result in serious retardation of the growth and development of affected children (Lebenthal, 1984) .

Table 9.1. Clinical Panorama of Pediatric Gastroenterology

1. Infectious gastrointestinal disorders
2. Malabsorptive disorders
3. Gastrointestinal intolerance/allergy
4. Inflammatory bowel disease
5. Nutritional problems
6. Psychosomatic disorders
7. Liver and pancreatic disorders
8. Various conditions, e.g. metabolic or endocrine disorders

Malabsorptive disorders may be caused by maldigestion and disturbed absorption across the intestinal mucosa, and may ultimately result in malnutrition. In developed countries, the appearance of primary malnutrition is rare and is linked to high-risk groups, but in developing countries, a variable but significant population suffers from malnutrition at some point in their lifetime, with infants being at the greatest risk. Malabsorption and malnutrition are often associated with gastrointestinal infections, and may be caused by viral, bacterial, or fungal infections. In developed countries, on the other hand, malabsorption is more rarely encountered, and is most often caused by chronic intestinal inflammatory processes, such as celiac disease or intestinal immunopathies, maldigestive processes, overgrowth of colonic bacteria in the small intestine, and intestinal dysmotility.

Gastrointestinal intolerance is commonly encountered in clinical pediatric gastroenterology and may be caused by enzyme deficiencies such as lactose intolerance or immunologically mediated syndromes such as cow's milk protein intolerance.

Inflammatory bowel diseases include a group of diseases, the most common of which are Crohn's disease (CD) and ulcerative colitis (UC). Although these diseases are not frequently encountered, most pediatricians will deal with inflammatory bowel disease at some point in their career, and inevitably will be faced with an extremely complex somatic and psychiatric clinical picture.

Nutritional problems in infancy and during childhood are fundamental in pediatric gastroenterology. Growth and development cannot proceed normally without adequate nutrition, and some diseases are primarily or secondarily linked to deficiencies in nutrition. Nutritional requirements must be estimated from established recommendations to optimize health care for patients with compromised gastrointestinal function. Special interest, knowledge, and experience in nutrition are needed to properly evaluate diet and growth, and to perform an adequate physical examination, as well as

obtain the proper laboratory testings. Specialized diets, formulas, or feeding routes are required by some patients with gastrointestinal and liver diseases.

Peptic ulcer, Helicobacter pylori ulcers, gastritis, and esophagitis, often associated with gastroesophageal reflux disease, are entities that are getting increasing attention in pediatric gastroenterology.

Gastrointestinal symptoms in the absence of evidence of physical disease are very common in pediatric gastroenterology. The most common clinical presentations include recurrent abdominal pain (RAP), irritable colon, and constipation. Chronic abdominal pain is one of the most commonly encountered physical symptoms in childhood and adolescence. There is a general agreement that abdominal pain becomes chronic when episodic attacks occur over a period of at least 3 months (Apley, 1975). This group of disorders accounts for a major portion of the clinical work within pediatric gastroenterology from a quantitative point of view. When dealing with these problems, the physician needs time and experience in order to perform a sound clinical evaluation. On the other hand, the need for sophisticated medical tests and investigations is most often limited, provided the primary clinical evaluation, including medical history and physical examination, has been carefully done. Determining which patients need further evaluation requires experience, as well as careful collaboration with others (i.e., schools, families, day care centers, nursery schools).

Liver and pancreatic disorders are relatively rare, but may require extensive workup when they are encountered.

Similarly, metabolic or endocrine disorders with gastrointestinal symptoms may demand special investigations, laboratory facilities, techniques, and sometimes highly specialized clinics. Very often, these needs can only be met in a few centers that specialize in these rarely encountered diseases.

For the mental health professional, recurrent abdominal pain of childhood and adolescence and inflammatory bowel disease (UC and CD) are representative disorders that highlight the major clinical problems encountered in pediatric gastroenterology. Consequently, the remainder of the chapter will focus on these disorders, with the general approach serving as a model for work with patients with other gastrointestinal disorders.

Recurrent Abdominal Pain (RAP)

The diagnostic term recurrent abdominal pain (RAP) refers to chronic abdominal pain with no demonstrated underlying physical disease. By definition, the syndrome is characterized by at least one episode of abdominal pain per month for 3 consecutive months severe enough to interfere with routine functioning, and separated by asymptomatic periods (Oberlander & Rappaport, 1993). The typical age at presentation is between 5 and 14 years. In the individual patient, pain episodes tend to cluster, alternating with pain-free episodes of variable length. The presentation of RAP varies widely in frequency, duration, intensity, location, and associated symptoms. Most episodes begin gradually and last less than 1 hour in 50 percent, and less than 3 hours in another 40 percent of children (Apley, 1975; Stone & Barbero, 1970). The pain is typically periumbilical or midepigastric in location. Radiation of pain is not typical. The pain rarely awakens the child, but it is not uncommon for the pain to affect the ability of the child to fall asleep. The parents describe the child as miserable during episodes of pain. Commonly associated symptoms are headache, pallor, nausea, dizziness, and fatigability. Weight loss, growth failure, joint pains, or rash are not symptoms of RAP and should engender a search for undiagnosed physical disease. The pathogenesis of the pain is unclear. Regarding prognosis, there is a high incidence of early resolution, but long-term studies have suggested that 30-50 percent of patients with functional abdominal pains in childhood experience pains as adults, although in most individuals normal activity is not limited (Christensen & Mortensen, 1975).

Ulcerative Colitis

In this disorder, the intestinal inflammation is limited to the colon. In at least 50 percent of the children, the UC is extensive, involving all the large intestine. In the other children, various lengths of the distal part of the colon are affected. The intestinal symptoms are similar to those in adults, with diarrhea, urgency to defecation, and blood and mucus mixed with the stools. Extraintestinal manifestations such as growth failure may precede the intestinal symptoms, which sometimes make it difficult to make a correct diagnosis (Berger, Gribetz, & Korelitz, 1975; Motil, Grand, & Davies-Kraft, 1983).

The clinical presentation is mild in 50 to 60 percent of patients, moderate in 30 percent, and severe in 10 percent, depending on the intestinal and systemic disturbances encountered, as well as the levels of hemoglobin, leukocytes, and albumin (Motil & Grand, 1987). The clinical severity of the attack most often correlates with the extent of disease involvement in the intestine. The initial attack does not necessarily reflect the sever-

ity of future attacks. Toxic megacolon, a medical and surgical emergency, is reported to occur in up to 5 percent of children with pancolitis.

Crohn's Disease

CD can affect any part of the intestinal tract from the mouth to the anus. The initial symptoms and signs of CD in childhood are often insidious, with non-specific features that may result in delay of diagnosis (Burbige, Huang, & Bayless, 1975). CD may present with only extraintestinal signs and possibly growth retardation. The intestinal manifestations are determined by the anatomic involvement. Small bowel CD or upper gastrointestinal involvement tend to result in obstructive symptoms, with abdominal pain and tenderness on palpation. Diffuse small bowel disease is often characterized by diarrhea and anorexia. Colonic involvement may result in symptoms similar to UC, with diarrhea, urgency, and rectal bleeding. Perianal fistulae, anal fissures, and tags strongly suggest diagnosis of CD (Burbige et al., 1975; Kelts & Grand, 1980).

EPIDEMIOLOGY

Recurrent Abdominal Pain (RAP)

Recurrent abdominal pain (RAP) is by far the most common disorder of the alimentary tract among children and adolescents. Between 10 and 20 percent of schoolchildren experience recurrent abdominal pain (Apley, 1975; Apley & Naish, 1958; Liebman, 1978). The highest incidence has been observed in children between ages 8 and 10 years. It may, however, occur as early as in 3-year-old children (Stevenson, Simpson, & Bailey, 1988). In a Danish study (Lundby, Sandbæk, & Juul, 1990), the prevalence among children 9 to 12 years of age was found to be 15 percent. In a recent Swedish study (Alfvén, 1993b) 19 percent of schoolchildren from the ages of 7 to 16 years fulfilled the criteria of RAP. Overall, girls seem to be more affected than boys, with a sex ratio of about 5:3 across most studies in the field (Oberlander et al., 1993). Whereas the prevalence among boys shows few variations from age 5 to 15, this is quite different among girls. The prevalence increases dramatically to about 30 percent at the age of 9 (Apley, 1975) and then drops back to 10–15 percent in 11- to 12-year-old girls. The aggregation of symptoms around the age of 9 has also been reported in other kinds of medically unexplained physical symptoms, and has been interpreted as a predictable consequence of Piagetian cognitive development (Oberlander et al., 1993). According to this theory, the latency period includes a capability of the child to view itself from an external point of view. This inevitably means that the child compares itself, its appearance, its capacities, and its performing abilities with other children. In this comparison process, the child may experience different shortcomings that may pave the road for a position of inferiority, leading to depressive or anxious feelings. For many children, these feelings are not made clear, but rather transform themselves into somatic symptoms. The reason for the gender differences in this developmental aspect, however, remains unclear.

These prevalence figures suggest that non-organic recurrent abdominal pain is the single most common presenting physical symptom in childhood. In no study has there been found any clear relation with socioeconomic class. It also seems to be equally distributed across European and North American countries. There is as of yet a lack of material from other continents concerning the epidemiology of RAP.

Inflammatory Bowel Disease

Approximately 20 percent of patients with UC and CD are diagnosed before 21 years of age (Michener & Wyllie, 1990). The incidence of IBD in the pediatric population is from 2 to 5 per 100,000 in the United States and Europe (Calkins, Lilienfeld, Garland, & Mendeloff, 1984; Hildebrand, Fredrikzon, Holmqvist, Kristiansson, & Lindquist, 1991; Michener et al., 1990), with males and females being equally represented. CD is considered to be more common than UC in childhood, although the reverse has been reported (Hildebrand et al., 1991).

UC may present in infancy, but it becomes more prevalent from 11 to 15 years, with a peak age at 16 to 20 years. The majority of cases of CD in childhood are diagnosed between 10 and 16 years. CD is rarely diagnosed during early childhood. Most infants with colitis have transient allergic colitis or Behcet's disease (Chong, Blackshaw, Morson, Williams, & Walker-Smith, 1986).

Some authors have reported a significant delay between onset of symptoms and diagnosis (Michener et al., 1990). Others have reported that the time period from when the patient seeks medical attention to diagnosis is short (Lindquist, Järnerot, & Wickbom, 1984). A delay of diagnosis might be an important concern, as early diagnosis of IBD in childhood or adolescence has been

suggested to prevent development of complications that affect prognosis, and require specific therapy. On the other hand, it is not clearly documented whether advanced disease responds less well to treatment and whether the long-term prognosis is worse, but it is conceivable that early diagnosis and initiation of therapy may lead to an earlier recovery and a better quality of life for the patient.

The clinical presentation of childhood IBD is highly variable, and the signs and the symptoms may be difficult to sort out due to the presence of extraintestinal complications. UC and CD can be distinguished in approximately 85 percent of affected children after evaluating the clinical, radiologic, endoscopic, and histologic findings. The remaining children have colonic involvement, but are designated indeterminate colitis because their endoscopic and histologic findings are not sufficiently clear to allow categorization as UC or CD.

ASSESSMENT APPROACHES

Medical Issues

RAP

The assessment of RAP should be based on a comprehensive and thorough integration of anamnestic facts and clinical findings. The assessment should begin with a complete history and physical examination. It is never enough to presume RAP just from the history. It is of utmost importance, for both medical and psychological reasons, to evaluate the child for evidence of physical disease.

Typically, the clinical presentation of RAP is characterized by

- Paroxysmal (unexpected) pain. Typically the pain has a gradual beginning and has a periumbilical or suprapubic location.
- The pain is nonradiating, dull, crampy or sharp, appears in clusters and usually lasts less than 1 hour. The pain behavior is often reinforced by rest periods, social attention, and medication.
- Usually the pain is not related to activity, meals, stress, or bowel habits.
- The symptoms interfere with or interrupt normal activities.
- Between episodes the child is doing quite well, with no symptoms or signs indicating pain.

- The physical examination is normal in all aspects. The gain of height and weight is normal and the psychomotor developmental characteristics are normal.
- Laboratory investigations are normal.

It is important to consider any deviations that may suggest a definite and more serious physical disease. Similarly, it is important to consider the possibility of psychiatric disorder in such children. Attention needs to be directed toward warning signals that may point to the need for further medical investigation.

Examples of such signals are:

- Well-localized pain and pain far from the umbilicus ("Apley's Law" states that the further the pain is from the umbilicus, the more likely that it represents identifiable disease)
- Permanent changes in bowel function (constipation, diarrhea, or incontinence)
- Night pains
- Vomiting
- Dysuria
- Rectal bleeding
- Age at presentation atypical (i.e., < 4 years or > 15 years of age).
- Family history of gastrointestinal or systemic disease.
- Pain radiation to the shoulder or to the back.

The initial clinical approach is extremely important, and the physician needs to make a sound evaluation considering what investigations need to be done. A typical but unfortunate approach to the evaluation of RAP attempts to make a diagnosis of exclusion by ruling out identifiable disease by performing various more-or-less complicated investigations. This approach may reinforce the idea that something is severely wrong with the child for the patient and the family. The absence of positive findings of disease may lead to parental anxiety that there may be some hidden physical illness that has been overlooked. Ideally, the diagnosis should be based on a careful integration of historical facts, physical findings, and an understanding of the social and emotional context in which the pain occurs. The diagnosis of RAP should thus be considered a positive diagnosis, not a diagnosis of exclusion (Oberlander et al., 1993). Ideally, and depending on the history and physical findings, the number of investigations could be limited greatly in the clinical evaluation of most children with RAP.

The following steps are suggested in the clinical investigation of a child with RAP:

1. Medical history that must be very detailed and carefully done, focusing upon details of the diet, sleep pattern, bowel habits, and the context in which the pain exists. A record of dietary intake should be kept, as well as a diary of pain.
2. Physical examination should be thoughtfully and comprehensively performed, and the child's height and weight plotted on a growth chart to document gain in weight and height.
3. Basic laboratory analyses should include complete blood count, sedimentation rate, and possibly C-reactive protein, as well as routine urinalysis with the purpose of excluding glucosuria, proteinuria, leukocyturia, and bacteriuria. Fecal analysis should be performed to exclude occult blood in the stool.

If the medical history, the physical examination, and the basic laboratory analyses support the diagnosis RAP, no further somatic investigations need to be performed. If, on the other hand, there are warning signals in the medical history, physical examination, or in the lab evaluation that fail to support a positive diagnosis of RAP and/or suggest serious physical disease, appropriate additional investigations must be performed.

In approximately 10 percent of cases presenting with chronic abdominal pain, an underlying physical disease or disorder is identified. These include:

- Cholelithiasis, which is a rare cause of abdominal pain in children, especially in children below 9 years of age. This should be suspected if the pain history is not typical for RAP, or if the family history includes a history of family members with hemolytic diseases (e.g., sickle cell anemia, thalassemia, and spherocytosis).
- Peptic ulcer occurs in children, and should be considered especially if the pain history reveals symptoms such as night pain, vomiting, or occult blood in the stools. On the other hand, the relief of pain with food is not characteristic of childhood peptic ulcer. Ulcerogenic factors include certain well-known medicines such as aspirin, corticosteroids, and nonsteroidal antiinflammatory drugs (NSAID) or other prostaglandin synthesis inhibitors. The relationship between Helicobacter pylori and ulcer disease has attracted increased attention in children, and appears to be a clinical reality in many countries (Sullivan et al., 1990; Wewer et al., 1994).
- Carbohydrate malabsorption leading to intolerance. Lactose intolerance is the most common example and frequently is associated with recurrent pain and

intestinal dysfunction (Webster, DiPalma, & Gremse, 1995). Primary ethnic lactase deficiency has a very high incidence (60–90 percent) in certain regions of the world (e.g., South-East Asia).

- Obstipation and bowel dysmotility are frequently associated with abdominal pains, intestinal contractions, gas formation, and painful defecations. These causes have to be considered when evaluating a child with chronic abdominal pain clinically.

Another syndrome, Irritable Bowel Syndrome (IBS), not rare in children, has been regarded as associated with intestinal dysmotility and characterized by abdominal pains, and chronic irregular episodes of diarrhea alternating with constipation and normal bowel movements. Sometimes it is impossible to make a clear distinction between RAP and IBS in children because the diagnoses often may refer to the same patients. Similarly, it is often difficult to distinguish between non-ulcer dyspepsia and IBS in a meaningful way in practice.

Inflammatory Bowel Disease

A careful medical history is essential in making the diagnosis of IBD. Families frequently seek medical attention because the child has recurrent abdominal pains, usually nonspecific or periumbilical in location, and it is sometimes very difficult to decide which children require more extensive and specific diagnostic evaluation. Is there a suspicion of IBD or is it a more typical case of RAP? To make this decision there is need for time, listening, and experience.

The intestinal symptoms of diarrhea, urgency to defecation, and blood and mucus in the stools are sometimes obvious, but not always. Early diagnosis is important because it provides an opportunity to prevent future complications both in the intestinal tract and in extraintestinal systems. A detailed medical history is mandatory for systematizing the symptoms and signs. In what way do the symptoms affect the child and the daily life? Are there symptoms during the night?

The physical evaluation must be very careful and specifically focused on physical maturation and gain in weight and height. Efforts must be made to rule out evidence of malabsorption or malnutrition. Generally speaking, systemic and extraintestinal manifestations occur more often in children than in adults in both UC and CD, and have been reported in at least 50 percent of children. Weight loss is common and is reported more frequently in CD than in UC. It is often accompanied by impaired linear growth, retarded bone development, and delayed sexual development at the time of presentation.

Delayed growth is an important and serious complication of childhood IBD, more often observed and more pronounced in CD than in UC.

The cause of growth failure has been extensively investigated and is considered to be multifactorial. In most cases, growth failure is observed in patients with chronic caloric insufficiency, with a combination of anorexia and inadequate intake. The growth failure may be reversed by nutritional support, either by enteral or parenteral means; this has been demonstrated in several studies. Malabsorption is also common in IBD in children, but other causes have been identified such as excessive protein losses from the gut, and increased metabolic requirements.

Deficiencies in certain important vitamins and trace elements, such as B-12, folate, iron, zinc, magnesium, calcium, and phosphorus are sometimes found at the time of clinical presentation or during the clinical course. Endocrine disturbances occur frequently, with delayed sexual maturation or secondary amenorrhea occurring simultaneously with growth failure in some cases, especially in CD. Most endocrine studies on pituitary, thyroid, adrenal, and growth hormone reveal normal values in children with growth retardation and IBD (Kirschner & Sutton, 1986).

Arthralgia is a frequently occurring extraintestinal manifestation of IBD in children. Usually large joints are affected, especially knees, ankles, and hips. Joint deformity is rare. Sometimes joint symptoms precede intestinal complaints for years, and may require specific therapy with nonsteroidal antiinflammatory drugs. Fever is reported in 40 percent of children at the time of presentation. It may occur more frequently, but go unrecognized. The liver and biliary tract are frequently affected in IBD in children as well as in adults, and such problems may precede the clinical appearance of bowel symptoms.

Based on the clinical medical history and the physical findings, the necessary investigations are planned. There is a need for extensive medical investigations in childhood IBD, and even if very careful preparations are used, the investigations may be quite troublesome and psychologically painful for the children. It is extremely important to offer every child optimal psychological preparation before being investigated. This may appear obvious, but nevertheless it is important to emphasize it. The diagnosis of UC and CD in childhood is based upon the same set of investigations as adult patients. Upper (esophago-gastro-duodenoscopy) and lower (colonoscopy) endoscopies with biopsies are routinely used in children and essential to confirm the diagnosis. In addition, radiologic investigation of the small intestine is essential in the investigation. Blood tests are helpful, but cannot be used to confirm or exclude IBD in childhood. However, erythrocyte sedimentation rate, C-reactive protein, and orosomucoids in the serum are useful indicators of disease activity in UC as well as in CD in childhood .

Psychological and Psychiatric Issues

Recurrent Abdominal Pain

It is known from many studies that an organic etiology can be identified in 10 percent or less of children who report frequent abdominal pain (Graham, 1991). This leaves around 90 percent in whom no certain organic cause may be found. This group, with negative findings in the medical evaluation, are diagnosed as "recurrent abdominal pain" (RAP). By exclusion, these children are often assumed to have an emotional disturbance. It may be argued, however, that the absence of organic findings does not necessarily indicate the presence of a psychological disorder. The proportion between those with pain associated with psychiatric symptoms or disorders and those with so-called nonspecific or idiopathic pain is therefore uncertain. Different clinicians and researchers have found varying results concerning this matter. The majority of studies on this matter strongly suggest an association between RAP and emotional disorders. Although the hypothesis that children with RAP have emotional problems needs to be tested further, there is, however, increasing evidence to support this view (Crossley, 1982; Faull & Nicol, 1986). Children with RAP have been found to have higher levels of anxiety (Apley, 1975; Hodges, Kline, Barbero, & Flanery, 1985; Hodges, Kline, Barbero, & Woodruff, 1985; Wasserman, Whitington, & Rivara, 1988) and, to a lesser extent, depression (Hughes, 1984; Kashani, Barbero, & Bolander, 1981; Lesse, 1981) than community samples of healthy children. There are, however, studies available that in fact suggest a rather weak relationship between abdominal pain and psychiatric disorders (McGrath, Goodman, Firestone, Shipman, & Peters, 1983).

It is worth noting that the available studies have been done primarily on children seen by pediatric gastroenterologists in tertiary care settings. It is unclear whether psychiatric disorders will be as prevalent in community samples of RAP.

There are hitherto very few controlled studies in the area. In only a handful of studies have specific psychiatric diagnoses been assessed in children with RAP. In

a controlled study by Garber, Zeman, & Walker (1990), children with RAP were compared with children with an organic diagnosis for their abdominal pains and with healthy children. The results showed that children with RAP have more emotional symptoms than do healthy children. They particularly exhibit anxiety and depressive disorders. However, the children with organic abdominal disorders also had a significant degree of anxiety and depression that was not significantly different from that noted in the RAP group. Thus, the presence of emotional disorders may not be used to differentiate between so-called organic and non-organic abdominal pains.

RAP often occurs simultaneously with pain in other sites (Alfvén, 1993b). As an example, the co-occurrence of stomachache and headache among 10-year-old children is reported to be around 20 percent (Borge, Nordhagen, Moe, Botten, & Bakketeig, 1994).

The fact that different pains often exist concurrently leads to the question of whether there may be a general pain pattern in children that most often presents as RAP, but also often presents with other types of pain. This hypothesis is supported by findings that the pressure pain threshold is significantly lower in children with RAP compared with healthy controls (Alfvén, 1993a). This may indicate an increased pain sensitivity in the myofascial elements of the abdominal wall, as well as to muscular tension and tenderness in other muscles. It is therefore important in the assessment to establish whether the child has a more general pain syndrome or abdominal symptoms only.

The history should be taken very carefully and thoroughly. This is important for several reasons. Of primary importance is to reach an understanding of the social and emotional context in which the symptom occurs. Another reason is to convey to the child and the family that every possible aspect of the disorder is being taken into consideration. It is also well known that when psychosocial aspects are brought into discussion too late (e.g., after the medical investigation is completed), it is very hard to reach the family and discuss such matters. It is therefore much better to present the possibility of physical as well as psychosocial factors to the family from the very beginning, thus ensuring a sense of trust between the family and the doctor.

Details of the child's diet, sleep patterns, and bowel habits should be explored. The situations in which the symptoms occur should be mapped. The child as well as the parents are often unaware of possible connections between situations and symptoms. They seldom present a clear-cut picture of the symptom pattern at first. A pain diary may therefore be of great help in demonstrating the pattern of the symptoms. A simple registration, preferably done by the child, if mature enough, may be done in two to four weeks' time, registering the level of pain at certain intervals during the day. Four times a day usually works well. The child (and/or the parents) are also instructed to keep track of possible situations that may trigger the symptoms.

The assessment should also include such factors as family function, school performance, availability and adequacy of social interaction with peers, and the exploration of any anxiety about the meaning of the pain. An empathic communication with the child and the parents is necessary to convey a sense of interest and belief in the reality of the problem.

It is important to identify emotional distress in children with abdominal pain for several reasons. The history taking concerning psychiatric symptoms and problems may lead to important clues regarding the precipitation, predisposition to, or maintenance of the symptoms. It is also important to try to understand whether the symptoms themselves give rise to emotional distress. In both cases, the assessment of anxiety or depression increases the likelihood that these children will receive appropriate psychiatric treatment. There is also evidence that treating psychiatric symptoms in children with abdominal pain may also benefit the physical symptoms (Sanders, Shepherd, Cleghorn, & Woolford, 1994).

The psychological assessment may also be supported by standardized measures of psychological variables such as the Child Behavior Checklist (CBCL) (Achenbach, 1991a) and the Youth Self Report (YSR) (Achenbach, 1991b), or more specific instruments such as the Children's Depression Inventory (CDI) (Kovacs, 1982) or the State-Trait Anxiety Inventory for Children (STAIC) (Spielberger, 1973).

Inflammatory Bowel Disease

The unpleasantness of the symptoms of IBD is well recognized. Pains, bleeding, mucus discharge, and diarrhea are all connected with negative feelings and may also have an impact on social relations. It is not surprising that children and adolescents may feel ashamed of their disease due to the nature of its manifestations (Engström, 1992). It is therefore easy to understand how children with IBD become anxious or frightened, sad or depressed, angry or stubborn.

While it is relatively easy to recognize that a disease like IBD may have emotional sequelae like anxiety, depression, or despair, it is not generally understood that stress can aggravate or even play a part in the causality of the disease.

It is well established that children and adolescents with inflammatory bowel disease have high rates of psychiatric symptoms (Engström, 1992; Engström & Lindquist, 1991; Wood et al., 1987). Earlier studies stated that psychological factors had etiological importance (Grace & Wolff, 1951), but modern, controlled studies have not been able to replicate these findings. It has also been stated that IBD only affects certain personalities (McDermott & Finch, 1967). There is, however, no evidence in controlled studies that children with IBD have particular personality features (Lask, 1986).

The preponderance of controlled studies of children and adolescents with IBD find a high rate of psychiatric symptoms in this group. In one study, 56 percent of the children with IBD compared to 18 percent in the control group, had a psychiatric disorder, almost exclusively emotional disorders (Steinhausen & Kies, 1982). Engström (1992) found that 60 percent of the children and adolescents with IBD had a psychiatric disorder, predominantly depressive and anxiety disorders according to DSM-III-R criteria. Several other studies have found depressive disorders and lower self-esteem to be more common in the IBD group than in healthy control subjects (Burke et al., 1989a; Raymer, Weininger, & Hamilton, 1984). Obsessive-compulsive symptoms have also been found to be common (Burke et al., 1989b). Behavioral problems have been found to be significantly more common in children and adolescents with IBD compared to their siblings (Wood et al., 1987).

In a meta-analytic review of different chronic diseases, IBD seems to have the most profound effect on mental health of all medical diseases reviewed (Lavigne & Faier-Routman, 1992). In the absolute majority of studies, children with IBD have shown psychiatric disorders according to DSM-III-R in more than 50 percent of the cases. Since the IBD group differs significantly from children with other diseases, it seems clear that this is not a general effect of having a chronic disease, but rather is more specifically related to the specific clinical features of inflammatory bowel disease.

In most studies, there are no clear differences between UC and CD with respect to psychiatric disorders.

The question of how stress affects the course of the IBD should be assessed routinely. Stress is here used to mean an event or stimulus that is sufficiently intense to produce an emotional response of some kind. It is important to view this issue from the child's own point of view, since stresses for children can be subtle and far from clear from the perspective of others, especially adults. Stress in children and adolescents, however, has no generic attributes. This means that the conceptualization of stress is heavily based on individual factors.

The child's experiences of stress should therefore be reviewed individually in each case since the stress pattern is unique to the individual.

It has been reasonably clearly shown that stress can at least aggravate existing gastrointestinal pathology (Lask, 1986; MacDonald & Bouchier, 1980). In a study on adult patients with CD (Garrett, Brantley, Jones, & McKnight, 1990), a clear relation between daily stress and self-rated disease severity was shown. This was true even when the effects of major life events were controlled. There are no studies in children on this issue. It may be reasonable to believe that this can be true for children and adolescents. Efforts should therefore be made to periodically register the course of the disease in combination with registering daily stresses. The aim should be to identify how different kinds of stresses affect the disease in order to design models for stress management training specific to the individual patient.

The coping strategies used by the child with IBD should be explored in every case. According to Lazarus (1980), problem solving and regulation of emotional distress are the two major functions of coping, and coping makes the major difference in adaptational outcome in chronic diseases. A problem in assessing coping to date is the variability in the ways in which coping strategies have been categorized, thereby limiting the extent to which comparisons can be made across studies. One of the best inventories to date seems to be KIDCOPE (Spirito, Stark, & Tyc, 1989), which assesses the frequency and perceived efficacy of ten commonly used cognitive and behavioral strategies. It has been shown (Kinash, Fischer, Lukie, & Carr, 1993) that problem-oriented coping patterns usually are favorable to a preponderance of affect-oriented strategies.

TREATMENT STRATEGIES

Overview of Medical Management

RAP

There are no conclusive data supporting an effect of pharmacological agents on RAP. In some controlled studies fibers have been found to be useful (Feldman, McGrath, Hodgson, Ritter, & Shipman, 1985), but there are contradictory data on this point. Therefore no medicines are prescribed routinely to patients with RAP. If, on the other hand, the patient presents with additional symptoms, such as constipation or irritable colon, these conditions may require specific medication.

Inflammatory Bowel Disease

UC, unlike CD, can be cured by removing the colon. However, most patients of all ages with UC can be managed medically throughout their lives without operation. Both diseases are characterized by acute exacerbations and variable periods of remission. The aim of the therapy is twofold, to treat acute attacks effectively and to maintain remission.

Three key elements of the treatment can be recognized:

- Medical therapy, including pharmacological agents and nutritional support
- Surgical therapy
- Psychological intervention

Concerning medical management of IBD in children, some important factors are considered continuously:

- *Disease activity.* Is disease activity diminishing during the course of treatment? Several clinical indices of disease activity are used for follow up and evaluating the outcome of the treatment program, including the nutritional status.
- *Compliance with medication.* Some of the medicines may have pronounced side effects that have to be considered. Allergic reactions to medication may be seen, especially to sulfasalazine. Other agents may cause diarrhea. Corticosteroids are commonly used in the treatment of IBD during relapses. From the pediatric point of view, growth retardation is one major problem with corticosteroids. Therefore, the length of the treatment course is limited, or the medication is prescribed on an every other day regimen as much as possible. On the other hand, the child may not grow during clinical relapse, but may start gaining in height and weight as soon as the inflammatory activity begins to diminish, even if the child is still receiving steroids. Another problem with the steroids is that the child on steroids may experience muscle pains as well as abdominal pains. This clinically well-known dose-related side effect may affect the compliance among children.

Psychological side effects have been found to occur in children taking corticosteroids. Altered mood and negative feelings have been documented (Bender, Lerner, & Kollasch, 1988) in asthmatic children, and it seems that girls are more susceptible to these effects than boys (Bender, Lerner, & Poland, 1991). It is, however, noteworthy that emotional instability in children or their families predisposes the children to steroid-related psychologic problems (Bender et al., 1991). Psychiatric disturbances of a deeper kind are rarely seen in children, compared to adults, but there are case reports of hyperactivity, aggressiveness, uninhibited behavior, and impaired concentration (Meyboom, 1988). These reports have, however, most often been in response to inhaled budesonide. There are no reports of psychological steroid side effects in children with IBD and the use of steroids should not be precluded by the risk of psychological side effects. However, enhanced recognition of this aspect of steroid therapy will lead to optimal therapy.

- *Development.* One of the main purposes of medical treatment is to promote normal development from both somatic and psychological points of view, and to achieve normal sexual maturation.
- *Psychosocial adjustment to the disease.* Treatment is designed to control the symptoms, to secure a normalization of growth and development as much as possible, and to prevent relapses. Another key purpose is to help the child adjust psychosocially to the disease as much as possible. In order to accomplish this, it is often wise to establish a therapeutic team consisting of various experts, such as a pediatrician, pediatric surgeon, nutritionist/dietician, psychologist, psychiatrist, and social worker.

Pharmacological treatment is a key element in the medical management of IBD in children (Korelitz, 1989; Lake, 1988), with different strategies depending on type and severity of illness.

- *Mild ulcerative colitis.* The first pharmacological agent to be recommended is oral sulfasalazine, which has documented efficacy in controlling disease and preventing relapse. Unabsorbable salicylates have been formulated, but so far the experience with these new preparations in childhood is limited. Many authors advocate regular use of folate supplementation for children receiving sulfasalazine. Topical corticosteroid enemas are administered at bedtime for a 2-week period if there is rectal involvement of the disease. Retention may be improved with the use of a foam formulation.
- *Moderate ulcerative colitis.* Corticosteroids such as oral prednisolone are used initially in addition to sulfasalazine. It is recommended to start with a high dose of prednisolone, usually as a single morning dose.

The majority of children will respond within 2 weeks. After clinical response, the dose of steroids is tapered slowly and finished within 8 weeks if possible.
- *Severe ulcerative colitis.* Hospitalization is required, with intensive daily medical supervision to recognize early signs of toxic megacolon. Intravenous administration of corticosteroids is needed. It is not possible to predict which children will respond to aggressive medical intervention and avoid colectomy. Immunosuppressive medications have been used in children with intractable disease, especially as adjuncts to steroid therapy. Although the number of reports in childhood is limited, azathioprine and its active metabolite 6-mercaptopurine have been used successfully. Applications in IBD suggest that more than 2 months of therapy are required to demonstrate clinical efficacy.
- *Remission therapy in ulcerative colitis.* Children with extensive colitis in sustained remission should continue to take sulfasalazine for at least 5 years with careful monitoring of growth, development, and laboratory parameters (Meyers & Sachar, 1990). After 5 years of disease, endoscopic surveillance with colonoscopy on a yearly basis is warranted. Routines and recommendations for endoscopic follow-up have not been established in children with distal colitis.
- *Crohn's Disease.* Sulfasalazine is usually not effective in small bowel disease, but has been documented to be useful in inducing remission in patients with colonic involvement. The effect of alternative preparations of 5-aminosalicylic not linked to sulphapyridine has not been sufficiently tested. Clinical studies are ongoing, aiming to elucidate whether these new preparations are effective in children with CD involving the small intestine as well as the colon. Prednisolone has been shown to be the most effective form of therapy in small bowel and ileocolonic disease, whereas the combination of prednisolone and sulfasalazine may be more effective in colonic disease.

Metronidazole has been demonstrated to be effective, especially in perianal disease and Crohn's colitis, and may be recommended in children if the disease is not responding to sulfasalazine. Immunosuppressive agents such as azathioprine and 6-mercaptopurine have also been used in children especially if there is involvement of the perianum or fistulae. These agents sometimes allow a reduction in the steroid dose. Because of the potential side effects, these kind of therapies are recommended in selected cases of childhood CD not suited for operation. There are no convincing data on the beneficial effects of medical maintenance therapy in childhood

CD. However, some children have a continuous inflammatory activity that partially responds to medication and thus motivates prolonged medication therapy.

Nutritional treatment (support) in IBD in children is critical. The importance of nutritional rehabilitation and nutritional therapy in IBD in childhood is increasingly recognized, and nutrition therapy should be considered as a complement to the pharmacological therapy (Lake, 1988; Motil & Grand, 1985).

There is considerable data to document the effect of nutritional support in CD. Studies have demonstrated the beneficial effect of nutrition in decreasing disease symptoms, resolving inflammatory masses, closing fistulae, and reducing postoperative morbidity.

It is more difficult to evaluate the nutrition factor per se in UC in childhood. It is never possible to predict which patient with UC will respond to aggressive medical treatment including nutrition support. It is important to supervise and follow the nutritional status in a child with IBD in order to assure optimal growth and development. Oral supplementations should be done to provide at least 140 percent of the recommended daily allowance for protein and energy. This is, of course, a major problem because the diseased child often has a poor appetite. Often these children need a nasogastric silastic catheter to provide enough food. Most children tolerate nasogastric feeding through catheters very well, and some children use this method only during the night.

If it is not possible to use the enteral route for nutrition, the child may receive total parenteral nutrition intravenously. Total parenteral nutrition is used to decrease disease activity in chronic symptoms unresponsive to conventional therapy, partial bowel obstruction, growth failure, severe perianal disease, or fistulae.

Psychological and Behavioral Treatments

RAP

The overall goal for treatment in RAP is primarily to keep the pain confined as a "simple syndrome" (Barr, 1983). This means that even if the child continues to experience pain, the symptoms should not extend into the rest of daily life, nor should they interfere with daily functioning in any profound way.

This means that in the absence of a definite physical etiology, treatment must be directed toward restoring normal daily functioning despite pain symptoms. In order to make this possible, the child and the family should be assured that the child will be followed regularly and that sufficient medical surveillance will be undertaken. Such assurance almost always makes further medical investigations unnecessary unless specifically indicated. If the family still questions the validity of the diagnosis, a second opinion should be addressed.

It is very important to elucidate the pattern of pain-triggering situations and stress that may influence the symptom presentation. Particular attention should be directed toward what happens when the pain occurs. This includes activity before and during the painful episode, the use of medication, and coping strategies used by the child. If environmental factors that reinforce the symptom are identified, these should be addressed, with effort being directed toward minimizing any gain associated with the symptom.

Stressful situations that the pain allows the child to avoid should be identified. It is then necessary to determine whether the best approach initially is to allow the child to avoid such situations, or whether the goal should be to develop stress management skills that make the child less vulnerable to stress. In general, the latter approach tends to be superior. Unfortunately, there is a relative lack of treatment studies on this topic.

The RAP patient may also be assessed regarding the coping responses used. The style of coping response has been shown to mediate the impact of pain (Siegel & Smith, 1989). Active coping responses, like trying to function despite pain or to distract oneself from pain, are connected to an increased sense of control in the child, whereas passive coping responses, like depending on others for help or restricting activities, more often may lead to social withdrawal and greater pain (Flor, Birhaumer, & Rudy, 1990; Sanders et al., 1994; Siegel et al., 1989). Despite the paucity of controlled research studies in the RAP area, clinical experience and research from other pediatric pain syndromes suggest that children with RAP may have inadequate coping styles and feel that they have little control over their symptoms (Branson & Craig, 1988; Dunne-Geier, McGrath, Rourke, Latter, & D'Astous, 1986).

Clinical case reports (Linton, 1986) have suggested that behavior techniques aimed at training coping skills in children may be useful. Other studies (Miller & Kratochwill, 1979; Sank & Biglan, 1974) have shown that intervention programs aimed at modifying the social consequences of RAP are effective in reducing the symptoms. Systematic cognitive-behavioral therapy for RAP, including training in self-management skills and training the parents to prompt and reinforce children's use of their skills has been demonstrated to be successful (Sanders et al., 1989). The long-term effects of the treatment, however, were not evaluated. A recent controlled study (Sanders et al., 1994) has shown cognitive-behavioral family intervention to be superior over standard pediatric care with regard to pain elimination and relapse prevention. This program included a comprehensive functional analysis of the child's behavior and family interactions, teaching active skills training by instructions, modeling, rehearsal and feedback, and homework assignments that train parents to implement behavior change strategies with children in their home.

It is also important to assess the parents' own needs for help. Several studies have found higher levels of anxiety and depression in mothers of children with RAP than in mothers of children without RAP, and somewhat more anxiety, although not depression, in the fathers of children with RAP (Hodges, Kline, Barbero, & Flanery, 1985; Hodges, Kline, Barbero, & Woodruff, 1985; Walker & Greene, 1989; Zuckerman, Stevenson, & Bailey, 1987). It has also been found that approximately half the children in one RAP sample had one or more first-degree relatives who met criteria for somatization disorder (Routh & Ernst, 1984).

These findings may be interpreted in several ways. First, the distress of the parents may be an effect of having a disturbed child. On the other hand, the symptoms of the parents may play a causal role in the symptoms of the child either through genetic transmission, modeling, or through parent-child interaction. In all likelihood, the relationship between parental symptoms and the child's difficulties is complex, reciprocal, and multidetermined.

This fact highlights the importance of involving the parents in the treatment, preferably by using family therapy techniques concurrent with medical surveillance. There are hitherto few studies of the effects of systematic family therapy intervention programs in the treatment of RAP.

IBD

Treatment of inflammatory bowel disease should always include both medical and psychological approaches (Prugh, 1983). Careful explanation by the pediatrician of the joint medical-psychological approach is important in helping to reduce stigma and in preventing the family from feeling "blamed" for the illness. It is important to convey to the family that the psychological approach aims at two goals. The first is to provide support for the child and the parents in coping with a serious disease. The second is to map, understand, and alleviate stresses that may hinder recovery or cause exacerbations of the disease.

It is of utmost importance to create an atmosphere that permits both the child and the parents to express their concerns about the physical and the psychological aspects of the disease. It has been shown that children with IBD commonly have difficulties in expressing emotions (Engström, 1992). It is unlikely that they will share their worries and concerns with the medical staff in the beginning. As time goes by, a close and empathic relationship between the medical team and the patient may enhance the likelihood of emotional expression.

It is a common experience that children with IBD show a tendency to deny their problems, both with regard to the symptoms of the disease and with regard to coexisting psychological problems (Bruce, 1986). They may evidence a dissimulating style in communicating with their doctor. A high level of sensitivity regarding the message from the patient is therefore needed. Careful observation of non-verbal communications can help in the recognition of difficulties previously unexpressed (Lask, 1986).

It is important to see the child alone in order to make psychological communication easier. It is also important to educate the child about the disease, since a well-informed child may be more likely to develop active coping strategies. The problems that may be elicited from such an approach can be handled in several ways. The coping strategies that the child uses should be developed, and if they are found to be inappropriate, they should be discussed with the child. Cognitive-behavioral training has not been used systematically in this disease group, but the general effects of such training in other diseases suggests that it could be of good use also in IBD.

If the child is found to be overanxious, self-relaxation techniques should be taught in order to lower the anxiety level. Other psychotherapeutic strategies, including cognitive behavioral therapy, may also be helpful.

Depressive disorders are commonly encountered in children and adolescents with IBD. These problems may be detectable at the beginning of the disease, but more often develop after some period of time, perhaps when the child realizes that they will have to live with a chronic disease. There are some indications that this psychiatric comorbidity is more pronounced in cases with an intermittent type of IBD compared to chronic continuous types (Engström & Lindquist, 1991). When the course of the disease is unpredictable, the patients may have great difficulties in adapting accordingly. A continuous type of disease, however, may actually enhance the possibilities of a sound adaptation, despite the severe physical symptoms

The depressive disorder should be dealt with psychotherapeutically, either with the child or with the whole family, depending on the kind of problems envisaged. In certain cases, especially those that are refractory to psychotherapy, psychotropic medication such as antidepressants should be considered.

Pharmacological Treatments

If the assessment of the child yields evidence of any associated psychiatric disorder, such as depression or anxiety, it is necessary to give appropriate treatment for the disorder. In some cases, this may include pharmacological treatment with antidepressants or anxiolytic agents.

The results of treating adults having Irritable Bowel Syndrome (IBS) with antidepressant medication have been somewhat encouraging. This has led to the question of whether RAP in children may be treated with antidepressants. There is as of yet no scientific proof that this is beneficial, but further studies may give more clues to whether antidepressant medication has any place in the therapeutic arsenal concerning RAP.

CASE ILLUSTRATION

Clinical Presentation

A Swedish boy, the youngest of three children, appeared as an outpatient in the pediatric clinic, at the age of 8 years, with symptoms and signs that were compatible with intestinal inflammation.

His birth and perinatal period was completely without problems. He was weaned at the age of 3 months. His psychomotor development was normal and he began to walk at the age of 11 months. There were no feeding problems in infancy, nor any signs of colic. During childhood, he had been completely healthy with no evidence of intestinal or other disorders. There were no data indicating such disorders in his family or in his first- or second-degree relatives.

Psychologically, he was described by his parents as a normal child, with no clear signs of psychiatric problems or symptoms. He was, however, very ambitious and was very self-demanding concerning achievements in school as well as in sports. There were no negative life events in the period preceding the start of the disease.

When he came to the hospital, he complained of abdominal pains intermittently, with periumbilical localization and sometimes radiation to the right fossa. He had lost weight, 10 lbs during the last two months, and he had experienced loose stools with watery and mucoid

characteristics for one week. The boy was tired and his appetite was poor. His height was normal for age and his weight was 59.2 lbs (i.e., 1 SD below Swedish standards). He looked pale and appeared as an unhappy child. There was slight diffuse abdominal tenderness.

Assessment Findings

Laboratory investigations revealed normal blood chemistry including electrolytes, liver values, creatinine, and urea. Hemoglobin and leukocytes were normal. Phase reactants were elevated with sedimentation rate 40 mm/h and elevated orosomucoids. The platelets were increased in numbers (538×10^9/l). The serum albumin was low (34 g/l). There was no evidence of infection. Fecal cultures as well as parasitic investigations were negative. Rectoscopy, colonoscopy including multiple biopsies, and small intestinal radiological investigation documented the diagnosis of Crohn's disease, with extensive small intestinal involvement, but without obstruction. In addition, small mucosal lesions were documented endoscopically in the cecum and colon ascendens. These lesions are frequently encountered endoscopically in CD. In addition, microscopic changes, typical for CD, were found in rectal biopsies, with chronic inflammation in the rectal mucosa and epithelioid cell granulomas.

In conclusion, the boy was diagnosed having Crohn's disease involving large segments of the small intestine as well as segments of colon and rectum. There was no evidence of extraintestinal involvement.

Treatment Selection and Course

The boy received medical therapy with sulfasalazine and steroids and the disease went into remission. Both medicines could be tapered when clinical as well as laboratory investigations had been normalized. In addition, he received nutritional support in order to provide optimal amounts of energy, proteins, and other nutritional components. Great care was taken to ensure the boy and his parents an optimal psychosocial caretaking. Continuity of medical surveillance was ensured and plenty of time was used to educate and inform both the boy and his parents about his disease. The clinical course was characterized by relapsing phases with diarrhea, weight loss, and abdominal pains, and the boy needed to be treated in the hospital 3 times during the coming years. The disease could, however, be brought into remission every time with the help of aggressive intravenous pharmacological and nutritional therapy. In addition he had minor periods of deterioration when he could be treated as an out-patient. Between the relapses, his general condition was acceptable and the laboratory values were normal. His growth, height increase, and pubertal development were normal.

Initially, the boy was unhappy and sometimes angry at having to live with this disease. He often asked his mother the "why me?" question. Very soon, however, he tried in every way to avoid speaking of the disease. He tried to live a completely normal social life. He even exaggerated his "normality" and wanted to participate in sports and other activities to a large extent, even when he was not feeling well.

The boy appeared to develop psychologically within the normal framework, but he was often considered depressive and anxious. He never complained to the pediatrician about any gastrointestinal symptoms, not even when objective medical findings clearly demonstrated an active disease period. He was found to dissimulate to a large extent and tried to play a healthy role, even when he was seriously afflicted with the disease.

When he was sixteen years of age, he was assessed more extensively with regard to psychiatric aspects by partaking in a research project. Several questionnaires and inventories were used, both with the boy and with his parents. The boy and his mother were interviewed in depth concerning the disease and general mental health.

On the CBCL (Child Behavior Checklist), the mother indicated behavior problems, mostly in the area of internalizing symptoms. The mean results of the findings from healthy control groups are given next to the patients' scores in parentheses in order to provide some means of comparison. The mother scored a total of 22 points on the CBCL for him (8 pts.), consisting of 14 pts. for internalizing symptoms and 8 pts. for externalizing. On the CDI (Child Depression Inventory), he scored 10 points (5 pts.), indicating a relatively high level of depressive symptoms. On the RCMAS (Revised Children's Manifest Anxiety Scale), he showed quite low scores, 3 points (4.5 pts.), but the built-in "lie scale" showed 7 points (3 pts.), which indicated a high degree of denial in the answers. The Frisk well-being scale (Frisk, 1986), which was given to both the boy and his mother, showed quite different answers from the two respondents. The boy indicated a normal degree of general well-being, whereas the mother indicated a quite low degree of well-being, especially in the areas of self-esteem and social competence. This is a common finding in this diagnostic group, which is not common in groups with other chronic medical conditions. The most

probable explanation of this finding may be that because of the denial of the disease and its practical implications in everyday life, the children don't admit any psychological problems, whereas the mothers often report such problems.

In the interview, the boy was quite reluctant to talk about his disease. He was hard to interview, especially concerning emotional areas. He gave short and concrete answers and showed signs of apparent alexithymia. This corresponds with the patient's denial, which can be an adaptive way of handling the initial diagnosis, but which may be negative for the child's further development over time. Using the CAS (Child Assessment Schedule) (Hodges, 1985), the boy was found to have a major depressive disorder.

The parents completed the SCL-90 (Symptom Checklist-90) (Derogatis, Lipman, & Covi, 1973) instrument as a measure of their mental health. The mother scored 49 points (17 pts.), with high scores in the depressive subscale. The father scored 0 points (22 pts.), which may indicate a superior mental health or a denial pattern, just like the son. In the ISSI (Interview Schedule for Social Interaction) (Henderson, Byrne, & Duncan-Jones, 1982), both parents indicated a well-functioning social network, both with regard to social interaction and to attachment.

Termination and Follow-Up

The boy needed careful medical follow-up with close and frequent laboratory and clinical investigations, including intestinal investigations on a regular basis. He also received psychosocial support in order to develop good coping strategies with regard to his chronic medical condition.

Our conclusion of the psychological findings is that the boy showed signs of a depressive disorder. His own perception of his mental health was, however, quite different from our findings. The high degree of persisting denial is an indication of a crisis process that has not been worked through adequately. The depression may therefore be a consequence of this denial process. The optimal treatment for this boy was considered to be a respectful, supportive therapy in which his perceptions of his disease were thoroughly worked through.

Despite his psychological status, the course of the disease has so far been rather benign. The case, however, illustrates well the fact that having a chronic medical condition like CD is as much a state of mind as a state of the intestine.

SUMMARY

Gastrointestinal disorders are common in childhood. Such disorders frequently affect both somatic and psychological development. Gastrointestinal symptoms in the absence of evidence of physical disease are also very common in childhood. In this chapter, two gastrointestinal disorders, recurrent abdominal pain (RAP) and inflammatory bowel disease (ulcerative colitis and Crohn's disease) are described as representative disorders that highlight major clinical problems encountered in pediatric gastroenterology.

Recurrent abdominal pain (RAP) refers to a chronic abdominal pain with no demonstrated underlying physical disease. It is by far the most common gastrointestinal disorder in childhood. Between 10 and 20 percent of schoolchildren experience RAP. It may occur from ages 3 to 16, with an incidence peak around 9 to 12 years of age. The diagnosis should be based on a comprehensive medical and psychological assessment and considered as a positive diagnosis, not just a diagnosis of exclusion. In 10 percent or less of children with frequent abdominal pain, an organic etiology may be identified. RAP often occurs simultaneously with pain in other sites. Children with RAP may have a significantly lower pain threshold than other children.

It is important to assess children with RAP medically and psychologically simultaneously. There is no specific medical treatment of RAP. Treatment must be directed toward restoring normal daily functioning despite pain symptoms. Pain-triggering situations and stress should be elucidated, and whenever possible, alleviated. Behavior techniques aimed at training adequate coping skills may be useful, as well as cognitive-behavioral therapy, including training in self-management skills. It is also important to identify deeper emotional distress in these children. Children with RAP often have high levels of anxiety and depression, for which they may need specific psychiatric treatment.

Inflammatory bowel diseases (IBD) are not frequently encountered, but when they do occur, they often present with an extremely complex somatic and psychiatric clinical picture. The incidence is from 2 to 5 per 100,000 children. The diagnostic procedures, which may be troublesome and psychologically painful, include upper and/or lower endoscopies with biopsies together with radiologic investigations. IBD is medically treated with a combination of pharmacological agents, nutritional support, and sometimes surgical therapy.

Children with IBD have extremely high rates of psychiatric comorbidity. In several studies, around 60 percent have been found to have a psychiatric disorder, predominantly depressive and anxiety disorders. It has been shown that stress can aggravate the existing psychopathology. The patients should therefore be given stress management training. Measures directed toward training adequate coping strategies may also be helpful. Children and adolescents with IBD may show a general tendency toward denying their symptoms and disease. This is probably due to the characteristics of the disease. Depressive disorders should be dealt with psychotherapeutically, in some cases together with adequate antidepressant medication.

Treatment of IBD should always include both medical and psychological approaches. A multidisciplinary team is mandatory for this comprehensive treatment design.

REFERENCES

Achenbach, T. (1991a). *Manual for the Child Behavior Checklist/4-18 and 1991 Profile*. Burlington, VT: University of Vermont Department of Psychiatry.

Achenbach, T. (1991b). *Manual for the Youth Self Report and 1991 Profile*. Burlington, VT: University of Vermont Department of Psychiatry.

Alfvén, G. (1993a). The pressure pain threshold (PPT) of certain muscles in children suffering from recurrent abdominal pain of non-organic origin. An algometric study. *Acta Pædiatrica, 82,* 481–483.

Alfvén, G. (1993b). The covariation of common psychosomatic symptoms among children from socioeconomically differing residential areas. An epidemiological study. *Acta Pædiatrica, 82,* 484–487.

Apley, J., & Naish, N. (1958). Recurrent abdominal pains: a field survey of 1000 school children. *Archives of Diseases in Childhood, 33,* 165–170.

Apley, J. (1975). *The child with abdominal pains.* (2nd ed.). Oxford: Blackwell Scientific Publications.

Barr, R. (1983). Recurrent abdominal pain. In C. W. Levine, A. C. Crocker, & R. T. Gross (Eds.), *Developmental and behavioral pediatrics*. Philadelphia: W.B. Saunders Company.

Bender, B., Lerner, J., & Kollasch, E. (1988). Mood and memory changes in asthmatic children receiving corticosteroids. *Journal of the American Academy of Child and Adolescent Psychiatry, 27,* 720–725.

Bender, B., Lerner, J., & Poland, J. (1991). Association between corticosteroids and psychologic change in hospitalized asthmatic children. *Annals of Allergy, 66,* 414–419.

Berger, M., Gribetz, D., & Korelitz, B. (1975). Growth retardation in children with UC: the effect of medical and surgical therapy. *Pediatrics, 55,* 459–467.

Borge, A., Nordhagen, R., Moe, B., Botten, G., & Bakketeig, L. (1994). Prevalence and persistence of stomach ache and headache among children. Follow-up of a cohort of Norwegian children from 4 to 10 years of age. *Acta Pædiatrica, 83*, 433–437.

Branson, S., & Craig, K. (1988). Children's spontaneous strategies for coping with pain: a review of the literature. *Canadian Journal of Behavioral Science, 20*, 402–412.

Bruce, T. (1986). Emotional sequelae of chronic inflammatory bowel disease in children and adolescents. *Clinics in Gastroenterology, 15*, 89–104.

Burbige, E., Huang, S., & Bayless, T. (1975). Clinical manifestations of Crohn's disease in children and adolescents. *Pediatrics, 55*, 866–871.

Burke, P., Meyer, V., Kocoshis, S., Orenstein, D., Chandra, R., Nord, D., Sauer, J., & Cohen, E. (1989a). Depression and anxiety in pediatric inflammatory bowel disease and cystic fibrosis. *Journal of the American Academy of Child and Adolescent Psychiatry, 28*, 948–951.

Burke, P., Meyer, V., Kocoshis, S., Orenstein, D., Chandra, R., & Sauer, J. (1989b). Obsessive-compulsive symptoms in childhood inflammatory bowel disease and cystic fibrosis. *Journal of the American Academy of Child and Adolescent Psychiatry, 28*, 525–527.

Calkins, B., Lilienfeld, A., Garland, C. F., & Mendeloff, A. (1984). Trends in incidence rates of UC and CD. *Digestive Diseases and Science, 29*, 913–920.

Chong, S., Blackshaw, A., Morson, B., Williams, C., & Walker-Smith, J. (1986). Prospective study of colitis in infancy and early childhood. *Journal of Pediatric Gastroenterology and Nutrition, 5*, 352–358.

Christensen, M., & Mortensen, O. (1975). Long-term prognosis in children with recurrent abdominal pain. *Archives of Diseases in Childhood, 50*, 110–114.

Crossley, R. (1982). Hospital admissions for abdominal pains in childhood. *Journal of Research in Social Medicine, 75*, 772–776.

Derogatis, L., Lipman, R., & Covi, L. (1973). SCL-90: An outpatient psychiatric rating scale. *Psychopharmacological Bulletin, 9*, 13–28.

Dunne-Geier, B., McGrath, P., Rourke, B., Latter, J., & D'Astous, J. (1986). Adolescent chronic pain: the ability to cope. *Pain, 26*, 23–32.

Engström, I., & Lindquist, B. (1991). Inflammatory bowel disease in children and adolescents: a somatic and psychiatric investigation. *Acta Pædiatrica Scandinavica, 80*, 640–647.

Engström, I. (1992). Mental health and psychosocial functioning in children and adolescents with inflammatory bowel disease: a comparison with children having other chronic illnesses and with healthy children. *Journal of Child Psychology and Psychiatry, 33*, 563–582.

Faull, C., & Nicol, A. (1986). Abdominal pains in six-year olds: an epidemiological study in a new town. *Journal of Child Psychology and Psychiatry, 27*, 251–260.

Feldman, W., McGrath, P., Hodgson, C., Ritter, H., & Shipman, R. (1985). The use of dietary fiber in the management of simple, idiopathic, recurrent, abdominal pain. Results in a prospective, double blind, randomized, controlled trial. *American Journal of Diseases in Children, 139*, 1216–1218.

Flor, H., Birhaumer, N., & Rudy, D. (1990). The psychobiology of chronic pain. *Advances in Behavioral Research and Therapy, 12*, 47–84.

Frisk, M. (1986). *The Frisk well-being scale for children.* Uppsala, Sweden: Uppsala University Department of Child and Adolescent Psychiatry (in Swedish).

Garber, J., Zeman, J., & Walker, L. (1990). Recurrent abdominal pain in children: Psychiatric diagnoses and parental psychopathology. *Journal of the American Academy of Child and Adolescent Psychiatry, 29*, 648–656.

Garrett, V., Brantley, P., Jones, G., & McKnight, G. (1991). The relation between daily stress and CD. *Journal of Behavioral Medicine, 14*, 87–96.

Grace, W., & Wolff, H. (1951). Treatment of UC. *Journal of the American Medical Association, 146*, 981–987.

Graham, P. (1991). *Child psychiatry: A developmental approach.* (2nd ed.). Oxford: Oxford University Press.

Henderson, S., Byrne, D., & Duncan-Jones, P. (1982). *Neurosis and the social environment.* Sydney: Academic Press.

Hildebrand, H., Fredrikzon, B., Holmqvist, L., Kristiansson, B., & Lindquist, B. (1991). Chronic inflammatory bowel disease in children and adolescents in Sweden. *Journal of Pediatric Gastroenterology and Nutrition, 13*, 293–297.

Hodges, K. (1985). *Manual for the Child Assessment Schedule.* Columbia, MO: University of Missouri.

Hodges, K., Kline, J., Barbero, G., & Flanery, R. (1985). Depressive symptoms in children with recurrent abdominal pain and in their families. *Journal of Pediatrics, 107*, 622–626.

Hodges, K., Kline, J., Barbero, G., & Woodruff, C. (1985). Anxiety in children with recurrent abdominal pain and their parents. *Psychosomatics, 26*, 859–866.

Hughes, M. (1984). Recurrent abdominal pain and childhood depression: Clinical observations of 23 children and their families. *American Journal of Orthopsychiatry, 54*, 146–155.

Kashani, J., Barbero, G., & Bolander, F. (1981). Depression in hospitalized pediatric patients. *Journal of the American Academy of Child and Adolescent Psychiatry, 20*, 123–134.

Kelts, D., & Grand, G. (1980). Inflammatory bowel disease in children and adolescents. *Current Problems in Pediatrics, 10*, 1–40.

Kinash, R., Fischer, D., Lukie, B., & Carr, T. (1993). Coping patterns and related characteristics in patients with IBD. *Rehabilitation and Nursing, 18*, 12–19.

Kirschner, B., & Sutton, M. (1986). Somatomedin C-levels in growth-impaired children and adolescents with inflammatory bowel disease. *Gastroenterology, 91*, 830–836.

Korelitz, B. (1989). Immunosuppressive therapy. In T. Bayless (Ed.), *Current management of inflammatory bowel disease* Philadelphia: B.C. Decker.

Kovacs, M. (1982). *The Children's Depression Inventory: A self-rated depression scale for school-aged youngsters.* Pittsburgh, PA: University of Pittsburgh.

Lake, M. (1988). Recognition and management of inflammatory bowel disease in children and adolescents. *Current Problems in Pediatrics, 18*, 377–437.

Lask, B. (1986). Psychological aspects of inflammatory bowel disease. *Wiener Klinische Wochenschrift, 98*, 544–547.

Lavigne J., & Faier-Routman, J. (1992). Psychological adjustment to pediatric physical disorders: a meta-analytic review. *Journal of Pediatric Psychology, 17*, 133–157.

Lazarus, R. (1980). The stress and coping paradigm. In R. J. Bond (Ed.), *Competence and coping during adulthood* (pp. 28–74). Hanover, NH: University Press of New England.

Lebenthal, E. (1984). *Chronic diarrhea in children.* New York: Raven Press.

Lesse, S. (1981). Hypochondriacal and psychosomatic disorders masking depression in adolescents. *American Journal of Psychotherapy, 33*, 356–367.

Liebman, M. (1978). Recurrent abdominal pains in children. A retrospective survey of 119 children. *Clinical Pediatrics, 1*, 548–551.

Lindquist, B., Järnerot, G., & Wickbom, G. (1984). Clinical and epidemiological aspects of CD in children and adolescents. *Scandinavian Journal of Gastroenterology, 19*, 502–506.

Linton, S. (1986). A case study of the behavioural treatment of chronic stomach pain in a child. *Behavior Change, 3*, 70–73.

Lundby, L., Sandbæk, A., & Juul, S. (1990). Recurrent abdominal pain in schoolchildren aged 9–12 years. *Ugeskrift for Læger, 152*, 2851–2854.

MacDonald, A., & Bouchier, I. (1980). Non-organic gastrointestinal illness: A medical and psychiatric study. *British Journal of Psychiatry, 136*, 276–283.

McDermott, J., & Finch, S. (1967). UC in children. Re-

assessment of a dilemma. *Journal of the American Academy of Child Psychiatry, 6*, 512–525.

McGrath, P., Goodman, J., Firestone, P., Shipman, R., & Peters, S. (1983). Recurrent abdominal pain. A psychogenic disorder? *Archives of Diseases in Childhood, 58*, 888–890.

Meyboom, R. (1988). Budesonide and psychic side effects. *Annals of Internal Medicine, 109*, 683.

Meyers, S., & Sachar, D. (1990). Medical management of CD. *Hepatogastroenterology, 37*, 42–55.

Michener, W., & Wyllie, R. (1990). Management of children and adolescents with inflammatory bowel disease. *Medical Clinics of North America, 74*, 103–117.

Miller, A., & Kratochwill, T. (1979). Reduction of frequent stomach complaints by time out. *Behavioral Therapy, 10*, 211–218.

Motil, K., & Grand, R. (1985). Nutritional management of inflammatory bowel disease. *Pediatric Clinics of North America, 32*, 447–469.

Motil, K., & Grand, R. (1987). UC and CD in children. *Pediatrics in Review, 9*, 109–120.

Oberlander, T., & Rappaport, L. (1993). Recurrent abdominal pain during childhood. *Pediatrics in Review, 14*, 313–319.

Prugh, D. (1983). *The psychosocial aspects of pediatrics.* Philadelphia: Lea & Febiger.

Raymer, D., Weininger, O., & Hamilton, J. (1984). Psychological problems in children with abdominal pain. *Lancet, I*, 439–440.

Routh, D., & Ernst, A. (1984). Somatization disorder in relatives of children and adolescents with functional abdominal pain. *Journal of Pediatric Psychology, 9*, 427–437.

Sanders, M., Rebgetz, M., Morrison, M., Bor, W., Gordon, A., Dadds, M., & Shepherd, R. (1989). Cognitive-behavioral treatment of recurrent nonspecific abdominal pain in children: An analysis of generalization, and maintenance side effects. *Journal of Consulting and Clinical Psychology, 57*, 294–300.

Sanders, M., Shepherd, R., Cleghorn, G., & Woolford, H. (1994). The treatment of recurrent abdominal pain in children: A controlled comparison of cognitive-behavioral family intervention and standard pediatric care. *Journal of Consulting and Clinical Psychology, 62*, 306–314.

Sank, L., & Biglan, A. (1974). Operant treatment of a case of recurrent abdominal pain in a 10-year-old boy. *Behavior Therapy, 5*, 677–681.

Siegel, L., & Smith, K. (1989). Children's strategies for coping with pain. *Pediatrician, 16*, 110–118.

Snyder, J., & Merson, M. (1982). The magnitude of the global problem of acute diarrheal disease: A review of active surveillance data. *Bulletin of the WHO, 60,* 605–613.

Spielberger, C. (1973). *Manual for the State-Trait Anxiety Inventory for Children.* Palo Alto, CA: Consulting Psychologists Press.

Spirito, A., Stark, L., & Tyc, V. (1989). Common coping strategies employed by children with chronic illness. *Newsletter of the Society of Pediatric Psychology, 13,* 3–8.

Steinhausen, H., & Kies, H. (1982). Comparative studies of UC and CD in children and adolescents. *Journal of Child Psychology and Psychiatry, 23,* 33–42.

Stevenson, J., Simpson, J., & Bailey, V. (1988). Research note: Recurrent headaches and stomachaches in preschool children. *Journal of Child Psychology and Psychiatry, 29,* 897–900.

Stone, R., & Barbero, G. (1970). Recurrent abdominal pain in childhood. *Pediatrics, 45,* 732–738.

Sullivan, P., Thoma, J., Wright, D., Neale, G., Eastham, E., Corah, T., Lloyd-Evans, N., & Greenwood, B. (1990). Helicobacter pylori in Gambian children with chronic diarrhoea and malnutrition. *Archives of Diseases in Childhood, 65,* 189–191.

Walker, A., Durie, P., Hamilton, R., Walker-Smith, J., & Watkins, J. (1991). *Pediatric gastrointestinal disease.* Philadelphia: B.C. Decker.

Walker, L., & Greene, J. (1989). Children with recurrent abdominal pain and their parents: More somatic complaints, anxiety, and depression than other patient families? *Journal of Pediatric Psychology, 14,* 231–243.

Wasserman, A., Whitington, P., & Rivara, F. (1988). Psychogenic basis for abdominal pain in children and adolescents. *Journal of the American Academy of Child and Adolescent Psychiatry, 27,* 179–184.

Webster, R., DiPalma, J., & Gremse, D. (1995). Lactose maldigestion and recurrent abdominal pain in children. *Digestive Diseases and Sciences, 40,* 1506–1510.

Wewer, V., Christiansen, K., Andersen, L., Henriksen, F., Hart Hansen, J., Tvede, M., & Krasilnikoff, P. (1994). Helicobacter pylori infection in children with recurrent abdominal pain. *Acta Paediatrica, 83,* 1276–1281.

Wood, B., Watkins, J., Boyle, J., Nogueira, J., Zimand, E., & Carroll, L. (1987). Psychological functioning in children with CD and ulcerative colitis: Implications for models of psychobiological interaction. *Journal of the American Academy of Child and Adolescent Psychiatry, 26,* 774–781.

Zuckerman, B., Stevenson, J., & Bailey, V. (1987). Stomachaches and headaches in a community sample of preschool children. *Pediatrics, 79,* 677–682.

CHAPTER 10

NEUROLOGICAL DISORDERS

Wun Jung Kim
Michael P. Carey

DESCRIPTION OF DISORDERS

Pediatric psychologists and psychiatrists are frequently consulted for assessment and treatment of children suffering from a neurological disorder with concomitant psychological or psychiatric symptoms. Representative pediatric neurological disorders include epilepsy, cerebral palsy, neurodegenerative and neuromuscular disorders, and brain tumors (Williams, Pleak, & Hannesian, 1992). Seizure disorders are one of the most common neurological disorders experienced by children and adolescents, and are the primary focus of this chapter since pediatric psychologists and psychiatrists are likely to encounter a significant number of affected children and adolescents.

A *seizure* is defined as a sporadic disturbance of the central nervous system (CNS) due to sudden, excessive discharges of cortical neurons (Scheur & Pedley, 1990). *Epilepsy* is the term used to describe the state of recurrent and chronic seizures. Of all epilepsy cases, roughly 75 percent occur before the age of 20 (Cowan, Bodensteiner, Leviton, & Doherty, 1989). Between 28.6 percent and 58.3 percent of epileptic children or adolescents experience some form of concomitant psychiatric disorder (Rutter, Graham, & Yule, 1970) that may necessitate psychiatric and/or psychological assessment and intervention. Seizure disorders cannot be viewed as a single disorder but rather as a group of neurological disorders that can be loosely grouped into two major categories: partial and generalized. By far the most serious complication of seizures is status epilepticus, which involves a prolonged seizure episode (i.e., 20 minutes or more) or repeated seizures with the child or adolescent not regaining consciousness. Status epilepticus exemplifies a medical emergency that can be fatal or result in permanent brain damage without appropriate emergency medical treatment.

Seizure Disorder
Symptom Stages

In regard to seizure disorders there are four phases of symptoms (Kaplan, Sadock, & Grebb, 1994). First, the *ictal* phase is the actual occurrence of the seizure. Nonictal periods of time are classified as *preictal*, *postictal*, and *interictal*. For instance, in complex partial seizures, preictal symptoms include auras such as autonomic sensations (e.g., a fullness in the stomach, flushing, and respiration changes). Cognitive preictal symptoms may include a sense of déja vu and dreamy states. Affective preictal states might consist of fear, panic, depression, or elation, whereas psychomotor symptoms involve lip smacking, rubbing, and chewing. The postictal phase is depicted by a slow, gradual restoration of consciousness and cognitive functioning. In contrast, the interictal phase, the period between seizures, may involve changes in personality in such aspects as sexual behavior, religiosity, advent of psychotic behavior, in rare cases violence, and changes in mood states (i.e., depression, mania) that are unrelated to seizures per se, but that often require psychiatric and/or psychological intervention (Kaplan, Sadick, & Grebb, 1994).

Therefore, ictal and interictal symptoms often complicate accurate diagnosis and may lead to a premature functional psychiatric diagnosis unless a diagnosis of epilepsy is first ruled out (Stores, Williams, Styles, & Zaiwalla, 1992). This is especially the case with pseudo-seizures or non-epileptic seizures, where the patient may mimic signs and symptoms of a seizure. A classification of seizures is discussed below (see Commission on Classification and Terminology of International League Against Epilepsy, 1981).

Partial Seizures

Partial seizures involve activity in a localized portion of the brain. Areas affected include the motor area of a cerebral hemisphere, sensory cortex, or the limbic system. Partial seizures also are subdivided into complex and simple partial seizures.

Simple partial seizures usually begin in a localized area and customarily do not involve any impairment in consciousness. Classic Jacksonian seizures begin with a discharge in the motor cortex, often beginning with twitching in the mouth or eyes followed with spasms in the face, arm, trunk, or leg muscles. In some cases the other side of the body becomes involved, with transient postictal paralysis occasionally occurring after the seizure.

Simple partial seizures localized in the sensory cortex are typified by paresthesias, numbness, tingling, prickling or pain in the extremities or face, and may spread to other portions of the body (Griffin, & Ch'ien, 1984). Motor and sensory seizures can also occur together in a compound form of seizure. Other focal seizures occur in the autonomic nervous system (ANS), with the child experiencing melancholy or flushing, changes in heart rate, and nausea and vomiting. Focal seizures in the ANS are often related to electrical discharges in the frontotemporal cortex.

Complex partial seizures, formerly called temporal lobe or psychomotor seizures, differ from simple partial seizures. They usually involve impairment in consciousness. During the seizure the child may engage in confused, repetitive, and purposeless actions with limited knowledge or memory.

Seizures of this type most often occur due to diffuse cerebral disease. Symptoms consistent with complex partial seizures include complex motor movements, lip smacking, body rubbing, chewing, swallowing, walking, running in circles, mumbling, vomiting, flushing

and pallor. Postictal symptoms may include headache, lethargy, vomiting, hunger, thirst, and speech impairment. Focal or generalized paresis also may occur briefly or for several hours.

Generalized Seizures

Generalized seizures tend to involve the entire brain with bilateral symmetry. *Absence* or *petit mal seizures* occur for relatively brief periods of time (i.e., 5 to 30 seconds) and are characterized by staring or repetitive blinking, but also occasionally by lip smacking, mouth twitching, and a loss of balance or falls. These symptoms increase the difficulty of clinically distinguishing absence seizures from complex partial seizures. However, absence seizures are also most likely to be observed in prepubertal children.

Infantile spasms (infantile myoclonus) usually take place in infants between the age of one month and 3 years of age, with the symptoms consisting of sudden, brief, symmetrical flexion of the head or trunk with mild clonus of the legs and arms. The child's eyes may roll inward or upward with a sudden extension of the child's head and trunk, while the child's arms and legs are flexed or extended. In some children the convulsions occur in groups, numerous times daily. In such cases postictal sluggishness or sleep usually does not occur.

Clonic seizures involve rhythmic jerking motor movements following the loss of consciousness and posture. In contrast, *tonic seizures* consist of a stiffening of all the child's extremities associated with a loss of consciousness and loss of posture. Typically, an individual experiencing a tonic seizure without clonic seizures will fall backward.

Tonic-clonic (grand mal) seizures result in a sudden loss of consciousness and posture associated with both tonic and clonic features. Initially there may be a stiffening of muscles in the extremities with rhythmic twitching. Moreover, during the tonic phase the jaw muscles may be clenched tightly, resulting in the individual's tongue being bitten; respiration may be labored or cease for a brief period of time. Other features of tonic-clonic seizures include incontinence of feces or urine during or after the seizure. In the postictal phase the person may appear disoriented and lethargic, with full consciousness not being regained for several minutes to hours.

Atonic seizures involve a quick loss of posture and consciousness. In many cases the seizure may be very brief in duration. However, distinguishing atonic and myoclonic seizures is often difficult. Other seizures include neonatal convulsions, which usually occur in the first 10 days after birth. Neonatal convulsions are often poorly organized and may involve multifocal, focal clonic or tonic seizures.

Febrile Seizures

Febrile seizures occur between the age of 3 months and 5 years of age with children experiencing a fever. Febrile seizures are the most common type of seizure, occurring in 2 to 4 percent of all children; approximately one-third of these children have recurrent febrile seizures (Hauser & Kurland, 1975). However, care must be taken to distinguish febrile seizures from epileptic seizures. Fever lowers seizure threshold, and can be a trigger for patients with epilepsy across the life span. Essentially, simple febrile seizures are considered to be a common, self-limited condition, with affected children becoming seizure free by age six and never experiencing a seizure in the absence of fever. Only approximately two percent of children whose first seizure occurs with fever will develop true epilepsy by age seven (Nelson & Ellenberg, 1976). The chance of the child with febrile seizures later developing non-febrile seizures is low unless two or three of the following factors are present: a family history of non-febrile seizures, atypical febrile seizures, and/or abnormal neurological or developmental delays prior to the onset of the first febrile seizure.

Other Seizures

There are numerous rare seizure forms, most of which are the reflex seizures. Sensory stimuli such as light, sound, and touch may evoke seizures in vulnerable individuals. Cases of visual reflex epilepsy have been recently reported in relation to video games and television. Another type of recent interest to pediatric clinicians is Landau Kleffner syndrome or acquired epileptic aphasia that manifests usually between the ages of 3 to 6 years with deterioration of previously acquired language skills, EEG abnormalities (usually temporal lobe spikes) and, in some cases, seizures (Deonna, 1991).

Non-Epileptic Seizures (Pseudoseizures)

Pseudoseizure is a term often used when an individual exhibits signs and symptoms that are commonly associated with epileptic seizures in the absence of EEG changes, and psychological factors are presumed to be etiologic. Pseudoseizures are sometimes also referred to as "hysterical seizures" or "nonepileptic seizures." Pseudoseizures are often difficult to diagnose since they mimic the symptoms of epilepsy. Furthermore, epileptic children also sometimes exhibit pseudoseizures. Frequently children with pseudoseizures suffer from psychiatric conditions such as depressive or anxiety disorders, as well as histrionic personality features. They also may require further assessment to determine whether the pseudoseizure should be understood as representative of a somatoform disorder, factitious disorder, or malingering (Williams & Hirsch, 1988).

Transitory Cognitive Impairment (TCI)

Deonna (1993) alerted clinicians to emerging evidence of *transitory cognitive impairment* (TCI) in epileptic children, which occurs in addition to the well-documented cognitive and behavioral toxicity of AEDs. TCI is characterized by a temporary decrease in cognitive performance coincident with EEG epileptic discharges without any other clinical changes or typical seizures. While it may be difficult to distinguish TCI from inherent underlying cognitive deficits or AED toxicity without intensive laboratory testing, clinicians should keep in mind the possibility of non-convulsive cognitive dysfunction and the need for optimal control of epileptic discharges in vulnerable patients.

EPIDEMIOLOGY

Prevalence

Crude prevalence rates of epilepsy in the general population for the 1950s yielded a rate of 4 to 6 per 1000 persons from Rochester, Minnesota (Kurland, 1959) and the southwestern region of England (Pond, Bidwell, & Stein, 1959). These estimates have been found consistently throughout the world and over time (Cowan et al., 1989; Gudmundsson, 1966; Silanpaa, 1973; Tsubio, 1988). However, the different epidemiological surveys of childhood epilepsy have varied widely from 4.6/1000 to 20/1000 (Shamanski & Glaser, 1979). Case definitions, methods of case ascertainment, and the method of estimation have contributed to the variability of prevalence rates. The widely cited Isle of Wight study by Rutter and colleagues (1970) reported an overall 7.2/1000 prevalence rate of epilepsy and a 5.4/1000 prevalence rate of "idiopathic" (of unknown cause) epilepsy. Another methodologically sound study in the United States

(Cowan et al., 1989) reported a 5.2/1000 rate for children age 0–4 and a 4.6/1000 rate for children age 5–19. The point prevalence rate of epilepsy is higher in the early years of life than in adulthood and decreases over the life span. Hauser and Kurland (1975) estimated that the lifetime prevalence rate of epilepsy is about 6 percent for a single afebrile seizure and about 4 percent for recurrent seizures. Febrile convulsions are not uncommon in children under age 5, occurring in about 3 percent (Millichap, 1968), and often are not included in the epidemiologic studies of epilepsy.

Epilepsy is, indeed, the most common neurological disorder in the general population and is primarily a disorder of childhood. At least 75 percent of epilepsy begins before the age of 20, and 50 percent of epilepsy with an onset in childhood occurs in the first five years of life (Cowan et al., 1989; Gudmundsson, 1966; Silanpaa, 1973). As to the type of seizures, there is a great deal of variation among different studies due to the problems with the reliability of the classification system, not unlike the situation in psychiatry. Although the reliability of the classification system is problematic, generalized seizures appear to be the most frequent type, followed by partial seizures and other seizure types. There is a slightly higher incidence of epilepsy for males and for African-Americans (Cowan et al., 1989; Shamanski & Glaser, 1979). Idiopathic type without structural brain lesions constitutes about 70 percent of childhood epilepsy. Idiopathic seizure types often are associated with nonspecific minor to gross physical anomalies.

The rate of epilepsy is markedly higher in certain defined groups of the medically and mentally handicapped than in the general population. For instance, Michelucci, Forte, Rubboli, and Plasmati (1989) reported a prevalence rate of 50 percent for epilepsy in profoundly mentally retarded children.

Prognosis

Epilepsy often begins with seizures during sleep or wakefulness; its course varies greatly from complete recovery to fatal outcome. For example, the benign epilepsy of childhood with rolandic foci remits completely after puberty. In stark contrast, neonatal seizures and infantile spasms have about a 20 percent mortality rate during childhood and early adulthood (Dennis, 1979). In general, the majority of epileptic children recover fully. For instance, Suurmeijer (1991) in a five-year follow-up study of 136 epileptic children found that at least one-half were seizure-free and did not require any medical care. Several long-term follow-up studies of patients who have remained seizure-free for at least two years while on antiepileptic drugs (AED) following an initial seizure have reported up to a 75 percent remission rate after withdrawal of medication (Annegers, Hauser, Elveback, & Kurland, 1980; Medical Research Counsel Antiepileptic Drug Withdrawal Study Group, 1991). One-third to one-quarter of epileptic children, however, experience a poor prognosis with uncontrolled seizures and a host of psychosocial complications. In general, absence seizures, minor motor seizures, and generalized tonic-clonic seizures have a better prognosis than complex partial seizures. Factors favoring better prognosis include (a) normal intelligence, (b) absence of brain lesion, (c) onset after infancy and before puberty, (d) fewer seizures before treatment and a lower rate of seizure occurrence, and (e) normal neurological examination and a less abnormal EEG.

Psychiatric Comorbidity

Since epilepsy involves the CNS, it is not surprising emotional, behavioral, and cognitive complications may be associated with CNS dysfunction per se, in addition to the psychosocial problems that may be associated with adjusting to a chronic illness. The cognitive/behavioral toxicity of AEDs, social prejudice, and family adjustment problems may further compound the psychiatric complications. Epileptic children attending pediatric neurology clinics exhibit a higher rate of "behavioral" and "psychological" problems than community samples of epileptic children—about 50 percent versus 20 percent (Hinton & Knights, 1969; Holdsworth & Whitmore, 1974). Rutter and associates' (1970) classic Isle of Wight study reported that in comparison to a 6.6 percent rate of psychiatric disorders for physically healthy children, the rate of psychiatric disorders for children with neuro-epileptic disorders was 34.3 percent. Similarly, the rate of psychiatric disorder for idiopathic epilepsy was 29.6 percent and the rate for epilepsy with demonstrable CNS lesion was much higher at 58.3 percent. Focal EEG abnormalities and temporal lobe epilepsy (TLE) are associated with a high rate of psychiatric disorder.

In terms of specific child psychiatric syndromes, disruptive behavioral and impulse control disorders have been cited most frequently in relation to epilepsy. Inattentiveness, overactivity, aggression, rage attacks, and antisocial behaviors have been identified in numerous studies (e.g., Ounsted & Lindsay, 1981), especially in boys with TLE. Related to these impulsive, disruptive, and inattentive behavioral problems, educational under-achievement and learning deficits are also found in many epileptic children of normal intelligence (Stores, 1978). Brent (1986) also has reported an overrepresentation of epilepsy, especially TLE, among child and adolescent suicide attempters. This is congruent with findings of a high rate of depressive disorders and suicides in adult epileptics. Although anxiety, social withdrawal, and "neurotic" or "emotional" disorders have been reported, the diagnostic classification systems employed in earlier studies do not provide information sufficient to identify specific psychiatric disorders in keeping with current classification. However, it is plausible to assume that there is probably an over-representation of specific disorders such as affective disorders in epileptic children and adolescents (Kim, 1991). Similarly, although an association with so called "epileptic personality" and schizophrenia-like psychosis has been found in adult epileptics, it has not firmly been established in childhood epilepsy. However, there is the suggestion that psychosis may be more common in children with epilepsy and CNS lesions and/or mental retardation (Corbett & Trimble, 1983).

ASSESSMENT APPROACHES

Medical Issues

Diagnosis of epilepsy is primarily a clinical one, unless seizures are secondary to underlying medical conditions. There are numerous metabolic and structural lesions that cause seizures and require appropriate laboratory investigations after careful history taking and physical examination. While epileptic children and adolescents may present with minor physical and neurological abnormalities, physical evaluation often reveals few clues to the diagnosis of epilepsy, as about two-thirds of all epilepsies are of an idiopathic type (Cowan et al., 1989).

Blood chemistries, including serum glucose and calcium levels, are routinely done in the initial laboratory investigation. When developmental disorders are associated with seizures, metabolic screening of amino acids, organic acids, heavy metals and/or cytogenetic tests may be ordered. Unless an infectious origin is suspected, lumbar puncture is not a routine procedure for patients with seizure disorders. Electroencephalographies (EEG) are routinely ordered and various types of neuroimaging techniques increasingly are employed in the investigation of seizure disorders. EEG or neuroimaging may be helpful in differentiating epilepsy from other episodic disorders such as myoclonus, various types of sleep disorders, paroxysmal dystonia, paroxysmal dyskinesia, paroxysmal vertigo, syncope, migraine, tic disorders, breath-holding spells, and pseudoseizures that may mimic epilepsy (Morrell, 1993).

EEG

In addition to the above episodic disorders, pediatric psychiatric disorders are often accompanied by paroxysmal symptoms and episodic frequency. The nature of symptom manifestation is determined by psychogenic and physiological interplay with environmental provocation. However, clinicians are often confronted with the task of ruling out an "organic" etiology, particularly epilepsy, as a direct cause of emotional and behavioral problems. Therefore, the EEG has been extensively utilized in the study of childhood behavioral disorders.

Certain groups of patients with pediatric psychiatric disorders such as extremely aggressive delinquents and autistic children have a high incidence of associated epileptic disorders (Lewis, Pincus, Shanok, & Glaser, 1982). Up to one-third of patients with autism also suffer from epilepsy (Volkmar & Nelson, 1990). However, controlled studies do not indicate any diagnostic utility of EEG in most pediatric psychiatric disorders such as attention deficit disorders, conduct disorders, learning disabilities, tic disorders, or psychosis (Ritvo, Ornitz, Walter, & Hanley, 1970). Instead, the EEG should be employed only as the clinical situation dictates.

Compounding the diagnostic difficulties in epilepsy and pediatric psychiatric disorders are the validity and reliability of EEG. There is a high rate of EEG abnormalities (8 to 15 percent) in normal children, with the rate being higher in younger children (Eeg-Olofsson, 1970). One reason for this is that the immature brains of young children often send out dysrhythmic electrical impulses and artifactual factors complicate the interpretation of EEG tracings. On the other hand, a high false negative rate is often obtained when a single routine EEG is employed in patients with epilepsy, ranging from 30 to 70 percent depending on the type of seizure (Lee, 1983). Repeated EEG, provocation by sleep deprivation and pharmacological agents, and localizing techniques such as sphenoidal electrodes reduce the false negative rate. When epileptic disorders are strongly suspected despite normal findings on routine EEG, ambulatory cassette EEG records are often utilized and/or the patient may be admitted to a hospital for continuous long-term EEG monitoring. EEG telemetry and video monitoring techniques clarify the nature of epileptic attacks, seizure-type and other diagnostic issues such as differential diagnosis of true seizures and pseudoseizures (Duchowny, 1985; Duchowny, Resnick, Deray, & Alvarez, 1988). Continuous EEG monitoring may also uncover epileptiform discharges not accompanied by obvious clinical events that cause transitory cognitive impairment (TCI) with concomitant educational and behavioral dysfunction (Binnie, 1993).

Computerized EEG (CEEG) is designed to simplify the massive data generated by EEG tracings by mathematical algorithms, and depict a topographical brain map that displays the EEG wave form over time. CEEG has also been known as BEAM (brain electrical activity mapping). It has generated much interest for psychiatric clinicians as a potential psychiatric diagnostic tool of the future for investigation of genetic markers in children of schizophrenic and alcoholic parents, and for abnormal findings in attention deficit disorders, learning disabilities, and Tourette Syndrome (Kuperman, Gaffney, Hamdan-Allen, Preston, & Venkatesh, 1990).

Neuroimaging

The diagnosis of idiopathic epilepsy is made by ruling out possible primary causes such as brain tumor. An initial diagnostic workup of epilepsy invariably includes modern neuroimaging procedures. Computerized axial tomography (CT) has replaced skull films or ventricular pneumoencephalography in the last two decades since its introduction in the mid-1970s. Although CT has improved the resolution of brain structure, a newer brain imaging technique, magnetic resonance imaging (MRI), has further enhanced the resolution power and spatial configuration.

For example, a retrospective study of children with an initial presentation of seizures who later were found to have a brain tumor suggested that a delay in the use of appropriate brain imaging studies resulted in misdiagnosis (Sjors, Blennow, & Lantz, 1993). This is particularly worth noting since many of the children had normal physical examinations and normal findings on EEG. Williams, Abbott, and Manson (1992) reported that even CT was not diagnostic in 40 percent of cases, and that MRI was more reliable in detecting tumors. Although not widely available, functional studies by positron emission tomography (PET) or single photon emission computerized tomography (SPECT) have been found to be useful in detecting the foci of seizures when structural abnormalities are not evident by CT or MRI. Functional neuroimaging has not been demonstrated to be useful in

the assessment of most child psychiatric patients as a tool for differential diagnosis, but has been generating research interest, especially in developmental disorders (Kuperman et al., 1990; Peterson, 1995). However, judicious employment of such sophisticated neuroimaging techniques may be warranted in cases of episodic seizure-like behavioral disturbances with or without positive EEG findings.

Psychological and Psychiatric Issues

The role of psychological assessment is quite varied with regard to the assessment of children and adolescents with epilepsy. The primary areas in which psychological assessments have proven helpful include assessment of intellectual abilities and academic achievement in order to identify specific learning disabilities that might be evidenced by epileptic children and adolescents, formal assessment of emotional, behavioral, and personality functioning, evaluation of the psychosocial adjustment of epileptic children and their families to a chronic illness, and neuropsychological assessment related to the location of brain dysfunction and the toxicity of antiepileptic medications.

Intellectual, Academic Achievement, and Learning Difficulties

The findings concerning intellectual capabilities of children with epilepsy have been mixed. The vast majority of children with epilepsy do not evidence a decline in intellectual abilities unless the child had neurological abnormalities prior to their first seizure episode (Ellenberg, Hirts, & Nelson, 1986; Kim, 1991). For instance, the strongest evidence for intellectual decline has been with mentally retarded children who also have epilepsy (Corbett & Harris, 1974; Michelucci et al., 1989). Similarly, children with Lennox-Gastaut Syndrome or Infantile Spasms are more prone to evidence intellectual deficits. Furthermore, Hartlage and Telzrow (1984) reviewed studies of a wide range of epileptic children and found a mean Full Scale IQ of 87. Similarly, Renier (1990) found that approximately 60 percent of children with epilepsy had average intellectual abilities. Thus, it appears that seizure type (more generalized), earlier age of onset, longer duration of illness, greater frequency of seizure episodes, and lack of responsiveness to treatment may contribute to a greater risk of intellectual decline although the evidence is still relatively weak (Dodrill, 1981).

In stark contrast, there are a number of studies that have indicated that children with epilepsy perform poorly on academic achievement tests, with the deficits being static rather then progressive. For instance, Mitchell, Chavez, and Guzman (1991) found that in a sample of 78 epileptic children between 5 and 13 years of age, 16 percent evidenced underachievement in Reading Recognition and 50 percent in General Knowledge. The authors also found that recently diagnosed and/or untreated epileptic children were underachieving at an equivalent proportion as compared to children with a long duration of epilepsy and who were on antiepileptic medication. A study by Camfield, Camfield, Smith, Gordon, and Dooley (1993) examined the social outcomes of 337 patients from age 7 to 28 years over a 7 1/2 year time period and found a school failure rate of 34 percent, with an additional 34 percent of the sample having utilized special education resources. The authors also found that unfavorable outcomes for epileptic patients were predicted by the presence of a learning disability and a history of more than 21 seizures before initiating treatment.

Given the relatively stable findings concerning academic underachievement of epileptic children, it seems advisable to formally assess children with epilepsy individually with standardized intellectual and academic achievement tests in order to assure receipt of appropriate educational resources. Examples of such assessment instruments include the Wechsler Intelligence Scale for Children–Third Edition (WISC-III, Wechsler, 1991), Wechsler Adult Intelligence Scale-Revised (WAIS-R, Wechsler, 1980), Wechsler Intelligence Scale for Preschool and Primary School (WIPPSI-R, Wechsler, 1989), Wechsler Individual Achievement Test (WIAT, Wechsler, 1991), and the Kaufman Test of Educational Achievement (KTEA; Kaufman & Kaufman, 1985).

Psychosocial Adjustment of Epileptic Children and their Families

A study of children 6 to 16 years of age with epilepsy using the Child Behavior Checklist–Parent form (CBCL-P, Achenbach, 1991) found more social withdrawal and more difficulties with social functioning in epileptic children, but no evidence of more behavioral problems (Dorenbaum, Cappelli, Keene, & McGrath, 1985). Similarly, Batzel et al. (1991) found that adolescents with epilepsy had psychosocial problems based on a relatively new assessment instrument titled the

"Adolescent Psychosocial Seizure Inventory" (APSI). The CBCL-P and the APSI may be useful assessment tools for assessing epileptic children's adjustment to their chronic illness.

An assessment of the epileptic child/adolescent's parents also is advised to determine how well the parents are coping with their child being diagnosed with a chronic illness. For instance, one of the few studies to examine this area found that mothers of epileptic children who were newly diagnosed evidenced unusually high levels of anxiety and depression for approximately two months after diagnosis (Berg, Butler, Ellis, & Foster, 1993). Therefore, a thorough assessment of family psychiatric history should be conducted, particularly since Brent, Crumrine, Varna, Brown, & Allen (1990) found that those epileptic children with a positive family psychiatric history for affective disorder were at greater risk for developing a mood disorder on phenobarbital or carbamazepine, though the risk appeared greatest on phenobarbital. Anxiety and/or depression may lead to the parents being overly protective or rejecting, thus increasing the child's social isolation (Hoare, 1987) and possibly contributing to increased marital discord (Silanpaa, 1973).

Personality, Emotional, and Behavioral Functioning

Given the higher prevalence of specific psychiatric disorders in children with epilepsy such as Attention Deficit Hyperactivity Disorder (ADHD), disruptive behavior disorders, and impulse control disorders (Ounsted & Lindsay, 1981; Rutter et al., 1970), one area where psychological assessment can make a substantial impact is in the assessment of personality, emotional, and behavioral difficulties.

The use of standardized personality instruments such as the Millon Adolescent Clinical Inventory (MACI; Millon, 1993) and the Minnesota Multiphasic Personality Inventory for Adolescents (MMPI-A; Butcher et al., 1992) can prove useful in assessing an adolescent's current personality functioning, particularly when combined with information obtained from the adolescent's parents to determine whether personality functioning has changed since the diagnosis and treatment of the youth's epilepsy. With younger children the clinician will have to rely more heavily on the parents' report, due to cognitive developmental factors and limited reading skills. One useful assessment instrument is the Personality Inventory for Children–Revised (PIC-R; Wirt, Lachar, Klinedinst, Seat, & Broen, 1984). The PIC-R is completed by the parent or guardian and gives an estimate of the child's personality structure and functioning. Another advantage of such instruments is that they may yield information in a standardized manner concerning the child/adolescent's premorbid functioning and may aid in the development and implementation of psychiatric/psychological intervention.

The use of screening instruments for depression, anxiety, ADHD, behavior problems, and social skills also may aid children with epilepsy in receiving appropriate mental health referral and adequate treatment for such conditions. Representative instruments might include the Reynolds Adolescent Depression Scale (RADS; Reynolds, 1987), Children's Depression Inventory (CDI; Kovacs, 1983), the Revised Children's Manifest Anxiety Scale (RCMAS; Reynolds & Richmond, 1985), Conners's Rating Scales (CPRS, CTRS; Conners, 1989), Child Behavior Checklists (CBCL-T, CBCL-Y; Achenbach, 1991), and the Stony Brook Child Symptom Inventory (Gadow & Sprafkin, 1994).

In addition to the use of specific personality, emotional, and behavior rating scales, the use of a standard diagnostic interview to assist in the identification of psychiatric problems of children with epilepsy is essential. For instance, a thorough clinical interview addressing the reason for referral, present episode, and additional history (e.g., developmental, medical, social, school, family, and family psychiatric histories), as well as a formal mental status exam of the child are necessary to determine an accurate diagnosis and develop an effective treatment plan. Moreover, the use of semi-structured interviews, such as the Schedule for Affective Disorders and Schizophrenia for School Age Children (K-SADS; Puig-Antich & Chambers, 1978), the Child Assessment Schedule (Hodges, 1990), or the Diagnostic Interview for Children–Revised (Reich, Welner, & Herjanic, 1994) may also assist in the quantification of the type and degree of psychopathology of children and adolescents with epilepsy.

Neuropsychological Assessment

In addition to formal psychological assessment of intellectual and academic achievement, psychosocial adjustment of child and parent, and evaluation of personality, emotional, and behavioral status, neuropsychological assessment may also be warranted as a means of evaluating for adverse effects of antiepileptic drugs (AED) or the localization of brain dysfunction. Several studies have been conducted indicating that long-term phenobarbital therapy can contribute to a child's im-

paired learning ability, whereas long-term valproate therapy has not been shown to have the same adverse side effects on learning (Calandre, Dominguez-Granados, Gomez-Rubio, & Molina-Font, 1990). Other investigators have found that withdrawal of AEDs resulted in significant improvement attributable to drug withdrawal in terms of psychomotor speed (Aldenkamp et al., 1993). Furthermore, the use of neuropsychological testing with epileptic youth has also been found to be useful in terms of establishing priorities for identifying vocationally at risk teenagers and developing rehabilitative treatment programs.

TREATMENT STRATEGIES

Overview of Medical Management

The initial stage of medical management is to establish a valid diagnosis of epilepsy. The medical assessment includes careful history taking, physical examination, clinical observation, and appropriate laboratory tests. It may vary in its intensity depending on the kind of seizure manifestation. Secondary seizures resulting from a myriad of metabolic, structural, and iatrogenic causes may be readily relieved by identifying and treating the primary medical conditions.

Another dilemma pediatric clinicians often face is the differential diagnosis of pseudoseizures versus true seizures (Table 10.1). Diagnosis of pseudoseizures is not uncommon in tertiary care settings (Gross, 1983), but quite uncommon in community samples of children. It is also complicated by the high rate of pseudoseizures in diagnosed epileptic patients with estimates ranging from 5 to 50 percent (Gumnit & Gates, 1986). Misdiagnosis of epilepsy as pseudoseizures and vice versa is common. Not surprisingly, patients with mixed epileptic seizures and pseudoseizures are a very difficult group to manage and are at risk for inappropriate use of AEDs (Kim, 1991). Once the diagnosis of pseudoseizure is established, a careful review of AEDs in epileptic patients who have also evidenced pseudoseizures and discontinuation of AEDs in non-epileptic patients, as well as aggressive mental health interventions, are warranted.

When the diagnosis of idiopathic seizure is established, the mainstay of treatment is AED treatment. The selection of AEDs is based on the type of seizure and the side effect profile of AEDs. However, some clinicians stress the importance of the side effect profile rather than seizure type in considering the choice of AEDs.

Table 10.1. Differential Diagnosis of Pseudoseizures

CLINICAL PRESENTATION	PSEUDOSEIZURES	SEIZURES
I. Convulsions		
onset	often gradual	sudden
aura	variable with anxious or angry affect	present in some types
manifestation	inconsistent, bizarre	generally consistent
duration	variable; longer than a few minutes	generally short, less than a few minutes
frequency	in cluster, frequent	generally infrequent
time	only during wakefulness	anytime including during sleep
place	stressful location in the presence of people	any place
incontinence	rare	sometimes
injury	rare	sometimes
II. Neurological/Medical		
sensorium	conscious	unconscious
pupillary reflex	normal	abnormal
pain reflex	present	absent
Babinski sign	normal	sometimes abnormal
postictal amnesia	seldom	invariably
postictal disorientation confusion, somnolence	rare	often
neurodevelopmental abnormality	sometimes	often
EEG	normal or nonspecific abnormality	epileptic discharges
postictal prolactin	no rise	rise
III. Psychiatric		
primary gain	often identifiable	not present
secondary gain	conspicuous	seldom
suggestibility	high	average
personality/emotional disorders	invariably	not infrequent
alexithymia	rare	sometimes
cognitive deficits	infrequent	not infrequent
emotional/stressful precipitants	invariably	sometimes
postictal affect	pleasant or labelle indifference	blunted

The goal of drug treatment is to control seizures using the least number of AEDs with the fewest possible side effects. Monotherapy (single drug treatment) has been advocated, along with serum concentration measurement and standard, weight-adjusted starting and maintenance regimens to guide initial therapy and subsequent dose titration. Complex pharmacodynamics in growing human beings (i.e., children), the frequent cognitive and behavioral side effects of most AEDs, and the narrow margin of safety and therapeutic indices of AEDs warrant careful clinical observation and careful drug monitoring during the course of treatment.

A sizable number of epileptic children require combination drug therapy, especially institutionalized or difficult-to-manage epileptic children; many patients require the use of other psychotropic medications (Beghi et al., 1987). Complex drug interactions and pharmacokinetic complications render polytherapy a risk for increased behavioral and cognitive toxicity and even for worsening of seizures.

For a small group of children with medically intractable seizures, surgical treatment can be a viable option, especially when there is a circumscribed and resectable structural abnormality. Cortisectomy, lobectomy, callosotomy, and lesionectomy have been found to be effective in seizure control, and do not result in significant cognitive deficits in the majority of carefully selected children (Ribaric, Nagulic, & Djurovic, 1991).

In addition to standard AED treatment, various experimental approaches have been used when AEDs are ineffective in intractable seizures. For instance, the ketogenic diet, developed in the 1920s, which restricts protein and carbohydrate and supplies 80 percent of caloric intake through fats, continues to be an effective alternative, especially for young children with intractable seizures (Kinsman, Vining, Quaskey, Mellits, & Freeman, 1992). Vitamin B6, steroids, and immunoglobulins have been tried and produced equivocal results in infantile spasms (Pietz et al., 1993) and Lennox-Gastaut syndrome (Illum et al., 1990).

Psychological and Behavioral Treatments

While seizure control is a primary goal of medical treatment, clinicians have to be sensitive to the developmental and psychosocial needs of epileptic children. While there are common issues and dynamics in coping with a chronic illness on the part of both epileptic children and their families, there are clinical features unique to epileptic children that require specific psychiatric, psychosocial, and educational attention.

Unfortunately, many children with chronic illness do not receive effective mental health interventions for their associated behavioral difficulties, depression, anxiety, social withdrawal, and problems relating to peers (Gortmaker, Walker, Weitzman, & Sobol, 1990). In general, psychosocial interventions for children with epilepsy fall into five categories: individual and family therapy, school interventions, biofeedback, behavior therapy, and interventions focused on improving compliance with the medical treatment regimen.

Individual and Family Therapy

Individual therapy with epileptic children and adolescents may focus on the alleviation of stressors that can contribute to the development of anxiety and depressive disorders, particularly in light of the increased risk for suicide by epileptic patients (Barraclough, 1981; Brent,

1986). As such, children, adolescents, and their families may benefit from involvement in empirically derived interventions for depression and anxiety such as interpersonal psychotherapy (Mufson et al., 1994) and cognitive-behavioral individual psychotherapy (Lewinsohn, Clarke, Hops, & Andrews, 1990; Reynolds & Coats, 1986). Psychotherapy may help the patient deal with stressors associated with the diagnosis of epilepsy, such as the fear of dying, injury, potential for ridicule by peers, and recognizing the link between stress and seizures in some cases. Other functions of psychotherapy may include addressing subtle changes in intellectual ability, educational performance, or personality that are sometimes associated with epilepsy (Taylor, 1989). Family interventions may be needed in order to deal with issues such as enmeshment, parental overprotection, rigidity, and poor conflict resolution, that have been reported in so-called psychosomatic families (Liebman, Minuchin, Baker, & Rosman, 1976). Family therapy also may be needed to inquire about the child and parents' level of understanding of epilepsy, with psychoeducational work discounting any myths or inaccuracies regarding the disease (Livingston, 1972). An overall assessment of the parents' adjustment to their child's epilepsy is important, particularly in light of Austin, McBride, and Howard's (1984) findings that a child's control of their seizures was positively related to parents' adjustment.

School Interventions

Another area where intervention is needed is with the epileptic child/adolescent's school. Teachers and other school personnel may benefit from a formal inservice to familiarize them with the type of epilepsy the student is experiencing and how this might affect not only school performance, but also the reaction of peers and school personnel to the youth should the child experience a seizure while on school grounds. A useful resource is the "School Alert Kit" developed by the Epilepsy Foundation of America (Gourley, 1990). The "School Alert Kit" provides fundamental medical information concerning epilepsy to teachers and students.

Every effort should be made to provide the youth with educational services within the least restrictive setting. Depending on whether the epileptic youth evidences significant deficits in intellectual and educational achievement, it may be wise to consider whether the youth may be a candidate for a vocationally oriented educational program. In some cases adolescents with epilepsy may be best served by steering them toward a vocational educational track, particularly given the findings of Clemmons and Dodrill (1983). Specifically, Clemmons and Dodrill conducted a follow-up study of 42 epileptic adolescents approximately 6.4 years after neuropsychological testing and found that 57 percent reported being unemployed, with 31 percent receiving federal aid; 43 percent reported being employed or were pursuing further education; and 36 percent of the 43 percent had received vocational rehabilitation services. Had a larger percentage of these youths been steered toward a vocational educational track, the percentage of youths who were either unemployed or on federal assistance might have been reduced.

Biofeedback

Another promising intervention is the use of EEG biofeedback with treatment refractory epileptic children. Although many of the published studies have involved case studies, more than 50 studies have demonstrated the utility of the use of EEG biofeedback training with children with poorly controlled seizures. Hartlage and Hartlage (1984) have recommended that the most effective EEG biofeedback involves training focused on at least two waveforms. Specifically, the child with epilepsy first is trained to increase the 12- to 15-Hz sensorimotor rhythm (SMR) and then trained to decrease the 4- to 7-Hz theta rhythm.

Behavior Therapy

Behavioral therapy also has been shown to be effective with refractory epileptic seizures in children. Dahl, Brorson, and Melin (1992) conducted an eight-year follow-up study of 18 children who were divided into three groups: behavior modification, attention control, and an inert control group. The investigators' purpose was to determine whether the addition of behavioral modification to the child's medical intervention regimen would result in a reduction in seizure activity. The investigators found that similar to an initial study, only the behavior modification group experienced a significant reduction in seizures at 10 weeks, 1 year, and at the 8-year follow-up. Other interventions that have been found to be useful include relaxation training and contingency management (Andrasik, Kabela, & Blake, 1988).

Improving Compliance

Another area where psychosocial interventions can be useful is that of improving the compliance of epileptic children with their medical treatment regimen. For instance, Friedman and colleagues (1986) found that epileptic children's non-compliance with taking their medication as prescribed was associated with a restriction of autonomous daily activity, family discord, and low self-esteem. This prompted the authors to encourage clinicians to be observant for such features and encourage the family's involvement in family counseling. Moreover, a study by Regan, Banks, and Beran (1993) found that a therapeutic recreation program for epileptic children was successful in improving self-esteem and involvement in daily activities, which resulted in improved compliance with the long-term medication regimen.

Pharmacological Treatments

In addition to the list of established AEDs, there have been exciting developments in the discovery and implementation of new AEDs during the past decade. Among some 14 new AEDs, those most extensively tested in humans include felbamate, gabapentin, lamotrigine, oxcarbazepine, vigabatrin, and zonisamide (Leppik, 1994). Felbamate, gabapentin, and lamotrigine have been recently marketed in the United States. These new drugs were initially thought to be safe and effective in treatment resistant complex partial seizures. However, new drugs are typically tested in adults and their safety and efficacy are less known in children. For instance, felbamate was found to have a serious side effect of bone marrow suppression and was withdrawn from the U.S. market soon after its introduction, although it became available later in a limited way for the treatment of Lennox-Gastaut Syndrome.

A judicious practice is to first try an AED with an established track record. Extensive review of the pharmacology of old and new AEDs is beyond the scope of this chapter and therefore is deferred to standard pediatric neurology textbooks. This section will focus on issues relevant to pediatric psychologists and psychiatrists: (a) developmental and behavioral/cognitive side effects of AEDs; (b) withdrawal of AEDs; (c) use of psychotropic drugs in epileptic children; and (d) drug interactions.

Developmental and Cognitive/Behavioral Side Effects

Clinical side effects of AEDs are frequent with the use of commonly utilized AEDs (Herranz, Armijo, & Arteaga, 1988), and occur often with phenyntoin (71 percent), phenobarbital (64 percent), carbamazepine (43 percent), and valproate (43 percent). Behavioral and cognitive side effects are especially troubling in epileptic children, as epilepsy itself is associated with a high incidence of behavioral and cognitive deficits.

Ounsted (1955) long ago observed the association of phenobarbital and hyperkinetic syndrome, and others have confirmed the excitable behavioral effects of phenobarbital such as irritability, insomnia, tantrums, and a high incidence of conduct disorder (Corbett, Trimble, & Nichol, 1985; Farwell et al., 1990). A higher rate of clinical depression was also reported with phenobarbital treatment, as compared with carbamazepine treatment or no AED treatment (Brent et al., 1990). A placebo controlled follow-up study by Farwell and associates (1990) elucidated suppression of cognitive development by phenobarbital in young children. Phenytoin has been implicated in cognitive deterioration (Corbett et al., 1985; Reynolds, 1975; Stores, 1978). It has also been reported to cause clinical or subclinical "encephalopathy" or "pseudodegenerative disease" resulting in confusion, delirium, psychosis, and cerebellar dysfunction (Logan & Freeman, 1969; Vallarta, Bell, & Reichert, 1974).

Endocrine side effects of AEDs are evident in hirsutism caused by phenytoin (Corbett et al., 1985; Herranz et al., 1988) and subclinical hypothyroidism caused by carbamazepine and phenobarbital (Yuksel, Kartal, Cenani, & Yalcin, 1993). Hirsutism and gum hyperplasia caused by long-term phenytoin therapy certainly raise aesthetic concerns in epileptic adolescents.

In contrast to phenobarbital and phenytoin, carbamazepine and valproate have been found to be relatively well tolerated and to cause fewer cognitive or behavioral side effects (Berg et al., 1993; Reynolds, 1975). Carbamazepine's potential bone marrow suppression is probably an overrated concern. Although it causes a benign leukopenia in 10 to 12 percent of cases, it appears to be minimally associated with aplastic anemia, which occurs in approximately 1 in 575,000 treated patients per year (Seetharam & Pellock, 1991). Hepatoxicity with valproate is probably another overrated concern, as it has been reported to be very rare in healthy children over age five (Herskowitz, 1987). A weight gain and an increase in total cholesterol may become a nutritional concern with carbamazepine and other AEDs (Franzoni et al., 1992). Valproate may cause sedation, irritability, hyperactivity, and labile mood initially in some cases (Herranz et al., 1988); like carbamazepine, it is an FDA-approved mood stabilizer and is becoming widely used with a variety of psychiatric disorders, particularly mania.

Given the high incidence of teen pregnancy in the United States, the use of AEDs in sexually active epileptic adolescents raises concerns about possible pregnancy and their potential teratogenic effects. It is generally agreed that the incidence of malformations in infants of mothers with epilepsy who are treated with AEDs is two or three times that of infants of mothers without epilepsy (Delgado-Escueta & Janz, 1992). There is a similar increase in risk in perinatal mortality. Teen pregnancy itself adds another risk, of course. It is not clear which of the four major AEDs is the most teratogenic, although hydantoin syndrome has been well described in the children of mothers on phenytoin. Valproate may be especially teratogenic (Koch et al., 1992). However, the fetal anomalies tend to be minor and they may be related more to the genetic predisposition of the parents than teratogenic effects of the AEDs. It should also be noted that despite the small, but significant risks, more than 90 percent of women with epilepsy who receive AEDs during pregnancy will have an uneventful course of pregnancy and labor, and will deliver children free of birth defects (Hiilesmaa, 1992; Delgado-Escueta & Janz, 1992). If AED treatment cannot be avoided, the first choice drug for the seizure type should be used as monotherapy at the lowest effective dose.

Drug Withdrawal

As mentioned before, the remission rate of epilepsy is high and certain types of epilepsy such as benign epilepsy of childhood may not require medical treatment. Adverse cognitive and behavioral effects of AEDs and the social stigma associated with their use have generated much interest in discontinuation of AEDs in selected patients after at least two years of a seizure-free period. Recommendations for tapering AEDs range from abrupt discontinuation to gradual tapering over a period of two years. Most epileptologists recommend a three to six month tapering. A recent study found no difference between tapering AEDs over six weeks or nine months in the risk of seizure recurrence during drug tapering or after discontinuation of the four major AEDs (Tennison, Greenwood, Lewis, & Thorn, 1994). Favorable results of AED discontinuation by numerous studies have yielded recurrence rates of less than 40 percent in stable seizures. Therefore, careful selection of candidates for drug withdrawal is warranted (Tennison et al., 1994).

Use of Psychotropic Drugs

The high prevalence of psychiatric comorbidity in epileptic children calls for comprehensive assessments, and epileptic children with severe behavioral and emotional problems should be considered for treatment with psychotropic drugs. However, the epileptogenic side effects and drug interactions of psychotropic drugs with AEDs are less studied in children than adults. Summaries of adult studies by Itil and Soldatos (1980) and Trimble (1981) are useful in understanding psychopharmacology in epileptic children when considering psychotropic drug treatment.

It is well established that neuroleptics can lower seizure threshold and may increase the seizure frequency in epileptic patients. As high as a 5 percent occurrence of seizures in clozapine treated nonepileptic patients has been reported (Physician Desk Reference; PDR, 1995). Risperidone, a new class of neuroleptic, has not been reported to cause such side effects. Clozapine and aliphatic and piperazine phenothiazines are more likely to lower seizure threshold than butyrophenones, pimozide, and risperidone.

Tricyclic antidepressants may lower seizure threshold, while newer antidepressants such as selective serotonin inhibitors (SSRI), venlafaxine, and nefazodone do not yet have long enough track records. A large-scale surveillance study reported the incidence of seizures for antidepressants was 3.0 percent for clomipramine, 0.7 percent for imipramine, and 0.2 percent for maprotiline (Trimble, 1981). Seizures or seizure-like events were reported at a rate of 0.2 percent for a large premarketing study of fluoxetine and at lower rates for fluvoxamine and paroxetine (Physician Desk Reference; PDR, 1995). Bupropion caused alarm for a high rate of epileptogenic side effects after its introduction in the United States, but this was later found to be dose related, especially in eating disordered patients. The effects on seizure frequency in patients with preexisting seizures are not known, as epileptic patients were invariably excluded from drug trial studies. However, in view of the negligible rate of epileptogenic side effects with fluoxetine and similar drugs, SSRIs should be relatively safe drugs for use in epileptic patients when clinically indicated, though one needs to be watchful of drug interactions with AEDs and AED levels need to be carefully monitored.

Lithium may produce some EEG changes and Ghadirian and Lehmann (1980) reported that lithium treatment caused an increase of seizure frequency in epileptic patients. Others also have reported the safe and effective use of lithium in epileptic patients (Erwin, Gerber, Morrison, & James, 1973).

Use of stimulants should be of interest in view of their theoretical antiepileptic properties (Trimble, 1977; Kim, 1991) and the high incidence of disruptive and inattentive behavior observed in epileptic children. Dextroamphetamine produced a dramatic but transient improvement of EEG in one child with Landau-Kleffner syndrome (Marescaux et al., 1990) and behavioral improvement in a quarter of epileptic children (Ounsted, 1955).

Benzodiazepines such as clonazepam may be used safely for both anxiety-related symptoms and seizure control. Epileptogenic effects of illicit psychotropic drugs such as alcohol, marijuana, and cocaine have not been well studied, although alcohol is clearly epileptogenic (Kim, 1991).

Drug Interactions

Studies on drug interactions are rather scarce. Carbamazepine and phenobarbital cause autoinduction of enzymatic systems and hepatic enzyme induction (Jatlow, 1987; Reynolds & Trimble, 1982). When multiple AEDs are used and/or AEDs are used with psychotropic drugs, pharmacodynamics and clinical effects become complicated. Competitions for plasma protein binding and metabolizing enzymes such as the cytochrome p450 isoenzyme result in complex, unpredictable interactions between drugs, producing inhibition or stimulation of bioavailability and metabolism of one drug or the other or both. For example, SSRIs such as fluoxetine, fluvoxamine, and sertraline act as inhibitors of the cytochrome enzyme known to metabolize phenytoin and carbamazepine (DeVane, 1994) and may increase anticonvulsant blood levels.

In addition to pharmacokinetic complications, potentiation of clinical side effects may occur as a result of drug interactions even below therapeutic levels, as evidenced by augmentation of neurotoxic side effects of lithium by carbamazepine and phenytoin (Reynolds & Trimble, 1982). Therefore, it is important to carefully monitor both blood levels and clinical effects when multiple drugs are used in epileptic children. Appropriate reduction of the number and the dose of both antiepileptic and psychotropic drugs has been reported to produce improvement of both seizures and behavioral symptoms (Beghi et al., 1987).

CASE ILLUSTRATIONS

A Case of Pseudoseizure: Jennifer

Clinical Presentation

Jennifer, a 15-year-old girl, was initially admitted to an adolescent psychiatric in-patient unit because of depression and suicidal threats and later developed seizure-like symptoms during hospitalization. She reported experiencing depressive symptoms and flashbacks for the past seven years, attributable to sexual molestation by a neighbor at age 5. She began to exhibit self-abusive behaviors and suicidal threats when angry at age 13. In spite of her depressed mood, she had functioned well both academically and behaviorally until two years prior to admission. She was a track athlete and basketball player at school, but sprained her ankle many times and received reconstructive surgery five months before her hospitalization. Her school performance also significantly deteriorated in the few months prior to admission.

Assessment Findings

Significant family background information included that her mother was a victim of incest and that a six-year-old half-brother of the patient suffered anoxic brain injury after accidentally choking on a toy, which resulted in severe mental and physical handicaps. The patient admitted to occasional alcohol use on weekends, but denied any other substance abuse, sexual promiscuity, or delinquency. Cognitive and educational assessments indicated average functioning. Physical examination and routine laboratory tests were all within normal limits, except for her reported ankle pain and limited mobility. Physical therapy was arranged for functional rehabilitation of her ankle.

The initial diagnostic impression was that of Major Depressive Disorder and Post-Traumatic Stress Disorder, and sertraline was prescribed. The patient remained quite depressed and angry the first two weeks and requested her discharge so that she could commit suicide. She argued for her freedom to choose suicide. The family's limited insurance benefits quickly ran out in less than two weeks of hospitalization.

While addressing family issues two weeks after admission, Jennifer demanded to know about her biological father, whom the mother had been reluctant to discuss. The mother broke down and stated that Jennifer was a product of rape and she did not even know the name of Jennifer's father. Jennifer used this information as another reason to commit suicide.

The patient also began to complain of more somatic symptoms. A few days later, she began to experience "fainting spells." She complained of dizziness and weakness and laid in her bed, appearing to fall asleep once or twice a day. After three such episodes, the patient had another sudden fainting spell with shivering of her body and extremities during the parents' visit. On the following day, the patient developed an episode resembling

intermittent convulsions. On examination, the patient had little pain reflex, but normal pupillary reflex. Her vital signs were within normal limits. Blood glucose and electrolytes were also within normal limits. A bedside EEG was performed that did not show any epileptic discharges. Serum prolactin level was normal. EKG and MRI also were not significant. The patient did not seem to be very concerned when she woke up.

Treatment Selection and Course

Once the family was informed, the stepfather was very concerned, blaming hospital staff for not taking prompt and serious action at the onset of her symptoms. Potential side effects of the sertraline and ibuprofen, which was used for ankle pain, were discussed, but did not appear to be causal factors. In fact, sertraline was increased from 50 mg to 75 mg and 100 mg over the next few days as a provocative test, as well as for improvement of her remaining depressive symptoms. Although psychogenic origin was suspected, the lack of any significant medical findings was stressed for reassurance, rather than interpretation of potential underlying dynamic reasons. Continuing supportive individual and family therapy addressing her sense of loss, family conflicts, and the increase of sertraline resulted in improving mood and cessation of her fainting and pseudoseizures.

Termination and Follow-Up

After discharge, her fainting and seizure-like symptoms recurred during stress, leading to an emergency room visit in a local hospital. Another similar episode led to an admission to a cardiac unit. Continuous EKG monitoring did not reveal any abnormal findings. It is of note that she had the episode after drinking a wine cooler with her stepfather. There was a suspicion of inappropriate interaction between the patient and the stepfather, but the patient steadfastly denied any sexual impropriety or abuse by anyone since age five. The treating psychiatrist strongly recommended that the family doctor not pursue further medical workup or readmission of the patient. Continuous out-patient treatment and temporary therapeutic foster care were recommended instead. The patient was ambivalent initially about out-of-home placement, but made good adjustments after outside placement took place. The pseudoseizures did not recur.

A Case of Psychiatric Complication: John

Clinical Presentation

An 11-year-old Caucasian boy with a history of complex partial seizures was referred to child psychiatry for "escalating behavioral problems" by his neurologist. John was in good health, was attending a gifted class, and was the best behaved of three children until two-and-a-half years ago, when he contracted a viral illness. Two days after his fever broke, he developed a grand mal seizure. He was admitted to an intensive care unit and was placed on phenytoin and valproate. He was diagnosed with encephalitis, although the type of virus was never confirmed. While his multiple seizures had improved to a degree with AED treatment, he was "like a zombie" on these drugs, according to the mother.

John became moody and began to threaten to hurt himself, resulting in psychiatric hospitalization six months later. On the WISC-R, his intelligence was found to be in the superior range (FSIQ = 138). AEDs were increased at that time, which resulted in a toxic reaction with confusion and ataxia. John was admitted to another hospital a few months later for a second opinion and seizure management. Over the next several months, a variety of AEDs were tried such as carbamezepine, mysoline, methsuximide, and gabapentin. Due to intractable seizures, a depth electrode probing was performed for possible surgical intervention. Bilateral temporolimbic epileptic discharges were found. It was decided that John was not a candidate for surgery because of multiple foci. In addition to recurrent seizures, John's behavior and school performance continued to deteriorate. Two years later the WISC-R showed a Full-Scale IQ of 90. In the two weeks prior to the second psychiatric referral, his behavior became increasingly more aggressive. He threatened to hurt himself or run away, and also attempted to stab children at school with pencils. He frequently provoked and fought with his 13-year-old brother and 9-year-old sister at home. He also had episodes of head-banging at school during which he stated "I want to smash my brains out."

Assessment Findings

A comprehensive child psychiatric evaluation was carried out following admission to a child psychiatric unit, although he had received various psychological and psychiatric evaluations over the previous two years as an out-patient or an in-patient on a general psychiatric unit. On the Stanford Binet Intelligence Scale, John obtained a full-scale test composite of 72, which was derived from a standard score of 70 in verbal reasoning, 85 in abstract visual reasoning, 89 in quantitative reasoning, and 63 in short-term memory. Continuing intellectual deterioration was evident. A neuropsychological assessment revealed multiple deficits, but especially in verbal and attentional areas. Physical examination and laboratory findings including metabolic screening and viral studies were unremarkable, and unable to account for his intellectual deterioration. Another EEG tracing showed multiple epileptic foci, but more prominently in the frontal and temporal regions of the left hemisphere, and the diffuse slowing of background rhythms, indicating metabolic or degenerative encephalopathy. Previous CT and MRI were within normal limits. A brain SPECT scan showed decreased activity in a large portion of the left temporal lobe extending into the occipital lobe and also in a small area of the right inferior and medial temporal lobe.

The intellectual decline was attributed to the uncontrolled epilepsy causing brain injury (non convulsive status epilepticus) and lack of age-appropriate learning. However, it was observed that John demonstrated better abilities than the test scores showed. AED side effects and emotional interference may have contributed to the possible under-estimation of his abilities.

Treatment Selection and Course

Diagnoses of Mental Disorder due to epilepsy with mood disorder and personality change and Attention-Deficit Hyperactivity Disorder were formulated. A theme of loss was addressed in both individual and family therapy. A behavioral modification program was devised, in addition to educational and supportive therapy for both John and his family. Both siblings were closely involved in family therapy. The mother, who exhibited significant depressive symptoms, was also referred for psychiatric consultation. She began to receive treatment for herself, including an antidepressant. In view of his uncontrolled epileptic discharges on EEG and clinical seizures, modification of therapy with AEDs in a high-dose strategy was instituted in collaboration with the neurologist. Dextroamphetamine was also added for attentional and impulsive symptoms. Furthermore, a referral to a support group of the local epilepsy foundation was made.

Termination and Follow-Up

An arrangement for a special education program following discharge and intensive follow-up, including adjustment of dextroamphetamine and individual and family therapy, resulted in a modest degree of improvement in his overall adjustment.

SUMMARY

The aforementioned cases illustrate representative samples of the diagnostic and treatment dilemmas encountered in dealing with children and adolescents with seizures. Epilepsy is a very heterogeneous disease with a diverse course of benign to severely debilitating illness. Children and adolescents with epilepsy have an increased vulnerability to develop emotional, behavioral, and educational complications. The increased vulnerability may be associated with several factors, including AED toxicity, genetic and environmental influences, family disturbance, the type of neurological lesion (e.g., site of brain damage), the degree of seizure control, and individual characteristics of the child (i.e., age, intelligence, and coping ability; Hoare, 1987). While disruptive behavioral disorders tend to occur more often, especially in boys, and there is ample evidence of general educational underachievement, the type of psychiatric and developmental disorders manifested in youths with epilepsy is quite varied. The multiple handicapping nature of epilepsy in children requires a multidisciplinary team approach in terms of the developmental assessment of intellectual, academic, and psychosocial progress and the delivery of appropriate medical interventions.

Although the access to such sophisticated team approaches may be limited by lack of availability and managed care constraints, the pediatric psychologist and psychiatrist play important roles in providing holistic care in collaboration with the neurologist or pediatrician. Their expertise in developmental and clinical assessments, family work, and detecting developmental and behavioral side effects of AEDs should be employed almost routinely in epileptic children and adolescents in view of the enormous monetary and nonmonetary burdens placed on the child, family, and society by less than satisfactory diagnostic accuracy and management of epilepsy (Kim, 1991). Additionally, there is a need for new research to develop an understanding of the mechanisms of cognitive, educational, and emotional dysfunction, and to develop appropriate interventions, including behavioral, cognitive, and psychopharmacological treatments.

REFERENCES

Achenbach, T. M. (1991). *Manual for the Child Behavior Checklist/4-18 and 1991 profile*. Burlington, VT: University of Vermont Department of Psychiatry.

Achenbach, T. M. (1991). *Manual for the Youth Self-Report and 1991 profile*. Burlington, VT: University of Vermont Department of Psychiatry.

Achenbach, T. M. (1991). *Manual for the Teachers Report Form and 1991 profile*. Burlington, VT: University of Vermont Department of Psychiatry.

Aldenkamp, A., Alpherts, W., Blennow, G., Elmqvist, D., Heijbel, J., Nilsson, H., Sandstedt, P., Tonnby, B., Wahlander, L., & Wosse, E. (1993). Withdrawal of antiepileptic medication in children—effects on cognitive function: The multicenter Holmfrid study. *Neurology, 43*, 41–50.

Andrasik, F., Kabela, E., & Blake, D. (1988). Pediatrics: Psychological Therapies. In J. Matson (Ed.), *Handbook of treatment approaches in childhood psychopathology* (pp. 429–466). New York: Plenum Press.

Annegers, J. F., Hauser, W. A., Elveback, L. K., & Kurland, C. T. (1980). Remission and relapses of seizures in epilepsy. In J. Wada & J. Penry (Eds.), *Advances in epileptology: The Tenth International Epilepsy Symposium* (pp. 145–147). New York: Raven Press.

Austin, J., McBride, A., & Howard, W. (1984). Parental attitude and adjustment to childhood epilepsy. *Nursing Research, 33*, 92–96.

Barraclough, B. (1981). Suicide and epilepsy. In E. Reynolds & M. Trimble (Eds.), *Epilepsy and psychiatry* (pp. 72). Edinburgh: Churchill Livingstone.

Batzel, L., Dodrill, C., Dubinsky, B., Zeigler, G., Connolly, J., Freeman, R., Farwell, J., & Vining, E. (1991). An objective method for the assessment of psychosocial problems in adolescents with epilepsy. *Epilepsia, 32*, 202–211.

Beghi, E., Bolini, P. B., DiMascio, R., Cerisola, N., Merloni, J., & Manghi, E. (1987). Effects of rationalizing drug treatment of patients with epilepsy and mental retardation. *Developmental Medicine and Child Neurology, 29*, 363–369.

Berg, I., Butler, A., Ellis, M., & Foster, J. (1993). Psychiatric aspects of epilepsy in children treated with carbamazepine, phenytoin or sodium valproate: A random trial, *Developmental Medicine and Child Neurology, 35*, 149–157.

Binnie, C. D. (1993). Significance and management of transitory cognitive impairment due to subclinical EEG discharges in children. *Brain & Development, 15*, 23–30.

Brent D. A. (1986). Overrepresentation of epileptics in a consecutive series of suicide attempters seen at a children's hospital. *Journal of the American Academy of Child and Adolescent Psychiatry, 25,* 242–246.

Brent, D. A., Crumrine, P. K., Varma, R., Brown, R. V., & Allan, M. J. (1990). Phenobarbital treatment and major depressive disorder in children with epilepsy: a naturalistic follow-up. *Pediatrics, 85* 1086–1091.

Butcher, J., Williams, C., Graham, J., Archer, R., Tellegen, A., Ben-Porath, Y., & Kaemmer, B. (1992). *Minnesota Multiphasic Personality Inventory–Adolescent.* Minneapolis: University of Minnesota Press.

Calandre, E., Dominguez-Granados, R., Gomez-Rubio, M., & Molina-Font, J. (1990). Cognitive effects of long-term treatment with phenobarbital and valproic acid in school children. *Acta Neurologica Scandinavia, 81,* 504–506.

Camfield, C., Camfield P., Smith, B., Gordon K., & Dooley, J. (1993). Biologic factors as predictors of social outcome of epilepsy in intellectually normal children: A population-based study. Journal of Pediatrics, 122, 869–873.

Clemmons, D., & Dodrill, C. (1983). Vocational outcomes of high school students with epilepsy. *Journal of Applied Rehabilitation Counseling, 14,* 49–53.

Commission on Classification and Terminology of International League Against Epilepsy. (1981). Proposal for revised clinical and electroencephalographic classification of epileptic seizures. *Epilepsia, 22,* 489.

Conners, K. (1989). *Conners' Rating Scales.* NY: Multi-Health Systems, Inc.

Corbett, J., & Harris, R. (1974). Epilepsy in children with severe mental retardation. In P. Woodford (Ed.), *Epilepsy and mental handicap* (Report of Symposium No. 16). London: Institute for Research into Mental and Multiple Handicap.

Corbett, J. A., & Trimble, M. R. (1983). Epilepsy and anticonvulsant medication. In M. Rutter (Ed.), *Developmental neuropsychiatry* (pp. 112–129). New York: Guilford Press.

Corbett, J. A., Trimble, M. R., & Nichol, T. C. (1985). Behavioral and cognitive impairments in children with epilepsy: The long-term effects of anticonvulsant therapy. *Journal of American Academy of Child Psychiatry. 24:* 17–23.

Cowan, L. D., Bodensteiner, J. B., Leviton, A., & Doherty, L. (1989). Prevalence of the epilepsies in children and adolescents. *Epilepsia, 30,* 94–106.

Dahl, J., Brorson, L., & Melin, L. (1992). Effects of a broad spectrum behavioral medicine treatment program on children with refractory epileptic seizures: An eight year follow-up. *Epilepsia, 33,* 98–102.

Delgado-Escueta, A. V., & Janz, D. (1992). Consensus guidelines: Preconception counseling, management, and care of the pregnant woman with epilepsy. *Neurology, 42,* Supplement, 149–160.

Dennis, J. (1979). The implications of neonatal seizures. In R. Korobkin & C. Guilleninault (Eds.), *Advances in perinatal neurology* (pp. 205–224). New York: Spectrum Publications.

Deonna, T. (1991). Acquired epileptiform aphasia in children (Landau-Kleffer syndrome). *Journal of Clinical Neurophysiology, 8,* 288–298.

Deonna, T. (1993). Annotation: Cognitive and behavioral correlates of epileptic activity in children. *Journal of Child Psychology and Psychiatry, 34,* 611–620.

DeVane, C. L. (1994). Pharmacokinetics of the newer antidepressants: Clinical relevance. *American Journal of Medicine, 97:*(64), 135–235.

Dodrill, C. (1981). Neuropsychology of epilepsy. In S. B. Filskov & T. J. Boll (Eds.), *Handbook of clinical Neuropsychology* (pp. 366–395). New York: John Wiley & Sons.

Dorenbaum, D., Cappelli, M., Keene, D., & McGrath, P. (1985). Use of the child behavior checklist in the psychological assessment of children with epilepsy. *Clinical Pediatrics, 24,* 634–637.

Duchowny, M. S. (1985). Intensive monitoring in the epileptic child. *Journal of Clinical Neurophysiolology, 2,* 203–219.

Duchowny, M. S., Resnick, T. J., Deray, T., & Alvarez, L. A. (1988). Video EEG diagnosis of repetitive behavior in early childhood and its relationships to seizures. *Pediatric Neurology, 4,* 162–164.

Eeg-Olofsson, O. (1970). The development of the electroencephalogram in normal children and adolescents from the age of 1 through 21 years. *Acta Paediatrica Scandinavica,* Suppl. 208.

Ellenberg, J., Hirts, D., & Nelson, K. (1986). Do seizures in children cause intellectual deterioration? *New England Journal of Medicine, 314,* 1085.

Erwin, C. W., Gerber, C. H., Morrison, S. D., & James, J. F. (1973). Lithium carbonate and convulsive disorders. *Archives of General Psychiatry, 28,* 646–648.

Farwell, J. R., Lee, Y. J., Hirtz, D. G., Salzbacker, S. I., Ellenberg, J. H., & Nelson, K. G. (1990). Phenobarbital for febrile seizures—effects on intelligence and on seizure recurrence. *New England Journal of Medicine, 322,* 364–369.

Franzoni, E., Govoni, M., D'Addato, S., Gualandi, S., Sangiorgi, Z., Descovich, G. C., & Salvioli, G. P. (1992). Total cholesterol, high-intensity lipoprotein cholesterol, and triglycerides in children receiving antiepileptic drugs. *Epilepsia, 33,* 932–935.

Friedman, I. M, Litt, I. F., King, D. R., Henson, R., Holtzman, P., Halverson, D., & Kraemer, H. C. (1986). Compliance with anticonvulsant therapy by epileptic youth: Relationships to psychosocial aspects of adolescent development. *Journal of Adolescent Health Care, 7,* 12–17.

Gadow, K. D., & Sprafkin, J. (1994). *Manual for the Stony Brook Child Symptom Inventories.* Stony Brook, NY: Checkmate Plus, Ltd.

Ghadirian, A. M., & Lehmann, H. E. (1980). Neurological side effects of lithium: Organic syndrome, seizures, extrapyramidal side effects and EEG changes. *Comprehensive Psychiatry, 21,* 327–335.

Gortmaker, S., Walker, D., Weitzman, M., & Sobol, A. (1990). Chronic conditions, socioeconomic risks, and behavioral problems in children and adolescents. *Pediatrics, 85,* 267–276.

Gourley, R. (1990). Educational Policies. *Epilepsia, 31,* 59–60.

Griffin, J., & Ch'ien, L. (1984). Seizure disorders. In J. Griffin & J. Griffith (Eds.), *Synopsis of pediatrics (Sixth Edition)* (pp. 805–812). St. Louis: C. V. Mosby Company.

Gross, M. (1983). *Pseudoepilepsy.* Lexington, MA: Lexington Books.

Gudmundsson, G. (1966). Epilepsy in Iceland. *Acta Neurologica Scandinavica, 43,* (suppl. 25), 1–124.

Gumnit, R. J., & Gates, J. R. (1986). Psychogenic seizures. *Epilepsia, 27(Suppl. 2),* 124–129.

Hartlage, L., & Hartlage, P. (1984). Neuropsychological aspects of epilepsy: Introduction and overview. In C. Reynolds & E. Fletcher-Janzen (Eds.), *Handbook of clinical child neuropsychology* (pp. 409–417). New York: Plenum Press.

Hartlage, L., & Telzrow, C. (1984). Neuropsychological aspects of childhood epilepsy. In R. Tarter & G. Goldstein (Eds.), *Advances in clinical neuropsychology* (Vol. 2, pp. 409–417). New York: Plenum Press.

Hauser, W. A., & Kurland, C. T. (1975). The epidemiology of epilepsy in Rochester, Minnesota, 1935 through 1967. *Epilepsia, 16,* 1–66.

Herranz, J. L., Armijo, J. A., & Arteaga, T. (1988). Clinical side effects of phenobarbital, primidone, phenytoin, carbamazepine and valproate during monotherapy in children. *Epilepsia, 29,* 794–804.

Herskowitz, J. (1987). Developmental neurotoxicity. In C. Popper (Ed.), *Psychiatric pharmacosciences of children and adolescents* (pp. 81–124). Washington, DC: American Psychiatric Press.

Hiilesmaa, V. K. (1992). Pregnancy and birth in women with epilepsy. *Neurology. 42* (4 Suppl. 5), 8–11.

Hinton, G. G., & Knights, R. M. (1969). Neurological and psychological characteristics of 100 children with seizures. In B. Richard (Ed.), *Proceedings of the First Congress for the International Association for the Scientific Study of Mental Deficiency* (pp. 351–356). London: Michael Jackson Publishing.

Hoare, P. (1987). Children with epilepsy and their families. *Journal of Child Psychology and Psychiatry, 28,* 651–655.

Hodges, K. (1990). Structured diagnostic interviews. In A. M. La Greca (Ed.), *Through the eyes of the child: Obtaining self-report from children and adolescents.* (pp. 109–149). Boston: Allyn and Bacon.

Holdsworth, L., & Whitmore, K. (1974). A study of children with epilepsy attending normal schools. I: Their seizure patterns, progress and behavior in school. *Developmental Medicine and Child Neurology, 16,* 759–765.

Illum, N., Taudorf, K., Heilmann, C., Smith, T., Wulff, K., Mansa, B., & Platz, P. (1990). Intravenous immunoglobulin: A single-blind trial in children with Lennox-Gastaut syndrome. *Neuropediatrics, 21,* 87–90.

Itil, T. M., & Soldatos, C. (1980). Epileptogenic side effects of psychotropic drugs: Practical recommendations. *Journal of American Medical Association, 224,* 1460–1463.

Jatlow, P. I. (1987). Psychotropic drug disposition during development. In C. Popper (Ed.), *Psychiatric pharmacosciences of children and adolescents* (pp. 29–44). Washington, DC: American Psychiatric Press.

Kaplan, H. I., Sadock, B. J., & Grebb, J. A. (1994). Cognitive disorders: Delirium, dementia and amnestic and other cognitive disorders and mental disorders due to a general medical condition. In H. Kaplan, B. Sadock, & J. Grebb (Eds.), *Synopsis of psychiatry (7th Edition)* (pp. 336–373). Baltimore, Maryland: Williams & Wilkins.

Kaufman, A., & Kaufman, N. (1985). *Kaufman Test of Educational Achievement.* Circle Pines, MN: American Guidance Service.

Kim, W. J. (1991). Psychiatric aspects of epileptic children and adolescents. *Journal of the American Academy of Child and Adolescent Psychiatry, 30,* 874–886.

Kinsman, S. L., Vining, E. P., Quaskey, S. A., Mellits, D., & Freeman, J. M. (1992). Efficacy of the ketogenic diet for intractable seizure disorders: Review of 58 cases. *Epilepsia, 33,* 1132–1136.

Koch, S., Losche, G., Jager-Roman, E., Jakob, S., Rating, D., Deichl, A., & Helge, H. (1992). Major and minor birth malformations and antiepileptic drugs. *Neurology, 42* (4 Suppl. 5), 83–88.

Kovacs, M. (1983). *The Children's Depression Inventory: A self-rated depression scale for school-aged youngsters.* Unpublished manuscript.

Kuperman, S., Gaffney, G. R., Hamden-Allen, G., Preston, D. F., & Venkatesh, L. (1990). Neuroimaging in child and adolescent psychiatry. *Journal of the American Academy of Child and Adolescent Psychiatry, 29*(2): 159–172.

Kurland, L. T. (1959). The incidence and prevalence of convulsive disorders in a small urban community. *Epilepsia, 1*, 143–161.

Lee, S. I. (1983). Electroencephalography in infantile and childhood epilepsy. In F. Dreifuss (Ed.), *Pediatric epileptology* (pp. 33–64). Boston: John Wright PSG, Inc.

Leppik, I. E. (1994). Antiepileptic drugs in development: Prospects for the near future. *Epilepsia, 35*, Suppl 4, 29–40.

Lewinsohn, P., Clarke, D., Hops, H., & Andrews, J. (1990). Cognitive-behavioral group treatment of depression in adolescents. *Behavior Therapy, 21*, 385–401.

Lewis, D. O., Pincus, J. H., Shanok, S. S., & Glaser, G. H. (1982). Psychomotor epilepsy and violence in a group of incarcerated adolescent boys. *American Journal of Psychiatry, 139*, 882–887.

Liebman, R., Minuchin, S., Baker, L., & Rosman, B. (1976). The role of the family in the treatment of chronic asthma. In P. Guerin (Ed.), *Family therapy: Theory and practice.* New York: Gardner.

Livingston, S. (1972). *Comprehensive management of epilepsy in infancy, childhood and adolescence* (pp. 123–166). Springfield, IL: Charles C. Thomas.

Logan, W. J., & Freeman, J. M. (1969). Pseudodegenerative disease due to diphenylhydantoin intoxication. *Archives of Neurology, 21*, 631–637.

Marescaux, C., Hirsch, E., Finck, S., Maquet, P., Schlumberger, E., Sellal, F., Metz-Lutz, M. N., Alembik, Y., Salmon, E., & Franck, G. (1990). Landau-Kleffner syndrome: A pharmacologic study of five cases. *Epilepsia, 31*, 768–777.

Medical Research Council Antiepileptic Withdrawal Study Group (1991). Randomized study of antiepileptic withdrawal in patients in remission. *Lancet, 337*, 1175–1180.

Michelucci, R., Forti, A., Rubboli, G., & Plasmati, R. (1989). Mental retardation and behavioral disturbances related to epilepsy: A review. *Brain Dysfunction, 2*, 3–9.

Millichap J. G. (1968). *Febrile convulsions.* New York: Macmillan.

Millon, T. (1993). *Millon Adolescent Clinical Inventory Manual.* Minneapolis: National Computer Systems.

Mitchell, W., Chavez, J., & Guzman, B. (1991). Academic under-achievement in children with epilepsy. *Journal of Child Neurology, 6*, 65–72.

Morrell, M. J. (1993). Differential diagnosis of seizures. *Neurological Clinics, 11*, 737–754.

Mufson, L., Moreau, D., Weissman, M., Wickramaratne, P., Martin, J., & Samoilov, A. (1994). Modification of inter-personal psychotherapy with depressed adolescents (IPT-A): Phase I and Phase II. *Journal of the American Academy of Child and Adolescent Psychiatry, 33*, 695–705.

Nelson, K. H., & Ellenberg, J. H. (1976). Predictors of epilepsy in children who have experienced febrile seizures. *New England Journal of Medicine, 295*, 1029–1033.

Ounsted, C. (1955). The hyperkinetic syndrome in epileptic children. *Lancet, 2*, 303–311.

Ounsted, C., & Lindsay, J. (1981). The long-term outcome of temporal lobe epilepsy in children. In E. Reynolds and M. Trimble (Eds.), *Epilepsy and psychiatry* (pp. 185–215). London: Churchill Livingstone, Inc.

Peterson, B. S. (1995). Neuroimaging in child and adolescent neuropsychiatric disorders. *Journal of the American Academy of Child and Adolescent Psychiatry, 34(12)*, 1560–1576.

Physicians' Desk Reference (49th edition). (1995). Montvale, NJ: Medical Economics Data Production Company.

Pietz, J., Benninger, C., Shafer, H., Sontheimer, D., Mittermaier, G., & Rating, D. (1993). Treatment of infantile spasms with high-dosage vitamin B6. *Epilepsia, 34*, 757–763.

Pond, D. A., Bidwell, B. H., & Stein, L. (1959/1960). A survey of epilepsy in fourteen general practices: I. Demographic and medical data. *Psychiatria, Neurologia, Neurochiargia, 63*, 217–236.

Puig-Antich, J., & Chambers, W. (1978). *The Schedule for Affective Disorders and Schizophrenia for School-Age Children (Kiddie-SADS).* New York: New York State Psychiatric Institute.

Regan, K., Banks, G., & Beran, R. (1993). Therapeutic recreation programs for children with epilepsy. *Seizure, 2*, 195–200.

Reich, W., Welner, Z., & Herjanic, B. (1994). *Diagnostic interview for children and adolescents–revised (for DSM-IV) Computer Program: Child/adolescent version and parent version.* New York: North Tonawanda, MHS.

Renier, W. (1990). Learning disabilities and behavioral problems in children with epilepsy. *Wiener Klinische Wochenschrift, 102*, 218–222.

Reynolds, C. R., & Richmond, B. O. (1985). *Revised Children's Manifest Anxiety Scale (RCMAS).* Los Angeles: Western Psychological Services.

Reynolds, E. H. (1975). Chronic antiepileptic toxicity: A review. *Epilepsia, 16*, 319–352.

Reynolds, E. H., & Trimble, M. R. (1982). The pharmacologic management of epilepsy associated with psychological disorders. *British Journal of Psychiatry, 141*, 549–557.

Reynolds, W., & Coats, K. (1986). A comparison of cognitive-behavioral therapy and relaxation training for the treatment of depression in adolescents. *Journal of Consulting and Clinical Psychology, 54,* 653–660.

Reynolds, W. M. (1987). *Assessment of depression in adolescents: Manual for the Reynolds Adolescent Depression Scale (RADS).* Lutz, FL: Psychological Assessment Resources, Inc.

Ribaric, I. I., Nagulic, M., & Djurovic, B. (1991). Surgical treatment of epilepsy: Our experiences with 34 children. *Childs Nervous System, 7,* 402–404.

Ritvo, E. R., Ornitz, E. M., Walter, R. D., & Hanley, J. (1970). Correlation of psychiatric diagnosis and EEG findings: A double blind study of 194 hospitalized children. *American Journal of Psychiatry, 126,* 988–996.

Rutter, M., Graham, P., & Yule, W. (1970). A neuropsychiatric study in childhood. *Clinics in Developmental Medicine* (pp. 35–36). London: Heinemann/Spastics International Medical Publications.

Scheur, M. L., & Pedley, T. A. (1990). The evaluation and treatment of seizures. *New England Journal of Medicine, 323,* 1468–1474.

Seetharam, M. N., & Pellock, J. M. (1991). Risk-benefit assessment of carbamazepine in children. *Drug Safety, 6,* 148–158.

Shamanski, S. L., & Glaser, G. H. (1979). Socioeconomic characteristics of childhood seizure disorders in the New Haven area: An epidemiologic study. *Epilepsia, 20,* 457–474.

Silanpaa, M. (1973). Medico-social prognosis of children with epilepsy: Epidemiological study and analysis of 245 patients. *Acta Paediatrica Scandinavica, 62,* 3–104.

Sjors, K., Blennow, G., & Lantz, G. (1993). Seizures as the presenting symptom of brain tumors in children. *Acta Paediatrica Scandinavica, 82,* 66–70.

Stores, G. (1978). School children with epilepsy at risk for learning and behavior problems. *Developmental Medicine and Child Neurology, 20,* 502–508.

Stores, G., Williams, P. L., Styles, E., & Zaiwalla, Z. (1992). Psychological effects of sodium valproate and carbamazepine in epilepsy. *Archives of Disease in Childhood, 67,* 1330–1337.

Suurmeijer, T. (1991). Eight-year outcome in infants with birth weight of 500 to 999 grams: Continuing regional study of 1979 and 1980 births. *Journal of Pediatrics, 118,* 761–767.

Taylor, D. (1989). Epilepsy problems in child psychiatry practice. Symposium: Epilepsy, learning and behavior. *Educational and Child Psychology, 6,* 74–77.

Tennison, M., Greenwood, R., Lewis, D., & Thorn, M. (1994). Discontinuing antiepileptic drugs in children with epilepsy. *The New England Journal of Medicine, 330*(20): 1407–1410.

Trimble, M. R. (1977). The relationship between epilepsy and schizophrenia: A biochemical hypothesis. *Biological Psychiatry, 12,* 299–304.

Trimble, M. R. (1981). Psychotropic drugs in the management of epilepsy. In E. Reynolds & M. Trimble (Eds.), *Epilepsy and psychiatry* (pp. 337–346). London: Churchill Livingstone, Inc.

Tsubio, T. (1988). Prevalence and incidence of epilepsy in Tokyo. *Epilepsia, 29,* 103–110.

Vallarta, J. M., Bell, D. B., & Reichert, A. (1974). Progressive encephalopathy due to chronic hydantoin intoxication. *American Journal of Diseases of Children, 128,* 27–34.

Volkmar, F. R., & Nelson, D. S. (1990). Seizure disorders in autism. *Journal American Academy of Child and Adolescent Psychiatry, 29,* 127–129.

Wechsler, W. (1980). *Wechsler Adult Intelligence Scale–Revised.* New York: The Psychology Corporation.

Wechsler, W. (1989). *Wechsler Preschool and Primary School Intelligence Scale–Revised.* New York: The Psychology Corporation.

Wechsler, W. (1991). *Wechsler Intelligence Scale for Children–Third Edition.* New York: The Psychology Corporation.

Wechsler, W. (1992). *Wechsler Individual Achievement Test.* New York: The Psychology Corporation.

Williams, B. A., Abbott, K. J., & Manson, J. I. (1992). Cerebral tumors in children presenting with epilepsy. *Journal of Child Neurology, 7,* 291–294.

Williams, D., & Hirsch, G. (1988). The somatizing disorders: Somatoform disorders, factitious disorders, and malingering. In C. Kestenbaum and D. Williams (Eds.), *Handbook of clinical assessment of children and adolescents (Vol. 2, p. 743).* New York: New York University Press.

Williams, D. T., Pleak, R. R., & Hannesian, H. (1992). Neurological disorder. In M. Lewis (Ed.), *Child and adolescent psychiatry: A comprehensive textbook* (pp. 629–646). Baltimore, MD: Williams & Wilkins Co.

Wirt, R., Lachar, D., Klinedinst, J., Seat, P., & Broen, W. (1984). *Personality Inventory for Children–Revised.* Los Angeles: Western Psychological Services.

Yuksel, A., Kartal, A., Cenani, A., & Yalcin, E. (1993). Serum thyroid hormones and pituitary response to thyrotropin-releasing hormone in epileptic children receiving anti-epileptic medication. *Acta Paediatrica Japonica, 35,* 108–112.

CHAPTER 11

ENDOCRINE DISORDERS

Alan M. Delamater
Margaret Eidson

The purpose of this chapter is to review medical, psychological, and behavioral aspects of endocrine disorders in children. Because the field of endocrine disorders is very broad, this review will focus only on the more common major disorders of metabolism, thyroid functioning, and growth, including diabetes mellitus, congenital hypothyroidism, and short stature. Diabetes will be reviewed more extensively and will follow the same presentation format as other chapters in this book; the other two disorders will be treated more briefly, considering epidemiology, medical issues, and psychological and psychiatric issues. After discussing these disorders, two case studies are presented to illustrate common issues for psychological and psychiatric assessment and management in diabetes and growth hormone deficiency. Disorders of sexual development, including congenital adrenal hyperplasia and Turner's syndrome, among others, will not be addressed in this chapter because of space limitations, although they are of considerable relevance for pediatric psychologists and psychiatrists.

DIABETES MELLITUS

Description of Disorder

Type I or insulin-dependent diabetes mellitus (IDDM) is a chronic disease reflecting an absolute lack of insulin secretion from the pancreas. In another form of diabetes, Type II or non-insulin-dependent diabetes mellitus, there is a relative deficiency of insulin action and/or insulin resistance. The onset of Type II diabetes is more common among older adults and is associated with obesity, hypertension, and hyperlipidemia. Occasionally adolescents may be diagnosed with Type II diabetes, particularly obese black females. In recent years, a third type of diabetes, maturity-onset diabetes of youths (or "Type I and a half") has been identified (Winter et al., 1987). This disorder has features of insulin resistance and appears to be more common among black youths.

The onset of IDDM is now thought to arise in genetically susceptible persons after immune-mediated destruction of the insulin secreting beta-cells of the pancreatic islets (Maclaren, Schatz, Drask, & Grove, 1989). Environmental factors such as viral infections are thought to contribute to the process of beta-cell destruction. Studies have shown immunological alterations in the form of islet cell antibodies in the period prior to diagnosis (Riley et al., 1990).

Epidemiology

About 10 percent of all people diagnosed with diabetes have Type I or IDDM. Because Type I diabetes generally appears in children or young adulthood, it has been referred to as juvenile diabetes. Diabetes mellitus is the most common metabolic disease affecting children. Approximately one in 700 children have IDDM, and the incidence increases with age, peaking between 11 and 14 years of age (Arslanian, Becker, & Drash, 1994). There is evidence that boys are more affected than girls, and in recent years, non-white males have shown an increasing incidence (Dokheel, 1993). There are also reports of increasing rates of diagnosis among very young children (Travis, Brouhard, & Schreiner, 1987).

Assessment Approaches

Medical Issues

The onset of the classic symptoms of IDDM usually occurs rapidly over a period of weeks, representing the end point of a progressive decline in beta-cell function, and includes polyuria, polydipsia, and polyphagia, accompanied by weight loss and fatigue. These symptoms are related to the inability to metabolize glucose and the subsequent utilization of fat as an alternative energy source. With severe insulin deficiency, fatty acids oxidized in the liver are converted to ketone bodies and become concentrated in the blood and urine. If untreated, this condition leads to diabetic ketoacidosis (DKA), with nausea and vomiting, abdominal pain, and eventually coma. Prior to the discovery of insulin that could be injected into the body, this condition always resulted in death.

Criteria established by the National Institutes of Health National Diabetes Data Group (NDDG) for the diagnosis of IDDM consists of a fasting plasma glucose greater than or equal to 140 mg/dl and a sustained elevated glucose level (greater than or equal to 200 mg/dl) two hours following a standard glucose dose administered orally (NDDG, 1979). According to the American Diabetes Association's Clinical Practice Recommendations (1996), IDDM can also be diagnosed by the classic symptoms of polyuria, polydipsia, polyphagia, ketonuria, rapid weight loss, and a random plasma glucose greater than 200 mg/dl.

A number of factors affect metabolic control. In the period after diagnosis of IDDM, children go through a "honeymoon" period during which their beta-cells produce some insulin (Madsbad, McNair, & Faber, 1980). During this time, generally lasting about 18–24 months after diagnosis, glycemic control is relatively easy to attain, but after the residual pancreatic activity subsides, good glycemic control becomes more challenging. Puberty represents another critical time during which biologic factors influence metabolic control. Studies indicate that the worsening of metabolic control typically seen during puberty can be attributed in part to decreased insulin sensitivity (Amiel, Sherwin, Simonson, Lauritano, & Tamborland, 1986; Bloch, Clemons, & Sperling, 1987).

Research indicates that poor metabolic control is eventually associated with serious health complications, including kidney disease, retinopathy, and neuropathy (Clark & Lee, 1995). Metabolic control has therefore been considered a very important factor in diabetes management and prevention of complications (Diabetes Control and Complications Trial Research Group [DCCT], 1993), with improved metabolic control shown to reduce risk of complications even among adolescents (DCCT, 1994). Studies have shown racial disparity in the complications associated with poor control of diabetes, with, for example, increased rates of end-stage renal disease among black adults (Cowie et al., 1989). Studies also indicate that black youths have greater metabolic control problems than white youths (Auslander, Anderson, Bubb, Jung, & Santiago, 1990; Delamater, Albrecht, Postelon, & Gutai, 1991; Hanson, Henggeler, & Burghen, 1987a).

Metabolic control is assessed by several methods. Patients can measure their blood glucose with a drop of blood obtained by finger-prick. Accurate results are available within two minutes, providing feedback to the patient and family about current blood glucose level. In recent years, reflectance meters became equipped with memory so that several hundred values could be stored and downloaded to personal computers for statistical and graphical evaluation. Generally, patients are prescribed to do two or more blood glucose tests each day. Urine tests for ketones may also be prescribed at certain times of high risk for DKA, such as during viral illness or after several days of hyperglycemia.

The "gold standard" of measurement for the past two decades has been the glycosylated hemoglobin A1 (or A1C) assay, reflecting the amount of glucose bound to hemoglobin in the blood (Gonen, Rachman, Rubenstein, Tanega, & Horwitz, 1977; Nathan, Singer, Hurxthal, & Goodson, 1984). Because the half-life of hemoglobin is about two months, this assay provides a measure of average blood glucose over that two month antecedent period. This blood test is generally conducted on a quarterly basis and has been increasingly used to determine the effectiveness of interventions. The glycohemoglobin test has typically required a venous blood sample, but new technologic advances have made it possible to attain via a finger-stick sample of blood.

It is important to note that this test does not reflect short-term changes and should not be used as a measure of regimen adherence (because metabolic control is affected by multiple biological, psychological, and behavioral factors). Norms for glycosylated hemoglobin A1 vary across assays and laboratories, but the range for most is 4–7 percent for individuals without diabetes; the value for patients with diabetes in good control is less than 9 percent, while those in poor control would have values greater than 12 percent. Although glycohemoglobin results are undoubtedly an important outcome measure, additional variables should be considered in evaluating control of diabetes, including number of blood glucose values (from self-monitoring) outside the target range both pre- and post-prandially, number of hypoglycemic episodes, and normal growth and development.

Psychological and Psychiatric Issues

Diagnosis of IDDM poses considerable challenges and stress for children and families (Delamater, 1990). Several longitudinal studies have been conducted. Kovacs and colleagues found 36 percent of newly diagnosed children had diagnosable psychiatric disorders soon after diabetes was diagnosed, most commonly being adjustment disorders (Kovacs, Feinberg, et al., 1985). However, 50 percent of these children had recovered by three months, and 93 percent had recovered by nine months post-diagnosis. In addition, high rates of depression have been observed in mothers soon after their children's IDDM diagnosis, but within six months there was a significant decline in depression and other symptoms (Kovacs, Finkelstein, et al., 1985).

Jacobson and colleagues have also investigated children with newly diagnosed IDDM. Evaluations conducted within the first five months after diagnosis showed no differences between the group of children with diabetes and a medical control on a variety of behavioral and psychological measures, with the exception of decreased school-related competence (Jacobson et al., 1986). Families of these children reported significantly more organization and recreational activities during the period after diagnosis (Hauser, Jacobson, Wertlieb, Brink, & Wentworth, 1985). Taken together, these findings indicate that most children and families adapt well to having diabetes. These authors also demonstrated that good coping and adjustment of children (Jacobson et al., 1990) and healthier family functioning (Hauser et al., 1990) in the months just after diagnosis were predictive of better regimen adherence over the first four years of having diabetes. Other studies indicate children from families of lower socioeconomic status have a higher risk of having metabolic control problems in the years following diagnosis (Auslander et al., 1990; Hamman et al., 1985).

Studies comparing children with established diabetes to other groups on psychological variables generally do not find significant differences (Johnson, 1995), although there is a report of boys with later onset of diabetes having more behavioral problems (Rovet, Ehrlich, & Hoppe, 1987). One study did indicate, however, that the rate of psychiatric problems was significantly higher among older adolescents with IDDM: by structured interviews, 33 percent of 93 IDDM adolescents had psychiatric disorders (mostly internalizing symptoms), compared with 10 percent of the subjects in the control group (Blanz, Rensch-Riemann, Fritz-Sigmund, & Schmidt, 1993).

Psychological and family factors have been associated with regimen adherence and metabolic control within samples of children with diabetes (Delamater, 1986; Johnson, 1995). Results from studies of psychosocial factors suggest youths in poor metabolic control have increased anxiety and lower self-concept (Anderson, Auslander, Jung, Miller, & Santiago, 1981), more peer relationship problems and depression (Simonds, 1977), and greater levels of stress (Chase & Jackson, 1981; Hanson, Henggeler, & Burghen, 1987b; Hanson & Pichert, 1986; Kager & Holden, 1992). Other studies indicate social competence appears to buffer the negative effects of stress on blood glucose (Hanson, Henggeler, & Burghen, 1987c). There is also data indicating that eating disorders are common among adolescent girls and young women with IDDM, and that disordered eating is associated with poor metabolic control (Rodin, Johnson, Garfinkel, Daneman, & Kenshole, 1987; Stancin, Link, & Reuter, 1989; Wing, Norwalk, Koeske, & Feingold, 1986).

Studies of attributional and coping styles suggest youths in poor metabolic control are more likely to use the learned helplessness style (Kuttner, Delamater, & Santiago, 1990) and engage in avoidance and wishful thinking in response to stress (Delamater, Kurtz, Bubb, White, & Santiago, 1987). Health beliefs (Brownlee-Duffeck et al., 1987) and self-efficacy (Grossman, Brink, & Hauser, 1987) have also been shown to be important correlates of metabolic control.

With children as patients, the effects of family functioning become very salient. Studies indicate families of youths in poor metabolic control have more conflict and financial problems, and less cohesion and stability than those of youths in good metabolic control (Anderson et al., 1981; Koski & Kumento, 1977). Better family communication and conflict resolution skills (Wysocki, 1993) and agreement about family responsibilities for diabetes management tasks (Anderson, Auslander, Jung, Miller, & Santiago, 1990) have been associated with improved levels of metabolic control among youths, as have more structured and controlling family environments (Weist, Finney, Barnard, Davis, & Ollendick, 1993). Research also suggests the effects of family functioning on metabolic control may depend on the duration of diabetes (Hanson, Henggeler, Harris, Burghen, & Moore, 1989). Clinical studies of adolescents selected for chronically poor metabolic control have revealed significant family dysfunction for the majority of families (Orr, Golden, Myers, & Marrero, 1983; White, Kolman, Wexler, Polin, & Winter, 1984).

Besides the effects of the family on metabolic control, there is growing evidence that family relations are linked with regimen adherence. In studies of adolescents, adherence levels have been associated with both general and regimen-specific family support (Hanson, DeGuire, Schinkel, Henggeler, & Burghen, 1992; Schafer, Glasgow, McCaul, & Dreher, 1983) as well as communication skills (Bobrow, AvRuskin, & Siller, 1985) and conflict (Miller-Johnson et al., 1994).

It is important to assess children's abilities to assume responsibility for various components of the regimen. Studies have shown that professionals often expect children to assume self-management responsibilities at relatively young ages (Wysocki, Meinhold, Cox, & Clarke, 1990), and that parents and professionals may differ in how they assess children's competence with respect to diabetes management (Wysocki et al., 1992). This is especially important in light of the finding that cognitive maturity among adolescents has been associated with more insulin self-adjustment and better glycemic control (Ingersoll, Orr, Herrold, & Golden, 1986). These findings call attention to the importance of good communication between families and health care providers, particularly regarding the goals of treatment (Marteau, Johnson, Baum, & Bloch, 1987).

A number of cross-sectional studies have investigated neuropsychological functioning in children with diabetes (Holmes, 1990). Ryan, Vega, and Drash (1985) found that children with early onset of diabetes had significantly poorer cognitive performance, particularly for visual-spatial functioning. Similarly, Rovet, Ehrlich, and Hoppe (1988) found that children with early onset performed more poorly than those with later onset on tests of visual-spatial skills. Their verbal skills, regardless of age of onset, were lower than children without diabetes. Regression analysis indicated that age of onset, diabetes duration, and history of hypoglycemic episodes were significant predictors of visual-spatial abilities.

Other studies provide additional data indicating children who develop diabetes early in life may be at increased risk for later neurocognitive deficits, both verbal and visual-spatial (Anderson et al., 1984; Holmes & Richman, 1985; Ryan, Vega, Longstreet, & Drash, 1984). Ryan, Longstreet, & Morrow (1985) found that children with diabetes missed twice as much school as their peers who did not have diabetes, and reading achievement was associated with school absences. Based on available data, it appears that visual-spatial deficits may be secondary to history of hypoglycemia, while verbal deficits may be attributed to more frequent school absences, particularly in children with early onset of diabetes.

Because blood glucose levels influence cognitive functioning (Holmes, Hayford, Gonzalez, & Weydert, 1983; Holmes, Koepke, Thompson, Gyves, & Weydert, 1984), and the above cited studies did not control for blood glucose of their subjects at the time of assessment, the findings concerning neuropsychological consequences of diabetes must be interpreted cautiously, particularly without more compelling longitudinal data. One study by Kovacs, Goldston, and Iyengar (1992) did examine neuropsychological functioning in a sample of newly diagnosed children. These investigators found that verbal intelligence and school grades were average shortly after diagnosis, but declined significantly over time. More recently they have suggested that this decline in verbal skill can be predicted in part by memory dysfunction (Kovacs, Ryan, & Obrosky, 1994).

Treatment Strategies

Overview of Medical Management

Medical treatment is aimed at maintenance of normal or near normal blood glucose levels, with prevention of hypoglycemia (less than 70 mg/dl) and hyperglycemia (greater than 180 mg/dl). Education and involvement of the family is a pre-requisite to good management of IDDM. The regimen requires adherence to a variety of medically prescribed behaviors, including daily insulin administration and glucose monitoring, planning and modification of diet and exercise, and timing of all these factors related to blood glucose levels. Children are typically prescribed two insulin injections each day (before breakfast and dinner), two blood glucose tests per day (generally before breakfast and dinner), and a balanced diet of meals and snacks with a daily caloric goal. While most physicians encourage their IDDM patients to exercise, specific exercise prescriptions are not routinely made.

Perfect adherence does not necessarily guarantee good metabolic control, however, as regimen prescriptions may be inappropriate and endogenous factors (e.g., residual beta-cell activity, insulin resistance) may exert independent effects on blood glucose. Conversely, poor adherence may still be associated with acceptable metabolic control in individual cases. Thus, the interaction between biological and behavioral factors in diabetes management is complex and difficult to predict. This may help explain why some studies have found significant associations between regimen compliance and metabolic control (e.g., Brownlee-Duffick et al., 1987; Hanson, Henggeler, & Burghen, 1987b; Johnson et al., 1992; Kuttner et al., 1990), while others have not (Johnson, Freund, Silverstein, Hanse, & Malone, 1990; Glasgow, McCaul, & Schafer, 1987).

With the results of the Diabetes Control and Complications Trial establishing that maintenance of normal glycohemoglobin levels by intensive insulin therapy delays the onset and slows the progression of retinopathy, neuropathy, and nephropathy (DCCT, 1993, 1994), "tight" control of blood glucose has become an important goal of medical management of IDDM. Intensive therapy requires multiple insulin injections and blood glucose measures each day (up to six or more), with utilization of blood glucose data for adjustments in insulin dose, physical activity, and diet. Regimen adherence is best considered a multivariate rather than unitary construct (Johnson, Silverstein, Rosenbloom, Carter, & Cunningham, 1986). Four separate factors or components have been identified from empirical study, including injection, diet type, eating/testing frequency, and exercise, with total calories and consumption of concentrated sweets considered separate, single-indicator constructs (Johnson, Tomer, Cunningham, & Henretta, 1990).

Studies have generally shown relatively low rates of adherence to various aspects of the regimen, especially among older children and adolescents (Johnson, Silverstein, Rosenbloom, Carter, & Cunningham, 1986). Insulin administration is of obvious importance in preventing ketoacidosis, and has been identified as a major compliance problem among the subgroup of patients hospitalized recurrently for poor metabolic control (White et al., 1984); however, studies indicate the vast majority of patients do take their insulin shots on a daily basis. While glucose testing is commonly prescribed 2–4 times per day, studies indicate adherence rates and utilization of blood glucose data are fairly low (Delamater et al., 1989; Wing et al., 1985). Furthermore, blood glucose testing is not necessarily associated with improved metabolic control (Daneman et al., 1985; Mann, Noronha, & Johnston, 1984). Dietary adherence is very problematic for young patients (Christensen, Terry, Wyatt, Pichert, & Lorenz, 1983; Delamater, Smith, Kurtz, & White, 1988; Lorenz, Christensen, & Pichert, 1985) and has been associated with metabolic control (Delamater, Smith, et al., 1988). Exercise levels are generally low among diabetic youths (Johnson et al., 1986), but as noted above, exercise is not usually prescribed in a very specific manner.

Psychological and Behavioral Treatments

Diabetes knowledge and skills are of obvious importance in successful management, yet studies have shown substantial deficits (Johnson et al., 1982). Improving knowledge and skills has been assumed to lead to better adherence and metabolic control, but studies have shown this not to be the case (Bloomgarden et al., 1987). In fact, studies have indicated children in poor metabolic control actually have high levels of diabetes knowledge (Weist, Finney, Barnard, Davis, & Ollendick, 1993). Because knowledge and skills are necessary but not sufficient to predict good adherence and metabolic control, interventions that target behavioral change are necessary.

A number of single case and controlled adherence intervention studies have been published (Delamater, 1993). Results from single case studies have shown that the use of goals, memos, and parent administered contingent praise and behavioral contracts improve adherence to various aspects of the regimen (mostly focusing on blood glucose testing) during brief (5- to 10-week) interventions (Carney, Schechter, & Davis, 1983; Lowe & Lutzker, 1979; Schafer, Glasgow, & McCaul, 1982).

Studies utilizing randomized group designs have used a number of approaches. For example, individual clinic-based behavioral contracting (Wysocki, Green, & Huxtable, 1989) and computer-assisted feedback (Marrero et al., 1989) have improved blood glucose testing adherence, but without improvements in glycemic control. However, other intervention programs utilizing peer groups for problem solving related to social situations associated with nonadherence (Kaplan, Chadwick, & Schimmel, 1985) and utilization of blood glucose data in combination with parent training (Anderson, Wolf, Burkhart, Cornell, & Bacon, 1989) have led to improvements in both adherence and glycemic control. Peer group interventions targeting structured physical exercise have shown improved short-term glycemic control in children (Campaigne, Gilliam, Spencer, Lamplman, & Schork, 1984) and adolescents (Stratton, Wilson, Endres, & Goldstein, 1987). Improvements have also been observed in an intervention consisting of multi-family groups and parent simulation of diabetes management tasks (Satin, La Greca, Zigo, & Skyler, 1989).

Most diabetes education is typically provided during hospitalization at diagnosis, but because of the stress associated with diagnosis this is not an ideal time for the family to assimilate all the complex information needed for effective diabetes management. Therefore, behavioral interventions may be particularly beneficial in the months after diagnosis. In a randomized prospective study of family-based self-management training conducted with newly-diagnosed children, treated patients showed significantly improved glycemic control two years after diagnosis (Delamater et al., 1990). This intervention emphasized utilization of blood glucose data (Delamater et al., 1989) for problem solving, as well as parent training in behavior management and consisted of seven outpatient sessions in the four months after diagnosis.

In summary, several types of behavioral interventions have led to improved adherence and glycemic control. The targets have included social risk factors for nonadherence, utilization of blood glucose data for problem solving, and exercise. The interventions incorporated the use of peer groups for exercise or problem solving, and family problem solving, support, and parent training in the use of contingent reinforcement and contracts with clear behavioral goals. Although stress has been shown to play a role in diabetes, few controlled studies have evaluated the effects of relaxation and stress management interventions with children and adolescents (Delamater, 1992). In one study employing a peer group approach, stress management training resulted in reduced disease-specific stress without improvement in glycemic control (Boardway, Delamater, Tomakowsky, & Gutai, 1993).

In general, however, the intervention literature is limited by studies of relatively small samples of youths, fairly brief interventions, and lack of long-term follow-up evaluations. More studies are needed that can clarify the roles of behavior and emotional problems, parent-adolescent relationships, and family functioning in relation to adherence and metabolic control. Further, studies that can identify paths of influence on metabolic control would be informative and helpful in planning interventions. Such studies require both theoretically based hypotheses of paths of influence and appropriate statistical methodologies to handle the complex relationships among these variables.

Pharmacological Treatments

Pharmacologic treatments may sometimes be indicated for psychiatric problems in children with IDDM. Given the base rate of IDDM in the pediatric population and within that group the expected rate of psychiatric disorders requiring pharmacologic treatment (similar to or slightly elevated compared to the general population), it is not surprising that controlled studies of the use of psychopharmacologic agents with such children are not available. With attention deficit hyperactivity, anxiety, depression, and obsessive-compulsive disorders, among others for which pharmacological treatments are efficacious, the clinician should consult the *Physician's Desk Reference* (PDR) concerning the possible effects of the medications on glucose metabolism. For example, among imipramine hydrochloride's adverse reactions, elevation or depression of blood sugar levels is noted. Similarly, the PDR notes that fluoxetine hydrochloride may alter glycemic control in patients with diabetes. Although rarely used for psychiatric disorders in children, beta-blockers can mask the symptoms of hypoglycemia. Therefore, for all cases requiring psychopharmacological interventions in children with diabetes, increased monitoring for glycemic side effects is clinically indicated, particularly during the initial phases of dosage adjustments.

CONGENITAL HYPOTHYROIDISM

Description of Disorder

Congenital hypothyroidism (CH), referred to in the past as cretinism, is a relatively common disease affecting newborns. The cause of CH is a deficiency in the production of thyroid hormone, which is necessary for normal growth and development. Diagnosis of CH could be considered a medical emergency since thyroid hormone is critical for proper maturation of the rapidly developing infant brain. If untreated early in infancy, CH results in irreversible brain damage and mental retardation.

Epidemiology

Epidemiologic studies in modern industrialized countries indicate CH has an incidence of approximately one in 4,000 newborns (Fisher et al., 1979), with three times as many females as males affected (Tunbridge et al., 1977). Approximately 1,400 infants with CH are detected annually in North America out of more than 5 million screened. Higher rates of CH have been reported in developing countries, due to iodine insufficiency in the populations (Ermans, Boudoux, Lagasse, Delange, & Thilly, 1980).

Medical Issues

Children can appear to be normal for several weeks after birth before symptoms gradually develop that suggest a lack of adequate thyroid hormone. By this time, permanent brain damage can result. The clinical picture of severe CH includes lethargy, poor feeding, poor growth, puffy features, large fontanelles, large tongue, flat nose and sunken nasal bridge, abundant hair, hypotonia, mottling and dryness of skin, constipation, umbilical hernia, and persistent neonatal icterus. Unfortunately, treatment of CH at this late stage does not reverse all the features, particularly the poor mental prognosis and often associated neurological findings of spasticity and incoordination.

In the past two decades, as programs have been implemented to screen newborns, the diagnosis of CH has become easy. Screening for CH is now routine throughout the United States and Canada, and most other modern industrialized countries. The screening involves obtaining a few drops of blood from the infant on a filter paper and mailing the sample to a central facility for analysis using radioimmunoassay techniques. Most programs test initially for T4, which if low, is repeated along with TSH. If the repeat test is abnormal with either low T4 or elevated TSH, the regional program physician in charge of screening is notified as well as the infant's physician to contact the family and evaluate the child more completely with physical examination, laboratory evaluation of thyroid function, and thyroid scan. Treatment is started immediately with replacement L-thyroxine before results from confirmatory tests are available, as data indicate the best outcomes are obtained when treatment is initiated in the first weeks of life and the T4 level is maintained in the upper normal range during the first three years of life.

There are two major types of hypothyroidism: primary hypothyroidism, caused by a defect or absence of the thryoid gland; and diseases of the hypothalamus and pituitary that affect the secretion of thyrotropin releasing hormone (TRH) and thyroid stimulating hormone (TSH) (Foley, 1990). Primary hypothyroidism is by far more common and is usually due to a missing thyroid gland (agenesis), a structurally malformed or incomplete gland (hypoplastic), or a gland located in an abnormal position (ectopic). Another cause of CH is a deficiency of an enzyme necessary for adequate synthesis of thyroid hormone within the gland (familial dyshormonogenesis). This problem is hereditary (occurring as an autosomal recessive trait) and accounts for about 10 percent of cases.

In a small number of cases, primary hypothyroidism can be transient, generally occurring in infants whose mothers have thyroid inhibitory antibodies that cross the placenta and inhibit fetal thyroid activity until some months after birth when the antibodies can be excreted. These infants need treatment initially but may be weaned off treatment during their first year. Transient CH also occurs in infants exposed to iodine in excess or from intrauterine exposure to antithyroid drugs taken by the mother.

An important medical issue concerns severity of CH, which is related to both type of CH and timing of the onset of CH. More severe CH is thought to be associated more with agenesis and prenatal onset. Type of CH can be determined by radiologic and hormonal analyses. Timing of onset can be assessed by determination of skeletal maturity using bone age. Delayed bone age suggests prenatal onset of CH, as in utero skeletal maturation is compromised.

Medical treatment of CH involves once daily ingestion of synthetic oral replacement hormone (L-thyroxine), which can be taken orally. Studies have shown that better prognosis of infants is obtained when treatment is initiated within the first month after birth (Grant, 1995). The dosage is adjusted periodically based on clinical examination and serum thyroid hormone determinations. Clinical examination, including assessment of growth and development, is an important component of follow-up. In contrast to older children, infants need more frequent laboratory evaluation of thryoid levels because of their rapid growth and exceptional need for adequate replacement therapy.

The development of radioimmunoassay techniques used in infant screening programs has allowed for earlier diagnosis and treatment of CH, preventing mental retardation and other difficulties. Even with the screening programs, however, treatment in some cases may not be initiated until infants are about one month of age, and euthyroidism may not be attained until another month, raising concerns about more subtle effects on neurocognitive function. Thus one of the most important medical treatment issues concerns timing and dosage of hormone replacement therapy.

Psychological and Psychiatric Issues

Most often results of newborn screening abnormalities are available only after the infant is at home with the family and thought to be well. It can sometimes be difficult to convince a parent that their child has a serious problem that will require thorough evaluation and life-long treatment, especially if they have no familiar family physician or pediatrician with whom they can discuss the diagnosis of CH. Reassurance that life can be carried out in a normal fashion with expectation of excellent outcome, contingent on adherence to daily medication, is needed and particularly helpful in the family's acceptance of their child's CH.

Several controlled longitudinal studies of neurocognitive development have been conducted and are ongoing, including studies in Quebec, Toronto, and New England. In the Quebec program, which began in 1975, findings indicated that at age 18 months, 77 CH children had lower scores in hearing and speech performance than 45 normal control children. Comparing 59 CH and 40 normal children at 36 months of age, the CH children also had lower scores on a test of practical reasoning, leading to a lower overall score for intelligence using the Griffiths Mental Development Scales (Glorieux, Dussault, Letarte, Guyda, & Morissette, 1983).

This team of investigators found that at age 5 years, CH children still had a lower score for overall intelligence, but it is important to note their mean score was within normal limits (102 for 36 CH children vs. 106 in 45 control children) (Glorieux et al., 1985). Using the WISC-R, the mean IQ for 25 children at age 7 years with CH was 101. Further, children identified as having more severe CH by bone age ($<.05$ cm^2) and T4 concentrations (<2 ug/dl) had lower global intelligence at ages 3 (means of 91 vs. 103), 5 (means of 88 vs. 104), and 7 years (means of 86 vs. 102) than those with less severe hypothyroidism (Glorieux, Desjardin, Letarte, Morissette, & Dussault, 1988). At age 7, 10 of 13 children with IQs less than 90 had severe CH by the above criteria. More recently, Glorieux, Dussault, and Van Vliet (1991) reported that at age 12, 12 children with severe CH still had significantly lower global intelligence than 15 children with less severe hypothyroidism (means of 89 vs. 104). Comparisons of the more severe children with their siblings also showed lower scores, indicating the differences could be attributed to disease severity.

In the late 1970s, Rovet and colleagues in Toronto also began longitudinal studies of CH children (Rovet, 1990). They examined the effects of prenatal onset of CH by grouping children on the basis of bone age at the time of diagnosis (Rovet, Ehrlich, & Sorbara, 1987). The delayed group had a bone age less than 36 weeks. Forty-five children in the delayed group (with athyrosis) were compared to 35 non-delayed CH children in a prospective

study with yearly neurocognitive evaluations from age 1 to 5 years of age. Results indicated the delayed group had significantly lower scores on various measures. Perceptual-motor, visuospatial, and language abilities were most affected, contributing to lower overall intelligence. However, it is important to note that mean scores for the delayed group were within the normal range.

In one of their most recent reports, Rovet and colleagues (Rovet, Ehrlich, & Sorbara, 1992) compared 108 children with CH and 71 of their normal siblings on a variety of neurodevelopmental measures in a longitudinal study from age 1 to 5 years. The number of children compared at each age varied from 68 to 94 CH and 13 to 30 sibling control children. Differences between CH and control children began to appear at age 3, with CH children exhibiting poorer receptive language skills, persisting until age 5. On measures of global intelligence, as well as verbal and performance IQ and mazes, CH children performed significantly poorer than their siblings, but mean scores were well within the normal range.

When the performance of CH subgroups was examined, results indicated children with athyrosis scored significantly lower on overall intelligence than sibling controls and the other CH subgroups at almost every age. Similarly, tests of specific neurocognitive abilities revealed lower performance for the subgroup with athyrosis, compared with both other CH subgroups and sibling controls. The specific deficits of these children included motor and visuomotor delays at age 1, speech and perceptual deficits at age 2 and 3, receptive language and quantitative skills at age 4, and visuomotor skills at age 5. Results also indicated that regardless of etiology, children with intrauterine CH (as indicated by delayed bone age at diagnosis) showed a similar pattern of deficits in language, visuomotor, and motor skills.

Regression analyses were performed to identify predictors of poorer outcomes at each of the five age groups for global intelligence as well as composite scores for language, visuomotor, motor, memory, spatial, and auditory discrimination skills. After accounting for the effects of gender, parent IQ and socioeconomic status, predictors included intrauterine hypothyroidism (determined by bone age at diagnosis), severity of hypothyroidism at birth (determined by T4 levels), and timing and duration of hypothyroidism. In general, these analyses indicated in utero hypothyroidism was an important predictor of later outcomes in visuomotor and motor development, with language skills being affected by both pre- and postnatal hypothyroidism. Hypothyroidism later in infancy was associated more with auditory discrimination abilities, consistent with previous studies indicating abnormalities of brainstem auditory evoked responses in children with CH (Herbert et al., 1986).

The other major developmental study has been conducted by the New England Congenital Hypothyroidism Collaborative Study (NECHCS). This team of investigators reported on the status of 56 CH children at age 6 years, compared with 31 sibling controls and 28 euthyroid children with low T4 levels (NECHCS, 1985a). A variety of neurocognitive tests were conducted, including measures of intelligence, academic achievement, perceptual speed, sensory perception, motor, and psychomotor function. No differences were found between the groups on intellectual, achievement, and neuropsychological tests, with the exception of slower motor functioning in CH children. Mean scores for full-scale IQ (using the WISC-R) were 109 for CH children and 110 for the combined control group.

The NECHCS (1985b) also reported on the elementary school performance of 72 children at ages 9 or 10 years after completion of 3rd grade. They were compared with 96 normal classmates and 32 siblings matched for age. No differences could be detected on measures of intelligence (WISC-R mean IQs of 106 for CH and 109 for controls), academic achievement, neuropsychological functioning, or school histories (repeating grades or requiring special educational placement), leading the authors to conclude that CH children have no learning problems. The correlations of IQ and academic achievement were similar for each of the three groups. It is of note that only 29 percent of this sample of CH children had atrophic glands. In discussing their results, the authors speculated that the lack of differences in their study relative to the differences obtained in the Canadian studies may be due to less adequate treatment in the latter, where a much longer time was needed to attain serum T4 levels in the normal range.

Few studies have focused on psychological aspects other than neurocognitive functioning in children with CH. Rovet, Ehrlich, and Sorbara (1989) examined temperament in 50 6-month-old infants with CH and also evaluated them at 12, 18, 24, and 26 months of age. Their findings indicated that more children were considered as having "difficult" temperament than would be expected in the normative population. Difficult temperament persisted until at least 2 years of age and was associated with higher T4 and TSH levels, and also with increased central nervous system arousal. The authors observed that higher levels of thyroid hormone may increase temperamental difficulties in these infants, although better perceptual motor skills at age 3 were associated with higher T4 levels. These findings suggest that proper dosage of hormone replacement in infants should consider behavior as well as circulating hormone levels.

SHORT STATURE

Description of Disorder

Stature is an important point of reference for social recognition and position in our society. During childhood, social relationships, successful competition in athletics, and self-esteem are often related to physical stature. It is not surprising then, that parents become concerned when their child is small in comparison with their peer group. Short stature is more likely to be of concern to boys and their parents than to girls, but girls are also becoming more aware of height, considering tall stature to be most desirable.

A variety of factors may be implicated in short stature, including intrinsic defects of growing tissues (e.g., skeletal dysplasias, autosomal abnormalities, abnormalities of the X chromosome, dysmorphic dwarfism), abnormalities in the environment of growing tissues (e.g., nutritional insufficiency, gastrointestinal disease, renal, and cardiac disease), and endocrine abnormalities (thyroid hormone deficiency, glucocorticoid excess, growth hormone deficiency) (Rieser & Underwood, 1990).

Growth hormone (GH) plays a significant role in promoting growth. It is secreted by the pituitary gland after stimulation by growth hormone releasing hormone from the hypothalamus. Growth hormone deficiency (GHD) or hypopituitarism is one cause of slow growth and severe short stature. The most common form of GHD is termed idiopathic hypopituitarism and is considered to be due to damage to the hypothalamus that results in a deficiency of secretion of growth hormone releasing hormone. Rather than a dichotomous classification of GHD or GH sufficient, current diagnostics consider variants of growth disorders, including inactive GH (Bright et al., 1983), GH resistance (Laron et al., 1993), and neurosecretory defects in GH secretion (Bercu & Diamond, 1986).

Other terms used to describe children with short stature include constitutional growth delay and psychosocial dwarfism. In the former, children are shorter than expected based on parental heights, but grow at a normal rate. They exhibit delayed bone age and have a late onset of puberty. Although their height throughout childhood and adolescence is at about the third percentile, their eventual adult height is generally consistent with parental heights.

The short stature of children with psychosocial dwarfism is thought to be related to severe psychosocial stress due to environmental deprivation, malnutrition, and poor parenting (particularly with feeding behaviors), resulting in disordered endocrine responses that account for deficient growth (Powell, Brasel, & Blizzard, 1967). Besides growth delay, behavioral abnormalities usually exist, including disordered eating, social withdrawal, irritability, self-injury and accident proneness, and parental psychopathology and physical abuse is often evident (Green, 1990). With appropriate intervention, psychosocial dwarfism can be reversed, with restoration of growth and improved psychosocial adjustment.

Epidemiology

There are approximately 2 million children in the United States who are considered to have short stature, because they are below the fifth percentile on the growth chart. Most of these children have normal variants of short stature, due to their genetic heritage (familial short stature), a constitutional delay of growth, or a combination of these. Constitutional growth delay is apparently more common in boys than girls, and is often associated with a family history of delayed growth and puberty in male relatives. Pathologic etiologies of short stature account for the remainder. Approximately 1 in 4,000 children have GHD (Rieser & Underwood, 1990).

In a recent report of 258 children evaluated for short stature at a large regional children's hospital, Sandberg, Brook, and Campos (1994) identified 14 separate etiologies using standardized criteria for diagnoses (Underwood & Van Wyk, 1992). Although not an epidemiologic study, the sample was considered representative of those children referred clinically for evaluation of short stature. Fifty-four percent were considered normal variants, 32.4 percent were pathologic, and 13.6 percent could not be conclusively determined. Among the pathologic etiologies, GHD accounted for 14.4 percent of cases, idiopathic growth failure accounted for 7.8 percent, and undernutrition for 4.7 percent, with 1.9 percent due to intrauterine growth retardation, and less than 1 percent each due to skeletal dysplasia, chromosomal abnormality, chronic disease, psychosocial dwarfism, dysmorphic syndrome, and hypothyroidism. Normal variants were associated with smaller height deficits than pathologic deficits. Boys had relatively more constitutional growth delay and GHD, while there were more girls with undernutrition, intrauterine growth retardation, chromosomal abnormality, chronic disease, psychosocial short stature, and hypothyroidism.

Medical Issues

Genetics, psychosocial factors, and state of health influence growth and maturation. Abnormal growth can be recognized when the pattern of one's growth does not follow the standards expressed on the typical growth curve and growth velocity curve. It is not unusual for an infant or toddler to fluctuate between percentiles to some extent, but after the age of three years, children who are growing normally will be at or near the same percentile each year. During puberty, there is normally an acceleration of growth in height, but significant changes across percentiles is a cause of concern.

The evaluation of short stature includes accurate measurements of height over time, calculation of growth velocity, determination of skeletal maturity (by x-ray of the hand to measure bone age), and consideration of family size. It is also critical to determine whether short stature is caused by an underlying physical condition. Therefore, a medical history from birth to the present is obtained. A number of physical conditions and their treatment may be associated with short stature, including inflammatory bowel disease, brain tumors, thyroid deficiency, severe asthma (with glucocorticoid treatment), sickle cell disease, and renal disease, to name a few.

If inadequate growth is found, medical evaluation includes serum chemistries, complete blood count, erythrocyte sedimentation rate, urinalysis, thryoid hormone level, and bone age. If these do not reveal another illness, a screening test for GH adequacy, IGF-1 (insulin-like growth factor-1), is done. IGF-1 is produced in response to GH and acts at the tissue level to stimulate growth. If IGF-1 is low, a more definitive test for GH adequacy is done using a pharmacologic stimulus to cause release of GH from the pituitary gland into the blood stream so that it can be measured. Positive tests are usually followed by confirmatory tests using a different stimulus. If this also results in abnormally low GH levels, imaging of the brain is done (usually with MRI) to ascertain that there is no anatomical anomaly of the pituitary or hypothalamus. Lesions are rare but must be ruled out prior to initiation of GH replacement therapy.

Medical intervention for short stature due to GHD involves GH replacement therapy, aimed at allowing catch-up growth and achievement of a reasonable adult height without causing problems associated with excessive levels of GH. In the past GH was obtained from cadavers but new recombinant technology has made synthetic GH available. GH is administered by subcutaneous injection, usually given on a daily basis for several years. Side effects are uncommon for synthetic GH, but may include hyperinsulinism, insulin resistance, and impaired glucose tolerance. The child must be evaluated every three to four months to assess the response to treatment and adjust the dose of GH if necessary.

Results depend on several factors, including the target height based on parental heights, bone maturation (i.e., how much growth potential is left), how far from the norm height the time treatment is initiated, and whether other health or psychological problems are present. GH replacement treatment is discontinued when the bones show maturation so that no further growth can occur or when the individual achieves an acceptable height. GH replacement therapy has been given to short stature children without evidence of GHD, although this practice is controversial (Allen & Fost, 1990; Hopwood et al., 1993; Lantos, Siegler, & Cuttler, 1989). In general, children report fairly good satisfaction and compliance with GH replacement therapy (Leiberman et al., 1993).

Psychological and Psychiatric Issues

A number of studies have evaluated the psychological and academic functioning of short stature children (Holmes, 1990; Siegel, 1990; Stabler, 1986; Young-Hyman, 1990). The results of these studies generally indicate that growth delay is associated with socially immature behaviors and academic problems, possibly related to attention deficits and learning disabilities. Several representative studies are reviewed below.

Psychological Functioning

Deficient social problem-solving skills and a tendency to internalize feelings were identified by Drotar, Owens, and Gotthold (1980) in a sample of children with GHD. Similarly, Stabler and colleagues (Stabler et al., 1980) reported that children with GHD scored lower on a test of social awareness. In other reports, short stature children have been described as showing more social withdrawal and somatic complaints and less aggressive behavior than normal height peers (Gordon, Crouthamel, Post, & Richman, 1982; Holmes, Hayford, & Thompson, 1982). In a longitudinal study of 47 short stature youths (17 with GHD, 21 with constitutional delay, and 9 with Turner's syndrome), Holmes, Karlsson, and Thompson (1985) observed an age-related decline in social competence beginning in early adolescence, apparently related to greater social isolation (fewer friendships and social contacts).

In a more recent study of 56 GHD children evaluated at a mean age of 10 years, Allen, Warzak, Greger, Berno-

tas, and Huseman (1993) found increased behavior problems and decreased social competence only among older children (12 and over) in the sample compared with nonclinical norms. Mean behavioral and social competence scores were not significantly different from clinical norms. There were no differences between younger children and nonclinical norms, however. Interestingly, scores on measures of personality, self-concept, anxiety, and social competence correlated significantly with the magnitude of height discrepancy with normal peers.

In one of the most recent and largest studies of psychosocial aspects of short stature, Sandberg, Brook, and Campos (1994) reported on 180 boys and 78 girls evaluated at a large regional children's hospital. Etiology of short stature was hetereogenous in the sample, with 54 percent of the children having normal variants of growth. The mean age for boys and girls was 11.4 and 10.4 years, respectively. Children and their parents completed standardized behavioral and self-concept scales.

Parent ratings indicated boys were less competent socially and had more behavioral and emotional problems, compared both to non-clinical norms and to girls with short stature. The most significant differences were for internalizing problems such as social withdrawal, somatic complaints, and anxious/depressed. However, their problems were not as great as a clinical sample of children referred for psychiatric problems. On self-report measures, boys also indicated reduced social competence and decreased self-concept in athletic and job competence (particularly among older boys). Although degree of height deficit was greater in children with pathologic versus normal variants of growth, etiology and height deficit were unrelated to psychosocial problems.

Academic Functioning

Holmes, Thompson, and Hayford (1984) reported that 31 percent of GHD children had been retained in a grade, compared with 20 percent of girls with Turner's syndrome and 19 percent of those with constitutional growth delay. Retained children exhibited decreased academic achievement and increased behavioral and emotional problems than short children who had not been retained. Siegel and colleagues (Siegel & Hopwood, 1986; Siegel, 1990), have reported that about half of GHD children in their sample had significant academic problems and nearly one-third had failed at least one grade in school. Among underachievers, 40 percent evidenced low cognitive abilities and 36 percent had specific learning disabilities, with a significant number of these children exhibiting deficits in attention, visual-spatial skills, and memory. The rest had normal intelligence with no evidence of cognitive deficits. The authors attributed the poor academic performance of the latter group to environmental and psychosocial factors.

Voss, Bailey, Mulligan, Wilkin, and Betts (1991) found no differences in academic achievement between a large nonreferred sample of children with short stature and their normal height peers. In addition, these children showed no differences in behavioral adjustment and self-esteem. When academic problems were observed, they were attributable more to lower socioeconomic status than to stature.

Long-Term Follow-Up

Few studies are available concerning the prognosis of children with short stature. Available evidence suggests that individuals with GHD may continue to experience difficulties with their social adjustment, in terms of psychosexual and marital behavior (Clopper, 1990; Dean, McTaggert, Fish, & Friesen, 1985). In a follow-up study of children with constitutional growth delay who were not treated by growth hormone replacement, no differences with control subjects were observed on measures of self-esteem, social and marital adjustment, and employment status, despite the fact that many felt their short stature interfered with their success at school, athletics, and socially.

CASE ILLUSTRATIONS

Two case examples are presented below, illustrating common issues for psychological intervention in diabetes and short stature.

Case One

Clinical Presentation

The patient was a 13-year-old Hispanic boy who had been diagnosed at age 6 with insulin-dependent diabetes. In the past few years he began having poor metabolic control. The referral was made to pediatric psychology because of sad affect, academic difficulties, problems with anger control, few peer interactions, and poor regimen adherence and metabolic control. The pattern of social withdrawal, depression, and anger control problems began following the death of the patient's father seven years before, just prior to his diagnosis of diabetes one

month later. He lived with his mother, who had little formal education and whose income was limited.

Assessment Findings

Assessment procedures included measurement of general and diabetes specific behaviors. The mother completed a standardized behavior rating scale, which indicated significant elevations (all T-scores above 73) in withdrawn, anxious/depressed, conduct problems, and psychosomatic problems. Both the mother and child completed a checklist of diabetes specific family behaviors, revealing high levels of negative and few positive interactions around diabetes management tasks. In terms of responsibilities for diabetes management tasks, the mother reported having primary responsibility for the majority of tasks, while the patient reported either sharing or having responsibility for most tasks. There were several tasks that each denied having responsibility for. Measurement of regimen adherence indicated blood glucose monitoring and dietary adherence were the most significant problems, the latter characterized by binge eating when feeling angry or depressed. Glycosylated hemoglobin was 13 percent.

Treatment Selection and Course

After completing assessment procedures, a session was held with the patient and his mother identifying the various problem areas and providing a formulation for them. A diagram was drawn in which links between the problem areas were identified. For example, the issues of poor adherence and metabolic control were related to each other, and also to the withdrawn behavior and depressed feelings, which in turn were linked with conflict with mother, few friends, and refusal to do homework, resulting in poor academic achievement.

One of the keys to this formulation was the issue of control: as long as the mother felt responsible for the patient's diabetes care, the patient could not assume age-appropriate responsibilities. His nonadherence was related to the anger he felt about having diabetes and the conflict he experienced with his mother over management tasks. The patient's developmental need for more independence was thwarted by mother's need to involve herself in all aspects of diabetes care. The patient could thus use regimen nonadherence as a way to manipulate his mother and indirectly express his anger toward her.

Therapeutic goals were then set, defining an increased role in self-care responsibilities for the patient, improved affect, more positive interactions with mother, and acceptance of diabetes and increased peer interactions.

The intervention consisted of weekly sessions with the patient and his mother to address the issues of self-care responsibilities and relationship conflict. In addition, the patient was encouraged to attend the monthly peer group for youths with diabetes to enhance acceptance of diabetes and increase peer interactions.

Regarding self-care, control was given to the patient, who decided how much responsibility he wanted to assume. A hierarchy was set up with eight steps listed from very dependent behavior (with mother assuming all responsibilities) to very independent behavior (with the patient assuming all responsibilities). Self-care was framed as independent behavior that was under the patient's control. Independent self-care behavior was monitored on a daily basis, with points earned for each occurrence of appropriate behaviors. Points were backed-up by rewards given weekly. The mother was instructed to praise his self-care behaviors and, if he did not meet his goal, to comment in a non-judgmental fashion that he was not ready for his independence at that particular time.

Over about three months of intervention, the patient was able to assume more self-care responsibilities, eventually doing his morning blood glucose test and insulin injections by himself, reaching the sixth step on the eight step hierarchy. During this time the patient reported less conflict with his mother and his affect was improved. He attended the monthly group for teens with diabetes and seemed more accepting of his disease. The glycosylated hemoglobin test indicated improved glycemic control, decreasing from 13 percent to 9 percent.

Termination and Follow-Up

The patient missed several appointments and was seen by the psychologist at a regular out-patient clinic appointment with his physician. At that time he indicated that he was angry with his mother, who was not following through on her part of the contract. The mother was not providing consistent rewards contingent on his appropriate self-care behaviors; further, at times she gave him extra rewards on a non-contingent basis. In addition, the mother continued to watch the patient give himself insulin injections, not trusting him to do it correctly. This served to anger the patient, who felt his mother still did not trust him to care for himself in a responsible manner. Therefore, they had discontinued the behavioral program. An attempt was made to schedule another out-patient session with the psychologist to address these issues, but the patient refused. Assessment using the same battery of instruments indicated that they

had reverted to pre-treatment levels of problems with adherence and lack of supportive behavior from the mother, with the mother assuming responsibility for most self-care tasks. The patient also reported continuing to binge whenever he felt angry and depressed. In addition, the patient began to be more rebellious in other areas, such as skipping school. The patient did not show up for the next teen group.

This case illustrates a number of diabetes-specific and more general issues in a complex case. First, it shows the short-term effectiveness of developmentally appropriate behavioral interventions and the important role of family relationships in influencing health behaviors of adolescents. However, in order for behavioral interventions to be effective for more than a brief period of time, it is important to deal with more general developmental and psychological issues. In this case, normal development and diabetes management tasks became intertwined and problematic: the mother's anxiety regarding her son's diabetes was great enough to interfere with the son assuming age-appropriate responsibilities for self-care. Although well meaning, her overprotective behaviors undermined the son's efforts toward more independent functioning.

In the last clinic visit, the nurse observed the patient draw up and administer an insulin injection and reassured the mother that his technique was fine. Despite this demonstration, the mother remained firm in her conviction that she needed to be responsible for giving her son daily injections. Because they terminated therapy abruptly, a number of other issues were not adequately addressed, including the patient's unresolved grief concerning his father's death, the mother's anxiety regarding diabetes and her son's emergence into puberty, the problem of dietary nonadherence and binge eating, and the goal of developing more effective responses in coping with negative affect.

In cases such as these, it is important to provide continuity of care, with the physician, psychologist, nurse, and other team members communicating with each other about the patient's status, and for the team to continue demonstrating their concern for the patient and their issues. Often, despite initial treatment failures, the stage can be set for later treatment gains. This case serves well in illustrating the point that often in chronic disease when many issues complicate psychological adjustment and health outcomes, it is important for health professionals to realize that "quick fixes" are often not possible. Rather, therapeutic interventions must be refined over time in the context of an ongoing relationship with the health care team.

Case Two

Clinical Presentation

The patient was a 9-year-old white, non-Hispanic boy with short stature (at the 2nd percentile), who was from an intact, upper-middle-class family. The family had taken their son to several pediatric endocrinologists who all determined that his short stature was due to GHD, and who all recommended GH replacement therapy. The presenting problem was that the boy refused to begin treatment, reporting that he was afraid of injections. At that point he was referred for psychological evaluation by the pediatric endocrinologist. Almost two years had elapsed from the time of the first endocrinologist's recommendation to begin GH replacement therapy and the time of the psychological consultation.

Assessment Findings

The parents completed a standardized behavior rating form indicating no significant behavioral or emotional concerns. He was well adjusted socially and was doing very well in school. The only significant finding clinically was an intense fear of having an injection. For that reason alone, the patient claimed he was not interested in the GH replacement therapy, and would rather be short than subject himself to pain every day for years.

A clinical interview with the parents revealed them to be very concerned and loving parents who were at their wits end as to how to get their son to comply with the treatment plan. They were very distressed by the boy's refusal to begin therapy. The father had actually tried to give an injection to his son on one occasion in the preceding year before, but the attempt failed as the son panicked, and thrashed about resulting in a bent needle and a bleeding and bruised arm. They indicated they had a democratic parenting style in which they wanted their son to assume responsibility for the decision to begin treatment.

Treatment Selection and Course

The initial formulation was that the patient had developed an anxiety reaction conditioned by previous needle sticks for inoculations and the more recent attempt by the father to inject the first dose of GH. A treatment plan was proposed by the therapist and accepted by the patient and parents in which the patient would (1) be taught physical relaxation and cognitive

coping skills to manage his anxiety, and (2) follow an in vivo desensitization hierarchy of systematically handling the GH bottle and injection materials, practice giving saline injections to an orange, practice giving "pretend" injections to himself (i.e., putting the syringe against his body without the needle), followed by actually giving a GH injection. It was explained that after substantial rehearsal and exposure to the anxiety-provoking stimuli, and mastery of relaxation and coping skills, he would be able to receive the injection, after which he would be able to handle the daily regimen with much less anxiety.

In the next session, the patient was taught a simple relaxation technique and self-statements to cope with his anxiety. He handled all the injection materials and practiced giving injections to an orange. By the end of the session he reported a significant reduction in anxiety and agreed to take the first injection later that evening when they got home. Telephone contact with the parents the next morning revealed, however, that the boy once again panicked and refused to take the injection. The therapist encouraged them to practice the anxiety reduction techniques and try again the following day. This did not work either.

In a treatment session conducted by phone, the therapist explored with the parents alone how they presented the problem and the recommended treatment to their child. It was pointed out that they were essentially giving all decision-making responsibility to their son, allowing him to avoid his anxiety now but suffer the later consequences of delayed puberty and short stature. The therapist challenged them to reconsider their approach, asking them to evaluate whether it was fair to give a 9-year-old child this much power. After all, given a choice between pain now and eventual rewards later, most children will choose to avoid pain. After only a little discussion, they decided to assert their parental decision that he take the recommended treatment. They were then encouraged to explain to their son the reasons for their decision. Another session was scheduled for the following week, in which the parents would again reiterate their decision and give their rationale, after which the first GH injection would be given in the therapist's office.

In the session the parents communicated very clearly what they had decided about their son's medical treatment. The boy was then told to prepare for the injection given by the father, with the mother out of the room (at both mother's and the patient's request). The therapist helped the patient to relax himself and modeled effective coping statements to reduce anxiety. He was told by his father that the injection would be given, even if he had to be held down to get it. At the moment the father prepared to give the injection, the boy panicked and began to scream, at which point the therapist held him down so that the injection could be given. As soon as the injection was given, the boy immediately stopped screaming and calmly remarked, "That wasn't so bad!"

Termination and Follow-Up

The family was incredibly relieved, congratulations were given all around, and the therapist made a plan to call the parents a few days later to check on their progress. The parents reported the first few injections were given at home with no problems. Therapy was terminated at that point. Long-term follow up was obtained by telephone contact one and a half years later. The mother reported that they had no problems at all since the intervention. The boy was taking the GH injections every day without fail, and had grown four inches the first year, and so far in the second year had grown another inch. His adjustment was excellent both socially and academically, and he was enjoying playing on the school soccer team.

This case dramatically demonstrates how simple behavioral interventions may be insufficient on their own. Although relaxation, coping skills training, and exposure with behavioral rehearsal are effective intervention tools, the family system analysis resulted in a far more powerful and efficient intervention. In this case, the parents simply had to be reminded of their parental responsibility and encouraged to assert themselves in the best interest of their child.

SUMMARY

A substantial literature now exists on medical and psychological issues in the management of diabetes in children. With the results of the DCCT indicating that good glycemic control reduces the risk of health complications even among adolescents, studies must now address how to attain such levels of glycemic control in young patients. This is a formidable challenge for health care professionals, given the number of studies that have documented the high occurrence of regimen adherence problems in older children and adolescents. Intervention approaches can be guided by the literature, which has shown that poor glycemic control is associated with a number of psychological and family factors. Data is already available indicating that regimen adherence and glycemic control can be improved by behavioral interventions using positive family involvement. Further intervention research is needed, especially addressing how to intervene effectively with patients at high risk for metabolic control problems.

Due to advances in radioimmunoassay techniques and implementation of large-scale screening programs, CH can be easily diagnosed in infancy and hormone replacement therapy begun within the first month, thereby preventing mental retardation. A fairly large literature now exists concerning intellectual functioning of children with CH. For the most part this literature indicates that children with CH show lower intelligence than control children, but their intelligence is still within normal limits. More subtle neuropsychological deficits have begun to appear in recent studies, however, suggesting the possibility of nonverbal learning disabilities. In general, studies indicate severity of CH and treatment factors (i.e., at what age treatment is initiated and dosage of replacement hormone) are related to neuropsychological outcomes. More studies addressing the behavioral features associated with timing and dosage of hormone replacement are needed, as well as studies focusing on other aspects of psychological development.

A number of studies indicate that children with short stature are at increased risk for difficulties with social adjustment, particularly during early adolescence. Inconsistent findings have emerged with regard to the importance of height deficit and etiology of short stature, but some studies indicate more problems among children with GHD and more severe height deficits. Children with short stature are also apparently at risk for academic achievement problems, with a significant number exhibiting cognitive and learning problems. Conclusions are difficult to reach given the fact that most of the available literature is limited by small samples of heterogeneous subjects.

Children with endocrine disorders often present clinically with significant psychological or psychiatric disorders that may complicate their psychosocial adjustment, physical health, and adaptive functioning. The pediatric psychologist or psychiatrist, as well as other mental health professionals skilled in behavioral health issues for children, all may play an important role in the comprehensive care of these children.

REFERENCES

Allen D. B., & Fost, N. C. (1990). Growth hormone therapy for short stature: Panacea or Pandora's box? *Journal of Pediatrics, 117,* 16–21.

Allen, K. D., Warzak, W. J., Greger, N. G., Bernotas, T. D., & Huseman, C. A. (1993). Psychosocial adjustment of children with isolated growth hormone deficiency. *Children's Health Care*, 22, 61–72.

Alm, J., Larsson, A., & Zetterstrom, R. (1981). Congenital hypothyroidism in Sweden: Psychomotor development in patients detected by clinical signs and symptoms. *Acta Paediatrics Scandanavia, 70*, 907–912.

American Diabetes Association: Clinical Practice Recommendations. (1996). *Diabetes Care, 19 (Suppl. 1)*, S4.

Amiel, S. A., Sherwin, R. S., Simonson, D. C., Lauritano, A. A., & Tamborland, W. V. (1986). Impaired insulin action in puberty: A contributing factor to poor glycemic control in adolescents with diabetes. *New England Journal of Medicine, 315*, 215–219.

Anderson, B., Hagen, J., Barclay, C., Goldstein, G., Kandt, R., & Dacon, G. (1984). Cognitive and school performance in diabetic children. *Diabetes, 33, (Supp)*, 21A.

Anderson, B. J., Auslander, W. F., Jung, K. C., Miller, J. P., & Santiago, J. V. (1990). Assessing family sharing of diabetes responsibilities. *Journal of Pediatric Psychology, 15*, 477–492.

Anderson, B. J., Miller, J. P., Auslander, W. F., & Santiago, J. V. (1981). Family characteristics of diabetic adolescents: Relationship to metabolic control. *Diabetes Care, 4*, 586–594.

Anderson, B. J., Wolf, R. M., Burkhart, M. T., Cornell, R. G., & Bacon, G. E. (1989). Effects of peer-group intervention on metabolic control of adolescents with IDDM: Randomized outpatient study. *Diabetes Care, 12*, 179–183.

Arslanian, S., Becker, D., & Drash, A. (1994). Diabetes mellitus in the child and adolescent. In D. Wilkens (Ed.), *The diagnosis and treatment of endocrine disorders in childhood and adolescence (4th Ed.)* (pp. 969–971). Springfield, MA: Charles C. Thomas.

Auslander, W. F., Anderson, B. J., Bubb, J., Jung, K. C., & Santiago, J. V. (1990). Risk factors to health in diabetic children: A prospective study from diagnosis. *Health and Social Work, 15*, 133–142.

Bender, B., Linden, M., & Robinson, A. (1993). Neuropsychological impairment in 42 adolescents with sex chromosome abnormalities. *American Journal of Medical Genetics, 48*, 169–173.

Bercu, B. B., & Diamond, F. B. (1986). Growth hormone neurosectory dysfunction. *Clinical Endocrinology and Metabolism, 15*, 537–590.

Blanz, B., Rensch-Riemann, B., Fritz-Sigmund, D., & Schmidt, M. (1993). IDDM is a risk factor for adolescent psychiatric disorders. *Diabetes Care, 16*, 1579–1587.

Bloch, C. A., Clemons, P. S., & Sperling, M. A. (1987). Puberty decreases insulin sensitivity. *Journal of Pediatrics, 110*, 481–487.

Bloomgarden, Z., Karmally, W., Metzger, M., Brothers, M., Nechemias, C., Bookman, J., Faierman, D., Ginsberg-Fellner, F., Rayfield, E., & Brown, W. (1987). Randomized controlled trial of diabetes patient education. *Diabetes Care, 10*, 263–272.

Boardway, R., Delamater, A., Tomakowsky, J., & Gutai, J. (1993). Stress management training for adolescents with diabetes. *Journal of Pediatric Psychology, 18*, 29–45.

Bobrow, E. S., AvRuskin, T. W., & Siller, J. (1985). Mother-daughter interaction and adherence to diabetes regimens. *Diabetes Care, 8*, 146–151.

Bright, G. M., Rogol, A. D., Johnson, A. J., & Blizzard, R. M. (1983). Short stature associated with normal growth hormone and decreased somatomedin C concentrations, response to exogenous growth hormone. *Pediatrics, 71*, 576–580.

Brownlee-Duffeck, M., Peterson, L., Simonds, J. F., Goldstein, D., Kilo, C., & Hoette, S. (1987). The role of health beliefs in the regimen adherence and metabolic control of adolescents and adults with diabetes mellitus. *Journal of Consulting and Clinical Psychology, 55*, 139–144.

Campaigne, B. N., Gilliam, T. B., Spencer, M. L., Lampman, R. M., & Schork, M. A. (1984). Effects of a physical activity program on metabolic control and cardiovascular fitness in children with IDDM. *Diabetes Care, 7*, 57–62.

Carney, R. M., Schechter, D., & Davis, T. (1983). Improving adherence to blood glucose testing in insulin-dependent diabetic children. *Behavior Therapy, 14*, 247–254.

Chase, H. P., & Jackson, G. G. (1981). Stress and sugar control in children with insulin-dependent diabetes mellitus. *Journal of Pediatrics, 98*, 1011–1013.

Christensen, N. K., Terry, R. D., Wyatt, S., Pichert, J. W., & Lorenz, R. A. (1983). Quantitative assessment of dietary adherence in patients with insulin-dependent diabetes mellitus. *Diabetes Care, 6*, 245–250.

Clark, C. M., & Lee, D. A. (1995). Prevention and treatment of the complications of Diabetes mellitus. *New England Journal of Medicine, 332*, 1210–1217.

Clopper, R. R. (1990). Assessing the effects of replacement hormone treatment of psychosocial and psychosexual behavior in growth hormone deficient individuals. In C. S. Holmes (Ed.), *Psychoneuroendocrinology: Brain, Behavior, and Hormonal Interactions* (pp. 56–78). New York: Springer-Verlag.

Cowie, C., Port, F., Wolfe, R. A., Savage, P. J., Moll, P. P., & Hawthorne, V. M. (1989). Disparities in incidence of diabetic end-stage renal disease according to race and type of diabetes. *New England Journal of Medicine, 321*, 1074–1079.

Crowne, E. C., Shalet, S. M., Wallace, W. H. B., Eminson, D. M., & Price, D. A. (1990). Final height in boys with untreated constitutional delay in growth and puberty. *Archives of Disease in Childhood, 65*, 1109–1112.

Daneman, D., Siminerio, L., Transue, D., Betschart, J., Drash, A., & Becker, D. (1985). The role of self-monitoring of blood glucose in the routine management of children with insulin-dependent diabetes mellitus. *Diabetes Care, 5*, 472–478.

Dean, H. J., McTaggert, T. L., Fish, D. G., & Friesen, H. J. (1985). The educational, vocational and marital status of growth hormone deficient adults treated with growth hormone during childhood. *American Journal of Diseases of Children, 139*, 1105–1110.

Delamater, A. M. (1990). Adaptation of children to newly diagnosed diabetes. In C. S. Holmes (Ed.), *Neuropsychological and behavioral aspects of diabetes* (pp. 12–29). New York: Springer-Verlang.

Delamater, A. M. (1986). Psychological aspects of diabetes mellitus in children. In B. B. Lahey & A. E. Kazdin (Eds.), *Advances in clinical child psychology (Vol. 9)* (pp. 333–375). New York: Plenum Press.

Delamater, A. M. (1992). Stress, coping, and metabolic control among youngsters with diabetes. In A. La Greca, L. Siegel, J. Wallander, & C. Walker (Eds.), *Stress and coping in child health* (pp. 191–211). New York: Guilford Press.

Delamater, A. M. (1993). Compliance interventions for children with diabetes and other chronic diseases. In N. A. Krasnegor et al. (Eds.), *Developmental aspects of health compliance behavior* (pp. 335–358). Hillsdale, N.J.: Lawrence Erlbaum Associates, Inc.

Delamater, A. M., Albrecht, D., Postellon, D., & Gutai, J. (1991). Racial differences in metabolic control of children and adolescents with Type I diabetes mellitus. *Diabetes Care, 14*, 20–25.

Delamater, A. M., Bubb, J., Davis, S. G., Smith, J. A., Schmidt, L., White, N. H. & Santiago, J. V. (1990). Randomized prospective study of self-management training with newly diagnosed diabetic children. *Diabetes Care, 13*, 492–498.

Delamater, A. M., Bubb, J., Kurtz, S., Kuntze, J., White, N. H. & Santiago, J. V. (1988). Physiologic responses to acute psychological stress in adolescents with Type 1 diabetes. *Journal of Pediatric Psychology, 13*, 69–86.

Delamater, A. M., Davis, S. G., Bubb, J., Smith, J. A., White, N. H., & Santiago, J. V. (1989). Self-monitoring of blood glucose by adolescents with diabetes: Technical skills and utilization of data. *The Diabetes Educator, 15*, 56–61.

Delamater, A. M., Kurtz, S. M., Bubb, J., White, N. H., & Santiago, J. V. (1987). Stress and coping in relation to metabolic control of adolescents with Type 1 diabetes. *Journal of Developmental and Behavioral Pediatrics, 8*, 136–140.

Delamater, A. M., Kurtz, S. M., White, N. H., & Santiago, J. V. (1988). Effects of social demand on reports of self monitored blood glucose testing in adolescents with type I diabetes mellitus. *Journal of Applied Social Psychology, 18*, 491–502.

Delamater, A. M., Smith, J. A., Bubb, J., Davis, S. G., Gamble, T., White, N. H., & Santiago, J. V. (1991). Family-based behavior therapy for diabetic adolescents. In J. H. Johnson & S. B. Johnson (Eds.), *Advances in child health psychology* (pp. 293–306). Gainesville, Fla.: University of Florida Press.

Delamater, A. M., Smith, J. A., Kurtz, S. M., & White, N. H. (1988). Dietary skills and adherence in children with insulin-dependent diabetes mellitus. *The Diabetes Educator, 14*, 33–36.

Diabetes Control and Complications Trial Research Group (1993). The effect of intensive treatment of diabetes on the development and progression of long-term complications in insulin-dependent diabetes-mellitus. *New England Journal of Medicine, 329*, 977–986.

Diabetes Control and Complications Trial Research Group (1994). Effect of intensive diabetes treatment on the development and progression of long-term complications in adolescents with insulin-dependent diabetes mellitus, Diabetes Control and Complications Trial. *Journal of Pediatrics, 125*, 177–188.

Dokheel, T. M. (for the Pittsburgh Diabetes Epidemiology Research Group) (1993). An epidemic of childhood diabetes in the United States? Evidence from Allegheny County, Pennsylvania Pittsburgh Diabetes Epidemiology Research Group. *Diabetes Care, 16*, 1606–1611.

Drotar, D., Owens, R., & Gotthold, J. (1980). Personality adjustment of children and adolescents with hypopituitarism. *Child Psychiatry Human Development, 11*, 59–66.

Ermans, A. M., Boudoux, P., Lagasse, R., Delange, F., & Thilly, C. (1980). Congenital hypothyroidism in developing countries. In G. N. Burrow & J. H. Dussault (Eds.), *Neonatal thyroid screening*. New York: Raven Press.

Fisher, D. A., Dussault, J., Foley, T. P., et al. (1979). Screening for congenital hypothyroidism: Results of screening one million North American infants. *Journal of Pediatrics, 94*, 700–705.

Foley, T. P. (1990). Disorders of the thyroid: Medical overview. In C. S. Holmes (Ed.), *Psychoneuroendocrinology: Brain, behavior and hormonal interactions* (pp. 261–272). New York: Springer-Verlag.

Glasgow, R. E., McCaul, K. D., & Schafer, L. C. (1986). Barriers to regimen adherence among persons with insulin-dependent diabetes. *Journal of Behavioral Medicine, 9*, 65–77.

Glasgow, R. E., McCaul, K. D., & Schafer, L. C. (1987). Self-care behaviors and glycemic control in type I diabetes. *The Journal of Chronic Diseases, 40*, 399–412.

Glorieux, J., Desjardins, M., Letarte, J., Morissette, J., & Dussault, J. H. (1988). Useful parameters to predict the eventual mental outcome of hypothyroid children. *Pediatric Research, 24*, 6–8.

Glorieux, J., Dussault, J. H., Letarte, J., Guyda, H., & Morissette, J. (1983). Preliminary results on the mental development of hypothyroid infants detected by Quebec Screening Program. *Journal of Pediatrics, 102*, 19–22.

Glorieux, J., Dussault, J. H., Morissette, J., Desjardins, J., Letarte, J., & Guyda, H. (1985). Follow-up at ages 5 and 7 years on mental development in children with hypothyroidism detected by Quebec Screening Program. *Journal of Pediatrics, 107*, 913–915.

Glorieux, J., Dussault, J. & Van Vilet, G. (1992). Intellectual development at age 12 years of children with congenital hypothyroidism diagnosed by neonatal screening. *Journal of Pediatrics, 121*, 581–584.

Gonen, B., Rachman, H., Rubenstein, A. H., Tanega, S. P., & Horwitz, D. L. (1977). Hemoglobin A1C as an indicator of the degree of glucose intolerance in diabetics. *Lancet, 2*, 734–737.

Gordon, M., Crouthamel, D., Post, E., & Richman, R. (1982). Psychosocial aspects of constitutional short stature: Social competence, behavior problems, self-esteem, and family functioning. *Journal of Pediatrics, 101*, 477–480.

Grant, D. B. (1995). Congenital hypothyroidism, optimal management in the light of 15 years' experience of screening. *Archives in Disease in Childhood, 72*, 85–89.

Green, W. H. (1990). A theoretical model for classical psychosocial dwarfism (psychosocially determined short stature). In C. S. Holmes (Ed.), *Psychoneuroendocrinology: Brain, behavior and hormonal interactions* (pp. 92–112). New York: Springer-Verlag.

Grossman, H. Y., Brink, S., & Hauser, S. T. (1987). Self-efficacy in adolescent girls and boys with insulin-dependent diabetes mellitus. *Diabetes Care, 10*, 324–329.

Hamman, R. F., Cook, M., Keefer, S., Young, W., Finch, J., Lezotte, D., McLaren, B., Orleans, M., Klingensmith, G., & Chase, H. (1985). Medical care patterns at the onset of insulin-dependent diabetes mellitus: Association with severity and subsequent complications. *Diabetes Care, 8 (Suppl. 1)*, 94–100.

Hanson, C. L., De Guire, M., Schinkel, S., Henggeler, S. W., & Burghen, G. A. (1992). Comparing social learning and family systems correlates. *Journal of Pediatric Psychology, 17 (5)*, 555–572.

Hanson, C. L., Henggeler, S., & Burghen, G. A. (1987a). Race and sex differences in metabolic control of adolescents with IDDM: A function of psychosocial variables? *Diabetes Care, 10*, 313–318.

Hanson, C. L., Henggeler, S. W., & Burghen, G. A. (1987b). Model of associations between psychosocial variables and health-outcome measures of adolescents with IDDM. *Diabetes Care, 10*, 752–758.

Hanson, C. L., Hengeller, S. W., & Burghen, G. A. (1987c). Social competence and parental support as mediators of the link between stress and metabolic control in adolescents with insulin dependent diabetes mellitus. *Journal of Consulting and Clinical Psychology, 55*, 529–533.

Hanson, C. L., Henggeler, S. W., Harris, M., Burghen, G. A., & Moore, M. (1989). Family system variables and the health status of adolescents with insulin-dependent diabetes mellitus. *Health Psychology, 8*, 239–253.

Hanson, S. L., & Pichert, J. W. (1986). Perceived stress and diabetes control in adolescents. *Health Psychology, 5*, 439–452.

Hauser, S. L., Jacobson, A. M., Lavori, P., Wolsdorf, J. I., Herskowitz, R. D., Miley, J. E., Bliss, R., Wertlieb, D., & Stein, J. (1990). Adherence among children and adolescents with insulin dependent diabetes mellitus over a four-year longitudinal follow-up, II. Immediate and long-term linkages with the family milieu. *Journal of Pediatric Psychology, 15*, 527–542.

Hauser, S. T., Jacobson, A. M., Wertlieb, D., Brink, S., & Wentworth, S. (1985). The contribution of family environment to perceived competence and illness adjustment in diabetic and acutely ill adolescents. *Family Relations, 34*, 99–108.

Herbert, R., Laureau, E., Vanasse, M., Richard, J. E., Morissette, J., Glorieux, J., Desjardins, M., Letarte, J., & Dussault, J. H. (1986). Auditory brainstem response audiometry in congenitally hypothyroid children under early replacement therapy. *Pediatric Research, 20*, 570–573.

Holmes, C. (Ed.) (1990). *Psychoneuroendocrinology: Brain behavior and hormonal interactions*. New York: Springer-Verlag.

Holmes, C., & Richman, L. (1985). Cognitive profiles of

children with insulin-dependent diabetes. *Developmental and Behavioral Pediatrics, 6,* 323–326.

Holmes, C., Hayford, J., Gonzalez, J., & Weydert, J. (1983). A survey of cognitive function in different glucose levels in diabetic persons. *Diabetes Care, 6,* 180–183.

Holmes, C., Hayford, J., & Thompson, R. (1982). Parents' and teachers' differing views of short children's behavior. *Child: Care, Health and Development, 8,* 327–336.

Holmes, C., Karlsson, J., & Thompson, R. (1985). Social and school competencies in children with short stature: Longitudinal patterns. *Developmental and Behavioral Pediatrics, 6,* 263–267.

Holmes, C., Karlsson, J. A., & Thompson, R. (1986). Longitudinal evaluation of behavior patterns in children with short stature. In B. Stabler & L. E. Underwood (Eds.), *Slow grows the child* (pp. 1–13). Hillside, N.J.: Lawrence Erlbaum Associates, Inc.

Holmes, C., Koepke, K., Thompson, R., Gyves, P., & Weydert, J. (1984). Verbal fluency in naming performance in type I diabetes at different blood glucose concentrations. *Diabetes Care, 7,* 454–459.

Hopwood, N., Hintz, R. L., Gertner, J. M., et al. (1993). Growth response of children with non-growth-hormone-deficiency and marked short stature during three years of growth hormone therapy. *Journal of Pediatrics, 123,* 215–222.

Huisman, J., Slijper, F. M. E., Sinnema, G., et al. (1993). Psychosocial effects of two years of human growth hormone treatment in Turner Syndrome. *Hormone Research, 39 (S2),* 56–59.

Huttunen, N. P., Lankelaa, S. L., Knip, M., Lautala, P., Kaar, M. L., Laasonen, K., & Puukka, R. (1989). Effect of once-a-week training program on physical fitness and metabolic control in children with IDDM. *Diabetes Care, 12,* 737–739.

Ingersoll, G., Orr, D., Herrold, A., & Golden M. (1986). Cognitive maturity and self-management among adolescents with insulin-dependent diabetes mellitus. *Journal of Pediatrics, 108,* 620–623.

Jacobson, A. M., Hauser, S. T., Lavori, P., Wolfsdorf, J. I., Herskowitz, R. D., Miley, J. E., Bliss, R., Gelfand, E., Wertlieb, D., & Stein, J. (1990). Adherence among children and adolescents with insulin-dependent diabetes mellitus over a four-year longitudinal follow-up, I. The influence of patient coping and adjustment. *Journal of Pediatric Psychology, 15,* 511–526.

Jacobson, A. M., Hauser, S. T., Wertlieb, D., Woldsdorf, J., Orleans, J., & Viegra, M. (1986). Psychological adjustment of children with recently diagnosed diabetes mellitus. *Diabetes Care, 9,* 323–329.

Johnson, S. B. (1995). Diabetes mellitus in childhood. In M. Roberts (Ed.), *Handbook of pediatric psychology (second edition)* (pp. 263–285). New York: Guilford Press.

Johnson, S. B., Freund, A., Silverstein, J., Hansen, C. A., & Malone, J. (1990). Adherence-health status relationships in childhood diabetes. *Health Psychology, 9,* 606–631.

Johnson, S. B., Kelly, M., Henretta, J. C., Cunningham, W., Tomer, A., & Silverstein, J. (1992). A longitudinal analysis of adherence and health status in childhood diabetes. *Journal of Pediatric Psychology, 17,* 537–553.

Johnson, S. B., Pollak, T., Silverstein, J. H., Rosenbloom, A., Spillar, R., McCallum, M., & Harkavy, J. (1982). Cognitive and behavioral knowledge about insulin-dependent diabetes among children and parents. *Pediatrics, 69,* 708–713.

Johnson, S. B., Silverstein, J., Rosenbloom, A., Carter, R., & Cunningham, W. (1986). Assessing daily management in childhood diabetes. *Health Psychology, 5,* 545–564.

Johnson, S. B., Tomer, A., Cunningham, W. R., & Henretta, J. C. (1990). Adherence in childhood diabetes: Results of a confirmatory factor analysis. *Health Psychology, 9,* 493–501.

Kager, V., & Holden, W. (1992). Preliminary investigation of the direct and moderating effects of family and individual variables on the adjustment of children and adolescents with diabetes. *Journal of Pediatric Psychology, 17,* 491–502.

Kaplan, R. M., Chadwick, M. W., & Schimmel, L. E. (1985). Social learning intervention to promote metabolic control in Type I diabetes mellitus: Pilot experimental results. *Diabetes Care, 8,* 152–155.

Koski, M. L., & Kumento, A. (1977). The interrelationship between diabetic control and family life. *Pediatric Adolescent Endocrinology, 3,* 41–45.

Kovacs, M., Feinberg, T. L., Paulauskas, S., Finkelstein, R., Pollock, M., & Crouse-Novak, M. (1985). Initial coping responses and psychosocial characteristics of children with insulin-dependent diabetes mellitus. *Journal of Pediatrics, 106,* 827–834.

Kovacs, M., Finkelstein, R., Feinberg, T. L., Crouse-Novak, M., Paulauskas, S., & Pollock, M. (1985). Initial psychologic responses of parents to the diagnosis of insulin-dependent diabetes mellitus in their children. *Diabetes Care, 8,* 568–575.

Kovacs, M., Goldston, D., & Iyengar, S. (1992). Intellectual development and academic performance of children with insulin-dependent diabetes mellitus: A longitudinal study. *Developmental Psychology, 28,* 676–684.

Kovacs, M., Goldston, D., Obrosky, S., & Iyengar, S. (1992). Prevalence and predictors of pervasive noncompliance with medical treatment among youths with insulin-dependent diabetes mellitus. *Journal of the*

American Academy Child Adolescent Psychiatry, 31, 1112–1119.

Kovacs, M., Ryan, C., & Obrosky, D. S. (1994). Verbal intellectual and verbal memory performance of youths with childhood-onset insulin-dependent diabetes mellitus. *Journal of Pediatric Psychology, 19,* 475–483.

Kuttner, M. J., Delamater, A. M., & Santiago, J. V. (1990). Learned helplessness in diabetic youths. *Journal of Pediatric Psychology, 15,* 581–594.

Lantos, J., Siegler, M., & Cuttler, L. (1989). Ethical issues in growth hormone therapy. *Journal of the American Medical Association, 261,* 1020–1024.

Laron, Z., Blum, W., Chatelain, P., et al. (1993). Classification of growth hormone insensitivity syndrome. *Journal of Pediatrics, 122,* 241.

Leiberman, E., Pilpel, D., Carel, C., et al. (1993). Coping and satisfaction with growth hormone treatment among short-stature children. *Hormone Research, 40,* 128–135.

Lorenz, R. A., Christensen, N. K., & Pichert, J. W. (1985). Diet-related knowledge, skill and adherence among children with insulin dependent diabetes mellitus. *Pediatrics, 75,* 872–876.

Lowe, K., & Lutzker, J. R. (1979). Increasing compliance to a medical regime with a juvenile diabetic. *Behavior Therapy, 10,* 57–64.

Maclaren, N. K., Schatz, D., Drask, A., & Grove, G. (1989). The initial pathogenic events in insulin-dependent diabetes. *Diabetes, 38,* 534–539.

Madsbad, S., Faber, O. K., & Binder, C. (1978). Prevalence of residual beta cell function in insulin dependent diabetics in relation to age at onset and duration of diabetes. *Diabetes, 27, (Suppl. 1),* 262–264.

Madsbad, S., McNair, P., & Faber, O. K. (1980). Beta-cell function and metabolic control in insulin-treated diabetics. *Acta Endocrinology, 93,* 196–200.

Mann, N. P., Noronha, J. L., & Johnston, D. I. (1984). A prospective study to evaluate the benefits of long-term self-monitoring of blood glucose in diabetic children. *Diabetes Care, 7,* 323–326.

Marrero, D. G., Kronz, K. K., Golden, M. P., Wright, J. C., Orr, D. P. & Fineberg, N. S. (1989). Clinical evaluation of computer-assisted self-monitoring of blood glucose system. *Diabetes Care, 12,* 345–350.

Marteau, T. M., Johnson, M., Baum, J. D., & Bloch, S. (1987). Goals of treatment in diabetes, A comparison of doctors and parents of children with diabetes. *Journal of Behavioral Medicine, 10,* 33–48.

Miller-Johnson, S., Emery, R., Marvin, R., Clarke, W., Lovinger, R., & Martin, M. (1994). Parent-child relationships and the management of insulin-dependent diabetes mellitus. *Journal of Consulting and Clinical Psychology, 62,* 603–610.

Nathan, D., Singer, D. E., Hurxthal, K., & Goodson, J. D. (1984). The clinical information value of the glycosylated hemoglobin assay. *New England Journal of Medicine, 310,* 341–346.

National Diabetes Data Group. (1979). Classification and diagnosis of diabetes and other categories of glucose intolerance. *Diabetes,* 139–157.

New England Congenital Hypothyroidism Collaborative (1985a). Neonatal hypothyroidism screening: Status of patients at 6 years of age. *Clinical and Laboratory Observations, 107,* 915–919.

New England Congenital Hypothyroidism Collaborative (1985b). Elementary school performance of children with congenital hypothyroidism. *Journal of Pediatrics, 116,* 27–32.

Orr, D., Golden, M. P., Myers, G., & Marrero, D. G. (1983). Characteristics of adolescents with poorly controlled diabetes referred to a tertiary care center. *Diabetes Care, 6,* 170–175.

Powell, G. F., Brasel, J. A., & Blizzard, R. M. (1967). Emotional deprivation and growth retardation simulating idiopathic hypopituitarism. I. Clinical evaluation of the syndrome. II. Endocrinologic evaluation of the syndrome. *New England Journal of Medicine, 276,* 1270–1283.

Rieser, P. A., & Underwood, L. E. (1990). Disorders of growth and short stature: Medical overview. In C. S. Holmes (Ed.), *Psychoneuroendocrinology: Brain, behavior and hormonal interactions* (pp. 10–16). New York: Springer-Verlag.

Riley, W. J., Maclaren, N. K., Krischer, J., Spillar, R. P., Silverstein, J., Schatz, D. A., Schwartz, S., Malone, J., Shah, S., Vadheim, C., & Rotter, J. I. (1990). A prospective study of the development of diabetes in relatives of patients with insulin-dependent diabetes. *New England Journal of Medicine, 323,* 1167–1172.

Rodin, G. M., Johnson, L. E., Garfinkel, P. E., Daneman, D., & Kenshole, A. B. (1986–1987). Eating disorders in female adolescents with insulin dependent diabetes mellitus. *International Journal of Psychiatry in Medicine, 16,* 49–57.

Rovet, J. (1990). Congenital hypothyroidism: Intellectual and neuropsychological functioning. In C. S. Holmes (Ed.), *Psychoneuroendocrinology: Brain, behavior and hormonal interactions* (pp. 273–322). New York: Springer-Verlag.

Rovet, J., & Holland, J. (1993). Psychological aspects of the Canadian randomized controlled trial of human growth hormone and low-dose ethinyl oestradiol in children with Turner Syndrome. *Hormone Research, 39,* 60–64.

Rovet, J., Ehrlich, R., & Hoppe, M. (1987). Behavior problems in children with diabetes as a function of sex and age of onset of disease. *Journal of Child Psychology and Psychiatry, 28*, 477–491.

Rovet, J., Ehrlich, R., & Hoppe, M. (1988). Specific intellectual deficits associated with the early onset of insulin-dependent diabetes mellitus in children. *Child Development, 59*, 226–234.

Rovet, J., Ehrlich, R., & Sorbara, D. L. (1987). Intellectual outcome in children with fetal hypothyroidism. *Journal of Pediatrics, 110*, 700–704.

Rovet, J., Ehrlich, R., & Sorbara, D. L. (1989). Effect of thyroid hormone level on temperament in infants with congenital hypothyroidism detected by screening of neonates. *Journal of Pediatrics, 114*, 63–68.

Rovet, J., Ehrlich, R., & Sorbara, D. L. (1992). Neurodevelopment in infants and preschool children with congenital hypothyroidism, Etiological and treatment factors affecting outcome. *Journal of Pediatrics, 2*, 187–213.

Ryan, C., Longstreet, C., & Morrow, L. (1985). The effects of diabetes mellitus on the school attendance and school achievement of adolescents. *Child: Care, Health and Development, 11*, 229–240.

Ryan, C., Vega, A., & Drash, A. (1985). Cognitive deficits in adolescents who developed diabetes early in life. *Pediatrics, 5*, 921.

Ryan, C., Vega, A., Longstreet, C., & Drash, A. (1984). Neuropsychological changes in adolescents with insulin-dependent diabetes. *Journal of Consulting and Clinical Psychology, 52*, 335–342.

Sandberg, D., Brook, A., & Campos, S. (1994). Short stature: A psychosocial burden requiring a growth hormone therapy? *Pediatrics, 94*, 832–840.

Satin, W., La Greca, A. M., Zigo, M., & Skyler, J. S. (1989). Diabetes in adolescence: Effects of multifamily group intervention on parent simulation of diabetes. *Journal of Pediatric Psychology, 14*, 259–276.

Schafer, L. C., Glasgow, R. E., & McCaul, K. D. (1982). Increasing the adherence of diabetic adolescents. *Journal of Behavioral Medicine, 5*, 353–362.

Schafer, L. C., Glasgow, R. E., McCaul, K. D., & Dreher, M. (1983). Adherence to IDDM regimens: Relationship to psychosocial variables and metabolic control. *Diabetes Care, 6*, 493–498.

Siegel, P. T. (1990). Intellectual and academic functioning in children with growth delay. In C. S. Holmes (Ed.), *Psychoneuroendocrinology: Brain, behavior and hormonal interactions* (pp. 17–39). New York: Springer-Verlag.

Siegel, P. T., & Hopwood, N. J. (1986). The relationship of academic achievement and the intellectual functioning and affective conditions of hypopituitary children. In B. Stabler & L. E. Underwood (Eds.), *Slow grows the child* (pp. 57–71). Hillside, N.J.: Lawrence Erlbaum Associates, Inc.

Simonds, S. (1977). Psychiatric status of diabetic youth matched with a control group. *Diabetes, 26*, 921–925.

Stabler, B., & Underwood, L. E. (Eds.) (1986). *Slow grows the child*. Hillsdale, N.J.: Lawrence Erlbaum Associates, Inc.

Stabler, B., Whitt, J. K., Moreault, D. M., et al. (1980). Social judgements by children of short stature. *Psychological Reports, 46*, 743.

Stancin, T., Link, D. L., & Reuter, J. M. (1989). Binge eating and purging in young women with IDDM. *Diabetes Care, 12*, 601–603.

Stratton, R., Wilson, D. P., Endres, R. K., & Goldstein, D. E. (1987). Improved glycemic control after supervised 8-week exercise program in insulin-dependent diabetic adolescents. *Diabetes Care, 10*, 589–593.

Travis, L. B., Brouhard, B. H., & Schreiner, B. J. (Eds.) (1987). The child less than three years old. In *Diabetes mellitus in children and adolescents* (pp. 187–192). Philadelphia: W.B. Saunders Company.

Turnbridge, W. M. G., Evered, D. E., Hall, R., et al. (1977). The spectrum of thyroid disease in a community: The Wickham survey. *Clinical Endocrinology, 7*, 481–493.

Underwood, L. E., & Van Wyk, J. J. (1992). Normal and aberrant growth. In J. D. Wilson & D. W. Foster (Eds.), *Williams textbook of endocrinology*, 8th edition, (pp. 1079–1138). Philadelphia: W.B. Saunders Company.

Voss, L. D., Bailey, B. J. R., Mulligan, J., Wilkin, T. J., & Betts, P. R. (1991). Short stature and school performance: The Wessex Growth Study. *Acta Paediatrics Scandanavia, 377 (Supp)*, 29–31.

Weist, M., Finney, J., Barnard, M., Davis, C., & Ollendick, T. (1993). Empirical selection of psychosocial treatment targets for children and adolescents with diabetes. *Journal of Pediatric Psychology, 18*, 11–28.

White, K., Kolman, M., Wexler, P., Polin, G., & Winter, R. J. (1984). Unstable diabetes and unstable families: A psychosocial evaluation of diabetic children with recurrent ketoacidosis. *Pediatrics, 73*, 749–755.

Williams, J., Richman, L. C., & Yarbrough, D. B. (1991). A comparison of memory and attention in Turner syndrome and learning disability. *Journal of Pediatric Psychology, 16*, 585–593.

Wing, R. R., Koeske, R., New, A., Lamparski, D., & Becker, D. (1986). Behavioral skills in self-monitoring of blood glucose: Relationship to accuracy. *Diabetes Care, 9*, 330–333.

Wing, R. R., Lamparski, D. M., Zaslow, S., Betschart, J., Siminerio, L., & Becker, D. (1985). Frequency and accuracy of self-monitoring of blood glucose in children: Relationship to glycemic control. *Diabetes Care, 8,* 214–218.

Wing, R. R., Norwalk, M. P., Marcus, M. D., Koeske, R., & Feingold, D. (1986). Subclinical eating disorders in children and adolescents with type I diabetes. *Diabetes Care, 9,* 162–167.

Winter, W. E., Maclaren, N. K., Riley, W. J., Clarke, D. W., Kappy, M. S., & Spillar, R. P. (1987). Maturity-onset diabetes of youth in black Americans. *New England Journal of Medicine, 316,* 285–291.

Wolter, R., Noel, P., De Cock, P., Craen, M., Ernould, C., & Malvaux, P. (1979). Neuropsychological study in treated thyroid dysgenesis. *Acta Paediatrica Scandanavia, 277 (Supp.),* 41–46.

Wysocki, T. (1993). Associations among teen-parent relationships, metabolic control, and adjustment to diabetes in adolescents. *Journal of Pediatric Psychology, 18,* 441–452.

Wysocki, T., Green, L., & Huxtable, K. (1989). Blood glucose monitoring by diabetic adolescents: Compliance and metabolic control. *Health Psychology, 8,* 267–284.

Wysocki, T., Meinhold, P. A., Abrams, K. C., Barnard, M. U., Clarke, W. L., Bellando, B. J., & Bourgeois, M. J. (1992). Parental and professional estimates of self-care independence of children and adolescents with IDDM. *Diabetes Care, 15,* 43–52.

Wysocki, T., Meinhold, P. A., Cox, D. J., & Clarke, W. L. (1990). Survey of diabetes professionals regarding developmental changes in diabetes self-care. *Diabetes Care, 13,* 65–68.

Young-Hyman, D. L. (1990). Psychological functioning and social competence in growth hormone deficient, constitutionally delayed and familial short stature children and adolescents. In C. S. Holmes (Ed.), *Psychoneuroendocrinology: Brain, behavior, and hormonal interactions* (pp. 40–55). New York: Springer-Verlag.

CHAPTER 12

PULMONARY DISORDERS

Marianne Z. Wamboldt
Leslie Gavin

DESCRIPTION OF DISORDERS

Reactive Airways Disease (Asthma)

Asthma is a lung disease characterized by the following features: (1) *airway obstruction*, or narrowing that is reversible (but not completely so in some patients), either spontaneously or with treatment; (2) *airway inflammation*; and (3) *airway hyperreponsiveness* to a variety of stimuli (Sheffer, 1991a). Clinically, it is diagnosed when episodic wheeze and/or cough occurs where asthma is likely and other rarer conditions have been excluded (Warner, 1992). Pathologically, it is characterized as a chronic inflammatory disease of the airways, with a granulocytic-lymphocytic submucosal infiltration, epithelial cell desquamation, and mucus gland hypertrophy and hyperplasia. Secondary to this inflammatory process, and also in part on a genetic basis, the airways of patients with asthma are hyperresponsive to bronchoconstrictors, such as histamine and methacholine. Several factors may contribute to the inflammatory response and others may trigger airway response. Conditions contributing to inflammation in the airways include allergy, exposure to cigarette smoke, and viral infections. In addition, these conditions contribute to pathology that leaves the airways sensitive to noninflammatory triggers, such as exercise, cold air, environmental irritants, and central nervous system pathways, such as emotions. Clinically, asthma presents as airway obstruction secondary to mucus accumulation, thickening and edema of the bronchial walls, and contraction of the smooth muscle surrounding the airways. All elements of this obstruction are capable of reversal, hence the characteristic feature of asthma is airway narrowing that changes in severity either spontaneously or as a result of therapy (American Thoracic Society Committee on Diagnostic Standards, 1962).

Current consensus views asthma as a multifactorial illness with both genetic and environmental (i.e., infectious, allergic, mechanical, and psychosocial) factors involved in its development and course. Although asthma is fairly heritable (there is a two- to four-fold difference in the concordance rates for monozygotic and dizygotic twins), the concordance rate in monozygotic twins is only 20 percent (Edfors-Lubs, 1971; Hopp, Bewtra, Watt, Nair, & Townley, 1984). Hence, phenotypic expression of the genetic component for asthma appears dependent on substantial environmental influence. This conclusion remains unchanged despite data indicating that propensity towards atopy (e.g., as reflected by total serum IgE level) is the major genetic risk factor for asthma (Hopkin, 1993; Hopp et al., 1984).

Asthma is unlikely to be a single-gene disorder. Indeed, in a recent review of the genetics of asthma, Mrazek and Klinnert (1991) proposed an oligogenetic model that provides a good fit for our current knowledge. Their three-gene model includes: (1) an immunologic regulator, (2) an airway sensitivity regulator, and (3) an autonomic nervous system regulator. To the degree to which this assumption is true, one can expect that there are different kinds of asthma, each of which have qualitative and quantitative differences in the role of psychosocial factors.

(1) *Role of the immunologic regulator:* Pertubations in this system are revealed phenotypically by the presence of allergies or atopic illness. The term "atopy" refers to a group of diseases linked by their tendency to occur in the same subjects, to have a genetic predisposition, and to be associated with spontaneous sensitivity to common environmental allergens. Asthma, along with allergic rhinitis, was one of the diseases included in the original definition of this term by Coca and Cooke (Nelson, 1985). Other associated atopic illnesses include eczema and food allergies. Renewed interest in the role of allergy in bronchial asthma resulted from the demonstration that bronchial allergen challenge results in a late recurrence of airway narrowing, an influx of inflammatory cells, and a prolonged increase in bronchial hyperresponsiveness to nonspecific stimuli such as histamine and methacholine. In community studies of children, presence of bronchial hyperresponsiveness correlates with the presence and number of positive prick skin tests to inhalant allergens (Salome, Peat, Britton, & Woolcock, 1987; Woolcock, et al., 1987). Prospective studies of infants born of allergic parents have demonstrated a correlation between development of positive skin tests first to ingestants and later to inhalants, and development of bronchial asthma (Van Asperen & Kemp, 1989). Asthma severity in childhood has also been shown to correlate with the number of positive prick skin tests, (Zimmerman, Feanny, & Reisman, 1988).

Although these data are suggestive, it does not prove a causal connection. The possibility that there is more than a chance association is supported by studies of asthma prevalence in relation to house dust mite exposure. A survey of residents of Marseilles (sea level) and Briancon, France (elevation over 4,000 feet), revealed that at high elevation (where dust mites do not thrive) there was a significant reduction in both skin test reactions to mite and asthma prevalence (Van Asperen & Kemp, 1989). A 10-year follow-up of children in England demonstrated that persistent asthma at age 11 years was significantly correlated with the level of house dust mite antigen exposure in infancy (Sporik, Holgate, Platts-Mills, & Cogswell, 1990). Finally, prevalence of bronchial asthma has increased from 0.1 percent to 7.3 percent in the adult population of the South Fore region of Papua, New Guinea over a period of 10 years, and 90 percent of the adult asthmatics were skin test positive to house dust mites (Dowse, Turner, Stewart, Alpers, & Woolcock, 1985). Increase in asthma was temporally associated with the introduction of cotton blankets, which have been shown to be heavily infested with house dust mites. Therefore, it is very important to consider the role of environment allergens in both the prevention of asthma and in evaluating the efficacy of therapeutic interventions.

(2) *Role of the airway sensitivity regulator:* There is evidence for the role of bronchial hyperresponsivity on a genetic basis apart from airway inflammation. Lang et al., (1987) demonstrated that asymptomatic relatives of asthmatics have an increased probability of being sensitive to low concentrations of inhaled methacholine compared to members of families in whom there have been no asthmatics for three generations.

(3) *Role of the autonomic nervous system regulator:* Finally, there are data suggesting that labile autonomic reactivity is associated with asthma. Taguchi and colleagues (1992) have shown that afferent vagal activity from the lung is one component in determining the sensation of breathlessness. Additionally, several groups have demonstrated an increase in anxiety disorders among children with asthma (Kashani, Konig, Shepperd, Wilfley, & Morris, 1988; Wamboldt, Weintraub, Settle, & Krafchick, 1994). Two groups (Biederman, Milberger, Faraone, Guite, & Warbuton, 1994; Wamboldt & Wamboldt, 1995) have also shown an increase in anxiety disorders among the first degree genetic relatives of asthmatic children with anxiety disorders, indicating a possible shared genetic connection between anxiety disorders and asthma. This could theoretically be mediated through a similar dysfunction in the autonomic nervous system, or through a shared central nervous system mechanism. Neurophysiologically, the increased incidence of panic disorder in asthmatic patients has been related to common projections from the respiratory centers to hypothesized panic centers in the brain (Klein, 1993; Yellowlees & Kalucy, 1990).

Children whose asthma is more or less affected by each of these three genetically determined systems may have different degrees and types of psychological difficulties. For example, children who either do not report clear allergic triggers for their asthma, or report emotional and family stress triggers, appear to have higher rates of psychosocial problems than those who report only allergic triggers (Block, Jennings, Harvey, & Simpson, 1964; Mrazek, 1984; Mrazek & Klinnert, 1989; Purcell, 1963).

There have been few prospective studies of the role of environmental factors in the initial onset of childhood asthma. Most of these have not found global psychosocial factors to be important influences, supporting instead early infections with parainfluenza or respiratory syncytial viruses, parental smoking habits, and specific antigen exposure leading to clinical atopy as major risk factors (Arshad & Hide, 1992; Horwood, Fergusson, Hons, & Shannon, 1985). In contrast, a recent study suggests that more specific psychosocial factors may be of importance. Klinnert and associates (Klinnert, Mrazek, & Mrazek, 1994) have demonstrated an interactive effect of quality of parenting and family stress on asthma onset by 3 years of age in a group of infants at high genetic risk to develop asthma. Specifically, high family stress only increased asthma incidence by age 3 when the stress occurred in the context of deficient parenting practices. In children who developed asthma between the ages of 3 and 6 years, however, behavioral problems in the children at ages 4 and 6 were associated with development of asthma (Klinnert, personal communication). This may be a somewhat independent mechanism, and more directly linked to poorer parenting practices affecting regulation of the autonomic nervous system in the child.

Comorbid medical conditions that are often found in children with asthma include gastroesophageal reflux, sinusitis, rhinitis and upper airways infections, and vocal cord dysfunction. If these conditions are active and untreated, they may precipitate asthma symptoms and complicate management (Sheffer, 1991b).

Vocal Cord Dysfunction

Vocal cord dysfunction (VCD), also referred to as laryngeal stridor, factitious asthma, or Munchausen Stridor, is characterized by a paradoxic adduction of the vocal cords during inspiration. It has at times been thought to be a conversion disorder, potentially representing a symbolic "cry for help." Of importance, patients with VCD often receive intensive treatment and medication for their symptoms before an accurate diagnosis is made. Initial surveys of adults with this disorder found high percentages of women who had been

sexually abused, which was consistent with the psychogenic hypothesis (Freedman, Rosenberg, & Schmaling, 1991). However, more recent reviews suggest that this case is greatly overstated, and that there is considerable heterogeneity of psychological health among VCD patients (Newman & Dubester, 1994). The pediatric population appears to be similarly heterogeneous. Brugman and colleagues (1994) reviewed 37 pediatric patients diagnosed with VCD. The majority of the group (78 percent) had documented concurrent asthma. Only 11 percent had a history of sexual abuse, although another 16 percent had suspected abuse. However, the majority were characterized as high achievers (84 percent academic scholars and 61 percent successful athletes). The children with VCD also had a higher occurrence of depression, anxiety, and family dysfunction than the general pediatric population. It is important to diagnose VCD even if there is comorbid asthma, as hospitalizations and medication requirements (and thus functional severity of asthma) can be markedly reduced with ancillary treatments of speech therapy and/or psychosocial intervention (Newman & Dubester, 1994).

EPIDEMIOLOGY

Prevalence

Prevalence of asthma in the United States increased an estimated 29 percent from 1980 through 1987, from 31.2 to 40.1 per 1,000 population (from 6.8 to 9.6 million). The greatest increase occurred in persons less than 20 years of age. Prevalence of asthma in American children 18 years or younger rose from 3.2 percent in 1981 to 4.3 percent in 1988—an increase of nearly 40 percent, which translates into approximately 2.7 million children (Taylor & Newacheck, 1992; Weitzman, Gortmaker, Sobol, & Perrin, 1992).

Although asthma may begin at any age, highest incidence is in the first 4 years of life (Broder, Higgins, Mathews, & Keller, 1974a; Broder, Higgins, Mathews, & Keller, 1974b). This results in a high prevalence of childhood asthma, followed by a declining prevalence during the late teens and early twenties, and a rise during mid and late adulthood (Broder et al., 1974a, 1974b; Bronnimann & Burrows, 1986). The decline in prevalence during the teens reflects not only a sharp drop in new cases, but also a tendency for remission in childhood asthma. Overall, about half of the children who begin wheezing before age 7 years will be symptom free in early adulthood (Jansson, Boe, & Berlin, 1987; Martin, Landau, & Phelan, 1981).

A number of factors affect the prognosis of childhood asthma. Chronic, persisting asthma and severe asthma correlate with onset prior to age 3 years and multiple episodes of wheezing in the first year of life, occurrence or persistence of eczema, coexistence of allergic rhinitis, lower peak flow rates in childhood, parental asthma, and presence of positive skin tests (Blair, 1977; Jansson et al., 1987; Martin et al., 1981; Martin, McLennan, Landau, & Phelan, 1980; Zimmerman et al., 1988). The more severe the asthma in childhood, the more likely it is to persist (Blair, 1977; Linna, 1985; Martin et al., 1981). Childhood asthma is also more persistent in girls (Martin et al., 1980). Unfortunately, no studies have evaluated the effect of treatment intervention on persistence of symptoms. It would be particularly important to identify the effect of early intervention on patients at highest risk for persistent asthma or asthma in adulthood.

Prevalence of asthma in children is highly variable within a genetically homogeneous population depending upon the living conditions under which the children are raised. An example of the effect of the environment are the differing rates of asthma in Zimbabwean children raised in native villages, urban slums, or middle-class neighborhoods of the capital city of Harare (Keeley, Neill, & Gallivan, 1991). Prevalence of asthma has also increased over time. Examples are the marked increase in Aberdeen, Scotland over the last 25 years (Ninan & Russell, 1992) or the increasing prevalence in Finnish Army recruits over a similar period of time (Haahtela, Lindholm, Bjorksten, Koskenvuo, & Laitinen, 1990). In the United States, prevalence of asthma began to increase in the late 1970s and continues through the most recent statistics. A careful study of the incidence of asthma in a county in Minnesota where records are available on all residents, confirms the increasing prevalence in children under age 14 years (Yunginger et al., 1992). Recent studies in Australian children indicate a similar rise in prevalence in that country (Peat & Woolcock, 1994).

Many factors have been implicated in the world-wide rise in asthma prevalence, including outdoor air pollution (Abbey, Petersen, Mills, & Beeson, 1993). However, the most important factor appears to be the decreasing quality of indoor environments. In epidemiologic studies in New Zealand (Sears et al., 1989), Australia (Peat, Tovey, Gray, Mellis, & Woolcock, 1994), and the United States (Gergen & Turkeltaub, 1992), there is an increased odds risk of a child developing asthma if they are sensitive to a number of indoor allergens, including house dust mites and animal dander. There is also an increased risk of developing asthma with a high level of house dust mite exposure in infancy (Sporik et al., 1990). In adults, increased levels of house dust mite exposure are associated with increased asthma medication requirement (Vervloet et al., 1991).

Exposure to maternal smoking is the second major indoor environmental risk factor associated with asthma risk. The limitation to maternal rather than parental smoking is presumably related to the proximity of the exposure. Maternal smoking has been associated with a number of deleterious effects on the respiratory health of the child, including increased wheezy bronchitis in the first year of life (Arshad & Hide, 1992) and increased risk of wheezing in older children (Gortmaker, Walker, Jacobs, & Ruch-Ross, 1982). In addition to allergens and passive cigarette smoke, other irritants in the indoor environment can cause increased asthma symptoms (Ostro, Lipsett, Mann, Wiener, & Selner, 1994). Cooking with a gas stove and burning wood in a stove or fireplace can both cause increased cough, shortness of breath, and nocturnal awakening.

Mortality

Not only is asthma prevalence increasing, but the severity and mortality associated with this disease are also on the rise. Despite considerable improvement in the many aspects of asthma treatment, from 1980 to 1987 the asthma mortality rate increased 31 percent from 1.3 to 1.7 per hundred thousand population—that is, nearly 1,500 more people died from asthma in 1987 than 1980. The greatest increase (42 percent) occurred in those under age 20, with the highest increase in poor, urban, minority children (Evans, 1992; Weiss, Gergen, & Crain, 1992; Weiss & Wagener, 1990). In addition to the risk of death, there is a high risk for morbidity from pediatric asthma. Asthma accounts for 30 percent (Gortmaker & Sappenfield, 1984) of pediatric hospitalizations, approximately one third of school absences (Weitzman et al., 1992; Weitzman, Klerman, Lamb, Menary, & Alpert, 1982), and numerous other psychosocial complications, including reduced participation in sports and extracurricular activities (Nocon, 1991).

A number of case reports and studies have suggested that psychosocial and family factors are powerful predictors of asthma deaths (Carswell, 1985; Fritz, Rubenstein, & Lewiston, 1987; Kravis, 1987; Kravis & Kolski, 1985; Lanier, 1989; Rubenstein, Hindi, Moss, Blessing-Moore, & Lewiston, 1984; Sears, 1988; Sears & Rea,

1987; Sears et al., 1986; Strunk, Mrazek, Fuhrmann, & LaBrecque, 1985; Strunk, 1987). In a case-controlled study, Strunk and associates (1985) compared 21 children with severe asthma who were previously hospitalized on a tertiary asthma care pediatric in-patient unit and who subsequently died of asthma, with 21 still-living control children matched for age at time of hospitalization, sex, and asthma severity. Of the 57 physiologic and psychosocial variables evaluated by review of hospital records, only those presented in Table 12.1 were found to be significantly different across the groups. As can be seen, psychosocial risk factors were prominent in severely ill asthmatic children who subsequently died. Epidemiologically, children at high risk for death from asthma include those who have had previous life-threatening exacerbations of asthma and those with a lack of adequate and ongoing medical care (Sheffer, 1991a). Non-adherence to treatment was also associated with asthma death.

Associated Psychological Disorders

Although early work by Graham and colleagues (Graham, Rutter, Yule, & Pless, 1967) and McNichol and colleagues (McNichol, Williams, Allan, & McAndrew, 1973) found that the incidence of emotional disturbance in asthmatics was not significantly higher than in controls, other more recent studies have documented a higher level of adjustment difficulties than in control children. For example, elevated levels of psychopathology have been found in asthmatic preschoolers (Mrazek, Anderson, & Strunk, 1985) as well as in older children (Kashani et al., 1988). Several studies have suggested that psychopathology is related to disease severity, with severely asthmatic children demonstrating more psychosocial difficulties than controls or those with a milder form of the illness (Graham et al., 1967; MacLean, Perrin, Gortmaker, & Pierre, 1992; Mrazek, 1988; Norrish,

Table 12.1. Variables That Distinguished Asthma Death Group from Control Group

	NO. OF PATIENTS		STATISTICAL COMPARISON (P)
	DEATH GROUP	CONTROL GROUP	
Physiologic Variables			
History of seizures during asthma attack	9	1	.01
Inhaled beclomethasone dipropionate	13	6	.05
Prednisone decreased ≥ 50% initial dose during hospitalization	13	5	.01
More asthma symptoms in week prior to discharge compared with 4 wk prior to discharge	8	2	.05
Psychosocial Variables			
Disregard of perceived asthma symptoms	7	2	.06
Self-care in hospital not appropriate for age	15	5	.01
Emotional disturbance	18	9	.01
Depressive symptoms	16	9	.05
History of emotional/behavioral reactions to separation or loss	15	6	.01
Patient-staff conflict	15	6	.01
Parent-staff conflict	15	6	.01
Patient-parent conflict	12	5	.05
Manipulative use of asthma	19	12	.01
Family dysfunction	17	11	.05

Adapted from Strunk, et al. *Journal of the American Medical Association, 254,* 1193–1198, 1985, Copyright 1985, American Medical Association, reprinted with permission.

Tooley, & Godfrey, 1977). Caution must be taken in interpreting these data, however, as much of the work documenting psychosocial problems in asthmatic children has relied on either clinical impressions or parent self-report questionnaires of child psychosocial adjustment, such as the Child Behavior Checklist (Achenbach, 1991). Parental psychological states are well known to influence their ratings of their children's behavior (Achenbach, 1991; Brody & Forehand, 1986; Richman, Stevenson, & Graham, 1982), and in cases where the parent is depressed, their child's psychopathology rating may be falsely elevated. A particularly obvious weakness is the paucity of studies that have collected research-based psychiatric diagnostic information from direct observation or interviews with the child.

It is difficult to assess whether psychosocial problems are associated more with physiologically severe asthma as opposed to mild or moderate asthma, in part because the ratings of severity often include a functional component. The NHLBI guidelines for severity (Sheffer, 1991b) include information as to frequency and severity of symptoms, as well as medication requirements. In fact, the number of symptoms reported by the patients (or their parents), the number of days missed from school or work, and the amount of "as needed" medications utilized may all have psychological components to them. Patients with difficulty identifying respiratory sensations may confuse anxiety with bronchoconstriction and report more symptoms. Patients who are depressed or having interpersonal difficulties may be more likely to miss school or work and attribute this to increased asthma symptoms. Patients less compliant with anti-inflammatory medications may utilize more rescue medications. Physicians assessing the need for medications may take these functional symptoms into account and prescribe more medications, thus making it appear that the patient requires more medication, another component of rating asthma severity (Dirks, Horton, Kinsman, Fross, & Jones, 1976). Until there is a set laboratory or physiologic "gold standard" of asthma severity (Stein et al., 1987) it will be difficult to definitely establish whether increased psychopathology is only associated with physiologic severe asthma.

Nonetheless, patients with concurrent asthma and psychosocial problems have been found to be more difficult to treat medically in a variety of ways. Children with more psychosocial problems have been shown to (1) require more concurrent anti-asthma medication, especially corticosteroids (Fritz & Overholser, 1989); (2) require a greater number of hospitalizations in the prior year (Baron et al., 1986; Fritz & Overholser, 1989); (3) exhibit poorer compliance with oral theophylline (Christiaanse, Lavigne, & Lerner, 1989); (4) have longer hospitalizations (Dirks et al., 1977); (5) require a greater number of hospitalizations, emergency room and urgent office visits, and longer hospitalizations in the year post-discharge from an asthma treatment center (Strunk, Fukuhara, LaBrecque, & Mrazek, 1989); and (6) more frequently die of asthma (Kravis, 1987; Kravis & Kolski, 1985; Sears & Rea, 1987; Strunk et al., 1985; Strunk, 1987).

There is now solid evidence documenting the heterogeneity of personality styles and psychosocial difficulties found in patients with asthma (Kinsman, Dirks, & Jones, 1982; Mrazek, 1988). In general, internalizing disorders, particularly anxiety, are found more often than externalizing disorders. Kinsman and associates (Dirks et al., 1977; Dirks, Schraa, Bron, & Kinsman, 1980; Kinsman et al., 1982) developed an assessment of anxiety levels from the MMPI that they labeled the panic-fear profile. They have shown that adult asthmatics who were either low or high on this dimension had more hospitalizations for asthma than those who scored in the moderate range (Dirks & Kinsman, 1981; Dirks et al., 1980). They hypothesized that too little anxiety was associated with denial of symptoms and delay in seeking treatment. High levels of anxiety were associated with poor discernment of respiratory versus anxiety symptoms, leading to overutilization of medical treatment. (Kashani et al., 1988) and Wamboldt and Taylor (1995) have found an increased incidence of anxiety disorders in children with moderate to severe asthma using structured diagnostic interviews.

ASSESSMENT APPROACHES

Medical Issues

Asthma is a multifactorial disease, the severity of which varies across individuals. Because the disease can be triggered in a variety of ways, the assessment process is a mosaic of procedures, the goal of which is to characterize the individual along a number of dimensions. These include physical and laboratory findings, allergic status, bronchial reactivity, and reactivity to exercise.

History and Physical Examination

Evaluation of asthma begins with a history and physical examination of the patient presenting with a recurrent cough or wheeze, and shortness of breath. In infants, asthma can present somewhat differently, with shortness of breath, excessive secretions, noisy breathing, cough, and chest retractions. As outlined in the report from the International Pediatric Asthma Consensus Group (Warner, 1992), features that support an asthma diagnosis include periodicity of symptoms, nocturnal attacks, seasonal variations, symptoms that are produced by allergen exposure or physical exertion, and a family history of atopy. Improvement after being given a bronchodilator is also supportive of the diagnosis, as reversible airway obstruction is a defining characteristic of asthma. Division of asthma into mild, moderate, and severe categories is generally based on the frequency, chronicity, and severity of the asthma symptoms, along with information about lung functions and response to treatment. Status asthmaticus refers to acute, increasingly severe asthma not responsive to drugs that are normally effective.

Pulmonary Function Testing

Pulmonary function testing (PFT) involves equipment into which the patient performs various breathing maneuvers. This can aid in the assessment of lung function, and help to clarify the differential diagnosis. In general, asthma is related to increased airway resistance, decreased flow rates, decreased vital capacity, and hyperinflation with increased residual volume in the lungs. Due to the accuracy of the test being dependent on effort, pulmonary function testing is most useful in children above 4 to 5 years of age, although special equipment is available in some specialty institutions for testing infants and young children.

Pulmonary function equipment varies in complexity from a simple hand-held peak flow monitor to highly complex computerized machines. The spirometer is the most common form of PFT equipment available in clinics. Here the patient takes a long full breath and then exhales suddenly and forcefully into a tube, sustaining the exhalation for several seconds. This tube is connected to a computer, which calculates several functions, including the forced vital capacity (FVC), or total amount of air that is exhaled from maximum inspiration, the forced expiratory volume in the first second of the exhalation (FEV1), and the FEV/FVC ratio, which should be greater than 0.8 in children and young adults with normal unobstructed airflow (Larsen, Abman, Fan, White, & Accurso, 1991). These tests aid in differentiating between obstructive processes (asthma, bronchitis) and interstitial lung diseases.

The hand-held peak flow monitor is a basic device that can be easily used by the patient at home. The patient blows forcefully into the tube, which provides the peak expiratory flow rate (PEFR). The patient can use this to measure pulmonary functions daily, and can track the course of a chronic illness over time to see trends and identify a worsening course before a severe exacerbation. This can be used as a therapeutic tool in individuals who have poor body awareness and have difficulty identifying early warning signs of an exacerbation (Larsen et al., 1991).

In asthma, chest X-rays or CT scans may indicate hyperinflation of the lungs, thickening of the airways, and peribronchial infiltration.

Allergy Evaluation

Elevated serum IgE level is a gross indication of atopy in an individual, and high levels of cord IgE in infants has been associated with onset of asthma before age three (Mrazek & Klinnert, 1989). More specific identification of allergies requires testing, which can be accomplished through in vitro blood tests (radioallergosorbent test, or RAST) or through immediate skin testing. Skin testing is considered more accurate than RAST testing, and can be accomplished through epicutaneous (prick or scratch) or intracutaneous (interdermal) skin testing methods. Allergy extracts are applied to the arm or back, and an erythematous reaction of 3mm or greater is accepted as positive (Nelson, 1989). It should be noted that the accuracy of skin testing can be compromised by the patient taking steroids, antihistamine medications, and tricyclic antidepressants that have significant antihistamine effects. In order to determine the clinical importance of positive allergy tests, open or double blind challenges can be performed. This can be particularly helpful when food allergies are in question.

Inhalant Provocation Testing

The degree of airway reactivity can be assessed through inhalant challenges, employing an irritant such as methacholine or histamine. The patient inhales the substance in increasing dosages, and the reactivity of their airways is measured. Although this provides some objective measure of airway reactivity, it does have shortcomings. Airway reactivity is not exclusive to asthma, and it is possible to have reactive airways when provoked but be otherwise asymptomatic. In addition, being on asthma medications can affect reactivity during inhaled provocation, thus obscuring results.

Exercise Provocation Testing

Exercise testing can be used to evaluate objectively the degree to which individuals are affected by physical exertion. This can be done using a free run or treadmill. Exercise testing can also be employed to assess the general conditioning of the patient and to track the effect of the chronic illness on the individual's overall health over time.

Differential Diagnosis

Asthma can be confused with a number of disorders. These include but are not limited to middle and lower respiratory tract infections, presence of a foreign body in the esophagus or airway, hypersensitivity pneumonitis, immunologic deficiency disease, allergic bronchopulmonary aspergillosis, cystic fibrosis, immobile cilia syndrome, and vocal cord dysfunction.

Vocal Cord Dysfunction

Vocal Cord Dysfunction (VCD) can present alone or in conjunction with asthma. Thus, it is crucial to assess whether this disorder is playing a role in symptom presentation. The "gold standard" of VCD assessment is laryngoscopy in which the vocal cords are observed to close paradoxically on inspiration. VCD is also associated with a loud inspiratory wheeze coming from the larynx, and truncated inspiratory loops on spirometry. However, these latter signs are suggestive and not definitive. It should be noted that videotapes of the laryngoscopic findings can provide an excellent teaching tool for the patient and the family in helping them understand this little known and confusing disorder.

Psychological and Psychiatric Issues

The comprehensive assessment of psychosocial functioning of the asthmatic child includes not only the child's adjustment to the illness, but also an assessment of the context in which the illness occurs. Important variables include the individual's and family's adherence to the medical regimen, family functioning, and school and family support networks.

Individual Functioning

Asthma and Psychopathology. Having a chronic illness such as asthma has a dramatic effect on the developing child, affecting self-esteem, body image, and involvement in age-appropriate activities. As noted above, anxiety and depressive symptoms are commonly found, and

complicate management of the illness. A family history of antisocial personality disorder and/or substance abuse, as well as a family history of anxiety disorders, are associated with children who have more severe asthma (Wamboldt & Wamboldt, 1995).

Coping Styles. It is important to identify what coping styles the child utilizes. Some children use illness symptoms for secondary gain, seeking special attention from others or using symptoms to exit from daily challenges. Others tend to be highly sensitized to physiologic changes, and become anxious about changes in respiratory status, which can at times exacerbate symptoms. Still others tend to ignore symptoms that will curtail their desired involvement in activities, thereby placing themselves at risk by not identifying symptoms early in the illness cycle. Each of these coping styles will have an impact on the patient's ability to adhere to medical recommendations and follow a treatment plan.

Perception of Symptoms. The child's ability to detect changes in respiratory sensations should be assessed. Approximately 15 percent of patients with asthma are unable to detect marked changes in airway obstruction (Rubinfeld & Pain, 1976). Lack of perception of dyspnea has been associated with near-fatal attacks of asthma (Kikuchi, Okabe, & Tamura, 1994; Zach & Karner, 1989). Fritz and Overholser (1990) found that children have a marked variability in their ability to perceive respiratory changes. How perception relates to other coping or defensive styles is still controversial. Steiner, Higgs, and Fritz (1987) reported an association between inability to detect respiratory sensations and a defensive style of repression, which is characterized by low anxiety despite being involved in stressful situations. Interestingly, however, Kinsman's high panic-fear group had the worst ability to detect changes in respiratory status, while the low anxiety group was more accurate (Hudgel, Cooperson, & Kinsman, 1982; Hudgel & Kinsman, 1983). Although this line of work is promising, it has been limited thus far by small sample sizes and imprecise measurements of respiratory perception accuracy. Nonetheless, determining clinically whether a child is relatively accurate in their perceptions is useful in determining how much emphasis to place on peak flow monitoring when designing a treatment plan, as peak flow monitoring can help provide data to the child who is a poor perceiver.

Functional Status. Functional status refers to the degree to which a child's daily activities and ability to function are affected by their illness. Of primary concern is the child's ability to participate fully in school, play, and athletic activities.

There are a variety of ways in which asthma may influence a child's ability to succeed in the school setting. Asthma may affect school absences, actual school performance, ability to participate in sports and activities, and social acceptance by peers. Effects in all of these areas have an impact on the child's self-esteem, which in turn can affect motivation to do well in school. Poor school achievement and/or poor social acceptance are often associated with symptoms of depression and anxiety. Medication side effects and chronic hypoxia can influence attention, concentration or memory, and may increase the possibility of learning disabilities. Additionally, children with poor control of nocturnal symptoms may fatigue easily from decreased sleep. Children with psychological symptoms in turn have more difficult to treat asthma (Fritz & Overholser, 1989; Mrazek, 1988). Thus, a negative cycle can be initiated that is often difficult to break without both medical and psychological interventions. It is much easier to prevent the negative side effects of illness than to manage them once they become entrenched.

Findings regarding the effect of asthma on school achievement have been mixed. In general, however, it appears that asthmatic children have more school absences (Freudenberg, Feldman, & Clark, 1980; O'Neil, Barysh, & Setear, 1985), have lower grades, and need to repeat grades more frequently than healthy children (Freudenberg et al., 1980). Some studies also suggest that the group at highest risk for poor school achievement are children who are also socially disadvantaged and who have psychologic difficulties. For example, in a study of 99 severely asthmatic children, Gustadt and colleagues (1989) found that, although severe asthmatics overall were not more likely to experience school failure, the main predictors of achievement were socioeconomic status, age, chronic oral steroid usage, and emotional problems. Psychological problems added increased predictability even when the other variables were controlled.

Medication Side Effects

In addition to the direct effects of illness on the child's functional status, it is important to assess the possible side effects of anti-asthma medications on cognitive and emotional functioning as well as school performance. Controlled investigations of neuropsychological

side effects have chiefly been limited to theophylline, oral corticosteroids, and beta agonists. In a survey of parents of asthmatic children, one-half reported side effects of hyperactivity and restlessness when their child was taking theophylline. Results from controlled studies generally do not support this claim (Bender, Lerner, Iklé, Conner, & Szefler, 1991; Bender & Milgrom, 1992). However, in a recent review of neuropsychologic studies done on and off of theophylline, Annett and Bender (Annett & Bender, 1994) have concluded that there are subtle changes in children on theophylline, including increased anxiety, improved attention, increased tremor, and diminished verbal comprehension, which are similar to the effects of caffeine.

Oral steroid usage has been shown to result in subtle neuropsychological changes in asthmatic children, characterized by decreased verbal memory and mood disruption. Stump (1986) reported that children taking at least 20 mg of prednisone every other day for two weeks or longer had significantly lower scores in mathematics than did children receiving lower dosages or theophylline alone; there was no difference between days on or off of steroid medication. Suess, Stump, Chai, and Kalisker (1986) demonstrated that oral steroid use was associated with deficits in memory, providing a possible mechanism for the relationship between steroid use and lower mathematical performance. Short-term use of oral steroids does not seem to impair academic functioning or behavior (Nall et al., 1992). Inhaled steroid use has not yet been examined, although concerns have been raised because of systemic absorption and varying levels of systemic effect (Kamada, Parks, & Szefler, 1992). Available evidence indicates that beta-agonists do not influence more complex psychological functions. In summary, children on theophylline are likely to be more anxious, although not more likely to have cognitive deficits. Children receiving corticosteroids for more than two weeks at a time are at increased risk for learning difficulties as a side effect of the medication. Based on the literature, however, parents may overestimate the impact of medication on their child's behavior.

Neuropsychologic Assessment

The possibility of neuropsychologic deficits in asthmatic children was first suggested (Dunleavy, Hansen, & Baade, 1981) in a study of 20 children attending an asthma camp. Based on the results from the Halstead Neuropsychological Test Battery for Children, it was concluded that one-third of the children with asthma exhibited some neuropsychological deficits, presumably induced from chronic or episodic hypoxemia. Since that initial report, there has been no more evidence to suggest that brain damage is common among children with mild to moderate asthma apart from medication side effects. For example, Bender, Belleau, Fukuhara, Mrazek, and Strunk (1987) studied 67 children with moderate to severe asthma and found no evidence of intellectual deficiencies. However, there have been case reports of asthmatic children who develop neuropsychological dysfunctions secondary to respiratory arrests and seizures (Annett & Bender, 1994), suggesting that those who have these serious complications may be at greater risk. In the one study that controlled for arrests and seizures, however, no association between these and cognitive deficits were found (Gustadt et al., 1989).

There is a small body of literature suggesting a link between asthma and reading difficulties. Children with dyslexia or verbal deficits have a higher rate than normal of asthma (Defries, Olson, Pennington, & Smith, 1991; Pennington, Smith, Kimberling, Green, & Haith, 1987; Smith, Meyers, & Kline, 1989). Although several older survey studies have suggested an increase in parental perceptions of learning difficulties among children with any allergic diseases (McLoughlin et al., 1983; Rawls, Rawls, & Harrison, 1971), more recent studies do not substantiate this claim (Celano & Geller, 1993). There is some suggestion that observed learning difficulties may be due to teacher and parent perceptions of children with asthma having more difficulties rather than any empirical evidence of such. Older reports substantiate that teachers often expected less-acceptable behaviors from children with asthma, in part out of fear of precipitating an asthma attack if they required them to behave, thus inadvertently rewarding behaviors unconducive to good learning skills (Creer & Yoches, 1971). In summary, there is no clear evidence that as a group children with asthma have more learning difficulties than healthy children, although some subsets of asthmatic children have a higher incidence of reading and verbal deficits. Interventions aimed at educating teachers and parents about reasonable expectations of asthmatic students may be useful.

Adherence to Treatment

Assessing how well asthmatic children and their families adhere to medical recommendations is critical. Some studies estimate that up to 90 percent of pediatric asthmatics are noncompliant to some degree with their prescribed medical regimen (Baum & Creer, 1986; Chryssanthopoulos, Laufer, & Torphy, 1983). Nonadherence has been identified as a major factor in asthma morbidity (Epstein & Cluss, 1982) and mortality (Strunk et al., 1985). Nonadherence problems include both underuse and overuse of medications. In fact, a common problem among children and adolescents is nonadherence with anti-inflammatory inhalers (e.g., steroid or cromolyn), which are prophylactic and do not yield an immediate improvement in symptoms, along with overuse of the rescue beta-adrenergics that do have an immediate effect. Some authors have cited overutilization of beta adrenergic inhaler medication as a potential risk factor for asthma death (Whitelaw, 1991).

It is important to consider not only whether the patient is taking their medications, but when they are taking them (e.g., pretreating before exercise in the patient with exercise-induced bronchospasm), and how they are taking them (i.e., are they using good inhaler technique, are they using an appropriate spacer device to maximize medication delivery such as an InspriEase or Aerochamber?).

Many techniques for measuring medication compliance have been used both clinically and empirically, but most have significant limitations. Methods such as medication usage diaries and self-report of compliance are highly unreliable, as patients tend to over-report their adherence (Mawhinney et al., 1991). Methods such as taking pill counts or measuring serum blood levels of medications such as theophylline are more objective, but are sometimes inaccurate. Perhaps the most accurate technique for measuring medication compliance per se is a new technology that has been developed in which electronic devices are attached to aerosol inhalers. These devices record the time at which the inhalers are actuated, and can track patterns of medication usage over a period of several months. Studies using electronic devices have been able to measure adherence with a much higher degree of accuracy than other systems such as self-report (Nides et al., 1993). These devices are gaining popularity in empirical research, although they are not yet commonly used clinically due to cost.

Although this is an impressive new advance in our ability to measure medication adherence, the problem remains that medical adherence in the case of a chronic illness requires far more than simply taking medication. In the pediatric patient, it is important to assess how well the family is able to develop an appropriate asthma management system in the home. Important questions include: Does the family keep records of symptoms and peak flow measurements? Does the family get prescriptions refilled on time? Do they keep physician office visits? Do they keep appropriate documentation on their child's illness in between visits? The degree to which the parent creates an appropriate asthma management system and models good compliance may be related not only to subsequent asthma severity and functional impairment, but also to the patient's attitudes toward illness and individual medical compliance.

Another important aspect of adherence is the patient's and family's ability to follow recommendations about environmental controls. As noted above, increased prevalence of asthma appears to be strongly related to quality of the indoor environment, including exposure to dust mites, animal dander, and smoking (Peat et al., 1994; Sears et al., 1989; Gergen & Turkeltaub, 1992). Thus, it is important to assess whether there is smoking in the home, what environmental controls they have in place, and whether they have removed pets from the home, for example. The family's willingness to make appropriate sacrifices is indicative of their commitment to manage the illness.

Family Factors

The chronic, recurrent nature of severe asthma creates a major burden for even the most well-functioning of families. Daily medication routines, frequent physician office visits, medically induced financial hardship, and lifestyle limitations based on the avoidance of asthma triggers create considerable difficulty for pediatric and adult patients and their families. The burden of these stressors may outweigh the coping resources of the family.

The exact nature of the family's role in the actual maintenance of asthma has long been the subject of controversy. In the 1940s, psychoanalysts in the school of French & Alexander described asthma attacks as an "inhibition of a cry" that arose from the child's fear of being separated from his or her mother (Gerard, 1948). In the 1960s, therapy for severe asthma sometimes involved separating children with intractable asthma from their parents as a means of reducing asthmatic symptoms. Working on the assumption that family interactional factors might be present for a subgroup rather than for all asthmatic children, Purcell and colleagues (1969) classified asthmatics by whether they reported emotional reactions as precipitants for their asthma. These investigators subsequently demonstrated that the emotionally triggered children showed symptom alleviation during an experi-

mental separation in which parents and siblings were removed from the home and the patient remained in his normal physical environment with a trained caretaker. The putative success of this intervention appeared to validate the notion that symptoms for these children were precipitated by exposure to some aspect of family functioning, such as family conflict. What was not considered, however, was the role of having a surrogate caretaker in the home who was a trained asthma manager and who may have been administering treatment at home more effectively than the parent.

Other investigators have attempted to examine aspects of the parent-child dyad among asthmatics that may distinguish them from normal children, and there is some evidence that asthmatic families have more negative characteristics when they are compared to nonasthmatic families. Block et al. (1964) obtained parent descriptions of asthmatic children and observed the behavior of the children alone with an examiner, as well as in interaction with their mothers. These investigators noted increased interactional difficulties between mothers and their asthmatic children. Mrazek et al. (1985) studied severely asthmatic preschoolers and their interactions with their mothers, and compared them with healthy children. The asthmatic children were more likely to be oppositional, and the affective climate of the interactions with their mothers was more negative than those of healthy controls. In studies of slightly older children, mothers report more stress, overindulgence and overprotectiveness in their relationships with their children (Carson & Schauer, 1992). In observational studies, families with asthmatic children have been found to have inadequate problem-solving and conflict-resolution skills (Wikran, Faleide, & Blakar, 1978), as well as more chaos and difficulty making decisions than control families (Di Blasio, Molinari, Peri, & Taverna, 1990).

Recent evidence has mounted that critical parental affect may be the important component linking family process to asthma outcome. Using a methodology borrowed from research on the relapse rate of chronic psychiatric patients (Miklowitz, Goldstein, Falloon, & Doane, 1984), investigators have explored the effect of parental expressed emotion (specifically parental criticism and emotional overinvolvement) on asthma status in children. Using the Five Minute Speech Sample (FMSS; Magana, Goldstein, Miklowitz, & Falloon, 1986), and a mother-child dyadic problem discussion, Hermanns, Florin, Dietrich, Rieger, and Hahlweg (1989) found that mothers of moderate asthmatics demonstrated more criticism of their child and had more negative verbal exchanges with their child than control mother-child dyads. In addition, they found that the amount of criticism was correlated with asthma severity. In a similar study of father-child dyads, Schöbinger, Florin, Zimmer, Lindemann, and Winter (1992) demonstrated more criticism in the FMSS, and more critical exchanges in the dyadic observational context. However, they did not replicate Hermanns and colleagues' correlation of criticism with asthma severity.

Investigators studying parental criticism tend to favor the interpretation that such criticism functions as a chronic stressor for asthmatic children, affecting severity and possibly the course of the disease through immunological mechanisms. However, other explanations are possible. For example, Wamboldt, Wamboldt, Gavin, Roesler, and Brugman (1995) also found that parental criticism was prevalent among severely asthmatic adolescents. Higher rates of criticism were linked to noncompliance upon admission and greater improvement in asthma symptoms during hospitalization (and separation from parents). However, it is unclear whether symptoms remitted because the adolescents were removed from the chronic stressor of parental criticism, or whether parents were critical in response to medical nonadherence of their teenagers, whose asthma improved during an intensive intervention period.

Family Social Support and Resources

How a family manages a chronic illness may be significantly affected by their financial and social support resources. Financially disadvantaged families often have difficulty accessing consistent, timely medical care with a personal physician who can track the course of the illness and the family's ability to manage it. Having continuity in medical care is crucial for families with chronically ill children, who when disconnected from the medical system may delay or avoid necessary care in a way that precipitates an illness crisis. Financially disadvantaged or uninsured families may rely on emergency room treatment for their primary care, leading to inconsistency in medical recommendations and poor follow-up. The family's relationship with their physician should be assessed in order to determine whether there is an adequate working relationship for maximal care of the child. In cases where medical neglect is suspected, it is important to assess how well the child's needs are being attended to, and whether there is a history of social services involvement.

TREATMENT STRATEGIES

Overview of Medical Management

Education

Since asthma is a chronic disease that waxes and wanes in response to environmental pertubations, it is essential that the patient and their family be taught how to manage the day-to-day symptoms of the illness. Education, a working partnership with the physician, and self-charting of symptoms and medication usage are essential. There are many good educational programs available for children with asthma and their families, and these have been shown to be effective at increasing self-management knowledge and skills (Wigal, Creer, Kotses, & Lewis, 1990). Patients should minimally understand the use of inhaled drugs and peak flow meters and the difference between medications for relief of symptoms and those taken to prevent episodes. A written action plan for what to do when symptoms occur should be developed by the physician and given to the patient, parents and school officials. As with any chronic disease, education is necessary, though not sufficient, for good self-management.

In a review of all pediatric asthma education programs up to 1988, Howland, Bauchner, and Adair (1988) summarized the effect of 13 programs on school absences, acute care visits, and hospitalizations. One of these programs was carried out in the school, but most were clinic based. The total duration of interventions ranged from 3 to 24 hours, with most programs providing 8 to 12 hours of instruction. Although it was difficult to combine the results of these studies due to methodological differences and limitations, most of the studies reviewed reported a lessening of school absences. In an example of one large, well-controlled study, Clark, Feldman, Evans, Wasilewski, and Levison (1984) provided 6 one-hour group sessions on asthma education, focused separately on parents, children aged 8 to 14 years, and children aged 4 to 7 years. Subjects were recruited from pediatric allergy clinics at four large hospitals in New York City, as well as a private practice maintained by the clinic physicians. The majority of the subjects were non-Caucasian. Of the 274 children agreeing to participate, two-thirds were given the active intervention. Those in the intervention group had fewer emergency visits and hospitalizations than the control group at one-year follow-up. Additionally, children participating in the groups maintained better grades in math, reading, and science. There were no statistically significant differences in school absences, adjustment behaviors in school, or participation in physical education classes between the two groups. Thus, in this sample, some aspects of school performance (grades) improved, while other aspects (attendance, behaviors) did not change.

Prevention

Practicing environmental control can decrease the risk of developing asthma in genetically at-risk children and decrease the severity of symptoms in children with active asthma. Parents should be educated about smoking risk and be supported in quitting. Since it is often difficult for parents to stop smoking, the usual approach is to not allow smoking in the house. Parental report of cigarette smoking appears to be fairly reliable (Chilmonczyk, Salmun, & Megathlin, 1993). More objective data on passive tobacco smoke exposure can be obtained by measuring the levels of cotinine, a stable metabolite of nicotine, in the child's urine, serum, or saliva (Jarvis et al., 1985; Jarvis, Tunstall-Pedoe, Feyerabend, Vesey, & Saloojee, 1987).

Reducing house dust mite exposure has been shown to decrease asthma symptoms, medication requirements, and non-specific bronchial hyperresponsiveness (Platts-Mills & Chapman, 1987). Reduction in house dust mite levels can be accomplished both by generally reducing the indoor environmental humidity (Korsgaard, 1983) and by specifically limiting exposure to mite antigens in the bedding (Ehnert et al., 1992). Removing carpets and drapes from the bedroom and encasing mattresses and pillows in plastic is recommended. Although the most effective means of avoiding animal dander exposure is to eliminate pets from the home, this is often not possible. In this case, reduction in animal dander exposure can still be accomplished by not allowing the pet in the bedroom and by washing the pet weekly.

Medications

Anti-asthma medications improve pulmonary function via three primary mechanisms: bronchodilation, protection of the airways from allergen or histamine challenge, and resolution of airway hyperresponsiveness via anti-inflammatory properties. The individual medications may be grouped into those that are primarily bronchodilators (e.g., ß agonists, theophylline, anti-

cholinergics) and those that are considered nonbronchodilator antiasthma medications (e.g., cromolyn, nedocromil, glucocorticoids).

Most of these medications can be delivered via inhalation, either with a nebulizer, face mask, or metered dose inhaler. More than 50 percent of children receiving medication with a metered dose inhaler have little or no benefit from the prescribed medication because of poor medication technique (Pedersen & Mortensen, 1990). It is essential that children be taught proper technique, including use of a spacer device with a valve system attached to the metered dose inhalers. This should allow children as young as 2 to 3 years old to administer inhaled medications properly. The spacer devices also reduce oral deposition and swallowed drug, thus reducing systemic absorption and side effects.

Bronchodilators. Although bronchodilators used to be the first-line treatment for asthma, they are currently viewed as supplementary to the nonbronchodilator medications. Increased frequency of use could be an indicator of the need for additional anti-inflammatory therapy. The *beta-agonist medications* evolved from those that are relatively short acting (epinephrine, isoproterenol) to those of longer duration of action (albuterol, terbutaline, pirbuterol), but still lasting only 4 to 6 hours (Joad, Ahrens, Lindgren, & Weinberger, 1987). Their greatest advantage is a rapid onset of effect in the relief of acute bronchospasm via smooth muscle relaxation. They are also excellent bronchoprotective agents for pretreatment prior to exercise, perhaps related to their effect of blocking release of mediators from mast cells. Prior to allergen exposure, they effectively block the early pulmonary response, but are of insufficient duration of action to prevent the late phase pulmonary response and do not block the development of airway hyperresponsiveness (Cockroft & Murdock, 1987). All of these medications have potential side effects of tremors and nervousness, especially in younger children.

It has been demonstrated that bronchodilator drugs (e.g., ß-adrenergic agonists, theophylline, anti cholinergics) do not block the allergen-induced increase in bronchial hyperresponsiveness (Cockcroft, 1987) and do not reduce pre-existing bronchial hyperresponsiveness (Dutoit, Salome, & Woolcock, 1987). Several studies have demonstrated that the regular administration of ß-adrenergic bronchodilators may actually increase the level of bronchial hyperresponsiveness (Kraan, Koeter, Sluiter, & de Vries, 1985; Van Schayck, Visch, Van Weel, Van Herwaarden, & Dompeling, 1990). The use of regular inhaled ß-adrenergic agonists at more than three times a day has been implicated as a factor contributing to asthma deaths, and while not proven, discourages routine usage.

Two newly introduced ß-adrenergic agonists, formoterol and salmeterol, produce bronchodilation that persists well beyond 12 hours (Becker & Simons, 1989; Ullman & Svedmyr, 1988). Their prolonged effect overcomes several of the shortcomings of the ß-agonists presently available. They are particularly effective in preventing nocturnal asthma (Ullman, Hedner, & Svedmyr, 1990; Wallin, Melander, Rosenhall, Sandstrom, & Wahlander, 1990). They also block not only the early, but also the late bronchoconstrictor response to inhaled allergen challenge (Twentyman, Finnerty, Harris, Palmer, & Holgate, 1990).

Although *theophylline* is a weak bronchodilator when compared to ß-adrenergic agonists, the main advantage of theophylline is the long duration of action (10 to 12 hours with the use of sustained-release preparations), which is especially useful in the management of nocturnal asthma (Joad et al., 1987). Theophylline has moderate bronchoprotective effects during exercise and histamine challenge, and also attenuates the early and late phase pulmonary response to an allergen challenge (Pauwels, Van Renterghem, Van Der Straeten, Johannesson, & Persson, 1985). This may be related to potential anti-inflammatory properties, since it decreases microvascular leakage and macrophage activity. Doses of theophylline must be individualized to account for patient variability in absorption and elimination. There is a tendency for absorption to be slower at night as compared to the day, resulting in lower serum concentrations at night. A once daily preparation in the evening may be useful in patients with nocturnal symptoms (D'Alonzo et al., 1990; Kossoy, Hill, Lin, & Szefler, 1989; Martin, Cicutto, Ballard, Goldenheim, & Cherniack, 1989).

While the beneficial effects of theophylline have been a mainstay for management of chronic asthma, the narrow margin of safety and risk for significant adverse effects are a continuing concern for patients and their physicians. With the increased emphasis on anti-inflammatory medication as first-line therapy in chronic asthma, the role of theophylline has been reduced to a second- or even third-line agent, even in the guidelines proposed by the National Institutes of Health (Sheffer, 1991b).

The *anticholinergic* group of medications has been shown to provide a modest additional bronchodilator effect to that obtained with optimal ß-adrenergic agonist therapy in patients with acute severe asthma. There are ongoing attempts to define the role of anticholinergic drugs in the treatment of chronic or persistent asthma. While they would empirically seem to be beneficial, their actual clinical effect is not impressive. Perhaps newer agents with a longer duration of action when administered in a sufficient bronchodilator dose will result in increased use of this class of medications. At the present time, anticholinergics are not approved for the treatment of asthma in the United States.

Anti-inflammatory agents include the glucocorticoids, cromolyn, and nedocromil. In studies of reversal of airway hyperresponsiveness by anti-inflammatory drugs, there is often a plateau of hyperresponsiveness reached which is greater than normal and persists despite continued anti-inflammatory therapy (Kerrebijn, Neijens, & Van Essen-Zandvliet, 1987; Woolcock, Yan, & Salome, 1988). It is clear, however, that exposure to allergens to which an asthmatic is sensitive can result in increased bronchial hyperresponsiveness associated with increased airway inflammation. Finally, it has been shown that inhaled corticosteroids and to a lesser degree cromolyn (Svendsen et al., 1987) can block this allergen-induced increase in bronchial hyperresponsiveness and over time reduce the existing level of bronchial hyperresponsiveness, especially in patients with allergic asthma.

Cromolyn blocks both the early and late phase pulmonary response to allergen challenge as well as preventing the development of airway hyperresponsiveness (Cockroft & Murdock, 1987). The precise mechanism of action is not known. The primary advantage of cromolyn is the minimal incidence of adverse effects, making it a safe medication for all age groups including young children. The beneficial effects of cromolyn relate to its prophylactic effect for allergen and exercise-induced asthma. While cromolyn reduces airway hyperresponsiveness when administered on a regular basis, especially during seasonal exposure to an allergen in sensitized patients, most studies are limited to at most one year.

Similar to cromolyn, *nedocromil* can block the early and late phase pulmonary response to an allergen challenge as well as the resultant increased airway hyperresponsiveness. However, the manufacturer claims nedocromil has certain advantages over cromolyn, specifically greater potency and an extended mechanism of beneficial effect (Bel, Timmers, Hermans, Dijkman, & Sterk, 1990; Leung et al., 1988; Richards, Phillips, & Holgate, 1989). Like cromolyn, the precise mode of action of nedocromil is not known. It is suggested that nedocromil, similar to cromolyn, interrupts the inflammatory process and thus leads to long-term reduction in airway hyperresponsiveness.

Glucocorticoids represent the most potent anti-inflammatory agents available for the treatment of asthma. When administered prior to an allergen challenge in a sensitized patient, they block the late phase pulmonary response and the development of airway hyperresponsiveness (Cockroft & Murdock, 1987). Continued administration is also effective in reducing the immediate pulmonary response to an allergen challenge. They are also more effective than ß-adrenergic agonists, theophylline, and cromolyn in reducing airway hyperresponsiveness during maintenance treatment (Dutoit et al., 1987; Kerrebijn et al., 1987; Svendsen et al., 1987). However, given systematically at high doses over time, they can induce numerous side effects including weight gain, hypertension, Cushingoid appearance, acne, osteoporosis, growth suppression, and cataracts.

Unfortunately, dosing guidelines for systemic glucocorticoid therapy are poorly described. For severe acute asthma and status asthmaticus, high dose systemic glucocorticoids are combined with frequent administration of inhaled ß-adrenergic bronchodilator agents. Glucocorticoids can initially be administered intravenously (methylprednisolone sodium succinate, hydrocortisone sodium succinate), which provides a rapid systemic effect. Following resolution of severe obstruction, the steroid dose is reduced and administered orally (methylprednisolone or prednisone). The duration of treatment and tapering dose is based on the patient's response and past history.

Glucocorticoids are also recommended for treatment of impending episodes of severe asthma when bronchodilator therapy is inadequate (Harris et al., 1987). Prednisone, approximately 1–2 mg/kg per day, is administered orally in two to three divided doses for 3 to 7 days. Once again, dose and duration of treatment is based on the patient's response and past history.

Recent emphasis has been placed on the development of inhaled glucocorticoids. The key concept is how much topical activity they can exhibit with the least amount of systemic absorption. The available inhaled glucocorticoids in the United States, beclomethasone dipropionate, triamcinolone acetonide, and flunisolide, appear to have similar topical to systemic potency ratios. All three are administered by a metered dose inhaler. The best characterized inhaled glucocorticoid is budesonide, with high topical anti-inflammatory potency and low systemic bioavailability. An attempt was made to derive prednisone equivalents for the topical administration of budesonide (Toogood, Baskerville, Jenning, Lefcoe, & Johansson, 1989). From these studies, a 1 mg per day dose of budesonide produces an anti-asthmatic effect equivalent to 35 mg per day prednisone in patients previously receiving steroid therapy and 58 mg per day in patients who have not received steroids. This dose of inhaled budesonide also produces a systemic effect on serum cortisol concentration equivalent to 8.7 mg

per day prednisone. Given in high doses, up to 2.0 mg inhaled budesonide per day, it may eliminate recurrent episodes of severe bronchospasm even in patients with moderate to severe asthma, but may also produce systemic side effects, such as hypertension, osteoporosis, cataracts, disturbed carbohydrate and lipid metabolism, weight gain, and growth suppression in children.

More information is needed on prednisone equivalents, comparative efficacy and toxicity for the inhaled glucocorticoids available in the United States, especially with long-term treatment. In the meantime, patients requiring doses of the inhaled glucocorticoids approaching or exceeding 2 mg per day should be monitored for adverse effects.

Current recommendations for treatment are to use inhaled bronchodilators as needed for acute symptoms of cough or wheezing. For mild asthmatics, this may be all that they need. If use is greater than three times a week, however, it is recommended that an anti-inflammatory agent, usually cromolyn, be added to the regimen. If after six weeks of cromolyn the patient is still requiring more than three times a week of beta-agonists, then inhaled steroids should be added. In severe cases, it may be necessary to add scheduled beta-agonists and/or oral steroids (Warner, 1992).

Immunotherapy. Immunotherapy ("allergy shots") has been established to be superior to placebo in many controlled trials (Bousquet, Hejjaoui, & Michel, 1990). However, there have not been controlled studies comparing immunotherapy to pharmacotherapy. Therefore, its place in asthma management shows considerable variations in different areas of the world. It should only be used when a clear, unavoidable allergic trigger has been identified. It appears to be most effective in patients with seasonal rhinoconjunctivitis and mild asthma.

Psychological and Behavioral Treatments

Prevention

Many of the preventive efforts aimed at children at genetic risk for asthma (i.e., with at least one parent with asthma) require commitment by parents to avoid passive smoke exposure, certain allergens, and to maintain good parenting practices. These interventions are straightforward for well-educated and psychologically healthy parents. For parents with intellectual limitations, antisocial disorders, substance abuse, or other major psychiatric problems, these can be difficult practices to implement. It is not surprising that a large percentage of children with moderate to severe asthma in adolescence have a family history of substance abuse and/or antisocial disorder. It may be that the chaos in the family during their critical early childhood years left them exposed to many allergens, to passive smoke, and to numerous viral infections. Klinnert and colleagues' (1994) finding that stress and poor parenting skills lead to increased incidence of asthma in genetically at-risk children suggests that these parents are also unable to regulate their child's stress appropriately. It is important for a consulting mental health professional to identify these high-risk families early and supply behavioral interventions aimed at promoting more consistent parenting, avoidance of major triggers, and prompt medical attention for infections.

Education

As stated above, education is a primary intervention for children with asthma. One of the most difficult aspects for parents to determine is how much responsibility their child should take for their medication regimen at a particular age. Providing developmentally appropriate expectations for parents is useful, and helps them to gauge whether their child is on a trajectory toward independence. One such set of guidelines, developed by Klinnert and Lum Lung, is shown in Table 12.2.

Family Support

Various illness groups, including asthmatics, have created strong self-help networks across the country that provide support, information, and resources for individuals and families. Groups such as Mothers of Asthmatics and the American Lung Association can provide invaluable information to families about the illness and its treatment, as well as specialty services and financial resources. Groups such as the Asthma and Allergy Foundation of America disseminate research findings and support education and service programs. The National Jewish Center for Immunology and Respiratory Medicine is a national referral center for patients with asthma and other respiratory illnesses, and provides community outreach services in the form of literature and a toll free LUNG-LINE™ information service for patients, families and professionals.

Individual Therapy

Behavior Therapy. In the 1970s and 1980s, efforts were made to develop behaviorally oriented approaches focused on anxiety reduction through muscle relaxation, with the assumption that constriction of the airway was the primary problem in asthma. Research focused on relaxation, biofeedback, and hypnosis, with mixed results. Some studies using general relaxation with asthmatic children demonstrate that relaxation can lead to increased in peak expiratory flow rate (Alexander, 1972) and increased lung tolerance to an inhaled irritant during a provocation test (Philipp, Willde, & Day, 1972). There is some evidence in both of these studies that children with more emotionally triggered asthma demonstrate the most benefit from relaxation.

Studies of autosuggestion and hypnosis highlight the power of suggestion in both symptom induction and symptom reversal in certain asthmatics. Separating extrinsic (allergic) from intrinsic (non-allergic) asthmatics, Philipp and colleagues (1972) found that intrinsic asthmatics were more easily triggered by suggestion than extrinsic asthmatics, and that their symptoms were reversed by placebo. In a review of studies using hypnosis to increase lung function, DePiano and Salzberg (1979) concluded that hypnosis may have more effect on symptom perception and symptom control than on actual lung function.

Studies of biofeedback have generated some provocative results. Davis, Saunders, Creer, and Chai (1973) compared biofeedback-enhanced relaxation with traditional Jacobsonian relaxation and studied the effects on airway resistance in asthmatic children. They found that biofeedback was significantly more effective than traditional relaxation, but only in mild, not severe, asthmatics. In a study of chronic asthmatics in a summer camp setting, Scherr, Crawford, Sergent, and Scherr (1975) trained children in muscle relaxation biofeedback 1½ hours per week for 6 weeks. They found that children using biofeedback had fewer infirmary visits, fewer asthma attacks, and higher peak flow measures than control children. In a case study with 4 asthmatic children, Feldman (1976) used biofeedback to reduce airway resistance. Unlike other studies that focused on muscle relaxation, Feldman trained asthmatic children to change their breathing pattern using biofeedback, resulting in decreased respiratory resistance. As with studies of relaxation and hypnosis, however, the mechanism of effect and the clinical utility of biofeedback remain unclear. Further research needs to identify more clearly which

Table 12.2. Developmentally-Based Self-Care for Asthmatic Children

AGE IN YEARS	ASTHMA SELF-CARE EXPECTATIONS
1 $\frac{1}{2}$ to 3	**Step 0: Cooperation** • Cooperate in taking respiratory treatments and medications • Respond to adult guidance to slow down or sit down
3 to 5	• Learn body awareness with verbal labels for wheezing/tightness • Learn to swallow pills • Begin using peak flow meter correctly with adult reminders
6 to 7	**Step 1: Learn Basic Skills** • Take medications and respiratory treatments correctly when adults remind • Use peak flow meter correctly with adult reminders • Demonstrate "listening to self" (the internal stethoscope) so can report wheezing to adults and treat asthma attacks early
7 to 8	**Step 2: Beginning Decision-Making** • Request medications within 30 minutes of scheduled time • Request and do peak flow meter, spirometry, and respiratory treatments at scheduled time. Record date, time and results of peak flow, graph if appropriate • Notice, report, and record triggers and if appropriate early warning signs • Request pretreatments before exercise if ordered • Demonstrate proper cleaning of equipment
8 to 9	**Step 3: Beginning Responsibility of Managing Symptoms** • Recognize and report wheezing/tightness • Rest and relax at the first sign of wheezing/tightness • Continue to record peak flow meter values at scheduled times • Demonstrate and use breathing exercises • Begin learning about medications • Continue "listening to self"
9 to 10	**Step 4: Knowledge of Illness and Medications** • Know medications: including dose, times taken, action, indications, contraindications, and side effects • Parents and adults provide emotional backup and assistance with care when ability to self-manage is limited due to increasing symptoms • Learn to take and record pulse
11 to 12	**Step 5: Advance Decision-Making and Responsibility** • Prepare respiratory treatments with supervision • Demonstrate use of Epi pen if appropriate • Assess condition before and after respiratory treatments • Continue taking and recording pulse before and after respiratory treatments when scheduled • Update medication records regularly to reflect any changes in orders • Practice waking (with alarm clock) for nighttime medications and treatments
13 to 14	**Step 6: Practice Independence Skills and Planning** • Prepare respiratory treatments without supervision • Pack medication for 24 hours or one week at a time with supervision • Demonstrate good preparation and judgment by making arrangements for medications and treatments needed if away from home during a scheduled medication time • Continue reporting all wheezing episodes and demonstrating wheezing protocol
14 to 15	**Step 7: Demonstrate Preparation for Independence in Treatment and Management of All Aspect of Care** • Pack medications for one week with supervision • Keep written records of medications, peak flow, and pulse, with supervision • Prepare and take respiratory treatments independently • Awaken for nighttime medications and treatments • Continue to report all episodes of wheezing
16+	**Step 8: Independent Functioning** • Prepare and take medication and respiratory treatments independently • Continue packing medications • Arrange for refill of prescribed medications when low • Assess condition before and after respiratory treatments • Keep accurate records (medications, RTs pulse, peak flows, symptoms diary)

Klinnert, Tedesco, 1985. Revised 1991, Klinnert and Lum Lung. Reprinted with permission from Strunk, 1991.

subpopulations are most likely to respond to biofeed-back, what the precise mechanism of effect in biofeed-back is, and whether it is useful in an acute crisis as well as the nonacute, research paradigm situation.

More recent behavioral approaches have focused on helping children with symptom recognition, appropriate responses to symptoms, and anxiety management, and there is some empirical support for this more comprehensive approach. In one recent study (Dahl, Gustafsson, & Melin, 1990), children on chronic beta-agonist therapy were taught discrimination training of asthma signals, counterconditioning of learned fear responses, contingency management of asthma-related behavior, and compliance training. Data indicated that children undergoing this treatment had reduced need for PRN albuterol treatments and missed fewer days of school when compared to the control group, although the children did not demonstrate any differences in objective measures such as lung functions when compared to controls. The authors concluded that behavioral strategies such as these can be helpful in reducing functional morbidity, particularly when the degree of handicap is affected by psychosocial factors.

In summary, research on behavioral approaches such as relaxation, biofeedback, and autosuggestion have suggested that at least some subgroups of asthmatics may benefit from these techniques. Mild asthmatics and those who have intrinsic, emotionally triggered asthma appear to benefit most. Emotion-triggered asthmatics also appear to be more suggestible, both in terms of symptom induction and reversal. Whether these approaches actually help improve lung function directly or indirectly through increasing the child's ability to perceive breathing changes, avoid panic, and take effective action more quickly, is unclear from the literature. It is important to note that these approaches target one aspect of asthma pathology, bronchoconstriction, and do not address inflammation, which has gained increasing attention as a primary factor in asthma pathology in the past ten years (Sheffer, 1991b).

Supportive Psychotherapy. The use of long-term, psychodynamic therapy as a modality to treat asthmatic children has long been debated, and little empirical work has been done to validate its efficacy. However, we would suggest that there is a role for goal-oriented supportive psychotherapy with this population. Specifically, children with a chronic illness often develop deficits in self-esteem, become isolated socially, and in some cases develop coping styles in which they use asthma symptoms for secondary gain in the family and at school. A comprehensive problem-focused therapeu-tic approach combining behavioral, cognitive and supportive techniques to address the child's adjustment to chronic illness, teach useful coping strategies and explore emotional issues that may be triggering the illness may have a role in a modern treatment regimen, particularly for the severe asthmatic. However, controlled studies need to be done to support this use of psychotherapy and to identify which children might benefit from which components.

Group Therapy

Groups for Asthmatics. There are few empirical studies of group psychotherapy for children with asthma. One study investigated the cost effectiveness of a "psychosomatic coping group therapy" in adults with asthma and found that those in the treatment group had fewer days missed from work and fewer days hospitalized than controls (Deter, 1986). The group met weekly for a year and focused on psychological aspects of coping behavior and disease management. The study concluded it was cost effective (i.e., reduced costs of hospitalizations and loss of work time), but did not address whether asthma improved.

Multifamily Groups. Research suggests that multifamily treatment groups, employing a time-limited psychoeducational model, can be effective in extending the remission rate of psychiatric patients (Falloon, McGill, Boyd, & Pederson, 1987; McFarlane, 1982). It has also been demonstrated to be effective in helping families of adolescents with eating disorders (Slagerman & Yager, 1989), substance abusers (Kosten, Hogan, Jalali, Steidl, & Kleber, 1986) and schizophrenia (Anderson, Reiss, & Hogarty, 1986).

In chronic illness populations, Gonzales, Steinglass, and Reiss (1989) described a multifamily group outpatient program for adolescents and adults with chronic medical illness and their families. This program included eight structured sessions focusing on ways in which the illness had disrupted family identity, ways in which communication of feelings about the illness could be enhanced, and helping the family "put illness in its place." Others have reported the benefits of using multifamily groups in populations with rheumatoid arthritis, developmental disabilities, and oncologic illnesses (Strelnick, 1977; Szymanski & Kiernan, 1983; Wellisch, Mosher, & Van Scoy, 1978). In juvenile-onset diabetes, multifamily group therapy has actually been demonstrated to affect medical outcome. In a report by Satin,

LaGreca, Zigo, and Skyler (1989), adolescents in multi-family group treatment demonstrated significant decreases in hemoglobin A1 six months post-treatment, while the control group did not.

Wamboldt and Levin (1995) have developed a model for multifamily psychoeducation with asthmatic children that is effective in improving the therapeutic alliance with the health care team, as well as helping families explore the psychological aspects of the child's asthma and its effects on the family. Common parenting pitfalls (e.g., not disciplining a child because their crying precipitates an asthma attack or allowing a child to avoid chores due to fear of asthma precipitation) can be talked about in an educational and preventive manner. This model of therapy deserves more research with the asthma population.

Family Therapy

Intervention in the family has been found to have important influences on psychosocial and medical status in children and adolescents with asthma. Early studies demonstrated that children with intractable asthma could improve dramatically when separated from their families and provided with a surrogate caretaker in the home (Purcell et al., 1969). Whether this "parentectomy" approach was successful due to the child being separated from some pathologic family dynamic or due to the surrogate caretaker providing more structured and consistent illness management remains unclear.

Studies of family therapy per se have demonstrated that therapy with severely asthmatic children and their families improved the child's asthma status. In a report of a structural family therapy approach with seven case examples of children with severe "psychosomatic asthma," Liebman, Minuchin, and Baker (1974) reported significant improvement in each of the seven children, with decreases in asthma symptoms and days of school missed. The length of therapy varied from five to ten months, and focused both on dysfunctional family interaction as well as medical management issues. In a study by Gustafsson, Kjellman, and Cederbald (1986), a therapeutic approach similar to that of Liebman and associates was used with a more rigorous empirical design. In this study, 17 severely ill children and adolescents were followed for a period of eight months, then were randomly assigned to either family therapy or medical management. The treatment group received treatment for eight months, then both groups were assessed in a blind fashion. The experimental group showed greater clinical improvement than the medical management group. Lask and Matthew (1979), in a well-controlled trial, contrasted families receiving 6 hours of family therapy over 4 months to a no treatment control group. The therapeutic focus in this therapy was on coping with the illness and talking about emotional issues related to the disease. At one-year follow-up, children of the families in the treatment group demonstrated lower daily wheezing scores and lower thoracic gas volumes when compared to the control group. In sum, the few studies that have been performed on family therapy outcome in relation to asthma demonstrate positive effects. Although the mechanism of these effects has not been elucidated, two primary candidates are helping families develop better asthma-related coping skills, including compliance, and helping families manage emotional issues around the illness.

In-Patient Treatment

There is a long history of residential treatment for asthmatic children. This was perhaps first initiated by Peshkin (1930), who advocated the use of long-term hospitalization for severely asthmatic children who could not be managed in the home. This treatment approach was further supported by research demonstrating the benefits of the "parentectomy" approach (Purcell et al., 1969). However, with the advent of more potent and effective medication regimens in the past fifty years, severe asthma has become more easily controlled on an out-patient basis. In addition, the notion of separating a child from the family as a long-term solution has fallen out of favor for both philosophic and financial reasons. However, there continue to be cases in which the child's asthma is life threatening and there is deemed a need for intensive hospitalization to address the disabling condition.

One advantage of in-patient treatment is that ancillary services (e.g., physical therapy and art therapy) are available. Often children with asthma reduce their participation in sports and physical activities. If exercise-induced bronchospasm is undetected or undertreated, children will have experienced shortness of breath with exertion, causing them to avoid physical activity. If they are taking chronic steroids, they also may be overweight and have muscle pains. Helping them to develop a safe physical activity program is difficult, and an intensive intervention program can help children learn to detect respiratory symptoms during exercise, to pace activities to avoid these symptoms, and encourage them into a routine exercise program. The overall benefits of improved cardiovascular function and body tone, as well as the social aspects of sports participation, help to improve self-esteem. Children with moderate to severe asthma often have difficulty identifying and expressing their emotions. Art therapy is a modality that is often easier for them to approach than verbal therapies, and it is helpful in initiating a therapeutic process. For children with moderate to severe asthma that is poorly controlled, a specialized in-patient or partial hospitalization program can provide these rehabilitative services in addition to medical management and psychotherapy. Outcome data on 103 children discharged consecutively from one such in-patient treatment program for asthma showed that use of medical resources, including hospitalizations, emergency room visits, and acute physician visits, decreased significantly in the two years following discharge (Strunk et al., 1989). A second study of 44 consecutive patients admitted to a short-term in-patient treatment program (11–52 days) that emphasized family participation and included out-patient psychotherapy, showed similar results, with a reduction in hospitalizations, emergency visits, and steroid doses (Weinstein, Faust, McKee, & Padman, 1992). Given that children admitted to either of these programs had a combination of moderate to severe asthma and significant psychological and family problems, there is support that these intense interventions are helpful for this subset of asthmatic children.

Therapeutic Approaches for Vocal Cord Dysfunction

The primary therapeutic approaches to VCD include hypnotherapy, speech therapy focused on relaxed breathing techniques, and psychotherapy. There are several case reports describing successful intervention in VCD using hypnosis. For example, Smith (1983) reported the successful use of self-hypnosis to treat psychogenic stridor in a male adolescent athlete. The boy was instructed in a mental imagery technique in which he visualized his vocal cords relaxing and having complete ease of inspiration. In a seminal article on paradoxical vocal cord motion, Martin, Blager, Gay, and Wood (1987) outline a different but related therapeutic approach. Here the therapeutic techniques include validating the disorder instead of attacking it as "all in the patient's head," and using a behavioral approach to teaching diaphragmatic awareness, open throat breathing exercises, and a slow exhalation techniques. These authors advocate supportive psychotherapy as an adjct to behavioral treatments used to provide symptom relief.

Pharmacological Treatments

Antidepressants

Given that children with asthma tend to have more internalizing problems, antidepressant therapy targeting depressive and/or anxiety symptoms would seem to be useful. However, child psychiatrists may be reluctant to prescribe antidepressants to children with asthma due to concern about interactive side effects with anti-asthma medications. For example, in a controlled prospective study of imipramine in a group of children with intractable asthma, Kanner, Klein, Rubinstein, and Mascia (1989) suspended their pilot study after encountering serious side effects in 4 of 5 patients. The side effects causing discontinuation were increased motor activity, impulsive behavior, premature atrial contractions, diastolic hypertension, and a generalized seizure. The children included four with separation anxiety disorder and one with major depression. Parenthetically, all four children with separation anxiety improved clinically on imipramine.

Recent reports of sudden, unexplained deaths associated with desipramine also suggest the need for caution (Abramowicz, 1990; Riddle, Geller, & Ryan, 1993) in the use of tricyclic antidepressants with children in general. The concern is greatest with regard to cardiac effects. The most common effects of tricyclics on electrocardiograms are prolongation of PR intervals, increase in QRS intervals, and increased QTc. Other common side effects are tachycardia, diastolic hypertension, and orthostatic hypotension. Many of these same side effects are seen in children on asthma regimens. The bronchodilating drugs produce decreases in peripheral vascular resistance and cardiac stimulation resulting in tachycardia, palpitations, nervousness and tremor (Rall, 1990). The more selective beta agonists (e.g., albuterol) have fewer of these effects than the less selective medications (e.g., theophylline). Cardiac side effects of oral steroids include hypertension (Haynes Jr., 1990; Sanders, Portman, Ramey, Hill, & Strunk, 1992), which may be additive to the hypertension possible with tricyclics. Often, children with asthma are also treated with decongestants (e.g., phenylpropanolamine, ephedrine, pseudoephedrine) for chronic rhinitis. The common mechanism is alpha-adrenergic stimulation. Toxic effects of these medications also include hypertension (Goodman, Wright, Barlascini, McKenney, & Lambert, 1986). Thus, adding a tricyclic antidepressant to other anti-asthma medications may exacerbate the cardiac effects of all of these medications.

Despite the risks, Wamboldt, Roesler, and Yancey, Jr. (1995) demonstrated that antidepressants can be safely administered to children with moderate to severe asthma if introduced slowly and with monitoring of vital signs. Additionally, the newer SSRI antidepressants generally do not have cardiac side effects.

There have been no published studies on the use of anti-anxiety medications, such as the shorter acting benzodiazepines, in children or adolescents with asthma. As benzodiazepines can depress ventilation and be addictive, they are contraindicated for acute asthma attacks or for chronic use in children with asthma. The non-benzodiazepine, buspirone, may be safer for long-term use in chronically anxious children with asthma. However, to date there are no studies looking at the effectiveness or safety in children with asthma (Rosenberg, Holttum, & Gershon, 1994). The non-selective betablockers such as propranolol, which are sometimes used to treat anxiety, are contraindicated for patients with asthma. Whether the newer selective beta-blockers such as atenolol are safer has yet to be tested.

Neuroleptics

There are no contraindications to using neuroleptics with anti-asthma medications. Some of the more common indications in children with asthma include steroid-induced psychosis, brief psychotic episodes occurring with borderline personality disorder, and manic episodes.

Stimulants

Stimulants may be used to treat ADHD in children with asthma. There are some children who cannot tolerate certain side effects (e.g., anorexia, nervousness) associated with stimulants, particularly if they also have these side effects with beta agonist medications. Buproprion is often a good choice, as it is effective for symptoms of ADHD and generally does not interact with the asthma medications.

Lithium

Lithium is indicated for children with comorbid bipolar disorder and asthma. Lithium does increase theophylline clearance, and thus levels of both drugs must be monitored closely.

CASE ILLUSTRATION

Clinical Presentation

The patient was a three-year-old Caucasian female who was transferred to the National Jewish Center for Immunology and Respiratory Medicine from a local children's hospital, where she had been air evacuated after a near death asthma episode. The child lived with her mother in a rural area that was three hours away from the nearest major medical center. This was a single mother supported by public assistance who had no car or telephone. The mother had a history of alcohol abuse but was not actively drinking, and appeared to be of below average intelligence.

The patient began having respiratory problems at 11 months of age, and by the age of three she had five hospitalizations and 3 intensive care unit admissions for severe asthma. On each occasion the child presented to the hospital in severe respiratory distress. On three occasions she presented in respiratory failure, and required intubation with mechanical ventilation. Despite months of regular physician visits and frequent home visiting nurses, there were continued problems with poor compliance, inadequate maternal recognition of early warning signs, and delays in seeking medical attention. These factors placed the child at extremely high risk for asthma morbidity and mortality.

The child and mother were transferred to the tertiary care facility to treat the asthma, educate the mother, and assess medical neglect. During the course of hospitalization, the patient and her mother were assigned to a multidisciplinary treatment team consisting of a physician, a psychologist and a primary nurse. Clear expectations were laid out for the mother, who was asked to care full time for the patient, including daily self-care and medications. She was also expected to participate in intensive education and would be observed in her performance of the medication regimen. A formal treatment contract was drawn up and signed by the parent and the treatment staff.

Assessment Findings

Maternal Behavior

From the outset, mother complained that too much was expected of her. Upon admission, her greatest concerns were where she could watch television, when she could leave the unit to smoke cigarettes, and whether she could go to Bingo games three nights a week in a neighboring town. She watched television throughout the day, and became angry when staff asked her to watch her daughter more closely. On one occasion when the patient had an acute asthma exacerbation at night, the mother refused to get up to carry out the necessary treatments, then became angry about the noise being made while she was trying to sleep. She later got up, refused to take her child to X-ray, and stormed out to have a cigarette. This episode was highly concerning, as the child regularly became acutely ill at night, and her illness was observed to quickly progress to a life-threatening stage. This and other similar episodes of maternal behavior were documented in the medical chart.

Observations made of the parent-child relationship supported a DSM-IV diagnosis of reactive attachment disorder. The patient was noted to attach indiscriminately to strangers, while avoiding her mother. When given the choice of going to a nurse or her mother for play or for comfort, she often chose the nurse. The mother was regularly noted to show either an intrusive parenting style, in which she was impatient and punitive, or to ignore the child. She demonstrated little sensitivity to the child's needs, and she had little insight into the ways that her own behavior affected her daughter.

Although mother did show an ability to administer medications, she did not demonstrate knowledge about the different medication actions, and her behavior during medication times was inappropriate. During administration of nebulized medications, mother would walk away from the child and not return for several minutes, instead of sitting by and ensuring that proper technique was used.

Child Functioning

Upon admission, it was evident that the patient was developmentally delayed. She had no speech, and demonstrated a significant impairment in affect regulation. On the Bayley Scales of Infant Development, she was found to be significantly developmentally delayed. Whether these delays were a reflection of brain insults secondary to respiratory arrests was unclear. Neurologic and genetic evaluations performed during the hospitalization were unremarkable, and it was judged that her delays were caused by a neglectful parenting style that precluded the stimulation necessary to promote normal growth and development.

There was some evidence during the hospitalization that the patient was having some post-traumatic symptoms from her invasive medical procedures. She was noted to wake up during the night, and on occasion to be inconsolable as if she were having nightmares. She was also observed to have unprovoked emotional outbursts where she would kick, scratch and bite. Because of her inability to communicate, the origin of this behavior pattern was difficult to assess.

Treatment Selection and Course

Treatment focused on providing mother with skills necessary to take care of her child and gathering support services necessary to bolster her development and keep her alive. The question of the mother's ultimate ability to keep the child safely was assessed throughout.

Asthma Education

Mother participated in a course of asthma education classes designed to teach her about the illness, medication actions, and illness assessment. The fact that her child was at high risk for asthma death was underlined. The mother was also enrolled in CPR classes.

Smoking Cessation

Mother was enrolled in a smoking cessation class. She was counseled about behavioral strategies, and provided with nicotine patches. The mother was ambivalent about quitting smoking, and was not willing to continue wearing the patches after one day. She restarted smoking after two days.

Parent-Child Counseling

The mother was provided with information about child development and the emotional and supervisory needs of her child. Parent-child tasks were observed, and the mother was provided feedback about ways she could be more emotionally responsive and encourage language development.

Follow-Up Services

A number of support services were arranged for this family. First, a phone was placed in the home through the help of a national program run through local telephone companies that provides financial aid to pay for telephone hook-ups in the home of handicapped individuals. This facilitated access to medical care that might save the child's life. Next, mother was guided through the process of applying for Social Security benefits for her daughter. In addition, mother was instructed in how to connect this child with educational and rehabilitation services in her community that would address developmental delays. It was also recommended that the child be reevaluated on an ongoing basis to track her development.

Medically, contact was made with the home physician to arrange for regular physician visits. The need for the physician to create an ongoing positive working relationship with this mother was emphasized. In addition, it was arranged that a visiting nurse come to the home to assess the child's condition and document the home situation two to three times per week.

Child Protective Services

One of the goals of the hospitalization was to assess whether this mother was capable of taking care of this child appropriately, and considerable effort was made to provide mother with every possible tool and support to enable her to manage her daughter at home. After two weeks, however, it became clear that mother had considerable difficulty understanding and meeting the needs of her child. When child protective services was contacted at the outset of the hospitalization, they felt they did not have adequate documentation of neglect to take custody of the child. Assessments made during the hospitalization of poor parenting skills, poor supervision of the child during medication administration, maternal mood swings, maternal inability to quit smoking, and inability to create a treatment alliance with the staff was all carefully documented and provided to social services. In turn, social services developed an intensive intervention plan that included the child remaining in the home, but having a family support service provider being in the home three to four times per week to work on adherence with the medical regimen, transportation to medical and other special services, aid in connecting with community resources and education about proper child care, nutrition, discipline, and parent child activities. It was made clear to the mother that her cooperation with these services would determine her ability to keep custody of her child.

Termination and Follow-Up

The child and her mother were hospitalized for one month. During the course of the hospitalization, the child's asthma stabilized completely, and all other potential complicating disorders were ruled out. The mother achieved an adequate level of asthma education, but continued to smoke and was in continual conflict with the staff. The family was sent home under the care of social services.

At the three month follow-up point, the child was doing well medically, and the mother had made significant gains in her parenting ability. An excellent working relationship with social services had been established, and home visitors were in the home several times per week. The mother continued to smoke, although had decreased her number of cigarettes per day and only smoked outside the home.

The above case illustrates a child at high risk for serious psychological problems and asthma morbidity and mortality. Some of the high-risk variables noted at the outset of treatment were severe asthma, as indicated by several respiratory arrests; a parent who had limited understanding of her child's early warning symptoms and appropriate action to take, was not able to help her child avoid triggers (i.e., smoke), and seemed to lack appropriate parenting skills to help the child regulate her affect or develop appropriately; and early signs of affective dysregulation in the child. In addition, the parent had a conflicted relationship with the health care team and was unable to develop a working alliance with health care professionals. If untreated, one might anticipate problems for this dyad in the future that would include the development of inadequate discipline strategies leading to cycles of negative criticism from the mother and oppositional behavior from the child. In these cases, chronic noncompliance often becomes one of the child's oppositional behaviors, which in turn further compromises the child's health. Her asthma exacerbations may keep her out of school, so that she might fall further behind in overall development and educational achievement. It is clear that early intervention was crucial in this case.

The initial goals of intervention in such a system may well be to stabilize the health of the child by using outside resources (e.g., visiting nurse). When the child reached school age, treatments and medications could be arranged to be given her within the school system, with a focus placed on maximizing her attendance in school. In the meantime, considerable work would need to be done to develop a therapeutic alliance with the mother. A multifamily group for parents of medically ill children may be a good beginning, to help her feel understood and encourage her to learn from other parents and develop a support network. Giving her simple behavioral strategies to use in parenting (e.g., medication delivery and time out strategies) may be able to prevent the more difficult to interrupt cycle of criticism and noncompliance. Such interventions may not only decrease the psychological problems the child may develop, but lessen asthma severity and risk for asthma death.

SUMMARY

Asthma, or reactive airways disease, is a common chronic illness of childhood. The phenotypic disease has a heterogeneous etiology, and thus there are different subtypes, with varying degrees of psychological problems associated with the illness. Most children and families manage to control the illness with minimal adverse psychological effects for the child. However, there are some common pitfalls these children and their parents may experience, and the role of the pediatric psychologist or psychiatrist may be educational to help prevent adverse outcomes for the child. There are other children who are at higher risk for psychological sequelae, by virtue of having a comorbid psychiatric disorder themselves, or, more commonly, a family history of psychiatric disorders or a family system that has dysfunctional dynamics. These are the children the pediatric psychologist and psychiatrist will often be called to consult with and treat. Overall, family education, support and therapy have been shown to be useful in helping families manage their child's asthma with less interruption to normal development. In more difficult cases, combinations of individual or group therapy, or an in-patient or partial hospitalization rehabilitative program, may be necessary to interrupt a dysfunctional pattern and restart the child on a course of normal psychological development.

REFERENCES

Abbey, D. E., Petersen, F., Mills, P. K., & Beeson, W. L. (1993). Long-term ambient concentrations of total suspended particulates, ozone, and sulfur dioxide and respiratory symptoms in a nonsmoking population. *Archives of Environmental Health, 48*, 33–46.

Abramowicz, M. (1990). Sudden death in children treated with a tricyclic antidepressant. *The Medical Letter on Drugs and Therapeutics, 32*, 53.

Achenbach, T. M. (1991). *Manual for the child behavior checklist/4-18 and 1991 profile.* Burlington, Vt: Department of Psychiatry, University of Vermont.

Alexander, A. B. (1972). Systematic relaxation and flow rates in asthmatic children. *Journal of Psychosomatic Research, 16*, 405–410.

American Thoracic Society Committee on Diagnostic Standards. (1962). Definitions and classification of chronic bronchitis, asthma and pulmonary emphysema. *American Review of Respiratory Disease, 85*, 762.

Anderson, C. M., Reiss, D. J., & Hogarty, G. (1986). Schizophrenia and the family. Parenting stress and the mother-child relationship. *Psychological Reports, 71*, 1139–1148.

Annett, R. D., & Bender, B. G. (1994). Neuropsychological dysfunction in asthmatic children. *Neuropsychology Review, 4*, 91–115.

Arshad, S. H., & Hide, D. W. (1992). Effect of environmental factors on the development of allergic disorders in infancy. *Journal of Allergy and Clinical Immunology, 90*, 235–241.

Baron, C., Lamarre, A., Veilleux, P., Ducharme, G., Spier, S., & Lapierre, J. G. (1986). Psychomaintenance of childhood asthma: A study of 34 children. *Journal of Asthma, 23*, 68–79.

Baum, D., & Creer, T. L. (1986). Medication noncompliance in children with asthma. *Journal of Asthma, 23*, 49–59.

Becker, A. B., & Simons, F. E. R. (1989). Formoterol, a new long-acting selective ß-2 adrenergic receptor agonist: Double-blind comparison with salbutamol and placebo in children with asthma. *Journal of Allergy and Clinical Immunology, 84*, 891–895.

Bel, E. H., Timmers, M. C., Hermans, J., Dijkman, J. H., & Sterk, P. J. (1990). The long-term effects of nedocromil sodium and beclomethasone dipropionate on bronchial responsiveness to methacholine in nonatopic asthmatic subjects. *American Review of Respiratory Disease, 141*, 21–28.

Bender, B. G., Belleau, L., Fukuhara, J., Mrazek, D., & Strunk, R. (1987). Psychomotor adaptation in children with severe chronic asthma. *Pediatrics, 79*, 723–727.

Bender, B. G., Lerner, J. A., Iklé, D., Conner, C., & Szefler, S. (1991). Psychological change associated with theophylline treatment of asthmatic children: A six-month study. *Pediatric Pulmonology, 11*, 233–242.

Bender, B. G., & Milgrom, H. (1992). Theophylline-induced behavior change in children: An objective evaluation of parents' perceptions. *Journal of the American Medical Association, 267*, 2621–2624.

Biederman, J., Milberger, S., Faraone, S. V., Guite, J., & Warbuton, R. (1994). Associations between childhood asthma and ADHD: Issues of psychiatric comorbidity and familiality. *Journal of the American Academy of Child and Adolescent Psychiatry, 33*, 842–848.

Blair, H. (1977). Natural history of childhood asthma: 20 year follow-up. *Archives of Diseases in Children, 52*, 613–619.

Block, J., Jennings, P. H., Harvey, E., & Simpson, E. (1964). Interaction between allergic potential and psychopathology in childhood asthma. *Psychosomatic Medicine, 26*, 307–320.

Bousquet, J., Hejjaoui, A., & Michel, F. B. (1990). Specific immunotherapy in asthma. *Journal of Allergy and Clinical Immunology, 86*, 292–305.

Broder, I., Higgins, M., Mathews, K., & Keller, J. (1974a).

Epidemiology of asthma and allergic rhinitis in a total community, Tecumseh, Michigan. IV. Natural history. *Journal of Allergy and Clinical Immunology, 54*, 10–110.

Broder, I., Higgins, M. W., Mathews, K. P., & Keller, J. B. (1974b). Epidemiology of asthma and allergic rhinitis in a total community, Tecumseh, Michigan. III. Second survey of the community. *Journal of Allergy and Clinical Immunology, 53*, 127–138.

Brody, G. H., & Forehand, R. (1986). Maternal perceptions of child maladjustment as a function of the combined influences of child behavior and maternal depression. *Journal of Consulting and Clinical Psychology, 54*, 237–240.

Bronnimann, S., & Burrows, B. (1986). Prospective study of the natural history of asthma: Remission and relapse rates. *Chest, 90*, 480–484.

Brugman, S. M., Howell, J. H., Mahler, J. L., Rosenberg, D. M., Blager, F. B., & Lack, G. (1994). The spectrum of pediatric vocal cord dysfunction. In *Conference Proceedings of the American Thoracic Society*, Miami, Florida.

Carson, D. K., & Schauer, R. W. (1992). Mothers of children with asthma: Perceptions of parenting stress and the mother-child relationship. *Psychological Reports, 71*, 1139–1148.

Carswell, F. (1985). Thirty deaths from asthma. *Archives of Diseases in Children, 60*, 25–28.

Celano, M. P., & Geller, R. J. (1993). Learning, school performance and children with asthma: How much at risk? *Journal of Learning Disabilities, 26*, 23–32.

Chilmonczyk, B. A., Salmun, L. M., & Megathlin, K. N., (1993). Association between exposure to environmental tobacco smoke and exacerbations of asthma in children. *New England Journal of Medicine*, 1665–1669.

Christiaanse, M. E., Lavigne, J. V., & Lerner, C. V. (1989). Psychosocial aspects of compliance in children and adolescents with asthma. *Developmental and Behavioral Pediatrics, 10*, 75–80.

Chryssanthopoulos, C., Laufer, P., & Torphy, D. E. (1983). Evaluation of compliance and combined drug therapy. *Journal of Asthma, 20*, 35–38.

Clark, N. M., Feldman, C. H., Evans, D., Wasilewski, Y., & Levison, M. (1984). Changes in children's school performance as a result of education for family management of asthma. *Journal of School Health, 54*, 143–145.

Cockroft, D. W. (1987). Airway hyperresponsiveness: Therapeutic implications. *Annals of Allergy, 59*, 405–414.

Cockroft, D. W., & Murdock, K. Y. (1987). Comparative effects of inhaled salbutamol, sodium cromoglycate, and beclomethasone dipropionate on allergen-induced early asthmatic responses, late asthmatic responses, and increased bronchial responsiveness to histamine. *Journal of Allergy and Clinical Immunology, 79*, 734–740.

Creer, T., & Yoches, C. (1971). The modification of an inappropriate behavioral pattern in asthmatic children. *Journal of Chronic Diseases, 24*, 507–513.

Dahl, J., Gustafsson, D., & Melin, L. (1990). Effects of a behavioral treatment program on children with asthma. *Journal of Asthma, 27*, 41–46.

D'Alonzo, G. E., Smolensky, M. H., Feldman, S., Gianotti, L. A., Emerson, M. B., Staudinger, H., & Steinijans, V. W. (1990). Twenty-four hour lung function in adult patients with asthma: Chronoptimized theophylline therapy once-daily dosing in the evening versus conventional twice-daily dosing. *American Review of Respiratory Disease, 142*, 84–90.

Davis, M. H., Saunders, D. R., Creer, T. L., & Chai, H. (1973). Relaxation training facilitated by biofeedback apparatus as a supplemental treatment in bronchial asthma. *Journal of Psychosomatic Research, 17*, 121–128.

Defries, J. C., Olson, R. K., Pennington, B. F., & Smith, S. D. (1991). Colorado reading project: An update. In D. D. Duane & D. B. Grey (Eds.), *The reading brain: The biological basis of dyslexia*. Parkton, MD: York Press.

DePiano, F. A., & Salzberg, H. G. (1979). Clinical applications of hypnosis to three psychsomatic disorders. *Psychological Bulletin, 86*, 1223–1235.

Deter, H. C. (1986). Cost-benefit analysis of psychosomatic therapy in asthma. *Journal of Psychosomatic Research, 30*, 173–182.

Di Blasio, P., Molinari, E., Peri, G., & Taverna, A. (1990). Family competence and childhood asthma. *Family Systems Medicine, 8*, 145–149.

Dirks, J. F., Horton, D. J., Kinsman, R. A., Fross, K. H., & Jones, N. F. (1976). Patient and physician characteristics influencing medical decisions in asthma. *The Journal of Asthma Research, 15*, 171–178.

Dirks, J. F., & Kinsman, R. A. (1981). Clinical prediction of medical rehospitalization: Psychological assessment with the battery of asthma illness behavior. *Journal of Personality Assessment, 45*, 608–613.

Dirks, J. F., Kinsman, R. A., Jones, N. F., Spector, S. L., Davidson, P. T., & Evans, N. W. (1977). Panic-fear: A personalilty dimension related to length of hospitalization in respiratory illness. *The Journal of Asthma Research, 14*, 61–71.

Dirks, J. F., Schraa, J. C., Bron, E. L., & Kinsman, R. A. (1980). Psycho-maintenance in asthma: Hospitalization rates and financial impact. *British Journal of Medical Psychology, 53*, 349–354.

Dowse, G. K., Turner, K. J., Stewart, G. A., Alpers, M. P.,

& Woolcock, A. J. (1985). The association between der-matophagoides mites and the increasing prevalence of asthma in village communities within the Papua New Guinea highlands. *Journal of Allergy and Clinical Immunology, 75*, 75–83.

Dunleavy, R. A., Hansen, J. L., & Baade, L. E. (1981). Discriminating powers of Halstead battery tests in assessment of 9 to 14-year-old severely asthmatic children. *Clinical Neuropsychology, 3*, 9–12.

Dutoit, J. I., Salome, C. M., & Woolcock, A. J. (1987). Inhaled corticosteroids reduce the severity of bronchial hyperresponsiveness in asthma but oral theophylline does not. *American Review of Respiratory Disease, 136*, 1174–78.

Edfors-Lubs, M. (1971). Allergy in 7000 twin pairs. *Acta Allergologica, 26*, 249–285.

Ehnert, B., Lau-Schadendorf, S., Weber, A., Bluettner, P., Schou, C., & Wahn, U. (1992). Reducing domestic exposure to dust mite allergen reduces broncial hyperreactivity in sensitive children with asthma. *Allergy, 90*, 135–138.

Epstein, H. H., & Cluss, P. A. (1982). A behavioral medicine perspective on adherence to long-term medical regimens. *Journal of Consulting and Clinical Psychology, 50*, 960–971.

Evans, I. R. (1992). Asthma among minority children: A growing problem. *Chest, 101*, 368S–371S.

Falloon, I., McGill, C., Boyd, J., & Pederson, J. (1987). Family management in the prevention of morbidity of schizophrenia: Social outcome of a two-year longitudinal study. *Psychological Medicine, 17*, 59–66.

Feldman, J. M. (1976). The effect of biofeedback training on respiratory resistance of asthmatic children. *Psychosomatic Medicine, 38*, 27–35.

Freedman, M. R., Rosenberg, S. J., & Schmaling, K. B. (1991). Childhood sexual abuse in patients with paradoxical vocal cord dysfunction. *Journal of Nervous and Mental Disease, 179*, 295–298.

Freudenberg, N., Feldman, C. H., & Clark, N. M., et al. (1980). The impact of bronchial asthma on school attendance and performance. *Journal of School Health, 50*, 522–526.

Fritz, G. K., & Overholser, J. C. (1989). Patterns of response to childhood asthma. *Psychosomatic Medicine, 51*, 347–355.

Fritz, G. K., & Overholser, J. D. (1990). Accuracy of symptom perception in childhood asthma. *Developmental and Behavioral Pediatrics, 11*, 69–72.

Fritz, G. K., Rubenstein, S., & Lewiston, N. J. (1987). Psychological factors in fatal childhood asthma. *American Journal of Orthopsychiatry, 57*, 253–257.

Gerard, M. W. (1948). Bronchial asthma in children. In F. Alexander & T. M. French (Eds.), *Studies in psychomatic medicine: An approach to the cause and treatment of vegetative disturbances*, (pp. 243–248). New York: Ronald Press.

Gergen, P. J., & Turkeltaub, P. C. (1992). The association of individual allergen reactivity with respiratory disease in a national sample: Data from the second National Health and Nutrition Examination Survey, 1976–80 (NHANES II). *Journal of Allergy and Clinical Immunology, 90*, 579–588.

Gonzalez, S., Steinglass, P., & Reiss, D. (1989). Putting the illness in its place: Discussion groups for families with chronic medical illnesses. *Family Process, 28*, 69–87.

Goodman, R. P., Wright, Jr., J. T., Barlascini, C. O., McKenney, J. M., & Lambert, C. M. (1986). The effect of phenylpropanolamine on ambulatory blood pressure. *Clinical Pharmacology and Therapeutics, 40*, 144–147.

Gortmaker, S., & Sappenfield, W. (1984). Chronic childhood disorders: Prevalence and impact. *Pediatric Clinics of North America, 31*, 3–18.

Gortmaker, S. L., Walker, D. K., Jacobs, F. H., & Ruch-Ross, H. (1982). Parental smoking and the risk of childhood asthma. *American Journal of Public Health, 72*, 574–579.

Graham, P. J., Rutter, J. L., Yule, W., & Pless, I. B. (1967). Childhood asthma: A psychosomatic disorder: Some epidemiological considerations. *British Journal of Preventive Social Medicine, 21*, 78–85.

Gustadt, L. B., Gillette, J. W., Mrazek, D. A., Fukuhara, J. T., LaBrecque, J. F., & Strunk, R. C. (1989). Determinants of school performance in children with chronic asthma. *American Journal of Diseases of Children, 143*, 471–475.

Gustafsson, P. A., Kjellman, N. M., & Cederbald, M. (1986). Family therapy in the treatment of severe childhood asthma. *Journal of Psychosomatic Research, 30*, 369–374.

Haahtela, T., Lindholm, H., Bjorksten, F., Koskenvuo, K., & Laitinen, L. A. (1990). Prevalence of asthma in Finnish young men. *British Medical Journal, 301*, 266–268.

Harris, J. B., Weinberger, M. M., Nassif, E., Smith, G., Milavetz, G., & Stillerman, A. (1987). Early intervention with short courses of prednisone to prevent progression of asthma in ambulatory patients incompletely responsive to bronchodilators. *Journal of Pediatrics, 110*, 627–630.

Haynes Jr., R. C. (1990). Adrenocorticotropic hormone; adrenocortical steroids and their synthetic analogs; inhibitors of the synthesis and actions of adrenocortical hormones. In A. G. Gilman, T. W. Rall, A. S. Nies, & P.

Taylor (Eds.), *The pharmacological basis of therapeutics* (pp. 1431–1462). New York: Pergamon Press.

Hermanns, J., Florin, I., Dietrich, M., Rieger, C., & Hahlweg, K. (1989). Maternal criticism, mother-child interaction, and bronchial asthma. *Journal of Psychosomatic Research, 33*, 469–476.

Hopkin, J. M. (1993). Genetics of asthma. *Archive of Diseases in Children, 68*, 712–723.

Hopp, R. J., Bewtra, A. K., Watt, G. D., Nair, N. M., & Townley, R. G. (1984). Genetic analysis of allergic disease in twins. *Journal of Allergy and Clinical Immunology, 73*, 265–270.

Horwood, L., Fergusson, D., Hons, B., & Shannon, F. (1985). Social and familial factors in the development of early childhood asthma. *Pediatrics, 75*, 859–868.

Howland, J., Bauchner, H., & Adair, R. (1988). The impact of pediatric asthma education on morbidity. *Chest, 94*, 964–969.

Hudgel, D. W., Cooperson, D. M., & Kinsman, R. A. (1982). Recognition of added resistive loads in asthma: The importance of behavioral styles. *American Review of Respiratory Disease, 126*, 121–125.

Hudgel, D. W., & Kinsman, R. A. (1983). Interactions among behavioral style, ventilatory drive, and load recognition. *American Review of Respiratory Disease, 128*, 246–248.

Jansson, J. A., Boe, J., & Berlin, E. (1987). The long-term prognosis of childhood asthma in a predominently rural Swedish county. *Acta Paediatrica Scandinavia, 76*, 950–954.

Jarvis, M. J., Russell, M. A. H., Feyerabend, C., Eiser, J. R., Morgan, M., Gammage, P., & Gray, E. (1985). Passive exposure to tobacco smoke: Saliva cotinine concentrations in a representative population sample of non-smoking schoolchildren. *British Medical Journal, 291*, 927–929.

Jarvis, M. J., Tunstall-Pedoe, H., Feyerabend, C., Vesey, C., & Saloojee, Y. (1987). Comparison of tests used to distinguish smokers from nonsmokers. *American Journal of Public Health, 77*, 1435–1438.

Joad, J. P., Ahrens, R. C., Lindgren, S. D., & Weinberger, M. W. (1987). Relative efficacy of maintenance therapy with theophylline, inhaled albuterol, and the combination for chronic asthma. *Journal of Allergy and Clinical Immunology, 79*, 78–85.

Kamada, A. K., Parks, D. P., & Szefler, S. J. (1992). Inhaled glucocorticoid therapy in children: How much is safe? *Pediatric Pulmonology, 12*, 71–72.

Kanner, A. M., Klein, R. G., Rubinstein, B., & Mascia, A. (1989). Use of imipramine in children with intractible asthma and psychiatric disorders: A warning. *Psychotherapy and Psychosomatics, 51*, 203–209.

Kashani, J. H., Konig, P., Shepperd, J. A., Wilfley, D., & Morris, D. A. (1988). Psychopathology and self-concept in asthmatic children. *Journal of Pediatric Psychology, 13*, 509–520.

Keeley, K. J., Neill, P., & Gallivan, P. S. (1991). Comparison of the prevalence of reversible airways obstruction in rural and urban Zimbabwean children. *Thorax, 46*, 549–553.

Kerrebijn, K. F., Neijens, H. J., & Van Essen-Zandvliet, E. E. (1987). Effect of long-term treatment with inhaled corticosteroids and beta-agonists on the bronchial responsiveness in children with asthma. *Journal of Allergy and Clinical Immunology, 79*, 653–659.

Kikuchi, Y., Okabe, S., & Tamura, G. (1994). Chemosensitivity and perception of dyspnea in patients with a history of near-fatal asthma. *New England Journal of Medicine, 330*, 1329–1334.

Kinsman, R. A., Dirks, J. F., & Jones, N. F. (1982). Psychomaintenance of chronic physical illness. In T. Millon & C. J. Green (Eds.), *Handbook of clinical health psychology* (pp. 435–465). New York: Plenum Press.

Klein, D. F. (1993). False suffocation alarms, spontaneous panics, and related conditions: An integrative hypothesis. *Archives of General Psychiatry, 50*, 306–317.

Klinnert, M. D., Mrazek, P. J., & Mrazek, D. A. (1994). Early asthma onset: The interaction between family stressors and adaptive parenting. *Psychiatry, 57*, 51–61.

Korsgaard, J. (1983). House-dust mites and absolute indoor humidity. *Allergy, 38*, 85–92.

Kossoy, A. F., Hill, M. R., Lin, F. L., & Szefler, S. J. (1989). Are theophylline "levels" a reliable indicator of compliance? *Journal of Allergy and Clinical Immunology, 84*, 60–65.

Kosten, T. R., Hogan, I., Jalai, B., Steidl, J., & Kleber, H. D. (1986). The effect of multiple family therapy on addict family functioning: A pilot study. *Advances in Alcohol and Substance Abuse, 5*, 51–62.

Kraan, J., Koeter, G. H., Sluiter, H. J., & de Vries, K. (1985). Changes in bronchial hyperreactivity induced by 4 weeks of treatment with antiasthmatic drugs in patients with allergic asthma: A comparison between budesonide and terbutaline. *Journal of Allergy and Clinical Immunology, 76*, 628–636.

Kravis, L. P. (1987). An analysis of fifteen childhood asthma fatalities. *Journal of Allergy and Clinical Immunology, 80*, 467–472.

Kravis, L. P., & Kolski, G. B. (1985). Unexpected death in childhood asthma: A review of 13 deaths in ambulatory patients. *American Journal of Disease in Childhood, 139*, 558–563.

Lang, D. M., Hopp, R. J., Bewtra, A. K., Nair, N. M., Watt, G. D., & Townley, R. G. (1987). Distribution of methacholine inhalation challenge response in a selected adult population. *Journal of Allergy and Clinical Immunology, 79,* 533–540.

Lanier, B. (1989). Who is dying of asthma and why? *Journal of Pediatrics, 115,* 838–840.

Larsen, G. L., Abman, S. H., Fan, L. L., White, C. W., & Accurso, F. J. (1991). Respiratory tract and mediastinum. In W. E. Hathaway, J. R. Groothuis, W. W. Hay, & J. W. Paisley (Eds.), *Current pediatric diagnosis and treatment* (10 ed., pp. 361–411). East Norwalk, CT: Appleton & Lange.

Lask, B., & Matthew, D. (1979). Childhood asthma. A controlled trial of family psychotherapy. *Archives of Diseases in Children, 54,* 116–119.

Leung, K. B., Flint, K. C., Brostoff, J., Hudspith, B. N., McJohnson, N., Lau, H. Y. A., Liu, W. L., & Pearce, F. L. (1988). Effects of sodium cromoglycate and nedocromil sodium on histamine secretion from human lung mast cells. *Thorax, 43,* 756–761.

Liebman, R., Minuchin, S., & Baker, L. (1974). The use of structural family therapy in the treatment of intractable asthma. *American Journal of Psychiatry, 131,* 535–540.

Linna, O. (1985). A 5-year prognosis of childhood asthma. *Acta Paediatric Scandinavica, 74,* 442–445.

MacLean, W. E., Perrin, J. M., Gortmaker, S., & Pierre, C. B. (1992). Psychological adjustment of children with asthma: Effects of illness severity and recent stressful life events. *Journal of Pediatric Psychology, 17,* 159–171.

Magana, A. B., Goldstein, M. J., Miklowitz, D. J., & Falloon, J. J. (1986). A brief method for assessing expressed emotion in relatives of psychiatric patients. *Psychiatric Research, 17,* 203–212.

Martin, A., Landau, L., & Phelan, P. (1981). Natural history of allergy in asthmatic children followed to adult life. *Medical Journal of Australia, 2,* 470–474.

Martin, A. J., McLennan, L. A., Landau, L. I., & Phelan, P. D. (1980). The natural history of childhood asthma to adult life. *British Medical Journal, 280,* 1397–1400.

Martin, R. J., Blager, F. B., Gay, M. L., & Wood, R. P. (1987). Paradoxic vocal cord motion in presumed asthmatics. *Seminars in Respiratory Medicine, 8,* 332–337.

Martin, R. J., Cicutto, L. C., Ballard, R. D., Goldenheim, P. D., & Cherniack, R. M. (1989). Circadian variations in theophylline concentrations and the treatment of nocturnal asthma. *American Review of Respiratory Disease, 139,* 475–478.

Mawhinney, H., Spector, S. L., Kinsman, R. A., Siegel, S. C., Rachelefsky, G. S., Katz, R. M., & Rohr, A. S. (1991). Compliance in clinical trials of two nonbronchodilator, antiasthma medication. *Annals of Allergy, 66,* 294–299.

McFarlane, W. R. (1982). Multiple family therapy in the psychiatric hospital. In H. Harbin (Ed.), *The psychiatric hospital and the family.* (pp. 103–130). New York: Spectrum.

McLoughlin, J., Nall, M., Isaac's, B., Petrosko, J., Karibo, J., & Lindsey, B. (1983). The relationship of allergies and allergy treatment to school performance and student behavior. *Annals of Allergy, 51,* 506–510.

McNichol, K. N., Williams, H. E., Allan, J., & McAndrew, I. (1973). Spectrum of asthma in children—III, Psychological and social components. *British Medical Journal, 4,* 16–20.

Miklowitz, M. G., Goldstein, M. J., Falloon, I. R. H., & Doane, J. (1984). Interactional correlates of expressed emotion in the families of schizophrenics. *British Journal of Psychiatry, 144,* 482–487.

Mrazek, D. (1984). Effects of hospitalizations on early child development. In R. Emde & R. Harmon (Eds.), *Continuities and discontinuities in development* (pp. 211–225). New York: Plenum Press.

Mrazek, D. (1988). Asthma: Psychiatric considerations, evaluation, and management. In E. Middleton, C. E. Reed, E. F. Ellis, N. F. Adkinson, & J. W. Yuninger (Eds.), *Allergy principles and practice* (pp. 1176–1196). Washington, D.C.: C.V. Mosby.

Mrazek, D., Anderson, I., & Strunk, R. (1985). Disturbed emotional development of severely asthmatic preschool children. In J. E. Stevenson (Ed.), *Recent research in developmental psychopathology* (pp. 81–94). New York: Pergamon Press.

Mrazek, D. A., & Klinnert, M. (1991). Asthma: Psychoneuroimmunologic considerations. In R. Ader, D. L. Felten, & N. Cohen (Eds.), *Psychoneuroimmunology* (pp. 1013–1035). New York: Academic Press.

Mrazek, D. A., & Klinnert, M. D. (1989). Asthma and serum levels of IgE. *New England Journal of Medicine, 320,* 1696.

Nall, M., Corbett, M., McLoughlin, J., Petrosko, J., Garcia, D., & Karibo, J. (1992). Impact of short-term oral steroid use upon children's school achievement and behavior. *Annals of Allergy, 69,* 218–220.

Nelson, H. (1985). The atopic diseases. *Annals of Allergy, 55,* 441–447.

Nelson, H. (1989). Clinical application of immediate skin testing. In S. L. Spector (Ed.), *Provocative challenge procedures: Background and methodology* (pp. 639–666). Mount Kisco, NY: Futura Publishing.

Newman, K. B., & Dubester, S. N. (1994). Vocal cord dysfunction: Masquerader of asthma. *Seminars in Respiratory Critical Care Medicine, 15,* 161–167.

Nides, M. A., Tashkin, D. P., Simmons, M. S., Wise, R. A., Li, V. C., & Rand, C. S. (1993). Improving inhaler adherence in a clinical trial through the use of the nebulizer chronolog. *Chest, 104*, 501–507.

Ninan, T. K., & Russell, G. (1992). Respiratory symptoms and atopy in Aberdeen schoolchildren: Evidence from two surveys 25 years apart. *British Medical Journal, 304*, 873–875.

Nocon, A. (1991). Social and emotional impact of childhood asthma. *Archives of Diseases in Children, 66*, 458–460.

Norrish, M., Tooley, M., & Godfrey, S. (1977). Clinical, physiological, and psychological study of asthmatic children attending a hospital clinic. *Archives of Diseases in Children, 52*, 912–917.

O'Neil, S. L., Barysh, N., & Setear, S. J. (1985). Determining school programming needs of special population groups: A study of asthmatic children. *Journal of School Health, 55*, 237–239.

Ostro, B. D., Lipsett, M. J., Mann, J. K., Wiener, M. B., & Selner, J. (1994). Indoor air pollution and asthma. *American Journal of Respiratory and Critical Care Medicine, 149*, 1400–1406.

Pauwels, R., Van Renterghem, D., Van Der Straeten, M., Johannesson, N., & Persson, C. G. A. (1985). The effect of theophylline and enprofylline on allergen-induced bronchoconstriction. *Journal of Allergy and Clinical Immunology, 76*, 583–590.

Peat, J. K., Tovey, E., Gray, E. J., Mellis, C. M., & Woolcock, A. J. (1994). Asthma severity and morbidity in a population sample of Sydney schoolchildren: Part II—Importance of house dust mite allergens. *Australian and New Zealand Journal of Medicine, 24*, 270–276.

Peat, J. K., & Woolcock, A. J. (1994). New approaches to old problems. Why not prevent asthma? *Medical Journal of Australia, 160*, 604–605.

Pedersen, S., & Mortensen, S. (1990). Use of different inhalation devices in children. *Lung, 168*(suppl.), 653–657.

Pennington, B. F., Smith, S. D., Kimberling, W. J., Green, P. A., & Haith, M. M. (1987). Left-handedness and immune disorders in familial dyslexics. *Archives of Neurology, 44*, 634–639.

Peshkin, M. M. (1930). Asthma in children, IX. Role of environment in the treatment of a selected group of cases: A plea for a "home" as a restorative measure. *American Journal of Diseases of Children, 39*, 774.

Philipp, R. L., Willde, G. J., & Day, J. H. (1972). Suggestion and relaxation in asthmatics. *Journal of Psychosomatic Research, 16*, 193–204.

Platts-Mills, T. A., & Chapman, M. D. (1987). Dust mites: Immunology, allergic disease, and environmental control. *Journal of Allergy and Clinical Immunology, 80*, 755–75.

Purcell, K. (1963). Distinctions between subgroups of asthmatic children: Children's perceptions of events associated with asthma. *Pediatrics, 31*, 486.

Purcell, K., Brady, K., Chai, H., Muser, J., Molk, L., Gordon, N., & Means, J. (1969). The effect of asthma in children of experimental separation from the family. *Psychosomatic Medicine, 31*, 144–164.

Rall, T. W. (1990). Drugs used in the treatment of asthma. In A. G. Gilman, T. W. Rall, A. S. Nies, & P. Taylor (Eds.), *The pharmacologic basis of therapeutics* (pp. 618–637). New York: Pergamon Press.

Rawls, D. J., Rawls, J. R., & Harrison, C. W. (1971). An investigation of six- to eleven-year-old children with allergic disorders. *Journal of Consulting and Clinical Psychology, 36*, 260–264.

Richards, R., Phillips, G. D., & Holgate, S. T. (1989). Nedocromil sodium is more potent than sodium cromoglycate against cyclic AMP-induced bronchoconstriction in atopic asthmatic subjects. *Clinical Experiments in Allergy, 19*, 285–291.

Richman, N., Stevenson, J., & Graham, P. (1982). *Preschool to school: A behavioral study*. London: Academic Press.

Riddle, M. A., Geller, B., & Ryan, N. (1993). Another sudden death in a child treated with despiramine. *Journal of the American Academy of Child and Adolescent Psychiatry, 32*, 792–797.

Rosenberg, D. R., Holttum, J., & Gershon, S. (1994). *Textbook of pharmacotherapy for child and adolescent psychiatric disorders*. New York: Brunner/Mazel, Inc.

Rubenstein, S., Hindi, R. D., Moss, R. B., Blessing-Moore, J., & Lewiston, N. J. (1984). Sudden death in adolescent asthma. *Annals of Allergy, 53*, 311–318.

Rubinfeld, A., & Pain, M. (1976). Perception of asthma. *The Lancet, 1*(7965), 882–884.

Salome, C., Peat, J., Britton, W., & Woolcock, A. (1987). Bronchial hyperresponsiveness in two populations of Australian school children. I. Relation to respiratory symptoms and diagnosed asthma. *Journal of Clinical Allergy, 17*, 271–281.

Sanders, P. S., Portman, R. J., Ramey, R. A., Hill, M., & Strunk, R. C. (1992). Hypertension during reduction of long term steroid therapy in young subjects with asthma. *Journal of Allergy and Clinical Immunology, 89*, 816–821.

Satin, W., LaGreca, A., Zigo, M., & Skyler, J. (1989). Diabetes in adolescence: Effects of multifamily group intervention and parent simulation of diabetes. *Journal of Pediatric Psychology, 14*, 259–275.

Scherr, M. S., Crawford, P., Sergent, C. B., & Scherr, C. (1975). Effect of biofeedback techniques on chronic asthma in a summer camp environment. *Annals of Allergy, 35*, 289–295.

Schöbinger, R., Florin, I., Zimmer, C., Lindemann, H., & Winter, H. (1992). Childhood asthma: Paternal critical attitude and father-child interaction. *Journal of Psychosomatic Research, 36*, 743–750.

Sears, M. (1988). Fatal asthma: A perspective. *Immunology and Allergy Process, 9*, 259.

Sears, M. J., Herbison, G. P., Holdaway, M. D., Hewitt, C. J., Flannery, E. M., & Silva, P. A. (1989). The relative risks of sensitivity to grass pollen, house dust mite and cat dander in the development of childhood asthma. *Clinical and Experimental Allergy, 19*, 419–424.

Sears, M. R., & Rea, H. H. (1987). Patients at risk for dying of asthma: New Zealand experience. *Journal of Allergy and Clinical Immunology, 80*, 477–481.

Sears, M. R., Rea, H. H., Fenwick, J., Beaglehole, R., Gilles, A. J. D., Holst, P. E., O'Donnell, T. V., Rothwell, R. P. G., & Sutherland, D. C. (1986). Deaths from asthma in New Zealand. *Archives of Diseases in Children, 61*, 6–10.

Sheffer, A. L., Chair (1991a). *Executive summary: Guidelines for the diagnosis and management of asthma.* Bethesda, MD: U.S. Dept. Health and Human Services.

Sheffer, A. L., Chair (1991b). *Guidelines for the diagnosis and management of asthma.* Bethesda, MD: National Institutes of Health.

Slagerman, M., & Yager, J. (1989). Multiple family group treatment for eating disorders: A short term program. *Psychiatric Medicine, 7*, 269–283.

Smith, B. D., Meyers, M. B., & Kline, R. (1989). For better or for worse: Left handedness, pathology, and talent. *Journal of Clinical and Experimental Neuropsychology, 11*, 944–958.

Smith, M. (1983). Acute psychogenic stridor in an adolescent athlete treated with hypnosis. *Pediatrics, 72*, 247–248.

Sporik, R., Holgate, S. T., Platts-Mills, T., & Cogswell, J. J. (1990). Exposure to house-dust mite allergens (Der p1) and the development of asthma in childhood. A prospective study. *New England Journal of Medicine, 323*, 502–507.

Stein, R. E. K., Perrin, E. C., Pless, B. I., Gortmaker, S. L., Perrin, J. M., Walker, D. K., & Weitzman, M. (1987). Severity of illness: Concepts and measurements. *Lancet* (December), 1506–1509.

Steiner, H., Higgs, C., & Fritz, G. K. (1987). Defense style and the perception of asthma. *Psychosomatic Medicine, 49*, 34–44.

Strelnick, A. H. (1977). Multiple family group therapy: A review of the literature. *Family Process, 16*, 307–325.

Strunk, R., Mrazek, D., Fuhrmann, G., & LaBrecque, J.

(1985). Physiologic and psychological characteristics associated with deaths due to asthma in childhood. *Journal of the American Medical Association, 254*, 1193–1198.

Strunk, R. C. (1987). Asthma deaths in childhood: Identification of patients at risk and intervention. *Journal of Allergy and Clinical Immunology, 80*, 472–477.

Strunk, R. C. (1991). Asthma-related death: Can it happen to you? In S. Spector & N. Sander (Eds.), *Understanding asthma: A blueprint for breathing* (pp. 185–201). Milwaukee: American College of Allergy and Immunology.

Strunk, R. C., Fukuhara, T., LaBrecque, J. F., & Mrazek, D. A. (1989). Outcome of long-term hospitalization for asthma in children. *Journal of Allergy and Clinical Immunology, 83*, 17–25.

Stump, N. (1986). Effects of steroid medication on school performance in asthmatic children. In *Conference Proceedings of Rocky Mountain Psychological Association Meeting*, Denver, Colorado.

Suess, W. M., Stump, N., Chai, H., & Kalisker, A. (1986). Mnemonic effects of asthma medication in children. *Journal of Asthma, 23*, 291–296.

Svendsen, U. G., Frolund, L., Madsen, F., Nielsen, N. H., Holstein-Rathlou, N. H., & Weeke, B. (1987). A comparison of the effects of sodium cromoglycate and beclomethasone dipropionate on pulmonary function and bronchial hyperreactivity in subjects with asthma. *Journal of Allergy and Clinical Immunology, 80*, 68–74.

Szymanski, L., & Kiernan, W. (1983). Multiple family group therapy with developmentally disabled adolescents and young adults. *International Journal of Group Psychotherapy, 33*, 521–535.

Taguchi, O., Kikuchi, Y., Hida, W., Iwase, N., Okabe, S., & Chonan, T. (1992). Prostaglandin E2 inhalation increases the sensation of dyspnea during exercise. *American Review of Respiratory Disease, 145*, 1346–1349.

Taylor, W. R., & Newacheck, P. W. (1992). Impact of childhood asthma on health. *Pediatrics, 90*, 657–662.

Toogood, J. H., Baskerville, J., Jenning, B., Lefcoe, N. M., & Johansson, S. A. (1989). Bioequivalent doses of budesonide and prednisone in moderate and severe asthma. *Journal of Allergy and Clinical Immunology, 84*, 688–700.

Twentyman, O. P., Finnerty, J. P., Harris, A., Palmer, J., & Holgate, S. T. (1990). Protection against allergen-induced asthma by salmeterol. *Lancet, 336*, 1338–1342.

Ullman, A., Hedner, J., & Svedmyr, N. (1990). Inhaled salmeterol and salbutamol in asthmatic patients: An evaluation of asthma symptoms and the possible development of tachyphylaxis. *American Review of Respiratory Disease, 142*, 571–575.

Ullman, A., & Svedmyr, N. (1988). Salmeterol, a new long acting inhaled ß-2 adrenoceptor agonist, comparison with salbutamol in adult asthmatic patients. *Thorax, 43*, 674–678.

Van Asperen, P. P., & Kemp, A. S. (1989). The natural history of Ig E sensitization and atopic disease in early childhood. *Acta Paediatric Scandinavica, 78*, 239–245.

Van Schayck, C. P., Visch, M. B., Van Weel, C., Van Herwaarden, C. L. A., & Dompeling, E. (1990). Increased bronchial hyperresponsiveness after inhaling salbutamol during one year is not caused by desensitization to salbutamol. *Journal of Allergy and Clinical Immunology, 86*, 793–800.

Vervloet, D., Charpin, D., Haddi, E., N'guyen, A., Birnbaum, J., Soler, M., & Van der Brempt, A. (1991). Medication requirements and house dust mite exposure in mite-sensitive asthmatics. *Allergy, 46*, 554–558.

Wallin, A., Melander, B., Rosenhall, L., Sandstrom, T., & Wahlander, L. (1990). Formoterol, a new long acting beta 2 agonist for inhalation twice daily, compared with salbutamol in the treatment of asthma. *Thorax, 45*, 259–261.

Wamboldt, F. S., Wamboldt, M. Z., Gavin, L. A., Roesler, T. A., & Brugman, S. M. (1995). Parental expressed emotion and treatment outcome in adolescent hospitalized for severe, chronic asthma. *Journal of Psychosomatic Research, 39*, 995–1005.

Wamboldt, M. Z., & Levin, L. (1995). Utility of multifamily psychoeducational groups for medically ill children and adolescents. *Family Systems Medicine, 13*, 151–161.

Wamboldt, M. Z., Roesler, T. A., & Yancey Jr., A. G. (1995). Antidepressants and childhood asthma: Do they mix? Manuscript submitted for publication.

Wamboldt, M. Z., & Taylor, J. L. (1995). Psychiatric comorbidity in children with moderate to severe asthma. Manuscript in preparation, University of Colorado Health Sciences Center.

Wamboldt, M. Z., & Wamboldt, F. S. (1995). Psychosocial aspects of severe asthma in children. In S. J. Szefler & D. Y. M. Leung (Eds.), *Severe asthma: Pathogenesis and clinical management* (pp. 465–495). New York: Marcel Dekker.

Wamboldt, M. Z., Weintraub, P., Settle, J., & Krafchick, D. (1994). Psychiatric family history of severe asthmatic adolescents. In N. Alessi & S. Porter (Eds.), *American Academy of Child and Adolescent Psychiatry, X* (p. 74).

New York: American Academy of Child and Adolescent Psychiatry.

Warner, J. O. (1992). Asthma: A follow up statement from an international paediatric asthma consensus group. *Archives of Disease in Childhood, 67*, 240–248.

Weinstein, A. G., Faust, D. S., McKee, L., & Padman, R. (1992). Outcome of short-term hospitalization for children with severe asthma. *Journal of Allergy and Clinical Immunology, 90*, 66–75.

Weiss, K. B., Gergen, P. J., & Crain, E. F. (1992). Inner-city asthma. The epidemiology of an emerging U.S. public health concern. *Chest, 101*, 362S–367S.

Weiss, K. B., & Wagener, D. K. (1990). Changing pattern of asthma mortality: Identifying target populations at risk. *Journal of the American Medical Association, 264*, 1683–1687.

Weitzman, M., Gortmaker, S. L., Sobol, A. M., & Perrin, J. M. (1992). Recent trends in the prevalence and severity of childhood asthma. *Journal of the American Medical Association, 268*, 2673–2677.

Weitzman, M., Klerman, L. V., Lamb, G., Menary, J., & Alpert, J. (1982). School absence: A problem for the pediatrician. *Pediatrics, 69*, 739–746.

Wellisch, D. K., Mosher, A. B., & Van Scoy, C. (1978). Management of family emotional stress: Family group therapy in a private oncology practice. *International Journal of Group Psychotherapy, 28*, 225–231.

Whitelaw, W. A. (1991). Asthma deaths. *Chest, 99*, 1507–1510.

Wigal, J. K., Creer, T. L., Kotses, H., & Lewis, P. (1990). A critique of 19 self-management programs for childhood asthma: Part I. Development and evaluation of the programs. *Pediatric Asthma, Allergy and Immunology, 4*, 17–39.

Wikran, R., Faleide, A., & Blakar, R. M. (1978). Communication in the family of the asthmatic child. *Acta Psychiatrica Scandinavica, 57*, 11–26.

Woolcock, A. J., Peat, J. K., Salome, C. M., Yan, K., Anderson, S. D., Schoeffel, R. E., McCowage, G., & Killalea, T. (1987). Prevalence of bronchial hyperresponsiveness and asthma in a rural adult population. *Thorax, 42*, 361–368.

Woolcock, A. J., Yan, Y., & Salome, C. M. (1988). Effect of therapy on bronchial hyperresponsiveness in the long-term management of asthma. *Clinical Allergy, 18*, 165–176.

Yellowlees, P. M., & Kalucy, R. S. (1990). Psychobiological aspects of asthma and the consequent research implications. *Chest, 97*, 628–634.

Yunginger, J. W., Reed, C. E., O'Connell, E. J., Melton 3d, L. J., O'Fallon, W. M., & Silverstein, M. D. (1992). A community-based study of the epidemiology of asthma. Incidence rates, 1964–83. *American Review of Respiratory Diseases, 146*, 888–894.

Zach, M. S., & Karner, U. (1989). Sudden death in asthma. *Archives of Diseases in Children, 64*, 1446–1451.

Zimmerman, B., Feanny, S., Reisman, J., Hak, H., Rashed, N., McLaughlin, F. J., & Levison, H. (1988). Allergy in asthma. I. The dose relationship of allergy to severity of childhood asthma. *J Allergy Clin Immunol, 81*, 63–70.

CHAPTER 13

HEMATOLOGIC DISORDERS

Robert J. Thompson, Jr.
Kathryn E. Gustafson
Russell E. Ware

DESCRIPTION OF DISORDERS

The hematologic system is comprised of several different types of cells and proteins that must function properly for normal childhood growth and development. Red blood cells (erythrocytes) function primarily to carry oxygen to the body; erythrocyte disorders therefore typically manifest with signs and symptoms of anemia (fatigue, pallor, shortness of breath) and/or hemolysis (jaundice, dark urine, gallstones). White blood cells are critical for a healthy immune system; disorders of neutrophils and lymphocytes lead to recurrent infections and poor growth and development. Circulating blood platelets ensure proper hemostasis; disorders of these components lead to excessive mucocutaneous bleeding and bruising. Finally, the fluid phase coagulant/anticoagulant proteins carefully balance blood clotting; abnormalities in this system can lead to serious bleeding or thrombotic events.

Hematologic disorders in children can be classified in several different ways, including by the cell of origin, clinical manifestations, whether the disorder is quantitative or qualitative, or other parameters. In this chapter, we have chosen to separate the disorders based on whether they are congenital or acquired. Congenital hematologic disorders are summarized in Table 13.1, and include abnormalities within a single cell line or multiple lineages, as well as deficiencies of coagulation factors. Each of these disorders is generally believed to

be an inherited condition, although the actual gene(s) involved is not well understood in each case. In contrast, transient or acquired disorders (Table 13.2) have a less clear genetic basis, and often result from environmental causes (e.g., viral infections, medications, toxins). In addition, some acquired hematologic disorders result from dysregulation of the immune system, with formation of autoantibodies against specific blood components such as erythrocytes or platelets.

In this chapter, we will focus on two common childhood hematologic disorders with medical and psychological manifestations: sickle cell disease and hemophilia. Appropriate care for children afflicted with these conditions involves attention to both the medical and psychologic/psychiatric aspects of the disease. We will begin the description with an overview, followed by a discussion of the pathogenesis and pathophysiology of each disorder.

Sickle Cell Disease

Overview

The phrase "sickle cell disease" is actually a misnomer, as it does not describe a single disease entity, but

Table 13.1. Congenital Hematologic Diseases in Children

I. Erythrocytes
   - A. Red Cell Aplasia (Blackfan-Diamond Anemia)
   - B. Quantitative Hemoglobinopathies (Thalassemia)
   - C. Qualitative Hemoglobinopathies (Sickle Cell Disease)
   - D. Enzyme Disorders (G6PD, Pyruvate Kinase Deficiency)
   - E. Membrane Abnormalities (Spherocytosis, Elliptocytosis)
   - F. Sideroblastic Anemia
   - G. Porphyria

II. Neutrophils
   - A. Granulocyte Aplasia (Kostmann's Syndrome)
   - B. Leukocyte Adhesion Deficiency
   - C. Lazy Leukocyte Syndrome

III. Platelets
   - A. Thrombocytopenia Absent Radius (TAR) Syndrome
   - B. Amegakaryocytic Thrombocytopenia
   - C. Alpha Granule Deficiency (Gray Platelet Syndrome)
   - D. Dense Granule Deficiency (Storage Pool Defect)
   - E. Glycoprotein Deficiency (Glanzmann, Bernard-Soulier)

IV. Multiple Cell Lines
   - A. Fanconi's Anemia
   - B. Karotypic Abnormalities (Monosomy 7)

V. Coagulation Factors
   - A. Von Willebrand Disease
   - B. Procoagulant Deficiency (Factor VIII, IX, XI)
   - C. Anticoagulants (Protein C and S, Antithrombin III, Factor V)

Table 13.2. Acquired Hematologic Diseases in Children

I. Erythrocytes
   - A. Red Cell Aplasia (Parvovirus, Transient Erythroblastopenia)
   - B. Nutritional Deficiencies (Iron, B12, Folate Deficiency)
   - C. Lead Poisoning
   - D. Autoantibodies, Alloantibodies

II. Neutrophils
   - A. Viral Suppression
   - B. Medications
   - C. Autoantibodies, Alloantibodies

III. Platelets
   - A. Viral Suppression
   - B. Medications
   - C. Autoantibodies, Alloantibodies

IV. Multiple Cell Lines
   - A. Aplastic Anemia
   - B. Paroxysmal Nocturnal Hemoglobinuria

V. Coagulation Factors
   - A. Autoantibodies

instead refers to a collection of hematologic disorders. Sickle cell anemia, sickle-thalassemia, and sickle-hemoglobin C disease are examples of sickle cell disease; each is characterized by the presence of an abnormal hemoglobin (Hb S) that causes the red blood cell to adopt a rigid (sickled) shape. The clinical manifestations of sickle cell disease result from premature breakdown of the red blood cells (hemolytic anemia) as well as acute and chronic organ damage from repeated sickling events and hypoxia (Kinney & Ware, 1988).

Pathogenesis

Normal adult hemoglobin (Hb A) is a tetrameric molecule composed of two alpha globin chains and two beta globin chains. When an amino acid mutation occurs at the sixth position of the beta globin gene (glutamic acid is changed to valine), the abnormal Hb S molecule is formed. A child inherits one beta globin gene from each parent; when both inherited beta globin genes have the sickle mutation, the child has homozygous sickle cell anemia (Hb SS). Other forms of sickle cell disease, such as sickle-thalassemia and sickle-hemoglobin C disease, occur when the child inherits a sickle beta globin gene from one parent, and another abnormal beta globin gene from the other parent.

Pathophysiology

In its fully oxygenated state, Hb S functions normally to deliver oxygen to the body. After unloading oxygen, however, Hb S can polymerize within the erythrocyte to form large insoluble structures known as tactoids; these Hb S polymers bind to the red cell membrane and induce a rigid shape which often resembles a "sickle." As the red blood cell circulates repeatedly from the lungs (oxygenated state) to the distal capillaries (deoxygenated state) and back again to the lungs, it undergoes a series of reversible sickling processes, which eventually lead to a dense and irreversibly sickled erythrocyte. As a consequence of repeated sickling events, the erythrocyte has a shortened life span and the patient has a hemolytic anemia. In addition, chronic sickling within the lungs, kidneys, and brain leads to damage within these organs.

Hemophilia

Overview

Similar to the phrase "sickle cell disease," the term "hemophilia" does not refer to a single entity but instead refers to a collection of inherited diseases characterized by a deficiency of a specific clotting factor, which results in the inability to generate normal fibrin clots. Patients with hemophilia are often called "free bleeders" due to their tendency to have spontaneous and/or prolonged bleeding. In most cases, a plasma protein important in clot formation is quantitatively or qualitatively abnormal, which leads to a lifelong bleeding diathesis (Levine & Brettler, 1991).

Pathogenesis

As a consequence of a genetic mutation, the patient has a quantitative or qualitative abnormality in a specific coagulation factor. If the functional activity of the factor is <1 percent of normal, by definition the patient has severe hemophilia; a level of 1–5 percent represents moderate hemophilia with fewer hemorrhagic problems, while a level of 5–15 percent is considered mild hemophilia. As a genetic condition, hemophilia "runs true" within a family, with similar penetrance and expression of the gene within affected members of a family. The most common disorders, Factor VIII and Factor IX deficiency, are X-linked and are therefore carried by females and expressed only in males.

Pathophysiology

The formation of a clot requires the action of multiple circulating plasma proteins known collectively as the coagulation cascade. Following trauma to a blood vessel, the coagulation factors work in a sequential fashion to generate fibrin, which interacts with platelets and red blood cells to form a stable clot. If one of the coagulation proteins is missing, fibrin formation is greatly impaired. Patients with hemophilia have quantitative or qualitative abnormalities of specific coagulation factors, and therefore have significant bleeding episodes. The most common sites of bleeding in hemophilia are within the muscles and joints. Many boys have repeated bleeding events into a particular joint, such as the knee or elbow; over time the joint may develop limited range of motion and become severely damaged. Bleeds into the head or neck may be life-threatening, due to the surrounding vital structures. Similarly, bleeds in the abdomen are dangerous due to the large amount of blood that may be lost before symptoms develop.

EPIDEMIOLOGY

Sickle Cell Disease

Sickle cell disease is a congenital, inherited genetic disorder that affects over 50,000 black Americans. Approximately 1 in every 650 newborn black infants is affected with sickle cell disease, making it a major public health concern. Currently, 42 states utilize newborn screening for the early detection of infants with sickle hemoglobinopathies.

Hemophilia

The most common forms of hemophilia are congenital deficiencies of Factor VIII or Factor IX. Each of these proteins is encoded by a gene located on the X chromosome, and therefore abnormalities are most frequently identified in males. The estimated incidence of Factor VIII deficiency is 1 in 10,000 males, while Factor IX deficiency occurs once in 40,000 males. Factor XI deficiency is a more rare autosomal recessive disorder with similar clinical manifestations.

ASSESSMENT APPROACHES

Medical Issues

Sickle Cell Disease

The clinical consequences of erythrocyte sickling can be divided into two large categories. The first is chronic hemolytic anemia, due to a shortened life span of the erythrocytes within the blood stream. The child with sickle cell disease typically has a hemoglobin concentration of 6–9 gm/dL (normal:12–15 gm/dL), and therefore often has strain on the cardiovascular system and mild exercise intolerance. Jaundice may be clinically apparent, and chronic red cell hemolysis frequently leads to bilirubin gallstone formation (Ware, Filston, Schultz, & Kinney, 1988). Due in large part to the anemia, growth and development are also stunted, and sexual maturity typically is delayed at least 2–3 years.

The second clinical consequence of sickling is acute and chronic organ damage due to vaso-occlusion of erythrocytes within the vasculature. The abnormally rigid sickled erythrocyte is unable to flow freely through the capillaries, and this frequently leads to a blockage of blood flow and hypoxia of the distal tissues. In the acute setting, such vaso-occlusion often occurs within the bone and bone marrow, and leads to a "painful event" that is typically described as a severe gnawing pain of the back and/or extremities (Platt et al., 1991). Acute sickling can also lead to other serious clinical conditions, including the acute chest syndrome (pneumonia with infarction of pulmonary blood vessels), acute splenic sequestration (sudden enlargement of the spleen due to blocked splenic drainage), and priapism (painful undesired erection lasting over 12 hours). On a chronic basis, vaso-occlusion may lead to hypoxic damage of multiple organ systems, including the brain (thrombotic infarct and stroke), spleen (autoinfarction and subsequent susceptibility to infection with encapsulated bacterial organisms), kidney (hyperfiltration followed by renal failure), lung (restrictive pulmonary disease), eyes (retinal neovascularization), and skin (leg ulcers). Children with sickle cell disease are particularly susceptible to bacterial infections due to splenic infarction, and are therefore prescribed twice daily penicillin at least for the first five years of life (Gaston et al., 1986).

Hemophilia

The major medical issues with regard to hemophilia are the prevention and management of bleeding episodes. Bleeding for children with hemophilia is typically musculoskeletal, that is, in the muscles and joints. Frequently, the child will bleed following events such as circumcision, immunization, dental work, and trauma. Bleeding in patients with hemophilia is very painful, especially when there is expansion of the joint capsule. Depending upon the degree of coagulation factor deficiency, the bleeding ranges from spontaneous hemorrhage in a child with severe hemophilia, to exaggerated hemorrhage only after a surgical procedure in a child with mild disease. Bleeding episodes often recur within the same joint, and can lead to physical deformity with limited range of motion and irreversible destruction of the joint.

Psychological and Psychiatric Issues

Assessment of Children's Adjustment

The assessment of adjustment in children with hematological disorders includes two primary domains: psy-

chosocial functioning and neurocognitive functioning. Within each domain, the major assessment issues will be discussed. Findings from empirical studies are reviewed in terms of sickle cell disease and hemophilia.

Psychosocial Functioning. Included in this domain are behavioral and emotional adjustment that can be understood in terms of the presence or absence of specific symptoms such as anxiety or abnormal activity level, as patterns of behavioral/emotional functioning such as internalizing or externalizing syndromes, or as psychiatric disorders such as overanxious disorder or oppositional disorder. Psychosocial adjustment also includes self-esteem, as well as social functioning in terms of skill in interpersonal relationships, quality of peer relationships, or participation in activities and organizations. Neurocognitive functioning can be conceptualized specifically as brain-behavior patterns, or broadly as intellectual functioning or school achievement.

Strategies for assessing psychosocial adjustment have included checklists and interviews completed by the children themselves or by parents about their children, or more infrequently by teachers or peers. It is necessary to utilize multiple informants to assess psychosocial functioning in children because there is a relatively low level of agreement among different informants regarding child adjustment (Achenbach, McConaughy & Howell, 1987) and concordance among informants varies as a function of age of the child and type of symptoms (Edelbrock, Costello, Dulcan, Conover, & Kalas, 1986). Low agreement between parent report and child report of child adjustment is due in part to the impact of parental mental state on perceptions of child adjustment (Angold et al., 1987). Mothers' levels of stress and psychological distress have been found to influence their perceptions of their children's behavior (Middlebrook & Forehand, 1985; Webster-Stratton, 1990). Mothers' stress and distress are related not only to maternal reports of children's adjustment, but also to children's self-reported symptoms, indicating that the relationship between children's adjustment and parent psychological distress is not merely a function of parent perceptions (Thompson, Gustafson, Hamlett, & Spock, 1992; Thompson, Merritt, Keith, Murphy, & Johndrow, 1993).

In addition to the issues discussed above regarding adjustment in children in general, there are several issues specific to assessment of adjustment in children with chronic illness. First, most of the frequently used instruments did not include children with chronic illness in the standardization sample. In addition, some checklists, such as the Child Behavior Checklist (CBCL; Achenbach & Edelbrock, 1983), were not developed to be sensitive to milder forms of adjustment problems that may be present in children with chronic illness, and the inclusion of somatic items on checklists can lead to scale elevations that reflect physical rather than psychological difficulties (Perrin, Stein, & Drotar, 1991).

Second, many studies have not comprehensively examined the range of potential difficulties, but have focused only on internalizing difficulties such as anxiety or depressive symptoms. Yet, when the range of difficulties is more comprehensively assessed, there is the potential for other difficulties, including externalizing problems, to emerge (Thompson, Gustafson, & Gil, 1995).

Third, relatively few studies have assessed for behavioral and emotional problems based on DSM-III-R diagnostic criteria (e.g., Thompson, Gil, Burbach, Keith, & Kinney, 1993; Thompson et al., 1995). Understanding the types of adjustment problems in children with chronic physical disorders requires the level of specificity inherent in diagnoses, as this will guide intervention efforts.

Knowledge about psychosocial adjustment in children with chronic illnesses is based on epidemiological studies and clinical studies of specific disorders. The findings of several large population-based epidemiological studies of children with chronic physical conditions have provided strong evidence that these children demonstrate 1.5 to 3 times the risk of psychosocial adjustment difficulties relative to children without chronic illness (Cadman, Boyle, Szatmari, & Offord, 1987; Gortmaker, Walker, Weitzman, & Sobol, 1990; Pless, 1984). Clinic-based studies provide evidence for the type, as well as the frequency, of adjustment problems in children diagnosed with specific disorders.

The etiology of psychosocial adjustment problems in children with chronic illness is not entirely clear. It is likely that some adjustment problems reflect difficulties in adapting to the extraordinary stressors associated with illness. It is also likely that some adjustment problems reflect the co-morbidity (that is, independence) of behavioral and medical problems.

Sickle Cell Disease. Studies of children and adolescents with sickle cell disease have reported an array of adjustment problems (for review, see Thompson, Gil et al., 1993). These problems have included poor self-concept, social adjustment problems, behavior problems, and symptoms of depression. Adjustment problems seem to increase with age, and boys demonstrate more problems than girls; the severity of SCD contributes lit-

tle to psychosocial adjustment over and above the effects of age and gender.

Our own research program has demonstrated that about half of the children and adolescents assessed met criteria for one or more DSM-III diagnoses on a self-reported diagnostic interview, the Child Assessment Schedule (Hodges, Kline, Stern, Cytryn & McKnew, 1982). Internalizing diagnoses including anxiety, phobic, and obsessive-compulsive disorders were most frequent, whereas externalizing problems including conduct disorder and oppositional disorder were infrequent (Thompson, Gil et al., 1993; Thompson et al., 1995). Mother-reported behavior problems were evident in almost two-thirds of the children and adolescents, with internalizing problems again the most frequent (Thompson, Gil et al., 1993).

Despite the relatively high rates of adjustment problems seen in these cross-sectional studies, longitudinal studies of adjustment in children and adolescents with SCD have indicated relatively little stability in adjustment over time. Based on child report, 29 percent exhibited stable poor adjustment, 31 percent exhibited stable good adjustment, and 40 percent changed classification over time. Based on mother report, 49 percent exhibited stable poor adjustment, 20 percent exhibited stable good adjustment, and 31 percent changed classification (Thompson et al., 1994). Although internalizing diagnoses and problems were consistently the most frequent, there was little congruence over time in specific diagnosis. It is those children demonstrating stable poor adjustment that should be targeted for intervention programs.

Given that painful crises are a significant and persistent problem for children and adolescents with SCD, it is also important to address the influence of pain on adjustment. Gil and colleagues have demonstrated that pain coping strategies characterized by passive adherence and negative thinking (i.e., thinking patterns such as catastrophizing and self-statements of fear and anger) were associated with more frequent visits to the emergency room (ER), less activity during painful episodes, and higher levels of self-reported psychological distress. Active coping attempts, such as cognitive and behavioral strategies including diverting attention, calming self statements, and reinterpreting pain sensations, were associated with fewer visits to the ER and more activity during painful episodes (Gil, Williams, Thompson, & Kinney, 1991).

Moreover, passive adherence coping strategies were associated with more frequent health care contacts during the subsequent nine months, and increases in negative thinking over time were associated with further increases in health care contacts. Active coping attempts were associated with higher levels of school, household, and social activity during painful episodes (Gil et al., 1993).

Hemophilia. There have been relatively few studies of psychosocial adjustment in patients with hemophilia. Existing findings have indicated an increased risk for self-reported depressive symptoms (Klein & Nimorwicz, 1982), parent-reported defiance and hostility (Meijer, 1980), and internalizing and externalizing behavior problems (Wallander & Varni, 1986). Increased psychosocial adjustment difficulties have been found to be associated with increased age (Wallander & Varni, 1986), more severe physical handicap (Steinhausen, 1976), greater disease severity (Wallander & Varni, 1986) and lower levels of hemophilia-related knowledge (Klein & Nimorwicz, 1982). Although some early studies utilized general psychiatric observations, no studies to date have used more reliable structured diagnostic interviews to identify the types and frequencies of specific psychological diagnoses in children and adolescents with hemophilia.

In addition to the multiple stressors inherent in having a chronic illness, in the past decade patients with hemophilia and their families have also had to confront the fact that HIV could be transmitted through blood products. Thus, these families have had to cope with an entirely new set of psychosocial and medical challenges. Clinical reports have indicated that patients and family members initially responded to this threat with increased anxiety, but long-term adjustment reflected a return to daily living and a low level of anxiety (Mason & Olson, 1989). In addition, a multicenter study of the psychological impact of the risk of HIV infection and AIDS on older adolescents and adults with hemophilia and their families found that hemophiliacs were at risk for developing adjustment problems and decreasing their use of clotting factor concentrates for the treatment of bleeding episodes (Agle, Gluck, & Pierce, 1987). However, the recent availability of highly purified concentrate products has made the risk of HIV infection negligible, which may have subsequently resulted in a return to previous patterns of clotting factor usage.

Assessment of Neurocognitive Functioning

It is recognized that hematological disorders have potential consequences for the brain. Methods for assessing neurocognitive functioning include administration of standardized tests of intellectual, academic, visual-motor, speech and language, memory, attention,

and executive functioning. The findings regarding neurocognitive functioning are reviewed in terms of the specific disorders of sickle cell disease and hemophilia.

Sickle Cell Disease. Despite the fact that extant studies have revealed some variability in patterns of findings and have been plagued by methodological shortcomings, there is increasing evidence that children with sickle cell disease are at risk for neurocognitive difficulties secondary to central nervous system effects of the illness itself (Brown, Armstrong, & Eckman, 1993; Brown, Buchanan et al., 1993). Children and adolescents with sickle cell disease have been found to differ from control subjects on intellectual functioning, academic achievement, attention, and other neuropsychological abilities (for review see Brown, Armstrong, & Eckman, 1993). Cognitive impairment seems to be evident by age seven but does not appear to be associated with increased age. Etiological factors such as chronically-reduced oxygen delivery have been hypothesized, although the variability in cognitive functioning of these children and adolescents may also in part reflect socioeconomic status (Brown, Buchanan et al., 1993).

Hemophilia. Although children with hemophilia are at risk for focal learning difficulties secondary to bleeding episodes in the brain, there have been few studies of neurocognitive functioning in patients with hemophilia. However, intellectual functioning has been found in general to be normally distributed (Olch, 1971), and no differences in overall intelligence have been identified between hemophilia patients and healthy control subjects (Steinhausen, 1976).

Children and adolescents with hemophilia who are infected with HIV may also be at risk for the neurocognitive sequelae of HIV infection. However, the Hemophilia Growth and Development Study, a multi-center study of the long-term effects of HIV infection on pediatric patients with hemophilia, revealed no significant differences in neuropsychological performance between HIV[+] and HIV[-] patients with hemophilia (Loveland et al., 1994). Although mean scores for both groups were within the average range, academic and adaptive skills were lower than expected based on mean IQ scores. The investigators concluded that patients with hemophilia who were HIV[+] remained relatively free from HIV encephalopathy several years after seroconversion, and the difficulties in academic and adaptive skills seen in both HIV[+] and HIV[-] subjects are likely associated with the hemophilia or its secondary consequences (e.g., school absenteeism).

TREATMENT STRATEGIES

Overview of Medical Management

Sickle Cell Disease

The mainstay of therapy for sickle cell disease is early recognition and intervention. It is absolutely essential that patients and their families receive frequent education and counseling about the clinical manifestations of sickle cell disease. At the first signs and symptoms of an acute painful event, oral hydration and analgesia should be instituted promptly. Extra fluids should be taken at 150–200 percent of maintenance fluid intake, to improve intravascular blood flow and release the blockage within distal capillaries. Analgesia in the form of acetaminophen or ibuprofen will help reduce inflammation and swelling. Children who receive early intervention for painful events rarely require additional therapy; however, occasionally intravenous fluids and narcotics are required to relieve the painful vaso-occlusive event (Kinney & Ware, 1988).

The management of a febrile event also requires early recognition and intervention by the patient and family. An extra dose of oral penicillin and a prompt medical evaluation are essential to prevent overwhelming bacterial sepsis in young children with sickle cell disease. Other clinical events related to sickle cell disease, including splenic sequestration, gallstones, or stroke, similarly require early recognition by the patient and family for optimal treatment.

Hemophilia

Family education and counseling are essential for proper management of the child with hemophilia. Special precautions must be taken for routine childhood immunizations, including subcutaneous injection with concomitant administration of ice to reduce bleeding. Parents must be taught to provide extra padding for babies when they are learning to crawl and walk; toddlers are particularly susceptible to trauma. Dental care should be provided by personnel familiar with hemophilia, so that excessive bleeding does not occur. Comprehensive care in conjunction with physical therapy and orthopedics is ideal. Families are also taught to recognize the signs and symptoms of musculoskeletal bleeding, so that early intervention can occur.

The most common therapy for children with severe hemophilia is an intravenous infusion of the specific clotting factor, for example, Factor VIII concentrate. For patients with a significant hemorrhage, prompt replacement of the deficient coagulation factor is essential. Parents are encouraged to seek medical attention at the earliest signs of hemorrhage; a single dose of factor replacement is usually sufficient to control bleeding if administered early. In contrast, a delay in medical attention frequently leads to the need for repeated factor infusions and eventual destruction of the joint space. For this reason, many families are taught to infuse factor replacement at home, an approach that is both economical and convenient. Once the child is of school age, self-administration of factor becomes possible. While most patients receive factor replacement through a peripheral vein, a permanent subcutaneous central line also can be used safely in children (Schultz, Ware, Filston, & Kinney, 1988).

Currently, the majority of factor replacement products are purified from normal human donors, and therefore carry a risk of viral transmission. One of the great tragedies for this patient population is that the ready availability of concentrated coagulation factors initially led to a dramatic improvement in morbidity and mortality, but the subsequent transmission of hepatitis and the human immunodeficiency virus (HIV) has been devastating. It is estimated that over 90 percent of patients with hemophilia who received blood products prior to 1985 (when HIV testing became available) are HIV positive, and many are now developing the AIDS syndrome (Levine, 1985). For patients with mild Factor VIII deficiency, therapy with the synthetic compound (1-amino-8-D-arginine vasopressin) (DDAVP, or Desmopressin) can obviate the need for exposure to human blood products (Mannucci, 1988). DDAVP stimulates the release of Factor VIII and von Willebrand factor from the endothelium.

Psychological and Behavioral Treatments

The utility and efficacy of psychotropic medications with children with hematologic disorders has not yet been established. The clinical management of depression and/or pain may include antidepressant medications but efficacy has not been systematically studied. Furthermore, the distinction between depressive symptoms and clinical depression is important. For example, in contrast with controls, children with sickle cell disease (Yang et al., 1994) reported higher levels of symptoms commonly associated with depression, such as fatigue and physical complaints, but which also are common medical symptoms of sickle cell disease. Furthermore, clinical psychiatric interview did not reveal an increased prevalence of clinical depression.

The utility and efficacy of psychological and behavioral treatments are being systematically studied. In relation to the hematologic disorders discussed in this chapter, psychological and behavioral treatments have particular application to three domains: pain management, adherence, and stress management. Within each domain, attention is directed to enhancing children's adaptation and to the ability of parents to foster their children's development.

Pain Management

Pain is a complex, multidimensional experience involving two components. The sensory component is directly related to activity in neuro-pathway response to tissue damage (McGrath et al., 1990). The response component includes psychological, physiological, emotional, and behavioral responses to the sensory responses. There are a number of factors that affect this response dimension, including those intrinsic to the child, such as anxiety, depression, and previous experience with pain, and those that are extrinsic to the child, such as parental anxiety and response to the child's reaction to pain.

It is useful to distinguish three types of pediatric pain: acute, chronic, and recurrent (Varni et al., 1989). Acute pain has functional value as an adaptive biologic warning signal. Acute pain is characterized by intensity and associated anxiety. Chronic pain is characterized by a lack of anxiety and temporal proximity to a pathogenic stimulus, and reactive behaviors such as compensatory posturing and restrictions of normal activities. Recurrent pain typically has elements of both acute and chronic pain.

Approaches to pain management can involve analgesia, behavioral intervention, or a combination of these methods. The goal of analgesia is to obtain maximum pain relief with as few side effects as possible. Psychological approaches to pain management are predominantly cognitive-behavioral in nature.

Cognitive-behavioral treatment approaches to chronic and recurrent pain management have been characterized by two types of techniques (Varni, Walco, & Wilcox, 1990). One technique involves self-regulation of *pain perception* through techniques such as progressive muscle relaxation, meditation, and guided imagery. A second technique involves modification of *pain behavior* through the identification and modification of pain coping strategies and socio-environmental factors that influence pain expression (Sanders, Shepard, Cleghorn, & Woolford, 1994). In particular, the social-learning perspective calls attention to the role of caregivers in providing cues and selective reinforcement of pain management behaviors on the part of the child. This has led to intervention efforts to train parents to alter their behaviors in such a way as to support their children's active coping and self-management skills and to withhold reinforcement for pain behaviors. These treatment approaches have been applied to patients with hemophilia and sickle cell disease.

Patients with hemophilia may experience both the acute pain of internal hemorrhaging and chronic musculoskeletal pain as a result of arthropathy caused by bleeding into the joints (Varni, 1981). One goal of treatment has been to develop an effective intervention to reduce perceived arthritis pain while not interfering with the signal function of acute pain associated with bleeding (Varni, 1981). Varni and his colleagues (Varni, 1981; Varni et al., 1989) have developed and empirically verified the effectiveness of cognitive-behavior therapy techniques for the treatment of chronic arthritic pain in both children and adults with hemophilia. The self-regulation component consists of three phases. In the first phase, the child is taught a 25-step progressive muscle relaxation sequence. The child alternatively tenses and relaxes the major muscle groups. In the second phase, the child learns to inhale medium deep breath through the nose and to slowly exhale through the mouth. While exhaling, the child learns to say the word "relax" and to visualize it in warm colors written on a chalk board. In the third phase the child learns to use guided imagery through which he or she imagines actively participating in pleasant, distracting scenes.

In sickle cell disease, the manner in which pain is conceptualized affects treatment strategies (Walco & Dampier, 1987). Vaso-occlusive episodes lead to bone and/or joint pain that can last for several hours or days and are referred to as "painful crises." For approximately 95 percent of patients, hospitalizations occur one or less times per year, with an average length of stay of 7 days (Walco & Dampier, 1987). Acute pain intervention is appropriate and includes rest, immobilization, and analgesics. In some patients, chronic pain syndromes develop; painful crises in such patients are not independent events, but episodes in a series of crises that are maladaptive (Varni et al., 1989).

Walco and Dampier (1987) have developed a treatment strategy for patients with sickle cell disease that includes a fixed schedule of tapering analgesic dosages and a structured program to promote an adaptive lifestyle. The organic/psychogenic dichotomized way of thinking about pain is avoided. Recurrent pain is viewed as a lifelong problem, and cognitive and affective behaviors are viewed as mediating the ways in which the patient learns to tolerate the discomfort and to function. Coping is emphasized and the notion of curing the pain is de-emphasized. Patients are taught pain perception regulation and pain behavior regulation techniques. Positive clinical results of this treatment program have been reported (Walco & Dampier, 1987), but controlled trials have not yet been accomplished.

Cognitive-behavioral family intervention, with a dual emphasis on teaching children pain coping skills and parent training has been demonstrated to be efficacious in studies of children suffering from recurrent abdominal pain (Sanders, Rebgetz, & Morrison, 1989; Sanders, Shepherd, Cleghorn, & Woolford, 1994). These techniques have not yet been applied in a controlled study to children with hemophilia or sickle cell disease, but such a controlled trial would seem warranted.

In summary, while the majority of children function well socially and academically while dealing with pain associated with their chronic illness, there is a small subset who "miss school, withdraw from social activities, become pre-occupied with their pain, and begin early their careers as pain patients" (McGrath et al., 1986, p. 229). Considerable support has been provided for the efficacy of cognitive-behavioral intervention treatment programs for training children in pain management strategies and their parents to support active pain coping efforts. A focus on coping skills avoids both blame and self-pity and helps children not to be cut off from the pleasures and joys afforded by their normal daily activities.

Stress Management

Children with hematological disorders and their parents are confronted with dealing with the stress associated with chronic illness over substantial periods of their respective lives. Chronic illness can be viewed as a potential stressor that confronts children and their families with the threat of suffering and loss, as well as with illness tasks that need to be managed. These tasks include dealing with the symptoms and treatments, managing the impact on social relationships, and facing an uncertain future.

In addition to the stresses associated with chronic illness, stress also has been hypothesized to have a specific role in the spontaneous bleeding episodes experienced by children with hemophilia (Wyngaarden, Smith, & Bennett, 1992; Swirsky-Sacchetti & Margolis, 1986). Although the mechanism of effect is not yet clear, a review of the small number of extant empirical studies provides support for the likelihood of a relationship between stress and bleeding (Perrin, MacLean, & Janco, 1988). Both the general and specific contributions of stress to the adjustment of children with hematological disorders suggest the potential benefits of learning how to manage stress.

Stress management training programs combine a number of cognitive-behavioral therapy approaches to regulation of thoughts and feelings and their interrelationships. For example, cognitive restructuring and reframing techniques are useful in modifying cognitive appraisals that lead to perceptions of stressfulness and threat. The self-regulatory components of relaxation training described previously in relation to pain management are also utilized as a method of stress reduction. Finally, social problem-solving skill training is utilized to help children deal with school re-entry and teasing and/or rejection from peers.

It is likely that stress varies as a function of illness type, in terms of specific symptoms and treatments that must be dealt with, phase of illness course, and developmental issues. However, incorporating stress management components into the comprehensive care program for children with sickle cell disease and hemophilia may be one way to enhance quality of life and prevent psychological adjustment problems.

Adherence

Adherence to medical regimens is a component of the quality of life of children with chronic illnesses. Numerous studies have attempted to improve adherence to medical regimens and several excellent reviews are available (e.g., Epstein & Cluss, 1982). In general, there are educational, behavioral, and combined educational and behavioral approaches to improving adherence (Haynes, 1976). While knowledge of the therapeutic regimen is necessary, it is not sufficient in and of itself to assure adherence.

Evidence for the effectiveness of behavioral strategies for improving compliance is substantial. These behavioral strategies include three types of techniques. Stimulus control techniques modify the medical regimen to make it less aversive, for example, by increasing the acceptability of pills through flavoring or tailoring the drug regimen to specific situations in the patient's life. Self-control techniques focus on developing the patients' skills with self-monitoring of symptoms and corresponding self-regulation of dosage. Reinforcement methods focus on self and other reinforcement of symptom reduction and other behaviors that are consistent with the medical regimen. Self-monitoring and the process of tailoring treatment regimens are consistent with the increasing focus on the patient as an active decision maker in his/her treatment (Fink, 1976). Establishing and maintaining collaborative relationships among health care providers and their patients and families provides the context in which effective tailoring of treatment regimens in relation to the priorities of patients and families can take place. Such an approach affords the greatest probability of enhancing adherence, and thereby improving quality of life.

Fostering adherence is important for children with sickle cell disease or hemophilia, and behavioral strategies are beginning to be included in comprehensive care programs. For example, behavioral techniques have been used to foster adherence in patients with hemophilia. The recognition of the advantages of early treatment of each bleeding episode has prompted the creation of home care programs as a component of comprehensive care for hemophilia. Adherence to proper factor replacement techniques is essential. Behavioral techniques have been systematically applied to teaching parents and children home care factor replacement therapy. The impact on proficiency of treatment and adherence to proper technique has been evaluated (Sergis-Deavenport & Varni, 1983). A behavioral assessment checklist was developed to systematically and objectively record parental performance on 107 specific behaviors. Training sessions consisted of two-hour weekly visits over a four- to eight-week period. Behavioral intervention consisted of modeling, observational learning, behavioral rehearsal, corrective feedback, and social reinforcement. The behavioral training intervention increased the proficiency of the treatment group from a mean percentage correct performance of 15 percent during baseline to 92 percent. In terms of long-term adherence, the treatment group demonstrated 97 percent correct performance to the 65 percent correct performance of the comparison group.

Pharmacological Treatments

For hemophilia, genetically engineered recombinant factor VIII has recently become available, and appears to be as efficacious as the human product without the risk of viral transmission (Bray et al., 1994). As a result, many young patients are now receiving only the recombinant product. However, replacement of other coagulation factors still necessitates the infusion of human blood products. As the genes for the various deficient factors have been identified and cloned, the concept of gene therapy has become attractive. The placement of a normal gene into the cells of a patient with hemophilia may well become standard therapy within the next decade.

For sickle cell disease, the natural history study for sickle cell disease has shown that the amount of hemoglobin F (Hb F) is an important predictive marker for disease severity and mortality (Platt et al., 1994). Hb F is the primary hemoglobin of the fetus, constitutes approximately 80 percent of the total hemoglobin at birth, but gradually declines over the first year of life to the adult level of approximately 1 percent. While infants with sickle cell disease have Hb F levels at birth similar to those of normal infants, their rate of Hb F decline is slower and the nadir is often not reached until age 5 years. Several studies have demonstrated that patients with elevated Hb F levels have a milder clinical course, and those with Hb F greater than 20 percent have virtually no symptoms (Powars, Weiss, Chan, & Schroieder, 1984). The distribution of Hb F within erythrocytes, however, is perhaps more critical for preventing in vivo sickling than the absolute amount of Hb F.

Pharmacologic enhancement of Hb F can be achieved using several antineoplastic drugs, with hydroxyurea as the prototype due to its relatively safe track record and its modest and reversible toxicity. Hydroxyurea has been tested in adults with sickle cell disease, and in most patients can increase both the absolute amount of Hb F as well as the number of F cells (Charache et al., 1992). Toxicity is primarily bone marrow suppression (especially granulocytes) and is dose-dependent and reversible. Clinical trials on adults with sickle cell disease have yielded promising results, with improvement of hematologic parameters and amelioration of clinical symptoms. A multi-center pediatric hydroxyurea trial is currently under way.

Similarly, arginine butyrate has been demonstrated to increase Hb F production in patients with sickle cell disease (Perrine et al., 1993). Although the precise mechanism of action is not known, there appear to be few side effects. A multi-center trial using arginine butyrate in pediatric patients is currently under way. Finally, bone marrow transplantation is curative for patients with sickle cell disease, but the relatively high morbidity of this procedure makes its routine use unattractive. In addition, many patients with sickle cell disease do not have HLA-matched siblings who can provide compatible bone marrow. For now, bone marrow transplantation is a serious consideration only for children with sickle cell disease who have had a stroke, for whom the long-term prognosis is poor.

CASE ILLUSTRATION

Clinical Presentation

FM was diagnosed with sickle cell disease at birth through routine neonatal screening. FM experienced complications and symptomatology secondary to her disease starting at three months of age. She has had frequent pain crises and infections requiring multiple hospitalizations. FM was initially referred to the Pediatric Psychology Service when she was nine years of age during an admission for painful crisis. The referral was made to assess potential contributing factors to FM's difficulties in coping with her illness and her reluctance to be discharged to home.

The initial clinical interview with FM and her mother indicated that FM exhibited a generally pleasant demeanor, but was emotionally immature and physically thin and slender. She exhibited little understanding of her illness and was apprehensive about returning home because she didn't believe that she was "well enough."

At the time of the initial referral, FM lived with her mother and younger sister. Her mother and father had been divorced for approximately six years. FM's maternal grandmother was also involved in caretaking. FM was in a regular third grade classroom and reportedly did well academically. However, FM reported being embarrassed by critical comments made by her teacher subsequent to receiving a note from her mother asking for her to remain inside the classroom on cold days because of her sickle cell disease. In addition, FM reported being teased because of her thinness. In addition to a lack of understanding about her disease, FM also demonstrated regressed, demanding, and attention-seeking behavior during painful crises and at other times when she was feeling poorly. Consequently, she had poorly developed coping skills.

Support was provided to mother for her plans to meet with FM's teacher to clarify issues related to her disease. Arrangements were made to complete a more thorough psychological evaluation on an outpatient basis. However, FM's mother did not make arrangements for this out-patient evaluation. Continued contacts were made during in-patient hospitalizations and out-patient clinic visits in an effort to build rapport. It was not until 14 months later when FM was 10-years, 5 months of age that the out-patient psychological evaluation was completed.

Assessment Findings

Assessment focused on intellectual functioning, academic performance, and psychological adjustment. Methods included standardized individual psychological tests, mother-completed behavior checklists, and clinical interview. On the Wechsler Intelligence Scale for Children–Revised, FM obtained a Verbal Scale IQ score of 80, a Performance Scale IQ score of 96, and a Full Scale IQ score of 87. Verbally and overall, FM's functioning was within the Average range but nonverbally was in the Low Average range. At the time of testing, FM's grade placement was the 4.8 grade level. On the Woodcock-Johnson Psychoeducational Battery–Revised, FM obtained grade equivalency scores of 4.8 in reading and 4.6 in mathematics. Mother's responses to the Child Behavior Checklist indicated that she viewed FM as more depressed, socially withdrawn, dependent, and oppositional than other children her age and as having very poor self-esteem. Clinical interview indicated that FM's problem-solving and coping style was generally passive, dependent, and avoidant. Parent interview data indicated that FM's mother was angry with FM's demanding and dependent style and inadvertently reinforced passivity and dependency.

Treatment Selection and Course

Recommendations were for individual and parent counseling to focus on resolving feelings of mutual hostility and dependency. With improved interpersonal relationships, attention could then be focused on improving FM's ability to cope with the stresses associated with her illness and normal developmental tasks. It was recommended that these counseling services be obtained through the Mental Health Center in their local community. FM's mother was in agreement with the recommendations and signed a release of information form so that the assessment findings could be shared with the local Mental Health Center.

A follow-up telephone conversation a month later revealed that FM's mother was having a difficult time coordinating her work schedule to accommodate an appointment at the local Mental Health Center. However, she indicated that she believed that there could be a resolution to the scheduling conflict.

The Pediatric Psychology Service was reconsulted six months later, when FM was hospitalized for pneumonia, to again address issues related to coping and adjustment. FM's mother reported that she had been unable to arrange the out-patient counseling sessions through the local Mental Health Center. In addition, she had experienced a number of stressors including the death of her grandmother. Her responses to the Child Assessment Schedule–Parent Form (Hodges et al., 1982) indicated that she perceived FM as displaying symptoms that met the criteria for both separation anxiety and depression. Her responses to the Missouri Children's Behavior Checklist (Sines, Pauker, Sines, & Owen, 1969) resulted in an internal behavior problem profile (Thompson, Kronenberger, & Curry, 1989). Her responses indicated that she continued to see FM as more depressed, socially withdrawn, and inhibited than other children her age. Mother's responses to the SCL-90, a self-report measure of psychiatric symptomatology, indicated a clinically significant degree of psychological distress. In particular, FM's mother was acknowledging high levels of depression, hostility, interpersonal sensitivity, and anxiety. Recommendations again included obtaining individual and parent counseling through the Mental Health Center to be followed with specific focused intervention on coping with stress and pain in relation to her sickle cell disease.

The Pediatric Psychology Service was again contacted six months later during another hospitalization for pain management. FM's mother had not obtained the recommended counseling services and indicated a lack of interest in doing so. She expressed the belief that FM would "do fine if everyone would just leave her alone." The plan was to continue to be available to provide psychological services during FM's in-patient hospitalizations if and when requested by her mother.

FM was again referred to the Pediatric Psychology Service during an in-patient hospitalization 1½ years later. Assistance in fostering FM's coping with her illness and pain management was requested. FM reported that she had participated in one counseling session through the local Mental Health Center. Reportedly, additional counseling sessions were scheduled. Consequently, support was provided for the family as they continued to follow through with counseling services through their local Mental Health Center. Eight months later FM was again referred to the Pediatric Psychology Service for assistance in coping with her painful medical crises and use of analgesics. FM reported pain coping strategies that were largely passive in nature. When in painful crises, she sleeps, avoids others, goes to a quiet place where she will not be bothered, pretends that the pain is not there, prays that it won't last long, and tries to relax. She acknowledged feeling overwhelmed and that others do not understand what she is going through. She appeared depressed and withdrawn and her guard-

edness made more formal assessment of her mood difficult. Her use of guardedness and withdrawal allowed her to avoid direct confrontation of her difficulties. Her methods of coping continued to be palliative and passive. Development of more active-adaptive strategies of coping with stress and pain continued to be seen as necessary for more successful emotional and behavioral control, functioning at school, and overall adaptation to her illness. Given that FM was approaching 14 years of age and given the difficulties in obtaining family counseling services, individual therapy was recommended through the local Mental Health Center.

Termination and Follow-Up

Although FM clearly needed psychological intervention directed toward enhancing her pain management skills and ability to cope with the stresses associated with her illness, it was clear that her mother's resistance to engaging in counseling sessions was a continuing obstacle. Moreover, it was not clear that focusing on just individual work for FM would be any more acceptable to her mother. In retrospect, perhaps consideration should have been given to antidepressant medication, but the perceived need was for a change in her passive and palliative methods of coping with stress and pain. Continued efforts would be made during her hospitalizations and out-patient follow-up visits to encourage initiation of the counseling sessions. However, the poor prognosis for these efforts as well as the degree of functional impairment she was experiencing as a result of her illness led to consideration of other treatment avenues.

Because of the multiple painful episodes that led to numerous hospitalizations and missed school days, FM was electively started on hydroxyurea therapy. Her dose has been slowly escalated, with frequent monitoring of blood counts to identify any toxic effects. To date, her blood counts suggest a modest beneficial effect from hydroxyurea, with an improvement in hemoglobin concentration of 1 gm/dl, and an increase in her hemoglobin F percentage as well. Overall, FM feels slightly better while on hydroxyurea, but continues to have occasional painful episodes related to her sickle cell disease.

SUMMARY

Hematological disorders vary in their incidence, prevalence, manifestations, and treatments. This chapter has focused on two common hematologic disorders, sickle cell disease and hemophilia, that have medical and psychological manifestations. Comprehensive care for children afflicted with these conditions requires attention to both the medical and psychological-psychiatric aspects of these disorders. Furthermore, there is an interrelationship between the medical and psychosocial manifestations.

Considering hematological disorders as a potential stressor to which the child and his/her family need to adapt highlights the need for an integrated biopsychosocial approach to care. The specific stressors vary as a function of the specific clinical manifestations and corresponding treatments associated with the type of disorder, phase in the illness course, and whether the disorder has resulted in cognitive deficits. The stressors also vary as a function of developmental level and individual and family coping resources.

With hematological disorders, as with chronic childhood disorders in general, there is an increased risk for psychosocial adjustment difficulties and psychiatric disorders/psychopathology. However, effective pain management and stress management treatment programs have been developed and can be incorporated into the comprehensive care provided for children with hematological disorders to improve psychosocial adjustment. Furthermore, training in these coping skills may not only prevent psychological adjustment difficulties, but also can enhance disease management.

Fostering adherence to treatment regimens is another way in which disease management can be enhanced. Behavioral techniques have been developed that are effective in enhancing adherence and maintaining a collaborative relationship among the patient, family members, and health care providers.

There is a need to increase our understanding about how biomedical and psychosocial processes act together in hematological disorders. However, the knowledge base is currently sufficient to warrant incorporation of psychological/psychiatric assessment and treatment approaches into the comprehensive care of children with hematological disorders. Correspondingly, there needs to be systematic outcome research in terms of fostering disease management, preventing psychosocial adjustment difficulties, and enhancing quality of life.

REFERENCES

Achenbach, T., & Edelbrock, C. (1983). *Manual for the Child Behavior Checklist.* Burlington, VT: Queen City Printers.

Achenbach, T. M., McConaughy, S. H., & Howell, C. T. (1987). Child/adolescent behavioral and emotional problems: Implications of cross-informant correlations for situational specificity. *Psychological Bulletin, 101,* 213–232.

Agle, D., Gluck, H., & Pierce, G. F. (1986). The risk of AIDS: Psychologic impact on the hemophilic population. *General Hospital Psychiatry, 9,* 11–17.

Angold, A., Weissman, M. M., John, K., Merikangas, K. R., Prusoff, B. A., Wickramaratne, G., Gammon, D., & Warner, V., (1987). Parent and child reports of depressive symptoms in children at low and high risk of depression. *Journal of Child Psychology and Psychiatry, 28,* 901–915.

Bray, G. L., Gomperts, E. D., Courter, S., Gruppo, R., Gordon, E. M., Manco-Johnson, M., Shapiro, A., Scheibel, E., White, G., & Lee, M. (1994). A multicenter study of recombinant Factor VIII (Recombinate): Safety, efficacy, and inhibitor risk in previously untreated patients with hemophilia A. *Blood, 83,* 2428–2435.

Brown, R. T., Buchanan, I., Doepke, K., Eckman, J. R., Baldwin, K., Goonan, B., & Schoenherr, S. (1993). Cognitive and academic functioning in children with sickle cell disease. *Journal of Clinical Child Psychology, 22,* 207–218.

Brown, R. T., Armstrong, F. D., & Eckman, J. R. (1993). Neurocognitive aspects of pediatric sickle cell disease. *Journal of Learning Disabilities, 26,* 33–45.

Cadman, D., Boyle, M., Szatmari, P. & Offord, D. R. (1987). Chronic illness, disability, and mental and social well being: Findings of the Ontario Child Health Study. *Pediatrics, 79,* 805–813.

Charache, S., Dover, G. J., Moore, R. D., Eckert, S., Ballas, S. K., Koshy, M., Milner, P. F. A., Orringer, E. P., Phillips, G., Platt, O. S., & Thomas, G. H. (1992). Hydroxyurea: Effects on hemoglobin F production in patients with sickle cell anemia. *Blood, 79,* 2555–2565.

Edelbrock, C., Costello, A. J., Dulcan, M. K., Conover, N. C., & Kalas, R. (1986). Parent-child agreement on child psychiatric symptoms assessed via structured interview. *Journal of Child Psychology and Psychiatry, 27,* 181–190.

Epstein, L. H., & Cluss, P. A. (1982). A behavioral medicine perspective on adherence to long-term medical regimens. *Journal of Consulting and Clinical Psychology, 50,* 950–971.

Fink, D. L. (1976). Tailoring the consensual regimen. In D. L. Sackett & R. B. Haynes (Eds.), *Compliance with therapeutic regimens* (pp. 110–118). Baltimore, MD: The Johns Hopkins University Press.

Gaston, M. H., Verter, J. I., Woods, G., Pegelow, C., Kelleher, J., Presbury, G., Zarkowsky, H., Vichinsky, E., Iyer, R., Lobel, J. S., Diamonds, S., Holbrook, C. T., Gil, F. M., Ritchey, K., & Falletta, J. M. (1986). Prophylaxis with oral penicillin in children with sickle cell anemia: A randomized trial. *New England Journal of Medicine, 314*, 1593–1599.

Gil, K. M., Thompson, R. J., Jr., Keith, B. R., Tota-Faucette, M., Noll, S., & Kinney, T. R. (1993). Sickle cell disease pain in children and adolescents: Change in pain frequency and coping strategies over time. *Journal of Pediatric Psychology, 18*, 621–637.

Gil, K. M., Williams, D. A., Thompson, R. J., Jr., & Kinney, T. R. (1991). Sickle cell disease in children and adolescents: The relation of child and parent pain coping strategies to adjustment. *Journal of Pediatric Psychology, 16*, 643–663.

Gortmaker, S. L., Walker, D. K., Weitzman, M., & Sobol, A. M. (1990). Chronic conditions, socioeconomic risks and behavioral problems in children and adolescents. *Pediatrics, 85*, 267–276.

Haynes, R. B. (1976). Strategies for improving compliance: A methodologic analysis and review. In D. L. Sackett and R. B. Haynes (Eds.), *Compliance with therapeutic regimens* (pp. 69–82). Baltimore, MD: The Johns Hopkins University Press.

Hodges, K., Kline, J., Stern, L., Cytryn, L., & McKnew, D. (1982). The development of a child assessment interview for research and clinical use. *Journal of Abnormal Child Psychology, 10*, 173–189.

Kinney, T. R., & Ware, R. (1988). Advances in the management of sickle cell disease. *Pediatric Consult, 7*, 1–7.

Klein, R. H., & Nimorwicz, P. (1982). The relationships between psychological distress and knowledge of disease among hemophilia patients and their families: A pilot study. *Journal of Psychosomatic Research, 26*, 387–391.

Levine, P. H. (1985). The acquired immune deficiency syndrome in persons with hemophilia. *Annals of Internal Medicine, 103*, 723–726.

Levine, P. H., & Brettler, D. B. (1991). Clinical aspects and therapy for hemophilia A. In R. Hoffman, E. J. Benz, S. J. Shattil, B. Furie, & H. J. Cohen (Eds.), *Hematology: Basic principles and practice* (pp. 1290–1304). New York: Churchill Livingstone, Inc.

Loveland, K. A., Stehbens, J., Contant, C., Bordeaux, J. D., Sirois, P., Bell, T. S., Hill, S., Scott, A., Bowman, M., Schiller, M., Watkins, J., Olson, R., Moylan, P., Cool, V., & Belden, B. (1994). Hemophilia growth and development study: Baseline neurodevelopmental findings. *Journal of Pediatric Psychology, 19*, 223–240.

Mannucci, P. M. (1988). Desmopressin: A nontransfusional form of treatment for congenital and acquired bleeding disorders. *Blood, 72*, 1449–1455.

Mason, P. J., & Olson, R. A. (1989). Psychosocial aspects of AIDS and HIV infection in pediatric hemophilia patients. In J. M. Seibert & R. A. Olson, *Children, ado-lescents, and AIDS*. Lincoln, NB: University of Nebraska Press.

McGrath, P. J., Beyer, J., Cleeland, C., Eland, J., McGrath, P. A., & Portenoy, R. (1990). Report of the subcommittee on assessment and methodologic issues in the management of pain in childhood cancer. *Pediatrics* (Supplement), *86*, 814–817.

McGrath, P. J., Dunn-Geier, J., Cunningham, S. J., Brunette, R., D'Astoris, J., Humphreys, P., Latter, J., & Keene, D. (1986). Psychological guidelines for helping children cope with chronic benign intractable pain. *Clinical Journal of Pain, 1*, 229–233.

Meijer, A. (1980). Psychiatric problems of hemophilic boys and their families. *International Journal of Psychiatry in Medicine, 10*, 163–172.

Middlebrook, J. L., & Forehand, R. (1985). Maternal perceptions of deviance in child behavior as a function of stress and clinic versus nonclinic status of the child: An analogue study. *Behavior Therapy, 43*, 601–622.

Olch, D. (1971). Effects of hemophilia upon intellectual growth and academic achievement. *Journal of Genetic Psychology, 119*, 63–74.

Perrin, E. C., Stein, R. K., & Drotar, D. (1991). Cautions in using the Child Behavior Checklist: Observations based on research about children with a chronic illness. *Journal of Pediatric Psychology, 16* (4), 411–422.

Perrin, J. M., MacLean, W. E., & Janco, R. L. (1988). Does stress affect bleeding in hemophilia? A review of the literature. *The American Journal of Pediatric Hematology/Oncology, 10*, 230–235.

Perrine, S. P., Ginder, G. D., Faller, D. V., Dover, G. H., Ikuta, T., Witkowska, H. E., Cai, S., Vichinsky, E. P., & Olivieri, N. F. (1993). A short-term trial of butyrate to stimulate fetal-globin-gene expression in the B-globin disorders. *New England Journal of Medicine, 328*, 81–86.

Platt, O. S., Brambilla, D. J., Rosse, W. F., Milner, P. F., Castro, O., Steinberg, M. H., & Klug, P. P. (1994). Mortality in sickle cell disease: Life expectancy and risk factors for early death. *New England Journal of Medicine, 330*, 1639–1644.

Platt, O. S., Thorington, B. D., Brambilla, D. J., Milner, P. F., Rosse, W. F., Vichinsky, E., & Kinney, T. R. (1991). Pain in sickle cell disease: Rates and risk factors. *New England Journal of Medicine, 325*, 11–16.

Pless, I. R. (1984). Clinical assessment: Physical and psychological functioning. *Pediatric Clinics of North America, 31*, 33–45.

Powars, D. R., Weiss, J. N., Chan, L. S., & Schroieder, W. A. (1984). Is there a threshold level of fetal hemoglobin that ameliorates morbidity in sickle cell anemia? *Blood, 63*, 921–926.

Sanders, M. R., Rebgetz, M., & Morrison, M. (1994). Cognitive-behavioral treatment of recurrent nonspecific abdominal pain in children: An analysis of generalization, maintenance and side effects. *Journal of Consulting and Clinical Psychology, 57*, 294–300.

Sanders, M. R., Shepherd, R. W., Cleghorn, G., & Woolford, H. (1994). The treatment of recurrent abdominal pain in children: A controlled comparison of cognitive-behavioral family intervention and standard pediatric care. *Journal of Consulting and Clinical Psychology, 62*, 306–314.

Schultz, W. H., Ware, R., Filston, H. C., & Kinney, T. R. (1988). Prolonged use of an implantable central venous access system in a child with severe hemophilia. *Journal of Pediatrics, 114*, 100–101.

Sergis-Deavenport, E., & Varni, J. W. (1983). Behavioral assessment and management of adherence to factor replacement therapy in hemophilia. *Journal of Pediatric Psychology, 8*, 367–377.

Sines, J. O., Pauker, J. D., Sines, L. K., & Owen, D. R. (1969). Identification of clinically relevant dimensions of children's behavior. *Journal of Consulting and Clinical Psychology, 33*, 728–734.

Steinhausen, H. C. (1976). Hemophilia: A psychological study in chronic disease in juveniles. *Journal of Psychosomatic Research, 20*, 461–467.

Swirsky-Sacchetti, T., & Margolis, C. G. (1986). The effects of a comprehensive self-hypnosis training program on the use of factor VIII in severe hemophilia. *The International Journal of Clinical and Experimental Hypnosis, 34*, 71–83.

Thompson, R. J., Jr., Gil, K. M., Keith, B. R., Gustafson, K. E., George, L. K., & Kinney, T. R. (1994). Psychological adjustment of children and adolescents with sickle cell disease: Stability and change over a 10-month period. *Journal of Consulting and Clinical Psychology, 62*, 856–860.

Thompson, R. J., Jr., Gil, K. M., Burbach, D. J., Keith, B. R., & Kinney, T. R. (1993). Role of child and maternal processes in the psychological adjustment of children with sickle cell disease. *Journal of Consulting and Clinical Psychology, 61*, 468–474.

Thompson, R. J., Jr., Gustafson, K. E., & Gil, K. M. (1995). Psychological adjustment of adolescents with cystic fibrosis or sickle cell disease and their mothers. In J. Wallander and L. Siegel (Eds.), *Advances in pediatric psychology: II. Behavioral perspectives on adolescent health* (pp. 232–247). New York: Guilford Press.

Thompson, R. J., Jr., Gustafson, K. E., Hamlett, K. W., & Spock, A. (1992a). Psychological adjustment of chil-

dren with cystic fibrosis: The role of child cognitive processes and maternal adjustment. *Journal of Pediatric Psychology, 17*, 741–755.

Thompson, R. J., Jr., Kronenberger, W., & Curry, J. F. (1989). Behavior classification system for children with developmental, psychiatric and chronic medical problems. *Journal of Pediatric Psychology, 14*, 559–575.

Thompson, R. J., Jr., Merritt, K. A., Keith, B. R., Murphy, L. B., & Johndrow, D. A. (1993). The role of maternal stress and family functioning in maternal distress and mother-reported and child-reported psychological adjustment of non-referred children. *Journal of Clinical Child Psychology, 22*, 78–84.

Varni, J. W. (1981). Self-regulation techniques in the management of chronic arthritic pain in hemophilia. *Behavior Therapy, 12*, 185–194.

Varni, J. W., Walco, G., & Katz, E. (1989). A cognitive-behavioral approach to pain associated with pediatric chronic disease. *Journal of Pain and Symptom Management, 4*, 238–245.

Varni, J. W., Walco, G. A., & Wilcox, K. T. (1990). Cognitive-biobehavioral assessment and treatment of pediatric pain. In A. M. Gross & R. S. Drabman (Eds.), *Handbook of clinical behavioral pediatrics* (pp. 83–97). New York: Plenum Press.

Walco, G. A., & Dampier, C. D. (1987). Chronic pain in adolescent patients. *Journal of Pediatric Psychology, 12*, 215–225.

Wallander, J. L., & Varni, J. W. (1986). *Psychosocial factors, adaptation, and bleeding episodes in hemophilic children.* Paper presented at the meeting of the Society of Behavioral Medicine, San Francisco.

Ware, R., Filston, H. C., Schultz, W. H., & Kinney, T. R. (1988). Elective cholecystectomy in children with sickle hemoglobinopathies: Successful outcome using a preoperative transfusion regimen. Annals of Surgery, 208, 17–22.

Webster-Stratton, C. (1990). Stress: A potential description of parent perceptions and family interactions. *Journal of Clinical Child Psychology, 19*, 302–312.

Wyngaarden, J. B., Smith, L. H., & Bennett, C. (Eds.) (1992). *Cecil textbook of medicine* (19th Edition). Philadelphia: W. B. Saunders Company.

Yang, Y., Cepeda, M., Price, C., Shah, A., & Mankad, V. (1994). Depression in children and adolescents with sickle cell disease. *Archives of Pediatric Adolescent Medicine, 148*, 457–460.

CHAPTER 14

ONCOLOGIC DISORDERS

James W. Varni
Ronald L. Blount
Daniel J. L. Quiggins

DESCRIPTIONS OF DISORDERS

Advances in biomedical science and technology have resulted in dramatic changes in the prognosis of children and adolescents who have been diagnosed with cancer. Although in the past, survival was measured in terms of months, today many children are surviving for five years and longer (Bleyer, 1990; Sposto & Hammond, 1985). Childhood cancer has gradually evolved from an inevitably fatal illness to a life-threatening chronic disease. With increased survival, quality of life issues have progressively assumed a more prominent role in the treatment protocols being developed for childhood cancer.

Pediatric oncology encompasses a myriad of childhood malignancies. For the purposes of this chapter, we will use the term pediatric cancer to describe the various childhood malignant diseases that involve the uncontrolled proliferation of abnormal cells. The most prevalent type of pediatric cancer is acute leukemia, followed by brain tumors, lymphoma (Hodgkin's disease and non-Hodgkin's lymphoma), neuroblastoma, soft tissue sarcomas (primarily rhabdomyosarcoma), Wilm's tumor, and bone tumors (osteosarcoma and Ewing's sarcoma) (Cecalupo, 1994).

The annual incidence of childhood cancer is approximately 12 per 100,000 children, or 11,000 newly diagnosed cases per year. Leukemia, tumors of the central nervous system, sympathetic nervous system, kidneys, bone, and lymphoma are the most frequent types (Bleyer, 1990; Pratt, 1985). Although rare, cancer accounts for the deaths of more children than does any other disease and is the second leading cause of death in children (Granowetter, 1994). However, because of the recent decline in deaths from childhood cancer, it is predicted that by the year 2000, one in 1,000 young adults aged 20 to 29 years will be a survivor of childhood cancer given a composite current cure rate of 60 percent (Meadows & Hobbie, 1986).

Concerns for the late effects of cancer treatment have become more salient with the increasing survival of children with cancer. Late effects on the cardiovascular, endocrine, gastrointestinal, musculoskeletal, nervous, pulmonary, and genitourinary systems as well as an increased risk of second malignancies, have become evident (Byrd, 1985; DeLaat & Lampkin, 1992). In addition, psychosocial, intellectual, and academic late effects also appear to be emerging in long-term survivors of childhood cancer (see, Copeland, 1992; Koocher, 1985; Lansky, List, Lanskey, Cohen, & Sinks, 1985; Varni & Katz, 1987). These findings indicate the need for more prospective longitudinal studies of the biological, psychological, social, and cognitive late effects of cancer treatment on the quality of life of pediatric cancer patients.

With the increased probability of long-term survival, psychosocial quality of life issues have progressively assumed a more prominent role in the interdisciplinary comprehensive treatment for pediatric cancer. The trend in survivability has led to a shift in psychological emphasis from crisis intervention confronting imminent death to facilitating coping with and adjustment to a serious life-threatening chronic disease (Katz, Dolgin, & Varni, 1990; Varni & Katz, 1987).

MEDICAL TREATMENT

After the diagnosis of cancer, medical treatment is begun as soon as possible since childhood cancer is inevitably fatal if left untreated. The goal of pediatric cancer treatment is to achieve remission, hopefully accompanied by consolidation and long-term maintenance without subsequent relapse of disease (Granowetter, 1994). The exact type of medical treatment that a child receives will depend on their presenting diagnosis. The three primary modalities for pediatric cancer are chemotherapy, radiation therapy, and surgery, which will vary across the different types of pediatric cancers.

Leukemia

Leukemia is the most common childhood malignancy, including acute lymphoblastic and nonlymphoblastic forms. In order to induce remission in acute lymphoblastic leukemia (ALL), the most common form of leukemia, a combination of chemotherapy agents is administered that are intended to prevent the uncontrolled proliferation and growth of cancer cells throughout the body. Vincristine, prednisone, and L-asparaginase are usually given to induce remission, typically followed by the administration of methotrexate and 6-mercaptopurine as consolidation therapy (to prevent central nervous system relapse). Maintenance chemotherapy may continue for two to three years in an effort to prevent relapse. Acute nonlymphocytic leukemia (ANLL) includes acute myelogenous leukemia and other hematologic malignancies that affect blood-forming cells other than lymphoblasts (Granowetter, 1994). The induction for ANLL is similar to ALL; however, because of its poor prognosis with chemotherapy alone, bone marrow transplantation after remission is increasingly becoming standard practice (Cecalupo, 1994).

Brain Tumors

Brain tumors are the second most common childhood malignancy, and include principally medulloblastoma, cerebellar astrocytoma, and brainstem glioma. Surgical resection, typically in combination with radiation and chemotherapy, have become the standard. The prognosis for brain tumor survival varies across the tumor subtypes, with the five-year survival of low-grade astrocytomas approaching 70 percent, and brain stem tumor survival 15 to 20 percent (Granowetter, 1994).

Lymphomas

Lymphomas are the third most common childhood malignancy, and include Hodgkin's and non-Hodgkin's lymphoma. Hodgkin's lymphoma most frequently involves the cervical lymph nodes (Cecalupo, 1994). Depending on the staging of the disease, radiation therapy and chemotherapy are administered in combination or alone. The non-Hodgkin's lymphomas are rapidly growing tumors that affect primarily the abdominal, head and neck, or mediastinum sites (Granowetter, 1994). Treatment includes multiple chemotherapy agents, typically vincristine, cyclophosphamide, prednisone, and methotrexate (Cecalupo, 1994).

Other Cancers

Neuroblastoma (sympathetic nervous tissue tumor), Wilm's tumor (kidney tumor), rhabdomyosarcoma (solid muscle tumor), retinoblastoma (eye cancer), osteosarcoma (bone tumor), and Ewing's sarcoma (bone tumor) are less common childhood malignancies that are treated with various regimens, alone or in combination, including surgical resection, radiation, and chemotherapy (Granowetter, 1994).

PSYCHOLOGICAL ADJUSTMENT

Adjustment of Newly Diagnosed Children

The significant improvement in survival rates has quite understandably resulted in an increased focus on the long-term adaptation of the survivors of childhood cancer (e.g., Gray et al., 1992; Varni, Katz, Colegrove, & Dolgin, 1994a). Although this trend is vital in addressing the quality of life of childhood cancer survivors, continued empirical investigation of children with newly diagnosed cancer is essential in order to assess their quality of life during the more intensive forms of chemotherapy regimens that now dominate current treatment protocols (Hays, 1993; Neglia & Nesbit, 1993; Robinson, 1993).

Empirical investigations of the psychological and social adjustment of pediatric cancer patients utilizing standardized assessment measures have resulted in mixed findings. While some studies suggest that children with cancer are at increased risk for psychological and social adjustment problems (e.g., Greenberg, Kazak, & Meadows, 1989; Katz, Rubenstein, Hubert, & Blew, 1988; Mulhern, Wasserman, Friedman, & Fairclough, 1989; Sawyer, Toogood, Rice, Haskell, & Baghurst, 1989), other studies have reported adjustment comparable to control samples and standardized norms (e.g., Brown et al., 1992; Kaplan, Busner, Weinhold, & Lenon, 1987). Although some null findings can be attributed to a lack of statistical power given small sample sizes (Cohen, 1988), a number of other methodological differences exist across studies that may explain in part the inconsistencies in findings.

One possible candidate that may partially explain the diversity of empirical findings in regards to the "average" adjustment of the child with cancer is the often extreme heterogeneity of patients in terms of time since diagnosis. It is not unusual for studies to combine groups of recently diagnosed children with children on treatment for several years and long-term survivors off treatment. This research strategy is certainly understandable for single site investigations, where accruing adequate numbers of recently diagnosed children may be a daunting task. However, this heterogeneity reduces the precision of the findings and may account for some of the inconsistencies reported in the literature.

In addition to the wide range of time since diagnosis indigenous to a large number of studies on the adaptation of pediatric cancer patients, the inconsistencies across studies may be further explained by the inherent disagreement observed among child, parent, and teacher report measures of adjustment (Achenbach, McConaughy, & Howell, 1987; Hodges, Gordon, & Lennon, 1990; Loeber, Green, Lahey, & Stouthamer-Loeber, 1991; Kashani, Orvaschel, Burk, & Reid, 1985; McConaughy, Stanger, & Achenbach, 1992; Varni & Setoguchi, 1992; Weissman et al., 1987; Worchel et al., 1990). Specifically, the assessment of physically healthy child adjustment based on independently derived information from child, parent, and teacher informants has rather consistently shown a lack of congruence among these three

sources. In a meta-analysis of published studies, a mean correlation of .28 between parents and teachers was found, with a mean correlation of .22 between children's self-ratings and ratings by parents, teachers, and mental health professionals (Achenbach et al., 1987). Agreement among observers has also been found to be lower for internalizing behavior problems (e.g., depression, anxiety, withdrawal) than for externalizing behavior problems (e.g., acting-out, hyperactivity, aggression). Correlations over time by the same informant (e.g., parent) have been shown to be in the $r = .50$ range (McConaughy et al., 1992), indicating greater agreement over time by the same informant than across informants. This discordance among observers of child adjustment has been termed "cross-informant variance" (Varni, Katz, Colegrove, & Dolgin, 1995a).

The findings with physically healthy children that children, parents, and teachers perceive child adjustment differently may help explain some of the disparate results on the adjustment of pediatric cancer patients. Cross-informant variance among child, parent, and teacher reports of child adjustment might account in part for the wide range of adaptation of newly diagnosed children with cancer described in the literature. Further, an empirical understanding of the variability shown across informants and settings (e.g., school versus hospital) in which children are assessed may enhance clinical practice by clarifying the role of child, parent, and teacher report in formulating a comprehensive psychosocial treatment plan.

Given the lack of agreement among reports of child adjustment, Varni et al. (1995a) investigated the concordance among child, parent, and teacher reports of child adjustment in newly diagnosed pediatric cancer patients. Based on the previous literature with physically healthy children, it was expected that the concordance among child, parent, and teacher report would be in the small ($r = .10$) to medium ($r = .30$) effect size range, as statistically defined by Cohen (1988), for internalizing problems, and in the medium to large ($r = .50$) effect size range for externalizing problems. A secondary objective of the study was to investigate the predictive abilities of within-informant report at Time 1 (at diagnosis) to Time 2 (6 months post diagnosis) and Time 3 (9 months post diagnosis). Based on the empirical literature, it was expected that these stability coefficients would be in the medium to large effect size range. This is the first study to investigate cross-informant variance and longitudinal predictive relations between child, parent, and teacher perceptions of child adjustment in newly diagnosed pediatric cancer patients.

Consistent with the general empirical literature for children, the results of the study generally demonstrated small to medium effect sizes ($rs = .10–.50$) across child, parent, and teacher report measures with larger effect sizes observed within informants. The findings indicate the need to take into consideration the perspective of multiple informants in determining the adjustment of children with newly diagnosed cancer. The results demonstrate the *a priori* hypothesized "cross-informant variance" as evidenced by the modest magnitude of correlational effect sizes among child, parent, and teacher perceptions of child adjustment. Predictive correlational stability coefficients within informants were substantially higher than concurrent correlations between informants. These results are consistent with a previous meta-analysis of physically healthy children's adjustment that demonstrated higher concurrent agreement between similar informants than between different types of informants (Achenbach et al., 1987).

Discordance among child, parent, and teacher perceptions of child adjustment has rather clear implications for determining the "true" or "correct" mean adaptation of newly diagnosed children with cancer. Simply put, no one informant should be considered more accurate than another. Rather, these disparate reports of child adjustment reflect differing perceptions based on logical/rational interpretations. For instance, parent and teacher perception of externalizing behavior problems may vary because of situational specificity of behavior between home and school environments. Likewise, variance between child self-perception of depressive and anxious symptoms with parent/teacher report of internalizing behavior problems may reflect the highly subjective intrapersonal nature of these internalizing disorders. Thus, since true differences exist in both children's behaviors in multiple environments and cross-informants' perceptions of child functioning, then the most parsimonious interpretation of these findings suggests that a complete assessment of adjustment must include data from more than one informant whenever possible in determining child adjustment to newly diagnosed cancer. In other words, there is no single source gold standard for determining the adjustment of children with newly diagnosed cancer; rather, the perception of adjustment is inevitably affected by source and situational variables.

These findings may in part explain the often disparate results in the literature on the "average" adjustment of children with cancer. Drawing conclusions of child adjustment from one informant clearly provides only a partial perception of a much more complex construct. The available psychosocial empirical literature has generally provided only single source perceptions of pediatric cancer patient's adjustment, and as the study by Varni et al. (1995a) indicates, this methodology greatly limits the generalizability and validity of any one given study.

The variance observed across child, parent, and teacher report of behavioral/emotional problems and social competence may be a function of not only the observable nature of the problem manifested (e.g., subtle depressive symptoms versus acting-out behavior), but also as a result of other factors such as the informant's familiarity with the child and confidence in his/her assessment (cf. Ines & Sacco, 1992). These factors need to be taken into consideration when evaluating the validity of an informant's perception of child adjustment.

The clinical implications of these findings suggest several paths. Achenbach (1993) has recommended multiaxial empirically based assessment (MEBA). MEBA is a comprehensive assessment of children that incorporates multiple informants such as the children themselves, parents, teachers, clinicians, and objective observers. Inherent informant disagreement is a function of situational variations in children's behavior, informant differences, and variations in the manifestation of internalizing and externalizing behavior problems. Consequently, the MEBA strategy emphasizes the utilization of standardized assessment instruments combining child, parent, and teacher report, as well as clinical interviews and direct observations.

MEBA can facilitate treatment interventions by documenting problems reported by different informants and by identifying problems as cross-situationally consistent or inconsistent. Those symptoms for which there is good agreement across informants would be good candidates for interventions targeting generalized change, for example, teaching children problem-solving skills and having parents and teachers reinforce these prosocial behaviors. Alternatively, disagreements across informants may reflect child behavior under different conditions (e.g., school versus home), or the under-identification by a particular informant (e.g., depressive symptoms missed by a teacher). Thus, the MEBA strategy suggests that problems reported by multiple informants can be targeted for cross-situational interventions (e.g., home and school), whereas those reported by a single source may warrant interventions specific to the situations reported by the informant (e.g., aggressive behavior toward patient's mother by the patient only in the home setting).

Treatment interventions may be designed that focus on adjustment problems identified as cross-situational, or targeted toward situationally specific problems such as classmates' interpersonal relationship difficulties (cf. Varni, Katz, Colegrove, & Dolgin, 1993; Varni, Katz,

Colegrove, & Dolgin, 1994b). Additionally, risk and protective factors conceptual models (cf. Varni & Wallander, 1988; Wallander & Varni, 1992), which often serve to empirically identify targets for treatment research, may be further enhanced by separately predicting child, parent, and teacher report outcome measures (Perrin, Ayoub, & Willett, 1993; Varni, Katz, Colegrove, & Dolgin, 1993; Varni et al., 1994b). Robust predictors may be delineated as those that are significant risk and resistance factors across multiple informant outcome measures. These factors may then be incorporated as targets for cross-situational treatment research. This research strategy of linking cross-informant assessments to conceptually driven treatment models promotes the aim of current psychosocial oncology interventions for children with newly diagnosed cancer, that is, treatment targeted toward enhancing multidimensional quality of life outcome domains (cf. Varni, Katz, & Waldron, 1993).

Family Functioning Predictors

Within the conceptual risk and resistance model proposed by Varni and Wallander (Varni & Wallander, 1988; Wallander & Varni, 1992), family functioning has been hypothesized to be a predictor of child psychological and social adaptation to a pediatric chronic physical disorder. A relatively extensive empirical literature has generally supported the hypothesized relationship between various dimensions of family functioning and child adaptation to chronic illness. However, although the assessment of family functioning in childhood cancer has been studied (e.g., Brown et al., 1992; Fife, Norton, & Groom, 1987), the concurrent and prospective predictive effects of family functioning on the adjustment of children with newly diagnosed cancer had not been previously empirically investigated. The objective of the study by Varni, Katz, Colgrove and Dolgin (1996) was to test the predictive effects of family functioning on the adjustment of children with newly diagnosed cancer. From previous family research by our group and others (Varni, Rubenfeld, Talbot, & Setoguchi, 1989c; Varni, Wilcox, & Hanson, 1988; Wallander, Varni, Babani, & Wilcox, 1989), it was hypothesized that (1) various dimensions of higher family functioning would statistically predict lower psychological distress and higher social competence, (2) among the three underlying domains of family functioning assessed, the relationship dimensions of cohesion, expressiveness, and conflict would be the most consistently predictive of child adaptation, and (3) concurrent family functioning would be more predictive of child adaptation at 6 and 9 months

postdiagnosis than the prospective prediction of child adaptation at these follow-up intervals by family functioning at diagnosis.

Results of the study provided support for the *a priori* conceptual model. Specifically, various dimensions of higher family functioning were significantly correlated with lower psychological distress and higher social competence after controlling for demographic variables. The relationship dimensions of cohesion and expressiveness were the most consistently predictive of child adaptation across both concurrent and prospective associations. Family functioning was more predictive of concurrent child adjustment than prospective child adjustment at six and nine months post diagnosis.

The pattern of results indicated that dimensions of the family psychosocial environment are statistically significant predictors of psychological and social adjustment in children with newly diagnosed cancer. The fact that concurrent prediction was more consistent than prospective prediction suggests that current family functioning is more important for children with newly diagnosed cancer at six and nine months post diagnosis than family functioning at the time of the cancer diagnosis.

The differential findings of the various dimensions of family functioning predictors on the children's adjustment to newly diagnosed cancer suggest the need to measure multiple domains of family functioning for their potential differential influence on psychological and social adjustment rather than simply reporting only a global index that may obscure important and unique associations. The relationship dimensions of family cohesion and expressiveness were the most consistently predictive of psychological adjustment and social competence in both concurrent and prospective analyses. Thus it appears that aspects of the family psychosocial environment that include commitment, help, support, and the open expression of feelings facilitate child adjustment to newly diagnosed cancer and biomedical treatment.

These findings have implications for primary and secondary prevention efforts. A major focus of the study was to attempt to identify potentially modifiable risk and protective factors that might enhance the adjustment of children with newly diagnosed cancer. The results suggest several paths in this regard. Empirical investigations in behavioral family therapy have developed cognitive-behavior therapy techniques with increasingly greater efficacy in resolving family conflict and enhancing family emotional support and problem-solving (Falloon, 1988; Varni & Corwin, 1993). Nonfamilial social support has also been found to significantly predict the adjustment of children with newly diagnosed cancer

(Varni et al., 1994b), and may be enhanced through interpersonal social skills training interventions (Varni, Katz, Colegrove, & Dolgin, 1993). Taken together, the findings emphasize the need to evaluate the adjustment of children with newly diagnosed cancer in the context of the familial and nonfamilial social environment. Families with identified multiple risk factors can be made aware of appropriate interventions to prevent or further treat dysfunction so as to maximize child adjustment to newly diagnosed cancer and biomedical treatment.

Adjustment of Long-Term Survivors

Concerns for the late effects of cancer treatment have become more salient with the increasing survival of children with cancer. Late effects on the cardiovascular, endocrine, gastrointestinal, musculoskeletal, nervous, pulmonary, and genitourinary system, as well as an increased risk of second malignancies, have become evident (Byrd, 1985; DeLaat & Lampkin, 1992). In addition, psychological, social, cognitive, and academic late effects are also emerging in long-term survivors of childhood cancer (see, Copeland, 1992; Koocher, 1985; Lansky, List, Ritter-Sterr, Klopovich, & Chang, 1985). These findings indicate the need for more longitudinal studies of both the medical and psychosocial status of the increasing number of survivors of childhood cancer who are now adolescents or young adults.

Until relatively recently, few data-based studies were published on the long-term psychological and social adjustment of children, adolescents, and young adults who had survived childhood cancer. In general, these empirical investigations suggest that long-term survivors of childhood cancer represent an at-risk group for psychological and social adjustment difficulties (Greenberg et al., 1989; Mulhern et al., 1989). However, the variability observed in adaptation suggests wide individual differences among long-term survivors. This at-risk status in combination with the observed individual variance in adaptation indicates the need to identify accurately the risk and protective factors that may explain these individual differences in adaptation among long-term survivors of childhood cancer.

With the emerging status of childhood cancer as a life-threatening chronic disease, the opportunity now exists to draw upon the relatively large empirical literature on the predictors of adaptation in pediatric chronic physical disorders in identifying the potential risk and protective factors that may be instrumental in determining the observed variability in adaptation among long-term childhood cancer survivors. Preeminent among the potentially *modifiable* risk factors in pediatric chronic physical disorders is the concept of perceived stress (Varni, Rubenfeld, Talbot, & Setoguchi, 1989a; Varni, Rubenfeld, Talbot, & Setoguchi, 1989b; Varni, Setoguchi, Rappaport, & Talbot, 1991). Varni and his associates have found that higher perceived stress predicted higher depressive symptoms and lower general self-esteem in children with chronic physical disorders. These findings of the association of greater levels of perceived stress with increased psychological distress is consistent with the empirical literature in physically healthy children, adolescents, and adults (Compas, 1987; Steptoe, 1991).

A major conceptual influence in the general stress literature has been the cognitive appraisal model set forth by Lazarus and his colleagues (Lazarus & Folkman, 1984). Specifically, in this theoretical framework, the perceived stress paradigm emphasizes the importance of cognitive appraisal in the determination of which events are perceived as stressful by individuals. Stressful appraisals are characterized by threat, challenge, or harm-loss. Thus, it is the meaning of the event, rather than its mere occurrence, that may result in its perception as stressful or benign for any given individual.

Studying the association of perceived stress with multiple adjustment parameters not only may lead to a better understanding of the individual variability in adaptation shown by long-term survivors of childhood cancer, but also may provide the empirical heuristic guidance needed in the development of stress treatment interventions designed to facilitate coping in pediatric cancer patients. Although in the adult cancer research literature perceived stress has been demonstrated to be a prominent factor in the adaptation to cancer (Andersen, 1992), no empirical investigation of perceived stress and adjustment in long-term survivors of childhood cancer had previously been conducted.

Consequently, the objective of the study by Varni, Katz, Colegrove, and Dolgin (1994a) was to investigate the hypothesized psychological adjustment correlates of perceived stress in long-term survivors of childhood cancer. Psychological adjustment factors selected for investigation were identified based on the extant empirical literature, as well as through a logical-rational approach based on experience with pediatric cancer patients. Measures were selected that were both theoretically and empirically related to the perceived stress construct. Based on previous research, it was hypothesized that higher perceived stress would statistically predict higher psychological distress and lower general self-esteem even after controlling for relevant demographic and disease variables.

The results indicated that demographic and medical variables generally explain only a small amount of the variance in the psychological adjustment of the cohort of long-term survivors of childhood cancer studied. Rather, it appeared that perceived stress, a potentially modifiable factor, did explain a significant amount of the variance in adaptation of long-term childhood cancer survivors. Higher perceived stress predicted higher psychological distress and lower general self-esteem after controlling for relevant demographic and medical variables.

The potentially modifiable nature of perceived stress portends well for the development of stress management interventions for long-term survivors of childhood cancer. In recent years, a growing number of stress management studies with adult cancer patients have demonstrated the relative efficacy of cognitive-behavior therapy treatment strategies in ameliorating psychological distress and stress-induced immunosuppression (Andersen, 1992; Bridge, Benson, Pietroni, & Priest, 1988; Davis, 1986; Fawzy, Cousins, Fawzy, Kemeny, Elashoff, & Morton, 1990; Fawzy, Kemeny, Fawzy, Elashoff, Morton, Cousins, Fahey, 1990; Greer et al., 1992; Sabbioni, 1991; Spiegel, Bloom, Kraemer, & Gottheil, 1989; Telch & Telch, 1986). Given that stressful events have been demonstrated to adversely affect a wide range of immune functions (Cohen, Tyrrell, & Smith, 1991; Cohen & Williamson, 1991; Irwin, Daniels, Bloom, Smith, & Weiner, 1987; Kiecolt-Glaser & Glaser, 1992), then adult cancer psychosocial research that has demonstrated enhanced immunocompetence in patients receiving stress management interventions seems particularly provocative for its potential to effect multiple biobehavioral outcomes (Cooper & Watson, 1991). While the emerging field of psychoneuroimmunology, as applied to cancer patients, is still in its early developmental stage, the beneficial effects that may result warrant continued well-controlled stress management research, including investigating the prediction of long-term survival (Fawzy et al., 1993; Spiegel et al., 1989).

Cognitive Functioning in Long-Term Survivors

Over the last 20 years, the introduction of prophylactic central nervous system (CNS) treatment in children with acute lymphocytic leukemia (ALL) has significantly increased survival rates (Sposto & Hammond, 1985). CNS prophylaxis has been a standard component of many ALL treatment protocols, usually consisting of chemotherapeutic agents administered directly into the spinal fluid (i.e., intrathecally) and radiation therapy to the head and spine. Such CNS treatment has proven useful in eliminating the proliferation of leukemia cells in an area that does not appear to be affected by systemically administered chemotherapy, due to the blood-brain barrier (Bleyer, 1981).

Although CNS prophylaxis has improved survival rates in childhood ALL, numerous studies have documented negative sequelae (i.e., late effects) of such treatment, including encephalopathy, neuroendocrine dysfunction, peripheral disturbances, and cognitive impairments (Byrd, 1985; Fletcher & Copeland, 1988; Varni & Katz, 1987; Lansky, List, Ritter-Sterr, Klopovich, & Chang, 1985). The degree to which cognitive functioning is impaired and the specific child characteristics related to the severity of impairment observed are areas of continuing investigation. Early studies evaluating the late effects of cranial radiation on cognitive functioning typically measured cognitive functioning immediately after treatment, whereas more recent studies have retrospectively evaluated long-term cognitive functioning.

In general, these retrospective studies have documented cognitive late effects after cranial irradiation at 2400 cGy (units of absorbed radiation), particularly in children diagnosed at a young age (Fletcher & Copeland, 1988). These cognitive late effects were most apparent three or more years after treatment. The most consistently identified cognitive impairments included visual-spatial difficulties, memory problems, quantitative ability problems, and gross and fine motor speed performance difficulties. Lower overall IQ scores on the Wechsler Intelligence Scales were reported, with significant discrepancies between Verbal and Performance IQs (Performance IQs typically significantly below Verbal IQs). A meta-analysis of the extant literature revealed a mean effect size of -0.67 for 20 studies, with a decrement of about two-thirds of a standard deviation following CNS prophylaxis that includes cranial irradiation (Cousins, Waters, Said, & Stevens, 1988). Other problems observed in these children after treatment included distractibility (short attention span), problem-solving deficits, and apparent learning disabilities (Fletcher & Copeland, 1988). However, since the children in these retrospective follow-up studies were generally not assessed prior to cranial irradiation, conclusions regarding any possible decrement in cognitive functioning scores must be viewed cautiously.

A long-term prospective design allows for more confidence in drawing conclusions regarding cognitive late effects of craniospinal radiation, since each patient serves as their own control. The first prospective study was conducted by Meadows et al. (1981). Twenty-three children with ALL diagnosed between the ages of 2½ and 15 years were administered neuropsychological tests at the time of their diagnosis and 1 to 3 years after their diagnosis. All of these children had received cranial irradiation of 2400 cGy. All the children were administered either the Stanford-Binet or the Wechsler Intelligence Scale for Children–Revised. Results revealed that 33 percent of the children evidenced a decrement of 10 or more points on the Full Scale IQ scores over time. Younger children and children with higher intelligence levels were found to be more at risk than older children and children with average to low intelligence levels. Several additional short-term prospective studies have also appeared in the literature (Moehle & Berg, 1985; Stehbens, Kisker, & Wilson, 1983; Stehbens & Kisker, 1984).

Whereas there is growing evidence that survivors of ALL exhibit cognitive impairment after CNS prophylaxis of 2400 cGy, controlled prospective studies of cognitive functioning four to five years after treatment would be useful in sorting out some of the discrepancies of earlier studies. The lack of control for time since treatment in many of the previous studies may account for the diverse findings reported. Although cognitive impairments may not be detected one year after treatment, cognitive late effects may be evident following a longer time interval posttreatment. If age, pretreatment IQ, and the pre/posttreatment interval relate to the magnitude of the cognitive impairments observed, children at risk for later learning problems may be identified at the most appropriate time for educational interventions.

A prospective longitudinal study by Rubenstein, Varni, and Katz (1990) was one of the first studies to measure long-term cognitive functioning in children receiving the newer protocols incorporating reduced craniospinal irradiation of 1800 cGy. The major research question guiding the design of the present study was whether long-term survivors of ALL who received 1800 cGy of craniospinal irradiation exhibited patterns of performance on a standardized measure of intellectual functioning four to five years after central nervous system treatment that would warrant special education services.

The findings of this long-term prospective study were generally consistent with earlier retrospective studies that documented cognitive impairments in survivors of acute lymphocytic leukemia (ALL) after 2400 cGy of craniospinal irradiation (Cousins et al., 1988; Fletcher & Copeland, 1988). Specifically an effect size of –0.59 was found for the Full Scale IQ scores, a finding quite similar to the –0.67 effect size of a recent meta-analysis of 2400 cGy studies (Cousins et al., 1988). To put these data into a relative magnitude of change perspective, Cohen (1988) has defined an effect size of 0.20 as small, 0.50 as medium, and 0.80 or greater as large. Thus, the major findings of the investigation indicated that, similar to a medium effect size found with 2400 cGy of craniospinal irradiation, 1800 cGy also resulted in cognitive late effects in long-term survivors of childhood leukemia, with a relative magnitude in the medium decrement range for Full Scale IQ over a four- to five-year time interval.

The results indicate the need, on an annual basis, to assess systematically the cognitive and academic achievement of children who have undergone central nervous system (CNS) prophylaxis in order to provide special education services as soon as possible. The pattern of results suggests that children who have received 1800 cGy of craniospinal irradiation are exhibiting specific learning difficulties similar to those of children who have received 2400 cGy. Whereas initial assessment of cognitive functioning is necessary, continued assessment at yearly intervals is crucial. The decrement in cognitive functioning and the signs of specific learning disabilities were not apparent at the one-year posttreatment follow-up but were apparent four to five years after CNS treatment. Clearly, many children who have received cranial irradiation for the treatment of ALL need access to special education services so as to maximize their academic achievement and overall quality of life.

School and Social Reintegration

In order to enhance rehabilitation and long-term adjustment to cancer and its treatment, children with newly diagnosed cancer are encouraged to return to their normal premorbid school and social experiences as soon as medically feasible. School represents the work of childhood and the opportunity for ongoing socialization and social support. Unfortunately, multiple impediments to optimal school and social reintegration have been documented. Following a cancer diagnosis, children face repeated absences from school and peers. They must endure visible side effects of cancer and its treatment, such as hair loss, weight gain or loss, and physical disfigurement, all of which can result in significant negative reactions from peers (Varni, Katz, Colegrove, & Dolgin, 1995b). Specialized academic needs may interact with school staff misconceptions regarding cancer and its medical treatment to negatively affect teacher reactions. The disruption of school participation and accompanying social experiences due to cancer and its treatment has been related to major problems in adjustment and adaptation to the disease (see reviews by Katz, Dolgin, & Varni, 1990; Varni & Katz, 1987) .

For the child newly diagnosed with cancer, continuation of social and academic activities provides an important opportunity to normalize as much as possible a very difficult and ongoing stressful experience. Previous research with pediatric chronic physical disorders suggests that perceived social support may attenuate the negative impact of stressful life events and ongoing chronic strain on psychological adjustment. Specifically, Varni and his associates have empirically demonstrated the importance of perceived social support from parents, teachers, and classmates as predictors of adjustment in children with chronic physical disorders (Varni et al., 1989a; Varni et al., 1989b; Varni & Setoguchi, 1991; Varni & Setoguchi, 1992; Varni & Setoguchi, 1993; Varni et al., 1991; Varni, Setoguchi, Rappaport, & Talbot, 1992). These investigations provide empirical evidence of the potentially powerful effects of the social environment of the school setting, with perceived classmate social support the most significant predictor of depressive symptoms, trait anxiety, and general self-esteem.

Based on these findings, Varni et al. (1993) hypothesized that social skills training may enhance the social competence of children with chronic physical disorders. Social skills training should facilitate positive social interactions with classmates and teachers, resulting ultimately in greater perceived social support from these two essential interpersonal resources in the school environment. Further, these investigators hypothesized that the experimentally induced increase in perceived social support would result in lower socioemotional distress and higher self-esteem. An analysis of the empirical literature indicates general support for the hypothesis that children with peer relationship difficulties are at risk for long-term adjustment problems (Ladd, 1990; Parker & Asher, 1987). Children with chronic physical disorders often experience a disruption in their social relations with classmates and teachers secondary to illness-imposed limitations and extensive medical treatments. The potential, therefore, exists that social skills training may overcome these disruptions in normal social development and potentially prevent later psychological and social adjustment problems.

Although social skills training was not formally investigated, Katz, Rubenstein, Hubert, and Blew (1988)

reported initial findings that suggested the potential efficacy of a school reintegration intervention in facilitating adaptation in children with newly diagnosed cancer. While the school reintegration intervention did include components targeting social interactions, no explicit social skills training program was tested. Thus, even though the Katz et al. (1988) study represents the first empirical investigation of a school reintegration intervention for childhood cancer, the results are tempered by the lack of a randomized controlled design and a wide age range (ages 5 to 17 years), with unequal representation at the different grade levels. The intervention group did score higher on social competence and lower on behavior problems than the no-treatment comparison group. However, the relatively large standard deviations on these measures suggested the presence of substantial individual differences among subjects within the intervention group, indicating the need for further refinement in the treatment intervention. Finally, the design of the study did not allow for a direct evaluation of the social interactions component from the overall school reintegration standard intervention. Nonetheless, the intervention was highly rated by the children, their parents, and teachers, providing support for the social validity of the school reintegration approach (Katz, Varni, Rubenstein, Blew, & Hubert, 1992).

Social skills training may be an important component of the comprehensive psychosocial care of children with cancer because many children have not typically acquired the social competence needed to cope with the stressors associated with their disease (Katz & Varni, 1993). Social skills training is hypothesized to facilitate the adaptation to childhood cancer by teaching the child a set of social skills that are particularly relevant to their current life situation of having to cope with cancer and its treatment. It is further hypothesized that social skills training early in the course of the child's illness and treatment may prevent later adjustment problems associated with the ongoing chronic strain of this life-threatening chronic disease.

It was the purpose of the investigation by Varni, Katz, Colegrove, and Dolgin (1993) to empirically evaluate an explicit social skills training component in facilitating the school reintegration of children with newly diagnosed cancer. The study was designed to address the following research questions: (1) Does explicit social skills training prospectively enhance the psychological and social adjustment of children with newly diagnosed cancer in comparison to the standard school reintegration; and (2) Does explicit social skills training enhance the perceived social support from classmates and teachers in children with newly diagnosed cancer?

Social Skills Training Intervention Program

A structured curriculum was presented, and the children were taught through modeling, behavioral rehearsal, and corrective feedback how to effectively improve their social interactions. The children were shown videotapes that provided concrete examples of the social skills concept being addressed. Parents were encouraged to support their child's attempts to improve their social relations with their peers. The curriculum was comprised sequentially of the following three content modules:

Social Cognitive Problem-Solving: In this module, the child was taught problem-solving skills needed to relate to peers, teachers, siblings, and parents. These skills included identifying the problem, considering the antecedents of the problem, and exploring possible resolutions to the problem.

Assertiveness Training: The child was taught effective communication in this module. Differences among being assertive, aggressive, and passive were demonstrated. Examples included situations involving medical care and treatment as well as school and home activities.

Handling Teasing and Name Calling: This module demonstrated how children can cope with verbal and physical teasing associated with changes in their physical appearance due to medical treatment. Strategies such as giving age-appropriate explanations for physical changes, going to an authoritative adult for support and assistance, and extinguishing inappropriate peer responses through lack of response were taught.

The findings of this empirical investigation indicated that social skills training provides incrementally greater therapeutic effects on child adjustment beyond those found for the standard school reintegration intervention for children with newly diagnosed cancer. Specifically, those children who received social skills training in addition to the standard school reintegration intervention evidenced significantly less internalizing, externalizing, and total behavior problems and significantly greater classmate and teacher social support at the nine-month follow-up compared to pretreatment. In contrast, those children who received the standard school reintegration intervention without social skills training exhibited no significant differences in adjustment between pretreatment and nine months follow-up.

In a subsequent analysis of the nine-month findings, Varni, Katz, Colegrove, and Dolgin (1994b), found that higher perceived classmate social support predicted lower depressive symptoms, lower state anxiety, lower trait anxiety, lower social anxiety, lower internalizing behavior problems, and lower externalizing behavior problems, while higher perceived teacher social support predicted lower externalizing behavior problems. Taken together, the clinical implications of these findings suggest that social skills training with children with newly diagnosed cancer may increase their perceived social support from classmates and teachers, which is associated with lower behavioral and emotional problems.

Psychopharmacologic Intervention

Psychopharmacologic intervention with pediatric cancer patients is indicated in cases of severe depression and anxiety, psychotic reactions, and intractable pain (Maisami, Sohmer, & Coyle, 1985; Pfefferbaum-Levine, DeTrinis, Young, & Van Eys, 1984). Because of the children's physically compromised status as a result of chemotherapy drugs that are toxic to the heart, liver, and kidney, psychotropic medications should be utilized cautiously, prescribed at the minimal effective dose, for short-term relief of severe symptoms, and reserved for patients who have not responded to psychotherapeutic intervention or are in the terminal stages of their disease (Maisami et al., 1985; Pfefferbaum-Levine, Kumor, Cangir, Choroszy, & Roseberry, 1983). Ideally, when psychotropic medications are indicated, they should be combined with an ongoing psychotherapeutic intervention to facilitate maximum effectiveness of the overall treatment plan. Further, potential behavioral side effects of the patient's chemotherapy regimen, such as emotional liability, listlessness, and depressed mood secondary to corticosteroids (Drigan, Spirito, & Gelber, 1992), are taken into consideration given the time-limited effects of these drugs. Finally, psychopharmacologic intervention is clearly indicated for severe procedural anxiety and pain (Green & Kowalik, 1994), and will be discussed in the section on acute procedural pain.

ACUTE PROCEDURAL PAIN

Children's coping and distress during acute painful medical procedures is determined by a host of variables. Each of these variables is a potential point for intervention to reduce child distress. A child with cancer must undergo many repeated acute painful medical treatments. These include finger sticks, intramuscular (IM) and intravenous (IV) injections, lumbar punctures (LP), and bone marrow aspirations (BMA). During an acute painful medical procedure, the child, parents, and medical staff who perform the procedure all have behavioral and psychological predispositions, abilities, physical conditions, and learning histories. These potentially important variables may combine, along with the social interactions and medical events in the treatment room, to influence the coping and distress of all parties involved. The child with a life-threatening illness is anticipating a painful treatment. The child may be influenced by his or her physical state or medications which were administered earlier that day. In addition, the child has a particular temperament, anxiety level, expectations about the procedure, and a history of effective or ineffective coping in similar situations.

Parents in these situations respond to their child and also influence their child by their own behaviors. In acute painful medical situations, we believe that many parents do not know what to do to help their child cope. Approaches that help children cope with a scraped knee on the playground or a disappointment at school may not be beneficial in the medical environment. Particularly during the more intense painful treatments such as the BMA and LP, parents may feel anxious for their child and about their lack of ability to help them. Other parents may manage their own emotions and behave in ways that help their child through the painful procedures. Add to this proximal social environment the potential influence of more distal factors, such as the quality of the parents' marriage, additional stressors on the family, general parenting skills for managing child behavior, and social support and it becomes clear that multiple factors may either directly or indirectly influence children's coping and distress during medical treatment.

Medical staff and treatments also play a role in the distress experienced by the children and parents. Medications administered to reduce children's acute distress may prove beneficial or have countertherapeutic results for any particular child. Staffs' influence also comes from their skill at performing the procedures, their style of interaction, and their own psychological and behavioral predispositions. They may be more or less confident, anxious, and skilled at helping parents and children cope. It should be noted that there are often few, and possibly even confusing, guidelines for parents and medical staff to use when attempting to promote coping by children. In the absence of empirical guidelines, adults often turn to what has worked in other situations when children were distressed, or to clinical lore. These informally selected procedures may prove helpful or may have iatrogenic effects in the medical treatment room.

A theoretical model of the influence of various factors on child coping and distress has been developed. These factors can be divided into more distal psychosocial factors, which exist prior to entering the medical environment, and the proximal social interactions, which occur in the treatment room. Proposed directional pathways are presented. Distal factors influencing parental behavior are also proposed. The exact associations among the factors will change depending on the phase of the medical procedure. Blount and associates' (e.g., Blount et al., 1989; Blount, Sturges, & Powers, 1990) and others' (e.g., Jacobsen et al., 1990) assessment and treatment research has helped clarify the influence of the social environment on children's coping and distress during the different phases of acute painful treatments. However, the influence of only a few of the more distal psychological variables, such as parental anxiety, on children's procedural distress have been explored (e.g., Jay, Ozolins, Elliott, & Caldwell, 1983). Thus far, no investigations in the pediatric oncology area, and few outside this area (Frank, Blount, Smith, Manimala, & Martin, 1995; Greenbaum, Cook, Melamed, Abeles, & Bush, 1988), have evaluated the influence of the more distal psychological variables on parents' behavior during their child's medical treatment. Further, an assessment of the combined effect of these possible predictors on child coping and distress has yet to be done. Such investigations may prove heuristic in the development of new approaches to reducing child distress. Additional treatment approaches may be particularly beneficial for pediatric oncology patients, a population that must undergo repeated painful medical procedures over several years.

Not every child who undergoes a painful medical procedure is in need of coping skills training. Both Zeltzer and LeBaron (1982), and Hilgard and LeBaron (1982) found that 25 percent to 30 percent of the children they assessed were coping satisfactorily with the LPs and BMAs. Our clinical work and research (Blount et al., 1992) supports this observation. Satisfactory coping does not mean an absence of distress during a medical procedure, although some children and parents seem to achieve this. Rather, satisfactory coping means that the event is seen as manageable for both the child and parents, even though it is unpleasant. Learning what distinguishes those children and parents who cope more effectively from those who are highly distressed should be a goal of much of the assessment work in this area.

Assessment Approaches

The focus of this section will be on recent research using direct observation methods. In the initial investigations using direct observation measures for oncology patients undergoing BMAs and LPs, higher distress and more diffuse anxious behaviors over a longer period were observed in younger children during each phase of the medical treatment (Katz, Kellerman, & Siegel, 1980). Around 6 to 7 years of age, children appeared to make a transition in their expression of distress. They, like adolescents, exhibited more self-control, fewer emotional outbursts and fewer anxious behaviors than younger children. No habituation to repeated procedures was evident. Jay et al. (1983) later found a positive association between parental anxiety and children's distress scores. Additionally, there was a positive correlation between children's anxiety and ratings of anticipated and experienced pain. Children displayed less distress after repeated BMAs, although two years was needed to show this effect for the younger children.

Expanding upon previous research that focused exclusively on child distress, the Child-Adult Medical Procedure Interaction Scale (CAMPIS; Blount et al., 1989) was developed to code the interactions of all the people present in the pediatric treatment room, including the staff (physician, nurse), parent (mother, father), and child. Sixteen child codes encompassing distress, coping behaviors and normal talk during a medical procedure and 19 adult behaviors including adult-adult and adult-child verbalizations were utilized on the CAMPIS. The thirty-five CAMPIS codes were combined into the 6 category CAMPIS-R, which includes child coping, distress and neutral behaviors, and adult coping promoting (behaviors associated with child coping), distress promoting (associated with child distress), and neutral behaviors that were not associated with either child coping or distress (Blount et al., 1990)

In the initial study using the CAMPIS (Blount et al., 1989), data were analyzed across phases of the BMA or LP procedures for pediatric oncology patients who were not trained in the use of coping behaviors. The results of sequential analyses indicated that adults' nonprocedural talk and humor *to* the child was most often followed by nonprocedural talk and humor *by* the child. Adults' commands to the child to use coping strategies (typically saying "Breathe") most often resulted in the children using deep breathing, which rarely occurred without repeated coaching. Child distress was most often preceded by adults' reassuring comments, empathic comments, apologies, criticism, and giving control to the child. Also, adults typically attempted to reassure following child distress. Reassurance was the highest frequency adult behavior directed toward the children. Also important to note, adults often took their cues from other adults as to how to interact with each other and with the child. For 11 of the 19 adult behaviors, the most frequent behavior to follow was another adult behaving in the same manner. For example, if a parent observed a nurse distracting the child, the parent often joined in and also distracted the child.

To elaborate, the association between child distress and adults' behaviors of reassurance, empathic comments and apologies to the child could be viewed as interacting with the child in an emotionally solicitous manner (also see Jay, 1988, p. 416). While these adult behaviors may be helpful in some situations, they may cue and reinforce child distress during painful medical procedures, particularly if adults do not prompt child coping behaviors. Bush, Melamed, Sheras and Greenbaum (1986) found a similar association between parental reassurance and child distress. The association between giving control to the child and child distress may initially appear counter-intuitive. Ross and Ross (1988, pp. 93–94) have distinguished between different types of control that may be offered a child. One type is decisional control, such as "would you like the shot in your left or right arm?" Decisional control has limits and does not easily allow for delays. We have not observed decisional control being offered by the adults in our research. Instead, the type of control offered has been behavioral control, usually in the form of "Tell me when you are ready (to begin or resume this painful LP or injection)." Behavioral control over the initiation or resumption of the painful procedure may overwhelm the child, particularly if the child is already distressed. Crying and other forms of distress may be negatively reinforced in this situation due to the temporary avoidance of the painful procedure. At this point, no one is in control. The type of control we advocate for children is cognitive control; children feeling like there are coping behaviors they can perform, probably with adults' prompting, that will help them manage their distress (also see Blount, Davis, Powers, & Roberts, 1991).

The second investigation examined child and adult behavioral variations by phase of medical procedure (Blount et al., 1990; Sturges, Blount, James, Powers, & Prater, 1991). Children's distress increased at the beginning of the anesthetic and did not decrease significantly until after the final painful procedure. Early anticipatory phase distress was highly correlated with distress during the BMA. Although the amount of coping did not vary significantly during the anticipatory, painful, and recovery phases, the types of coping varied dramatically. During the anticipatory phase, children used relatively high levels of distraction (nonprocedural talk and occasionally humor) and low levels of deep breathing. The reverse was true during the painful phases.

Very high correlations were obtained within medical phase between children's use of distraction and breathing, and adults' attempts to distract the child or coach them to breathe. Further, there was a negative association between adults' distracting or coaching the children to use a coping behavior and the children's distress during the anticipatory and painful phases, respectively. Therefore, children's and adults' coping and coping promoting behaviors tended to be phase-specific; distraction was used during the anticipatory phase and breathing during the painful phases.

In the final assessment study (Blount, Landolf-Fritsche, Powers, & Sturges, 1991), subjects were assigned to groups depending on whether the children engaged in high or low proportions of coping behaviors. Results indicated that (a) parents of high coping children engaged in more coping promoting behaviors than the parents of low coping children, (b) high coping children were more likely to cope following adults coping promoting prompts than were the low coping children, and (c) both the high and low coping children were more likely to cope following adult coping promoting behaviors (distraction and coaching) than following any other adult antecedents. Also, both groups were more likely to display distress following adult distress promoting behaviors (reassurance, apologies, empathic statements, criticism, and giving control to the child) than following any other adult statements. These latter findings indicated that the same conversational rules applied for both groups of children, regardless of the absolute level of coping or distress behavior.

The reliability and validity of each of the CAMPIS-R adult and child categories were supported by the correlations between them and the Observation Scale of Behavioral Distress (Jay et al., 1983), the Behavioral Approach-Avoidance and Distress Scale (Hubert, Jay, Saltoun, & Hayes, 1988), and various self-report, parental-report, and staff-report measures (Blount, Manimala, Frank, Bisson, & Smith, 1993). Morrow, Armstrong, Routh, Gay and Levy (1993) and Manne and her colleagues (1992) have adopted several CAMPIS codes, rather than the entire scale, for use in their investigations. In addition, we have used modifications of the CAMPIS in an interval coding format (Cohen, Blount, Panopoulos, & Manimala, 1995; Manimala et al., 1995) and when coding only from videotapes (Cohen et al., 1995).

In several assessment studies, Manne, Jacobsen, Redd, and their colleagues (Jacobsen et al., 1990; Manne et al., 1992) examined the dyadic interactions of parents and their children during their IV injections. Nurse behaviors during the medical procedures were not observed. The results of the first investigation (Jacobsen et al., 1990) indicated that the timing of parents giving procedural explanations (information) to the children may be important. Children who were distressed during the anticipatory phase who were given explanations did better during the injection phase than similarly distressed children who were not given explanations. However, children who were not distressed during the anticipatory phase and were not provided with explanations did better during the injection than similarly nondistressed children who were provided explanations. Explanations to distressed children during the injection did little good, and may have made the children more distressed. In the second assessment study from this group, Manne et al. (1992) found that distraction was the only parent behavior that was both positively related to child coping and negatively related to distress. Also, parents' praise was unlikely to be followed by distress. Giving decisional control to the child, such as "Which hand do you want me to look at first?" (p. 248), was associated with less crying and screaming during the injection.

In summary, the assessment of relevant variables during the BMAs, LPs, and IM and IV injections has become more complex and complete. Through pioneering work done in the early 1980s, valid and reliable measures of the intensity of acute child distress have been developed. However, child coping behaviors are also relevant dependent variables and, until recently, their occurrence during the medical procedure had not been monitored. In addition, the literature increasingly points to the influence of adults' behaviors in the treatment room on child distress and coping. However, the amount of effort required for comprehensive assessments might prove prohibitive for some investigations. Therefore, we recommend focusing on those parent and medical staff behaviors that have been shown to be associated with child distress and coping, as well as on child coping and distress behaviors, as the minimum requirements for a sufficiently comprehensive assessment instrument.

A primary goal of assessment research should be to aid in the development of better interventions to reduce child distress. This means that results from the assessment studies should be utilized in treatment intervention research in order to experimentally validate the findings. Assessment research that does not eventually assist in either the identification of children in need of training or in the design of therapeutic interventions is of limited clinical value (also see Roberts, 1992, p. 798). From the studies reviewed above, parent and child anxiety (Jay et al., 1983), reassurance, apologies, empathic statements, and criticism (Blount et al., 1989); giving the child different types of control (Blount et al., 1989; Manne et al., 1992; Ross & Ross, 1988); distraction and coaching the child to use coping behaviors (Blount et al., 1989; Blount et al., 1990; Manne et al., 1992), and explanations (Jacobsen et al., 1990) are potential behavioral variables influencing child distress that should be manipulated experimentally.

The movement of the field toward more comprehensive models of acute child distress means that the associations among additional variables will need to be examined. As the conceptual model broadens, additional proximal/social and distal/psychosocial variables may emerge as having some influence on child distress and coping. Some of these variables may have a direct effect on child behavior, while others may influence child distress and coping indirectly through parent or staff behavior.

Cognitive-Behavioral Treatment

In their Report of the Subcommittee on the Management of Pain Associated With Procedures in Children With Cancer, Zeltzer et al. (1990) recommended that "psychologic preparation of the child and parents for procedures should become part of the 'induction' phase of treatment" (p. 826). Psychological preparation includes information provision, coping skills for the parents and children, and behavioral rehearsal. We should note that there are no known physiological or psychological risks from psychological preparation and that there is now a considerable body of research supporting its efficacy. Brief reviews of the older research using hypnosis and cognitive-behavioral interventions will be presented first, followed by more recent research using cognitive-behavioral approaches. For reviews of the older treatment research, see Blount, Davis, et al. (1991) and Jay (1988).

There is no single hypnosis treatment for children's acute procedural distress. However, regardless of the hypnotic technique used, all seem to rely on concentrated imaginal involvement as a form of distraction. In addition, suggestions for mastery or particular cognitive coping behaviors are often provided. The consensus from the studies using hypnosis is that the techniques have been useful in reducing children's procedural distress. Hypnosis was shown to be as effective (Katz, Kellerman, & Ellenberg, 1987; Kuttner, 1988; Wall & Womack, 1989) or more effective (Zeltzer & LeBaron, 1982) than distraction or a nonmedical play condition. Distraction seemed to be more effective than hypnosis in only one study of 7- to 11-year-old children (Kuttner, Bowman, & Teasdale, 1988). The effects of hypnosis may be more immediate than those produced by dis-

traction, at least in some cases for younger children (Kuttner et al., 1988). However, any advantage for hypnosis over distraction seems to diminish or disappear after repeated training sessions, even for the younger children. This suggests that nonhypnotic distraction should be considered as a skill that children may develop more fully after several training sessions.

The best known cognitive-behavioral program for reducing children's distress was developed by Jay and colleagues (e.g., Jay, Elliott, Katz, & Siegel, 1987; Jay, Elliott, Woody, & Siegel, 1991). This treatment package combines filmed modeling, breathing exercises, imagery/distraction, incentives, rehearsal, and therapist's coaching during the medical treatment. Jay et al. (1987) compared the effectiveness of their training program to diazepam administration and a no-treatment condition. The coping skills program resulted in less child distress during BMAs when compared to the control condition. In contrast, children who were administered .3 mg/kg of diazepam 30 minutes before the BMA did not have lower distress scores than children in the control condition. However, diazepam was found to result in lower distress scores than the control condition during the anticipatory phase.

The combination of the cognitive-behavioral program plus .15 mg/kg of oral diazepam was later compared to the cognitive-behavioral program alone (Jay et al., 1991). Both interventions resulted in lower OSBD, heart rate, and self-reported pain scores during the BMAs and LPs when compared to baseline. There were no differences between the two conditions, indicating that small dosages of oral diazepam provide no measurable therapeutic benefit beyond that of the cognitive behavioral intervention alone. Trends in OSBD scores suggested that pre-procedural administrations of oral diazepam may have iatrogenic effects when compared to the cognitive-behavior therapy program alone. More research needs to be done to evaluate this possible outcome.

Manne et al. (1990) used a behavioral intervention to reduce distress for 23 3- to 9-year-old children undergoing venipuncture injections for chemotherapy. The treatment consisted of having the child blow a party blower while the parent counted to pace the rate of blowing, and giving stickers to the child for holding still during the IV and for using the party blower. The intervention was provided approximately 10 minutes before the injection. Results indicated that distress was lower than during baseline.

In Blount and associates' treatment research with leukemia patients undergoing painful medical procedures (Blount, Powers, Cotter, Swan, & Free, 1994; Powers, Blount, Bachanas, Cotter, & Swan, 1993), an empirically guided, matching-to-sample type of approach was used to aid in the selection of therapeutic interventions. The coping skills intervention was designed to teach the children to use the behaviors that the untrained children and parents in the assessment studies (e.g., Blount et al., 1989; Blount et al., 1990) found to be incompatible with distress. Training initially focused on promoting nonprocedural talk and deep breathing. However, nonprocedural talk proved difficult to train, with long silences ensuing even after a list of conversational topics had been prepared with parents' input. Also, these young children had a difficult time using deep breathing. Therefore, toys, books, and so on were used to prompt distracting interactions between the parent and child in the treatment room prior to the medical procedures. In addition, the use of a party blower was adopted to replace deep breathing. Training consisted of providing a rationale to the parents about the effects of distraction on distress; modeling of toy play, use of the blower, and parental distraction and coaching; and behavioral rehearsal of coping and coping promoting behaviors during a BMA/LP role play. Repeated role plays, feedback and praise were provided until the child and parent(s) were proficient and until the child ceased to flinch when touched on the back with pretend medical equipment during the role play. Results indicated that all children and parents changed in the therapeutic direction on all variables.

Powers and colleagues (1993) used a variation of the previously described training package to teach four 3- to 5-year-old oncology patients and their parents to use an active distraction procedure prior to, and blowing or counting during, IM or IV injections. A multiple baseline design was used. Coping skills training consisted of two to four intensive training sessions, followed by two to four maintenance promoting sessions and several true maintenance sessions. Intensive training lasted approximately 45 minutes and was taught through three components. First, a trainer modeled parent coping promoting behavior while another trainer held a doll and engaged in low distress and appropriate coping behaviors. Next, children gave the doll a pretend injection while the trainer held the doll and engaged in active distraction and use of the blower or counting aloud, depending on the child's preference. Finally, the parent and child practiced coping promoting and coping skills during three rehearsals. One trainer coached the family while the other assumed the role of the nurse and performed the pretend medical procedures. In the maintenance promoting sessions, the trainers led the family through an abbreviated coping skills practice. In the true maintenance sessions, no training was provided. Trainers did not accompany the families during the medical treatment. Toys, blowers,

books, and so on were available in the treatment room during each session. The CAMPIS-R, nurse ratings of distress and cooperation, and parents' ratings of their child's fear and pain served as dependent variables. Results indicated that parents' coaching and children's coping increased, while children's distress decreased. Also, nurses rated the children as more cooperative during and after training. Maintenance was assessed and found for three of the children. Although the treatments were successful, Powers and colleagues point out that not all trained children at all times maintained their behavior change following, or even during, training. They note that the "trying to cope most of the time and being distressed occasionally" pattern may be optimal outcome, given the multiple sources of variability that are inherent in the display of children's procedural distress.

In summary, cognitive-behavioral techniques have proven useful for reducing procedural distress experienced by pediatric oncology patients. The interventions have included varieties of distraction, deep breathing, using a blower, filmed modeling, imagery, incentives, role play, feedback and praise. Also, desensitization likely results from the role play during the coping skills training programs. The range of dependent variables was broadened in some of the treatment studies to include child coping (Blount et al., 1994; Powers et al., 1993) and other parent behaviors such as coaching (Blount et al., 1994; Manne et al., 1990; Powers et al., 1993) during the medical treatment. Maintenance of treatment gains has been found in the studies by Manne et al. (1990), Powers et al. (1993), and Blount et al. (1994).

Research consistent with the model presented in the overview to this section may help identify other more distal psychosocial variables that either directly or indirectly influence child coping and distress. Some of these variables may be modifiable, resulting in additional positive effects on child coping and distress. In addition to the possibility of further reductions in children's procedural distress, a broader treatment approach may lead to greater maintenance, more efficient treatment delivery, the availability of alternative treatment approaches for some children, and reduced distress for parents and staff. Therefore, research in this area should seek both to refine current coping skills treatment approaches and to consider broader paradigms of pediatric pain in the design of therapeutic interventions.

There has been a move from hypnosis to more behaviorally oriented coping skills programs as the treatments of choice. However, the results of the treatment comparison studies do not generally indicate the superiority of coping skills over hypnosis. Several hypotheses for this paradigm shift are apparent. First, there may be some negative mystique associated with being hypnotized. Parents, medical staff, and even children may have misgivings about the technique. These misgivings, combined with the increased availability of more straightforward coping skills training programs, may have led to fewer investigations using hypnosis. Second, many of the people who were conducting the hypnosis studies are no longer involved in those areas of research. The research on acute pain experienced by pediatric oncology patients has been conducted by a small number of people. The paradigms of those few investigators help dictate the types of studies produced. Finally, teaching adults to use cognitive behavioral coping skills to coach children in the treatment room seems much more feasible than teaching those adults to be good hypnotherapists. By incorporating parents and staff as coaches, there is an increased likelihood of generalization of child coping across time and, potentially, to other settings. In terms used by Stokes and Baer (1977), adults can serve as the "common stimuli" to prompt the desired child behaviors when the experimenters are not present. However, achieving maintenance of adults' coaching behaviors is not necessarily an easy task.

Pharmacological Treatment

Various pharmacological and psychological interventions were suggested by the Subcommittee on the Management of Pain Associated With Procedures in Children With Cancer (Zeltzer et al., 1990) for children who must undergo LPs, BMAs, and IV and IM injections. Due to developmental factors, recommendations differ among the age groups. At the time of the subcommittee's report, local anesthesia in the form of a 1 percent lidocaine application was recommended across age groups and procedures. The following is a summarization of their recommendations for the LPs and BMAs. For children less than 6 months old, suggestions for preparation included assuring the infant was calm prior to the procedures. For 6- to 24-month-old children, parental contact during the procedure was recommended, along with sedation if necessary. Recommendations for the 2- to 5-year-old children were for distraction along with providing information to the child about what to expect during the procedures, and also sedation if necessary. After the first BMA for the 5- to 12-year-old children, sedation was suggested if necessary. However, a local anesthetic and behavioral intervention was deemed sufficient for many children in this age range. Similar recommendations were made for the

adolescents as for the older children. Despite the subcommittees' guidelines (Zeltzer et al., 1990), in our experience effective psychosocial interventions are often seen as more of an adjunctive, rather than as an integral, part of the treatment plan to reduce suffering during painful procedures.

Since the 1990 guidelines, another local anesthetic, EMLA, has been receiving increasing popularity (for a review, see Buckley & Benfield, 1993). EMLA is a 5 percent eutectic mixture of the local anesthetics lidocaine and prilocaine. It may be applied in cream or patch form and the general recommendations are that it remain in place for 60 minutes prior to the invasive procedure, though the time required for adequate anesthesia, as well as the duration of anesthesia, varies with the body site (Arendt-Nielsen, Bjerring, & Nielsen, 1988). In one study of 12 healthy adults, the maximum depth of anesthesia with EMLA applied to the dorsal side of the forearm was 5 mm (Bjerring & Arendt-Nielsen, 1990). There may be racial differences in the degree and rapidity of anesthesia obtained. Following application of EMLA, Hymes and Spraker (1986) found that African-Americans reported a higher amount of pain to a pin-prick than Caucasians when using self-reports of pain intensity. The most frequent physical complications include pallor or blanching of the skin and erythema. However, these effects typically resolve within 2 hours (Buckley & Benfield, 1993). There has been a case report of methemoglobinemia in a 3-month-old infant who, after a 5-hour application of EMLA, became cyanotic (Jakobson & Nilsson, 1985). Determining the cause of this reaction was difficult because the child was also receiving other medication at the time. However, because of iatrogenic effects, the use of EMLA is not recommended in infants less than 6 months of age (e.g. Buckley & Benfield, 1993).

The utility of EMLA has been supported in a number of investigations of children and adults undergoing a variety of acute painful medical procedures. For children, the bulk of the research has been conducted on pain responses to venipuncture or venous cannulation (e.g., Joyce, 1993; Molodecka, Stenhouse, Jones, & Tomlinson, 1994). There have been two investigations and one clinical report of children's reactions to LPs following EMLA-induced anesthesia. The clinical report (Price, 1988) indicated that in the six preceding years, EMLA had been used over 100 times and in over 75 percent of the LPs performed with pediatric oncology patients. No ill effects were noted. Halperin et al. (1989) also reported the use of EMLA during venipunctures, Port-A-Cath injections, and LPs for children with cancer. In their study of response to venipunctures, a double-blind placebo-controlled trial was conducted using 18 children, aged 6 to 12 years. The placebo or EMLA was placed 30 to 175 minutes prior to the venipuncture and then removed, wiped dry and sterilized 1 to 20 minutes prior to the IV. Pain was scored using a self-reported visual analogue scale (VAS) responses ranging from 0 (no sensation) to 10 (worst pain imaginable). Results for the EMLA and placebo treated groups were means of 2.8 and 6.8, respectively, with longer periods of EMLA application being associated with lower VAS pain scores. Eight children, ages 6 to 15 years, participated in the investigation of responses during Port-A-Cath injections. Each subject served as his or her own control in this double-blind investigation. The mean pain scores were 1.2 for EMLA and 3.9 for the placebo. For the investigation of responses to LPs, 14 children ages 5.5 to 15.3 years served as subjects. As in the previous investigation, a double-blind, crossover design was used, whereby each subject serves as his or her own control during successive LPs. The mean pain scores for the EMLA condition were 1.9 and for the placebo condition, 5.6. Twelve of the fourteen children preferred EMLA over the placebo. In about a third of the children, minor skin irritation following EMLA application occurred and persisted for up to 3 hours.

Kapelushnik, Koren, Solh, Greenberg, and DeVeber (1990) conducted two investigations of the efficacy of EMLA. In the first study, EMLA was compared to no-treatment for 18 children ranging in age from 5 to 15 years (mean = 9.2). EMLA was applied 45 to 60 minutes prior to the LP. All children gave their responses on a 100 mm VAS, with response options ranging from 0 (no pain) to 4 (most pain imaginable). Mean scores were 2.55 and 1.66 for the no-treatment and EMLA conditions, respectively. Parents and nurses also rated the EMLA condition as less painful for the children, although 6 parents and 5 nurses could not detect a difference. In the second study, a double-blind placebo-control was used, with 10 children serving as their own controls on successive LPs. In this investigation, the results still favored EMLA on self-report and nurse report measures of children's pain, though the differences were not as striking. For the 2 youngest of the 10 children, both they and the nurses rated the pain during the placebo condition as less than in the EMLA condition. The authors suggested that it is often difficult to separate pain from other forms of distress during medical procedures, particularly for younger children.

In summary, both of these investigations support the utility of EMLA as a topical anesthetic for pediatric oncology patients undergoing painful medical procedures. However, in each of the investigations, the efficacy of EMLA was supported only by self-report and global ratings by adults present during the procedures. The importance of a placebo control is indicated in the investigation by Kapelushnik et al. (1990). Thus far, for children with cancer, there has not yet been investigations of EMLA versus, or in combination with, behavioral coping skills interventions, such as were conducted by Jay and her colleagues (1987, 1991) when evaluating the effectiveness of diazepam. The only investigation of EMLA versus distraction, as well as a placebo condition, used 180 four- to 16-year-old children undergoing general anesthesia via intravenous cannulation (Arts et al., 1994). On self-report and global behavior ratings completed by the investigators, EMLA was superior to the placebo and the distraction condition, but only for the 4- to 6-year-old children. Statistically insignificant trends favored the EMLA condition for the 7- to 11-year-old children, with even smaller differences found for the 12- to 16-year-old children. Unfortunately, the distraction condition was relatively weak and consisted of the children listening to contemporary music through earphones. In fact, the weak distraction condition was not superior to the placebo condition on any measure for any age group. Use of a more potent coping skills intervention is called for in similar treatment comparison studies with pediatric oncology patients and other children undergoing painful procedures.

In some cases for highly distressed children, midazolam, a benzodiazepine, has been used to reduce the distress of children undergoing LPs and BMAs. Midazolam (Versed, Roche Laboratories) is a sedative with anterograde amnesic qualities (Public Health Service, 1994). It has a rapid onset, short duration, and short half-life of 1 to 4 hours (Sievers, Yee, Foley, Blanding, & Berde, 1991). It is not an analgesic, and is therefore sometimes used in conjunction with opioids such as morphine or fentanyl. Because of the possibility of respiratory suppression, it is important to follow published pediatric guidelines for the use of conscious sedation, including having available oxygen, suction, self-inflating resuscitation bag, naloxone, and other appropriate resuscitative equipment. In addition, a pulse oximeter should be used, along with someone to attend to the child's level of consciousness, respiratory rate and effort, skin color and oxygen saturation (Zeltzer et al., 1990).

Midazolam has been compared in a double-blind study to a placebo in 23 children with acute lymphocytic leukemia undergoing LPs or BMAs (Friedman et al., 1991). All children had previously experienced high levels of pain from the procedures. Patients, physicians and parents judged the midazolam group to be less distressed than controls during and after the procedures. Observers coded fewer pain and anxiety-related behaviors prior to and after the procedures for the midazolam condition, but not during the procedures. As indicated by a visual recall/recognition test, the amnestic effects of midazolam seemed to be responsible for the beneficial effects. No adverse reactions were noted.

In a double-blind crossover study (Sandler et al., 1992), midazolam was compared in safety and efficacy with fentanyl. The twenty-five 3- to 21-year-old patients were diagnosed with leukemia or lymphoma and were to undergo LPs or BMAs. There were statistically insignificant changes in preprocedural anxiety, adverse behavioral symptoms, anticipated pain, and VAS pain scores in most patients in either medication condition from prior to the introduction of midazolam or fentanyl. In fact, OSBD distress scores actually increased somewhat for the midazolam condition and decreased only slightly for those subjects receiving fentanyl. Of the 25 subjects, 72 percent preferred midazolam. Total amnesia was obtained following 91 percent of the procedures using midazolam and 35 percent of the procedures using fentanyl. Two patients (8 percent) experienced hallucinations while receiving midazolam.

In another investigation of both beneficial and undesirable effects, midazolam was used either alone or in combination with fentanyl or morphine (Sievers et al., 1991). Twenty-four 1.5- to 15.5-year-old pediatric cancer patients undergoing 70 LPs or BMAs served as subjects. The OSBD was used to monitor distress upon entry into the treatment room. Distress scores were insignificantly higher for the combined medication group with OSBD means of approximately 11 (range from near 0 to 21). For the midazolam only group, the mean was approximately 8 with a range from 0 to approximately 16. While the OSBD was not coded *during* the procedure, 20 percent of the subjects required "much" restraint while 35 percent of the children required "some" restraint. Although no comparison sample was provided, these figures seem relatively high. No indication is given as to the distribution of restraint between the experimental conditions. The mean oxygen saturation in each of the 70 procedures was 95 percent, with a range of 67 percent to 100 percent. There was a 13 percent incidence of hypoxemia (oxygen saturation $\leq$ 90 percent) during the procedures. In 14 percent of the procedures, verbal stimulation to take deep breaths was needed. Two patients (8 percent of sample) required face-mask oxygen due to decreased oxygen saturation and lack of response to verbal stimulation. For these two children, their lowest oxygen saturation was 67 per-

cent and 82 percent. Hypoxemia was unrelated to opioid use. Hypoxemia appeared to be related to total midazolam dose, and it could occur even with normal respiratory rate. There was a significant mean decrease in systolic blood pressure of 7.9 to 8.9 mmHg at each 15-min interval following the last dose of midazolam. However, no instances of hypotension were noted. Total amnesia was reported in 62 percent of the cases, partial amnesia in 28 percent, and full recall in 10 percent. The level of amnesia was not related to total dose of midazolam adjusted for weight.

As is true with EMLA, to our knowledge no test of the effectiveness of midazolam versus or in combination with coping skills programs has been undertaken. Such investigations should include multiple sources of measurement of behavior prior to, during, and after the procedure, as well as during the hours that follow. Also, physiological and behavioral data should be obtained. The side-effects from midazolam primarily include hypoxemia and apnea, with some patients reporting hallucinations. In addition, there have been a number of deaths associated with the use of midazolam, often in combination with opioids (Bailey et al., 1990). Further, one of the recommendations of the subcommittee presented above (Zeltzer et al., 1990) was that sedation or general anesthesia should be used for the first BMA for the 5- to 12-year-old children. The utility of this recommendation for reducing anticipatory anxiety during subsequent procedures should be investigated empirically.

Future Directions

There are a number of directions for future research in the area of acute pain experienced by pediatric oncology patients and by other pediatric populations. The most obvious is to develop more effective interventions. Cognitive refocusing is a common component and one of the essential ingredients of all the cognitive-behavioral treatments reviewed. Developing treatments that help assure greater distraction during the painful procedure seems to be a promising approach. Second, incorporating medical staff as coaches for the child or parent should be attempted. Staff might cost-effectively coach children and cue parents to do the same. Third, consistent with previous guidelines (Zeltzer et al., 1990), it should become a priority in pediatric oncology clinics that coping skills programs should be available for children who need them. Fourth, evaluating the effects of medications, such as EMLA and midazolam, for children undergoing painful treatments should be done when they are used in conjunction with, and when compared to, the effects of potent coping skills programs. These types of investigations might result in the development of criteria for matching particular pharmacological and/or psychological treatments to the unique characteristics of the child and family. It is possible that some children may cope better and some worse when under the influence of a sedative. It will be especially important in investigations using pharmacological interventions that children's responses be assessed for longer periods in order to determine side effects. Thus far, behavioral researchers have focused on the several minutes before, during, and after the medical procedure. That discrete time frame has made treatment and assessment research more feasible. However, longer follow-up is needed in general, but especially when evaluating the effects of pharmacological interventions. Further, an evaluation of physiological side effects is particularly important when comparing coping skills programs versus midazolam and/or fentanyl. Hypoxemia, apnea, and hallucinations (Sievers et al., 1991), as well as death (Bailey et al., 1990), have been associated with the use of midazolam, but not with coping skills interventions. These unwanted events may be considered as low frequency, but high impact, iatrogenic events. Because of these events, guidelines such as those proposed by the Subcommittee on the Management of Pain Associated With Procedures in Children With Cancer (Zeltzer et al., 1990) should be revised periodically as new data become available on the costs, risks and effectiveness of various psychological and pharmacological treatment approaches.

An additional goal of the cognitive behavioral treatment research should be the promotion of the long-term maintenance of adults' coping promoting and children's coping behaviors during acute painful procedures, particularly with pediatric oncology patients who undergo many painful procedures over long periods of time. Similarly, there are other dimensions of generalization, such as children and parents using their coping and coping promoting skills during other painful medical treatments, which should be promoted and assessed. Finally, after the eventual development of safe, cost-effective, empirically validated coping skills programs and guidelines, interventions should be widely disseminated to oncology and other medical clinics in order to assist a greater number of children (Blount, 1987).

Children's coping and distress during acute painful medical procedures is determined by a host of variables. Each of these variables is a potential point for intervention to reduce child distress. A child with cancer must undergo many repeated acute painful medical treatments. These include finger sticks, intramuscular (IM) and intravenous (IV) injections, lumbar punctures (LP), and bone marrow aspirations (BMA). During an acute painful medical procedure, the child, parents, and medical staff who perform the procedure all have behavioral and psychological predispositions, abilities, physical conditions, and learning histories. These potentially important variables may combine, along with the social interactions and medical events in the treatment room, to influence the coping and distress of all parties involved. The child has a life-threatening illness and is anticipating a painful treatment. The child may be influenced by his or her physical state or medications that were administered earlier that day. In addition, the child has a particular temperament, anxiety level, expectations about the procedure, and a history of effective or ineffective coping in similar situations.

Case Illustration

Clinical Presentation

Nicole was a 4.5-year-old black girl from a lower SES group who had been diagnosed as having acute lymphocytic leukemia for approximately 1 month. She had received one BMA and two LPs prior to beginning baseline observations. She was referred for training by medical staff because she displayed more distress than other leukemia patients during BMAs and LPs.

Assessment Findings

During four baseline sessions, Nicole and her family were observed. Typically, there was little interaction between her and her parents prior to the medical procedures. When the staff entered, the parents usually would focus on the staff member and interact with him or her. During the invasive medical procedure, her parents might help in positioning Nicole or attempt to offer some support and stand near her while she was held.

Treatment Selection and Course

For five sessions, coping skills training was conducted in an area away from the medical treatment room on the morning prior to the medical treatment. During the first day of training, Nicole and her parents were provided a rationale for training, and were provided modeling, rehearsal, guided feedback, and praise for their performance. Initially, the trainers tried to teach Nicole and her parents to talk about topics related to their daily lives and to use deep breathing. However, long silences occurred, thus the family was instructed to interact around toys, coloring and reading books, and other conversation as desired. Also, Nicole could not easily use deep breathing techniques, nor would she blow on a pinwheel, even with prompting. For that reason, a party blower was substituted.

Two trainers were used during the first training session. One stayed with the family and prompted and praised their performance. The other wore a lab coat and assumed the role of the physician or nurse who performed the procedure. An attempt was made to interact in a way consistent with medical personnel. The trainer pretending to be the medical staff member left the family to allow them to practice interacting in a distracting manner with the toys, books, and so on for several minutes. That person returned with a toy syringe and a wet paper towel. The "staff member" then greeted the family, made small talk for a few seconds, and asked Nicole to get on the couch for the pretend procedures. Nicole was told that no real needles would be used and was shown the materials. Her shirt or dress was pulled up, the area on the back was cleaned, the pretend shot given, a needle was supposedly inserted for the LP, the drops of spinal fluid were collected, chemotherapy was injected, the needle was withdrawn, and a Band-Aid was supposedly applied. Nicole and her family were told what was happening at each point, mimicking the talk from the medical personnel. During this time, the other trainer coached the family to distract Nicole, to minimally attend to the staff member when they entered the room and to tell Nicole to "breathe" or "blow" during the pretend procedures (at least until the spinal fluid was collecting, during which time the family was usually quieter). Even though Nicole was assured that the staff member was not using real medical equipment, she would flinch and withdraw, sometimes dramatically, from the cloth and pretend needle during the first trial. Training continued from 30–45 minutes over several trials until she ceased to flinch noticeably and until the family members performed the desired coping or coping promoting behaviors. At the conclusion of the first training session, Nicole was given a small gift-wrapped toy. On subsequent training sessions, an abbreviated training program was used that lasted 10–25 minutes.

During the actual medical procedures, one trainer accompanied the family while the medical treatment occurred. He typically stood in the corner and provided a few prompts to the parents or child to perform the desired coping behaviors. Toys, coloring books, dolls, and a blower for the child and parent(s) were placed in the medical treatment room.

Two maintenance sessions were conducted 1.5 and 4 months following training. These sessions consisted of making toys, books, and blowers available in the medical treatment room as before. No training occurred and the trainer did not accompany the family during the medical procedures.

Results indicated that Nicole's parents engaged in fairly low rates of Coping Promoting (CP) behaviors during baseline (X = 2.6/minute; Range = 1.9 to 3.2). For the most part, baseline coping promoting behaviors consisted of Nicole's mom saying "Breathe, Nicole." However, this was ineffectual, as Nicole never demonstrated the ability to breathe deeply during the baseline phase. It is likely that this behavior helped her mother manage her own distress. Nicole's parents showed an immediate increase in their rate of CP behaviors during training (X = 8.35/minute; Range = 3.7 to 18.5). The rate of CP during maintenance sessions remained high, with rates of 8.7 and 12.2 per minute.

Nicole engaged in near zero rates of coping during baseline (X = .38/minute; Range = 0 to .9). She showed an increase in coping during the first three training sessions, but that increase was smaller than desired. Her rates during those sessions were 3.2, .95, and 2.7 Coping behaviors per minute, respectively. She was a young child and had difficulty using the party blower during these sessions. She used the party blower easily and readily during the fourth and remaining sessions, with a substantial increase in her rate of Coping behaviors. The rates were 17 and 11.8 per minute during the next two training sessions. During maintenance, she continued to increase her rate of Coping, with rates of 17.8 and 23 times per minute.

Nicole's baseline mean OSBD distress score was 15.8 (Range = 10.3 to 20.7) and her baseline mean rate of CAMPIS Distress behavior was 11.7/minute (Range = 6.8 to 16). During training, she showed an immediate and fairly consistent drop to a mean OSBD score of 6.3 (Range = 3.1 to 11.7) and a mean rate of CAMPIS Distress of 5.9 (Range = 3.3 to 8.7). Nicole's distress maintained below baseline levels during the maintenance phase. Physical restraint was required in the following percentage of 15-sec. intervals from session 1 to 11: 14, 18, 15, and 34 percent (the four baseline sessions); 3, 0, 21, 8, and 0 percent (the five treatment sessions); and 8 and 6 percent (maintenance sessions). Thus, the coping skills intervention proved to be helpful in reducing Nicole's distress to tolerable levels.

ANTICIPATORY NAUSEA AND VOMITING

Accompanying the increased survival rate associated with pediatric cancer treatment have been side effects that have resulted from cytotoxic treatment protocols. The most serious and distressing side effects of pediatric cancer treatment are nausea and vomiting (Coates, 1986; Zeltzer, Dolgin, LeBaron, & LeBaron, 1991; Zeltzer, LeBaron, & Zeltzer, 1984). Nausea and vomiting (NV) not only cause physical changes such as dehydration, electrolyte imbalance, and poor nutrition (Cotanch, Hockenberry, & Herman, 1985; Zoubek, Dronberger, Puschmann, & Gadner, 1993), but may also produce psychological/behavioral sequelae (Burish, Snyder, & Jenkins, 1991; Carey & Burish, 1988; Carr et al., 1985). Perhaps the most important behavioral side effect resulting from therapy-related nausea and vomiting is *anticipatory* nausea and vomiting (AN/AV).

Anticipatory nausea and vomiting appears approximately 24 hours before children receive chemotherapy and results from the association of emetogenic chemotherapeutic agents and postchemotherapy nausea and vomiting associated with these treatments (Blasco, 1994). Specifically, according to the classical conditioning paradigm, after one or more pairings, an association is established between the pharmacological side effects of nausea/vomiting (unconditioned response or UCR) produced by the chemotherapy (unconditioned stimulus or UCS) and the sights, smells, and tastes (conditioned stimulus or CS) associated with the treatment setting. As a result of repeated pairings of the CS and UCS, the CS (e.g., sights and smells of the treatment setting) elicits nausea and vomiting (conditioned response or CR) in the absence of the chemotherapy (UCS) (Carey & Burish, 1988). Specific conditioned stimuli may include clinic odors, the color of chemotherapeutic drugs, the nurse's voice, and the sight of the oncologist (Andrykowski & Redd, 1987; Divgi, 1989), as well as cognitively generated stimuli such as thoughts and images of chemotherapy (Dobkin, Zeichner, & Dickson-Parnell, 1985; Redd, Andresen, & Minagawa, 1982). The classical conditioning explanation of the development of AN/AV has received wide support in the psychosocial oncology literature relating to children and adults (Redd, Dadds, Futterman, Taylor, & Bovbjerg, 1993).

Epidemiology of AN/AV

Results from studies reporting on the incidence of AN/AV indicate that it occurs in approximately 10–15 percent of children receiving chemotherapy (Dolgin, Katz, Zeltzer, & Landsverk, 1989), while separate incidence figures of anticipatory nausea (AN) and anticipatory vomiting (AV) suggest rates of approximately 30 percent and 20 percent, respectively (Dolgin & Katz, 1988; Dolgin, Katz, McGinty, & Siegel, 1985). Although these figures are based on relatively few studies, similar findings have been demonstrated in the adult literature (Andrykowski et al., 1988; Lindley, Gernard, & Fields, 1989). These findings notwithstanding, the pediatric literature would benefit from incidence studies that focus on pediatric populations and report separately on AN and AV. In addition, future studies may address the differences in AN/AV incidence between adults and children. Although previous studies have suggested that children experience more problems with AN/AV than adults (e.g., Terrin, McWilliams, & Maurer, 1984), recent investigations have found similar rates of AN/AV among adults and children (Blasco, 1994).

Knowledge of the individual markers that predict pediatric patients' susceptibility to AN/AV may lead to important and significant improvements in the efficacy of prophylactic pharmacological and psychological interventions for AN/AV (Hursti et al., 1992; Kvale et al., 1991). Within the past decade, there has been an effort to identify the individual difference variables that mediate the relationship between treatment and development of AN/AV. Variables that have been investigated may be divided into two groups: pharmacological and nonpharmacological. Studies that have investigated the pharmacological mediators of AN/AV have focused on the following variables: emetogenic potential of treatment protocol (Dolgin & Katz, 1988; Dolgin, Katz, McGinty, & Siegel, 1985), degree of post-chemotherapy nausea and vomiting (PNV) (Dolgin, Katz, McGinty, & Siegel, 1985), chemotherapy type (LeBaron, Zeltzer, LeBaron, Scott, & Zeltzer, 1988; Zeltzer et al., 1984), number of treatment cycles (Dolgin & Katz, 1988), and use of antiemetics to control AN/AV (LeBaron et al., 1988). Among the nonpharmacological factors to be examined are age (Dolgin, Katz, McGinty, & Siegel, 1985; Dolgin, Katz, Zeltzer, & Landsverk, 1989; LeBaron et al., 1988), gender (Dolgin, Katz, McGinty, & Siegel, 1985; LeBaron et al., 1988), anxiety (Dolgin & Katz, 1988; Dolgin, Katz, McGinty, & Siegel, 1985), taste aversions (Dolgin & Katz, 1988), and stimulus screening (Dolgin & Katz, 1988), which refers to the ability to selectively filter environmental stimuli.

Results from these studies are preliminary and suggest that both pharmacological and nonpharmacological factors play a role in the development of AN/AV.

Specifically, from the few studies conducted in the pediatric literature, it appears that PNV, emetic potential, and age are the strongest mediators of AN/AV; that is, increased PNV after initial courses of chemotherapy, drugs with higher emetic potential, and being an adolescent (versus a younger child) are associated with a higher frequency and severity of AN/AV. In addition, Dolgin et al. (1989) found that girls were more likely to develop AN/AV than boys; however, this gender difference was only found for severity of nausea and is inconsistent with findings from Dolgin et al. (1985).

Results from the adult literature also demonstrate support for PNV (Albá, Bastús, De Andrés, et al., 1989; Andrykowski, Redd, & Hatfield, 1985; Andrykowski et al., 1988; Morrow, 1982; Morrow, Lindke, & Black, 1991; Olafsdottir, Sjoden, & Westling, 1986) and emetic potential (Morrow, 1982; Redd & Andrykowski, 1982) as mediators of AN/AV, upholding PNV as the best predictor of AN/AV. Other variables that have been shown to be strong mediators of AN/AV in adults include autonomic reactivity (Challis & Stam, 1992; Fredrikson et al., 1993; Hursti et al., 1992; Kvale et al., 1991), anxiety (Andrykowski & Redd, 1987; Andrykowski et al., 1985; Burish & Carey, 1986; Nerenz, Leventhal, Easterling, & Love, 1986; Redd, Burish, & Andrykowski, 1985), and history of motion sickness (Hursti et al., 1992; Morrow, 1984a; Morrow, 1984b). Studies investigating these variables need to be conducted with children and adolescents in order to elucidate the relationships between potential mediating variables and AN/AV. Results from these studies will make it possible to identify children at risk for developing AN/AV, which may lead to improved prevention and treatment in this area.

Assessment of AN/AV

The development of effective cognitive-behavioral and pharmacological interventions for AN/AV depends on the reliable and valid assessment of nausea and vomiting (Tyc, Mulhern, Fairclough, et al., 1993). The problem that has hampered the assessment of AN/AV in pediatric populations is similar to the challenge that faces all researchers who conduct research with children—designing an assessment instrument that is developmentally appropriate and understandable to children of various ages. This task is particularly demanding in the case of AN/AV, because the most common form of cancer is acute lymphocytic leukemia, which has its highest incidence in children from 3 to 5 years of age (Tyc et al., 1993). The two fundamental questions to answer in evaluating AN/AV assessments are the following: (1) what should be assessed, and (2) how should it be assessed.

With regard to the first question, there is universal agreement that nausea and vomiting are distinct concepts and therefore should be measured independently from one another. In addition, future assessment instruments in pediatric oncology should include questions relating to the mediators of AN and AV, such as emetogenic potential of chemotherapy regimen, degree of PNV, and age. Pending future studies examining the mediating effects of autonomic reactivity, anxiety, and motion sickness on AN and AV in pediatric samples, researchers may also find it useful to include these variables as part of a comprehensive assessment of AN and AV. This comprehensive assessment may help professionals establish risk status profiles for individual children/adolescents. These profiles will not only aid in the prevention of AN/AV, but will also be a step toward individualizing treatment decisions based on a child's AN/AV profile.

Most investigators in the field agree that the assessment of AN and AV should be an interdisciplinary process, including information not only from behavioral scientists but also from nursing specialists, who are in an optimal position to collect information from pediatric patients receiving chemotherapy (Hockenberry-Eaton & Benner, 1990). Specifically, nursing assessment should include the child's rating of nausea and vomiting, oral intake after treatment, and the frequency and volume of emesis (Cotanch et al., 1985). Moreover, from the nursing standpoint, the key to effective symptom control is assessing the child's risk of AN/AV before chemotherapy begins (Zeltzer & LeBaron, 1986) and assessing a child's nausea and vomiting associated with each chemotherapy course (Hockenberry-Eaton & Benner, 1990). This process may both enable nurses to effectively decrease one important side effect of cancer treatment on children and provide information regarding the development of AN/AV and delayed-onset nausea and vomiting (Hockenberry-Eaton & Benner, 1990).

Regarding the process by which AN/AV should be measured in children and adolescents, most investigators agree that state-of-the-art measurement includes both observational data and patient self-report (e.g., Jay et al., 1987; LeBaron & Zeltzer, 1984a; Varni, Jay, Masek, & Thompson, 1986). Although there are currently very few standardized observational assessments published in the AN/AV literature, there are several self-report measures that have demonstrated good validity and reliability when utilized with children and adolescents. The most recent and successful AN/AV assessment efforts are based on work by Varni et al. (1986) conducted with pediatric pain patients, which involved the development of the Visual Analogue Scale (VAS). This work has been extended to the AN/AV literature by Zeltzer and colleagues (e.g., Zeltzer et al., 1988), who have designed specific vignettes to measure the subjective frequency and severity of nausea and vomiting symptoms. During prechemotherapy, chemotherapy, and post-chemotherapy parents and children read the vignettes and separately rate the child's nausea and vomiting by marking the appropriate place on a 10-cm line, which is anchored by verbal descriptions (0=no vomiting; 10=constant or extremely frequent vomiting or nausea). Ratings of severity or bother utilize this same method but add faces of children showing increasing amounts of distress.

Results from studies conducted by LeBaron et al. (1988), Zeltzer et al. (1984), and Zeltzer et al. (1988), utilizing this type of measurement, suggested that child ratings were significantly correlated with parent ratings. In addition, Zeltzer et al. (1988) found that children's ability to rate symptoms of nausea and vomiting, as measured by correlation to parent ratings, increased with age. Correlations between ratings of 5-year-olds and parents ranged from .38 to .66 for AN and AV, whereas correlations between ratings by 12- to 18-year-olds and parents ranged from .84 to .92. Results from Tyc et al. (1993) suggested that child ratings are significantly correlated to parent self-report ratings of frequency and severity of *nausea,* but are not significantly correlated to subjective parent-report or parental behavioral observations of frequency and severity of *vomiting.* Tyc et al. (1993) indicated that the low interrater reliability between parents and children may be explained in part by parental tendencies to base their perceptions on their child's overt behavior rather than on the subjective meaning of their child's symptoms.

These findings suggest that the study of AN/AV in children with cancer would benefit both from further examination of the relationship between parent and child reports of nausea and vomiting, and from the development of assessment instruments that could be utilized with children younger than 5 years of age. In addition, results from Tyc et al. (1993), Zeltzer & LeBaron (1986), and LeBaron et al. (1988) underscore the necessity of assessing children when measuring nausea and vomiting, because parents often overlook children's subjective experience. Thus, although observational data has been demonstrated to be quite useful in the assessment of children and adolescents (i.e., Jay et al., 1987), studies in the AN/AV literature underscore the superior statistical and clinical validity of direct, subjective child reports (Hockenberry-Eaton & Benner,

1990; LeBaron et al., 1988; Tyc et al., 1993; Zeltzer & LeBaron, 1986).

Pharmacological Treatment of AN/AV

The pharmacological treatment of nausea and vomiting in pediatric oncology patients has dramatically improved over the past 3 years, despite the fact that a majority of research in this area has been conducted with adults and is focused on the management of chemotherapy-induced nausea and vomiting rather than the *prevention* and treatment of *anticipatory* nausea and vomiting. This improvement is based upon advancements in the understanding of the physiology and pharmacology of emesis.

Results from multiple studies indicate that the mechanisms of cytotoxic chemotherapy- and radiotherapy-induced nausea and vomiting involve a release of serotonin from cells in the gastrointestinal tract (Zoubek et al., 1993). It has been demonstrated that high concentrations of serotonin activate the 5-HT$_3$ receptors located on vagal visceral afferent fibers. This information from the vagus nerve (the tenth cranial nerve) then activates the vomiting reflex by stimulating the chemoreceptor trigger zone (CTZ) and the vomiting center, which are located in the medullary lateral reticular formation (Zoubek et al., 1993; Frankiewicz & Farrington, 1992).

Based on these research findings, drugs that inhibit 5-HT$_3$ serotonin receptors (serotonin receptor antagonists) have been developed and researched in pediatric patients over the past several years. The serotonin receptor antagonist that has received the most attention is ondansetron (Zofran). Results from the efficacy studies indicate that ondansetron completely controlled acute nausea in 61–90 percent of cases and acute vomiting in 50–92 percent of cases (Carden, Mitchell, Waters, Tiedemann, & Ekert, 1990; Hewitt, Cornish, Pamphilon, & Oakill, 1991; Jurgens & McQuade, 1992; Matera, et al., 1993; Pinkerton, Williams, Wooton, Meller, & McElwain, 1990; Roberts & Priestman, 1993; Sullivan, Abbott, & Robison, 1992; Zoubek et al., 1993). Moreover, not only has ondansetron been demonstrated to be highly effective against nausea and vomiting but it is also associated with infrequent and mild side effects (most notably headache and constipation), which have been demonstrated to occur in approximately 15 percent of children (Hewitt, McQuade, & Stevens, 1993; Jurgens & McQuade, 1992).

Of the antiemetics that had been studied before the introduction of ondansetron, metoclopramide had received the most empirical support for controlling nausea and vomiting (Gralla, 1992). At conventional doses, metoclopramide has been demonstrated to antagonize dopamine D_2 receptors and facilitates the release of acetylcholine from nerve endings in the stomach. This antagonism of D_2 receptors not only leads to emesis control, but also to undesirable side effects, most notably extrapyramidal side effects such as akathisia (restlessness) and dystonia (Allen, Gralla, Reilly, Kellick, & Young, 1985; Carr et al., 1985; Chevallier, 1990; Tabona, 1990; Taylor, Proctor, & Bateman, 1984; Zambetti, Bajetta, Bidoli, & Verusio, 1985). Although studies investigating the relative efficacy and safety of ondansetron versus metoclopramide have not been conducted in the pediatric literature, findings from the adult literature indicate that ondansetron is more efficacious, safer and more cost-effective than conventional-dose metoclopramide (Cox & Hirsch, 1993; Hainsworth, Omura, Khojasteh, Bryson, & Finn, 1991; Rath et al., 1993; Roberts & Priestman, 1993; Roila, 1993). When metoclopramide is used in higher doses not only is ondansetron still at least equally as effective, but it is also associated with many fewer side effects (Tabona, 1990).

Concurrent with its recent advances, however, are areas in which the pharmacological treatment for AN/AV may improve; these areas include: (1) focusing on *anticipatory* nausea and vomiting, (2) studying delayed nausea and vomiting and its relationship to AN/AV, and (3) formulating guidelines delineating both the emetogenicity of single drugs and drug combinations and recommendations for antiemetics based on the emetic potential of the chemotherapy and/or radiation regimens. Currently, only one study (Ninane, Ozkaynak, Kurtin, & Siegel, 1995) has addressed all of these concerns. Ninane and colleagues classified emetic potential of chemotherapeutic agents into four classes (Class A=very high emetic potential; Class D=low emetic potential) and give separate recommendations for children receiving drugs within the different classes. To briefly summarize their recommendations, ondansetron was suggested for children receiving drugs in classes A and B. Additional recommended medications were low- to medium-dosed metoclopramide and diphenhydramine (Benadryl). The authors recommend more frequent and durable drug administration for class A medications (4 days) than for classes B, C, and D (3, 3, and 0 days, respectively). Moreover, they give options to physicians, such as moving to the next higher class schedule if a child's symptoms are refractory to the previous antiemetic, and prescribing lorazepam both on the evening before chemotherapy and on the day of chemotherapy for children with AN/AV.

Although the study by Ninane et al. (1995) represents an improvement in the pediatric AN/AV literature, its findings also demonstrated insufficient agreement among physicians on the emetic potential of chemotherapeutic agents. To date, only one study (Matera et al., 1993) has published the emetic potentials of chemotherapy drugs, not only placing them into classes based on emetic potential, but also naming the medications that belong in the different classes. An even better table is published in the Pediatric Drug Handbook and Formulary of Children's Hospital of Orange County (Stringham, 1993). Such a classification system is the foundation for decreasing the variability in physicians' prescriptions. The next steps that need to be taken are formulating a similar classification system for antiemetics, creating a systematic way to match antiemetics with chemotherapeutic agents (as Ninane et al., 1995, have done), and then applying this formula not only to manage existing nausea and vomiting but also to prevent AN/AV.

Cognitive-Behavioral Treatment of AN/AV

Cognitive-behavioral interventions involving hypnosis, guided imagery, progressive muscle relaxation, and systematic desensitization have been demonstrated to be very effective in decreasing AN/AV symptomatology in children (LeBaron & Zeltzer, 1984b; Zeltzer, Kellerman, Ellenberg, Dash, & Rigler, 1983). Historically, however, although these techniques have been associated with significant decreases in AN/AV symptoms, they have also been shown to be time-consuming (Kolko & Rickard-Figueroa, 1985), limited in their cost-effectiveness (Kolko & Rickard-Figueroa, 1985), and implemented exclusively by clinical psychologists (Morrow, Asbury, Hammon, et al., 1992).

Given these limitations, current efforts in pediatric psychology have focused on conducting and testing AN/AV interventions that are easier to administer and understand, less time-consuming, and more cost-effective in their implementation. Specifically, recent investigations have concentrated on the development and evaluation of cognitive distraction techniques (more recently termed cognitive refocusing; Varni, 1995). This change in scope is due not only to the aforementioned reasons, but also to hypotheses that hypnosis and relaxation exert at least part of their effects via cognitive refocusing. Moreover, recent investigations have focused on the relative efficacy of cognitive refocusing and hypnosis, which theoretically involves both relaxation and cognitive refocusing.

The two studies that have examined the effectiveness of cognitive refocusing in pediatric cancer patients were conducted by Kolko & Rickard-Figueroa (1985) and Redd et al. (1987), who have operationalized cognitive refocusing as active participation in video games. Both studies instructed children in the use of an Atari Video Computer System with various games (i.e., Asteroids, Frogger) and gave children unlimited access to the games before chemotherapy administration. Results from these two studies showed that cognitive refocusing was not only associated with more than a 50 percent decrease in nausea/vomiting symptoms, but also was associated with decreases in anxiety and distress related to chemotherapy.

Investigations comparing the effectiveness of cognitive refocusing to hypnosis have yielded inconsistent results. Zeltzer, LeBaron, and Zeltzer (1984), examining nausea and vomiting in children and adolescents receiving chemotherapy, demonstrated both interventions to be quite effective in decreasing nausea, vomiting, and bother related to those symptoms, and found no differences between the two treatment conditions. On the other hand, Zeltzer and colleagues (1991) found significant differences between the hypnosis (31 percent improvement from baseline) and cognitive refocusing (13 percent improvement from baseline) groups with regard to total symptomatology, which included duration and severity of nausea and vomiting, as well as measures of functioning with regard to school, social functioning, eating, and sleeping. However, it is important to note that both groups showed significantly more improvement in total symptoms than the control group, which demonstrated a 50 percent decrement in functioning.

One plausible explanation for these inconsistent results is the definition of cognitive refocusing in the two studies. Although Zeltzer et al. (1984) did not report on the percent of improvement of the two groups, the cognitive refocusing intervention in the Zeltzer et al. (1991) study was more passive in the sense that it only involved establishing rapport and teaching children skills that they could use on their own (i.e., refocusing techniques such as counting objects). In contrast, in the Zeltzer et al. (1984) study, the supportive intervention had an interactive emphasis, refocusing the child's attention by helping them to focus on interesting objects, telling them jokes, or playing guessing games with the child.

Findings from these four studies are preliminary. More research is necessary to elucidate the relationship between cognitive refocusing, relaxation, and hypnosis, and their efficacy in decreasing symptoms in children with AN/AV. However, one consistent finding from all four studies was that children in an intervention group (i.e., cognitive refocusing) always improved, whereas children in control groups always remained the same or got worse. Moreover, these findings indicate that effective cognitive-behavioral treatment for AN/AV may be relatively simple, and suggest the desirability of training various professionals (e.g., nurses) to implement cognitive refocusing strategies as cost-effective interventions for pediatric oncology patients. One such study, conducted by Morrow et al. (1992) with adult subjects, found significant decreases in AN/AV symptoms for all treatment groups led by either psychologists or nurses, with no statistical differences based on population.

One additional future direction for cognitive-behavioral AN/AV interventions comes out of the cognitive appraisal literature. In contrast to the classical conditioning explanation for the development of AN/AV, cognitive appraisal theory describes a process in which an individual's ability to cope (in this case with chemotherapy treatment) is based upon their attribution of the situation as either controllable (challenging or nurturing) or uncontrollable (threatening or harmful) (Burish et al., 1991; Pickett, 1991). In a study with adults, Burish et al. (1991) demonstrated increases in coping ability and knowledge and decreases in distress in response to a 90-minute, pre-chemotherapy coping intervention, which involved touring the oncology clinic, a videotape presentation about chemotherapy, a question/answer session, and a booklet for patients/families to take home. Future research in pediatric AN/AV may benefit from comparing the cost-effectiveness of similar interventions to hypnosis and cognitive refocusing.

Overall, anticipatory nausea and vomiting (AN/AV) is a common problem among pediatric cancer patients, for whom pharmacological and cognitive-behavioral interventions may be very effective. In fact, it is likely that the most effective treatment for AN/AV would include pharmacological and cognitive-behavioral components, although further research is needed to determine which symptoms are amenable to the various interventions. This review also clearly demonstrates the necessity to clarify and systematize assessment and treatment procedures for AN/AV in order to compare results across studies (within and between disciplines) and ultimately to develop state-of-the-art treatment for anticipatory nausea and vomiting.

SUMMARY

Inconsistencies in the literature on the adjustment of children with cancer can be attributed to a number of methodological differences across studies, including a general lack of theoretically driven investigations on the potentially modifiable predictors of individual differences in adaptation. Pediatric chronic physical disorders have been conceptualized within the stress and coping theoretical framework proposed by Varni and Wallander (1988) and Wallander and Varni (1992) as a chronic strain for both the children and their families. Chronic strains are defined as persistent objective conditions that require continual readjustment, repeatedly interfering with the adequate performance of ordinary role-related activities (Pearlin, Lieberman, Menaghan, & Mullan, 1981). The chronic strains of childhood cancer, such as treatment-related pain; nausea and vomiting; visible side effects such as hair loss, weight gain or loss, and physical disfigurement; and repeated absences from school and peers may interact to negatively impact psychological and social adjustment. By developing conceptually-driven research, the risk and resistance factors that determine individual differences in adjustment can be identified, potentially leading to enhanced treatment interventions for children with cancer and their families.

REFERENCES

Achenbach, T. M. (1993). Implications of multiaxial empirically based assessment for behavior therapy with children. *Behavior Therapy, 24,* 91–116.

Achenbach, T. M., McConaughy, S. H., & Howell, C. T. (1987). Child/adolescent behavioral and emotional problems: Implications of cross-informant correlations for situational specificity. *Psychological Bulletin, 101,* 213–232.

Albá, E., Bastús, R., De Andrés, L., Sotá, C., Paredes, A., & López, J. J. (1989). Anticipatory nausea and vomiting: Prevalence and predictors in chemoptherapy patients. *Oncology, 46,* 26–30.

Allen, J. C., Gralla, R., Reilly, L., Kellick, M., & Young, C. (1985). Metoclopramide: Dose-related toxicity and preliminary antiemetic studies in children receiving cancer chemotherapy. *Journal of Clinical Oncology, 3,* 1136–1141.

Andersen, B. L. (1992). Psychological interventions for cancer patients to enhance the quality of life. *Journal of Consulting and Clinical Psychology, 60,* 552–568.

Andrykowski, M. A., Jacobsen, P. B., Marks, E., Gorfinkle, K., Hakes, T. B., Kaufman, R. J., Curie, V. E., Holland, J. C., & Redd, W. H. (1988). Prevalence, predictors and course of anticipatory nausea in women receiving adjuvant chemotherapy for breast cancer. *Cancer, 62,* 2607–2613.

Andrykowski, M. A., & Redd, W. H. (1987). Longitudinal analysis of the development of anticipatory nausea. *Journal of Consulting and Clinical Psychology, 55,* 36–41.

Andrykowski, M. A., Redd, W. H., & Hatfield, A. K. (1985). Development of anticipatory nausea: A prospective analysis. *Journal of Consulting and Clinical Psychology, 53,* 447–454.

Arendt-Nielsen, L., Bjerring, P., & Nielsen, J. (1988). Regional variations in analgesic efficacy of EMLA cream. Quantitatively evaluated by argon laser stimulation. *Acta Dermato-Venereologica, 70,* 314–318.

Arts, S. E., Abu-Saad, H. H., Champion, G. D., Crawford, M. R., Fisher, R. J., Juniper, K. H., & Ziegler, J. B. (1994). Age-related response to lidocaine-prilocaine (EMLA) emulsion and effect of music distraction on the pain of intravenous cannulation. *Pediatrics, 93,* 797–801.

Bailey, P. L., Pace, N. L., Ashburn, M. A., Moll, J. W. B., East, K. A., & Stanley, T. H. (1990). Frequent hypoxemia and apnea after sedation with midazolam and fentanyl. *Anesthesiology, 78,* 826–830.

Bjerring, P., & Arendt-Nielsen, L. (1990). Depth and duration of skin analgesia to needle insertion after topical application of EMLA cream. *British Journal of Anaesthesia, 64,* 173–177.

Blasco, T. (1994). Anticipatory nausea and vomiting: Are psychological factors adequately investigated? *British Journal of Clinical Psychology, 33,* 85–100.

Bleyer, W. A. (1981). Neurologic sequelae of methotrexate and ionizing radiation: A new classification. *Cancer Treatment Reports, 65,* 89–98.

Bleyer, W. A. (1990). The impact of childhood cancer on the United States and the world. *Cancer Journal for Clinicians, 40,* 355–367.

Blount, R. L. (1987). The dissemination of cost-effective psychosocial programs for children in health care settings. *Children's Health Care, 15,* 206–213.

Blount, R. L., Bachanas, P. J., Powers, S. W., Cotter, M. C., Franklin, A., Chaplin, W., Mayfield, J., Henderson, M., & Blount, S. D. (1992). Training children to cope and parents to coach them during routine immunizations: Effects on child, parent and staff behaviors. *Behavior Therapy, 23,* 689–705.

Blount, R. L., Corbin, S. M., Sturges, J. W., Wolfe, V. V., Prater, J. M., & James, L. D. (1989). The relationship between adults' behavior and child coping and distress during BMA/LP procedures: A sequential analysis. *Behavior Therapy, 20,* 585–601.

Blount, R. L., Davis, N., Powers, S., & Roberts, M. D. (1991). The influence of environmental factors and coping style on children's coping and distress. *Clinical Psychology Review, 11,* 93–116.

Blount, R. L., Landolf-Fritsche, B., Powers, S. W., & Sturges, J. W. (1991). Differences between high and low coping children and between parent and staff behaviors during painful medical procedures. *Journal of Pediatric Psychology, 16,* 795–809.

Blount, R. L., Manimala, M. R., Frank, N. C., Bisson, J. A., & Smith, J. A. (1993, April). *The Child-Adult Medical Procedure Interaction Scale-Revised: An examination of reliability and validity.* Paper presented at the Florida Conference on Child Health Psychology, Gainesville, FL.

Blount, R. L., Powers, S. W., Cotter, M. W., Swan, S. C., & Free, K. (1994). Making the system work: Training pediatric oncology patients to cope and their parents to coach them during BMA/LP procedures. *Behavior Modification, 18,* 6–31.

Blount, R. L., Sturges, J. W., & Powers, S. W. (1990). Analysis of child and adult behavioral variations by phase of medical procedure. *Behavior Therapy, 21,* 33–48.

Bridge, L. R., Benson, P., Pietroni, P. C., & Priest, R. G. (1988). Relaxation and imagery in the treatment of breast cancer. *British Medical Journal, 297,* 1169–1172.

Brown, R. T., Kaslow, N. J., Hazzard, A. P., Madan-Swain, A., Sexson, S. B., Lambert, R., & Baldwin, K. (1992). Psychiatric and family functioning in children with leukemia and their parents. *Journal of the American Academy of Child and Adolescent Psychiatry, 31,* 495–502.

Buckley, M. M., & Benfield, P. (1993). Eutectic lidocaine/prilocaine cream: A review of the topical anaesthetic/analgesic efficacy of a eutectic mixture of local anesthetics (EMLA). *Drugs, 46,* 126–151.

Burish, T. G., & Carey, M. P. (1986). Conditioned aversive responses in cancer chemotherapy patients. Theoretical and developmental analysis. *Journal of Consulting and Clinical Psychology, 54,* 593–600.

Burish, T. G., Snyder, S. L., & Jenkins, R. A. (1991). Preparing patients for cancer chemotherapy: Effect of coping preparation and relaxation interventions. *Journal of Consulting and Clinical Psychology, 59,* 518–525.

Bush, J. P., Melamed, B. G., Sheras, P. L., & Greenbaum, P. E. (1986). Mother-child patterns of coping with anticipatory medical stress. *Health Psychology, 2,* 137–157.

Byrd, R. (1985). Late effects of treatment of cancer in children. *Pediatric Clinics of North America, 32,* 835–857.

Carden, P. A., Mitchell, S. L., Waters, K. D., Tiedemann, K., & Ekert, H. (1990). Prevention of cyclophosphamide/cytarabine induced emesis with ondansetron in children with leukemia. *Journal of Clinical Oncology, 8,* 1531–1535.

Carey, M. P., & Burish, T. G. (1988). Etiology and treatment of the psychological side effects associated with cancer chemotherapy: A critical review and discussion. *Psychological Bulletin, 104,* 307–325.

Carr, B. I., Bertrand, M., Browning, S., Doroshow, J. H., Presant, C., Pulone, B., & Hill, R. L. (1985). A comparison of the antiemetic efficacy of prochlorperazine and metoclopramide for the treatment of cisplatin-induced emesis: A prospective, randomized, double-blind study. *Journal of Clinical Oncology, 3,* 1127–1132.

Cecalupo, A. (1994). Childhood cancers: Medical issues. In R. A. Olson, L. L. Mullins, J. B. Gillman, & J. M. Chaney (Eds.), *The source book of pediatric psychology* (pp. 90–97). Boston: Allyn and Bacon.

Challis, G. D., & Stam, H. J. (1992). Longitudinal study of the development of anticipatory nausea and vomiting in cancer chemotherapy patients: The role of absorption and autonomic perception. *Health Psychology, 11,* 181–189.

Chevallier, B. (1990). Efficacy and safety of granisetron compared with high-dose metoclopramide plus dexamethasone in patients receiving high-dose cisplatin in a single-blind study. *European Journal of Cancer, 26,* S33–S36.

Coates, A. (1986). Coping with cytotoxic therapy. In B. A. Stoll & A. D. Weisman (Eds.), *Coping with cancer* (pp. 39–44). Dordrecht: Martinus Nijhoff Publishers.

Cohen, J. (1988). *Statistical power analysis for the behavioral sciences.* Hillsdale, NJ: Lawrence Erlbaum Associates, Inc.

Cohen, L., Blount, R. L., Panopoulos, G., & Manimala, M. R. (1995). *Training nurses to administer coping skills program to parents and children undergoing immunizations.* Manuscript submitted for publication.

Cohen, S., Tyrrell, D. A., & Smith, A. P. (1991). Psychological stress and susceptibility to the common cold. *New England Journal of Medicine, 325,* 606–612.

Cohen, S., & Williamson, G. M. (1991). Stress and infectious disease in humans. *Psychological Bulletin, 109,* 5–24.

Compas, B. E. (1987). Stress and life events during childhood and adolescence. *Clinical Psychology Review, 7,* 275–302.

Cooper, C. L., & Watson, M. (Eds.). (1991). *Cancer and stress: Psychological, biological and coping studies.* New York: John Wiley & Sons.

Copeland, D. R. (1992). Neuropsychological and psychosocial effects of childhood leukemia and its treatment. *Cancer Journal for Clinicians, 42,* 283–295.

Cotanch, P., Hockenberry, M., & Herman, S. (1985). Self-hypnosis as antiemetic therapy in children receiving chemotherapy. *Oncology Nursing Forum, 12,* 41–46.

Cousins, P., Waters, B., Said, J., & Stevens, M. (1988). Cognitive effects of cranial irradiation in leukemia: A survey and meta-analysis. *Journal of Child Psychology and Psychiatry, 29,* 839–852.

Cox, F., & Hirsch, J. (1993). Ondansetron: A cost-effective advance in anti-emetic therapy. *Oncology, 50,* 186–190.

Davis, H. (1986). Effects of biofeedback and cognitive therapy on stress in patients with breast cancer. *Psychological Reports, 59,* 967–974.

DeLaat, C. A., & Lampkin, B. C. (1992). Long-term survivors of childhood cancer: Evaluation and identification of sequelae of treatment. *Cancer Journal for Clinicians, 42,* 263–282.

Divgi, A. B. (1989). Oncologist-induced vomiting: The IGVID syndrome? *New England Journal of Medicine, 320,* 189–190.

Dobkin, P., Zeichner, A., & Dickson-Parnell, B. (1985). Concomitants of anticipatory nausea and emesis in cancer chemotherapy. *Psychological Reports, 56,* 671–676.

Dolgin, M. J., & Katz, E. R. (1988). Conditioned aversions in pediatric cancer patients receiving chemotherapy. *Developmental and Behavioral Pediatrics, 9,* 82–85.

Dolgin, M. J., Katz, E. R., McGinty, K., & Siegel, S. E. (1985). Anticipatory nausea and vomiting in pediatric cancer patients. *Pediatrics, 75,* 547–552.

Dolgin, M. J., Katz, E. R., Zeltzer, L. K., & Landsverk, J. (1989). Behavioral distress in pediatric patients with cancer receiving chemotherapy. *Pediatrics, 84,* 103–110.

Drigan, R., Spirito, A., & Gelber, R. D. (1992). Behavioral effects of corticosteroids in children with acute lymphoblastic leukemia. *Medical and Pediatric Oncology, 20,* 13–21.

Falloon, I. R. H. (Ed.). (1988). *Handbook of behavioral family therapy.* New York: Guilford Press.

Fawzy, F. I., Kemeny, M. E., Fawzy, N. W., Elashoff, R., Morton, D., Cousins, N., & Fahey, J. L. (1990). A structured psychiatric intervention for cancer patients: II. Changes over time in immunological measures. *Archives of General Psychiatry, 47,* 729–735.

Fawzy, F. I., Cousins, N., Fawzy, N. W., Kemeny, M. E., Elashoff, R., & Morton, D. (1990). A structured psychiatric intervention for cancer patients: I. Changes over time in methods of coping and affective disturbance. *Archives of General Psychiatry, 47,* 720–725.

Fawzy, R. I., Fawzy, N. W., Hyun, C. S., Elashoff, R., Guthrie, D., Fahey, J. L., & Morton, D. L. (1993). Malignant melanoma: Effects of an early structured psychiatric intervention, coping, and affective state on recurrence and survival 6 years later. *Archives of General Psychiatry, 50,* 681–689.

Fife, B., Norton, J., & Groom, G. (1987). The family's adaptation to childhood leukemia. *Social Science and Medicine, 24,* 159–168.

Fletcher, J. M., & Copeland, D. R. (1988). Neurobehavioral effects of central nervous system prophylactic treatment of cancer in children. *Journal of Clinical Experimental Neuropsychology, 10,* 495–538.

Frank, N. C., Blount, R. L., Smith, A. J., Manimala, M. R., & Martin, J. K. (1995). Parent and staff behavior, previous child medical experience, and material anxiety as they relate to child distress and coping. *Journal of Pediatric Psychology, 20,* 277–289.

Frankiewicz, V., & Farrington, E. (1992). Ondansetron HC: Zofran™. *Pediatric Nursing, 18,* 385–386.

Fredrikson, M., Hursti, T., Salmi, P., Borjeson, S., Furst, C. J., Peterson, C., & Steineck, G. (1993). Conditioned nausea after cancer chemotherapy and autonomic nervous system conditionability. *Scandanavian Journal of Psychology, 34,* 318–327.

Friedman, A. G., Mulhern, R. K., Fairclough, D., Ward, P. M., Baker, D., Mirro, J., & Rivera, G. K. (1991). Midazolam premedication for pediatric bone marrow aspiration and lumbar puncture. *Medical and Pediatric Oncology, 19,* 499–504.

Gralla, R. J. (1992). Serotonin antagonist antiemetics: Progress and concerns. *Annals of Oncology, 3,* 677–678.

Granowetter, L. (1994). A medical overview. In D. J. Bearison & R. K. Mulhern (Eds.), *Pediatric psychooncology: Psychological perspectives on children with cancer* (pp. 9–34). New York: Oxford University Press.

Gray, R. E., Doan, B. D., Shermer, P., Fitzgerald, A. V., Berry, M. P., Jenkin, D., & Doherty, M. A. (1992). Psychologic adaptation of survivors of childhood cancer. *Cancer, 70,* 2713–2721.

Green, W. H., & Kowalik, S. C. (1994). Psychopharmacologic treatment of pain and anxiety in the pediatric patient. *Child and Adolescent Psychiatric Clinics of North America, 3,* 465–483.

Greenbaum, P., Cook, E., Melamed, B., Abeles, B., & Bush, J. (1988). Sequential patterns of medical stress: Maternal agitation and child distress. *Child and Family Behavior Therapy, 10,* 9–18.

Greenberg, H. S., Kazak, A. E., & Meadows, A. T. (1989). Psychologic functioning in 8- to 16-year-old cancer survivors and their parents. *Journal of Pediatrics, 114,* 488–493.

Greer, S., Moorey, S., Baruch, J. D., Watson, M., Robertson, B. M., Mason, A., Rowden, L., Law, M. G., & Bliss, J. M. (1992). Adjuvant psychological therapy for patients with cancer: A prospective randomized trial. *British Medical Journal, 304,* 675–680.

Hainsworth, J. D., Omura, G. A., Khojasteh, A., Bryson, J. C., & Finn, A. L. (1991). Ondansetron (GR 38032F): A novel antiemetic effective in patients receiving a multiple-day regimen of cisplatin chemotherapy. *American Journal of Clinical Oncology, 14,* 336–340.

Halperin, D. L., Koren, G., Attias, D., Pellegrini, E., Greenberg, M. L., & Wyss, M. (1989). Topical skin anesthesia for venous subcutaneous drug reservoir and lumbar punctures in children. *Pediatrics, 84,* 281–284.

Hays, D. M. (1993). Adult survivors of childhood cancer: Employment and insurance issues in different age groups. *Cancer, 71,* 3306–3309.

Hewitt, M., Cornish, J., Pamphilon, D., & Oakill, A. (1991). Effective emetic control during conditioning of children for bone marrow transplantation using ondansetron, a 5-HT$_3$ antagonist. *Bone Marrow Transplantation, 7,* 431–433.

Hewitt, M., McQuade, B., & Stevens, R. (1993). The efficacy and safety of ondansetron in prophylaxis of cancer chemotherapy induced nausea and vomiting in children. *Oncology Review and Collaborative Radiology, 5,* 11–14.

Hilgard, J., & LeBaron, S. (1982). Relief of anxiety and pain in children and adolescents with cancer: Quantitative measures and clinical observations. *International Journal of Clinical and Experimental Hypnosis, 30,* 417–442.

Hockenberry-Eaton, M., & Benner, A. (1990). Patterns of nausea and vomiting in children: Nursing assessment and intervention. *Oncology Nursing Forum, 17,* 575–584.

Hodges, K., Gordon, Y., & Lennon, M. P. (1990). Parent-child agreement on symptoms assessed via a clinical research interview for children: The child assessment schedule (CAS). *Journal of Child Psychology and Psychiatry, 31,* 427–436.

Hubert, N. C., Jay, S. M., Saltoun, M., & Hayes, M. (1988). Approach-avoidance and distress in children undergoing preparation for painful medical procedures. *Journal of Clinical Child Psychology, 17,* 194–202.

Hursti, T., Fredrikson, M., Borjeson, S., Furst, C., Peterson, C., & Steineck, G. (1992). Association between personality characteristics and the prevalence and extinction of conditioned nausea after chemotherapy. *Journal of Psychosocial Oncology, 10,* 59–77.

Hymes, J. A., & Spraker, M. K. (1986). Racial differences in the effectiveness of a topically applied mixture of local anesthetics. *Regional Anesthesia, 11,* 11–13.

Ines, T. M., & Sacco, W. P. (1992). Factors related to correspondence between teacher ratings of elementary student depression and student self-ratings. *Journal of Consulting and Clinical Psychology, 60,* 140–142.

Irwin, M., Daniels, M., Bloom, E., Smith, T. L., & Weiner, H. (1987). Life events, depressive symptoms, and immune function. *American Journal of Psychiatry, 144,* 437–441.

Jacobsen, P., Manne, S., Gorfinkle, K., Schorr, O., Rapkin, B., & Redd, W. H. (1990). Analysis of child and parent activity during painful medical procedures. *Health Psychology, 9,* 559–576.

Jakobson, B., & Nilsson, A. (1985). Methemoglobinemia associated with a prilocaine-lidocaine cream and trimetoprim-sulphamethoxazole: A case report. *Acta Anaesthesiologica Scandinavica, 29,* 453–455.

Jay, S. M. (1988). Invasive medical procedures: Psychological intervention and assessment. In D. K. Routh (Ed.), *Handbook of pediatric psychology* (pp. 401–425). New York: Guilford Press.

Jay, S. M., Elliott, C., Katz, E., & Siegel, S. (1987). Cognitive-behavioral and pharmacologic interventions for children's distress during painful medical procedures. *Journal of Consulting and Clinical Psychology, 55,* 860–865.

Jay, S. M., Elliott, C. H., Woody, P. D., & Siegel, S. (1991). An investigation of cognitive-behavior therapy combined with oral valium for children undergoing painful medical procedures. *Health Psychology, 10,* 317–322.

Jay, S. M., Ozolins, M., Elliott, C. H., & Caldwell, S. (1983). Assessment of children's distress during painful medical procedures. *Health Psychology, 2,* 133–147.

Joyce, T. H. (1993). Topical anaesthesia and pain management before venipuncture. *The Journal of Pediatrics, 122,* S24–S29.

Jurgens, H., & McQuade, B. (1992). Ondansetron as prophylaxis for chemotherapy and radiotherapy-induced emesis in children. *Oncology, 49,* 279–285.

Kapelushnik, J., Koren, G., Solh, H., Greenberg, M., & DeVeber, L. (1990). Evaluating the efficacy of EMLA in alleviating pain associated with lumbar puncture: Comparison of open and double-blinded protocols in children. *Pain, 42,* 31–34.

Kaplan, S. L., Busner, J., Weinhold, C., & Lenon, P. (1987). Depressive symptoms in children and adolescents with cancer: A longitudinal study. *Journal of the American Academy of Child and Adolescent Psychiatry, 26,* 782–787.

Kashani, J. H., Orvaschel, H., Burk, J. P., & Reid, J. C. (1985). Informant variance: The issues of parent-child disagreement. *Journal of the American Academy of Child Psychiatry, 24,* 437–441.

Katz, E., Kellerman, J., & Ellenberg, L. (1987). Hypnosis in the reduction of acute pain and distress in children with cancer. *Journal of Pediatric Psychology, 12,* 379–394.

Katz, E. R., Dolgin, M. J., & Varni, J. W. (1990). Cancer in children and adolescents. In A. M. Gross & R. S. Drabman (Eds.), *Handbook of clinical behavioral pediatrics* (pp. 129–146). New York: Plenum Press.

Katz, E. R., Kellerman, J., & Siegel, S. E. (1980). Distress behavior in children with cancer undergoing medical procedures: Developmental considerations. *Journal of Consulting and Clinical Psychology, 48,* 356–365.

Katz, E. R., Rubenstein, C. L., Hubert, N. C., & Blew, A. (1988). School and social reintegration of children with cancer. *Journal of Psychosocial Oncology, 6,* 123–140.

Katz, E. R., & Varni, J. W. (1993). Social support and social cognitive problem solving in children with newly diagnosed cancer. *Cancer, 71,* 3314–3319.

Katz, E. R., Varni, J. W., Rubenstein, C. L., Blew, A., & Hubert, N. (1992). Teacher, parent, and child evaluative ratings of a school reintegration integration for children with newly diagnosed cancer. *Children's Health Care, 21,* 69–75.

Kiecolt-Glaser, J. K., & Glaser, R. (1992). Psychoneuroimmunology: Can psychological interventions modulate immunity? *Journal of Consulting and Clinical Psychology, 60,* 569–575.

Kolko, D. J., & Rickard-Figueroa, J. L. (1985). Effects of video games on the adverse corollaries of chemotherapy in pediatric oncology patients: A single case analysis. *Journal of Consulting and Clinical Psychology, 53,* 223–228.

Koocher, G. P. (1985). Psychosocial care of the child cured of cancer. *Pediatric Nursing, 11,* 91–93.

Kuttner, L. (1988). Favorite stories: A hypnotic pain-reduction technique for children in acute pain. *American Journal of Clinical Hypnosis, 30,* 289–295.

Kuttner, L., Bowman, M., & Teasdale, M. (1988). Psychological treatment of distress, pain and anxiety for young children with cancer. *Journal of Developmental and Behavioral Pediatrics, 9,* 374–381.

Kvale, G., Hugdahl, K., Asbjornsen, A., Rosengren, B., Lote, K., & Nordby, H. (1991). Anticipatory nausea and vomiting in cancer patients. *Journal of Consulting and Clinical Psychology, 59,* 894–898.

Ladd, G. W. (1990). Having friends, keeping friends, making friends, and being liked by peers in the classroom: Predictors of children's early school adjustment. *Child Development, 61,* 1081–1100.

Lansky, L. L., List, M. A., Lanskey, S. B., Cohen, M. E., & Sinks, L. B. (1985). Toward the development of a play performance scale for children. *Cancer, 56,* 1837–1840.

Lansky, S. B., List, M. A., Ritter-Sterr, C., Klopovich, P., & Chang, P. (1985). Late effects: Psychosocial. *Clinics in Oncology, 4,* 239–246.

Lazarus, R. S., & Folkman, S. (1984). *Stress, appraisal, and coping.* New York: Springer Publishing Company, Inc.

LeBaron, S., & Zeltzer, L. (1984a). Assessment of acute pain and anxiety in children and adolescents by self-reports, observer reports, and a behavior checklist. *Journal of Consulting and Clinical Psychology, 52,* 729–738.

LeBaron, S., & Zeltzer, L. (1984b). Behavioral intervention for reducing chemotherapy-related nausea and vomiting in adolescents with cancer. *Journal of Adolescent Health Care, 5,* 178–182.

LeBaron, S., Zeltzer, L., LeBaron, C., Scott, S. E., & Zeltzer, P. M. (1988). Chemotherapy side effects in pediatric oncology patients: Drugs, age, and sex as risk factors. *Medical and Pediatric Oncology, 16,* 263–268.

Lindley, C. M., Gernard, S., & Fields, S. M. (1989). Incidence and duration of chemotherapy-induced nausea and vomiting in the outpatient oncology population. *Journal of Clinical Oncology, 7,* 1142–1149.

Loeber, R., Green, S. M., Lahey, B. B., & Stouthamer-Loeber, M. (1991). Differences and similarities between children, mothers, and teachers as informants on disruptive child behavior. *Journal of Abnormal Child Psychology, 19,* 75–95.

Maisami, M., Sohmer, B. H., & Coyle, J. T. (1985). Combined use of tricyclic antidepressants and neuroleptics in the management of terminally ill children: A report on three cases. *Journal of the American Academy of Child Psychiatry, 24,* 487–489.

Manimala, M. R., Blount, R. L., Panopoulos, G., Cohen, L., Pate, J., & Smith, A. (1995). *The effects of distraction and reassurance on the coping and distress of children undergoing immunizations.* Manuscript submitted for publication.

Manne, S., Redd, W. H., Jacobsen, P., Gorfinkle, K., Schorr, O., & Rapkin, B. (1990). Behavioral intervention to reduce child and parent distress during venipuncture. *Journal of Consulting and Clinical Psychology, 58,* 565–572.

Manne, S. L., Bakeman, R., Jacobsen, P. B., Gorfinkle, K., Bernstein, D., & Redd, W. H. (1992). Adult-child interaction during medical procedures. *Health Psychology, 11,* 241–249.

Matera, M. G., DiTullio, M., Lucarelli, C., Casale, F., Calabria, C., Lampa, E., Indolfi, P., & Rossi, F. (1993). Ondansetron, an antagonist of 5-HT$_3$ receptors, in the treatment of antineoplastic drug-induced nausea and vomiting in children. *Journal of Medicine, 24,* 161–170.

McConaughy, S. H., Stanger, C., & Achenbach, T. M. (1992). Three-year course of behavioral/emotional problems in a national sample of 4- to 16-year-olds: I. Agreement among informants. *Journal of the American*

Academy of Child and Adolescent Psychiatry, 31, 932–940.

Meadows, A. T., & Hobbie, W. L. (1986). The medical consequences of cure. *Cancer, 58,* 524–528.

Meadows, A. T., Massari, D. J., & Fergusson, J. (1981). Declines in IQ scores and cognitive dysfunctions in children with acute lymphocytic leukemia treated with cranial irradiation. *Lancet, 2,* 1015–1018.

Moehle, K. A., & Berg, R. A. (1985). Academic achievement and intelligence test performance in children with cancer at diagnosis and one year later. *Journal of Developmental and Behavioral Pediatrics, 6,* 62–64.

Molodecka, J., Stenhouse, C., Jones, J. M., & Tomlinson, A. (1994). Comparison of percutaneous anaesthesia for venous cannulation after topical application of either amethocaine or EMLA cream. *British Journal of Anaesthesia, 72,* 174–176.

Morrow, C. E., Armstrong, F. D., Routh, D. K., Gay, C., & Levy, J. (1993, April). *Correlates of child distress during lumbar punctures: Parent behavior and parenting characteristics.* Gainsville, FL.

Morrow, G. R. (1982). Prevalence and correlates of anticipatory nausea and vomiting in chemotherapy patients. *Journal of the National Cancer Institute, 68,* 585–588.

Morrow, G. R. (1984a). Susceptibility to motion-sickness and the development of anticipatory nausea and vomiting in cancer patients undergoing chemotherapy. *Cancer Treatment Reports, 68,* 1177–1178.

Morrow, G. R. (1984b). Susceptibility to motion-sickness and chemotherapy-induced side-effects. *Lancet, 52,* 1098–1099.

Morrow, G. R., Asbury, R., Hammon, S., Dobkin, P., Caruso, L., Pandya, K., & Rosenthal, S. (1992). Comparing the effectiveness of behavioral treatment for chemotherapy-induced nausea and vomiting when administered by oncologists, oncology nurses, and clinical psychologists. *Health Psychology, 11,* 250–256.

Morrow, G. R., Lindke, J., & Black, P. M. (1991). Anticipatory nausea development in cancer patients: Replication and extension of a learning model. *British Journal of Psychology, 82,* 61–72.

Mulhern, R. K., Wasserman, A. L., Friedman, A. G., & Fairclough, D. (1989). Social competence and behavioral adjustment of children who are long-term survivors of cancer. *Pediatrics, 83,* 18–25.

Neglia, J. P., & Nesbit, M. E. (1993). Care and treatment of long-term survivors of childhood cancer. *Cancer, 71,* 3386–3391.

Nerenz, D. R., Leventhal, H., Easterling, D. V., & Love, R. R. (1986). Anxiety and drug taste as predictors of anticipatory nausea in cancer chemotherapy. *Journal of Clinical Oncology, 4,* 224–233.

Ninane, J., Ozkaynak, M. F., Kurtin, P., & Siegel, S. E. (1995). Variation in the use of ondansetron as an antiemetic drug in children treated with chemotherapy. *Medical and Pediatric Oncology, 25,* 33–37.

Olafsdottir, M., Sjoden, P. B., & Westling, B. (1986). Prevalence and prediction of chemotherapy-related anxiety, nausea and vomiting in cancer patients. *Behavior Research and Therapy, 24,* 59–66.

Parker, J. G., & Asher, S. R. (1987). Peer relations and later personal adjustment: Are low-accepted children at risk. *Psychological Bulletin, 102,* 357–389.

Pearlin, L. I., Lieberman, M. A., Menaghan, E. G., & Mullan, J. T. (1981). The stress process. *Journal of Health and Social Behavior, 22,* 337–356.

Perrin, E. C., Ayoub, C. C., & Willett, J. B. (1993). In the eyes of the beholder: Family and maternal influences on perceptions of adjustment of children with a chronic illness. *Journal of Developmental and Behavioral Pediatrics, 14,* 94–105.

Pfefferbaum-Levine, B., DeTrinis, R. B., Young, M. A., & Van Eys, J. (1984). The use of psychoactive medications in children with cancer. *Journal of Psychosocial Oncology, 2,* 65–71.

Pfefferbaum-Levine, B., Kumor, K., Cangir, A., Choroszy, M., & Roseberry, E. A. (1983). Tricyclic antidepressants for children with cancer. *American Journal of Psychiatry, 140,* 1074–1076.

Pickett, M. (1991). Determinants of anticipatory nausea and anticipatory vomiting in adults receiving cancer chemotherapy. *Cancer Nursing, 14,* 334–343.

Pinkerton, C. R., Williams, D., Wooton, C., Meller, S., & McElwain, T. J. (1990). 5-HT$_3$ antagonist ondansetron—an effective outpatient antiemetic in cancer treatment. *Archives of Diseases in Children, 65,* 822–825.

Powers, S. W., Blount, R. L., Bachanas, P. J., Cotter, M. C., & Swan, S. C. (1993). Helping preschool leukemia patients and their parents cope during injections. *Journal of Pediatric Psychology, 18,* 681–695.

Pratt, C. B. (1985). Some aspects of childhood cancer epidemiology. *Pediatric Clinics of North America, 32,* 541–556.

Price, H. V. (1988). Lignocaine-prilocaine cream for lumbar puncture in children. *Lancet, 31,* 1174.

Public Health Service. (1994). Management of cancer pain. *AHCPR Publication No. 94–0592.*

Rath, U., Upadhyaya, B. K., Bockmann, H., Dearnaley, D., Droz, J. P., Fossa, S. D., Henriksson, R., Aulitzky, W. E., Jones, W. G., Weissbach, L., Paska, W., & Freeman, A. (1993). Role of ondansetron plus dexamethasone in fractionated chemotherapy. *Oncology, 50,* 168–172.

Redd, W. H., Andresen, G. V., & Minagawa, R. Y. (1982). Hypnotic control of anticipatory emesis in patients receiving cancer chemotherapy. *Journal of Consulting and Clinical Psychology, 50,* 14–19.

Redd, W. H., & Andrykowski, M. A. (1982). Behavioral intervention in cancer treatment: Controlling aversion reactions to chemotherapy. *Journal of Consulting and Clinical Psychology, 50,* 1018–1029.

Redd, W. H., Burish, T. G., & Andrykowski, M. A. (1985). Aversive conditioning and cancer chemotherapy. In T. G. Burish, S. M. Levy, & B. E. Meyerowitz (Eds.), *Cancer, nutrition and eating behavior: A biobehavioral perspective* (pp. 117–132). Hillsdale, NJ: Lawrence Erlbaum Associates, Inc.

Redd, W. H., Dadds, M. R., Futterman, A. D., Taylor, K. L., & Bovbjerg, D. H. (1993). Nausea induced by mental images of chemotherapy. *Cancer, 72,* 629–636.

Redd, W. H., Jacobsen, P. B., Die-Trill, M., Dermatis, H., McEvoy, M., & Holland, J. C. (1987). Cognitive/attentional distraction in the control of conditioned nausea in pediatric cancer patients receiving chemotherapy. *Journal of Consulting and Clinical Psychology, 55,* 391–395.

Roberts, J. T., & Priestman, T. J. (1993). A review of ondansetron in the management of radiotherapy-induced emesis. *Oncology, 50,* 173–179.

Roberts, M. C. (1992). Vale dictum: An editor's view of the field of pediatric psychology. *Journal of Pediatric Psychology, 17,* 785–805.

Robinson, L. L. (1993). Issues in the consideration of intervention strategies in long-term survivors of childhood cancer. *Cancer, 71,* 3406–3410.

Roila, F. (1993). Ondansetron plus dexamethasone compared to the standard metoclopramide combination. *Oncology, 50,* 163–167.

Ross, D. M., & Ross, S. A. (1988). *Childhood pain: Current issues, research, and management.* Baltimore, MD: Urban & Schwarzenberg.

Rubenstein, C. L., Varni, J. W., & Katz, E. R. (1990). Cognitive functioning in long-term survivors of childhood leukemia: A prospective analysis. *Journal of Developmental and Behavioral Pediatrics, 11,* 301–305.

Sabbioni, M. E. (1991). Cancer and stress: A possible role for psychoneuroimmunology in cancer research? In C. L. Cooper & M. Watson (Eds.), *Cancer and stress: Psychological, biological and coping studies* (pp. 3–26). New York: John Wiley & Sons.

Sandler, E. S., Weyman, C., Conner, K., Reilly, K., Dickson, N., Luzins, J., & McGorray, S. (1992). Midazolam versus fentanyl as premedication for painful proceduresin children with cancer. *Pediatrics, 89,* 631–634.

Sawyer, M. G., Toogood, I., Rice, M., Haskell, C., & Baghurst, P. (1989). School performance and psychological adjustment of children treated for leukemia. *American Journal of Pediatric Hematology/Oncology, 11,* 146–152.

Sievers, T. D., Yee, J. D., Foley, M. E., Blanding, P. J., & Berde, C. B. (1991). Midazolam for conscious sedatin during pediatric oncology procedures: Safety and recovery parameters. *Pediatrics, 88,* 1172–1179.

Spiegel, D., Bloom, J. R., Kraemer, H. C., & Gottheil, E. (1989). Effect of psychosocial treatment on survival of patients with metastatic breast cancer. *Lancet,* October 14, 888–891.

Sposto, R., & Hammond, G. D. (1985). Survival in childhood cancer. *Clinics in Oncology, 4,* 195–204.

Stehbens, J. A., & Kisker, C. T. (1984). Intelligence and achievement testing in childhood cancer: Three years postdiagnosis. *Journal of Developmental and Behavioral Pediatrics, 5,* 184–188.

Stehbens, J. A., Kisker, C. T., & Wilson, B. K. (1983). Achievement and intelligence test-retest performance in pediatric cancer patients at diagnosis and one year later. *Journal of Pediatric Psychology, 8,* 47–56.

Steptoe, A. (1991). The links between stress and illness. *Journal of Psychosomatic Research, 35,* 633–644.

Stokes, T. F., & Baer, D. M. (1977). An implicit technology of generalization. *Journal of Applied Behavior Analysis, 10,* 349–367.

Stringham, D. (Ed.). (1993). *Pediatric drug handbook and formulary—Children's Hospital of Orange County.* Ohio: Lexi-Comp, Inc.

Sturges, J. W., Blount, R. L., James, L. D., Powers, S. W., & Prater, J. M. (1991). Analysis of child distress by phase of medical procedure. In J. H. Johnson & S. B. Johnson (Eds.), *Advances in child health psychology* (pp. 63–76). Gainesville, FL: University of Florida Press.

Sullivan, M. J., Abbott, G. D., & Robison, B. A. (1992). Ondansetron antiemetic therapy for chemotherapy and radiotherapy induced vomiting in children. *New Zealand Medical Journal, 105,* 369–370.

Tabona, M. V. (1990). An overview on the use of granisetron in the treatment of emesis associated with cytostatic chemotherapy. *European Journal of Cancer, 26,* S37–S41.

Taylor, W. B., Proctor, S. J., & Bateman, D. N. (1984). Pharmacokinetics and efficacy of high-dose metoclopramide given by continuous infusion for the control of cytotoxic drug-induced vomiting. *British Journal of Clinical Pharmacology, 18,* 679–684.

Telch, C. F., & Telch, M. J. (1986). Group coping skills instruction and supportive group therapy for cancer patients: A comparison of strategies. *Journal of Consulting and Clinical Psychology, 54,* 802–808.

Terrin, B. N., McWilliams, N. B., & Maurer, M. H. (1984). Side effects of metoclopramide as an antiemetic in childhood cancer chemotherapy. *Journal of Pediatrics, 104,* 138–140.

Tyc, V. L., Mulhern, R. K., Fairclough, D., Ward, P. M., Relling, M. V., & Longmire, W. (1993). Chemotherapy induced nausea and emesis in pediatric cancer patients: External validity of child and parent emesis ratings. *Developmental and Behavioral Pediatrics, 14,* 236–241.

Varni, J. W. (1995). Pediatric pain: A decade biobehavioral perspective. *Behavior Therapist, 18,* 65–70.

Varni, J. W., Blount, R. L., Waldron, S. A., & Smith, A. J. (in press). Management of pain and distress. In M. C. Roberts (Ed.), *Handbook of pediatric psychology (2nd ed.).* New York: Guilford Press.

Varni, J. W., & Corwin, D. G. (1993). *Growing up great.* New York: Berkley Books.

Varni, J. W., Jay, S. M., Masek, B. J., & Thompson, K. L. (1986). Cognitive-behavioral assessment and management of pediatric pain. In A. D. Holzman & D. C. Turk (Eds.), *Pain management: A handbook of psychological treatment approaches* (pp. 168–192). New York: Pergamon Press.

Varni, J. W., & Katz, E. R. (1987). Psychological aspects of cancer in children: A review of research. *Journal of Psychosocial Oncology, 5,* 93–119.

Varni, J. W., Katz, E. R., Colegrove, R., & Dolgin, M. (1993). The impact of social skills training on the adjustment of children with newly diagnosed cancer. *Journal of Pediatric Psychology, 18,* 751–767.

Varni, J. W., Katz, E. R., Colegrove, R., & Dolgin, M. (1994a). Perceived social support and adjustment of children with newly diagnosed cancer. *Journal of Developmental and Behavioral Pediatrics, 15,* 20–26.

Varni, J. W., Katz, E. R., Colegrove, R., & Dolgin, M. (1994b). Perceived stress and adjustment of long-term survivors of childhood cancer. *Journal of Psychosocial Oncology, 12,* 1–16.

Varni, J. W., Katz, E. R., Colegrove, R., & Dolgin, M. (1995a). Adjustment of children with newly diagnosed cancer: Cross informant variance. *Journal of Psychosocial Oncology, 13,* 23–38.

Varni, J. W., Katz, E. R., Colegrove, K., & Dolgin, M. (1996b). Family functioning predictors of adjustment in children with newly diagnosed cancer: A prospective analysis. *Journal of Child Psychology and Psychiatry, 37,* 321–328.

Varni, J. W., Katz, E. R., Colegrove, R., & Dolgin, M. (1995b). Perceived physical appearance and adjustment of children with newly diagnosed cancer: A path analytic model. *Journal of Behavioral Medicine, 18,* 261–278.

Varni, J. W., Katz, E. R., & Waldron, S. (1993). Cognitive-behavioral treatment interventions in childhood cancer. *The Clinical Psychologist, 46,* 192–197.

Varni, J. W., Rubenfeld, L. A., Talbot, D., & Setoguchi, Y. (1989a). Determinants of self-esteem in children with congenital/acquired limb deficiencies. *Journal of Developmental and Behavioral Pediatrics, 10,* 13–16.

Varni, J. W., Rubenfeld, L. A., Talbot, D., & Setoguchi, Y. (1989b). Family functioning, temperament, and psychological adaptation in children with congenital/acquired limb deficiencies. *Pediatrics, 84,* 823–830.

Varni, J. W., Rubenfeld, L. A., Talbot, D., & Setoguchi, Y. (1989c). Stress, social support, and depressive symptomatology in children with congenital/acquired limb deficiencies. *Journal of Pediatric Psychology, 14,* 515–530.

Varni, J. W., & Setoguchi, Y. (1991). Correlates of perceived physical appearance in children with congenital/acquired limb deficiencies. *Journal of Developmental and Behavioral Pediatrics, 12,* 171–176.

Varni, J. W., & Setoguchi, Y. (1992). Screening for behavioral and emotional problems in children and adolescents with congenital or acquired limb deficiencies. *American Journal of Diseases of Children, 146,* 103–107.

Varni, J. W., & Setoguchi, Y. (1993). Effects of parental adjustment on the adaptation of children with congenital or acquired limb deficiencies. *Journal of Developmental and Behavioral Pediatrics, 14,* 13–20.

Varni, J. W., Setoguchi, Y., Rappaport, L. R., & Talbot, D. (1991). Effects of stress, social support, and self-esteem on depression in children with limb deficiencies. *Archives of Physical Medicine and Rehabilitation, 72,* 1053–1058.

Varni, J. W., Setoguchi, Y., Rappaport, L. R., & Talbot, D. (1992). Psychological adjustment and perceived social support in children with congenital/acquired limb deficiencies. *Journal of Behavioral Medicine, 15,* 31–44.

Varni, J. W., & Wallander, J. L. (1988). Pediatric chronic disabilities. In D. K. Routh (Ed.), *Handbook of pediatric psychology* (pp. 190–221). New York: Guilford Press.

Varni, J. W., Wilcox, K. T., & Hanson, V. (1988). Mediating effects of family social support on child psychological adjustment in juvenile rheumatoid arthritis. *Health Psychology, 7,* 421–431.

Wall, V. J., & Womack, W. (1989). Hypnotic versus active cognitive strategies for alleviation of procedural distress in pediatric oncology patients. *American Journal of Clinical Hypnosis, 31,* 181–191.

Wallander, J. L., & Varni, J. W. (1992). Adjustment in children with chronic physical disorders: Programmatic research on a disability-stress-coping model. In A. M. La Greca, L. J. Siegel, J. L. Wallander, & C. E. Walker (Eds.), *Stress and coping in child health* (pp. 279–298). New York: Guilford Press.

Wallander, J. L., Varni, J. W., Babani, L., & Wilcox, K. T. (1989). Family resources as resistance factors for psychological maladjustment in chronically ill and handicapped children. *Journal of Pediatric Psychology, 14,* 157–173.

Weissman, M. M., Wickramaratne, P., Warner, V., John, K., Prusoff, B. A., Merikangas, K. R., & Gammon, G. D. (1987). Assessing psychiatric disorders in children: Discrepancies between mothers' and children's reports. *Archives of General Psychiatry, 44,* 747–753.

Worchel, F. F., Hughes, J. N., Hall, B. M., Stanton, S. B., Stanton, H., & Little, V. Z. (1990). Evaluation of subclinical depression in children using self-, peer-, and teacher-report measures. *Journal of Abnormal Child Psychology, 18,* 271–282.

Zambetti, M., Bajetta, E., Bidoli, P., & Verusio, C. (1985). Antiemetic activity of metoclopramide versus alizapride during cancer chemotherapy. *Tumori, 71,* 609–614.

Zeltzer, L., Dolgin, M. J., LeBaron, S., & LeBaron, C. (1991). A randomized, controlled study of behavioral intervention for chemotherapy distress in children with cancer. *Pediatrics, 88,* 34–42.

Zeltzer, L., Kellerman, J., Ellenberg, L., Dash, J., & Rigler, D. (1983). Hypnosis for reduction of vomiting associated with chemotherapy and disease in adolescents with cancer. *Journal of Adolescent Health Care, 4,* 77–84.

Zeltzer, L., & LeBaron, S. (1986). Assessment of acute pain and anxiety and chemotherapy-related nausea and vomiting in children and adolescents. *Hospice Journal, 2,* 75–98.

Zeltzer, L., LeBaron, S., Richie, D. M., Reed, D., Schoolfield, J., & Prihoda, T. J. (1988). Can children understand and use a rating scale to quantify somatic symptoms? Assessment of nausea and vomiting as a model. *Journal of Consulting and Clinical Psychology, 56,* 567–572.

Zeltzer, L., LeBaron, S., & Zeltzer, P. M. (1984). The effectiveness of behavioral intervention for reduction of nausea and vomiting in children and adolescents receiving chemotherapy. *Journal of Clinical Oncology, 2,* 683–690.

Zeltzer, L. K., Altman, A., Cohen, D., LeBaron, S., Munuksela, E. L., & Schechter, N. L. (1990). Report of the subcommittee on the management of pain associated with procedures in children with cancer. *Pediatrics, 86,* 826–833.

Zeltzer, L. K., & LeBaron, S. (1982). Hypnosis and nonhypnotic techniques for reduction of pain and anxiety during painful procedures in children and adolescents with cancer. *Journal of Pediatrics, 101,* 1032–1035.

Zoubek, A., Dronberger, M., Puschmann, A., & Gadner, H. (1993). Ondansetron in the control of chemotherapy-induced and radiotherapy-induced emesis in children with malignancies. *Anti-Cancer Drugs, 4,* 17–21.

CHAPTER 15

INFECTIOUS DISEASES

John P. Glazer
Johanna Goldfarb
Regina Smith James

DESCRIPTION OF DISORDERS

The role of infectious diseases in producing altered mental status and abnormal behavior is well known to pediatricians. Historically, the acutely ill, febrile, agitated child with neck stiffness presenting to a hospital emergency room with bacterial meningitis exemplified the urgent management of serious pediatric illness. Prompt stabilization of vital functions, diagnostic lumbar puncture, institution of appropriate antimicrobials, with gradual resolution of presenting signs and symptoms and full recovery typified the management of acute, life threatening but curable pediatric disease. In the setting of acute bacterial meningitis, altered mental status and behavior were universal but were treated appropriately because it was known that full recovery of both the acute infectious process and its central nervous system effects could be expected. The risk of secondary infection in household and other close contacts was a factor easily managed with standardized chemoprophylactic measures. Long-term neurodevelopmental effects of bacterial meningitis, including auditory and cognitive impairment and other sequelae, were carefully studied and documented in children recovering from bacterial meningitis. However, serious, permanent, and adverse effects on neurodevelopment were rare, and mortality even rarer. With the recent licensure of Hemophilus influenzae type b vaccine and the subsequent adoption of routine pediatric immunization, the preva-

lence of the most common cause of bacterial meningitis in children has plummeted, further contributing to the trend by which children with acute, curable illness in pediatric in-patient settings have been displaced by those with acute exacerbations of chronic and/or incurable conditions (Glazer, 1990).

Human immunodeficiency virus infection (HIV) is by far the most important contemporary infectious disease for pediatric psychiatrists, psychologists, and other specialists in pediatric mental health. The importance lies in its sweeping effects on mental status, behavior, neurocognitive and physical development, family functioning and structure, and the crucial role of sexual and other risk-taking behaviors in its acquisition. Also, its epidemiology creates unique ethical dilemmas and patterns of vulnerability to bereavement, separation, and loss as challenging to diagnosis and treatment as the medical management of AIDS itself.

Since the onset of the HIV epidemic in 1981, an estimated 18 million adults and 1.5 million children have been infected worldwide (Nozyce et al., 1994); by 1994, an estimated 330,000 to 385,000 American men and women had died of AIDS, resulting in the orphaning of about 24,000 children and 21,000 adolescents (Adnopoz, Forsyth, & Nagler, 1994). The vast majority of HIV-infected infants acquire the virus vertically from their mothers during pregnancy, labor, and/or delivery. While the pathophysiology of transplacental transmission of HIV is not unlike that of classical congenital infectious diseases such as cytomegalovirus (CMV), toxoplasmosis, and rubella, the transplacental route accounts for a minority of HIV infections in infants. Although HIV is presumably always a fatal disease, a minority of patients with perinatally-acquired HIV infection have been reported to survive without symptoms as long as into the early adolescent years (Bussing & Burket, 1993).

After the perinatal period, adolescents are at uniquely high risk of acquiring HIV infection because of the prominence of sexual contact and, to a lesser extent, injection drug use in this population. By age 19, 79 to 86 percent of male adolescents and 66 to 74 percent of female adolescents in the United States have had sexual intercourse, with a majority of boys initiating sexual activity by age 16 or 17 and a majority of girls by age 17 or 18 (Seidman & Rieder, 1994). Moreover, American adolescents, both male and female, frequently have multiple sex partners: 46 percent of sexually experienced girls aged 12 to 19, and 21 to 60 percent of experienced boys reported two or more partners in recent studies (Orr, Langefeld, & Katz, 1992; Centers for Disease Control, 1992), and only 10 to 20 percent of adolescents consistently used condoms (Mosher & McNally, 1991; Aral, 1991). The presence of psychiatric disorder among adolescents is relevant to HIV risk since disturbed adolescents are more likely than their healthy counterparts to be sexually active with multiple partners, to be substance abusers, and to engage in self-mutilation with shared sharp objects (Ponton, DiClemente, & McKenna, 1991).

HIV infection and disease are perhaps most devastating psychosocially because of the patterns of bereavement, separation, and loss they engender. Because HIV is a stigmatized, fatal, vertically transmitted infectious disease, HIV-infected children and their uninfected siblings may face (1) episodic suspension of maternal caretaking secondary to HIV-related hospitalization or incapacity; (2) maternal or sibling death; (3) episodic or permanent institutional, foster, or adoptive placement; (4) ostracism and discrimination by peers, schools, health professionals, and the community; (5) the psychological burdens of keeping family secrets hidden from the outside world and a "conspiracy of silence" regarding HIV-related issues within the family. Permanency and consistency of nurturant caregiving are essential to the normative psychological and social development of infants and children (Goldstein, Freud, & Solnit, 1979). Pediatric psychiatrists and psychologists, given their traditional expertise in dealing with developmental psychopathology, disordered behavior, impulse dyscontrol, separation, loss, and family disruption, are uniquely situated to respond to the impact of the HIV epidemic on family functioning, behavior, and neurodevelopment. In this regard, HIV is uniquely challenging to the field of pediatric mental health in that not only are all of these difficult problems in clinical practice likely to be present in every case, but, in addition, psychiatric disorders may themselves predispose to HIV acquisition through substance abuse, promiscuity, and other high-risk behaviors.

Until late in the course of infection, the child with HIV infection generally can and should be cared for as an out-patient. Intensive, long-term management delivered within the matrix of a multidisciplinary, team-based service delivery system encompassing medical, psychiatric, nursing, social, community outreach, and home-based services is essential. As with any chronic pediatric illness, it is incumbent upon the pediatric AIDS caregiving team to assure as normative a developmental trajectory as possible for the HIV-infected child, siblings, and family, a goal that presents unprecedented challenges. This chapter reviews the epidemiology, medical diagnosis and treatment, behavioral contributions, and the neurocognitive, psychiatric, and developmental impact of HIV infection in infants, children, adolescents, and families.

EPIDEMIOLOGY

Global Epidemiology

Worldwide, the World Health Organization estimates that there are now about 18 million adults and 1.5 million children infected with the Human Immunodeficiency Virus-1 (HIV) (World Health Organization, 1995). Each year the number increases with the vast majority of new cases occurring in the developing world. While the epidemic was first described in the United States, the largest number of cases and the majority of women and children with HIV infection are now recognized in sub-Saharan Africa. HIV infection has only recently been recognized in southern Asia, but a major epidemic is expected to unfold there in the next decade and is predicted to rival the African epidemic in numbers. In Latin America, the epidemic began well after that in North America, but already the numbers of cases are similar. In most of the world, heterosexual transmission accounts for the majority of cases. Wherever heterosexual transmission occurs, women are affected and disease in children has followed.

Pediatric AIDS was first described in this country shortly after the disease was recognized in adults in the

early 1980s. Since then, the disease in children has followed the AIDS pandemic throughout the world. Most
children with AIDS now live in sub-Sahraran Africa,
paralleling the spread of HIV infection in women of
child-bearing age. In endemic urban areas, sexually active adults can have seroprevalence rates as high as 40
percent. The epidemic's impact on the social and economic stability of the area is staggering. The most productive members of society are affected, and social
systems are overburdened by the care of adults and children with this fatal disease. The epidemic threatens to reverse the efforts of the last decade in preventive care and
may make the goals of the World Health Organization
for the promotion of child health unattainable (Goldfarb, 1993a).

In the United States, the AIDS epidemic began in
the homosexual male population, and most of the early
cases occurred in young men. Over the past decade the
epidemic has moved into the heterosexual population
and is spreading out from the northeast and the west
coasts into the southern and Midwestern parts of the
country. While most cases of AIDS are still in the male
population, women, children, and adolescents are now
the groups with the fastest-growing rate of new infections in the United States (Centers for Disease Control,
1995). The overall seroprevalence rate in this country is
still relatively low at 1.5/1000, but the rate in urban areas,
as estimated from anonymous studies of child-bearing
women, can be as high as 8/1000 in inner-city populations (Hoff, Berardi, & Weiblen, 1988).

The exact number of Americans infected with HIV is
unknown, but it is estimated to be about 1 million, with
about 20,000 to 30,000 of these children, based upon
Centers for Disease Control (CDC) estimates. There
were over 500,000 cases of AIDS reported in the United
States as of October, 1995. This number vastly underes-
timates the numbers of individuals infected, as most are
unrecognized. Statistics are based on CDC case definitions of disease in adults and children. A revised classification system for HIV infection in children less than 13
years old takes into account the variations in disease
that distinguish children from adults with HIV infection, as well as the stages of disease that occur in the
child with HIV (U.S. Department of Health and Human
Services, 1994) (see Table 15.1).

Epidemiology of Pediatric AIDS

The epidemiology of pediatric AIDS parallels the epidemic in women because HIV infection in children is
predominantly acquired during the perinatal period by

Table 15.1. Centers for Disease Control Classification
System for Diagnosis of HIV in Children Less than 13 Years
of Age*

Diagnosis: HIV infected

1. *A child < 18 months of age who is HIV seropositive or born
   to an HIV-infected mother and:*
- has positive results on two separate determinations (excluding
  cord blood) of one or more of the following:
  —HIV culture
  —HIV polymerase chain reaction
  —HIV p24 antigen
  OR
- meets criteria for AIDS: CDC clinical definition of AIDS

2. *A child > 18 months of age born to an HIV-infected mother or
   any child infected by blood, blood products or other modes of
   transmission who:*
- is HIV-antibody positive by EIA and a confirmatory test such
  as Western blot or immunofluorescence assay,
  OR
- meets any of the criteria in 1 above.

Diagnosis: Perinatally exposed

A child who does not meet the criteria for HIV infection who:
- is HIV seropositive and is < 18 months old
  OR
- has unknown antibody status, but was born to a mother known
  to be infected with HIV.

Diagnosis: Seroreverter

A child who is born to an HIV-infected mother and who
- has been documented as HIV-antibody negative by EIA in two
  consecutive determinations at 6 to 18 months of age or one
  determination after 18 months of age.
- has had no other laboratory evidence of HIV infection
- has not had an AIDS defining clinical illness.

*HIV = Human Immunodeficiency Virus; AIDS = Acquired Immune Defi-
ciency Syndrome; CDC = Centers for Disease Control; EIA = Reactive Enzyme Immunoassay (CDC, 1994).

means of transmission from mother to infant (Peckham &
Gibb, 1995). Therefore, any attempt to understand pediatric AIDS requires understanding the epidemic in
women. While AIDS and HIV infection in women
worldwide are overwhelmingly related to heterosexual
transmission, in the United States injection drug abuse by
women or their sexual partners was much more common
early on. As the epidemic has matured in the United
States, injection drug abuse is less often a factor, with
heterosexual contact the only risk factor that can be identified in an increasing proportion of cases. In any case,
the AIDS epidemic in the United States has been concentrated among the urban minority poor because of the
concentration of injection drug abuse and promiscuity in

that socioeconomic setting. Even for the monogamous woman in an urban setting, the risk of HIV acquisition is significant given the high prevalence of injection drug use and promiscuity in prospective male partners.

Transmission

The risk of transmission of HIV infection during the perinatal period from infected mother to her infant is estimated to be between 20 and 40 percent, depending on the population studied (Andiman & Simpson, 1990; Blanche, Rozioux, & Moscato, 1989; European Collaborative Study, 1992; Lepage, Van de Perre, & Msellati, 1993). Factors such as maternal immune status, severity of maternal illness, and timing of maternal infection appear to influence the rate of transmission (Hutto, Parks, & Lai, 1991; Thomas, Weedon, & Krasinski, 1994). Transmission in the perinatal period appears to occur predominantly during labor and delivery, but in utero transmission also occurs. Children infected in utero are likely to have a positive viral culture at birth (Luzariaga, Mcuilken, & Alimenti, 1993) and to develop symptomatic disease early, often within the first year of life. Transmission in utero is thought to be most likely when the mother experiences primary infection during pregnancy; under these circumstances, the rate of maternal-fetal transmission approaches 50 percent (Van de Perre, Simonon, & Msellati, 1991), most likely because of the high grade viremia that characterizes acute primary HIV infection (Daar, Mmoudgil, Meyer, & Ho, 1991).

Children infected during labor and delivery, probably the majority of perinatal cases, are infected by exposure to maternal blood during the birth process (Mofenson, 1995). These infants are likely to have a negative viral blood culture at birth, becoming viremic in the first months of life. These children present with signs of infection later than children infected in utero and live longer. Risk factors favoring perinatal transmission include severe maternal immunocompromise, obstetrical complications, prolonged rupture of the fetal membranes, and first born twins (Dulliege, Amos, Felton, Biggar, & Goedert, 1995), of which the common feature is presumed to be the quantity of maternal virus to which the newborn is exposed.

While most children with perinatal infection will be ill by 2 years of age, as the epidemic matures there will be increasingly older children with apparent perinatal infection who are mildly ill or asymptomatic into adolescence. Factors such as virulence differences among viral strains and specific host immunity factors are presumably responsible for this spectrum of clinical severity. Whether children with long-term asymptomatic HIV infection are capable of transmission vertically to the next generation is unknown.

Breast-feeding has also been associated with transmission of HIV, but can be proven only in cases in which the mother becomes infected after the birth of an infant (Goldfarb, 1993b). During acute infection, viremia is high grade, and virus can be cultured from breast milk. Infection appears more likely to be transmitted by breast milk during acute infection in the mother, prior to the development of an immunological response, rather than from the chronically infected mother. In the developing world, the risks of not breast-feeding include life-threatening malnutrition and infection with enteric pathogens; these risks appear to significantly outweigh the morbidity associated with transmission of HIV by breast-feeding (Lederman, 1992), such that WHO policy stipulates that HIV-infected mothers in the developing world should breast-feed. In the developed world, such as in the United States, where safe formulas are available and hopefully affordable, the HIV-infected mother is urged not to breast-feed in order to decrease the likelihood of HIV transmission.

Infants and children, like adults, can become infected by transfusion of infected blood or blood products, but this route of infection is increasingly less frequent as our blood supply is screened, and methods of processing blood products such as coagulation factor for treatment of hemophilia are improved. Rare cases of transmission to young children related to sexual abuse have probably occurred and should be considered in suggestive clinical settings.

Adolescents, latecomers to the United States epidemic, are an increasingly significant epidemiologic reservoir of HIV, and are infected by heterosexual and homosexual contact, as well as through injection drug use (Gayle & D'Angelo, 1991). Again, the preponderance of adolescent cases are in the inner-city population where adolescents of color are over-represented. However, with 75 percent of graduating high school seniors in the United States reporting at least one sexual encounter and many reporting multiple partners, it is not surprising that the epidemic is reaching broadly into the young adult population. No group is excluded and the occurrence of significant HIV-seroprevalence on college campuses illustrates the volatility of the epidemic and emphasizes the risk of acquisition of the HIV infection for all young adults regardless of ethnic or socioeconomic background.

ASSESSMENT APPROACHES

Medical Issues

Diagnosis of HIV infection is difficult in the first months of life because maternal antibody crosses the placenta and all children born to seropositive women will have antibody for many months after birth. HIV culture and polymerase chain reaction (PCR) are currently used to confirm infection in the young infant (Husson, Comeau, & Hoff, 1990); p24 antigen detected by immune complex dissociation may also be useful in this setting (Miles, Balden, & Magpantay, 1993). After the first 18 months of life, transplacental HIV antibody is no longer an issue, such that standard testing for HIV-seropositivity is the most efficient and least costly method of documenting infection. At least two confirmatory tests should be done prior to accepting the diagnosis of infection at any age in any given case (see Table 15.1).

A small proportion of infected older infants and children are seronegative (Goetz, Hall, & Harbison, 1988). These children have low levels of immunoglobulin, appear to be unable to produce HIV antibody, and are usually ill with clear signs of HIV infection. A viral culture, PCR or p24 antigen is required to confirm the infection in these children.

Most infants born to HIV-infected mothers are well at birth, though subtle differences in birth weight and gestational age have been suggested in some studies, and there are progressive adverse effects on growth and development that become apparent over time (Moye, Rich, & Kalish, 1996). Illness may begin within the first months of life with failure to thrive, with recurrent infection, or with an episode of *Pneumocystis carinii* pneumonia (PCP), the latter often life-threatening. In general, children who present early progress more rapidly and often die in infancy, especially if untreated. Children who present later may appear to be completely well with normal growth and development until the onset of signs of HIV infection such as lymphadenopathy, organomegaly, anemia, thrombocytopenia, neutropenia, or other signs and symptoms. (See Table 15.2.)

Many children present with recurrent infections such as otitis media that mimic those of normal children at first. However, recurrent serious bacterial infections, especially recurrent pneumococcal infections, bacteremia, lower respiratory infections, meningitis, or osteomyelitis, should suggest the possibility of HIV infection, especially if risk factors are present. Two such serious infections in a child should prompt an investigation for HIV infection. Opportunistic infections such as *Candida albicans* esophagitis or severe infections due to *Herpes simplex* virus do not occur in normal children and should prompt consideration of HIV infection at their first occurrence. Early in the epidemic, lymphocytic interstitial pneumonitis (LIP) was frequently a presenting sign of infection, but with earlier identification of HIV-infected children and the advent of early antiretroviral therapy, LIP is often seen later in the course of disease. Still, in some instances, it remains a presenting manifestation.

Neurological presentations of HIV infection in childhood occur in about 10 percent of children with AIDS. HIV encephalopathy in the child, as in the adult, appears to be due to direct invasion of the central nervous system (CNS) by HIV (Epstein, Goudsmit, & Paul, 1987; Ho, Rota, & Schooley, 1985), but with a very different clinical presentation than in the adult, in whom dementia is the usual clinical picture (Epstein, Scharer, & Oleski, 1986). Typically, the HIV-infected child has developed normally until the onset of the encephalitis, often with achievement of normal weight, height, and developmental milestones. The child begins to lose milestones and becomes hypertonic. The child who was walking begins to toe walk, hypertonicity worsens, and the child ultimately reverts to crawling. This is a progressive syndrome that proceeds in a caudocephalad fashion, ultimately with loss of motor strength and function of legs, arms, and finally the muscles of the head and neck. Routine examination of the cerebrospinal fluid is often unremarkable in children with HIV encephalopathy, but is indicated to rule out other opportunistic and potentially treatable infectious causes of CNS disease. Neuroimaging findings in pediatric HIV encephalopathy include cortical atrophy on computerized axial tomography (CT) and white matter abnormalities and basal ganglia calcification on magnetic resonance imaging (MRI) (Belman, 1990). Treatment with zidovudine (AZT) has been shown to slow the progression and even reverse the neurological manifestations of HIV disease in some infants and children, at least temporarily (Piaao, Eddy, & Falloon, 1988).

Other HIV-infected infants fail to thrive early in infancy and exhibit developmental retardation and decreased velocity of head growth without the hypertonia described above. Children with severe HIV disease are invariably affected neuro-developmentally with malnutrition, wasting, and profound somatic and developmental failure (Nozyce et al., 1994). Complicating the assessment of infants and children with AIDS with neurodevelopmental impairment are the elements of severe

Table 15.2. Children with HIV Infection: Symptomatic Classification

Category N: Not Symptomatic

Children who have no signs or symptoms related to HIV infection or who have only one of the signs or symptoms of mildly symptomatic infection in category A.

Category A: Mildly Symptomatic

Children with two or more of the conditions listed below but none of the conditions listed in categories B and C:

- Lymphadenopathy > 0.5 cm at more than two sites (bilateral nodes are considered one site)
- Hepatomegaly
- Splenomegaly
- Dermatitis
- Parotitis
- Recurrent or persistent upper respiratory infection, sinusitis, or otitis media

Category B: Moderately Symptomatic

Children who have symptomatic conditions other than those in category A or C that are due to HIV infection such as:

- Anemia, neutropenia, thrombocytopenia persisting > 30 d, bacterial meningitis, pneumonia or sepsis (single episode)
- Cardiomyopathy
- CMV, onset before 1 month of age
- Diarrhea, recurrent or chronic
- Hepatitis
- HSV stomatitis, recurrent (>2 episodes/year)
- HSV bronchitis, pneumonitis or esophagitis onset, < 1 month of age
- *Herpes zoster*: >2 episodes or >1 dermatome
- Leiomyosarcoma

- Lymphoid interstitial pneumonia
- Nephropathy
- Nocardiosis
- Persistent fever for > 1 month
- Toxoplasmosis, onset < 1 month of age
- *Varicella*, disseminated

Category C: Severely Symptomatic

Children who have clinical AIDS:

- Serious bacterial infections, recurrent and confirmed
- Candidiasis, esophageal or pulmonary
- Coccidioidomycosis, disseminated
- Cryptococcosis, extrapulmonary
- Cryptosporidiosis or isosporiasis with diarrhea
- CMV disease, onset > 1 month (not lymph nodes, liver, spleen)
- Encephalopathy*
- HSV > 1 month, in children > 1 month old
- Histoplasmosis, disseminated
- Kaposi's sarcoma
- Lymphoma, primary, CHS
- Lymphoma, HIV-associated
- Mycobacterium tuberculosis, disseminated or extrapulmonary
- Mycobacterium, other species, disseminated
- *Pneumocystis carinii* pneumonia
- Progressive multifocal leukoencephalopathy
- *Salmonella* septicemia, recurrent (nontyphoidal)
- Toxoplasmosis of the brain, onset > 1 month old
- Wasting syndrome[+]

HIV = Human Immunodeficiency Virus; CMV = Cytomegalovirus infection; HSV = Herpes simplex virus

*Defined as at least one of the following progressive findings present for at least 2 months in the absence of a concurrent illness other than HIV that could explain: failure to attain milestones, loss of milestones, or loss of cognitive functioning; impaired brain growth or acquired microcephaly or brain atrophy on CT or MRI; acquired symmetric motor deficit (two or more of the following: paresis, pathologic reflexes, ataxia, or gait disturbance)

[+]Defined as either persistent weight loss of more than 10 percent of baseline or downward, crossing at least two weight percentile lines on the weight for age chart (age > 1 year) or as less than 5th percentile absolute weight (CDC, 1994a).

---

psychosocial adversity so often accompanying HIV infection in a pediatric setting. This complication only adds to the fact that pediatric HIV infections themselves are recognized causes of failure to thrive and neurodevelopmental impairment. It is crucial to thoroughly assess the complex family, socioeconomic, and community factors in every pediatric AIDS case, identifying and intervening intensively in adverse environmental circumstances that may be responsible for adverse outcomes over and above those due to AIDS itself.

Encephalopathy may occur in 20 percent of children with HIV infection over the course of their illness (Lobato, Caldwell, Ng, & Oxtoby, 1995). Terminally it may be very difficult to differentiate the exact etiology of a progressive encephalopathy in a particular child. Many opportunistic infections can produce an encephalopathic picture; it is often neither humane nor relevant to med-

ical management to attempt to differentiate, for example, CMV from atypical mycoplasma infection or other opportunistic pathogens in the HIV-infected child with severe cachexia who is wasting and terminally ill.

While most HIV infections are initially asymptomatic, a seroconverting illness can occur and may correlate with severity of viral burden. This chain of events is most often described in the adolescent who is infected by sexual contact. A mononucleosis-like illness occurs with fever, rash, pharyngitis and malaise, lasting days to weeks. Aseptic meningitis may also occur. Although individuals are usually seropositive within 3 to 4 weeks of infection, often exhibiting a transient high level viremia during this phase of infection, seroconversion after infection with HIV may not occur for several months (Daar et al., 1991). HIV culture, PCR or p24 antigen positivity can often be demonstrated, confirming the HIV infection prior to achievement of seropositivity by the ELISA and Western blot tests (Cooper, Gold, & Maclean, 1985).

In summary, pediatric AIDS is a fatal infectious disease with protean clinical manifestations and a highly variable clinical course, which almost always affects multiple family members, especially the mother. These fundamental epidemiologic features help create an unpredictable environment (Andiman, 1995) in which an HIV-seropositive pregnant woman is unable to know whether her baby will have AIDS for several months after birth, and multiple HIV-infected family members cannot know in whom and in which generation illness and death will occur first. As such, the psychosocial impact of pediatric AIDS is profound, and will be considered in the next section.

Psychological and Psychiatric Issues

Chronic medical illness in children and youth is an established risk factor for psychiatric disturbance, and central nervous system involvement enhances this risk (Pless & Nolan, 1989). Several models have been proposed to account for adverse psychosocial outcome in medically ill children and youth, including a "stress and coping" model and the proposition that serious medical illness may serve as a trigger for post-traumatic stress disorder (Glazer, 1991). HIV infection of mothers, infants, and children is not only a chronic illness involving multiple family members, but it also poses additional, unique psychosocial challenges to affected families including (1) isolation from family members and community due to stigma, (2) repeated separation of children from primary caretakers, (3) parental death, and (4) contagion. The psychosocial sequelae of childhood cancer, for example, have been well characterized (Glazer, 1991). Despite a significant risk of psychiatric disturbance and family dysfunction in pediatric oncology settings, cancer is not a contagious disease and is not acquired through stigmatized behaviors such as injection drug abuse and homosexuality. The parents of children with cancer are rarely ill, the disease itself is often curable, and there is no unique association with socioeconomic hardship. In "HIV-affected" families, an increasingly common and appropriate term, the effects of drug addiction, poverty, single parent households, separation, loss, and stigmatization beyond the medical and neuropsychiatric effects of HIV infection themselves pose a profound developmental challenge. This section will explore the neurodevelopmental and psychiatric effects of the AIDS epidemic and approaches to therapeutic intervention.

Neuropsychiatric Manifestations of HIV Infection in Adults

The neuropsychiatric manifestations of adult HIV infection have been well characterized and include AIDS-dementia complex (ADC), aseptic meningitis, vacuolar myelopathy, and peripheral neuropathy (Summergrad, Rauch, & Neal, 1993).

ADC typically presents as an insidious dementing process with impaired short-term memory, attention, and concentration as common initial complaints. These in turn are often accompanied by dysphoria and social withdrawal. This constellation of signs and symptoms can represent the first expression of HIV infection in as many as one-third of adult cases. Although precise figures are not available, it is estimated that up to 70 percent of adult AIDS patients will develop ADC at some point during their illness; along with progression of disease, severe dementia accompanied by marked cognitive slowing, incontinence, weakness, and hyper-reflexia with a paraplegic, mute state occurring pre-terminally often supervenes (Summergrad et al., 1993).

A wide spectrum of psychiatric disturbances has been reported in individual case reports and series of adults with AIDS, including depression, anxiety, mania, and psychosis (Summergrad et al., 1993). In their review of the published literature, Harris, Gleghorn, and Jeste (1989), found that in 31 percent of adults who experienced psychosis during the course of HIV infection, psychosis was the presenting clinical manifestation. With respect to psychological aspects of testing for HIV positivity, several studies have shown a decrease in depression, anxiety, and/or suicidal ideation after completion of testing, even in those found to be seropositive (Summergrad et al., 1993). Appropriate counselling support at the time of notification of serologic status is essential.

Several recent studies have addressed the prevalence of specific psychiatric disorders in HIV-positive adult populations. Perkins et al. (1994) found no statistically significant differences in the lifetime (29 percent vs. 45 percent), initial cross-sectional (8 percent vs. 3 percent), or six-month follow-up (9 percent vs. 11 percent) prevalence of major depressive disorder in a comparison of asymptomatic HIV-positive and HIV-negative gay men in a non-HIV endemic region. Moreover, symptom severity in study subjects with major depression was comparable in both groups. Current major depression in study subjects in both groups was associated with a lifetime history of major depression but not with neuropsychological functioning, suggesting that major depressive disorder in asymptomatic HIV-positive homosexual men is not due to HIV effects on the central nervous system. Finally, somatic complaints such as fatigue and insomnia in the study cohort of 98 asymptomatic HIV-positive homosexual men correlated with dysphoria and major depression but were not associated with CD4 cell counts or neuropsychological functioning. This study highlighted the importance of surveillance and intervention for depressive disorders in HIV-positive patients with these complaints.

Sewell et al. (1994) studied clinical, cerebrospinal fluid, neuropsychological, and magnetic resonance imaging findings in a group of 16 HIV positive men with new onset psychosis in comparison to non-psychotic HIV-positive controls. While this study did not address the prevalence of psychosis, the authors found a significantly greater occurrence of past stimulant and sedative abuse and a higher mortality rate in the group with psychosis than in controls. Using the Halstead-Reitan battery, the authors found a trend toward greater neuropsychologic impairment in the psychotic subjects compared to the non-psychotic subjects, but they found no between-group differences in CSF or MRI findings. Of 11 psychotic subjects who died during the course of the study, three of the six available for autopsy demonstrated high burdens of HIV in the brain. Unlike the study of mood disorders in HIV-positive men (Perkins et al., 1994), the present authors suggest that new-onset psychosis in HIV-positive men may be a manifestation of HIV-associated organic mental disorder (Sewell et al., 1994).

Finally, a high prevalence of axis II disorders has been reported in a sample of 260 adults volunteering for HIV testing, with 37 percent in the subsample who were subsequently determined to be seropositive, compared to 20 percent of the seronegatives (Jacobsberg, Frances, & Perry, 1995). Dramatic cluster and borderline disorders were particularly frequent in the HIV-positive group, suggesting a link between the impulsive behaviors that typify these axis II disorders and the risk for transmission of HIV.

Of interest with regard to the relationship between psychosocial stress and immunocompetence in HIV-infected adults, Evans et al. (1995) reported that "severe stress" was associated with significant reductions in natural killer cell populations and in the number of CD8+ and CD57 antigen-bearing T-cells, the latter thought to represent cytotoxic T-effector cells in HIV-positive homosexual men. No comparable cellular immunosuppression was found in stressed HIV-negative homosexual controls.

Neurodevelopmental Sequelae

The early North American pediatric AIDS literature reported prevalence rates for neurological involvement among symptomatic HIV-positive infants and children of 50–88 percent (Belman, Diamond, & Dickinson, 1988; Belman, Ultmann, & Horoapian, 1985; Epstein et al., 1986), while European studies reported neurological syndromes in only 24–29 percent (Tardieu, Blanche, & Rouzioux, 1987). Differences in prevalence estimates have been attributed to retrospective study design, insufficient length of follow-up in prospective studies, and varying degrees of comorbidity, particularly prenatal drug exposure and other accompaniments of poverty and social disadvantage (Tardieu et al., 1987). While the true prevalence of HIV-related neurodevelopmental sequelae is unknown, more recent prospective longitudinal studies have helped to define this major problem more clearly (Bale et al., 1993; Gay et al., 1995; Levenson, Mellins, Zawadzki, Kairam, & Stein, 1992; Loveland et al., 1994; Mellins, Levenson, & Zawadski, 1994; Nozyce et al., 1994; Tardieu et al., 1995; Whitt et al., 1993).

The age prevalences of the two most severe complications of pediatric AIDS, encephalopathy and opportunistic infection, follow a bimodal distribution (Mok & Newell, 1995). It is increasingly clear that pediatric HIV infection follows two distinct clinical, infectious, and immunological trajectories. In 15–20 percent of perinatally acquired cases, HIV infection is associated with heavy virus burden, severe immunocompromise, rapid clinical progression with a high mortality rate in the first months of life, and few survivors beyond the age of 4 years; most of these children have encephalitis. In contrast, a larger proportion of vertically infected infants are minimally symptomatic or asymptomatic for long periods and without encephalopathy, some with potentially reversible manifestations such as generalized lymphadenopathy, parotitis, lymphocytic interstitial pneumonitis, and more gradually progressive immunodeficiency, usually without overt neurological manifestations. Overall, the mortality rate by age 18 months approximates 10 percent in prospective studies in the developed world, with subsequent annual mortality of 3 to 4 percent per year, accounting for the documented survival of some congenitally infected individuals into early adolescence (Bussing & Burket, 1993). As with other perinatal infections such as cytomegalovirus (Glazer, 1990), however, significant neurocognitive morbidity less fulminant than that of early-onset HIV encephalopathy may be associated with congenital HIV infection of the more slowly progressive type.

Tardieu et al. (1995) prospectively assessed school achievement at age 6 years, using blinded teacher reports in 33 vertically HIV-infected children, and in 24 of these, formal neurocognitive and psychiatric symptom measures were also administered. Of 57 children in the original cohort, 15 had died before the 6th birthday, five died after age 6 but did so before the study or were too ill for testing, and four were lost to follow-up. Thirty of the 33 study subjects were neurologically normal and had normal head circumference when assessed; a pseudobulbar disorder and buccolingual dyspraxia, generalized CMV infection, and leiomyosarcoma metastatic to the brain, respectively, were present in the other three children. Twenty-two of the 33 subjects exhibited age-expected academic performance (including one child who performed well until her death at age 7), five were judged "borderline" and six had "failed." Of the 24 subjects undergoing formal cognitive assessment, mean scores on the Stanford-Binet (95) and the similarities subtest of the WISC-R (11) were considered "normal," with only one child showing "abnormal" (i.e., below the "low average" range) results on each instrument, respectively. However, 10 children exhibited deficits in visual-spatial organization, 10 exhibited time concept disorientation, and seven showed deficits in both areas. Three of 10 patients undergoing language assessment exhibited a range of abnormalities that included disarticulation, speech delay, or stuttering. Study subjects were scored psychiatrically by being assigned a Global Assessment of Functioning (GAF) score based upon results of the Child Behavior Checklist and clinical interview of 24 subjects. None of the 24 children were judged "severely" affected (GAF <30), seven were judged "intermediate" (GAF 31–50), and 17 were judged "mildly" affected (GAF >51) or asymptomatic. The authors note that the finding of two-thirds of the subjects exhibiting normal academic functioning is more optimistic than in a previous report of a 44 percent prevalence of "mental retardation" among 5-year-old HIV-infected children. The school failure rate, however, was higher than estimates of 10–15 percent in the general population. Also, there was a trend linking lower CD4+ lymphocyte counts with poorer neurocognitive functioning in this study, possibly indicating greater viral burden in the brains of the more immunocompromised subjects. Prenatal drug exposure is not described in this study, and there was no control group.

Gay et al. (1995) administered the Bayley Scales of Infant Development (BSID) every 3 months for the first 24 months of postnatal life to 28 HIV-infected and 126 uninfected infants of 126 nondrug-using HIV-positive Haitian women. There were no differences in gestational age, birth weight, or rates of maternal death among the two groups. Mean scores on the "performance" BSID subscale showed "no delay" (>85) in 50 percent of the HIV group and 91 percent of controls, "mild or moderate delay" (50–84) in 21 percent of HIV-positive and 8 percent of controls, and "severe" (<50) delay in 28 percent of HIV-positive and none of the controls, at all age intervals tested. Statistical analysis of these data are not reported by the authors due to the small sample of HIV-positive infants, but the trend toward HIV-associated developmental delay is clear, and prenatal drug exposure in this study was not a factor. Again, though neurodevelopmental sequelae were detected, 32 percent and 50 percent of HIV-positive infants, respectively, exhibited no delays on the "mental" and "performance" subscales of the BSID.

In a similar study using the BSID, Mellins et al. (1994) compared neurodevelopmental performance in HIV-infected and non-HIV infected prenatally drug exposed infants, concluding that congenital HIV infection and prenatal drug exposure are independent neurodevelopmental risk factors. However, the small number of non-drug exposed, HIV-infected subjects in this study limits conclusions regarding relative causality. HIV-infected infants with neurodevelopmental sequelae may be much more likely to exhibit abnormalities on neurological examination, including microcephaly, hypotonia, and weakness, compared to non-developmentally delayed HIV-infected controls (Mellins et al., 1994).

Studies of neurocognitive functioning among HIV-positive hemophiliacs (Bale et al., 1993; Loveland et al., 1994; Whitt et al., 1993) infected postnatally during the 1981–1984 "window" between the start of the epidemic and implementation of routine heat treatment of factor VIII suggest that hemophilia itself is responsible for significant neurocognitive deficits but that HIV infection confers little additional risk. Loveland et al. (1994) assessed IQ, neuropsychological functioning, academic achievement, and adaptive functioning in 207 HIV-positive and 126 HIV-negative 6 to 18-year-old males with hemophilia. Functioning in all four categories did not differ significantly relative to HIV status, but was relatively impaired in both groups compared to the general population. Despite these differences, 75 percent of the hemophilia group overall demonstrated normal cognitive functioning. Frank HIV encephalopathy appears to be uncommon in postnatally infected youth with hemophilia, resembling the course of CNS involvement in HIV-positive adults more than the more fulminant course seen in some vertically infected infants. One study did find a higher prevalence of neurologic abnormalities in muscle-stretch reflexes and muscle bulk, but no significant neurocognitive differences in HIV-positive compared to HIV-negative youth with hemophilia were found (Bale et al., 1993).

The Child and Family

By 1994, an estimated 50,000–75,000 women in the United States had been infected with HIV, 7,500 infants infected perinatally, and 350,000 men and women had died. Maternal HIV deaths alone may have accounted for the orphaning of as many as 24,000 children and 21,000 adolescents. In HIV-affected families with living parents, the risk of extended separation of children from biologic parents, which may have profound psychological sequelae, is common, as reported in one study in which 61 percent of cases concerned an HIV-positive mother who was an injection drug user (Adnopoz et al., 1994).

Systematic surveys of categorical psychiatric diagnosis in children with AIDS have not been reported to the authors' knowledge, but prevalence estimates are available. Adnopoz and colleagues (1994) reported that in a cohort of 126 uninfected children of HIV-positive mothers, 36 percent were judged to meet criteria for psychiatric intervention, a figure dramatically greater than that in the general population. The authors have astutely summarized the psychosocial forces impinging upon HIV-infected and uninfected infants, children, and parents in HIV-affected families. Themes include (1) non-disclosure of the HIV diagnosis because of fear of economic, employment or insurance discrimination; (2) disordered mother/infant attachment related to the mother's uncertainty as to the infection status, and thus the prognosis of her infant; (3) mother's guilt regarding her role in HIV transmission and her anxiety about her own longevity; (4) episodic inability of infected mothers to function in parental tasks with exacerbation of AIDS, along with affected young children falsely attributing parental incapacity or absence to their own wrongdoing; (5) for infected adolescents, the collision between needed restrictions imposed by HIV infection upon activities of daily living, and the teenager's developmentally normative strivings for sexual expression, independence, and a sense of immortality.

Grubman et al. (1995) recently summarized the clinical, immunologic, and psychosocial status of 42 surviving perinatally infected children at a mean age of 11.3 years at follow-up, with a mean age at diagnosis of 7.3 years. 23.8 percent of this cohort of 9 to 16-year-old HIV survivors were medically asymptomatic, 57 percent had developed AIDS, 76 percent had been orphaned due to maternal death, and most optimistically, 76 percent were attending regular school classes. However, despite the association between full disclosure of diagnosis of a serious illness and favorable psychological adjustment of affected children (Koocher & O'Malley, 1981), in only 57 percent of cases had the HIV diagnosis been disclosed to the infected child. In 33 percent of cases, school officials had been informed of the child's HIV positivity, but this is a different issue (see below). With regard to neurological status, 25 of the 42 subjects (59 percent) had normal neurological examinations and were symptom-free; five subjects each exhibited progressive encephalopathy, developmental regression, and attention deficit hyperactivity disorder, respectively.

Hein et al. (1995) reported no significant differences in self esteem, anxiety, depression, and "emotional distress" among 72 HIV-positive compared to 1142 HIV-negative 13 to 31-year-olds, all of whom were sexually active, seeking out-patient or in-patient medical services in an urban hospital in New York City.

Several recent studies have addressed psychosocial adaptation and coping in HIV-positive youth with hemophilia (Brown, Schultz, & Gragg, 1995; Colegrove & Huntziger, 1994; Drotar, Agle, Eckl, & Thompson, 1995). All of these studies document significant psychological resilience in this population and little difference in the prevalence of psychological distress or disturbance in comparison to HIV-negative counterparts with hemophilia. Drotar and colleagues, using a controlled cross-sectional design, administered the State-Trait Anxiety Inventory for Children (STAIC), the Weinberger Adjustment Inventory (WAI), the Friendship Questionnaire (FQ), and the Hemophilia Psychosocial Questionnaire (HPQ) to 91 HIV-seropositive and 92 HIV-seronegative adolescents with hemophilia at 33 hemophilia treatment centers throughout the United States. Mothers of each subject group were administered the Profile of Mood States (POMS) and the Family Relationship Inventory (FRI), which is derived from the Family Environment Scale (FES) and encompasses three dimensions of family functioning: "cohesion," "expressiveness," and "conflict." Differences in anxiety, depression, social withdrawal, and family adjustment between the HIV-positive and HIV-negative subject groups were assessed using analysis of variance (ANOVA) and group differences between the mothers' groups assessed using multivariate analysis of variance (MANOVA). The two groups of adolescents did not differ significantly on any of the general or hemophilia-specific measures of psychological adjustment except on a single subscale of the WAI showing "less positive affect" in the HIV-positive group. Moreover, the HIV-positive group was no more likely than the HIV-negative group to have utilized mental health services. However, the mothers of HIV-positive subjects demonstrated significantly greater psychological distress on the POMS (mean 46.3) than the mothers of HIV-negative subjects (mean 31.3; p <.008) and greater levels of depression (p <.0002) and confusion (p <.0001) on POMS subscales. Mothers' perceptions of overall family functioning did not differ between the two groups.

Drotar et al. (1995) note that the HIV-positive and negative groups in their study were demographically similar, socioeconomically advantaged, and recipients of ongoing psychosocial support through their local hemophilia treatment center; these results cannot be extrapolated to children and youth with congenitally acquired HIV infection and AIDS, of course, because of vast differences in socioeconomic status, psychosocial support, and family functioning, all of which are associated with psychological adjustment. On the other hand, demonstration of clinically significant levels of psychological distress among mothers of HIV-positive subjects with hemophilia underlines the importance of controlled studies in examining various aspects of psychosocial functioning and symptom formation in HIV-affected populations and their families, such that targeted interventions can be designed. In a three-way controlled study of anxiety disorders and familial stress in 23 children with hemophilia, 37 children with asthma, and 31 healthy children, using the Schedule for Affective Disorders and Schizophrenia for School-Age Children (K-SADS), Bussing and Burket (1993) found significantly higher rates of anxiety disorders, particularly separation anxiety disorder, in the group with hemophilia than in the other two groups. Little intrafamilial stress was found.

Finally, two recent case reports describe classical obsessive-compulsive disorder (OCD) in three prepubertal children (ages 10, 11, and 12; 2 girls, 1 boy) whose target symptom was fear of acquiring AIDS (Wagner & Sullivan, 1991; Fisman & Walsh, 1994). Two pathophysiologic mechanisms are suggested: first, that misinformation about AIDS, which has been documented in prepubertal children (Fassler, MacQueen, & Duncan, 1990), led to obsessive-compulsive behavior in a child who might not otherwise have been symptomatic (Wagner & Sullivan, 1991); second, that obsessive-compulsive symptom formation was likely in any case, in the context of genetic predisposition and developmental stage, with frequent exposure to AIDS-related material in the media and in educational settings serving as a "trigger incident" for OCD (Honjo, Hirano, & Murase, 1989), much as "syphilophobia" was described in the pre-penicillin era (Hoerr & Osol, 1956). Whether these cases reflect an increase in the incidence of OCD in response to the AIDS epidemic, or if they are specific symptom formations in individuals predisposed to OCD has not been determined; the latter hypothesis is more plausible.

TREATMENT STRATEGIES

Overview of Medical Management

Background

HIV infection is often a disease of the poor and underserved inner-city child. Sometimes there is no parent capable of providing day-to-day care, either because of parental illness, substance abuse, or other psychosocial factors. This care may then become the responsibility of older relatives who may not be prepared for the complex issues these children present. A home too chaotic to care for a child with HIV infection is often first recognized by the professionals when appointments are missed or medications not given. More common, however, is the loving mother who is overwhelmed. Diagnosis of HIV in a child is often the vehicle for diagnosis of infection in the mother. As both become ill, several issues arise, including the ill mother's concern over who will care for her child if she dies first, and issues pertaining to a father who may be absent, ill, or have died from AIDS himself. If there are uninfected siblings, planning for their care is also an important issue that will frequently concern the mother alone. Despite these profound psychosocial stressors, mothers of HIV-infected children in the urban inner city have mastered home intravenous antibiotic therapy and other medical interventions that allow their children with AIDS an optimal quality of life in outpatient settings well into the course of disease progression. Caring for the mother and child in the same facility with shared staff has many advantages. Communication among caregiving teams for child and mother is of immeasurable help in facilitating and coordinating the quality and efficiency of medical, psychiatric, and community-based care.

Pregnancy

AZT given to women with mild HIV infection during the last trimester of pregnancy, continued intravenously through labor, and continued orally in the infant at birth and through early infancy decreases the rate of vertical transmission (CDC, 1994b). The transmission rate of HIV infection in one multicenter prospective blinded study was decreased from 25.5 percent to 8.3 percent (Connor, Sperling, & Gelber, 1994). Women with severe infection have not been studied. Long-term effects of therapy are unknown for both the mother and infant; it should be noted that the use of newly released drugs with unknown fetal effects during pregnancy is unprecedented and must be studied.

In order for prophylaxis to be effective, women must be identified by at least mid-third trimester. Since voluntary screening fails to identify most pregnant women with HIV infection, the demonstrated efficacy of AZT administration during pregnancy upon favorably influencing vertical transmission adds urgency to the ethical debate over mandatory screening, as well as raises the issue of when in pregnancy women should be screened. Early screening could influence mothers' decisions to terminate a pregnancy, and mandatory screening could serve as a disincentive to seek prenatal care in the first place. While it is likely that most pregnant women found to be HIV-positive will elect to receive AZT prophylaxis, prophylaxis cannot realistically be mandatory (see below).

The Infant of an HIV-Positive Mother

Recently the CDC has recommended that PCP prophylaxis be started at about 1 month of age in all children born to HIV-infected mothers (CDC, 1995). This policy presumes recognition of infected mothers at least by the time of delivery. It aims at preventing early deaths from PCP in children who present in infancy, prior to diagnosis of infection. Clearly, once diagnosed as HIV infected, all infants should be placed on PCP prophylaxis.

Asymptomatic children born to an HIV-infected mother should be followed closely with periodic screenings of immune function, blood count, and general health. CD4 counts and percentages should be followed at least at 1, 3, and 6 months of age and then at 3-month intervals until the HIV status of an infant is determined. The uninfected child needs no further immunological surveillance. It is the authors' practice to screen HIV-infected infants clinically and neurologically at baseline and every 6 months thereafter. A baseline CT scan or MRI is performed, with detected abnormalities followed as clinically indicated (U.S. Department of Health and Human Services, 1994).

Antiretroviral therapies presently available are palliative and currently recommended either for HIV-related illness or a sub-threshold absolute CD4 lymphocyte count. Normal CD4 levels vary as a function of age such that guidelines for initiation of pharmacotherapy are age-dependent (see Table 15.3).

At present, AZT monotherapy is the regimen of first choice (Working group on antiretroviral therapy, 1993), though pediatric clinical trials presently underway may

Table 15.3. CD4+ Levels at Which Antiretroviral Therapy Should Be Begun in Children with Early Human Immunodeficiency Virus Infection*

AGE	CD4+ LEVEL (CELLS/MCL)	CD4+/TOTAL LYMPHOCYTES (%)
0 to 12 months	<1750	<30%
13 to 24 months	<1000	<25%
2 to 6 years	<750	<20%
older than 6 years	<500	<20%

*U.S. Department of Health and Human Services. (1994). *Evaluation and management of early HIV Infection.* (AHCPR no. 94-05). Washington, DC: Author.

lead to amended recommendations for multidrug regimens with demonstrably greater efficacy in adult studies (Husson, Mueller, & Farley, 1994). Didanosine (DDI) is now available in liquid form for pediatric use, and agents such as zalcitabine (DDC), stavudine, and others soon to be standard in adult protocols are beginning to be studied in children. Children with HIV infection requiring more than AZT monotherapy should be entered whenever possible into available multi-center clinical trials.

Prevention of Infectious Complications

HIV-infected children should receive routine pediatric immunizations on schedule (see Table 15.4). These are most likely to be successful if given prior to the onset of symptomatic HIV disease. Once infection progresses and immune function is affected, children are less likely to respond normally to vaccination. However, immunization is recommended regardless of stage of HIV infection since there are no demonstrable adverse effects except for with BCG for tuberculosis prophylaxis, which is not routinely recommended in the United States. These guidelines include the live, attenuated virus vaccines for measles, mumps, and rubella, for which the medical risks of naturally acquired infection in HIV-infected infants and children greatly exceed those of the vaccines. With regard to poliomyelitis prophylaxis, the CDC recommends the inactivated ("Salk") vaccine to minimize the risk of vaccine-acquired polio from the live product in immunocompromised hosts, but in much of the world only the live vaccine is available and is recommended even for HIV-infected children.

Immune globulin administered intravenously (IVIG) on a monthly basis has been shown to decrease the num-

Table 15.4. Vaccination Schedule for Children with Human Immunodeficiency Virus Infection

VACCINE	VACCINATION SCHEDULE
Diptheria/ tetanus/ pertussis	As for healthy children
Hemophilus influenzae	As for healthy children
Hepatitis B	As for healthy children
Inactivated polio ("Salk")	After 12 months
Measles	After 12 months
Mumps	After 12 months
Rubella	After 12 months
Influenza	Every fall
Pneumonococcus	After 2 years of age

*U.S. Public Health Services. (1995). *USPHS/IDSA guidelines for the prevention of opportunistic infections in person with HIV: A summary.* (Publication No. RR-8). Washington, DC: Author.

Table 15.5. Center for Disease Control Guidelines for *Pneumocystis carinii* Prophylaxis for Children with Human Immunodeficiency Virus Infection*

Begin Prophylaxis in:
• All infants 1 to 4 months old born to HIV-infected women
• All infants younger than 12 months with positive or indeterminate HIV status
• HIV-infected children 1 to 5 years old with <500 CD4+ cells per mcL or a CD4+/total lymphocyte ratio <15 percent
• HIV-infected children 6 to 12 years old with <200 CD4+ cells per mcL or a CD4+/total lymphocyte ratio <15 percent

First Choice Prophylaxis:
• Trimethoprim/ sulfamethoxazole

Alternatives:
• Aerosolized pentamidine
• Dapsone (in infants > 1 month old)
• Intravenous pentamidine

*(CDC, 1995)

ber of bacterial infections in HIV-infected children whose CD4 counts exceed 200/mcL, but no effect on survival has been demonstrated. Comparable preventive efficacy has been established for orally administered prophylactic trimethoprim/sulfamethoxazole (TMP/SMX) (Mofenson & Moye, 1993). The use of IVIG varies by center, but its overall popularity appears to be waning. Moreover, a monthly infusion regimen usually requires permanent central venous access and precious time at the medical center or at home administering the infusion and providing surveillance for side effects.

Chemoprophylaxis for PCP in HIV-infected infants and children, usually with TMP/SMX, has a demonstrably positive effect on survival and is now routine for all such children. While some authorities recommend prophylaxis for all infants, since PCP in infancy is most severe and most frequently fatal, guidelines for prophylaxis based upon age-adjusted CD4 count have been published (see Table 15.5; CDC, 1995).

Rifabutin prophylaxis for infections due to *Mycobacterium avium* complex has also been recommended based on data from adult trials, but its efficacy in prolonging life is unclear, and many experts do not routinely recommend its use.

As other opportunistic infections occur, specific antimicrobial chemotherapy is added to an individual child's regimen. Once infection with an opportunistic pathogen occurs, such as with CMV, prophylaxis, in this instance with gancyclovir, is often required indefinitely as complete eradication of many such organisms cannot be achieved.

Psychological and Behavioral Treatments

The stigma, socioeconomic disadvantage, psychiatric co-morbidity, substance use disorders, and confidentiality issues in which the AIDS epidemic is embedded pose unique and formidable challenges to the pediatric behavioral health community, whose interventions must encompass medical, psychosocial, legal, and ethical issues in a comprehensive and systematic manner that is both integrative and respectful of boundaries. In this sense, the AIDS epidemic may represent the most cogent contemporary rationale for a consultation-liaison approach to the behavioral health care of a medically vulnerable population. The following specific service needs must be addressed: (1) separation, loss, and bereavement; (2) AIDS education for schools, the general child, adolescent, and family population, and the infected child, adolescent, parent, and uninfected family contacts; (3) management of specific high-risk behaviors; (4) confidentiality and discrimination; (5) allocation of scarce psychosocial and medical resources. Although systematic trials of psychopharmacologic, psychotherapeutic, educational, and other interventions for AIDS-affected families and their uninfected counterparts have not been reported, reports of specific program initiatives in several centers and individual case reports are informative (Shonfeld et al., 1995; Rawitscher, Saitz, & Freidman, 1995; Ponton, DiClemente, & McKenna, 1991; Glazer, 1990; Adnopoz et al., 1994; Mok & Newell, 1995).

The program developed in New Haven, Connecticut, by Adnopoz and colleagues (1994), richly detailed by the authors, illustrates several fundamental principles of psychosocial intervention in the AIDS epidemic:

1 *access*—integration of mental health services with pediatric services through the geographic presence of behavioral health clinicians at the pediatric AIDS clinic and free transportation to the medical center

2. *stigma, fear of non-acceptance and abandonment*—clinician-initiated treatment contact through home visits, telephone outreach, etc., as distinct from traditional client-initiated models of mental health care

3. *custody, permanency planning and placement issues*—collaboration of the public sector child protective services agency and provision of free legal services

4. *multiplicity of behavioral health service needs*—broad spectrum of clinical services (see below)

5. *countertransference issues*—clinical supervision

6. *resource scarcity*—federal funding.

Clinical services offered in the New Haven program include four services: home-based family support services focused on the HIV-infected child and the family, and staffed by bachelors and masters level individuals, often recruited from the local community (previously demonstrated by the authors to reduce the rate of out of home placement of HIV-affected children); psychological and psychiatric evaluation of individual children at the medical center or in the home; individual, family, and group psychotherapy, including support groups specifically directed to uninfected children of infected parents or siblings, and parents and other adult caregivers; and finally, a "shared parenting" program for HIV-affected children living in more than one household because of parental incapacity or death, with the goal of minimizing out of home placements and maintaining the attachment between child and biological parent (Adnopoz et al., 1994). Although not yet the subject of rigorous longitudinal outcome analysis, this program exemplifies a developmentally and psychologically informed approach to a population of children facing severe, chronic psychosocial stress and multiple risk factors for psychiatric disturbance.

The rich literature on the developmental acquisition of cognitive concepts pertaining to illness and death (Glazer, 1990), particularly that using the principles of Piaget, has been applied to children's understanding of AIDS and HIV infection in a recent report (Walsh & Bibace, 1991). Using the Concepts of AIDS Protocol to assess subjects' perceptions of definition, etiology, prevention, and treatment of AIDS at preoperational (5–7 years), concrete operational (8–10 years), and formal operational (11–13 years) stages of cognitive development, the authors' results paralleled previous studies of children's cognitive understanding of other medical conditions. Preoperational subjects dealt with AIDS by association: "AIDS comes from throwing up"; concrete operational children posit a mechanism: "You get AIDS from falling into a puddle that someone with AIDS fell into before and he had a cut"; while preadolescents utilize mature abstract reasoning: "You get AIDS from a virus that gets into your bloodstream. It causes your immune system to stop fighting germs. Then, when another germ gets into your system, like pneumonia, the immune system can't fight it and you get very sick and may even die from the pneumonia."

In contrast to this theoretical formulation is a school-based AIDS education program for elementary level urban children recently reported by Schonfeld et al. (1995). In a randomized controlled trial, these investigators assessed the impact of a three-week AIDS education program on factual understanding of and anxiety about HIV infection in 189 kindergarten through 6th graders, finding highly significant (p < .0001) gains in conceptual understanding and no increase in anxiety in the intervention group compared to controls. The authors take issue with Walsh and Bibace's (1991) recommendation that "... it makes little sense to teach children at this age (5–7 years) how to identify and explain causes of AIDS, to instruct them on internal working of the body, or to provide specific information about preventive behaviors," noting that the young children in their study did exhibit advances in precisely these conceptual areas.

The influence of educational interventions on adolescent attitudes regarding sexual and substance-related risk taking behaviors and the preferences of adolescents regarding HIV counselling and testing have also been reported in recent studies. Ponton et al. (1991) evaluated the effects of an 8-day AIDS education program in 76 psychiatrically hospitalized adolescents using a pretest/post-test single group design, with patients serving as their own controls. The intervention included videotapes, written essays, art and drama therapy, and a presentation by an individual with AIDS. Outcome measures included the Sexual Behaviors Questionnaire (lstructured interview), and the Risk Behavior Inventory and AIDS Information Survey (self-report measures). Using one-way analysis of covariance (ANCOVA), the authors detected significant reductions in misconceptions of HIV contagion from casual contact but no change in general knowledge about AIDS or in subjects' perceived risk of acquiring HIV. Subjects were also stratified according to which HIV-risk associated behaviors they acknowledged prior to hospitalization and what proportion of subjects acknowledging each behavior intended to cease that behavior following the AIDS intervention program. Results indicated that adolescent subjects were more likely to discontinue unprotected sex (50 percent) and sex with homosexual men (75 percent) than they were to discontinue substance-related high-risk behaviors: only 20 percent of injection drug users and 33 percent of subjects sharing needles reported they would discontinue these practices. Staff concerns that the program would not be accepted were unfounded, with 87 percent recommending such a program for all psychiatrically hospitalized adolescents. The need for inclusion of material pertaining to fundamentals of sexuality and sexual anatomy in an AIDS education program for this population is illustrated by the authors' report of a 12-year-old male subject whose basic ignorance was profound. The need for outreach to parents is also emphasized as a means of gaining their acceptance rather than opposition to the program.

In an anonymous, self-report survey of 845 9th and 12th graders in the Boston area, Rawitscher et al. (1995) found that adolescents frequently report discomfort regarding the initiation of discussion of homosexuality (78 percent), condoms (67 percent), and safe sex (59 percent) with their physician. Nevertheless, the majority of these students expressed a clear desire for their physicians to inquire of them and provide information to them regarding condoms (73 percent), safe sex (80 percent), and HIV (85 percent), illustrating the responsibility of care-givers to inform themselves about the tangible implications of their patients' attitudes about these crucial issues. There was also a trend in the present study for adolescents' preference of anonymous HIV testing sites.

Limited data are available pertaining to psychosocial intervention for HIV-infected adults. In one of the only studies of individual psychotherapeutic intervention published to date, Markowitz, Klerman, & Clougherty (1995) reported that non-medically ill HIV-positive adult subjects who scored 15 or higher on the Hamilton Depression Rating Scale and who were randomly assigned to a 16-week interpersonal psychotherapy intervention were more likely to improve psychiatrically than a comparison group receiving supportive psychotherapy. Hamilton and Beck Depression Inventory scores, however, fell significantly in both groups.

Targ et al. (1994) reported improvement in depressive symptomatology in a group of 20 medically asymptomatic HIV-positive subjects receiving a structured group therapy intervention; interestingly, a comparison group receiving both group therapy and fluoxetine did no better than those receiving group therapy alone.

Death and Dying

The extensive literature pertaining to the psychological effects, developmental understanding, and approaches to management of the seriously ill or dying child (Glazer, 1990) must be understood and adapted to the unique setting of pediatric AIDS. The classical literature, for example, does not specifically address the needs of children who simultaneously confront their own fatal illness and that of parents and other care-givers. Fundamental principles include (1) tailoring intervention to the child's unique level of cognitive and psychological development; (2) recognizing the harmful psychological effects of a "conspiracy of silence" regarding issues of illness, death, and dying; (3) addressing the needs of parents who insist on non-disclosure; (4) taking the child's lead in psychotherapeutic encounters; (5) assuring adequate pain control (Glazer, 1990). Inherent in these principles is recognition that within a family, the psychological needs of child and parents may differ, particularly when AIDS affects multiple members.

Regarding non-disclosure in the pediatric AIDS setting, Lwin notes ". . . it is not uncommon for . . . parents . . . to fear that knowledge of the seriousness of the (child's) illness will frighten their child and . . . even accelerate death. The agony of accepting that a child is going to die can inhibit communication with the child about death. It can also deter parents from discussing any aspect of the illness for fear that the conversation and their emotions may escalate out of their control. Parents sometimes take refuge in the protective adage: 'What children do not know, cannot harm them.' But, for children who are ill, hospitalized, facing frequent and sometimes painful medical procedures, ignorance is not bliss" (Lwin, 1995, p. 270).

The helplessness felt by pediatricians, psychiatrists, psychologists, and other care-givers in these settings must be understood for what it often is—a countertransference distortion. The therapeutic impact of medical professionals' roles in pain management, treatment of anxiety and depression, management of guilt engendered by the child's or parents' view of illness as retribution for wrongdoing, protection from separation due to parental absence, disability, or death, and other measures are well documented and favorably impact a family's long-term adjustment to the tragedy of the loss of a child. These issues pertain both to the mental health clinician's direct clinical care of the child and family and to consult-liaison function with the entire treatment team (Glazer, 1991).

Similar issues pertain to bereaved children, HIV-infected or uninfected, who lose parents and other family members to AIDS. Again, professionals' capacity for misinterpretation and avoidance of a crucial therapeutic role in fostering psychological adjustment and resumption of a normal developmental trajectory should not be underestimated (Furman, 1974). Hemmings has noted that "Childhood bereavement presents a threat to normal development, but the threat does not necessarily lie in the experience of death. The significant factor that determines whether this experience is a challenge or a trauma is the quality of care afforded the child in the months and years that follow the loss. . . . We need to be guided by the child's experience of his (or her) bereavement and allow him (or her) a greater part in the family's shared experience of mourning" (Hemmings, 1995, p. 283). Hemmings comments further on the "paradox that loving parents often present problems for young bereaved children," pointing out that the psychological suffering inherent to bereavement cannot be assuaged by the usual role of parents in reassurance and protection of children from danger or trauma. The parent who inhibits the expression of their own grief in the child's presence implies to the child that the open expression of strong, painful feelings needed for the working through of such a loss is inappropriate.

In their understanding of individual and family psychodynamics, pharmacologic approaches to anxiety, depression and analgesia, transference and counter-transference, child psychiatrists and psychologists have a unique and fundamental role to play in the management of the psychological complications of terminally ill, dying, and bereaved children and families and in the facilitation of normal psychological, social, and cognitive development. We await systematic, controlled longitudinal intervention studies of the psychotherapies and medication management of the psychosocial manifestations of the pediatric AIDS epidemic.

Ethics

Lederberg (1989) has noted the importance of maintaining clear distinctions among psychiatric, legal, and ethical issues in consultation-liaison settings, and the problems that arise in clinical practice when one of these is mistaken for another. Goldstein, Freud, and Solnit (1979) draw particular attention to this issue when child psychiatrists or psychologists are asked to abrogate their therapeutic role by rendering opinions about custody or placement. AIDS and HIV infection pose major ethical challenges for mental health clinicians, challenges which, as Etemad (1995) notes, are not new issues, but arise in clinical practice with particular intensity. Etemad proposes the following categories of ethical concern posed by the AIDS epidemic: (1) duty to treat, (2) confidentiality and right to privacy, (3) informed consent, and (4) duty to warn. Resolution has been achieved in some of these areas; others remain controversial.

The American Psychiatric Association and the American Academy of Child and Adolescent Psychiatry have clearly articulated policies regarding the duty of psychiatrists to treat children and adults in out-patient and in-patient settings without regard to HIV status (Krener & Miller, 1989). In the case of possible HIV exposure due to accidental needle puncture in a hospital, Etemad (1995, p. 823) states "the ethical view is that the right to privacy should be breached only if the result of the test would make a difference in the treatment of the injured party. Presumably, reassurance alone would provide insufficient justification for such a breach." However, in one major hospital, the policy in such cases stipulates that the injured party may insist on anonymous assessment of HIV serostatus of the source of the needle injury (Goldfarb, personal communication, 1996). The controversy over routine mandatory HIV testing of pregnant women takes on particular poignancy with the demonstration of reduced vertical transmission with antiretroviral therapy during pregnancy. Similar conflicts of values may pertain to sexual maltreatment cases.

It is crucial to recognize the value of psychodynamically informed psychiatric intervention in addressing these issues. The child psychiatrist or psychologist who learns that an HIV-positive patient is sexually active with an uninformed partner may feel faced with an insoluble conflict between the right to privacy and the duty to warn. Although the Tarasoff decision has yet to be tested in the AIDS arena, skillful psychotherapeutic intervention can resolve an "either/or" ethical dilemma, as in a case reported in which a sexually active HIV-positive adolescent non-coercively decided to share her serostatus with her sexual partner (Etemad, 1995). Adolescents may reveal high-risk HIV-related behavior to a therapist, choose to be tested, but insist that parents and/or health insurance carriers not be informed; such requests for confidentiality must be respected but pose logistical questions such as the availability of free, anonymous HIV testing sites, which may vary by community.

Finally, there is a consensus that HIV-positive children should attend school as usual and that such children retain the right to privacy regarding HIV-related information. Schools, like hospitals, should routinely practice universal precautions, such as having gloves readily available in the case of playground injury with bleeding, and so on. Withholding or delaying lifesaving treatment for an injured, bleeding child is unacceptable in any setting.

Pharmacological Treatments

The limited published experience describing pharmacologic intervention for behavioral and psychiatric concomitants of pediatric AIDS and AIDS encephalopathy includes two reports of response to AZT (Moss et al., 1989; Schmitt, Seeger, Kreuz, Enenkel, & Jacobi, 1991), a case report of successful treatment of "hyperactivity" with methylphenidate (Lifschitz, Hanson, Wilson, & Shearer, 1989), and a recent detailed case report of the successful use of clonidine (Cesena, Lee, Cebollero, & Steingard, 1995). In the latter report, a 4-year-old congenitally infected boy whose early developmental history was noteworthy for the absence of impulsive, hyperactive, or inattentive behaviors, exhibited the acute onset of impulsivity, hyperactivity, 3–5 hour initial insomnia, and aggression at age 4.1 years and was unresponsive to diphenhydramine. Concerns that AZT was etiologic led to its discontinuation, without an effect on the behavioral symptoms. Minor EEG abnormalities not requiring anticonvulsants were noted; a computerized tomographic scan of the brain was normal. This child's hyperactivity, impulsivity, and insomnia improved significantly, as reflected by a change in the Teacher Abbreviated Symptom Questionnaire from two standard deviations above the norm to the normal range in all domains, and by a change of the Clinical Global Impression Scale for ADHD (CGI-ADHD) from "extremely severe" to "moderate." These changes were concurrent with the initiation of clonidine, titrated to a dose of 0.025 mg TID. Clonidine, an alpha-two adrenergic agonist, has been shown in several studies of healthy children with ADHD to improve target symptoms of hyperactivity and impulsivity, but not inattention (Steingard et al., 1993).

Rabkin, Rabkin, Harrison, and Wagner (1994) reported imipramine to be statistically significantly superior to placebo in a double blind controlled trial of the treatment of major depression and dysthymic disorder in a group of 80 HIV-positive adults, of whom 39 percent had AIDS. The response rate of 74 percent in the imipramine treated group and 26 percent in the placebo group is comparable to that in studies of non-HIV-positive adults with major depressive disorder. However, 20 percent of the imipramine responders elected to discontinue pharmacotherapy because of side effects, and it has been suggested that tricyclic agents may exacerbate the confusion of HIV encephalopathy. An open clinical trial of fluoxetine (Rabkin, Rabkin, & Wagner, 1994) in a comparable population found a lower frequency of side effects prompting discontinuation of treatment. Psychostimulants, particularly methylphenidate, have been reported to be efficacious in improving cognitive functioning in adults with HIV-encephalopathy (Summergrad et al., 1993).

CASE ILLUSTRATION

Clinical Presentation

The grandmother of an asymptomatic, HIV-infected five-year-old boy requested an out-patient pediatric visit because of cough and fever. On examination, the child was afebrile with a normal physical examination. However, upon entry of the physician into the examining room, the child was noted to be sitting under the table and refused to come out.

The grandmother had been awarded custody of the child four months previously because of the level of the mother's medical deterioration and inability to care for him alone. The father's whereabouts had been unknown for many years. The household also included a ten-year-old uninfected female sibling of the patient, also in the grandmother's custody. A maternal uncle had died of AIDS six months prior to this month's visit. The grandmother reported that since the death of the child's mother from AIDS 4 months previously, the child had been "out of control," crying or mute since the funeral.

Medically, the patient's HIV-infection had been documented in infancy and AZT and monthly IVIG had been begun, with no recent complications or hospitalizations. The family had not explicitly discussed the child's or the mother's AIDS diagnosis with the patient, nor had they made special efforts to keep the diagnosis secret, including during multiple visits to the AIDS clinic at the hospital.

Assessment Findings

Urgent child psychiatric consultation was requested and immediately conducted in the pediatric examining room. The psychiatric consultant had fully reviewed the child's and family's history with the attending pediatrician before entering the room and meeting the child. The psychiatric consultant sat on the floor adjacent to the patient and used an unobtrusive approach, taking nonverbal cues from the child. The child became much less anxious and spontaneously came out from under the table. Although remaining mute, the child listened intently as the psychiatric consultant shared what she knew about the events of the child's recent days, the loss of his mother and uncle, and so on. There was no history of attention deficit hyperactivity disorder or suicidality, and growth, development, and maternal attachment had been normal until the mother's final months of life. There was no evidence of delirium or cognitive impairment.

Treatment Selection and Course

Acknowledgement by the child psychiatrist not only of the child's recent loss but also of his fear that he might die was associated with a dramatic improvement in the child's overall functioning during the consultation. By the end of a 45-minute interview, the child accepted his grandmother's comfort, sitting on her lap and beginning to speak quietly and appropriately. The grandmother, pediatrician, and psychiatrist were reassured that he was not acutely ill and was able to return home with his grandmother. This urgent consultation was followed by weekly individual child psychotherapy and parent guidance for the grandmother.

Termination and Follow-up

During the ensuing weeks, the child was able to utilize both play and speech in addressing his losses and his fears. Although he continued to be somewhat socially isolated from peers, his acute symptoms of crying, behavioral discontrol, and muteness resolved completely.

SUMMARY

Krener and Miller (1989) have aptly cited several key clinical challenges arising in child and adolescent psychiatry practice in the context of the AIDS epidemic: a sexually active gay youth with uncertain risk of HIV-positivity who insists that his sexual orientation be withheld from his family; a toddler with AIDS and pneumonia whose mother dies of AIDS during the infant's hospitalization and whose bereaved grandparents reject the infant because of conflicts with the father who is bisexual and alcoholic; an adolescent hemophiliac with major depression triggered by notification of HIV positivity; and an adolescent prostitute being seen in a community mental health center who is found to be HIV positive.

The AIDS epidemic touches every aspect of child and adolescent psychiatry and psychology, encompassing psychiatric and developmental assessments, psychopharmacologic, psychotherapeutic, cognitive/behavioral, group, family, and systems interventions, forensics, and ethics. The need for multidisciplinary assessment, treatment planning, implementation of multimodal intervention strategies, and the crucial need for collaboration across professional disciplines informed by a biopsychosocial perspective are dramatically illustrated by the psychosocial, medical, legal, and ethical challenges facing clinicians in this setting. Metaphorically, one might compare the current state of knowledge regarding the characterization of the psychiatric/psychological effects of HIV on infants, children, and families, and the design of intervention strategies to that of the state of HIV vaccine development—in neither case are clear solutions at hand, but considerable progress has occurred in both arenas. The child psychiatrist and psychologist must call upon every facet of their individual expertise in psychopharmacology, the psychotherapies, consultation, forensics and ethics. As such, child and adolescent psychiatrists and psychologists are uniquely suited, with their pediatric colleagues, to work actively with this burgeoning population in the facilitation of normal development, the relief of suffering, and hopefully, in time, a cure.

In the meantime, it is essential that infants, children, and adolescents with HIV infection and AIDS have ready access to clinical trials protocols of existing and newly developed experimental antiretroviral therapies. Indeed, in the United States, AIDS dramatically illustrates the link between development of systems for provision of routine care and enrollment in controlled clinical trials, which allow many patients access to treatments years earlier than would otherwise be possible. Andiman (1995) has noted the stresses that befall pediatric AIDS patients even as promising new treatments are made available, including the awareness by young patients of the uncertain efficacy of experimental treatments, multiple medical procedures and trips to the medical center, and so forth. Challenging questions remain unanswered, from the effects of administration of antiretroviral agents to pregnant women on the neurological development of the infant AIDS survivor (Connor, personal communication, 1996) to the design of optimal pharmacologic, psychotherapeutic, and systems interventions for the infected child and parent, uninfected siblings, and the AIDS-bereaved. The only way to assure that neither medical, psychiatric, nor social needs of children and families affected by AIDS receive insufficient resource support is to insist that epidemiologic and intervention studies be informed by the biopsychosocial model and that reductionistic thinking, whether "medical vs. psychiatric" or "biological vs. psychological," be avoided at all costs.

ACKNOWLEDGMENTS

The authors gratefully acknowledge Mr. Howard Jung for his expert editorial assistance, and Ms. Anne Bakos, and Ms. Lillian Parmertor for their expert manuscript preparation.

REFERENCES

Adnopoz, J. A., Forsyth, B. W .C., & Nagler, S. F. (1994). Psychiatric aspects of HIV infection and AIDS on the family. *Child and Adolescent Psychiatric Clinics of North America, 3,* 543–555.

Andiman, W. A. (1995). Medical aspect of AIDS: What do children witness? In S. Geballe, J. Gruendel, & W. Andiman (Eds.), *Forgotten children of the AIDS epidemic* (pp. 32–49). New Haven, CT: Yale University Press.

Andiman, W. A., & Simpson, B. J. (1990). Rate of transmission HIV infection from mother to child and short-term outcome of neonatal infection. *American Journal of Diseases of Children, 144,* 758–766.

Aral, S. O. (1991). Sexual behavior and risk for sexually transmitted infections. *Sexually Transmitted Diseases Bulletin, 10,* 3–10.

Bale, J. F., Contant, C. F., Garg, B., Tilton, A., Kaufman, D. M., & Wasiewski, W. (1993). Neurologic history and examination results and their relationship to human immunodeficiency virus type 1 serostatus in hemophilic subjects: Results from the Hemophilia Growth and Development Study. *Pediatrics, 91,* 736–741.

Belman, A. L. (1990). AIDS and pediatric neurology. *Neurologic Clinics, 8,* 571–603.

Belman, A. L., Ultmann, M. H., & Horonpian, D. (1985). Neurological complications in infants and children with AIDS. *Annals of Neurology, 18,* 560–566.

Belman, A. L., Diamond, G., & Dickson, D. (1988). Pediatric acquired immunodeficiency syndrome—Neurologic syndromes. *American Journal of Diseases of Children, 142,* 29–55.

Blanche, S., Rozioux, C., & Moscato, M. L. F. (1989). A prospective study of infants born to women seropositive for human immunodeficiency virus type I. *The New England Journal of Medicine, 320,* 1643–1648.

Brown, L. K., Schultz, J. R., & Gragg, R. A. (1995). HIV-infected adolescents with hemophilia: Adaptation and coping. *Pediatrics, 95,* 459–663.

Bussing, R., & Burket, R. C. (1993). Anxiety and intrafamilial stress in children with hemophilia after the HIV crisis. *Journal of the American Academy of Child Adolescent Psychiatry, 93,* 562–566.

Centers for Disease Control. (1992). Selected behaviors that increase risk for HIV-infection among high school students—United States, 1990. *MMWR Morb Mortal Weekly Report, 41,* 231–240.

Centers for Disease Control. (1994). Revised classification system for HIV infection in children less than 13 years of age. *MMWR, 43* (No. RR-12), 1–19.

Centers for Disease Control. (1994b). Ziduvudine for the prevention of HIV transmission from mother to infant. *MMWR, 43,* 285–287.

Centers for Disease Control. (1995). Revised guidelines for prophylaxis against PCP for children infected with or perinatally exposed to HIV. *MMWR, 44* (4), 1–11.

Cesena, M., Lee, D. O., Cebollero, A. M., & Steingard, R. J. (1995). Case study: Behavioral symptoms of pediatric HIV-1 encephalopathy successfully treated with clonidine. *Journal of the American Academy of Child Adolescent Psychiatry, 95,* 302–306.

Colegrove, R. W., & Huntziger, R. M. (1994). Academic, behavioral, and social adaptation of boys with hemophilia/HIV disease. *Journal of Pediatric Psychology, 4,* 457–473.

Connor, E. M., Sperling, R. S., & Gelber, R. (1994). Reduction of maternal-infant transmission of HIV type I with zidovudine treatment. *The New England Journal of Medicine, 331,* 1173–1180.

Cooper, D. A., Gold, J., & Maclean, P. (1985). Acute AIDS retrovirus infection: Definition of a clinical illness associated with seroconversion. *Lancet, 1* (8428), 1537–1540.

Daar, E. S., Mmoudgil, T., Meyer, R. D., & Ho, D. D. (1991). Transient high levels of viremia in patients with primary HIV infection. *The New England Journal of Medicine, 324,* 961–964.

Drotar, D., Agle, D., Eckl, C. L., & Thompson, P. A. (1995). Psychological response to HIV positivity in hemophilia. *Pediatrics, 95,* 1062–1069.

Dulliege, A. M., Amos, C. I., Felton, S., Biggar, R. F., & Goedert, J. J. (1995). International registry of HIV exposed twins, birth order, delivery route and concordance in the transmission of HIV from others to twins. *The Journal of Pediatrics, 126,* 625–632.

Epstein, L. G., Goudsmit, J., & Paul, D. A. (1987). Expression of HIV in CSF of children with progressive encephalopathy. *Annals of Neurology, 21,* 397–401.

Epstein, L. G., Scharer, L. R., & Oleski, J. M. (1986). Neurologic manifestations of HIV infection in children. *Pediatrics, 78,* 678–687.

Etemad, J. G. (1995). Children, adolescents, and HIV: Ethical issues. *Child and Adolescent Psychiatric Clinics of North America, 4,* 823–835.

European Collaborative Study. (1992). Risk factors for mother to child transmission of HIV. *Lancet, 339,* 1007–1012.

Evans, D. L., Leserman, J., Perkins, D. O., Stern, R. A., Murphy, C., Tamul, K., Liao, D., van der Horst, C. M., Hall, C. D., Folds, J. D., Golden, R. N., & Petitto, J. M. (1995). Stress-associated reductions of cytotoxic T lymphocytes and natural killer cells in asymptomatic HIV infection. *The American Journal of Psychiatry, 152,* 543–550.

Fassler, D., McQueen, K., & Duncan, P. (1990). Children's perceptions of AIDS. *Journal of the American Academy of Child Adolescent Psychiatry, 29,* 459–462.

Fisman, S. N., & Walsh, L. (1994). Obsessive-Compulsive Disorder and Fear of AIDS contamination in childhood. *Journal of the American Academy of Child Adolescent Psychiatry, 94,* 349–353.

Furman, E. (1974). *When a child's parent dies.* New Haven: Yale University Press.

Gay, C. L., Armstrong, F. D., Cohen, D., Lai, S., Hardy Swales, T. P., Morrow, C. J., & Scott, G. B. (1995). The effects of HIV on cognitive and motor development in children born to HIV-seropositive women with no reported drug use: Birth to 24 months. *Pediatrics, 96,* 1078–1082.

Gayle, H. D., & D'Angelo, L. J. (1991). Epidemiology of acquired immunodeficiency syndrome and human immunodeficiency virus infections in adolescents. *Pediatric Infectious Diseases Journal, 10,* 322–328.

Glazer, J. P. (1990). Life-threatening pediatric illness in a high technology age: The paradigm of childhood cancer. In R. Michels, J. O. Cavenar, Jr., & H. K. Brodie (Eds.), *Psychiatry: A comprehensive textbook,* Vol. 2, Section 1, 75: (pp. 1–10). New York: J. B. Lippincott Company.

Glazer, J. P. (1991). Psychiatric aspects of cancer in childhood and adolescence. In M. Lewis (Ed.), *Child and adolescent Psychiatry: A comprehensive textbook* (pp. 964–976). Baltimore, MD: Williams & Wilkins.

Goetz, D. W., Hall, S. E., & Harbison, R. W. (1988). Pediatric acquired immunodeficiency syndrome with negative human immunodeficiency virus antibody response by ELISA and Western blot. *Pediatrics, 81,* 356–359.

Goldfarb, J. (1993a). The acquired immunodeficiency syndrome in African children. *Advances in Pediatric Infectious Diseases, 8,* 145–157.

Goldfarb, J. (1993b). Breastfeeding. AIDS and other infectious diseases. *Clinics in Perinatology, 20,* 225–243.

Goldstein, J., Freud, A., & Solnit, A. J. (1979). *Before the best interests of the child.* New York: Macmillan Publishing.

Grubman, S., Gross, E., Lerner-Weiss, N., Hernandez, M., McSherry, G. D., Hoyt, L. G., Boland, M., & Oleski, J. M. (1995). Older children and adolescents living with perinatally acquired human immunodeficiency virus infection. *Pediatrics, 95,* 657–663.

Harris, J. J., Gleghorn, A., & Jeste, D. V. (1989). *HIV-related psychosis.* Presented at the 142nd meeting of the American Psychiatric Association, San Francisco, CA.

Hein, K., Dell, R., Futterman, D., Rotheram-Borus, M. J., & Shaffer, N. (1995). Comparison of HIV+ and HIV– adolescents: Risk factors and psychosocial determinants. *Pediatrics, 95,* 96–104.

Hemmings, P. (1995). The bereaved child. In J. Y. Q. Mok & M. L. Newell (Eds.), *HIV infection in children: A guide to practical management* (pp. 283–297). Melbourne, Australia: Cambridge University Press.

Ho, D. D., Rota, T. R., & Schooley, R. T. (1985). Isolation of HTLV-III from cerebrospinal fluid and neural tissue of patients with neurologic syndrome related to AIDS. *The New England Journal of Medicine, 313,* 1493–1497.

Hoerr, N. L., & Osol, A. (1956). *Blakistons New Gould Medical Dictionary.* New York: McGraw-Hill.

Hoff, R., Berardi, V. P., & Weiblen, B. J. (1988). Seroprevalence of HIV among childbearing women. *The New England Journal of Medicine, 318,* 525–530.

Honjo, S., Hirano, C., & Murase, S. (1989). Obsessive-compulsive symptoms in childhood and adolescence. *Acta Psychiatric Scandanavia, 80,* 83–91.

Husson, R. N., Comeau, A. M., & Hoff, R. (1990). Diagnosis of HIV in infants and children. *Pediatrics, 86,* 1–10.

Husson, R. N., Mueller, B. U., & Farley, M. (1994). Zidovudine and didanosine combination therapy in children with HIV infection. *Pediatrics, 93,* 316–322.

Hutto, C., Parks, W. P., & Lai, S. (1991). A hospital based

prospective study of perinatal infection with HIV. *The Journal of Pediatrics, 118,* 347–353.

Jacobsberg, L., Frances, A., & Perry, S. (1995). Axis II diagnoses among volunteers for HIV testing and counseling. *American Journal of Psychiatry, 152,* 1222–1224.

Koocher, G., & O'Malley, J. (1981). *The Damocles Syndrome.* New York: McGraw-Hill.

Krener, P., & Miller, F. B. (1989). Psychiatric response to HIV spectrum disease in children and adolescents. *Journal of the American Academy of Child and Adolescent Psychiatry, 28,* 596–605.

Lederberg, M. (1989). The confluence of psychiatry, the law, and ethics. *Handbook of psycho-oncology: Psychological care of the patient with cancer* (pp. 694–702).

Lederman, S. A. (1992). Estimating infant mortality from HIV and other causes in breastfeeding and bottle feeding population. *Pediatrics, 89,* 290–296.

Lepage, P., Van de Perre, P., & Msellati, P. (1993). Mother to child transmission of HIV and its determinants: A cohort study in Kigali, Rwanda. *American Journal of Epidemiology, 137,* 589–599.

Levenson, R. L., Mellins, C. A., Zawadski, R., Kairam, R., & Stein, Z. (1992). Cognitive assessment of human immunodeficiency virus-exposed children. *American Journal of Diseases of Children, 146,* 1479–1483.

Lifschitz, M., Hanson, C., Wilson G., & Shearer, W. T. (1989). Abstract 316. *Behavioral changes in children with human immunodeficiency virus (HIV) infection.* Presented at Fifth International Conference on AIDS, Montreal.

Lobato, M. N., Caldwell, M. B., Ng, P., & Oxtoby, M. J., Pediatric Spectrum of Disease Clinical Consortium. (1995). Encephalopathy in children with perinatally acquired human immunodeficiency virus infection. *The Journal of Pediatrics, 126,* 710–715.

Loveland, K. A., Stehbens, J., Contant, C., Bordeaux, J. D., Sirois, P., Bell, T. S., Hill, S. (1994). Hemophilia growth and developmental study: Baseline neurodevelopmental findings. *Journal of Pediatric Psychology, 19,* 223–239.

Luzariaga, K., Mcuilken, P., & Alimenti, A. (1993). Early viremia and immune responses in vertical human immunodeficiency virus type I infection. *Journal of Infectious Diseases, 167,* 1008–1013.

Lwin, R. (1995). Talking with the dying child. In J. Y. Q. Mok & M. L. Newell (Eds.), *HIV infection in children: A guide to practical management* (pp. 270–282). Melbourne, Australia: Cambridge University Press.

Markowitz, J. C., Klerman, G. L., & Clougherty, K. F. (1995). Individual psychotherapies for depressed HIV-positive patients. *The American Journal of Psychiatry, 152* (10), 1504–1509.

Mellins, C. A., Levenson, R. L., & Zawadzki, R. (1994). Effects of pediatric HIV infection and prenatal drug exposure on mental and psychomotor development. *Journal of Pediatric Psychology, 19,* 617–628.

Miles, S. A., Balden, E., & Magpantay, L. (1993). Rapid serologic testing with immune complex dissociated HIV p24 antigen for early detection of HIV infection in neonates. *The New England Journal of Medicine, 328,* 297–302.

Mofenson, L. M. (1995). A critical review of studies evaluating the relationship of mode of delivery to perinatal transmission of HIV. *Pediatric Infectious Diseases Journal, 14,* 169–177.

Mofenson, L. M., & Moye, J. (1993). Intravenous immune globulin for the prevention of infections in children with symptomatic HIV infection. *Pediatric Research, 33,* 88–89.

Mok, J. Y. Q., & Newell, M. L. (1995). Living with HIV. In J. Y. Q. Mok & M. L. Newell (Eds.), *HIV infection in children: A guide to practical management* (pp. 298–305). Melbourne, Australia: Cambridge University Press.

Mosher, W. D., & McNally, J. W. (1991). Contraceptive use at first intercourse: United States, 1965-1988. *Family Planning Perspectives, 23,* 108–116.

Moss, H., Wolters, P., Eddy, J., Weiner, J., Pizzo, L., & Brouwers, P. (1989). Abstract 248. *The effects of encephalopathy and AZT treatment on the social and emotional behavior of pediatric AIDS patients.* Presented at Fifth International Conference on AIDS, Montreal.

Moye, J., Rich, K. C., & Kalish, L. A. (1996). Natural history of somatic growth in infants born to woman infected by HIV. *The Journal of Pediatrics, 128,* 58–69.

Nozyce, M., Hittelman, J., Muenz, L., Durako, S. J., Fischer, M. L., & Willoughby, A. (1994). Effect of perinatally acquired human immunodeficiency virus infection on neurodevelopment in children during the first two years of life. *Pediatrics, 94,* 883–891.

Orr, D. P., Langefeld, C. D., & Katz, B. P. (1992). Factors associated with condom use among sexually active female adolescents. *The Journal of Pediatrics, 120,* 311–317.

Peckham, C., & Gibb, D. (1995). Mother-child transmission of the HIV. *The New England Journal of Medicine, 333,* 298–302.

Perkins, D. O., Stern, R. A., Golden, R. N., Murphy, C., Naftolowitz, D., & Evans, D. L. (1994). Mood disorders in HIV infection: Prevalence and risk factors in a nonepicenter of the AIDS epidemic. *The American Journal of Psychiatry, 151,* 233–236.

Piaao, P. A., Eddy, J., & Falloon, J. (1988). Effect of continuous intravenous infusion of AZT in children with symptomatic HIV injection. *The New England Journal of Medicine, 319,* 880–896.

Pless, I., & Nolan, T. (1989). Risks for maladjustment associated with chronic illness in childhood. In D. Shaffer, I. Philips, & N. Enzer (Eds.), *Prevention of mental disorders, alcohol and other drug use in children and adolescents* (pp. 191–244). Washington, D.C.: U.S. Department of Health and Human Services.

Ponton, L. E., DiClemente, R. J., & McKenna, S. (1991). An AIDS education and prevention program for hospitalized adolescents. *Journal of the American Academy of Child Adolescent Psychiatry, 91,* 729–734.

Rabkin, J. G., Rabkin, R., Harrison, W., & Wagner, G. (1994). Effect of imipramine on mood and enumerative measures of immune status in depressed patients with HIV illness. *The American Journal of Psychiatry, 151,* 516–523.

Rabkin, J. G., Rabkin, R., & Wagner, G. (1994). Effects of fluoxetine on mood and immune status in depressed patients with HIV illness. *Journal of Clinical Psychiatry, 55,* 92–97.

Rawitscher, L. A., Saitz, R., & Friedman, L. S. (1995). Adolescents' preferences regarding human immunodeficiency virus (HIV)-related physician counseling and HIV testing. *Pediatrics, 95,* 52–58.

Schmitt, B., Seeger, J., Kreuz, W., Enenkel, S., & Jacobi, G. (1991). Central nervous system involvement of children with HIV-infection. *Developmental Medicine and Child Neurology, 33,* 535–540.

Schonfeld, D. J., O'Hare, L. L., Perrin, E. C., Quackenbush, M., Showalter, D. R., & Cicchetti, D. V. (1995). A randomized, controlled trial of a school-based, multifaceted AIDS education program in the elementary grades: The impact on comprehension, knowledge and fears. *Pediatrics, 95,* 480–486.

Seidman, S. N., & Rieder, R. O. (1994). A review of sexual behavior in the United States. *The American Journal of Psychiatry, 151,* 330–341.

Sewell, D. D., Jeste, D. V., Atkinson, J. H., Heaton, R. K., Hesselink, J. R., Wiley, C., Thal, L., Chandler, J. L., & Grant, I., San Diego HIV Neurobehavioral Research Center Group. (1994). HIV-associated psychosis: A study of 20 cases. *The American Journal of Psychiatry, 151,* 237–242.

Steingard, R., Biederman, J., Spencer, T., Wilens, T., & Gonzalez, A. (1993). Comparison of clonidine response in the treatment of attention deficit hyperactivity disorder with and without comorbid tic disorders. *Journal of the American Academy of Child Adolescent Psychiatry, 32,* 350–353.

Summergrad, P., Rauch, S., & Neal, R. (1993). Human immunodeficiency virus and other infectious disorders affecting the central nervous system. In A. Stoudemire & B. S. Fogel (Eds.), *Psychiatric care of the medical patient* (pp. 713–737). New York: Oxford University Press.

Tardieu, M., Blanche, S., & Rouzioux, C. (1987). Atteinte du systeme nerveux au cours des infections a HIV 1 chez le nourrisson. *Archive Francais Pediatrie, 44,* 495–499.

Tardieu, M., Mayaux, M. J., Seibel, N., Funch-Brentano, I., Straub, E., Teglas, J. P., & Blanche, S. (1995). Cognitive assessment of school-age children infected with maternally transmitted human immunodeficiency virus type 1. *The Journal of Pediatrics, 126,* 375–379.

Targ, E. F., Karasiz, D. H., Diefenbach, P. N., Anderson, D. A., Bystrinsky, A., & Fawzy, F. L. (1994). Structured group therapy and fluoxetine to treat depression in HIV-positive persons. *Psychosomatics, 35,* 132–137.

Thomas, P. A., Weedon, J., & Krasinski, K. (1994). Maternal predictor of perinatal human immunodeficiency virus transmission. *Pediatric Infectious Diseases Journal, 13,* 489–496.

U.S. Department of Health and Human Services. (1994). Evaluation and management of early HIV infection. *Clinical practice guideline number 7* (AHCPR publication No. 94-0572). Washington, D.C.: Author.

Van de Perre, P., Simonon, A., & Msellati, P. (1991). Postnatal transmission of HIV from mother to infant: A prospective cohort study in Kigali, Rwanda. *The New England Journal of Medicine, 325,* 593–598.

Wagner, K. D., & Sullivan, M. A. (1991). Fear of AIDS related to development of obsessive-compulsive disorder in a child. *Journal of the American Academy of Child Adolescent Psychiatry, 91,* 740–742.

Walsh, M. E., & Bibace, R. (1990). Children's conceptions of AIDS: A developmental analysis. *Journal of Pediatric Psychiatry, 16,* 273–285.

Whitt, J. K., Hooper, S. R., Tennison, M. B., Robertson, W. T., Gold, S. H., Burchinal, M., Wells, R., McMillan, C., Whaley, R. A., Combest, J., & Hall, C. D. (1993). Neuropsychologic functioning of human immunodeficiency virus-infected children with hemophilia. *The Journal of Pediatrics, 122,* 52–59.

Working group on antiretroviral therapy national pediatric HIV resource center. (1993). Antiretroviral therapy and medical management of the HIV infected child. *Pediatric Infectious Diseases Journal, 12,* 513–522.

World Health Organization. (1995). *The current global situation of the HIV/AIDS pandemic.* Geneva, Switzerland: Author.

CHAPTER 16

ORGAN TRANSPLANTATION

Margaret L. Stuber
Robert D. Canning

DESCRIPTION OF DISORDERS

During the past 15 years, organ and bone marrow transplantation in pediatric populations has moved from experimental therapy for a few severe disorders to the treatment of choice for many end-stage disorders. Although kidney transplantation was pioneered in the 1950s and heart replacement in the late 1960s, it was not until relatively safe and effective immunosuppressive agents became available in the early 1980s that the everyday application of solid organ transplantation began in both children and adults (Craven & Rodin, 1992; Fox & Swazey, 1992). Bone marrow transplantation (BMT) was attempted experimentally as early as the 1950s but has not been in wide usage until the last decade (Ramsay, 1989). The transplantation of kidneys, hearts, bone marrow, and livers is now commonplace in all age groups and makes news only if an unusual "human interest" issue arises. The transplantation of combinations of organs such as heart-lung, small bowel–liver, and multi-visceral transplantation of abdominal organs are procedures that remain experimental. In addition, the use of BMT as a first-line therapy for pediatric cancer continues to be controversial (Pinkel, 1993). End-stage disorders of childhood such as biliary atresia, acute lymphoblastic leukemia, idiopathic cardiomyopathies, cystic fibrosis, and kidney failure are now widely viewed as amenable to treatment by organ or bone marrow replacement. Cyclosporine-A (SandImmun®), once seen as almost miraculous, has been partially displaced by new immunosuppressant medications with fewer toxic side effects (Klintmalm, Husberg, & Starzl, 1991). The use of non-related bone marrow donors identified via computerized donor programs has increased the number of bone marrow procedures across the U.S. (Mangan, Klump, Rosenfield, & Shadduck, 1991).

For psychologists and psychiatrists, the transplant process affords a unique opportunity to evaluate, follow, and treat children and families as they move from the pre-transplant evaluation to the waiting period, through the transplantation process itself, and then on to recovery from surgery and the re-entry into home and school life. The psychological and ethical issues of living donors and the role of the family in caring for transplant patients present practitioners with numerous thorny dilemmas. With increasing numbers of patients undergoing these complex and taxing procedures, the psychological and ethical issues inherent in transplantation become more central, at times overshadowing the medical issues. This is particularly true of the youngest patients and those with disabilities. In addition, the interaction of medical treatment and development is particularly salient, since transplantation offers the chance of survival, but results in both long- and short-term morbidity. The personal and social costs of the transplantation procedures and the life-long immunosuppressant medication have sparked lively debate over this use of our limited health care dollars.

Kidney Transplantation

Kidney transplantation was the first transplantation technology developed, and remains the most widespread in both children and adults. However, it is performed much less frequently in children than adults, with children making up only 6.4 percent of all kidney transplants performed in the United States from 1988 through 1993. During this period, 3,804 pediatric kidney transplants were performed—almost 1,000 more than for liver transplants and three times the number of hearts. The major indication for kidney replacement in children is chronic renal failure caused by a variety of congenital conditions, infections, or disease processes. For the five-year period October 1987 through December, 1992, one-, two-, and three-year survival rates for both cadaveric and living-related kidneys were at least 90 percent, except for neonates who have slightly lower survival rates (UNOS, personal communication). As in other transplantation therapies, survival for subsequent transplantations is less than for first organs. Kidney transplantation remains the only solid organ transplantation technology that relies on living donors (most often immediate family members) for a significant number of its organs—almost 50 percent from 1988 through 1993.

Cardiovascular Transplantation

For the six years ending in 1993, 1,269 children and adolescents received heart transplants in the United States (approximately 10 percent of all heart transplants performed). Of those children transplanted, over 40 percent were less than one year of age. The most common indications for heart transplantation among children are cardiomyopathies and congenital malformations (mostly hypoplastic left heart syndrome). Congenital malformations predominate in neonates and cardiomyopathies in older children and adolescents. Smaller numbers of children are referred for coronary artery disease, myocarditis, graft rejection, and adriamycin toxic cardiomyopathy (Bernstein, Starnes, & Baum, 1989). From October, 1987 through December, 1992 survival for older children undergoing heart transplantation was approximately 80 percent at one year and near 70 percent at three years. Young children have a one year survival of 75 percent and 73 percent at three years. Infants have a survival rate of 69 percent at one-year and 62 percent at three years. Survival after retransplantation is lower for all age groups.

The frequency of lung transplantation and heart-lung transplantation among children remains low. During the six-year period ending in 1993, 120 pediatric patients underwent lung and 58 underwent heart-lung transplantation. These figures represent 6.2 percent and 16.5 percent of all lung and heart-lung transplants performed in the United States during these years. Among children, the major reasons for lung transplantation are cystic fibrosis and primary pulmonary hypertension (PPH). The major indications for heart-lung transplantation are congenital heart disease, PPH, and cystic fibrosis. One-year survival rates for lung transplants are generally between 60 percent and 70 percent, with three-year rates of less than 50 percent. Rates are substantially lower for neonates.

Liver, Pancreas, and Small Bowel Transplantation

Liver transplantation is the most common pediatric transplantation except for kidneys. From 1988 to 1993, 18 percent of all liver transplants were performed on individuals less than 18 years of age. Of these, 1,918, or two-thirds, were performed on children less than 5 years of age. The major indications for liver transplants in children are biliary atresia, inborn errors of metabolism (e.g., α_1-antitrypsin deficiency), or fulminant liver failure (most commonly caused by poisoning). One-, two-, and three-year survival rates for transplanted children are relatively stable for older children (80 percent), with three-year survival rates for younger children and infants nearer 70 percent.

Pancreas transplantation in children remains rare and is considered experimental therapy for severe diabetes mellitus. It is unique among solid organ transplants in that it is not used to save lives so much as it is to protect an insulin-dependent individual from the devastating indirect complications of their disorder (Tydén & Groth, 1991). From 1988 through 1993, 3,053 pancreas transplantations were performed in the United States, but only 15 were for patients less than 18 years of age. Some centers have performed combination kidney-pancreas transplants with good results.

Even more than pancreas transplantation, small bowel transplantation remains a rare and experimental procedure. Only a few centers attempt this operation and often in combination with a liver transplantation. The most common reason to consider a small bowel transplant is "short gut syndrome," which can be caused by absorptive insufficiency, motility disorders, or pseudo-obstruction of the small bowel (Reyes, Tzakis, Todo, Nour, & Starzl, 1993).

Bone Marrow Transplantation

BMT is used annually to treat several thousand children suffering from a heterogeneous group of hematologic and immune disorders (Mangan et al., 1991). Hematologic disorders treated with BMT include severe aplastic anemia, acute lymphoid and myeloid leukemia, and recently, severe sickle cell disease (Pinkel, 1993). Treatment of these diseases with BMT is usually considered when other therapies have failed or after the child has suffered relapses, although it is considered as treatment of choice for aplastic anemia if a matched, related donor is available. Although overall survival rates for BMT in these disorders are difficult to characterize because of differing protocols, divergent patient characteristics, and complications associated with the BMT conditioning regimens, survival after BMT is generally 10–30 percent below that for similar aged children receiving solid organ transplants (Mangan et al., 1991; Pinkel, 1993). On the other hand, the use of BMT for rare immune disorders has been more successful. When used to treat immune disorders such as severe combined immunodeficiency disease (SCID) survival rates approach those of solid organ transplants (Pinkel, 1993).

EPIDEMIOLOGY

The introduction of cyclosporine into regular use in 1981 ushered in the modern era of solid organ transplantation in both children and adults. Although the number of transplants as a whole has risen steadily, the proportion of solid organ transplants with children has shown a steady decline in the past half-decade. Thus, 9.4 percent of all transplants performed in 1988 were for children less than 18 years of age, while in 1993 the proportion of pediatric transplants had declined to 8.25 percent.[1] This trend is true for all organs except heart and lungs where there has been a rise in the past few years. The reason for this decline in the proportion of transplantation of children is probably only partly due to the increase in the sheer numbers of adult transplants. Other reasons may include changes in how organs are allocated (national to regional) and recent changes in state laws that have resulted in increased use and enforcement of child car seats and safety helmets (L. Siminoff, personal communication, November 18, 1994).

Although UNOS lists over 275 transplant centers in the United States, only a fraction of these perform pediatric transplantation on a regular basis. In the past six years, almost 200 centers have performed one or more pediatric kidney transplants, but only 35 have performed ten or more in any one year. For livers or hearts, the number of centers performing transplants on a regular basis is less than 25. Lung, heart-lung, pancreas, and intestinal transplantation are practiced at only a handful of centers. These figures are important because studies of transplantation of liver, heart and pancreas with adults have shown that centers that perform more transplants have significantly higher survival rates than centers with lower volume (Edwards, Hunsicker, Guo, Breen, & Daily, 1994; Hosenpud, Breen, Edwards, Daily, & Hunsicker, 1994; Hunsicker, Bennett, Breen, Sutherland, & Daily, 1994). As the technology of solid organ transplantation has progressed, the overall patient survival rates for the procedures have increased. In terms of the number of organs transplanted in children, most operations are performed to replace a kidney, liver, heart, lung, heart-lung, or pancreas. Intestinal transplants are not common and multi-visceral transplants of the intestinal organs are rare and considered experimental (Kocoshis, Tsakis, Todo, Reyes, & Nour, 1993).

Historically, the number of children awaiting transplantation has far exceeded the pool of available donors (although in raw numbers, the number of children on organ waiting lists is a small proportion—3.7 percent—of the total number of individuals waiting for transplantation). The median waiting time for an organ has increased in recent years for all organs and varies according to many factors including age and size of recipient, type of organ needed, medical urgency, and blood type compatibility. The median wait for a liver is approximately three to four months, a heart one to three months, and a kidney 9 to 18 months. Organs are currently allocated on a regional basis, which some in the transplant community believe adds needlessly to waiting time, and thus decreases survival. UNOS estimates that 10 percent of all those waiting for solid organ transplants will die before receiving an organ (UNOS, personal communication).

In the last 15 years the number of bone marrow transplants for pediatric cancer, immunodeficiency diseases, and rare hematologic disorders has risen dramatically (Ramsay, 1989). This has been due, in part, to the use of non-related donor programs and the use of BMT for more disorders and earlier in the disease process (Mangan et al., 1991; Pinkel, 1993). Because a donor's bone marrow is constantly regenerated, the waiting time for BMT depends only on finding a suitable donor. The first choice is an HLA matched family member, but if a suitable match within the family is not possible, a search of donor banks is initiated. With the advent of computerized searches, the search of donor registries is shorter than in the past but can still last from three to six months (Mangan et al., 1991).

The primary medical complications associated with solid organ transplantation are rejection of the organ, opportunistic infections secondary to immunosuppression, and the side effects of the numerous prescribed medications. Acute rejection can occur up to several months after the organ graft. Most patients experience at least one episode of rejection during the first year while chronic rejection appears over a period of years (Bernstein, Starnes, & Baum, 1989; Kocoshis et al., 1993; Kuo & Jenkins, 1993; Shapiro & Simmons, 1991). A significant threat to the long-term use of immunosuppressant medications is a chronic condition called post-transplant lymphoproliferative disease (PTLD) in which the patient experiences a lymphoma-like syndrome. This syndrome presents in slightly different forms in all solid organ transplants and requires the lowering of immunosuppression, thus increasing the chance of graft rejection and infection. The scenario is complicated by the fact that PTLD is associated with infection by Epstein-Barr virus, a common infectious agent (Kocoshis et al., 1993). Another complicating factor post-transplant is infection. Most opportunistic viral infections are caused by either the Epstein-Barr virus (EBV) or the cytomegalovirus (CMV), while a variety of bacterial agents can cause problems. Infections are treatable by reducing immunosuppression and/or the use of anti-viral or anti-bacterial therapies. The third major post-transplant complication is the long-term side effects of the immunosuppressant medications themselves. Cyclosporine-A (SandImmun®) and FK-506 or tacrolimus (ProGraf®) both have serious nephro- and neurotoxic effects. The steroid drugs have a multitude of negative side effects such as growth retardation, diabetes, depression, and weight gain that can complicate the long-term medical and psychological prognosis for pediatric transplant patients (Klintmalm, Husberg, & Starzl, 1991).

Once a BMT patient has survived the acute toxicity of the chemotherapy and /or radiation, and the infections of the time immediately post-transplant, the major dangers are relapse of the underlying disease or graft-versus-host-disease (GVHD) (Pinkel, 1993; Ramsay, 1989). GVHD is a syndrome that is conceptually similar to the rejection found in solid organ transplantation, except that in BMT it is the donor's immunological system that has been transplanted to the recipient. Thus, rather than the host's immune system rejecting the grafted organ, in GVHD the engrafted marrow tissue attacks the recipient's body, which is perceived as foreign. One-third or more of BMT patients suffer from acute GVHD and can experience skin disease, liver dysfunction, bronchitis, gastroenteritis, and stomatitis. Chronic GVHD occurs 3–6 months after the graft and is found in approximately 40 percent of patients (Pinkel, 1993; Ramsay, 1989). Other late sequelae of allogenic BMT include relapse, growth failure, endocrine disorders, renal insufficiency, pulmonary disease, and leukoencephalopathy (Pinkel, 1993; Ramsay, 1989). It is ironic that a rare late effect of some conditioning regimens for BMT is irreversible cardiomyopathy, requiring heart transplantation.

ASSESSMENT APPROACHES

Medical Issues

The principal type of assessment made by psychiatric consultants working with transplant teams is made at the time of the decision to transplant. However, medical assessment can be requested at any time in the transplant process. Although organ transplant recipients suffer from a variety of specific medical disorders, the usual medical factors of concern to the psychiatrist or psychologist are delirium or other organic brain disturbances that might interfere with the patient's ability to make an informed decision about the transplant or participate in care. These may be symptoms of the underlying medical condition, or may be responses to the various medications given to the child. Mental status changes secondary to hepatic failure or anoxia associated with heart failure may present with symptoms or signs that may initially be thought to represent depression. Careful assessment of level of consciousness and a mental status examination will distinguish between these possibilities (Smith, Breitbart & Platt, 1995). A review of current medications is also essential. It is not uncommon for a consultant to be asked to assess depression or confusion in a child who is receiving several psychoactive drugs, such as an anti-emetic, pain medication and an anxiolytic. These drugs can often be reduced, stopped or changed, with beneficial results.

Delirium or organic mental disturbances are less commonly diagnosed in children undergoing transplant than in adults (Sexson & Rubenow, 1992; Trzepacz, 1994). It is not clear whether this reflects a true decreased frequency of occurrence, or the tendency to overlook behavior in children that would be readily diagnosed in adults. For example, refusal to allow procedures or discussion of monsters in the hospital room would quickly result in a workup or psychiatric consultation on an adult service but may be interpreted as behavior problems or fantasy in a 6 year old. Often it is observant parents who let the staff know that the behavior is atypical and requires investigation. The fact that children are not the legal decision-makers regarding transplantation, and their need for adult assistance in following treatment protocols in any case, also reduces the urgency felt by some teams to have a confused child evaluated. However, anyone who has seen the distress of a child who is actively delusional as a result of delirium will appreciate the need to adequately assess this aspect of the child.

An additional problem in mental status assessment of pediatric transplant candidates is the lack of developmentally appropriate, standardized measures. A child's version of the Mini Mental Status Exam has been piloted, which evaluates basic orientation, memory, and concentration (Heiligenstein, personal communication, 1991). Careful evaluation, combined with a brief history from the parent, will usually allow the consultant to assess level of consciousness, reality testing, and basic motor coordination skills.

Another important aspect of assessment is evaluation of mood or anxiety disorders. Again, the current medication list must be carefully scrutinized before a diagnosis is made of depression or anxiety, as many commonly used medications can cause agitation or sedation. A careful interview and history are usually sufficient to differentiate between conservation withdrawal and true depression. However, the use of a structured diagnostic interview may be indicated in cases that remain unclear despite careful assessment of the child, parents, and medical record.

Psychological and Psychiatric Issues

Potential Recipients

Psychological assessment of a potential pediatric transplant recipient should always involve discussions with at least two people: the candidate and the responsible adult. Usually several additional people should also be seen, including but not limited to both parents, their partners or spouses, the siblings of the transplant candidate, and any other significant support people. For adolescents this may include a boyfriend or girlfriend. In some families the grandparents or other extended family members may play an essential role and should be included in the initial assessment.

The primary goals of the assessment are to establish whether there are any significant psychiatric contraindications to the transplant, and to understand the types of needs this family is likely to have during and after a transplant. Both goals require a certain amount of prediction. Unfortunately, there are few established data on which to base these predictions. Some of the data that do exist can be interpreted in ways that do not make practical sense. For example, the poor rate of adherence to medical recommendations of adolescents has led some to suggest that adolescence is a relative contra-indication to solid organ transplantation. Although this conclusion is supported by the data, it is not a useful interpretation. It is, however, useful to know that most if not all adolescents will experiment with their medications and will be resistant to adult advice at some point. This allows the consultant to make specific recommendations about necessary support and the utility of peer counseling for teens (Stuber, 1993a; Stuber & Nader, 1995).

Psychiatric consultation regarding selection of a potential recipient for the transplant list is a common part of the evaluation process for solid organ transplants. Adult and pediatric psychiatrists are generally members of the Selection Committee, and some payers may require psychiatric clearance before a patient is cleared as a candidate, and put on the list. BMT does not involve use of a regional list, since donors can be used more than once and because matching is more critical than for solid organs. Candidates are usually chosen by the BMT team, which is most likely to request consultation at the time of admission for BMT rather than months before. The assessment for BMT, although similar to that described below, emphasizes the prediction of needed services based on the assessment of the child and family's coping patterns, support system and psychopathology (Wolcott & Stuber, 1992). The actual hospitalization for BMT is much longer (averaging 45 to 60 days) and has a much higher mortality during initial transplant hospitalization (approximately 15 percent) than solid organ transplants (Mangan et al., 1991; Pinkel, 1993). Both of these factors tend to increase the stress on the child, family, and staff, and lead to a recommendation for routine follow-up by consultants from psychiatry or psychology.

A number of formal assessment instruments have been devised for adult transplant assessment (Levenson & Olbrisch, 1993; Olbrisch, Levenson & Hammer, 1989). Several recent review articles on pediatric transplantation have suggested outlines to be used in the initial transplant evaluation (Sexson & Rubenow, 1992; Slater, 1994; Stuber, 1993b). However, there is no formal pediatric instrument, at present. A summary of the types of issues considered by most instruments, adapted for pediatrics, leads to the following five basic areas of evaluation.

1. Does the patient and family (however that is defined) understand the reasons for the transplant, and have a realistic understanding of what will be required of them post-transplant?
2. Are the patient and at least one significant adult committed to having this transplant?
3. Do the patient and family have the basic support and skills to provide the necessary medical care after the transplant (e.g., telephone, transportation to the hospital or clinic, ability to administer a complex set of medications multiple times per day, judgment to perceive and respond to a medical emergency)?
4. Has the patient and responsible adult demonstrated an ability to adhere to medical instructions (e.g., compliance with medications, attendance at medical appointments)?
5. Are there any major psychiatric disturbances in this candidate or responsible adult?

The last question may appear to be the first concern to consultants trained to make psychiatric diagnoses and recommend appropriate treatment. However, in practice it is the impact of a psychiatric diagnosis on the other issues that determines whether or not that diagnosis is relevant to the transplant decision or to management of the patient and family during and after the transplant.

One of the most disturbing aspects of working with pediatric transplant decisions is the pivotal role of the responsible adult. Although it is obvious to anyone who has worked with children or adolescents that the family context is critical to the outcome of any intervention, be it medical or psychological, it is very difficult to make a determination that a child should not receive a donor organ because the parent is unreliable. However, to ignore the psychopathology of the parent is to allow a situation to develop that endangers the life of the child after depriving another child of the opportunity to receive that donor organ. In most cases this dilemma has been resolved by deciding that psychopathology in the responsible adult is an indication for intensive psychiatric intervention, or assistance from social work to find another adult to care for the child. The additional cost has not been considered a serious problem until recently, when staff reductions and managed care are raising questions about the feasibility of such decisions.

Psychopathology in an adolescent has been approached in different ways by different teams, to a large extent based on the experience of that team (Stuber, 1993a). For some teams who have dealt with the frustration of watching an adolescent "destroy" the donor organ with resistance to their instructions, experimentation with medication, or with use of illegal drugs, a candidate with a history of disruptive behavior raises serious concerns, and requires assurances from the consultant that this adolescent is "manageable." Other teams take an approach similar to that of the juvenile justice system, that anyone under 18 is still malleable, and it is inappropriate to condemn a minor to death for youthful indiscretions. The key variable for the consultant is to determine the level of support that can be elicited from the family or social service system. Unfortunately, adolescent and family psychopathology tend to co-vary, and the availability of resources is often slim for the most disturbed adolescents. A psychiatric hospitalization, either before or after the transplant, can be used to stabilize the situation and secure the best possible support system. However, it must be acknowledged at the onset that these patients will be high consumers of psychosocial resources, and a commitment must be made by the team to provide the requisite support.

Suicide attempts that result in a need for organ transplantation present difficult problems for the consultant. Often the situation is fulminant, requiring rapid decisions. The patient may be comatose, or sufficiently sedated or obtunded to be unable to provide a reliable history. From a purely medical point of view, these are appealing cases, since the absence of a chronic disease process generally means that other organ systems are intact. However, these are often impulsive adolescents from troubled homes, who are not good risks for medication adherence. Sometimes the transplant can be the impetus for a major positive life change, particularly if intensive in-patient psychiatric interventions can be provided before or after the transplant. However, these must be viewed as high-risk transplants, and be carefully monitored for years post-transplant.

Living Related Donors

The possibility of using relatives as living donors of needed organs has extended from kidneys to bone marrow and most recently to livers (Goldman, 1993; Kocoshis et al., 1993). Legal and ethical issues are most problematic when the potential donor is also a minor. This occurs primarily in bone marrow transplantation, for which siblings are generally the optimal donors.

Bone marrow donation offers no physical benefit to the donor, and inflicts mild suffering, as well as the potential for more serious harm through the need for general anesthesia. The question has therefore been raised whether parents should legally and ethically be able to make the decision to use one child to save the life of another. Some states appoint a legal advocate for the minor donor to protect against potential "abuse" by the parent who is eager to save another child. A recent case made the headlines when a middle-aged couple decided to reverse a vasectomy and conceive a child in hope that the newborn could serve as a matched donor for their teenage daughter (Chang, 1991). Generally, however, parents are expected to be able to weigh the risks and benefits and make appropriate decisions for both children. Consultants are frequently asked to make assessment as to the level of understanding the minor donor has about the transplant process, and to ensure that the minor has been actively prepared, and has not been coerced (Kinrade, 1987).

With the technology now available to perform successful liver transplants using one lobe of an adult liver for a child, parents can now serve as donors for their children (Kocoshis et al., 1993). Psychiatric assessment of these donors has raised interesting questions about the possibility of true informed consent for a serious, nontherapeutic operation when it has the potential to save the life of one's child (Goldman, 1993; Singer et al., 1989). It is inherently coercive to have to make a choice that has such an obviously socially correct alternative, and that is so emotionally laden. However, it is possible to determine whether someone is making an uninformed decision, or is terrified by the prospect of surgery, while feeling there are no options. Assessment is essential to providing appropriate interventions. In addition to the issues described above, which are discussed with parents of any type of transplant candidate, it is useful to discuss the decision-making process, checking specifically for coercion from or conflict with the other parent or family members. Potential donors must also be assessed as to their level of understanding of the procedures involved in the donation. Many parents, focused on their ill child, will underestimate the true extent of their own surgery and the need for post-operative recovery. Meetings with other donor parents, in person or by phone, will be more effective at conveying the reality of the surgery than any professional lectures. Plans for alternative care-providers for themselves, their spouses, and for their other children must be made. Assessment is best coordinated with social work and child life personnel to provide appropriate planning with and for the child and family.

TREATMENT STRATEGIES

Overview of Medical Management

Psychiatric interventions and treatment in organ transplantation vary with the phase of the transplant experience more than the type of transplant. Interventions must also be considered on at least two levels: the recipient and family, and the transplant team or clinical service caring for the recipient. In cases where the transplant involves a living, related donor, that person must also be considered. The phases can be roughly divided into three: (1) the time between the decision to transplant and the availability of a donor organ, (2) the transplant hospitalization, and (3) post-transplantation. As mentioned above, in cases where a living, related donor is used, the waiting time is decreased considerably, sometimes to a matter of days rather than months. Each of these phases will be considered first in terms of the medical problems that can be addressed by the psychiatric consultant. Then each of these phases will be considered in terms of psychological and behavioral management. Finally, some pharmacological interventions used by transplant consultants will be discussed.

Before Transplantation

The waiting period is a good time to prepare the child and family for the procedures that are ahead. Hypnosis, guided imagery and relaxation techniques are best learned when there is little time pressure and the participants are feeling relatively able to concentrate. A useful approach is to teach parents the technique, so they can use it and also facilitate the child's use of it. Many parents are surprised by the ease with which young children adopt these techniques. It is usually wise to introduce the topic using neutral terminology such as "relaxation techniques," since many people connect "hypnosis" with loss of control. There are a number of excellent references for professionals unfamiliar with these techniques (e.g., Fanning, 1988; Hilgard & LeBaron, 1984). However, it is best to have an experienced supervisor or teacher who can assist the novice, as the techniques are powerful and can unmask psychological issues for which the psychiatrist or psychologist must be prepared. Parents and children can be taught to use simple techniques on their own, using audiotapes or specific images or stories to relax or achieve pain control. Successful implementation of these techniques can help both parent and patient to feel more competent and in control.

Hospitalization

Adequate pain relief is frequently an issue for children in the immediate post-transplant period. The use of patient-controlled analgesia (PCA) is becoming more common. This system uses an indwelling catheter to deliver a constant infusion or regular boluses of intravenous medication. The patient or parent can also push a button to have additional, limited boluses delivered. In this way, an appropriate titration of medication can be made with minimal difficulty. Control of pain for children is historically poorer than for adults, largely due to the different verbal and non-verbal pain behaviors utilized by children (Ross & Ross, 1988). If relaxation or self-hypnotic techniques have been taught during the waiting period, they can be utilized for pain and anxiety control. However, the acute transplant hospitalization is a difficult time to first introduce such approaches.

Post-Transplant

Nonadherence to prescribed medications and follow-up care is the most common medical problem post-transplant requiring psychiatric or psychological consultation. Many solid organ recipients appear to assume that immunosuppressive medications are no longer needed after a few years, and become erratic about compliance with prescribed medications or stop them altogether (Didlake, Dreyfus, Kerman, VanBuren, & Kahan, 1988). Other survivors stop the medications to seek a return to normal appearance or to avoid the daily reminder of their transplant experience. Potentially lethal rejection episodes can result from these attempts to "put the transplant behind them." Nonadherence with medication is particularly frequent in adolescents, who are exquisitely sensitive to any deviation from what other adolescents are doing. Family conflict will exacerbate the normal tendency of adolescents to question the instructions of adults. "Scare techniques," in which adolescents are told all the terrible consequences of nonadherence, are rarely effective. Building an alliance that would allow the adolescent to discuss concerns and behaviors is a more useful therapeutic approach to work with a survivor at risk for nonadherence.

Medical complications of transplantation can also lead to depression or resistance to further medical interventions. Children with severe graft-versus-host disease or neurological impairment after bone marrow transplantation can become despondent and can cause the entire family to become distressed. The infertility that often results from bone marrow transplantation can also be demoralizing to adolescents, who may feel that they have nothing to offer a potential mate. Some adolescents will respond by attempting to test their fertility, potentially resulting in pregnancies for which they are unprepared. Survivors who have significant complications should be psychiatrically followed, and support offered to the family and child.

Psychological and Behavioral Management

Before Transplantation: Recipient and Family

The decision to transplant a child is made by both the family and the team, using somewhat different criteria. Although most children who undergo transplantation have had the underlying disease since birth or early infancy, and have been chronically ill, the recommendation of the medical team to transplant the child can be a major blow for the child and family. In most cases this signals the terminal phase of a progressive illness. In some cases, where the illness is disabling rather than fatal, the recommendation to transplant is more ambiguous, and involves a different type of gamble for the patient and family. Do they continue as they are, knowing that the disease is irreversible and progressive, or try a treatment that entails significant morbidity and mortality? In both situations, the decision is made more stressful by the wait that is usually required before a donor is found. The psychologist or psychiatrist can be extremely helpful to the family by working with them to clarify the decision-making process, and ensuring that all family members are getting information that is at the appropriate level of complexity. Families may have little idea of how to present the situation to siblings, including those who might be potential donors for bone marrow or kidney transplants. Parents may be protective of their children and spouses, and unintentionally complicate communication by keeping information from them that they think would be "upsetting." Cultural and language differences can also complicate the initial decision-making process, causing confusion if not antagonism between the team and the family. Use of professional translators, rather than family members will make it much more likely that the doctor's information is getting to the patient or parent directly, without modification.

Pre-transplant anxiety can also be greatly alleviated by an introduction to the actual places, procedures and machines that are a part of transplantation. Many hospitals will have child life programs that will provide tours and an opportunity to handle the lines and tubes that families will encounter. Viewing the OR, recovery room and ICU, and learning about the actual concrete steps of the transplant process will reduce the anxiety for parents, and allow them to better assist their children.

Many families attribute special meaning to various organs, and are concerned about the implications of having someone else's organ in their body. The most common example is the heart, which is seen by many as the origin of love or courage. Consultants are wise to explore such issues before the transplant, when there is time to consider the matter and come to some acceptable resolution. Racial prejudices may also affect emotional response to the donor organ, and are also best handled early.

Staff

Many transplant patients will spend extended periods in the hospital during the waiting period. This can be stressful for both staff and families, as they await the definitive treatment, the timing of which is outside their control. Education of the staff about the beliefs and coping style of a particular family or parent can save later confusion and conflict. Some parents are too emotionally overwhelmed by the hospital to spend extended time there. Other parents are unable to provide the support the child desires, due to personal, job-related or family responsibilities. While it is in the child's best interest to have the parent there if possible, and the consultant can sometimes facilitate this, there are times when staff must be helped to see that people are not necessarily bad parents if they are not at bedside 24 hours a day. Other parents may respond to the loss of usual parental functions by trying to exercise inappropriate control, which can conflict with medical and nursing staff. An extreme case of inappropriate expression of a need for control was that of a mother who wrote in the chart and made ventilator adjustments. In less severe cases, the hypervigilance and information-seeking that has worked well for parents as they sought treatment for their children may appear annoying and unnecessary to staff during the waiting period. Staff who are aware of the nature and reason for the problem can be helped to avoid power struggles and identify areas that can be returned to parental control, such as bathing or feeding.

HOSPITALIZATION

Recipient and Family

Despite the promise it entails, the actual transplant is often frightening for children and families. Many families find themselves reacting "I'm not ready!" when the call finally comes. Adequate preparation in the waiting period will reduce the ambivalence and panic of families at the time of admission.

General pediatric psychiatric consultation principles apply to work with families during the transplant hospitalization. Parents are to be encouraged to plan for a prolonged hospital stay. This means that they must get sleep and food at regular intervals, to maintain their health and strength to support their children. Social support networks, such as churches, can be mobilized to manage responsibilities at home or work. A useful service is to have a friend who serves as the news reporter for the network, so that the parent is not burdened with telling the story repeatedly. Parents can also be encouraged to use their support network to provide housing and logistical support for their other children. Attention to the siblings will reduce the tendency for acting out. However, parents may also need to hear that a certain amount of regression and anxiety or anger is to be expected, and does not indicate that their children are ungrateful or "bad."

Depression is a frequent reason for a request for psychiatric consultation. It is important to differentiate between the withdrawal often seen in children who are recovering from major medical problems and either demoralization or depression. Sometimes a child or adolescent will present with symptoms that are consistent with depression, which reflect a hopelessness that is not consistent with the true medical situation. Discovering and clearing up the misunderstanding can be a powerful antidepressant. For other children, activities and contact with peers can be extremely helpful in getting the child to be more energetic and hopeful. Child life specialists can offer trips to the playroom or teen lounge for those who are mobile, and room-based projects for those who must remain in isolation.

Although kidney transplants involve relatively short stays in the ICU, most transplants involve lengthy hospitalizations. The ICU is designed for acute care, and does not generally include the amenities found on the floor, such as chairs in the room that convert into beds for parents. Children and parents can become disoriented with the 24-hour activity of the ICU. Establishing some sort of expectable routine, which includes some time when the child is not examined, probed or poked, can be extremely helpful. Nurses can also be reminded of the need to explain all procedures to the child, and to provide regular orienting remarks (e.g., "It is morning now, time for breakfast.") even when the child appears unresponsive.

Sometimes families will request interaction with the family of the cadaveric donor when there is a solid organ transplant, or with the computer-matched living donor for BMT. To protect the privacy of all parties, policies have been developed that forbid the release of names, addresses, or phone numbers to either party. However, donors and recipients of solid organs may communicate anonymously through the regional donor coordinator. If both parties are willing, there can eventually be direct contact. Generally, however, a simple thank-you note is enough to provide the kind of feedback the donors want, and to express the recipients' feelings of gratitude. The principal danger to donors of more contact is that they may come to feel responsible for the outcome of the transplant, and therefore potentially involved in yet another tragic situation, after losing their own child.

Staff

Prolonged hospitalizations are hard on staff as well as families (Stuber, Caswell, Cipkala-Gaffin, & Billet, 1995; Stutzer, 1989). Boundary maintenance can be a problem when staff must work intensively with families for weeks or months. Transplant nurses have been known to take home laundry for families, or come in to visit on their days off. While not clearly inappropriate, such actions should alert the staff that the nurse is being pulled out of role. Ongoing rounds are the best way to address these issues, preventing splitting or inappropriate levels of involvement. Special staff meetings to process the death of a transplant patient who is well known or whose death was unexpected can also be extremely important in helping staff to regulate their emotional involvement with patients, and to avoid a sudden withdrawal from other patients in response to the loss.

Long-Term Survival

Follow-up studies of organ transplant survivors have indicated that they generally do well in terms of growth, ability to re-enter school, and number of life-threatening complications (Gersony, 1990; Pinkel, 1993; Simmons, Klein, & Simmons, 1977). Survivors and their families are told to try to return to a normal life. However, parents and children are often distressed to discover that transplantation does not return the survivor to "normal" in the sense that they had expected. Solid organ recipients must take daily medication for the rest of their lives. They must often undergo invasive procedures, such as cardiac biopsies, to monitor their graft's health. Side-effects of cyclosporine or steroids can cause alterations in appearance or lead to difficulties such as gum hyperplasia that may require surgical intervention. Schools

may be reluctant to accept the liability of having the transplant survivor return to the classroom. Some children will have missed enough school to preclude them from rejoining their peers, and they may be set back a year. Bone marrow transplant recipients find that their contact with the outside world and their diet are still restricted for months after the release from the hospital.

The wish to return to normal can also interfere with the cognitive processing of experience that children need to do in conjunction with their parents. Studies suggest that people who have undergone traumatic experiences, such as exposure to life-threat, benefit from opportunities to discuss their thoughts and feelings. However, such discussions are difficult for those who find themselves re-experiencing aspects of the event when they think or talk about what happened. Recent studies of bone marrow transplant survivors and their families have found that parents as well as survivors report symptoms of post-traumatic stress disorder years after successful transplantation (Pot-Mees, 1989; Stuber, Christakis, Houskamp, & Kazak, 1996; Stuber, Nader, Yasuda, Pynoos, & Cohen, 1991; Stuber and Nader, 1995). This suggests that parents will require assistance to comfortably discuss the transplant experience with their children, as they are limited by their own distress with the memories.

One of the most problematic long-term concerns is the psychiatrically disturbed parent. Generally, although the team may initially be more concerned about parents with Axis I conditions, these can be relatively well managed by the psychiatric consultant or an outside therapist. Parents with character pathology or who are substance abusers can be especially trying for the transplant team. The psychiatric consultant can assist the team to make specific management plans, such as naming one individual as the primary contact person and insuring good communication about treatment plans to prevent splitting. Reasonable limit-setting is also important, so that there are not recurrent calls to physicians' homes or hourly pages. In extreme cases, where the family pathology is adversely affecting the medical status of the survivor, placement outside the home may be considered. However, a trial of family therapy is usually warranted, in conjunction with close monitoring by the transplant team.

Pharmacological Treatments

The primary foci of consultation requiring pharmacological intervention are delirium, depression, anxiety or agitation, and pain. In cases of overt delirium, the psychiatric consultant can be most helpful by attempting to dissuade the team from giving large doses of benzo-diazepines, and recommending small, carefully titrated doses of high-potency neuroleptics. For example, it is common practice to give benzodiazepines for agitation. However, if the agitation is secondary to delirium, the benzodiazepines may worsen rather than improve the agitation, since the sedation may result in increased confusion. High-potency neuroleptics, carefully titrated, are effective in reducing the confusion, and, if given intra-venously, present little risk of extra-pyramidal side-effects (Trzepacz, DiMartini, & Tringali, 1993). These are also safer to use when the liver is compromised than are low-potency neuroleptics such as chlorpromazine. Most ICU teams will have experience with the use of droperidol in anesthesia, and may be more comfort-able with its use than haloperidol. Careful examination of psychotropic medications being used for other pur-poses is important in helping pinpoint an etiology for the delirium. Often the role of the psychiatric consultant is to try to persuade the attending team to reduce or dis-continue medications that are currently prescribed. Careful evaluation of the current medications is war-ranted to ensure that the depression is not a response to analgesics, sleeping medication, or anti-emetic drugs.

Low-dose tricyclic antidepressants are often given as an adjunct to a pain protocol. Less frequently, de-pression is found of sufficient severity to warrant treat-ment with full antidepressant levels of medication. Dosages must be carefully titrated, with consideration of the low tolerance generally seen in young children, and of the compromised organs that may interfere with me-tabolism or excretion. The specific drug used will vary with the medical circumstances, although selective serotonin reuptake inhibitors (SSRIs) are generally pre-ferred due to the minimal side-effect profile. Drug in-teractions are important to consider, especially given the narrow therapeutic index of the immunosuppresants cyclosporine and FK-506 or tacrolimus.

CASE ILLUSTRATIONS

The case illustrations that follow diverge from the es-tablished format used throughout the book in order to demonstrate the breadth of difficulties experienced by children and adolescents who have undergone organ transplantation.

Case 1

Jane was eight when she presented for her liver trans-plantation. She had done moderately well for years, de-spite congenital biliary atresia. However, she no longer had sufficient energy to function at school, and was be-ginning to show evidence of failure. When she was in-terviewed as part of the pre-transplant evaluation, she was friendly but clear that her major concern was that someone take care of her mother. The only child of a sin-gle mother, she was worried that her mother wasn't eat-ing and was smoking too much. Evaluation of the mother suggested that she suffered from a borderline character disorder, and was primarily concerned about how she could survive without her "best friend." The mother de-nied any contact with the child's father, and was not on good terms with any of her own relatives. The team dis-cussed the long-term risks in transplanting a child who had such a tenuous support system, but ultimately de-cided to put her on the list. She was successfully trans-planted. Her post-transplant course was marked by frequent calls from the team to the consultant, expressing concern about possible non-adherence, and conflict be-tween the mother and various members of the staff. In-tervention was needed to get the child to re-enter school, given the mother's anxiety. As the child grew to adoles-cence, conflict developed between her and her mother. Despite ongoing interventions from the psychiatric con-sultant, this ultimately led to the recipient being removed from the mother, and placed with another relative.

Case 2

Consultation was requested by the ICU regarding Jon, a 4-year-old boy who had received two heart trans-plants, and was being considered for a third. His father was seen as a major problem by the nurses, as he was changing respirator settings and writing notes in the pa-tient's chart. The nurses were also troubled by the pos-sibility that the boy would receive another transplant, as he had suffered a stroke after the second transplant, and had very little receptive and no expressive language. The neurology consultant thought that, given his age, the boy was likely to regain some, if not full language ca-pacity. However, the child was septic, and thus was not currently a candidate for transplantation. The different teams of doctors caring for the child were expressing widely varying opinions as to the next step, ranging from those who were advocating that the child be given a Do Not Resuscitate status, to those proposing retrans-plantation, which they were documenting in the chart. Consultation involved three levels of intervention. First, the father was seen, and work begun to help him express his need to have some control in ways that did not jeop-ardize his son's care. Second, the nurses met together to plan strategies for managing this family, and to express their mixed feelings about the appropriate treatment of this child. Third, a general meeting was held of all medical and nursing personnel involved with the care of this case, to discuss the plan for this child. There it was found that, despite the apparently contradictory approaches of the various teams working with this child, they actually had similar assessments of the current status of the child. A plan was made, and communication opened, allowing the team and parents to eventually agree on a DNR status for the child, who died peacefully.

Case 3

Cynthia, a 16-year-old girl with polycystic kidney disease, presented to the emergency room, having attempted to overdose on her steroids. She stated that she had become so ugly, and her life was so impaired by the need to have peritoneal dialysis, that she no longer wanted to live. She viewed transplantation as a solution to her problems. However, the renal transplant team was reluctant to consider her as a candidate, due to her erratic adherence to medical recommendations, and this "psychiatric problem." She was stabilized with a brief in-patient psychiatric visit, during which a therapeutic relationship was formed. Family therapy was begun to help her get the support she needed from her emotionally distant parents. She was eventually seen as an appropriate candidate for transplantation and received one of her brother's kidneys. She tolerated the surgery well. When she did have some later episodes of mild rejection connected with poor adherence to recommended immunosuppressive medications, she decided that she wanted to preserve the graft, and became much more compliant with medical advice. She went on to marry and successfully weather a high-risk pregnancy, and has a healthy child.

Case 4

Jackie was referred to the University Hospital for BMT for aplastic anemia, as she had been judged to be unmanageable by her local hospital, 400 miles away. This 8-year-old girl was very bright but aggressive, and had repeatedly assaulted nurses and doctors at the other hospital. She had been managed with neuroleptic medication, with difficulty. The BMT team set up a specific management group to plan and organize this girl's care. The attending child psychiatrist headed up this group, while a child psychiatry fellow served as the therapist for the child and family. The chief of the child life service

also met regularly with the girl, and worked with the nursing staff to give management suggestions. Nursing staff were selected for their willingness to work in a structured way, and with a great deal of communication to increase consistency and decrease burn-out. Weekly planning meetings were held to review the plan, educate the staff about the psychiatric issues, and provide support for those who had been targeted that week. Emergency meetings were also held as necessary. Although this planning did not entirely prevent attacks on the nurses, it did allow the BMT to be successfully carried out with minimal disruption to the unit, and maximal safety for the child.

Case 5

Jamie, a 6-month-old boy, was deteriorating rapidly, due to liver failure secondary to congenital biliary atresia. His parents had decided that they would like to be considered for the living-related liver donor program. At the time of the initial psychological evaluation of the mother, she barely got into the interview before she began to cry, and guiltily confessed that she and her husband were separated, and expected to divorce. They had not told anyone on the transplant team the truth about this, as she feared it might disqualify them from donating to their son. After establishing that adequate provision had been made for the post-transplant care of both donor and recipient, and that social support was sufficient, the parents were assured that there were no psychiatric contra-indications to using either of them as donors. The father was a better match, and became the donor. Two years later, all are doing well.

SUMMARY

Pediatric organ transplantation has brought the hope of life to a number of children with end-stage organ failure, cancer, or metabolic diseases. However, this dramatic intervention is costly in financial, personal, and social terms. New ethical issues arise with each technological advance, such as the capacity to use living-related liver donors. Consultation from psychiatry and psychology can help with the difficult decisions faced by families and transplant teams. Working as a member of the team, from initial evaluation, through the preparation period, hospitalization, and aftercare, the consultant is asked to predict and prevent problems with medical adherence, depression, or delirium. Consultants must be able to simultaneously work with children, families, and systems if they are to be effective. A good working knowledge of pain control techniques and psychopharmacology are also extremely useful in working with these complex patients. Probably the most demanding situations are those involving significant character pathology in parents or adolescent transplant candidates. Whether these cases will eventually be considered to be too high risk for negative outcome or too expensive in terms of need for professional support to warrant transplantation is a question that will undoubtedly be raised in an era of diminishing health care resources. It is incumbent upon those who do this work to begin to collect the outcome and intervention data to defend the selection decisions that are made. The alternative is that others will make these decisions, based on primarily financial issues. Another area deserving exploration is that of long-term psychological outcome of transplant survivors. The initial work with a PTSD model is intriguing, but is still in the very early stages, with little understanding of what the predictors or appropriate interventions might be.

The competing pressures of scientific advance and fiscal concern make the future of transplantation uncertain. However the role of psychiatric or psychological consultants may change with new health care models, the contribution they have to make will continue to be an important one. Consultants must be prepared to adjust their roles to best benefit the patients and families. Overall, transplantation continues to be an exciting area for both clinicians and researchers.

REFERENCES

Bernstein, D., Starnes, V. A. & Baum, M. D. (1989). Pediatric heart transplantation. *Advances in Pediatrics, 37,* 413–440.

Chang, I. (1991, June 5). Baby girl's bone marrow transplanted into sister. *Los Angeles Times,* p. 1.

Craven, J., & Rodin, G. M. (1992). *Psychiatric aspects of organ transplantation.* Oxford, UK: Oxford University Press.

Didlake, R. H., Dreyfus, K., Kerman, R. H., Van Buren, C. T., & Kahan, B. D. (1988). Patient noncompliance: A major cause of late graft failure in cyclosporine-treated renal patients. *Transplantation Proceedings, 20* (3), 63–69.

Edwards, E. B., Hunsicker, L. G., Guo, T., Breen, T. J., & Daily, O. P. (1994, October). *The impact of center volume on patient mortality following liver transplantation in the United States.* Paper presented at the XVth World Congress of the Transplantation Society, Kyoto, Japan.

Fanning, P. (1988). *Visualization for change.* Oakland, CA: New Harbinger Publications.

Fox, R. C., & Swazey, J. P. (1992). *Spare parts: Organ replacement in American society.* New York: Oxford University Press.

Gersony, W. M. (1990). Cardiac transplantation in infants and children. *Journal of Pediatrics, 116,* 266–268.

Goldman, L. S. (1993). Liver transplantation using living donors: Preliminary donor psychiatric outcomes. *Psychosomatics, 34,* 235–240.

Hilgard, J. R., & LeBaron, S. (1984) *Hypnotherapy of pain in children with cancer.* Los Altos, CA: Willia Kaufman.

Hosenpud, J. D., Breen, T. J., Edwards, O. P., Daily, O. P., & Hunsicker, L. G. (1994). The effect of transplant center volume on cardiac transplant outcome: A report of the United Network for Organ Sharing Scientific Registry. *Journal of the American Medical Association, 271,* 1844–1849.

Hunsicker, L. G., Bennett, L. E., Breen, T. J., Sutherland, D. E. R., & Daily, O. P. (1994, October). Impact of center volume on graft survival following pancreas transplantation in the United States. Paper presented at the XVth World Congress of the Transplantation Society, Kyoto, Japan.

Kinrade, L. C. (1987). Preparation of sibling donor for bone marrow transplant harvest procedure. *Cancer Nursing, 10*(2), 77–81.

Klintmalm, G. B. G., Husberg, B. S., & Starzl, T. E. (1991). The organ transplanted patient—immunological concepts and immunosuppression. In L. Makowka (Ed.), *The handbook of transplantation management* (pp. 72–108). Austin, TX: R. G. Landes.

Kocoshis, S. A., Tzakis, A. G., Todo, S., Reyes, J., & Nour, B. (1993). Pediatric liver transplantation: History, recent innovations, and outlook for the future. *Clinical Pediatrics, (32),* 386–392.

Kuo, P. C., & Jenkins, R. L. (1993). Liver transplantation. In B. A. Levine, E. M. Copeland, R. J. Howard, H. J. Sugarman, & A. L. Warshaw (Eds.), *Current Practice of Surgery,* Vol. 3 (pp. 2–19). New York: Churchill Livingstone, Inc.

Levenson, J., & Olbrisch, M. (1993). Psychosocial evaluation of organ transplant candidates: A comparative study. *Psychosomatics, 34,* 314–323.

Mangan, K. F., Klump, T. R., Rosenfield, C. S., & Shadduck, R. K. (1991). Bone marrow transplantation. In L. Makowka (Ed.), *The handbook of transplantation management* (pp. 322–400). Austin, TX: R. G. Landes.

Olbrisch, M. E., Levenson, J. H., & Hammer, R. (1989). The PACT: A rating scale for the study of clinical decision-making in psychosocial screening of organ transplant candidates. *Clinical Transplantation, 3,* 164–169.

Pinkel, D. (1993). Bone marrow transplantation in children. *Journal of Pediatrics, 122,* 331–341.

Pot-Mees, C. C. (1989). *The psychosocial effects of bone marrow transplantation in children.* Delft: Eburon Publishers.

Ramsay, N. K. C. (1989). Bone marrow transplantation in pediatric oncology. In P. A. Pizzo & D. G. Poplack (Eds.), *Principles and practice of pediatric oncology* (pp. 971–990). Philadelphia: J. B. Lippincott Company.

Reyes, J., Tzakis, A. G., Todo, S., Nour, B., & Starzl, T. (1993). Small bowel and liver/small bowel transplantation in children. *Seminars in Pediatric Surgery, 2,* 289–300.

Ross, D. M., & Ross, S. A. (1988). *Childhood pain, current issues, research, and management.* Baltimore-Munich: Urban & Schwarzenberg.

Sexson, S., & Rubenow, J. (1992) Transplants in children and adolescents. In J. Craven & G. M. Rodin (Eds.), *Psychiatric aspects of organ transplantation* (pp. 33–49). Oxford: Oxford University Press.

Shaffer, D. (1992). Pediatric psychopharmacology. *Psychiatric Clinics of North America, 15,* 1–15.

Shapiro, R., & Simmons, R. (1991). Kidney transplantation. In L. Makowka (Ed.), *The handbook of transplantation management* (pp. 168–191). Austin, TX: R. G. Landes.

Simmons, R. G., Klein, S. D., & Simmons, R. L. (1977). *Gift of life: The psychological and social impact of organ transplantation.* New York: John Wiley & Sons.

Singer, P. A., Siegler, M., Whittington, P. F., Lantos, J. O., Emond, J. C., Thistlethwaite, J. U. R., & Boelsch, C. E. (1989). Ethics of liver transplantation with living donors. *New England Journal of Medicine, 321*(9), 620–622.

Slater, J. A. (1994). Psychiatric aspects of organ transplantation in children and adolescents. *Child and Adolescent Psychiatric Clinics of North America, 3*(3), 557–598.

Smith, M. J., Breitbart, W., & Platt, M. (1995). A critique of instruments and methods to detect, diagnose and rate delirium. *Journal of Pain and Symptom Management, 10*(1), 35–77.

Stuber, M. L. (1993a). Psychologic care of adolescents undergoing transplantation. In E. R. McNarney, R. E. Kreipe, D. P. Orr, & G. D. Comerci (Eds.), *Textbook of Adolescent Medicine* (pp. 1138–1142). Philadelphia: W. B. Saunders Company.

Stuber, M. L., Christakis, D., Housekamp, B., & Kazak, A. Post trauma symptoms in childhood leukemia survivors and their parents. *Psychosomatics, 37,* 254–262.

Stuber, M. L. (1993b). Psychiatric aspects of organ transplantation in children and adolescents. *Psychosomatics, 34*(5), 379–387.

Stuber, M. L., Caswell, D., Cipkala-Gaffin, J., & Billett, B. (1995). Nursing concerns regarding liver transplantation: A case for more nursing involvement. *Nursing Management, 26,* 62–70.

Stuber, M. L., & Nader, K. (1995). Psychiatric sequelae in adolescent bone marrow transplant survivors: Implications for psychotherapy. *The Journal of Psychotherapy Practice and Research, 4*(1), 30–42.

Stuber, M. L., Nader, K., Yasuda, P., Pynoos, R. S., & Cohen, S. (1991). Stress responses after pediatric bone marrow transplantation: Preliminary results of a prospective, longitudinal study. *Journal of the American Academy of Child and Adolescent Psychiatry, 30,* 952–957.

Stutzer, C. A. (1989). Work-related stresses of pediatric bone marrow transplant nurses. *Journal of Pediatric Oncology Nursing, 3,* 70–78.

Trzepacz, P. T., DiMartini, A., & Tringali, R. (1993). Psychopharmacologic issues in organ transplantation. Part II: Psychopharmacologic medications. *Psychosomatics, 34,* 290–298.

Trzepacz, P. T. (1994). The neuropathogenesis of delirium: A need to focus our research. *Psychosomatics, 35:* 374–391.

Tydén, G. & Groth, C. G. (1991). Pancreas transplantation. In L. Makowka (Ed.), *The handbook of transplantation management* (pp. 300–321). Austin, TX: R. G. Landes.

United Network for Organ Sharing (UNOS) Organ Procurement and Transplantation Network (OPTN) Scientific Registry. Personal communication. UNOS is a non-profit organization that administers the solid organ procurement and distribution laws under contract to the United States Department of Health and Human Services.

Wolcott, D., & Stuber, M. L. (1992). Bone marrow transplantation. In J. Craven & G. Rodin (Eds.), *Psychiatric aspects of organ transplant* (pp. 189–204). New York: Oxford University Press.

AUTHOR INDEX

SUBJECT INDEX